The Oxford Handbook of Aphasia and Language Disorders

OXFORD LIBRARY OF PSYCHOLOGY

OXFORD LIBRARY OF PSYCHOLOGY

The Oxford Handbook of Aphasia and Language Disorders

Edited by

Anastasia M. Raymer

Leslie J. Gonzalez Rothi

OXFORD
UNIVERSITY PRESS

OXFORD
UNIVERSITY PRESS

Oxford University Press is a department of the University of Oxford. It furthers
the University's objective of excellence in research, scholarship, and education
by publishing worldwide. Oxford is a registered trade mark of Oxford University
Press in the UK and certain other countries.

Published in the United States of America by Oxford University Press
198 Madison Avenue, New York, NY 10016, United States of America.

© Oxford University Press 2018

Library of Congress Cataloging-in-Publication Data
Names: Raymer, Anastasia M., 1958– editor. | Gonzalez Rothi, Leslie J., editor.
Title: The Oxford handbook of aphasia and language disorders /
edited by Anastasia M. Raymer and Leslie J. Gonzalez Rothi.
Other titles: Handbook of aphasia and language disorders
Description: New York, NY : Oxford University Press, [2018] | Series: Oxford library of psychology |
Includes bibliographical references and index.
Identifiers: LCCN 2017022255 (print) | LCCN 2017024721 (ebook) |
ISBN 9780199773121 (UPDF) | ISBN 9780190669058 (EPUB) | ISBN 9780199772391 (hardcover : alk. paper)
Subjects: LCSH: Aphasia—Handbooks, manuals, etc. |
Language disorders—Handbooks, manuals, etc. Classification: LCC RC425 (ebook) |
LCC RC425 .O94 2018 (print) |
DDC 616.85/52—dc23
LC record available at https://lccn.loc.gov/2017022255

9 8 7 6 5 4 3 2 1

Printed by Sheridan Books, Inc., United States of America

This book is dedicated to all of those people with aphasia and their families.

Through their tragic circumstances we have learned about the brain and language, and the best ways to help those with this devastating condition.

SHORT CONTENTS

Anastasia M. Raymer

Anastasia Raymer, PhD, CCC-SLP, is Professor and Chair of the Department of Communication Disorders and Special Education at Old Dominion University in Norfolk, Virginia, and she is recognized for her research, supported by the National Institutes of Health (NIH) and the Department of Defense, to optimize rehabilitation of aphasia, limb apraxia, and agraphia. She is past president of the Academy of Neurologic Communication Disorders and Sciences, and a Fellow of the American Speech-Language-Hearing Association.

Leslie J. Gonzalez Rothi

Leslie Gonzalez Rothi, PhD, CCC-SLP, Professor Emeritus in the Department of Neurology at the University of Florida, is known for her work supported by the NIH and Veterans Administration (VA) examining neural and cognitive correlates of aphasia and related disorders and the integration of principles of neuroplasticity to maximize rehabilitation outcomes. She is past president of the International Neuropsychological Society and the Academy of Neurologic Communication Disorders and Sciences; is a Fellow of the American Psychological Association Division 40; and is a Fellow and recipient of Honors of the American Speech-Language-Hearing Association.

CONTRIBUTORS

A. M. Barrett
Stroke Rehabilitation Research
Kessler Foundation Research Center
East Hanover, New Jersey, USA

Annette Baumgaertner
University of Luebeck
Department of Neurology
Luebeck,
Germany

Pélagie M. Beeson
Department of Speech, Language, and
  Hearing Sciences
Department of Neurology
The University of Arizona
Tucson, Arizona, USA

Anastasia Bohsali
Department of Veterans Affairs
Rehabilitation Research and
  Development
Brain Rehabilitation Research Center
Malcom Randall VA Medical Center
Gainesville, Florida, USA

C. Elizabeth Brookshire
School of Communication Science and
  Disorders
Florida State University
Tallahassee, Florida, USA

Bruce A. Crosson
Brain Rehabilitation Research Center
Malcom Randall VA Medical Center
Gainesville, Florida, USA;
Departments of Neurology and Radiology
Emory University
Atlanta, Georgia, USA;
Department of Psychology
Georgia State University
Atlanta, Georgia, USA;
School of Health and Rehabilitation Sciences
University of Queensland
Brisbane, Australia

Elizabeth E. Galletta
Clinical Research Specialist
Speech Language Pathology Department
NYU Langone Medical Center
Clinical Assistant Professor of
  Rehabilitation Medicine
New York University School of Medicine

Leslie J. Gonzalez Rothi
Department of Neurology
University of Florida College of Medicine
Gainesville, Florida, USA

Margaret L. Greenwald
Department of Communication Sciences
  and Disorders
Wayne State University
Detroit, Michigan, USA

Stacy M. Harnish
Department of Speech and Hearing
  Science
The Ohio State University
Columbus, Ohio, USA

Kenneth M. Heilman
Department of Neurology
College of Medicine
University of Florida
Gainesville, Florida, USA

Yves Joanette
School of Speech Therapy and Audiology
Université de Montréal Medical School
Centre de recherche
Institute universitaire de gériatrie de
  Montréal
Montreal, Quebec, Canada

Diane L. Kendall
Department of Speech and Hearing
  Sciences
Veterans Administration Medical Center
  Puget Sound
University of Washington
Seattle, Washington, USA

Susan A. Leon
Veterans Affairs
RR&D Brain Rehabilitation
    Research Center
Department of Neurology
University of Florida
Gainesville, Florida, USA

Robert Lindenberg
Department of Neurology
Center for Stroke Research Berlin
Cluster of Excellence NeuroCure
Charite-Universitätsmedizin Berlin
Berlin, Germany

Lynn M. Maher
Department of Communication Sciences
    and Disorders
University of Houston
Houston, Texas, USA

Nadine Martin
Eleanor M. Saffran Center for Cognitive
    Neuroscience
Department of Communication Sciences
    and Disorders
Temple University
Philadelphia, Pennsylvania, USA

Marcus Meinzer
Center for Clinical Research
The University of Queensland
Brisbane, Australia;
Department of Neurology
Center for Stroke Research Berlin
Cluster of Excellence NeuroCure
Charite-Universitätsmedizin Berlin
Berlin, Germany

Janet P. Patterson
VA Northern California Health Care
    System
Martinez, CA

Anastasia M. Raymer
Department of Communication
    Disorders and Special Education
Old Dominion University
Norfolk, Virginia, USA

Ellyn A. Riley
Syracuse University
Elizabeth Brookshire Madden
Florida State University
Syracuse, New York, USA

Jamie Reilly
Eleanor M. Saffran Center for Cognitive
    Neuroscience
Department of Communication Sciences
    and Disorders
Temple University
Philadelphia, Pennsylvania, USA

Kindle Rising
Department of Speech, Language, and
    Hearing Sciences
The University of Arizona
Tucson, Arizona, USA

Amy D. Rodriguez
School of Health and Rehabilitation
    Sciences
University of Queensland
Brisbane, Australia;
Department of Veterans Affairs
Atlanta VA Rehabilitation Research and
    Development
Center of Excellence for Visual and
    Neurocognitive Rehabilitation
Atlanta VA Medical Center
Decatur, Georgia, USA

John C. Rosenbek
Department of Speech, Language, and
    Hearing Sciences
University of Florida
Gainesville, Florida, USA

Bernadette Ska
School of Speech Therapy
    and Audiology
Université de Montréal
    Medical School
Centre de recherche
Institute universitaire de gériatrie de
    Montréal
Montreal, Quebec, Canada

Lena Ulm
Department of Neurology
Center for Stroke Research Berlin
Cluster of Excellence NeuroCure
Charite-Universitätsmedizin Berlin
Berlin, Germany

Carolyn E. Wilshire
School of Psychology
Victoria University of Wellington
Wellington, New Zealand

Maximiliano A. Wilson
Université de Montréal
Medical School
Centre de recherche
Institut universitaire de gériatrie de
Montréal
Montreal, Quebec, Canada

TABLE OF CONTENTS

PART 1

Introduction

Aphasia Syndromes: Introduction and Value in Clinical Practice

Anastasia M. Raymer *and* Leslie J. Gonzalez Rothi

Abstract

Neurologic damage affecting the left cerebral hemisphere leads to impairments in comprehension and expression of language in the verbal modality (*aphasia*) and in the written modality (*dyslexia* and *dysgraphia*). Impairment patterns take various forms, differing in the fluency/nonfluency of verbal output and integrity of auditory comprehension, repetition, and word retrieval abilities. The divergent classifications of aphasia allow reflection on neural and psychological correlates of specific aspects of language processing in verbal and written modalities. Neurologic damage affecting the right cerebral hemisphere can lead to changes in social and prosodic communication, speaking to the role of the right hemisphere in language processing. Patterns of language breakdown following neurologic injury have implications for assessment and intervention for affected individuals. Whereas perspectives vary on interpretation of the language breakdown across disciplines, this volume's purpose is to facilitate interactions across disciplines to improve the lives of those with aphasia and related communication disorders.

Key Words: Aphasia, Broca's aphasia, Wernicke's aphasia, conduction aphasia, transcortical aphasia, aprosodia, social communication disorder

Introduction

Aphasia is a language disorder that is acquired as the result of damage or disease to the brain, most often the left cerebral hemisphere. Aphasia leads to difficulties understanding language and expressing thoughts and ideas with words and sentences. As with most neurobehavioral syndromes, aphasia is also defined by what it is not. It is not a communication problem explained by a possibly coexisting speech disorder such as apraxia of speech (an acquired disorder of the planning and sequencing of speech movements leading to articulatory struggle and misselection of speech sounds) or dysarthria (a disruption of articulatory execution pathways resulting in slurred or distorted speech pronunciations) (Duffy, 2013). When difficulty in formulating verbal utterances is accompanied by difficulty understanding words and sentences, the pattern suggests the presence of aphasia. Agnosia, a

perceptual disorder that represents the loss of ability to apply meaning to an incoming percept, also can be confused with aphasia. Again, co-occurring difficulties for comprehension and verbal expression lead back to aphasia as a likely defining problem. Difficulty interpreting and using the written mode of communication also typically accompanies the auditory–verbal difficulties of aphasia and may represent acquired dyslexia and dysgraphia. Observation of accompanying neurological symptoms, such as right hemiparesis or visual field cut, would further bolster the notion of a left hemisphere neurologic condition, leading to a primary diagnosis of aphasia. Yet, the other possibilities—dysarthria, apraxia of speech, and agnosia—remain as possible accompanying attributes of the devastating neurologic event that can lead to aphasia.

Clinicians who work with individuals with aphasia often come from a variety of disciplines, each with its own unique perspectives on the disorder. The neurologist and nursing staff have a medical and neurological perspective, the speech pathologist and neuropsychologist provide a cognitive–linguistic perspective, and the social worker has a psychosocial perspective. Yet, each of these professionals can be viewed as a clinical aphasiologist, someone who works with individuals with aphasia. Through each unique perspective can come diverging interpretations of what aphasia is and how it affects the individual with aphasia. Rosenbek (1982) decades ago eloquently reviewed the variety of definitions that have been proposed for aphasia. In that discussion, he clearly pointed out how definitions vary when considering slightly different viewpoints. Fundamental to this description is the assumption that aphasia occurs in someone who once had intact language abilities and then, because of some neurologic event, typically affecting the left cerebral hemisphere, loses language abilities.

On meeting individuals with aphasia, one quickly becomes impressed by the similarities and differences that can be observed from one person to the next. A good deal of the discussion and diverging perspectives on aphasia tend to center on how to interpret the similarities and differences. In his historical overview, Heilman (see Chapter 2 in this volume) describes how early on Wernicke, Lichtheim, Kussmaul, and their colleagues recognized that aphasia has many patterns, what are now called *aphasia syndromes*. Over the years, different groups have proposed unique but often overlapping systems for classifying aphasia (Ardila, 2010; Benson & Ardila, 1996).

Classifying Aphasia
Language Dimensions

The first distinction in looking across individuals with aphasia is the fluency with which they form an utterance. It is important to note that fluency in this context refers to sentence production, unlike the use of the term in neuropsychology to refer to the ease with which individuals think of individual words from a specific category (e.g., animals, words that start with *f*), that is, word fluency. Some individuals with aphasia are clearly restricted in the number of words they produce when attempting to construct a sentence. At times, they lack grammatical well-formedness in their utterances (e.g., dog . . . is black . . . chase . . . cat); struggle to produce prosodic, articulate utterances; or have limited ability to initiate even poorly formed utterances, any of which leads to nonfluent verbal expression

(Goodglass, Kaplan, & Barresi, 2001). This nonfluent verbal expression tends to occur in individuals with lesions that encompass left inferior frontal regions, often extending deep to include subcortical white matter (Damasio, 2008; Fridriksson, Guo, Fillmore, Holland, & Rorden, 2013). In contrast, there are those who are fluent in their verbal expression, as they fill time and linguistic space with many words in the shape of prosodic, fluid, sentence-like utterances. Yet, those utterances are sprinkled liberally with wrong words, incoherent words, or empty words, thereby markedly disrupting communication. Those with fluent verbal expression tend to have brain damage that spares left frontal regions and instead affects left postcentral regions of parietal or temporal cortex (Damasio, 2008).

Another dimension to consider among individuals with aphasia is auditory comprehension. Some individuals with aphasia have considerable difficulty understanding even basic words and messages spoken to them; the difficulty usually is associated with damage affecting the left superior temporal region, or Wernicke's area (Hillis et al., 2001). Others have relatively good abilities in understanding simple, direct sentences, yet experience breakdown when asked to process grammatically complex reversible sentences, such as passives (e.g., The dog is chased by the cat) or embedded clause constructions (e.g., The dog that was chased by the cat is brown) (e.g., Caramazza & Zurif, 1976). Instead, they may interpret grammatically complex utterances according to the order of the main content words in the sentence or the most common knowledge of the context, thereby misunderstanding the sentences (i.e., The dog chased the cat; the cat is brown). Grammatical comprehension difficulty is associated with circumscribed lesions situated throughout the left perisylvian region, including left inferior frontal, supramarginal, angular, and superior temporal gyri (Caplan, 2015).

Repetition abilities also can vary across individuals with aphasia. Although repetition performance will often parallel the impaired fluency pattern seen in spontaneous verbalizations, it is possible to find some individuals with aphasia who can easily and fluidly repeat even the most complex, lengthy linguistic input in a parrot-like, echolalic manner. The transcortical aphasias have retained repetition abilities and are typically associated with damage that spares the left perisylvian cortex (Damasio, 2008).

A final dimension often considered in individuals with aphasia is word retrieval abilities. Although word retrieval surely contributes to the ability to produce fluent verbal utterances, we often attend to word retrieval as a unique contribution to verbal output. Word retrieval difficulty or anomia is often tested with picture confrontation naming tests; thus, it is common to refer to "naming" difficulties in individuals with aphasia. When naming pictures or constructing sentences, individuals with aphasia often struggle to retrieve the desired noun or verb, instead selecting a related word or semantic paraphasia ("dog" for cat), a nonsensical word or neologism ("ersto" for cat), or no word at all. This complex process is mediated by multiple regions throughout the left hemisphere, including inferior temporal (Brodmann's area 37), anterior temporal, and inferior frontal cortex (Race & Hillis, 2015).

Aphasia Syndromes

Considering fluency of verbal expression, auditory comprehension for words and sentences, word and sentence repetition, and naming abilities, it is possible to distinguish several general patterns of language breakdown that emerge across individuals with aphasia. One of the most enduring aphasia syndrome classification schemes was proposed in Boston and referred to in common aphasia test batteries (Goodglass et al., 2001; Kertesz, 2007). Standing in contrast to one another on the fluency spectrum, the classification scheme starts with Broca's aphasia, a nonfluent aphasia, and Wernicke's aphasia, a fluent aphasia (Ardila, 2010). As shown in Table 1.1, there are several other nonfluent aphasias, including global, transcortical motor, and mixed transcortical aphasia, and several other fluent aphasias, such as conduction, transcortical sensory, and anomic aphasia. Within the fluent

and nonfluent varieties can be found some with profoundly impaired auditory comprehension abilities, that is, Wernicke's, transcortical sensory, global, and mixed transcortical aphasia. Likewise, there are those whose repetition is remarkably intact relative to their verbal expression (i.e., the transcortical aphasias). Anomic aphasia stands alone as a fluent form of aphasia with relatively intact comprehension and repetition, but with considerable word retrieval difficulties in isolation.

In addition to the general patterns of impairment noted in Table 1.1, each syndrome has unique characteristics in terms of typical patterns of errors and linguistic manifestations. Likewise, each syndrome tends to correspond to breakdown in fundamentally different components of the linguistic system and therefore reveals characteristics and principles of linguistic knowledge. Thus, each syndrome potentially serves as a backdrop for a discussion of unique components of linguistic knowledge and their neural representation. For example, Broca's aphasia sheds light on grammatical abilities, or syntax, the rules of word order in sentence construction (Maher, Chapter 8 in this volume). A consideration of transcortical sensory aphasia leads to a discussion of semantics, or meaning conveyed through words and sentences (Reilly & Martin, Chapter 6 in this volume). Anomic aphasia is best characterized within a discussion of lexical knowledge, the store of familiar words, whether spoken or written (Harnish, Chapter 7 in this volume). Conduction aphasia serves as a model for discussion of phonological mechanisms, that is, the speech sounds of language (Wilshire, Chapter 5 in this volume). Global aphasia, in contrast, informs discussions

Table 1.1 Traditional Aphasia Classification Scheme (Goodglass et al., 2001; Kertesz 2007)

Syndrome	Fluency	Auditory Comprehension	Repetition	Naming
Broca's	Nonfluent	+	–	–
Transcortical motor	Nonfluent	+	+	–
Global	Nonfluent	–	–	–
Mixed transcortical	Nonfluent	–	+	–
Wernicke's	Fluent	–	–	–
Transcortical sensory	Fluent	–	+	–
Conduction	Fluent	+	–	–
Anomic	Fluent	+	+	–

Note: + relatively intact; – impaired.

of the right hemisphere's contribution to language processing (Galetta & Barrett, Chapter 9 in this volume). Each aphasia syndrome, including its unique linguistic characteristics, the neural correlates, and implications for psycholinguistic theory, is described in great detail in the accompanying chapters.

In addition to aphasia, which encompasses language impairments affecting the auditory verbal modality, individuals with left hemisphere damage often experience significant difficulties dealing with written text, whether in reading or in writing. A discussion of aphasia therefore would be incomplete without a description of acquired dyslexia and dysgraphia. As reviewed in further chapters, it is clear that dyslexia and dysgraphia also can take on divergent patterns, correlating with the linguistic mechanisms of dysfunction characteristic of each aphasia syndrome (Beeson & Rising, Chapter 13 in this volume; Riley, Brookshire, & Kendall, Chapter 12 in this volume).

Other Communication Disorders
Atypical Forms of Aphasia

Although we have identified eight aphasia syndromes that form the core of this book, we recognize that this scheme does not include all possibilities. Sometimes referred to as atypical aphasias (Coppens, Lebrun, & Basso, 1998), other patterns of aphasia can be observed. For example, *optic aphasia* refers to language difficulties that emanate only for tasks that rely on object processing through the visual modality (e.g., picture naming, word/picture matching), while other modalities of language processing are presumably intact (e.g., naming to spoken definition, tactile naming, spoken definition to spoken word verification) (Coslett & Saffran, 1992; Marsh & Hillis, 2005; Raymer, Greenwald, Richardson, Rothi, & Heilman, 1997). This form of aphasia is sometimes discussed within the realm of associative agnosia, as it reflects dysfunction in activating semantic knowledge through visual input (De Renzi & Saetti, 1997).

Subcortical aphasia corresponds to language difficulties that follow damage affecting basal ganglia or thalamic circuitry on the left. Damage affecting the left thalamus leads primarily to a pattern consistent with anomic aphasia, with intact grammar and phonologic functions of language (e.g., Raymer, Moberg, Crosson, Nadeau, & Rothi, 1997). Nadeau and Rothi (2008), in their extensive review, noted that this pattern of deficits emerges because of the role of the thalamus in gated relaying

of information from one cortical region to others, particularly regions involved in declarative memory, including the lexical system. More variability has been noted in the patterns of language impairment described following left basal ganglia damage, ranging from severe global aphasia to milder anomic aphasia (Krishnan, Tiwari, Pai, & Rao, 2012; Nadeau & Crosson, 1997). Rather than arising from dysfunction of the basal ganglia directly, this variability in aphasia manifestations following nonthalamic subcortical damage has been attributed to hypoperfusion of cortical regions that occurs in many of the strokes that led to the aphasia (Hillis et al., 2004; Nadeau & Rothi, 2008).

Crossed aphasia is the unusual situation in which language impairments arise in a right-handed individual following *right* hemisphere damage (Coppens & Hungerford, 1998). More than 100 case studies have been reported. In their careful review, Marien, Paghera, De Deyn, and Vignolo (2004) summarized the findings of this disparate literature after ruling out cases whose language lateralization may have been confounded by factors such as forced right-handedness, family history of left-handedness, illiteracy, bilingualism, and tone language. Among the remaining 49 cases, patterns of aphasia varied, with an even split between fluent and nonfluent aphasias representing all eight aphasia syndromes mentioned in Table 1.1. In almost all individuals, crossed aphasia persisted into chronic stages. The majority had greater impairment for written language over oral language, and almost all had acalculia. Most also had typical impairments characteristic of right hemisphere damage, including aprosodia, visual neglect, and constructional apraxia. Analysis of lesion localization relative to expected clinicopathological correlates of the left hemisphere aphasias was possible for 38 cases. Among these cases, mirror image lesion locations were evident for 60 percent of cases and anomalous lesions were noted for the other 40 percent of cases.

Whereas aphasia is most often discussed in the context of an acute neuroetiology, such as stroke or brain injury, in recent years a good deal of attention has been devoted to individuals who progressively develop aphasia, known as *primary progressive aphasia* (PPA) (Duffy & McNeil, 2008; Mesulam, 1982). The premise in these cases is that language impairment occurs in isolation rather than as part of a broader degenerative dementia with accompanying memory and visuospatial impairments. As more and more cases were identified, it became evident that variations of PPA exist. It is now recognized that at least three PPA syndromes can be identified, which roughly correspond to perisylvian aphasia syndromes described previously: nonfluent/agrammatic, semantic, and logopenic (Gorno-Tempini et al., 2011). Presentation of PPA often heralds the onset of degenerative dementia, but for others can remain the defining symptom for some time.

Gorno-Tempini and colleagues (2011) delineated the diagnostic criteria for the three types of PPA. In the nonfluent/agrammatic variant of PPA, much like Broca's aphasia, these individuals have agrammatic verbal output and effortful distorted speech and possible difficulty understanding grammatically complex sentences. This variant can signal the onset of frontal–temporal dementia. The semantic variant of PPA is characterized by difficulty with picture naming and word comprehension in the presence of spared repetition. Reading and writing difficulties are also evident. Semantic PPA is associated with atrophy of the anterior temporal lobes. Finally, individuals with the logopenic variant of PPA have impaired word retrieval in naming and spontaneous speech and difficulty with sentence repetition. Phonologic errors in speech are also common, much like errors seen in conduction aphasia. Logopenic PPA is associated with left parietal atrophy and can presage onset of Alzheimer's dementia.

These atypical forms of aphasia can provide insights into the brain's mediation of language functions in unusual circumstances. Although specific chapters are not devoted to each of these atypical aphasias, they are woven into discussions that are seen in the core aphasia chapters.

Right Hemisphere Communication

While aphasia is a common concomitant of left hemisphere brain damage, communication impairments also can follow right hemisphere damage (Tompkins, 1995; Myers & Blake, 2008). Right hemisphere communication impairments tend to be more subtle, yet also debilitating. Discourse, figurative language, pragmatic functions involved in social communication, and linguistic and affective prosody all can be disrupted following damage affecting the right hemisphere. Detailed descriptions of the communication impairments and the theoretical implications of these right hemisphere disorders are provided in two other chapters of this text (Leon, Rodriguez, & Rosenbek, Chapter 15 in this volume; Wilson, Ska, & Joanette, Chapter 14 in this volume).

Varied Perspectives on Aphasia

We realize that some challenge the value of the aphasia classification system we incorporate in this text (Caramazza & Badecker, 1991; McNeil & Copland, 2011), yet the nomenclature continues to provide a means of communicating about the divergent patterns that arise related to neurologic damage affecting the cerebral cortex (e.g., Hoffmann & Chen, 2013; Marien et al., 2004). In addition to its historical value, each pattern allows us to focus on an aspect of language processing and mechanisms of language breakdown and their unique neural correlates.

Those who see individuals with the various forms of aphasia in clinical settings will benefit from use of syndrome classifications to guide their assessment and intervention for these individuals. Whereas the classification system may not always capture everything seen when working with individuals with aphasia, it gives clinicians a framework to guide the discussion and conceptualize what is happening to help individuals with aphasia deal with this devastating disorder.

Those who study aphasia from a theoretical perspective also have contributed to the discussion in important ways. For decades, researchers in the discipline of cognitive neuropsychology have investigated aphasia and its related disorders, dyslexia and dysgraphia, to understand the fundamental linguistic mechanisms that are damaged and to provide confirmation of theoretical models of language (Hillis, 2015). Theoretical models have then been used to guide assessment and intervention for individuals with aphasia (Hillis, 2015; Hillis & Newhart, 2008). Across several core chapters of this book, linguistic theories that relate to several of the aphasia syndromes are introduced (e.g., Baumgärtner, Chapter 11 in this volume; Greenwald, Chapter 4 in this volume; Reilly & Martin, Chapter 6 in this volume). Assessment tools and specific treatment approaches will often be guided by the theoretical perspective in an attempt to streamline clinical efforts to more efficiently identify and address the language breakdown (e.g., Beeson & Rising, Chapter 13 in this volume).

Some who examine aphasia have a neurologic perspective, trying to understand brain areas crucial to mediate aspects of language abilities (Damasio, 2008; Hillis et al., 2001). By understanding the neural basis for language breakdown, it can help to guide assessment choices and improve prognostic predictions (Crosson, Ford, & Raymer, Chapter 10 in this volume; Meinzer, Ulm, & Lindenberg, Chapter 16 in this volume). Further, principles of neuroplasticity and learning come into play as we address the impairment in clinical interactions (Raymer & Gonzalez Rothi, Chapter 17 in this volume), but the aphasia syndrome classification serves as a starting point to identify key methods and approaches.

One way of broadening our discussion to highlight the impact that aphasia has on the individuals who experience the disorder is to consider the World Health Organization (WHO) Model of Functioning, Disability, and Health (WHO, 2001). This model encompasses not only the structure/function components disrupted by a health condition, but also the impact of that disorder for functional daily activities and life participation. Most often in this volume, the health condition is a stroke that affects structures in the left cerebral hemisphere. Language functions mediated by the damaged regions then are disrupted, leading to various forms of aphasia. The presence of even the mildest forms of aphasia can pose serious limitations for daily life communication activities (e.g., talking with family, making phone calls, using the computer) and restrictions on economic and social life participation, also affecting those around them in their social circles. The WHO perspective leads to a broader aphasia assessment that goes beyond simply language testing to accounting for difficulties in daily communication activities for life participation (Patterson, Chapter 3 in this volume).

And beyond the WHO model, many discuss the implications of health conditions, including stroke-induced aphasia, for quality of life. Although this book centers on descriptions of the linguistic and neural implications of aphasia and related communication disorders, we cannot forget the impact that these disorders have on the individuals whose lives are disrupted by a tragic health event in terms of communication restrictions and undermined quality of life. Thus, most chapters in the book include sections that describe current evidence-based clinical procedures for assessment and treatment to improve communication for these individuals with aphasia and related disorders.

While there is substantial literature on aphasia characterization, assessment, and treatment, a variety of theoretical frameworks exist that make consolidation of evidence or even consensus opinion difficult. The difference in frameworks can involve differing assumptions regarding how the language system operates, a desire to link language operations with neural substrates, disciplinary perspectives (linguistic, neuropsychological, etc.), or

WHO granularity of behavioral target (impairment vs. participation). Clinicians are challenged to seek both specificity and comprehensiveness of understanding of the language system in a person with aphasia (Rapp, Caplan, Edwards, Visch-Brink, & Thompson, 2013). Serving as the basis for our approach to this book, we chose a "classical aphasia" framework that is most commonly used in the literature; it incorporates a common vocabulary and structure understood and shared (though not necessarily embraced) by much of the field, and it allows inclusion of the widest perspectives. We strategically extended the classifications to focus within each syndrome on a predominant language component or function and to allow linkage with other aspects of language as well as other cognitive functions, neural substrates, and clinical implications.

Although neurology, psychology, linguistic, and speech-language pathology researchers have written about aphasia for over 150 years, more recently the study of aphasia has captured the broader interests of additional fields, such as neuroscience, radiology, and genetics (Hamilton, 2016). Reasons for this are many, including the evolution of the view of the architecture of the language system from discrete center-based to a complex and nuanced systemic character. At the same time that neuroscientists have learned of the adaptive nature of the nervous system, influenced so profoundly by experience, advances in the neuroscience of language learning, loss, and recovery are yielding new insights for treatment targets and prognostic indicators.

Our goal in completing this volume is to bridge these complementary, interesting perspectives on aphasiology and facilitate interaction and discussion across disciplines studying aphasia. The neurologic events experienced by many individuals with aphasia can inform the neural and psychological underpinnings of language. In each area, additional research is needed to understand the complexity of language mechanisms, neural correlates, and effective means for clinical assessment and management of language breakdown. Through the breadth of perspectives provided in this book, it is our hope that individuals affected by aphasia and communication disorders would experience some positive benefit through improved communication and quality of life.

References

Ardila, A. (2010). A proposed reinterpretation and reclassification of aphasic syndromes. *Aphasiology*, 24, 363–394.

Benson, D. F., & Ardila, A. (1996). *Aphasia: A clinical perspective*. New York, NY: Oxford University Press.

Caplan, D. (2015). The neural basis of syntactic processing. In A. E. Hillis (Ed.), *The handbook of adult language disorders* (2nd ed., pp. 355–374). New York, NY: Psychology Press.

Caramazza, A., & Badecker, W. (1991). Clinical syndromes are not God's gift to cognitive neuropsychology: A reply to a rebuttal to an answer to a response to the case against syndrome-based research. *Brain and Cognition, 16*, 211–227.

Caramazza, A., & Zurif, E. (1976). Dissociation of algorithmic and heuristic processes in language comprehension. *Brain and Language, 3*, 572–582.

Coppens, P., & Hungerford, S. (1998). Crossed aphasia. In P. Coppens, Y. Lebrun, & A. Basso (Eds.), *Aphasia in atypical populations* (pp. 203–260). New York, NY: Erlbaum.

Coppens, P., Lebrun, Y., & Basso, A. (1998). *Aphasia in atypical populations*. New York, NY: Erlbaum.

Coslett, H. B., & Saffran, E. M. (1992). Optic aphasia and the right hemisphere: A replication and extension. *Brain and Language, 43*, 148–161.

Damasio, H. (2008). Neural basis of language disorders. In R. Chapey (Ed.), *Language intervention strategies in aphasia and related neurogenic communication disorders* (5th ed., pp. 20–41). Baltimore, MD: Lippincott Williams & Wilkins.

De Renzi, E., & Saetti, M. C. (1997). Associative agnosia and optic aphasia: Qualitative or quantitative difference? *Cortex, 33*, 115–130.

Duffy, J. R. (2013). *Motor speech disorders: Substrates: differential diagnosis, and management* (3rd ed.). St. Louis, MO: Elsevier Mosby.

Duffy, J. R., & McNeil, M. R. (2008). Primary progressive aphasia and apraxia of speech. In R. Chapey (Ed.), *Language intervention strategies in aphasia and related neurogenic communication disorders* (5th ed., pp. 543–564). Baltimore, MD: Lippincott Williams & Wilkins.

Fridriksson, J., Guo, D., Fillmore, P., Holland, A., & Rorden, C. (2013). Damage to the anterior arcuate fasciculus predicts nonfluent speech production in aphasia. *Brain, 136*, 3451–3460.

Goodglass, H., Kaplan, E., & Barresi, B. (2001). *The assessment of aphasia and related disorders* (3rd ed.). Philadelphia, PA: Lippincott, Williams & Wilkins.

Gorno-Tempini, M. L., Hillis, A. E., Weintraub, S., Kertesz, A., Mendez, M., Cappa, S. F., . . . Grossman, M. (2011). Classification of primary progressive aphasia and its variants. *Neurology, 76*, 1006–1014.

Hamilton, R. (2016). Neuroplasticity in the language system: Reorganization in post-stroke aphasia and in neuromodulation interventions. *Restorative Neurology and Neuroscience, 34*, 467–471.

Hillis, A. E. (2015). *The handbook of adult language disorders*. New York, NY: Psychology Press.

Hillis, A. E., Barker, P. B., Wityk, R. J., Aldrich, E. M., Restrepo, L., Breese, E. L., & Work, M. (2004). Variability in subcortical aphasia is due to variable sites of cortical hypoperfusion. *Brain and Language, 89*, 524–530.

Hillis, A. E., & Newhart, M. (2008). Cognitive neuropsychological approaches to treatment of language disorders: Introduction. In R. Chapey (Ed.), *Language intervention strategies in aphasia and related neurogenic communication disorders* (5th ed., pp. 595–606). Baltimore, MD: Lippincott Williams & Wilkins.

Hillis, A. E., Wityk, R. J., Tuffiash, E., Beauchamp, N. J., Jacobs, M. A., Barker, P. B., & Selnes, O. A. (2001). Hypoperfusion of Wernicke's area predicts severity of semantic deficit in acute stroke. *Annals of Neurology, 50*, 561–566.

Hoffmann, M., & Chen, R. (2013). The spectrum of aphasia subtypes and etiology in subacute stroke. *Journal of Stroke and Cerebrovascular Disease, 22*, 1385–1392.

Kertesz, A. (2007). *Western Aphasia Battery–Revised*. San Antonio, TX: Harcourt Assessment.

Krishnan, G., Tiwari, S., Pai, A. R., & Rao, S. N. (2012). Variability in aphasia following subcortical hemorrhagic lesion. *Annals of Neurosciences, 19*, 158–160.

Marien, P., Paghera, B., De Deyn, P. P., & Vignolo, L. (2004). Adult crossed aphasia in dextrals revisited. *Cortex, 40*, 41–74.

Marsh, E. G., & Hillis, A. E. (2005). Cognitive and neural mechanisms underlying reading and naming: Evidence from letter-by-letter reading and optic aphasia. *Neurocase, 11*, 325–337.

McNeil, M. R., & Copland, D. A. (2011). Aphasia theory, models, and classification. In L. L. LaPointe (Ed.), *Aphasia and related neurogenic language disorders* (pp. 27–47). New York, NY: Thieme.

Mesulam, M. M. (1982). Slowly progressive aphasia without generalized dementia. *Annals of Neurology, 11*, 592–598.

Myers, P., & Blake, M. L. (2008). Communication disorders associated with right-hemisphere damage. In R. Chapey (Ed.), *Language intervention strategies in aphasia and related neurogenic communication disorders* (5th ed., pp. 963–987). Baltimore, MD: Lippincott Williams & Wilkins.

Nadeau, S. E., & Crosson, B. (1997). Subcortical aphasia. *Brain and Language, 58*, 355–402.

Nadeau, S. E., & Rothi, L. J. G. (2008). Rehabilitation of subcortical aphasia. In R. Chapey (Ed.), *Language intervention strategies in aphasia and related neurogenic communication disorders* (5th ed., pp. 530–542). Baltimore, MD: Lippincott Williams & Wilkins.

Race, D. C., & Hillis, A. E. (2015). The neural mechanisms underlying naming. In A. E. Hillis (Ed.), *The handbook of adult language disorders* (2nd ed., pp. 151–160). New York, NY: Psychology Press.

Rapp, B., Caplan, D., Edwards, S., Visch-Brink, E., & Thompson, C. K. (2013). Neuroimaging in aphasia treatment research: Issues of experimental design for relating cognitive to neural changes. *Neuroimage, 73*, 200–220.

Raymer, A. M., Greenwald, M. R., Richardson, L., Rothi, L. J. G., & Heilman, K. M. (1997). Optic aphasia and optic apraxia: Case analysis and theoretical implications. *Neurocase, 3*, 173–183.

Raymer, A. M., Moberg, P., Crosson, B., Nadeau, S., & Rothi, L. J. G. (1997). Lexical-semantic deficits in two patients with dominant thalamic infarction. *Neuropsychologia, 35*, 211–219.

Rosenbek, J. C. (1982). When is aphasia aphasia? In R. Brookshire (Ed.), *Clinical aphasiology proceedings* (pp. 360–366). Minneapolis, MN: BRK.

Tompkins, C. A. (1995). *Right hemisphere communication disorders: Theory and management*. San Diego, CA: Singular.

World Health Organization. (2001). *International classification of functioning, disability, and health*. Retrieved from http://www.who.int/classifications/icf/en/

2

Aphasia Syndromes and Information Processing Models: A Historical Perspective

Kenneth M. Heilman

Abstract

This historical overview of aphasia represents the evolution in thought that has occurred over more than a century of studies of individuals with aphasia. The legacy of Broca and Wernicke live on in the syndromes that bear their names. We review the Wernicke–Lichtheim model that was used to predict several additional aphasia syndromes. We propose a model that encompasses modern perspectives on the Wernicke–Lichtheim models of aphasia. The aphasia syndromes that emanate from breakdown in that model also seem to be represented in recent studies of primary progressive aphasia. The framework continues to be an influential perspective for both theoretical and clinical activities to modern times.

Key Words: Aphasia, Broca's aphasia, Wernicke's aphasia, Conduction aphasia, Primary progressive aphasia, Transcortical aphasia

James Breasted, an early twentieth century Egyptologist, came into possession of the Edwin Smith papyrus (estimated to have been written in antiquity about 1700 BC) and in 1930 published translations of its detailed descriptions of 48 cases. Breasted reported that within the writings of this papyrus was the first reference to the brain and also the first rationalized, empirically based method for assigning treatment to disease. Charles Gross (1999) reported that the first to propose in writing that the brain was the seat of sensation, affect, and cognition was Alcmaeon (ca. 450), the Croton (in antiquity, one of three major centers of Greek medical thought). Alcmaeon apparently wrote that the heart provided no mental functions but instead stated: "It ought to be generally known that the source of our pleasure, merriment, laughter and amusement, as of our grief, pain, anxiety, and tears is none other than the brain. It is specially the organ which enables us to think, see, and hear, and to distinguish the ugly and the beautiful, the bad and the good, pleasant and unpleasant . . . " (Gross, 1999, p. 4). The first reported use of the term "aphasia" was Ogle in

1867, but descriptions and mechanisms of the variety of acquired language problems as a consequence of brain disease or injury have, like many other scientific inquiries, evolved over centuries. This chapter will focus on only a fraction of the themes that have emerged in the study of this remarkable brain–behavior relation.

The term phrenology comes from two stems, phren = "mind" and ology = "study of." The German physician and anatomist Franz Joseph Gall (1758–1828) was responsible for developing the postulates upon which phrenology was based (Sabbatini, 1997). His first postulate was that the brain is the organ that performs the functions that constitute the mind. His second postulate was that the brain is organized in a modular fashion such that different functions are mediated by different anatomic areas of the brain. Thus, a person's personality, behaviors, thoughts, and beliefs are very heavily dependent on the structure of their brain. His third postulate was that bigger is better, such that the larger the anatomic area or module responsible for mediating a function, the better it will perform this function.

Gall was aware that the shape of the skull is determined by the growth and size of different portions of the brain. Hence, skull measurements can provide information about the anatomic structure of the brain, and since anatomy plays a critical role in determining function, skull measurement can provide information about the brain's function.

Gall originally listed 27 characteristics that compose a person's personality (e.g., instinct for reproduction, love of one's children, affection and friendship, courage, brutality, guile–cleverness, covertness and honesty, pride, vanity, forethought, obstinacy, memory of words, sense of language, and others). He wrote that there was a specific brain area for each of these characteristics. According to Gall's postulates, the stronger the characteristic, the larger the brain area, and the larger a brain area, the larger the region of the skull that overlies this area. Thus, to determine which brain area determined each of these characteristics the phrenologists assessed peoples' personalities, made measurements of the overall size of the skull as well as specific regions, and developed causation correlations between anatomy and the personality characteristics mentioned above.

The scientific methods used by the phrenologists were weak and thus many of their conclusions were incorrect. Although phrenology was a pseudoscience, many of Gall's postulates were correct, as will be discussed below, including the postulate about anatomic modularity-specialization, the relationship between the size of a neurological network and its functional capacity, and even differences in skull growth. For example, in regard to modularity and size and shape of the skull, shortly after the introduction of computerized tomographic (CT) imaging, LeMay (1976) demonstrated that right-handed people had a different shape of the portion of the skull that covers the left hemisphere from the portion that covers the right hemisphere. The probable cause of this asymmetry is related to the anatomic asymmetries of the brain and these anatomic asymmetries are related to functional asymmetries that will be discussed in subsequent sections.

Broca's Aphasia
Background

Jean Baptiste Bouillaud (1796–1881), in part trained by Gall, published a paper in 1825 in which he wrote that clinical evidence supports Gall's frontal speech hypothesis that articulate language is mediated by human's frontal lobes. Earnest Auburtin, who was both Bouillaud's student and his son-in-law, also promoted the concept that

the frontal lobes were the organ of articulation. Auburtin offered a cash award to any person who could demonstrate a person with the loss of speech from a brain injury who did not have damage to their frontal lobe (Pearce, 2009; Stookley, 1963; Tesak & Code, 2008).

Syndrome

Leborgne was admitted to the hospital because of a gangrenous infection in his right lower extremity when Paul Broca first met his famous patient. Interestingly, Leborgne had lost his speech 21 years prior and was often called "Tan" because that was the only word he could speak. Leborgne's history was complicated, having developed right arm weakness 10 years after losing his speech, and several years later experiencing right leg weakness. Leborgne's speech at the time Broca met him was nonfluent, meaning that his ability to produce speech was limited, but he was able to comprehend other people's speech. Broca, who had heard Auburtin speak about Gall and Bouillaud's (1825) hypothesis of the frontal lobes' role in speech production, invited Auburtin to the hospital to see Leborgne. After seeing this patient with Broca, Auburtin stated with certainty that this patient's loss of speech must have been caused by damage that started in one of his frontal lobes (Pearce, 2009).

Pathophysiology

Leborgne died from the gangrenous cellulitis of his right leg several days after Auburtin saw him with Broca. Leborgne's brain was removed and the next day Broca exhibited the brain to the Société d'Anthropologic. There was a lesion that included the anterior portion of the left temporal lobe, the anterior portion of the parietal lobe, as well as the inferior portion of the frontal lobe. Leborgne's brain was never sliced to see how deep this lesion extended, but the brain was fixed in formalin and still can be viewed in the Museum of Man in Paris. Because the brain was never sliced and the depth of the lesion was unknown, when CT imaging became available, Signoret, Castaigne, Lhermitte, Abelanet, and Lavorel (1984) imaged Tan's brain and found that the lesion went very deep. Although Leborgne had an extensive lesion and multiple episodes of neurological deterioration, because he was aphasic after his first episode, Broca thought that the center of the lesion was the site that caused his aphasia. The site he thought was critical was the inferior portion of the left frontal lobe, including the pars opercularis and pars triangularis. Broca published the case report of Leborgne in 1861 and this paper was a major advance, being the first report attempting to understand the biological basis of a loss of language, that is, aphasia. Broca has several other reports, including a second patient, Lelong, with the same syndrome and with a lesion locus that was similar to that of LeBorgne. However, Broca's (1865) second major contribution was the report of eight patients who had aphasia and all eight of these patients had left hemisphere lesions. Whereas Broca did not report the probability of this being just a chance phenomenon, using the binomial theorem, the probability of this series of events occurring by chance would be less than 1%.

Broca's papers supported Gall's postulate of modularity and provided support for Gall, Auburtin, and Bouillaud's hypothesis that the frontal lobe is important for speech production. Was Broca's anatomic hypothesis correct? Not according to Mohr and co-workers (1978) who reviewed a series of patients who had lesions restricted to Broca's areas in the left frontal lobe and found that although these patients initially had impaired fluency, they improved rapidly except for perhaps having dyspraxic speech, and that a larger lesion was responsible for Broca's aphasia. Functional imaging studies have revealed that after an acute focal lesion, over a period of weeks to months the undamaged areas that surround the damaged area are often responsible for recovery observed in some patients (Heiss, Kessler, Karbe, Fink, & Pawlik, 1993). That some patients do recover from focal lesions suggests that other areas of the brain can compensate for the injured area. Recovery cannot be taken as evidence that an area such as Broca's area does not mediate the functions that are lost with injury.

The postulate that the nonfluent speech and speech errors observed with Broca's aphasia are related to a loss of the ability to program the movements needed to correctly make speech sounds, that is, an apraxia of speech, was first put forth by Alajouanine, Ombredane, and Durand (1939), who termed this a speech programming disorder, a term also subsequently used by Johns and Darley (1970). However, Arnold Pick (1913) noticed that patients with Broca's aphasia often do not use functional words, such as articles and prepositions, which are often important in making speech grammatically correct, but rather use only substantive words such as nouns, verbs, adjectives, and adverbs. This type of speech has been called telegraphic speech because when telegrams were used to deliver messages people paid per word, and not using function words

could save money. Some, such as Pick (1913), have thought the reason patients with Broca's aphasia use telegraphic speech is for this same reason; their production of speech is so difficult that they want to primarily use words that have strong content.

If the decreased fluency, speech errors, and telegraphic speech demonstrated by individuals with Broca's aphasia are all related to a motor programming deficit, perhaps the term aphasia is a misnomer and Broca's speech apraxia would be the correct term. Hughlings-Jackson (1879, 1880) wrote that when words are grouped together into larger structure, these structures are able to communicate more meaning than just the words by themselves. Another reason why a person with Broca's aphasia may use telegraphic speech is because they have lost the ability to meaningfully group words and use function words to aid this grouping. This grammatical impairment associated with Broca's aphasia was first noted by Arnold Pick (1913). Thus, it appears that Broca's aphasia is more than a motor programming deficit, but is truly an aphasic disorder.

Further evidence that the agrammatism cannot be fully explained by these individuals' attempts to increase the efficiency of their speech came from studies of the ability to understand the meaning of sentences based on syntax. Heilman and Scholes (1976) tested the ability of individuals with Broca's aphasia to understand sentences that differed by the presence of the direct versus indirect object (e.g., She showed her baby the pictures; She showed her the baby pictures). These sentences have the same substantive words, but the words were grouped differently and thus have different meanings. We showed the participants with Broca's aphasia four pictures: one picture was a woman showing her baby pictures and another had a woman showing her friend pictures of her baby. The two other pictures had an entirely different content. The examiner asked these individuals with Broca's aphasia to point to the correct picture for sentences such as "She showed her baby the pictures." Often the participants would point to the incorrect picture, such as the picture of a woman showing another woman a picture of a baby. They almost never pointed to a picture that had unrelated content.

Likewise, Caramazza and Zurif (1976) demonstrated that individuals with Broca's aphasia fail to comprehend semantically reversible relative clause (RC) constructions, in which both of the actors can act equally well as a grammatical agent or patient (e.g., The cat that the dog chased is black.). That is, based on the syntax of the sentence (subject/object), these patients could not understand the thematic roles to be assigned (agent/patient), thereby thinking that the dog is black rather than the cat is black.

The reason why the left frontal lobe lesion induces the syntactic deficit associated with Broca's aphasia is not fully known; however, syntax is based on the ordering of symbols, characterized by categories such as agent and patient. Individuals with frontal lobe dysfunction are often impaired at ordering and sequencing. In addition, whereas the left hemisphere appears to be dominant for mediating categorical relationships, the right hemisphere mediates continuous relationships. Thus, because syntax requires the ordering of categorical relationships, damage to the left frontal lobe would impair these processes and lead to the agrammatism associated with Broca's aphasia.

One of Gall's postulates about brain function was that bigger is better. Both the right and left hemisphere's motor regions have corticobulbar connections, but according to Foundas, Leonard, Gilmore, Fennell, and Heilman (1996), portions of the left Broca's area are larger than the homologous region on the right. In regard to the brain, if an area is larger there are many reasons why it can be larger. It may be larger because this area may contain more neurons and/or have greater connectivity with other neurons, and these increases may allow the storage of more representations or be able to have a richer repertoire of action programs.

Broca's aphasia is a syndrome and the word syndrome derives from the Greek word συνδρομή (sundromē), which means a concurrence of symptoms. Taubner, Raymer, and Heilman (1999) described a patient with a persistent nonfluent aphasia from a discrete primarily cortical, frontal-opercular lesion who, like individuals with Broca's aphasia, was nonfluent and also had impaired syntax, but had intact repetition and, therefore, did not conform to the traditional presentation because there was no phonetic disintegration of speech. Although it is possible that this patient's right hemisphere may have mediated repetition, based on this patient's behavior and a review of other cases, we divided the nonfluent aphasias with intact comprehension into four major subcategories and individuals with lesions in the same areas that Leborgne injured may have one or more of the following behavior disorders: (1) A verbal akinesia in which the individual has a diminished intention or drive

to speak. While lesions of the medial frontal lobe (supplementary motor area and cingulate gyrus) most commonly induce verbal akinesia, damage to the efferent projections from these medial areas to Broca's area may also reduce fluency. In addition, the supplementary motor and premotor areas have extensive connections with the basal ganglia and interruption of these networks can also reduce fluency. (2) Disorders of syntax, both an expressive disorder with telegraphic speech and agrammatic utterances as well as a receptive disorder in which the meaning of a sentence cannot be solely determined by the major lexical items such as nouns and verbs. These disorders of syntax may be associated with injury to the dominant pars opercularis. (3) Phonemic disintegration with a failure to correctly produce phonemes. This phonemic disintegration may be associated with injury to the opercular primary motor cortex or efferent projections from this area. (4) Defects of lexical access such that individuals struggle to find words and are impaired at timed word-generation tasks. Defects of lexical access may be associated with lesions of the pars triangularis and adjacent prefrontal cortex. According to this model, the traditional patient with Broca's aphasia would exhibit reduced fluency, disorders of syntax, phonemic disintegration, and defects of lexical access, whereas the patient with transcortical motor aphasia would have verbal akinesia or defects of lexical access or both. The patient reported by Taubner et al. (1999) had defects of lexical access and syntax, but no major problems with phonemic disintegration.

Wernicke's Aphasia
Background

Theodor Hermann Meynert, a nineteenth century German anatomist, was one of the first to study cortical cytoarchitectonics (Seitelberger, 1997). He noted that sensory input primarily projects to the posterior portions of the neocortex and the more anterior portions appear to control efferent motor output systems. Meynert must have also been an outstanding teacher because his students included Sigmund Freud, Sergei Korsakoff, and Carl Wernicke. Prior to Wernicke's description of what has been termed sensory aphasia, Bastian (1869) wrote about an auditory word center as well as a visual word center, and posited a modular network as well as a possible disconnection between the modules in this network. However, as discussed below, it was primarily Wernicke who described the syndrome that now bears his name.

Syndrome

In 1874, 13 years after Paul Broca wrote his classic paper, Carl Wernicke wrote *Der Aphasische Symptomencomplex*. Like the paper written by Paul Broca, Wernicke's paper was one of the most important papers written about aphasia. Consistent with Meynert's postulate that the anterior portions of the brain are motor-efferent and the posterior portions are sensory-afferent, in his classic article Wernicke contrasted Broca's (motor-efferent) aphasia caused by a left frontal lesion with a sensory-afferent type of aphasia that is currently called *Wernicke's aphasia*. Wernicke noted that whereas individuals with Broca's aphasia are impaired in producing speech (nonfluent), those with sensory aphasia display fluent speech. However, unlike individuals with Broca's aphasia who seem to comprehend speech input, those with Wernicke's aphasia are impaired at such comprehension. Although individuals with Wernicke's aphasia are fluent, their speech is not normal. Many with this disorder have excessive fluency and lose the ability to take turns; hence they continue speaking even when someone else is speaking to them, a sign called logorrhea. The spontaneous speech of these individuals is often incomprehensible. The words they speak, called neologisms, are often not words used in their native language (e.g., calling a table "chula"). Their fluent neologistic speech, at times, makes these people sound like they come from a country in which people speak a different language. Sometimes these individuals do produce words of native language, but often these words do not have the correct meaning, errors called semantic paraphasias (e.g., "chair" for table). Some other words they produce may have one or more incorrect phonemes, called phonemic paraphasias (e.g., "bable" for table). In addition to their deficit in comprehension, individuals with Wernicke's aphasia are also impaired when naming objects and when attempting to repeat. In both of these speech activities these individuals produce semantic and phonemic paraphasic errors as well as neologisms.

Pathophysiology

Wernicke (1874) suggested that the lesion that produces this deficit is in the posterior portion of the superior temporal gyrus in the left hemisphere. Since the studies by Meynert, this area was known to be an auditory association area. Wernicke thought that this area of auditory association cortex stored the memories of how previously heard words sounded (i.e., the sequence of phonemes or speech sounds that made up the word). This word sound dictionary is now called the phonological lexicon. In the absence of this phonological lexicon, when a person with Wernicke's aphasia hears someone speak, the words they hear sound like a foreign language that they never learned and thus they cannot understand speech.

In Wernicke's (1874) classical paper, not only did he suggest a second speech–language module, what is now considered as the phonological input lexicon, but he also introduced the concept of an information-processing network (Figure 2.1). He suggested that when a person normally attempts to

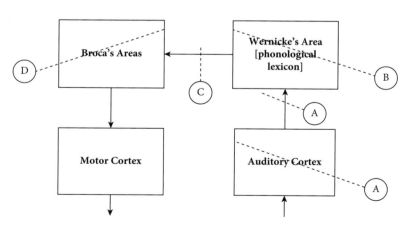

Figure 2.1 Wernicke's schema.

A = Pure Word Deafness: Impaired speech comprehension and repetition, normal spontaneous speech and naming; B = Wernicke's Aphasia: Fluent jargon speech, impaired naming, comprehension, and repetition; C = Conduction Aphasia: Fluent with phonemic paraphasic errors, impaired repetition, impaired naming, good comprehension; D = Broca's Aphasia: Nonfluent asyntactic (telegraphic) speech, impaired naming, impaired repetition, good comprehension.

speak, the area in the temporal lobe that contains the memories of how words sound (the phonological lexicon or Wernicke's area) provides information to the areas of the brain in which the sounds that comprise these words are phonetically programmed, namely Broca's area. Consequently, according to Wernicke, the posterior superior temporal lobe area, which stores the sounds that make up words, must be anatomically connected to Broca's area in the frontal lobe, allowing for fluent, accurate pronunciation of words. When people have an idea that they want to communicate or when they are attempting to name an object that they can recognize, these individuals with Wernicke's aphasia are unable to ascertain the set of speech sounds or phonemes in Wernicke's area that represents these thoughts or objects. Thus they cannot provide Broca's area with the phonological information that it needs to phonetically program the speech apparatus to produce the correct words. Hence, these individuals produce jargon in all speech tasks, whether repeating or producing spontaneous sentences or naming pictures.

One of the dramatic signs associated with individuals who have Wernicke's aphasia is their inability to be aware that they are producing jargon, a form of anosognosia. Because the area that would be able to monitor their output has been destroyed, they are unaware of their jargon and may even get upset that the person with whom they are speaking does not appear to understand their speech.

In regard to their logorrhea, since the time of Hughlings-Jackson (1879) it has been recognized that when an area of the nervous system that typically controls or helps to program another system fails, the system being controlled becomes disinhibited. Normally Wernicke's area provides Broca's area with information about the sound composition of words, and when Wernicke's area is damaged Broca's area becomes disinhibited and produces logorrheic jargon.

Pure Word Deafness
Syndrome

Pure word deafness was first described by Kussmaul in 1877, about 3 years after Wernicke (1874) described the form of aphasia now named after him. Like individuals with Wernicke's aphasia, persons with pure word deafness can neither comprehend spoken speech nor can they normally repeat spoken speech. However, unlike individuals with Wernicke's aphasia, they can speak normally and can also name seen or felt objects. This deficit, where the auditory system cannot access the

phonological lexicon in Wernicke's area (Figure 2.1), was predicted by Wernicke's schema.

Pathophysiology

The critical lesion in pure word deafness is in auditory cortex (Figure 2.1). This injury prevents auditory input from gaining access to Wernicke's area. Some individuals with word deafness can recognize the typical sounds that certain objects make and recognize the person speaking to them, and others cannot. The latter form is an example of pure word deafness with an auditory agnosia. Whereas the individuals with pure word deafness are more likely to have a lesion restricted to the left auditory cortex, those with associated auditory agnosia, who cannot recognize environmental sounds or the voices of familiar people, usually have bilateral lesions. Coslett, Brashear, and Heilman (1984), however, reported that with bilateral lesions of the primary cortex (Heschl's gyrus), people will demonstrate pure word deafness and that for the presence of a full auditory agnosia, in addition to the primary cortex, portions of the auditory association cortex must also be injured.

Conduction Aphasia
Background

Whereas Paul Broca (1861) was the first to provide evidence that the brain is organized in a modular fashion, it was Carl Wernicke (1874) who first put forth the proposal about the organization of a modular system and how dysfunction in different portions of this system would alter behavior (Figure 2.1). For example, Wernicke posited that if the connection between Broca's area and the posterior portion of the superior temporal gyrus (Wernicke's area) was disconnected by a lesion, the individual would also be aphasic, an aphasia now called conduction aphasia.

Syndrome

Wernicke posited that the store of word sound memories or Wernicke's area, now also called the phonological lexicon, is disconnected from Broca's area, the individuals with this disorder would also make phonological errors when speaking. Because these patients' word sound memories are intact they would be able to comprehend speech. This disorder is now called conduction aphasia.

Although many neurologists wrote about this disorder, it was Geschwind's classic 1965 paper that clearly defined the syndrome of conduction aphasia. Individuals with this disorder have fluent speech, but often make phonological paraphasic errors, have word finding difficulties, and circumlocute. In general, comprehension is relatively intact in these individuals, but their ability to repeat is especially impaired. Individuals with this disorder have the most trouble repeating sentences that use many function words (e.g., "No and ifs or buts.") as well as sentences made up of nonwords.

Pathophysiology

Individuals with a lesion that disconnects an intact phonological lexicon from Broca's area should be able to understand spoken words because their phonological lexicon is intact; however, because of the disconnection the phonological lexicon cannot entirely inform Broca's area about the speech–sound or phonemic composition of words. This disconnection would therefore produce a disorder in which, when attempting to speak or name objects, the person would make phonological errors. Because repetition uses this same system, the person with conduction aphasia should also have problems with correctly repeating words. But unlike the individuals with Wernicke's aphasia who cannot monitor their errors because they have lost the knowledge of how words should sound and thus appear to be unaware of their errors, individuals with this disconnection disorder have intact memories of word sounds and therefore should be able to monitor their errors and attempt to correct them, as is often seen in their "conduite d'approche" reattempts to correct phonemic errors.

Wernicke (1874) thought that the critical lesion inducing this conduction form of aphasia was injury to the insula. Pershing (1900) reported that it was a lesion of the supramarginal gyrus that caused this disorder and more recent cortical stimulation studies appear to support this hypothesis (Quigg, Geldmacher, & Elias, 2006). Anderson et al. (1999) induced dysfunction of the cortex of the posterior portion of the left superior temporal gyrus by electrical stimulation and found that this procedure led to signs of conduction aphasia. The arcuate fasciculus, however, travels under the cortex in the supramarginal gyrus and Konorski (1961) thought that the critical lesion was to the arcuate fasciculus, a white matter pathway that connects Wernicke's area with Broca's area, and Geschwind (1965) agreed with this localization. Catani and ffytche (2005) have delineated two dominant perisylvian pathways linking Wernicke's and Broca's areas, a direct one, corresponding to the arcuate fasciculus and an indirect one, projecting from Wernicke's area to the inferior parietal cortex (Brodmann's areas 39 and 40), with apparent relay to Broca's area by means of the superior longitudinal fasciculus (Makris et al., 2005).

Global Aphasia
Syndrome

Eleven years after Wernicke's (1874) influential report, Lichtheim (1885) published another landmark paper in which he elaborated on Wernicke's model (Figure 2.2). In this paper, Lichtheim mentioned a patient who, following typhoid fever, developed a form of Broca's aphasia, but with difficulty understanding complicated directions. Lichtheim referred to this pattern as "total aphasia." Individuals with what is now called global or mixed aphasia are nonfluent and cannot understand speech, repeat, or name (Benson, 1979; Goodglass & Kaplan, 1972; Nadeau, Rothi, & Crosson, 2000).

Pathophysiology

Global aphasia is usually caused by a large left hemisphere perisylvian lesion that destroys the inferior portion of the frontal and parietal lobes as well as the superior part of the temporal lobe (Damasio, 1981). This global aphasia from damage to multiple components of Wernicke's speech network (Figure 2.2) is a combination of Wernicke's aphasia and Broca's aphasia.

Transcortical Sensory Aphasia
Syndrome

In Lichtheim's (1885) influential paper, he predicted the existence of other forms of aphasia in which individuals have impaired comprehension of speech. These persons are different from the individuals with Wernicke's aphasia in that they would have normal repetition. Like individuals with Wernicke's aphasia, these other persons maintain fluent speech output. But they do make speech errors. Whereas those with Wernicke's aphasia produce frequent phonemic paraphasic errors as well as neologisms, individuals with transcortical sensory aphasia most often make semantic errors.

Pathophysiology

To help explain the possible pathophysiology of transcortical sensory aphasia, Lichtheim in his classic paper proposed some major modifications of Wernicke's (1874) schema (Figure 2.2). Lichtheim's information processing model or schema contained Wernicke's arc, including the primary auditory cortex, which performs an auditory analysis of incoming speech, and the posterior portion of the superior

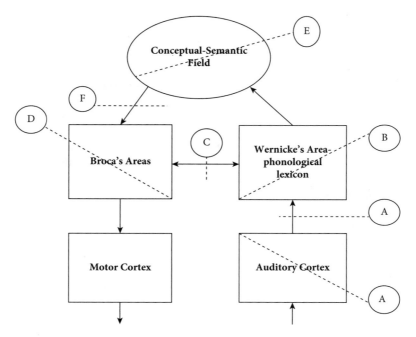

Figure 2.2 Lichtheim's schema.

A = Pure Word Deafness: Impaired speech comprehension and repetition, normal spontaneous speech and naming; B = Wernicke's Aphasia: Fluent jargon speech, impaired naming, comprehension, and repetition; C = Conduction Aphasia: Fluent with phonemic paraphasic errors, impaired repetition, impaired naming, good comprehension; D = Broca's Aphasia: Nonfluent, agrammatic, impaired repetition and naming, good comprehension; E = Transcortical Sensory Aphasia: Impaired comprehension and naming, intact repetition, fluent semantic jargon (empty speech); F = Transcortical Motor Aphasia: Nonfluent with intact repetition, impaired naming, good comprehension.

temporal gyrus (Wernicke's area), containing the acoustic representations of previously heard words. This module, which stores phonemic word representations, is now often called the phonological lexicon. Lichtheim posited that incoming speech, in addition to undergoing auditory and lexical processing, must access semantics. If a person is unable to access semantic representations or has a degradation of these representations, then this person will be unable to understand speech. Because the auditory cortex, Wernicke's area, and Broca's area are intact as well as connected, these individuals are able to repeat normally (Figure 2.2).

Transcortical Motor Aphasia
Syndrome

Lichtheim (1885), in this same article on transcortical sensory aphasia, also reported a patient who had a nonfluent aphasia, similar to that exhibited by individuals who have Broca's aphasia. Like those with Broca's aphasia, Lichtheim's patient could understand speech, but unlike individuals with Broca's aphasia, this patient was able to repeat speech normally. This individual's preserved ability

to repeat was related to an intact Wernicke's arc (auditory cortex, Wernicke's area, Broca's area) and their ability to comprehend was related to an intact auditory cortex, Wernicke's area, and conceptual–semantic networks (Figure 2.2). Many individuals with transcortical motor aphasia are also able to name objects.

Pathophysiology

Individuals who have transcortical motor aphasia most often may have injury to one of three areas, the left superior medial frontal lobe in the region of the supplementary motor area and anterior cingulate gyrus (Rubens, 1975), the left lateral frontal lobe in the middle frontal gyrus that is superior to Broca's area, and the left medial thalamus (McFarling, Rothi, & Heilman, 1982).

Lichtheim's model posited that transcortical motor aphasia was caused by a disconnection between the semantic–conceptual networks and Broca's area (Figure 2.2), but his model cannot explain why lesions of the medial thalamus or dorsomedial frontal lobe would cause a disconnection between semantic representations and Broca's

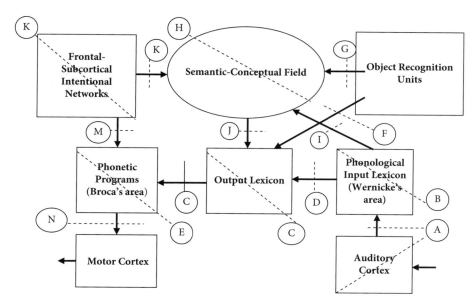

Figure 2.3 Updated Wernicke–Kussmaul–Lichtheim schema.

A = Pure Word Deafness: Impaired speech comprehension and repetition, normal spontaneous speech and naming; B = Wernicke's Aphasia: Fluent jargon speech, impaired naming, comprehension, and repetition; C = Conduction Aphasia: Fluent with phonemic paraphasic errors, impaired repetition, impaired naming, good comprehension; D = Deep Aphasia: Similar to conduction aphasia but makes semantic paraphasic errors with repetition; E = Broca's Aphasia: Nonfluent, agrammatic, impaired repetition and naming, good comprehension; F = Optic Aphasia: Impaired naming of visually presented stimuli. Speech and comprehension otherwise normal; G = Nonoptic Aphasia: Impaired naming to definition, intact visual naming, impaired comprehension; H = Transcortical Sensory Aphasia: Impaired comprehension and naming, intact repetition, fluent semantic jargon (empty speech); I = Transcortical Aphasia with Intact Speech: Impaired comprehension of speech, intact spontaneous speech, naming, and repetition; J = Anomic Aphasia: Spontaneous speech and naming with circumlocutions, repetition, and comprehension normal; K = Transcortical Motor Aphasia: Nonfluent with intact repetition, impaired naming, good comprehension; M = Speech Akinesia: Nonfluent, intact repetition and naming; N = Aphemia: Loss of speech with intact comprehension and writing.

area. In addition, if semantic representations are disconnected from Broca's area, how would these patients be able to name visually presented objects? Nielsen (1951) reported that individuals with bilateral dorsomedial frontal lesions are not only mute but also akinetic, such that they are impaired in self-activation. The medial thalamus projects to this dorsomedial frontal region and individuals with impairments in this frontal–basal ganglia–thalamic network who have transcortical motor aphasia may be impaired at self-activation of their lexical–semantic networks by intentional networks (Figure 2.3), leading to reduced fluency of spontaneous speech. With repetition and visual object naming, there is external activation and hence these individuals are able to perform these speech tasks that do not rely on self-activation.

Mixed Transcortical Aphasia
Syndrome

Individuals who have a combination of a transcortical sensory and transcortical motor aphasia

cannot understand speech, are nonfluent as well as being impaired at naming, but still can repeat. Sometimes when someone speaks with individuals who have this condition, that person will echo the speaker.

Pathophysiology

Individuals with mixed transcortical aphasia can normally repeat the words or sentences that they hear because their left perisylvian area (Wernicke' arc) is intact, but the lesions that cause this form of aphasia isolate this perisylvian area from the rest of the brain. Thus, Geschwind, Quadfasel, and Segarra (1968) called this disorder "Isolation of the speech area."

Deep Aphasia
Background and Syndrome

Michel and Andreewsky (1983) described an individual with an aphasic disorder that was somewhat similar to conduction aphasia. However, unlike those with conduction aphasia, this individual performed rather well repeating nouns, verbs, and adjectives, but was impaired when repeating function words (e.g., "No ifs, ands, or buts"), and completely failed to repeat nonwords. While this is a common finding in individuals with classical conduction aphasia, a remarkable feature of this person's repetition was the frequent production of semantic paraphasic errors. Subsequently, Katz and Goodglass (1990) essentially replicated Michel and Andreewsky's findings. The question was, what is the mechanism that can account for the production of these semantic errors?

Pathophysiology

Healthy people can repeat nonwords and this ability indicates that normally comprehension is not a requisite of repetition. Katz and Goodglass (1990) posited that the nonlexical route for repetition (Wernicke's arc) that functions without semantic mediation can be defective in individuals with this disorder. The modified Wernicke–Kussmaul's model (Figure 2.1) cannot account for this combination of aphasia signs; however, the Wernicke--Kussmaul–Lichtheim model (Figure 2.2) can. According to this model, individuals unable to repeat because there is a disconnection between the phonological lexicon (Wernicke's area) and the phonetic programs stored in Broca's area could use an alternative route. After words are processed by the phonological lexicon, they could activate their conceptual–semantic field and once activated these semantic representations could directly access the phonetic–articulatory programs stored in Broca's area. However, if this alternative semantic pathway can mediate repetition, this Wernicke–Kussmaul–Lichtheim model cannot explain the classical conduction aphasia in which individuals are impaired at repeating words as well as nonwords.

Explaining the repetition difficulties present in conduction aphasia and deep aphasia requires a modification of the Wernicke–Kussmaul–Lichtheim model in which there is a phonological input lexicon and a phonological output lexicon (Figure 2.3). In this revised model the phonological input lexicon receives and processes auditory phonological information and can transmit lexical (word) information to the semantic conceptual field, as well as to the phonological output lexicon. Thus this output lexicon receives input from both the phonological input lexicon as well as the semantic conceptual field and this output lexicon provides lexical (word) phonological information to phonetic processor (Broca's area). Based on this revised

Wernicke–Kussmaul–Lichtheim model, it can be posited that there are two loci of dysfunction that would allow a person to have fluent speech with relatively preserved comprehension (intact auditory processing with an intact phonological input lexicon and intact semantic–conceptual processing) but have impaired repetition. A dissociation–disconnection between the output lexicon and Broca's area (phonetic–articulatory module) could account for the production of phonemic paraphasic errors when speaking spontaneously, naming, and repeating, the signs that are characteristic of the classical conduction aphasia. A disconnection–dissociation between the phonological input lexicon and the output lexicon would still allow patients to repeat by using their intact input lexicon, which would activate semantic networks, and output from the semantic network could be processed by an intact output lexicon and phonetic programmer (Broca's area). When using this alternative semantic route, only real words that can be processed by the semantic–conceptual field could be repeated, and thus when relying solely on this route, a person should be unable to repeat nonwords, a sign that is associated with deep aphasia.

Anomic Aphasia
Syndrome

Almost all the forms of aphasia that have been discussed above are associated with impaired word retrieval or naming impairments, but individuals with anomic aphasia have a relatively isolated naming deficit that is not modality specific and may affect their spontaneous speech. Typically, these individuals remain fluent, but because they have trouble finding words such as the names of objects or actions, they often circumlocute, describing the objects or actions they cannot name. Individuals with anomia have intact comprehension and repetition.

Pathophysiology

Grashey (1885) was one of the first to describe a patient with anomic aphasia. Sigmund Freud (1891), who had a strong interest in aphasiology, noted that because these individuals are able to understand spoken words, he thought that in this disorder Wernicke's area and its connections with concept–semantic representations were intact. To explain why these individuals with anomia had problems with naming, Freud suggested that conceptual–semantic representations must have been unable to access Wernicke's area (the lexicon).

The model in Figure 2.2 where the conceptual–semantic representation must first access Wernicke's area (the phonological lexicon) was first put forth by Kussmaul (1877) a little more than a decade prior to Freud's postulate of the mechanism that might account for anomia.

The finding that individuals can have anomia in the absence of a transcortical sensory aphasia suggests that an efferent pathway from the stores of semantic–conceptual representations, that accesses the phonological lexicon in Wernicke's area, would be independent of the afferent pathways that permit activated phonological lexical representations, stored in Wernicke's area, to access semantics (Figure 2.3). Thus, based on this model, individuals who have transcortical sensory aphasia would have either degradation of their conceptual–semantic representations or have interruptions of both the pathways that bring lexical information to the areas that store semantic–conceptual representations and the pathways that allow these activated semantic representations to access the phonological lexical representations. But if this revised model set forth by Kussmaul helps to better understand disorders such as anomic aphasia, what would happen if only the pathway that allowed activated phonological lexical representation to access the semantic–conceptual representations was interrupted?

Transcortical Sensory Aphasia with Intact Naming and Spontaneous Speech

Syndrome

A patient with this disorder almost appeared to have word deafness (Heilman, Rothi, McFarling, & Rottman, 1981). His spontaneous speech was normal and he could name well, but he could not understand speech. However, unlike individuals with word deafness he could repeat normally.

Pathophysiology

What was unusual about the patient reported by Heilman et al. (1981) was that although he appeared to have a transcortical sensory aphasia with impaired repetition and intact naming, he was able to spontaneously speak and name well. These observations suggested that his phonological input lexicon could not access semantic representations, but his semantic representations could access his phonological output lexicon. These observations support the modification of Kussmaul's model (Figure 2.3) in which semantics accesses the phonological output lexicon rather than directly accessing Broca's area. As in Lichtheim's (1885) model (Figure

2.2) and as mentioned above, this modified model may also help explain the mechanisms that can account for anomia.

Optic Aphasia

Syndrome

Individuals with optic aphasia are impaired at naming objects they view. Unlike persons with anomic aphasia, they can name objects presented in the tactile and auditory modalities, as well as describe what they are viewing and correctly pantomime the use of those objects. Sometimes these activities of touching and pantomiming help these individuals with optic aphasia to find the correct name. Their speech is fluent when speaking spontaneously. Unlike individuals with anomic aphasia, they do not search for words or circumlocute. Like anomic aphasia, their comprehension and repetition are normal.

Pathophysiology

Optic aphasia is often confused with visual agnosia, because individuals with visual agnosia are also impaired at naming visually presented stimuli, but there is an important difference between optic aphasia and visual agnosia. The word agnosia comes from two morphemes, a = "without" and gnosis = "knowledge." Persons with visual agnosia, when viewing an object, cannot name the object, but they also do not appear to have any concept of the object. It is as if they had never seen it before and cannot describe its use, where it is found, or its superordinate category. If they are viewing a tool or implement, they cannot pantomime its use, but once they hold it, they may be able to correctly demonstrate its use.

Freund (1888), who first described optic aphasia in a patient with a tumor in the left occipital–parietal region leading also to a right hemianopia, thought this disorder was caused by a disconnection between the visual areas in the right hemisphere's occipital lobe and the language areas in the left hemisphere important for naming. While this disorder may be a disconnection between visual association areas and the left hemisphere areas that mediate language, it remains unclear how these individuals are able to describe verbally what they have seen. As will be discussed below, perhaps they have disconnected their visual association areas, which contain visual object recognition units, from their phonological output lexicon; however, their visual object recognition units still have access to their semantic–conceptual representations (Figure 2.3).

Nonoptic Aphasia
Syndrome

Several years ago we saw several patients who were adept at being able to name viewed pictures of objects and animals from the Boston Naming Test. In contrast to the individuals with optic aphasia, discussed above, who can name to definition, these patients with "nonoptic aphasia" were unable to name to definition (Shuren, Geldmacher, & Heilman, 1993). They were, however, able to repeat well, but when attempting to speak they primarily produced semantic jargon.

Pathophysiology

This nonoptic aphasia could be a form of mixed transcortical sensory aphasia with intact naming as discussed above; however, unlike the individual who had this disorder because of a stroke and had evidence of functioning semantic conceptual networks, the patients reported by Shuren et al. (1993) had some form of degenerative disease (possibly Alzheimer's disease or even semantic dementia) and these patients had no evidence of having intact semantic–conceptual networks.

Because individuals with nonoptic aphasia are able to name visually presented objects, their visual association areas, including their object recognition units, are intact and are able to access their phonological output lexicon, and this intact lexicon can access Broca's area. Because repetition was also intact in these individuals with nonoptic aphasia, their Wernicke's arc (primary auditory cortex—phonological input lexicon—phonological output lexicon—Broca's area-motor cortex) was also intact. These individuals' spontaneous speech was characterized by semantic jargon and they also had poor comprehension. Naming to definition, comprehension, and normal speech all require intact semantic–conceptual representations, and thus these patients' nonoptic aphasia was probably caused by degradation of their semantic–conceptual field with other portions of the speech network remaining intact.

Primary Progressive Aphasias
Background

The aphasic disorders discussed above for the most part have been described in individuals who have focal neurological lesions. However, recently there has been a greater interest in the aphasic disorders associated with degenerative diseases and these have been called the "primary progressive aphasias" (Mesulam, 1987). Although Pick (1892) as well as Dejerine and Sérieux (1897) described patients who

appeared to have these types of progressive aphasic disorders, these disorders were more recently brought to the attention of clinicians by Mesulam (1982, 1987). Although there is still considerable debate about the classification of the subtypes of progressive aphasia, most investigators have recognized three major subtypes: agrammatic-dysfluent also called primary progressive nonfluent aphasia, semantic dementia, and logopenic progressive aphasia (Gorno-Tempini et al., 2011). Each of these will be briefly described below.

Syndromes

Primary progressive nonfluent aphasia (PPNA): Typically individuals with this disorder have a progressive nonfluent aphasia with labored articulation and phonological errors. They have both expressive and receptive agrammatism. Although these individuals have relatively intact speech comprehension of single words, they are also impaired in naming and repeating (Mesulam, 1987).

Semantic dementia: Individuals with semantic dementia have a progressive anomia and a deficit in understanding single words. However, they are able to repeat and have intact fluency (Hodges & Patterson, 1996; Hodges, Patterson, Oxbury, & Funnell, 1992).

Logopenic primary progressive aphasia (LPPA): Individuals with this disorder have a progressive anomia, which interferes with their fluency. They make phonological paraphasic errors and also are impaired at repetition. However, their understanding of single words remains preserved (Gorno-Tempini et al., 2008).

Pathophysiology

These progressive syndromes are associated with a variety of degenerative neurological disorders that have different histopathologies, but these will not be discussed here. In some respects PPNA resembles Broca's aphasia, semantic dementia has similarities to transcortical sensory aphasia, and LPPA resembles conduction aphasia. In fact, when Hillis, Selnes, and Gordon (1999) described LPPA they called it "primary progressive conduction aphasia." Imaging studies attempting to learn what portions of the cortex have degenerated with these disorders have also found that individuals with PPNA often have degeneration of the left inferior frontal lobe, similar to Broca's aphasia, and those with LPPA have degeneration of the left parietal and temporal lobes, similar to conduction aphasia. The persons with semantic dementia have a cluster of signs that is very similar to those individuals with stroke who have a transcortical sensory aphasia. However, individuals with transcortical sensory aphasia often have damage to their parietal lobes, and persons with semantic dementia have atrophy of their left (or both) anterior temporal lobes. Whereas injury to the left anterior temporal lobe may cause an anomia, these individuals typically maintain their ability to understand speech. Even HM (Scoville & Milner, 1957), who had both anterior temporal lobes removed and was terribly amnesic, was able to normally understand speech. Thus, the reason that degeneration of the left anterior temporal lobe causes semantic dementia with anomia and comprehension disorders, but focal lesions of this area do not cause comprehension disorders, still needs to be determined.

Conclusions

This historical overview of aphasia represents the evolution in thought that has occurred over more than a century of studies of individuals with aphasia. The legacy of Broca and Wernicke live on in the syndromes that bear their names. In Figure 2.3, we propose a model that encompasses modern perspectives on the Wernicke–Lichtheim models of aphasia. The aphasia syndromes that emanate from breakdown in that model also seem to be represented in recent studies of primary progressive aphasia. The framework continues to be an influential perspective for both theoretical and clinical activities to modern times.

References

Alajouanine, T., Ombredane, A., & Durand, M. (1939). *Le syndrome de disintegration phonetique dans l'aphasie.* Paris: Masson.

Anderson, J.M., Gilmore, R., Roper, S., Crosson, B., Bauer, R.M., Nadeau, S., Beversdorf, D.Q., Cibula, J., Rogish, M., Kortencamp, S., Hughes, J.D., Gonzalez Rothi, L.J., & Heilman, K.M. (1999). Conduction aphasia and the arcuate fasciculus: A reexamination of the Wernicke-Geschwind model. *Brain and Language*, 70(1), 1–12.

Bastian, H.C. (1869). *Aphasia and other speech defects.* London: H. K. Lewis.

Benson, D.F. (1979). Aphasia. In K.M. Heilman & E. Valenstein (Eds.), *Clinical neuropsychology* (pp. 22–58). New York: Oxford University Press.

Bouillaud, J.B. (1825). Recherches cliniques propres à démonstrer que la perte de la parole correspond à la lésion des lobules anterieurs du cerveau. Et a confirmer l'opinion de M. Gall sur le siège de l'organe du language articulé. *Archives of Géneral Médicine (Paris)*, 8, 25–45.

Breasted, J.H. (1930). *The Edwin Smith surgical papyrus.* Oriental Institute Publications, III–IV. Chicago. *2 volumes.*

Broca, P. (1861). Remarques sur le siege de la faculte du language articule, suivies d'une observation d'aphemie. *Bulletin Société Anatomique (Paris)*, 2, 330–357.

Broca, P. (1865). Sur le siege de la faculte du langage articule. *Bulletin de la Societe d'anthropologie*, 6, 337–393.

Caramazza, A., & Zurif, E. (1976). Dissociations of algorithmic and heuristic processes in sentence comprehension: Evidence from aphasia. *Brain and Language*, 3, 572–582.

Catani, M., & ffytche, D.H. (2005) The rises and falls of disconnection syndromes. *Brain*, 128(Pt 10), 2224–2239.

Coslett, H.B., Brashear, H.R., & Heilman, K.M. (1984) Pure word deafness after bilateral primary auditory cortex infarcts. *Neurology*, 34(3), 347–352.

Damasio, H. (1981). Cerebral localization of the aphasias. In M.T. Sarno (Ed.), *Acquired aphasia* (pp. 27–50). New York: Academic Press.

Dejerine, J., & Sérieux, P. (1897). Un cas de surdite´ verbale pure terminée par aphasie sensorielle, suivie d'autopsie. *Comptes Rendues des Séances e la Société de Biologie (Paris)*, 49, 1074–1077.

Foundas, A.L., Leonard, C.M., Gilmore, R.L., Fennell, E.B., & Heilman, K.M. (1996). Pars triangularis asymmetry and language dominance. *Proceedings of the National Academy of Sciences USA*, 93(2), 719–722.

Freud, S. (1891). *On aphasia.* Leipzig: Deuticke.

Freund, C.S. (1888). Ueber optische Aphasie und Seelenblindheit. *Archiv fur Psychiatrie und Nervenbkhrankheit*, 20, 276–297.

Geschwind, N. (1965). Disconnexion syndromes in animals and man I & II. *Brain*, 88(2), 237–294; 88(3), 585–644.

Geschwind, N., Quadfasel, F.A., & Segarra, J.M. (1968). Isolation of the speech area. *Neuropsychologia*, 6, 327–340.

Goodglass, H., & Kaplan, E. (1972). *The assessment of aphasia and related disorders.* Philadelphia: Lea & Febiger.

Gorno-Tempini, M.L., Brambati, S.M., Ginex, V., Ogar, J., Dronkers, N.F, Marcone, A., Perani, D., Garibotto, V., Cappa, S.F., & Miller, B.L. (2008). The logopenic/phonological variant of primary progressive aphasia. *Neurology*, 71(16), 1227–1234.

Gorno-Tempini, M.L., Hillis, A.E., Weintraub, S., Kertesz, A., Mendez, M., Cappa, S.F,. . . Grossman, M. (2011). Classification of primary progressive aphasia and its variants. *Neurology*, 76(11), 1006–1014.

Grashey, H. (1885). Uber aphasie und ihre beziechunen zur Wahrnehmung. *Archiv fur Psychiatrie*, 16, 654–688.

Gross, C.G. (1999). *Brain, vision, memory: Tales in the history of neuroscience.* Cambridge, MA: MIT Press.

Heilman, K.M., Rothi, L., McFarling, D., & Rottmann, A.L. (1981). Transcortical sensory aphasia with relatively spared spontaneous speech and naming. *Archives of Neurology*, 38(4), 236–239.

Heilman, K., & Scholes, R.J. (1976). The nature of comprehension errors in Broca's, conduction and Wernicke's aphasics. *Cortex*, 12(3), 258–265.

Heiss, W.D., Kessler, J., Karbe, H., Fink, G.R., & Pawlik, G. (1993). Cerebral glucose metabolism as a predictor of recovery from aphasia in ischemic stroke. *Archives of Neurology*, 50(9), 958–964.

Hillis, A.E., Selnes, O.A., & Gordon, B. (1999). Primary progressive conduction aphasia: A cognitive analysis of two cases. *Brain and Language*, 69, 478–481.

Hodges, J.R., & Patterson, K. (1996). Nonfluent progressive aphasia and semantic dementia: A comparative neuropsychological study. *Journal of the International Neuropsychological Society*, 2, 511–524.

Hodges, J.R., Patterson, K., Oxbury, S., & Funnell, F. (1992). Semantic dementia. Progressive fluent aphasia with temporal lobe atrophy. *Brain*, 115, 1783–1806.

Hughlings-Jackson, J. (1879, 1880). On afflictions of speech from diseases of the brain. *Brain*, 1, 304–330; 2, 323–356.

Johns, D.F., & Darley, F.L. (1970). Phonemic variability in apraxia of speech. *Journal of Speech and Hearing Research*, 13(3), 556–583.

Katz, R.B., & Goodglass, H. (1990). Deep dysphasia: Analysis of a rare form of repetition disorder. *Brain and Language*, 39, 153–185.

Konorski, J. (1961). Pathophysiological analysis of various kinds of speech disorders and an attempt of their classification (in Polish). *Rozprawy Wydzialu Nauk Medycznych*, 2, 9–32.

Kussmaul, A. (1877). *Die Storungen der Sprache.* Leipzig: Vogel.

LeMay, M. (1976). Morphological cerebral asymmetries of modern man, fossil man, and nonhuman primate. *Annals of the New York Academy of Sciences*, 280, 349–366.

Lichtheim, L. (1885). On aphasia. *Brain*, 7, 433–484.

Makris, N., Kennedy, D.N., McInerney, S., Sorensen, A.G., Wang, R., Caviness, V.S., Jr., & Pandya, D.N. (2005). Segmentation of subcomponents within the superior longitudinal fascicle in humans: A quantitative, in vivo, DT-MRI study. *Cerebral Cortex*, 15(6), 854–869.

McFarling, D., Rothi, L.J., & Heilman, K.M. (1982). Transcortical aphasia from ischaemic infarcts of the thalamus: A report of two cases. *Journal of Neurology, Neurosurgery, & Psychiatry*, 45(2), 107–112.

Mesulam, M.M. (1982). Slowly progressive aphasia without generalized dementia. *Annals of Neurology*, 11, 592–598.

Mesulam, M.M. (1987). Primary progressive aphasia—differentiation from Alzheimer's disease [editorial]. *Annals of Neurology*, 22, 533–534.

Michel, F., & Andreewsky E. (1983). Deep dysphasia: An analog of deep dyslexia in the auditory modality. *Brain and Language*, 18, 212–223.

Mohr, J.P., Pessin, M.S., Finkelstein, S., Funkenstein, H.H., Duncan, G.W., & Davis, K.R. (1978). Broca aphasia: Pathologic and clinical. *Neurology*, 28, 311–324.

Nadeau, S.E., Rothi, L.J.G., & Crosson, B. (2000). *Aphasia and language.* New York: Guilford Press.

Nielsen, J.M. (1951). The cortical components of akinetic mutism. *Journal of Nervous & Mental Disorders*, 114(5), 459–461.

Ogle, W. (1867). Aphasia and agraphia. *St George's Hospital Reports*, 2, 83–122.

Pearce, J.M. (2009). Broca's aphasiacs. *European Neurology*, 61(3), 183–189.

Pershing, H.T. (1900). A case of Wernicke's conduction aphasia with autopsy. *Journal of Nervous & Mental Disease*, 279, 369–374.

Pick, A. (1892). Ueber die Beziehungen der senilen Hirnatrophie zur Aphasie. *Prager Medizinische Wochenschrift*, 17, 165–167.

Pick, A. (1913). *Die agrammatischen Sprachstörungen/1.* Berlin: Springer.

Quigg, M., Geldmacher, D.S., & Elias, W.J. (2006). Conduction aphasia as a function of the dominant posterior perisylvian cortex. Report of two cases. *Journal of Neurosurgery*, 104(5), 845–848.

Rubens, A.B., (1975). Aphasia with infarction in the territory of the anterior cerebral artery. *Cortex*, 11, 239–250.

Sabbatini, R.M.E. (1997, March). Phrenology: The history of brain localization. *Brain & Mind*, March. http://www.cerebromente.org.br/n01/frenolog/frenologia.htm.

Scoville, W.B., & Milner, B. (1957). Loss of recent memory after bilateral hippocampal lesions. *Journal of Neurology, Neurosurgery, & Psychiatry*, 20, 11–21.

Seitelberger, F. (1997). Theodor Meynert (1833–1892) pioneer and visionary of brain research. *Journal of the History of the Neurosciences*, 6, 264–274.

Shuren, J., Geldmacher D., &, Heilman, K.M. (1993). Non-optic aphasia. *Neurology*, 43, 1900–1907.

Signoret, J.L., Castaigne, P., Lhermitte, F., Abelanet, R., & Lavorel, P. (1984). Rediscovery of Leborgne's brain: Anatomical description with CT scan. *Brain and Language*, 22 (2), 303–319, 1900–1907.

Stookley, B. (1963). Jean-Baptiste Bouillaud and Ernest Auburtin. Early studies on cerebral localization and the speech center. *Journal of the American Medical Association*, 184, 1024–1029.

Taubner, R.W., Raymer, A.M., & Heilman, K.M. (1999). Frontal-opercular aphasia. *Brain and Language*, 70(2), 240–261.

Tesak, J., & Code, C. (2008). *Milestones in the history of aphasia.* New York: Psychology Press.

Wernicke, C. (1874). *Das Aphasiche Symptomenkomplex.* Breslau: Cohn and Weigart.

Aphasia Assessment

Janet P. Patterson

Abstract

Theoretically grounded aphasia assessment that matches clinical practice settings is critical to planning intervention and assisting individuals with aphasia and their family members. This chapter begins with an overview of aphasia assessment in three historical periods: clinical description prior to 1935, standardized testing into the 1960s, and the postmodern era of multifaceted assessment. Topics in this section include aphasia classification; screening; assessing specific linguistic ability, functional communication, and quality of life; and assessment within cognitive neuropsychological and information-processing models. The second section describes contemporary assessment practices including the purpose and models of assessment, personal and environmental factors influencing assessment decisions, assessing conversation and connected speech, and related assessment areas such as cognition, executive function, and emotional state. Finally, emerging trends in assessment are discussed including evidence-based practice, treatment candidacy and prognosis, psychosocial models of assessment, and telehealth. Successful aphasia assessment should be a principled, systematic, and dynamic component of managing and living with aphasia.

Key Words: Aphasia, Assessment, Standardized aphasia tests, Screening, Functional communication, Communication quality of life, Evidence-based practice, Assessment models, Telehealth

Assessment of aphasia is a cornerstone to successful treatment planning and to guiding an individual with aphasia, as well as family members and caregivers, to live with aphasia. Contemporary clinical practice demands assessment that addresses language abilities, functional communication, motor speech and praxis, and executive function processes such as attention and working memory, and considers the psychosocial consequences of aphasia. The assessment process can be constrained by factors such as linguistic or cultural barriers between a clinician and the individual with aphasia, the patient's medical status, or fee structure. The complex process that is contemporary aphasia assessment derives from a rich theoretical and empirical history, beginning well before the eighteenth century writings of respected clinical scholars such as Paul Broca and Carl Wernicke. In this chapter an overview of aphasia assessment is presented in three parts: an historical perspective of assessment efforts from case description to standardized tests, discussion of issues in contemporary clinical practice, and comments on emerging trends in assessment research and clinical practice.

An Historical Timeline of Aphasia Assessment Efforts

Aphasia Assessment Until 1935: The Age of Clinical Description

As noted in Chapters 1 and 2 of this book, a variety of aphasia classification schemes have been described since the dawn of time (Benton & Joynt, 1960; Kertesz, 1979, pp. 4–5). The interested reader can find several chronologies of the history of aphasia and its assessment tools and protocols dating back to ancient civilizations (e.g., Basso, 2003;

Benson & Ardila, 1996; Benton, 1981; Eling, 1994; Goodglass, 1993; Heilman, 2006; Roth & Heilman, 2002; Spreen & Risser, 2003; Tesak & Code, 2008). In the early reports of aphasia, assessment endeavors were idiosyncratic, incorporating a few common tasks (e.g., repetition), but consisting primarily of diagnostic activities specific to an individual examiner. Despite the idiosyncrasies many of these tasks were prescient to contemporary assessment. For example, Benton and Joynt (1960) described case reports that included assessment tasks such as reading, repetition, testing alternative forms of communication (e.g., a letter board), and analysis of spontaneous speech, all of which are familiar to contemporary clinical aphasiologists. Idiosyncratic assessment in the form of case presentation was conducted by individuals such as phrenologists, neurologists, anatomists, and philosophers who sought to describe symptoms of aphasia and to showcase their particular theory of aphasia. Some individuals even described individuals with aphasia as medical curiosities (Goodglass, 1993). Thus aphasia assessment was highly individualized and descriptive rather than clinically prescriptive. Nonetheless these case reports contributed to a rich literature that paved the way for the future development of a systematic assessment of aphasia.

Henry Head began the effort to systematize aphasia assessment into clinical protocols (Eisenson, 1973; Sarno & Höök, 1980). Head was a theorist opining on his observations and beliefs as a physician and an exacting scientist in his efforts to understand aphasia (Jacyna, 2008). He developed the Serial Tests of the language disturbance in aphasia including tasks examining naming, recognition, imitation, reading, and writing. The anticipated responses increased in complexity within each task and multiple repetitions of a response were required (Head, 1926). Although the Serial Tests did not stand the test of time, they were clinically useful in demonstrating a method of systematically describing a patient's language behavior (Worster-Drought & Allen, 1929) and laying a foundation for future work, particularly that of Weisenberg and McBride (1935). Somewhere between the publication of Head's Serial Tests and Weisenberg and McBride's work in 1935, the age of clinical description ended and the modern era of aphasia assessment emerged.

Aphasia Assessment from 1935 through the 1960s: The Age of the Standardized Test

Weisenberg and McBride published "Aphasia: A clinical and psychological study" in 1935 and it is generally considered to be the first aphasia test battery. Many of the tests in this battery had been used by other aphasiologists in case descriptions and in tests designed for children, however Weisenberg and McBride were credited as the first to produce a psychometrically sound protocol that was systematically administered to individuals with and without aphasia. The Weisenberg and McBride battery included tests of speaking, naming, repeating, reading, writing, arithmetic, language intelligence, imitation, and nonlanguage activities. Although this test battery was too lengthy for regular clinical use, it made an important contribution to aphasia assessment as a model for future standardized aphasia test batteries.

In the aftermath of World War II many standardized tests for aphasia appeared, in part to address the need to treat veterans returning from service with brain injuries and aphasia. Each test reflected the definition of aphasia espoused by its author(s); careful consideration of the test author's theoretical model of aphasia is an important precursor to understanding the test and incorporating it into clinical practice. One of the first of these aphasia batteries, Eisenson's (1954) Examining for Aphasia, was a clinically manageable assessment protocol based on the work of Weisenberg and McBride (1935). It included several subtests to evaluate language disturbance, such as those affecting auditory comprehension, automatic speech, repetition, naming, reading, writing, and arithmetic, as well as sections to evaluate agnosias and apraxias (see Chapter 1 for definitions). The report of results summarized performance as a predominantly receptive (evaluative) disturbance or a predominantly productive (expressive) disturbance and allowed for rating behavior in five severity levels. Examining for Aphasia-IV (Eisenson & LaPointe, 2008), the contemporary version of this test, maintains the subtest structure examining receptive and expressive language functions, and also includes assessment of cognitive and personality modifications associated with aphasia to address the impact on quality of life.

The period of time between 1955 and 1969 marked the publication of four important aphasia test batteries, the Minnesota Test for Differential Diagnosis of Aphasia (MTDDA, Schuell, 1965), the Language Modalities Test for Aphasia (LMTA, Wepman & Jones, 1961), the Porch Index of Communicative Ability (PICA, Porch, 1967), and the Neurosensory Centre Comprehensive Examination for Aphasia (NCCEA, Spreen & Benton, 1969). Of these the MTDDA and the

PICA have had considerable effect on aphasia assessment.

Schuell's colleagues, building on the work of Head, Weisenberg, McBride, and Wepman, and following exhaustive observation and testing of many individuals with aphasia, described their hypothesis of aphasia as a unitary language deficit crossing modalities such as speaking and writing, and with possible complications such as visual involvement (i.e., agnosia) or sensorimotor involvement (i.e., apraxia) (Jenkins, Jimenez-Pabon, Shaw, & Sefer, 1975, p. 103). They described the antecedents of what ultimately became the MTDDA as ". . . the first attempt to perform an explicit psychometric test of the hypothesis" (Jenkins et al., 1975, p. 104). The result was a test in five sections (auditory comprehension, visual and reading, speech and language, visuomotor and writing, and numerical relations) with an accompanying diagnostic scale and severity scale. MTDDA results placed an individual into one of seven aphasia diagnostic categories that Schuell and colleagues then compared to categories proposed by other theorists such as Wepman and Luria (1966) and to popular eclectic terminology. They suggested that unlike other systems that successfully classified individuals with aphasia into types less than half the time, more than 95% of individuals with aphasia could be classified using Schuell's system. They were careful to note, however, the differential bases of classification. For example, while Schuell (1965) based her classification on *patterns* of impairment, Wepman's classification system considered verbal output, Luria's system used cortical divisions and functional systems, and other systems were often based on classical localization (Jenkins et al., 1975, p. 155). These differences highlight the importance of understanding the theoretical foundation of a test before inserting it into clinical practice.

The MTDDA has been praised for its forward thinking, criticized for its length and lack of clinical utility, shortened for use as a screening test, and administered in pieces contrary to the theoretical hypothesis upon which it was created. While the MTDDA remains an important assessment tool, it is limited in contemporary aphasia testing and users are cautioned to consider the theoretical framework before adopting or adapting it.

In contrast to Schuell and colleagues (Schuell, 1965; Jenkins et al., 1975), Wepman and Jones (1961) constructed the LMTA based upon their perspective of aphasia as rooted in psycholinguistic processes and response modality, that is, the auditory and visual input and output channels involved in a language task. The LMTA relied upon scaled scoring of responses rather than pass/fail scoring, and included an examination of spontaneous speech and functional use of language, which were precursors to later scoring systems and tests of functional communication. Wepman and Jones (1961) proposed an aphasia classification system of five categories: semantic, syntactic, pragmatic or expressive, jargon, and global aphasia. The LMTA made a major contribution to aphasia assessment as a proponent of a differential scoring system for errors, permitting a detailed description of the nature of an individual's errors from a psycholinguistic perspective, thus providing fine-grained direction for treatment planning.

Porch published the PICA in 1967 (PICA-R, Porch, 2001) as a rigorously standardized test for aphasia. The PICA was designed to assess responsiveness in verbal, gestural, and graphic modalities across 18 subtests. A particularly important contribution of the PICA was the introduction of a multidimensional scoring system to capture response elements of accuracy, responsiveness, completeness, promptness, and efficiency. The scoring system used a 16-point scale, with additional sensitivity markings (i.e., for perseveration) to reflect response modality and quality. Porch (2001) suggested that the PICA was valuable for initial aphasia assessment and, given the sensitivity of multidimensional scoring, also useful in showing performance change over time. As important as the PICA has been in influencing assessment and treatment theory, research, and practice, it is not without criticism. In particular, the PICA has been criticized for the amount of clinician training required prior to use and for the complexity of the scoring system, which some see as cumbersome rather than informative (Odekar & Hallowell, 2005). Nonetheless, the PICA remains an important part of contemporary assessment in some arenas and Porch (2008) reported that test results provide valuable data in a systems analysis approach to treatment. The concept of multidimensional scoring has appeared in many aphasia assessment tools and the field is indebted to Porch for leading the way in this endeavor.

The NCCEA (Spreen & Benton, 1969; Spreen & Strauss, 1998) approached aphasia assessment from a neuropsychological perspective. Although it has not enjoyed the widespread popularity or longevity of the MTDDA or PICA, its contribution to aphasia assessment lies in the nature of its subtests, including verbal fluency. The subtests provided detailed descriptions of language performance that could be corrected for age and education, and compared to responses by neurologically intact adults as well as individuals with brain damage with or without accompanying aphasia. The NCCEA has 24 subtests, 20 that examine language comprehension and production, and reading and writing, and four devoted to visual and tactile functioning. Some subtests have two sets of stimuli to shorten administration time. If an individual makes no errors on the first set, administration of the subtest is discontinued. The NCCEA has been criticized for the low ceiling on many of its subtests, thus making it inappropriate for use for individuals with mild aphasia.

Taken together, the four comprehensive aphasia batteries, MTDDA, LMTA, PICA, and NCCEA, were instrumental in reframing aphasia assessment to a systematized, standardized endeavor to capture multiple aspects of an individual's language and communication skills. They induced order into a rigorous but individualized field of study.

Current Trends in Assessment: The Postmodern Era

Aphasia assessment since the 1970s unfolded in several directions, teasing apart symptoms and syndromes of aphasia. Six directions are notable: assessment to diagnose aphasia syndromes, screening tests for aphasia, tests of specific linguistic abilities, measures of functional communication, tests from cognitive neuropsychological and information-processing models of language, and measures of quality of life. Major influences on the development of assessment measures during this time were model-based perspectives, the emergence of neuroimaging techniques, the WHO ICF, sophistication in the fields of neuropsychology, neurolinguistics, and psycholinguistics, and psychosocial models of aphasia and rehabilitation.

Comprehensive Aphasia Batteries for Aphasia Syndrome Classification

Two tests stand alone for their enduring role in aphasia assessment and syndrome classification: the Boston Diagnostic Aphasia Examination, now in its third edition (BDAE-3, Goodglass, Kaplan, & Baressi, 2001; Goodglass & Kaplan, 1972), and the Western Aphasia Battery-Revised (WAB-R, Kertesz, 1977, 2007). Both tests have in common the goals of classifying an individual into a classical aphasia subtype and rating aphasia severity through response patterns on several subtests. The BDAE-3 contains five language-related sections and one praxis section

whereas the WAB-R has four language domain subtests and three performance domain subtests. The BDAE-3 arrives at a classification of aphasia through a z score profile and a five-point severity rating scale, whereas the WAB uses a quotient system (Aphasia Quotient, Performance Quotient, and Cortical Quotient). The resulting aphasia classification systems generally overlap, with one important difference. The WAB-R lists isolation aphasia in addition to seven other classical aphasia syndromes (global, Broca's, conduction, Wernicke's, anomic, transcortical motor, and transcortical sensory aphasia) and requires classification into one of the syndromes. In contrast, the BDAE-3 allows a mixed aphasia syndrome for those individuals who cannot be classified into the other seven classical aphasia syndromes, and does not include isolation aphasia. These tests share other attributes as well. Both are psychometrically rigorous, both have been updated and include a shortened version for bedside screening, both include an evaluation of spontaneous speech, both have been translated into languages other than English, and both have been criticized for the length of time required for administration, which is a drawback to their use in contemporary clinical settings. The BDAE and the WAB contributed to aphasia assessment by moving beyond clinical description and tests based solely on language behavior to relating brain and behavior through classic aphasia syndrome classification. Although the utility of the classic aphasia syndrome classification system in clinical practice has been criticized (Crary & Gonzalez-Rothi, 1989; Wertz, Deal, & Robinson, 1984), these aphasia syndromes remain a vital part of contemporary clinical parlance.

Many comprehensive aphasia assessment batteries have been published in the years following the appearance of the first versions of the BDAE and WAB; a selected list of contemporary comprehensive aphasia batteries appears in Table 3.1. Notably, several have been developed directly or indirectly through the efforts of speech–language pathologists working in the Veterans Administration (Freed, 2009). These test batteries differ on parameters such as scoring system and aphasia severity of the target population; however, they have in common the goal of producing a statement about the strengths and weaknesses of language comprehension and production abilities in persons with aphasia. Because of their length, comprehensive batteries often are not included in contemporary clinical assessment protocols, or are included only in part. For example, the NIH Stroke Scale (NIH Stroke Scale, 2003)

Table 3.1 Selected Comprehensive Aphasia Assessment Tests

Test	Author
Aachen Aphasia Test	Huber et al. (1984); Miller et al. (2000)
Aphasia Diagnostic Profiles	Helm-Estabrooks (1992)
Assessment for Living with Aphasia Toolkit	Aphasia Institute (2010)
Bilingual Aphasia Tests	Paradis & Libben (1987)
Boston Assessment of Severe Aphasia	Helm-Estabrooks et al. (1989)
Boston Diagnostic Aphasia Examination-3	Goodglass et al. (2001)
Assessment of Communicative Effectiveness in Severe Aphasia	Cunningham et al. (1995)
Examining for Aphasia—IV	Eisenson & LaPointe (2008)
Kentucky Aphasia Test	Marshall & Wright (2007)
Language Modalities Test of Aphasia	Wepman & Jones (1961)
Minnesota Test for Differential Diagnosis of Aphasia	Schuell (1965)
Multilingual Aphasia Examination	Benton et al. (1994)
Neurosensory Center Comprehensive Examination for Aphasia	Spreen & Strauss (1998)
Porch Index of Communicative Ability	Porch (1967, 2001)
The Comprehensive Aphasia Test	Swinburn, Porter, & Howard (2005)
Western Aphasia Battery (WAB-Revised)	Kertesz (2007)

includes the "cookie theft" picture description and three other stimulus sets from the BDAE as the language screening segment. Opinion on the propriety of administering portions of a comprehensive aphasia battery is mixed, suggesting that a clinician consider the purpose of an assessment session as well as the theoretical foundation and administration instructions for a comprehensive aphasia battery prior to selecting subtests for use. That said, some subtests have engendered independent clinical research endeavors. For example, Williams et al. (2010) created a corpus of spontaneous speech descriptions of the "cookie theft" picture from the BDAE, and Hux, Wallace, Evans, and Snell (2008) used a content analysis of responses to this picture description task to aid in the differential diagnosis of brain-injured individuals.

Screening Tests for Aphasia

Screening tests provide an efficient means of determining the presence or absence of aphasia in most individuals and suggesting the direction for additional assessment (Salter, Jutai, Foley, Hellings, & Teasel, 2006). They are most useful in the early poststroke stage when an individual is medically unable to tolerate a lengthy evaluation, in settings where length of stay is short, or when cost containment dictates rapid completion of aphasia testing. Aphasia screening is often performed through observation at bedside. An experienced clinician can be an astute observer and make maximal use of patient responses; however, even the best of clinicians must guard against using ". . . an unsystematic approach that may lead the examiner to miss important signs, and may invalidate comparisons of the patient's performance with that of other patients or with the same patient on subsequent visits" (Brookshire, 2003, p. 165).

Many comprehensive aphasia tests, such as the WAB-R (Kertesz, 2007), have shortened forms that can be used as screening tests. Tests of specific linguistic function may also have short forms or subtests that can be used as screening instruments; two examples are the Token Test (Spellacy & Spreen, 1969) and the Boston Naming Test (Del Toro et al., 2011; Fastenau, Denburg, & Mauer, 1998). Of importance when using the shortened form of a test is reliability and validity with respect to the full test (Koul, 2007), both of which have been established for the Token Test and Boston Naming Test.

Aphasia screening can also be accomplished by tests and scales specifically designed for this purpose, particularly for screening in an acute care setting. These instruments vary in design, intended outcome, and examiner training requirements. For example, the Frenchay Aphasia Screening Test (FAST, Enderby, Wood, & Wade, 2006; Enderby, Wood, Wade, & Hewer, 1987) can be administered in less than 10 minutes to individuals with acute or chronic aphasia by a clinician without training as a speech–language pathologist. The FAST claims to identify the presence or absence of aphasia, and direct further assessment, and is widely used in aphasia screening (Salter et al., 2006). In contrast, the ScreeLing (Doesborgh et al., 2003) requires expertise and training prior to administration as it examines three linguistic areas: semantics, phonology, and syntax. The administration time is 15 minutes and responses are scored correct/incorrect. Doesborgh et al. (2003) reported that the ScreeLing can detect the presence of aphasia from 2 to 11 days poststroke, and provides information on an individual's linguistic abilities in order to guide early treatment decisions. Table 3.2 lists selected aphasia screening tests.

Of perhaps less value to speech–language pathologists for aphasia screening, but potentially of value to other health professionals, are stroke screening scales, such as the NIH Stroke Scale (NIH, 2003),

Table 3.2 Selected Screening Tests for Aphasia

Test	Author
Acute Aphasia Screening Protocol (AASP)	Crary et al. (1989)
Aphasia Rapid Test	Azuar et al. (2013)
Aphasia Screening Test (3rd ed.)	Whurr (2011)
Bedside Evaluation Screening Test (2nd ed.)	Fitch-West & Sands (1998)
Frenchay Aphasia Screening Test (2nd ed.)	Enderby et al. (2006)
Language Screening Test	Flamand-Roze, Falissard et al. (2011)
Multimodal Communication Screening Task for Persons with Aphasia	Garrett & Lasker (2005)
Quick Assessment for Aphasia	Tanner & Culbertson (1999)
ScreeLing	Doesborgh et al. (2003)
Sheffield Screening Test for Acquired Language Disorders	Syder et al. (1993)
NIH Stroke Scale	http://www.ninds.nih.gov/doctors/NIHStrokeScale.pdf (revised 10/1/2003)

and language screening tools, such as the Language Screening Test (LAST, Flamand-Roze et al., 2011) and the Aphasia Rapid Test (ART, Azuar et al., 2013). These scales are designed to be used by medical professionals at bedside, in an acute medical or rehabilitation setting, and to monitor change in the early poststroke period. The NIH Stroke scale and other similar scales are broad in scope, cross several sensory, motor, and cognitive domains, and typically have only a few questions related to aphasia or language deficit. They are best used as an initial indicator of the likelihood of aphasia so as to inform medical professionals about a patient's communication potential during the first critical hours after a stroke. A list of scales intended for this use can be found at the Brain Attack Coalition (2014) or the Stroke Trials Registry (2014).

Language screening tests such as the LAST and ART are intended to rate language disorders and aphasia severity within 2–3 minutes in an emergency room or acute care setting. Both report validity, reliability, and sensitivity data as well as prediction of aphasia persistence at 3 months poststroke. Administration instructions and materials accompany reports of these tests and best practice would suggest that a speech–language pathologist be part of the team to select the preferred test.

Model-Based Assessment following Cognitive Neuropsychological Theory

Cognitive neuropsychology emerged in the 1970s as an extension of information-processing theory. Hillis and Newhart (2008) describe the field of cognitive neuropsychology as ". . . seek(ing) to understand normal human cognitive mechanisms through evidence from how cognitive mechanisms are modified by brain damage" (p. 595). Examples of cognitive neuropsychological models of language processing have been written for linguistic deficits such as naming, sentence production, and writing. In a review of historical and current information-processing models, Heilman (2006) wrote that despite a history of controversy, classic and current information-processing models can explain the major aphasic syndromes and many, but not all, of the symptoms associated with those syndromes (see Heilman, 2006, Figure 6).

Hillis and Newhart (2008) provide a clear description of the assumptions underlying cognitive neuropsychological assessment for aphasia, present examples of these models, note limitations of cognitive neuropsychological models of language and language disorders, particularly in relation to rehabilitation, and demonstrate the application of the models to the assessment and treatment of aphasia. In accounting for language behavior, cognitive neuropsychological models share three broad principles: individual behavior is important, error patterns are informative, and performance is interpreted in terms of the ability to process information rather than brain lesion (Whitworth, Webster, & Howard, 2005).

The importance of individual performance patterns in model-based assessment derived from cognitive neuropsychological theory suggests that a primary source of information about a person's language ability must be individual test results as they combine to produce a performance pattern. By assessing focused, specific task responses (e.g., naming high-frequency pictures) in both a pre-planned and error-driven manner, a clinician can create a statement of overall language functioning as well as identify specific strengths and weaknesses. Approaching assessment in this manner requires a clinician to select in advance tests of specific linguistic function, including subtests of comprehensive aphasia batteries, which are most likely to reveal language abilities and deficits. The assessment must also be flexible to accommodate unanticipated emerging error patterns. Error patterns and observations will lead to hypothesis formation about additional language abilities and require that additional tests of specific linguistic function be added to the assessment agenda. Examples of tests of specific linguistic function derived from a cognitive neuropsychological model are the Psycholinguistic Assessments of Language Processing in Aphasia (PALPA, Kay, Lesser, & Coltheart, 1992) and the ADA Comprehension Battery (Franklin, Turner, & Ellis, 1992). The PALPA contains 60 subtests in the areas of phonology, semantics, morphology, and syntax, and uses stimulus items that are often repeated across subtests. The ADA Comprehension Battery is similar to the PALPA in that subtests are selected for administration depending upon the symptom attributes of the individual with aphasia. Additional examples of the application of cognitive neuropsychological models to aphasia assessment can be found in Beeson and Henry (2008), Kerr (1995), Mitchum and Berndt (2008), and Raymer and Rothi (2008).

Tests of Specific Linguistic Function

Tests of specific language function serve multiple purposes in assessment: (1) supplementing a comprehensive aphasia battery to allow greater depth in evaluating a specific language behavior or response modality, (2) examining behavior in an individual who is likely to score at ceiling or floor on a comprehensive aphasia battery, (3) allowing the presentation of a greater range of stimulus items in an area than is typically included in a comprehensive aphasia battery, and (4) examining a coincident communication behavior, such as speech praxis. Normative data for some tests of specific linguistic functions are available in administration manuals or research literature (e.g., Walker & Schwartz, 2012; Philadelphia Naming Test: Short Form) while others are offered as alternatives or adjuncts to existing tests and report current participant data (e.g., Danek, Gade, Lunardelli, & Rumiati, 2013: Tomato and Tuna test). Selected tests of specific language functions appear in Table 3.3 and are grouped according to purpose: auditory comprehension, naming, syntax, reading comprehension, writing, and gesture.

Determining which tests of specific linguistic function to administer should be influenced by clinical setting and individual need as well as by the test length, training requirements for the examiner, and response abilities of the examinee. For example, the Revised Token Test (McNeill & Prescott, 1978) examines auditory comprehension deficits in individuals with mild to moderate aphasia and provides detailed information about the person's comprehension of simple and complex sentences. A drawback to its use in clinical practice is that it is lengthy and requires the examiner to use a complex multidimensional scoring system. In contrast, the Controlled Oral Word Association Task (COWAT, Benton, Hamsher, Rey, & Sivan, 1994), a word fluency test, requires little examiner preparation and has been shown to have value in the differential diagnosis of persons with neurogenic communication disorders. Scoring methods for the COWAT are straightforward and include the sum of productions consistent with target word class (i.e., action words or animals or letter categories such as FAS) and cluster and switching (e.g., the number of consecutive thematically related words that are produced before switching themes).

Critical to the successful use of data from a test of specific linguistic function or a comprehensive aphasia test is mindfulness of the psychometric properties of the test, including the theoretical foundation, reliability, validity, and standardization sample. A test should be carefully matched to the assessment needs of an individual with possible aphasia in order to achieve maximum benefit.

Table 3.3 Selected Tests of Specific Language Function

Test	Author
Auditory Comprehension	
Auditory Comprehension Test for Sentences	Shewan (1979)
ADA Comprehension Battery	Franklin et al. (1992)
Discourse Comprehension Test	Brookshire & Nicholas (1997)
Kissing and Dancing Test	Bak & Hodges (2003)
Peabody Picture Vocabulary Test-4	Dunn & Dunn (2007)
Pyramids and Palm Trees	Howard & Patterson (1992)
Revised Token Test	McNeil & Prescott (1978)
Test for Reception of Grammar—2nd Version	Bishop (2003)
Test of Adolescent and Adult Language (TOAL-4)	Hammill et al. (2007)
Psycholinguistic Assessments of Language Processes in Aphasia (also appropriate for other specific linguistic assessment)	Kay et al. (1992)
Tomato and Tuna Test	Danek et al. (2013)
Naming	
Action Naming Test	Obler & Albert (2009)
An Object and Action Naming Test	Druks & Masterson (2000)
Boston Naming Test	Kaplan et al. (2001)
Comprehensive Receptive and Expressive Vocabulary Test-Adult—2nd Version	Wallace & Hammill (2002)
Controlled Oral Word Association Test	Benton et al. (1994); Ruff et al. (1996)
Florida Semantics Battery	Raymer et al. (1990)
Philadelphia Naming Test	Roach et al. (1996)
Philadelphia Naming Test: Short Form (PNT30)	Walker & Schwartz (2012)
Test of Adolescent/Adult Word-Finding	German (1989)
The Word Test-2: Adolescent	Bowers et al. (2005)
Syntax	
Shewan Spontaneous Language Analysis	Shewan (1988)
Test of Adolescent and Adult Language (TOAL-4)	Hamill et al. (2007)
The Reporter's Test	DeRenzi & Ferrari (1978)
The SOAP (A Test of Syntactic Complexity)	Love & Oster (2002)
Reading Comprehension	
Gray Oral Reading Tests—4	Wiederholt & Bryant (2001)
Johns Hopkins University Dyslexia Battery	Goodman & Caramazza (1986b)

(*continued*)

Table 3.3 Continued

Test	Author
North American Adult Reading Test	Blair & Spreen (1989)
Reading Comprehension Battery for Aphasia-2	LaPointe & Horner (1998)
Kaufman Functional Academic Skills Test (K-FAST)	Kaufman & Kaufman (1994)
Test of Reading Comprehension-3	Brown et al. (1995)
Wechsler Test of Adult Reading	Wechsler (2001)
Writing	
Johns Hopkins University Dysgraphia Battery	Goodman & Caramazza (1986a)
Test of Adolescent and Adult Language (TOAL-4)	Hamill et al. (2007)
Written Language Assessment	Grill & Kirwin (1990)
Gesture	
Florida Apraxia Screening Test—Revised (FAST-R)	Rothi et al. (1997)
Florida Action Recall Test (FLART)	Schwartz et al. (1996)
Test of Apraxia	van Heutgen et al. (1999)
Test of Oral and Limb Apraxia	Helm-Estabrooks (1991)

Measures of Functional Communication

Sarno, in the late 1960s, challenged healthcare professionals to consider the impact of aphasia on the ability of persons to express themselves and also to consider the needs and capacities of family members and caregivers in their communication with their family member with aphasia. Sarno captured her ideas in the Functional Communication Profile (FCP, Sarno, 1969), which contains 45 common communication behaviors, each rated on a nine-point scale. The FCP overall score, although less frequently utilized in contemporary aphasiology, is said to be a measure of an individual's ability to effectively communicate in daily life.

Somewhat later, the Communication Activities of Daily Living (CADL, Holland, 1980) emerged from the foundation of speech act theory (Searle, 1969). The CADL and subsequently the CADL-2 (Holland, Frattali, & Fromm, 1999) were meant to be administered in an informal manner in a relaxed atmosphere of interaction between a person with aphasia and a clinician. The basis for selecting test items was to elicit everyday, functional communication behaviors in structured role-playing situations and encourage the use of any response modality. Responses are scored on a three-point scale and the overall sum score allows comparison of an individual's performance with that of the standardization sample of persons with neurogenic communication disorders. The CADL-2 has a rigorous and psychometrically sound assessment framework that can be efficiently used in a clinical setting. However, it has been criticized for attempting to standardize communication behavior that can best be observed only in a real-life context. The authors acknowledge that the CADL-2 results are a complement to and not a substitution for observation of interaction in context, and despite the constraint of administration within a clinical setting, the CADL-2 succeeds in its intent of providing an estimate of an individual's functional communication ability.

The publication of the CADL (Holland, 1980) was coincident with the release of the World Health Organization International Classification of Impairments, Disabilities, and Handicaps (ICIDH, WHO, 1980), which reframed thinking about how healthcare providers should view the health states of individuals. The ICIDH focused thinking on the consequences of a disease to an individual's daily life and activities as well as on disease state by identifying both activity and participation assessment measures and impairment measures. Diagnostic tests, whether comprehensive aphasia batteries or tests of specific linguistic function, describe the nature and severity of the aphasia that is, language impairment; however, the consequences of living with aphasia have been given short shrift (Spreen & Risser, 2003). Measures that examine functional communication and interaction outside the bounds of a test battery close this gap and complete the picture of aphasia and its effect on an individual and family.

Table 3.4 contains a list of selected measures of pragmatic abilities and functional communication. Some of these measures are structured tests examining a specific behavior set. For example, the Assessment of Language-Related Functional Activities (Baines, Heeringa, & Martin, 1999) examines an individual's ability to complete functional activities such as check writing despite the presence of communication impairment. Other measures are surveys or questionnaires, such as the Communication Inventory for Individuals with Complex Communication Needs and Their Partners (Blackstone & Berg, 2003). This inventory is based on social network theory and assesses the communication abilities and needs of an individual with communication impairment when interacting with partners who vary in familiarity, from family members (highly familiar) to paid workers and unfamiliar people. The Scenario Test (van der Meulen, van de Sandt-Koenderman, Duivenvoorden, & Ribbers, 2010) also includes communication partners in the assessment process. It is designed to assess the communication success of individuals with severe aphasia and their communication partners, focusing on supported communication. Another frequently used measure is the Functional Assessment of Communication Skills for Adults (ASHA-FACS, Frattali, Thompson, Holland, Wohl, & Ferketic, 1995), which contains 43 items in four domains and is designed to measure basic communication skills thought to be common to most adults. Each item is rated on a seven-point scale and each domain is rated on a scale for adequacy, appropriateness, promptness, and communication sharing.

Measures of Quality of Life

Quality of life (QOL), as a measurable concept, is both a broad scope term and an individualized experience. Definitions of QOL vary and encompass domains such as general health, communication satisfaction, sexual function, perceived self-efficacy, cultural and intellectual environment, and physical environment. The World Health Organization quality of life instruments, the WHOQOL-100

and WHOQOL-BREF (WHOQOL, 2001b), were developed to encourage individuals to express their opinions about their quality of life within the context of the culture and value systems in which they live and in relation to their goals, expectations, standards, and concerns, thus placing importance on the perceptions and beliefs of the individual respondent. The WHOQOL-100, with 100 items, and the shorter WHO-BREF, with 26 items, both contain six domains: physical health, psychological, level of independence, social relationships, environment, and spirituality/religion/personal beliefs. The WHOQOL instruments were developed cross-culturally and are appropriate for use in many settings and with individuals of varying ages and disorders. One drawback to assessing communicative quality of life, however, is that the WHOQOL items make it possible to infer communicative ability or satisfaction but do not directly measure it. For example, WHOQOL-BREF item 20 asks "How satisfied are you with your personal relationships?" The role that communication deficit plays in quality of life reports such as in the response to WHOQOL-BREF item 20 is not transparent, thus making judgment of communication quality of life difficult.

Three QOL instruments designed specifically for stroke survivors narrow this gap by including items that measure communication, the Burden of Stroke Scale (BOSS, Doyle, 2002; Doyle, McNeil, Hula, & Mikolic, 2003), the Stroke Impact Scale (SIS-2, 2014, Duncan et al., 1999), and the Stroke and Aphasia Quality of Life Scale (SAQOL, SAQOL-39, Cruice, Worrall, Hickson, & Murison, 2003; Hilari, Byng, Lamping, & Smith, 2003). These scales measure patient-reported difficulty in generalized domains such as mobility and physical health, but importantly also include communication domains. The BOSS in particular has two scales specific to communication, the communication difficulty scale (CD) and the communication-associated distress (CAD) scale.

Although not designed specifically for individuals with aphasia, the Quality of Communication Life Scale (ASHA QCL, Paul et al., 2005) measures the impact a communication disorder has on an adult's quality of life in psychosocial, educational, and vocational areas. Scales such as those noted above respect the principles of the WHO ICF (World Health Organization, 2001a) in examining the consequences of a deficit, in this case a communication deficit, on activities and participation in daily life. One or more of these scales should be

Table 3.4 Selected Measures of Pragmatic Abilities and Functional Communication

Measure	Author
Structured Tests	
Assessment of Language-Related Functional Abilities	Baines et al. (1999)
Communication Activities of Daily Living-2	Holland et al. (1999)
Functional Communication Therapy Planner	Worrall (1999)
The Amsterdam-Nijmegan Everyday Language Test	Blomert et al. (1994)
The "dice" game	McDonald & Pearce (1995)
Rating Scales and Inventories	
A Questionnaire for Surveying Personal and Communicative Style	Swindell et al. (1982)
Functional Assessment of Communication Skills for Adults (ASHA FACS)	Frattali et al. (1995)
Assessment Protocol of Pragmatic-Linguistic Skills	Gerber & Gurland (1989)
Communication Competence Rating Scale	Babbitt & Cherney (2010)
Communicative Competence Evaluation Instrument	Houghton et al. (1982)
Communicative Effectiveness Index	Lomas et al. (1989)
Communication Profile	Gurland et al. (1982)
Communicative Profiling System	Simmons-Mackie & Damico (1996)
Everyday Communicative Needs Assessment	Worrall (1992)
Functional Communication Profile	Sarno (1969)
Functional Outcome Questionnaire for Aphasia	Glueckauf et al. (2003)
Inpatient Functional Communication Interview	O'Halloran et al. (2004)
LaTrobe Communication Questionnaire	Douglas et al. (2000)
Pragmatic Protocol	Prutting & Kirchner (1987)
Profile of Communicative Appropriateness	Penn (1988)
Revised Edinburgh Functional Communication Profile	Wirz et al. (1990)
Social Networks: A Communication Inventory for Individuals with Complex Communication Needs and Their Communication Partners	Blackstone & Berg (2003)
The Communication Profile: A Functional Skills Survey	Payne (1994)
The Scenario Test	van der Meulen et al. (2010)

included in any assessment activity. However, as Eadie et al. (2006) noted in a study comparing six patient self-report instruments commonly used in speech–language pathology, none is solely dedicated to measuring communication participation, which may hinder a clinician's ability to identify outcome measures directly related to the ICF framework.

Quality of life concerns the individual with aphasia and also the family members or caregivers (Bond, Ware, & Young, 2011). Too often communication quality of life assessment efforts end with an assessment of the individual with aphasia and do not consider the quality of communication life for the family of a person with aphasia or education for families about aphasia and what to expect as they learn to live with aphasia (Avent et al., 2005). The Communicative Effectiveness Index (CETI, Lomas et al., 1989) and the LaTrobe Communication Questionnaire (Douglas, O'Flaherty, & Snow, 2000) are communication instruments that have family members or others as the focus of assessment and also are appropriate for use with individuals with aphasia. The CETI presents 16 communication situations and respondents are asked to use a 100-mm line to mark their perception of the current communication ability of the individual with aphasia as compared to the person's ability prior to the onset of aphasia. The LaTrobe Communication Questionnaire is a 30-item instrument that uses a four-point interval response scale for each item. Douglas et al. (2000) confirmed the utility of the LaTrobe Communication Questionnaire in reporting results of a study comparing responses by individuals with a communication disorder and individuals with whom they have close personal relationships. The perceptions of the two groups differed, emphasizing the importance of assessing quality of communication life with aphasia from multiple perspectives. A cautionary note is in order to advise clinicians to distinguish between a QOL assessment by the individual with aphasia, a proxy assessment by a caregiver about the QOL of the individual with aphasia, and a QOL assessment by a caregiver about himself or herself (Hilari, Owen, & Farrelly, 2007). Each result is important, but consistency may be observed and should be addressed.

Contemporary Aphasia Assessment

Theories and models of assessment guide assessment practice, yet the clinical work is influenced by factors such as practice setting, or patient status. Contemporary assessment practice can vary from the ideal and although experience teaches clinicians methods of managing the difference between theory and practice, experience can also lead to assessment activities that are not supported by evidence. Several considerations in managing the potential mismatch are presented below.

Purpose of Aphasia Assessment

Maintaining a balance between the desire to complete a thorough, psychometrically sound assessment using a comprehensive aphasia battery, relevant tests of specific linguistic function, pragmatic evaluation of functional communication, and measures of quality of life, and the real-life clinical need to complete the assessment in a timely and

cost-efficient manner is often not an easy task (Ellis, Lindrooth, & Horner, 2014; Boysen & Wertz, 1996). Determining the purpose of an assessment and understanding the mitigating factors that seek to constrain the assessment will help address this balance.

Spreen and Risser (2003) identified six purposes of assessment, considering the time course of an individual's aphasia and the type of information sought: (1) a screening, (2) a thorough diagnostic assessment of language and cognitive behavior to determine strengths and weaknesses, (3) a descriptive evaluation using a variety of procedures to assist in treatment and counseling decisions, (4) a progress evaluation to document change over time, (5) an assessment of functional communication, and (6) an evaluation of related disorders such as motor speech disorders. An assessment may include more than one purpose, thus requiring clinicians to be familiar with an array of tests, protocols, and procedures, and to carefully select those that will provide the desired measurement information within the allotted assessment time.

The importance of recognizing multiple factors in assessment decisions is nicely illustrated by Murray and Clark (2006) who proposed both general and specific frameworks for assessment. The general framework requires consideration of factors such as the setting in which the evaluation occurs (i.e., acute care setting or outpatient setting), the WHO ICF (2001) levels of functioning (e.g., impairment, activity/participation), lesion location and presenting symptoms, an individual's premorbid abilities, input from team members in related disciplines (i.e., audiology, neuropsychology, or physiatry; for a full listing see Murray & Clark, 2006, Table 4-2, p. 89), and caregiver perceptions. Within the general framework, Murray and Clark (2006) identify several specific frameworks for focused assessment in areas such as linguistic disorders, cognitive disorders, and quality of life.

The aphasia assessment process is viewed within the parameters of the scientific method by Patterson and Chapey (2008), who identified 11 specific assessment goals in three broad areas: etiologic goals; cognitive, linguistic, pragmatic, or life goals; and treatment goals (Patterson & Chapey, 2008, Table 4-1, p. 67). The general goal of determining the presence and severity of aphasia is subserved by the specific goals of completing a differential diagnosis of neurogenic communication disorders and identifying complicating conditions, evaluating cognitive functions, comprehension and production of language, and pragmatic abilities, and assessing the quality of life for both the individual with aphasia and his or her family members. Evidence from the assessment guides a decision about an individual's candidacy for and the direction of intervention.

The three models of aphasia assessment described above exemplify the variety of theoretical and practical approaches. Elements of historical approaches can be seen in these models, and individual variation according to practice setting is expected. Of importance, however, is allowing the theoretical model of aphasia and the purpose of aphasia assessment to guide decision making within practice parameters rather than the reverse.

Factors Influencing Assessment Decisions and Practice Parameters

To arrive at a decision about the presence of aphasia and to plan intervention, a clinician must have confidence in the data gathered through the assessment process. Although the tests and procedures listed in Tables 3.1–3.4 are psychometrically sound, their utility can be compromised by any one of several factors internal or external to the individual with aphasia and practice setting. Internal factors are those manifested by the individual with aphasia and may appear as physical status or psychosocial status variables. Physical status variables are often beyond an individual's control, for example, asthma. Psychosocial factors may or may not be within an individual's control. Examples of these factors are substance abuse, motivation, and perceived self-efficacy. Perceived self-efficacy is an individual's beliefs about his or her ability to produce effects and influence life events. It has been linked to general life achievement and perception of a positive quality of life (Bandura, 1977) and also to successful aphasia rehabilitation (Dunn, 2004). Information about internal variables is gathered largely through a review of medical and psychosocial history and through interviews with the person with aphasia and family members, co-workers, or friends. An individual with aphasia or a clinician may, or may not, have the power or resources to alter internal factors, but knowledge of the presence and extent of these factors will influence assessment decisions and ultimately the quality and interpretation of assessment data.

External factors also may or may not be under an individual's or clinician's sphere of influence. For example, external factors such as assessment setting or clinical administrative and fee structure are not within the ability of a clinician to control.

Nonetheless mindfulness of these factors and selecting assessment instruments accordingly to meet the assessment purpose will ensure results that are both representative of an individual's aphasia and in which a clinician has confidence. Examples of external factors that can be changed with little effort are environmental factors such as the temperature or lighting in a room. Other external factors, such as family structure and support, may not be altered but should be considered. Knowledge about the family structure surrounding an individual with aphasia is typically obtained through a case history or interview and may not have an effect on decisions prior to an assessment session, but can influence recommendations to aid a family in living with aphasia and in accessing community resources such as transportation systems. An example of an external factor that can easily be addressed during assessment is a family's knowledge about aphasia. Avent et al. (2005) reported that although families may obtain information about aphasia from healthcare providers, it is often insufficient or ill-timed for them to fully understand the nature of aphasia, the relevance of the information to their lives, or the time course of aphasia rehabilitation. Thus family members approach an assessment ill-equipped to be full partners in the process. Clinicians will likely not be aware of the extent of a family's knowledge about aphasia and so planning education as part of the assessment can influence the outcome by more fully engaging them.

Matching Assessment and Practice Settings

Aphasia assessment is typically viewed as an event that occurs within a discrete time frame and that carries a unique billing code or cost structure. Time frames vary according to the assessment setting, for example, they are shorter in an acute care setting than in an outpatient setting. The assessment protocol that provides most value is planned to meet two goals: (1) collect information in multiple areas following the WHO ICF (2001) or other theoretical model of assessment in order to provide a representative view of an individual's communicative status; and (2) fit within the allotted time frame. For example, in the acute care setting a short aphasia screening test can be used to indicate the possible presence of aphasia and lead to the recommendation for additional testing at a later time. Of primary importance in this setting is determining a patient's ability to communicate to healthcare providers and family members in the immediate environment to participate in healthcare decisions or to indicate health status such as pain. These observations may lead to a recommendation for and the format of a simple augmentative and alternative communication system that requires little user training and that can be used by many different people. Finally, discussion with family members and caregivers will begin the education process of living with aphasia.

Assessment completed in outpatient settings is typically allotted more time than in acute settings; however, it still requires planning to meet the two goals noted above. Three assessment models are useful in this setting. One is syndrome based and requires administration of a comprehensive test for aphasia, such as the WAB-R (Kertesz, 2007) or BDAE-3 (Goodglass et al., 2001), as well as tests of specific linguistic function. The second model represents a psychosocial view of aphasia, for example, Aphasia-Framework for Outcome Assessment (A-FROM; Kagan et al., 2008). Following the A-FROM model, a clinician creates an assessment protocol using outcome measures to examine abilities in four domains that contribute to an individual's being able to successfully live with aphasia: (1) communication and language environment; (2) participation in life situations; (3) personal identity, attitude, and feelings; and (4) language and related impairments. A-FROM is an ongoing, dynamic assessment of relevant outcome measures to demonstrate an individual's behavior change and success in learning to live with aphasia. Finally, a clinician might follow a cognitive neuropsychological model of aphasia assessment and include measures of information-processing ability (Kerr, 1995).

Assessing Spontaneous and Connected Speech

Connected speech in conversation and spontaneous speaking is for most people an important contribution to human communication; thus including a statement about an individual's ability to convey information verbally should be part of the assessment report. A sample of connected speech can be obtained through observation during general conversation and in responses to test items. An informal rating scale provides an overall judgment of success at conveying a message to a listener, including measures of content and intelligibility. For example, a clinician might use a three-point listener perceptual representation where 2 = message conveyed in an intelligible manner to all listeners/conversational partners; 1 = message conveyed but requires significant contextual support and conversational partner effort to understand; and 0 = message not

understood despite significant effort by conversational partner.

The success of conveying a message in connected speech or conversation can also be measured by analyzing discourse elements of connected speech (i.e., Cherney, Coelho, & Shadden, 1998) or using measures of content such as correct information units (CIUs, Brookshire & Nicholas, 1993) or efficiency (Yorkston & Beukelman, 1980). Bearing in mind that multiple discourse elements can be analyzed in a sample of connected speech, it is incumbent upon the clinician to carefully select those elements that match the purpose of the assessment. Cherney et al. (1998) presented a detailed description of methods to analyze elements such as cohesion, coherence, and syntactic structure. It is likely that analysis of more than one or two elements will be prohibitive in most assessment sessions given the time constraints; however, selecting at least one discourse element to assess initially and over time to document change is an important part of a dynamic assessment protocol. Brookshire and Nicholas (1993) created a standardized, rule-based system titled Correct Information Unit analysis, or CIUs, to evaluate two elements of connected speech production: informativeness and efficiency. A series of rules is applied to a sample of connected speech to identify those elements that contain information and to calculate a measure of efficiency in conveying that information. CIU analysis is a useful but time-intensive method of analysis that does not lend itself to online analysis of connected speech. Yorkston and Beukelman (1980) earlier proposed a method of content and efficiency analysis to mark connected speech characteristics of individuals with moderate aphasia as they recovered to mild aphasia. Three measures were calculated from a sample of connected speech: content units (amount of information conveyed), speaking rate (syllables per minute), and rate at which information was conveyed (content units per minute). Time constraints also limit the utility of this method; however, the rule system for determining content units is less complex than that of a CIU analysis.

Assessment of Related Abilities

Several other areas of assessment contribute to the overall diagnostic picture of a person with aphasia and assist in refining treatment goals and procedures. Tests of other cognitive functions are becoming increasingly important in aphasia assessment as individuals with aphasia may have cognitive deficits that adversely affect language and communication abilities during assessment (Hinckley & Nash, 2007). Cognitive systems that might be included in such an assessment include tests of memory, attention (i.e., divided and sustained), and executive functioning. A drawback to the use of many tests of such cognitive abilities is their heavy reliance on language.

Assessment of emotional state may be included to aid in the understanding of attributes such as an individual's coping ability or depressive state. Although several measures of depression exist (Salter, Bhogal, Foley, Jutai, & Teasell, 2007), many (e.g., the Geriatric Depression Scale, Yesavage et al., 1983) are inappropriate for use in individuals with aphasia because of the linguistic requirements of the scales. Aphasia-friendly depression scales such as the Visual Analog Mood Scales (Stern, Arruda, Hooper, Wolfner, & Morey, 1997) were created to surmount this issue.

Finally, a contemporary assessment protocol might include other tools to evaluate behavior that can affect performance on linguistic or aphasia tests, such as awareness of the language deficits. For example, to assess anosognosia for aphasia the Visual-Analogue Test for Assessing Anosognosia for Language Impairment (Cocchini, Gregg, Beschin, Dean, & Della Sala, 2010) might be used. Specific tests selected will be determined on a case-by-case basis.

Emerging Trends in Aphasia Assessment

In recent years several trends have emerged in aphasia assessment that hold promise for increasing effectiveness and efficiency. Among them are evidence-based practice, predicting treatment candidacy, incorporating psychosocial approaches to assessment, and assessment and treatment via telehealth.

Evidence-Based Practice

Evidence-based practice encourages clinicians to critically examine the evidence supporting diagnostic and treatment decisions (Klee, 2008). Quality scales are available to review the evidence about assessment and treatment protocols in order to make informed decisions about using them in clinical practice. One scale for reviewing the evidence for the diagnostic accuracy of a screening, diagnostic, or differential diagnostic measure is CADE: Critical Appraisal of Diagnostic Evidence (Dollaghan, 2007). CADE is a 13-point checklist that allows

the user to make a judgment about the quality of evidence relating to the accuracy of a diagnostic instrument in order to compare the test under evaluation to the current gold standard in that area. As a result, the user can make a clinical decision to support retaining the test in the clinical protocol or selecting another test. An important component of CADE is the clinical foreground question that focuses inquiry on the population, outcome, index measure, and reference standard.

Klee (2008) emphasized the importance of a systematic critical appraisal of assessment instruments, citing the roles of both test authors and end users as critical to the process. Among the scales of critical appraisal noted were CADE (Dollaghan, 2007), QUADAS (Quality Assessment Tool for Diagnostic Accuracy; Whiting et al., 2006), and STARD (STAndards for the Reporting of Diagnostic accuracy studies; Bossuyt et al., 2003; STARD, 2008). Whereas CADE and QUADAS have similar broad purposes, CADE was created for use with diagnostic tests of communicative disorders and QUADAS for evaluation of tests across medical fields; thus some QUADAS items may be of less value when examining the evidence for an aphasia test.

The general use of tools for critical appraisal of evidence of diagnostic accuracy is gaining ground in clinical settings but is not yet as commonplace as systematic reviews of treatment evidence. Klee (2008) illustrated the process by applying QUADAS to a published screening study in order to determine if ". . . the methodological quality was sufficiently high to warrant examining the study outcomes" (p. 40).

In contrast, STARD is a 25-point checklist designed for use by test authors in reporting their work. "The aim of the STARD initiative is to improve the accuracy and completeness of reporting of studies of diagnostic accuracy, to allow readers to assess the potential for bias in the study (internal validity) and to evaluate its generalisability (external validity)" (STARD, 2008). The STARD procedure has been adopted by several scholarly journals as a way to increase the use of evidence-based practice by holding authors to high standards of evidence in presenting information about diagnostic tools. Annually the National Center for Evidence-Based Practice of the American Speech-Language-Hearing Association (N-CEP; http://www.asha.org/members/ebp/EBSRs.htm) engages in systematic reviews of the evidence for assessment instruments and treatment protocols. Interested readers are referred to N-CEP for systematic reviews of assessment instruments and the procedure for requesting a systematic review of a diagnostic test or procedure.

Implementation science has emerged as a method for systematically examining the relationship between the evidence in a discipline and how it appears in performance (Sales, Smith, Curran, & Kochevar, 2006). A framework for implementation science suggests using the evidence and gaps in the evidence to pose questions that explore the feasibility of what to implement (e.g., which tests or protocols), what benefits or burdens might accrue to patients, and how closely the implementation matches the ideal. Implementation science is a natural extension of evidence-based practice and likely will inform future practice decisions.

Determining Candidacy for Treatment and Predicting Outcome

Predicting what the outcomes will be for a course of intervention for persons with aphasia is one of the first questions asked by patients and their family members, and represents an inexact clinical art at best. Multiple internal and external factors influence the success of assessment and treatment, as noted earlier, and honing prognostic skills is an ongoing endeavor. Many factors such as age, education, and gender that were previously thought to have prognostic value for recovery from aphasia have been shown to be unreliable. Other factors are emerging as promising.

Current research in prognosis is proceeding in three areas: neural imaging and neural plasticity studies, cognitive abilities, and results of language testing. Hillis (2007) included a discussion of neuroimaging studies in a review of progress in aphasia diagnosis and treatment over the past quarter century, citing their contribution to understanding the neural organization of language, which may assist in predicting recovery from aphasia. Fridriksson, Baker, and Richardson (2010) reviewed current research in neuroimaging and aphasia and examined brain activation associated with language behaviors. In considering picture naming, they suggested a relationship between cortical activation and severity of anomia (Fridriksson, Bonilha, Baker, Moser, & Rorden, 2010). They acknowledge that although neuroimaging studies have opened windows into understanding the relationship between brain and language behavior and in particular early recovery from stroke, the utility of these relationships to predict recovery from aphasia and to guide prescription of treatment type and dosage for an individual is an ongoing effort in its early stages.

The relationship of language and cognition is complex. Numerous studies have investigated cognitive abilities such as attention, memory, and executive functioning in persons with aphasia, but as yet, clear factors for predicting recovery and determining the best match of treatment and aphasia symptom have not emerged. Purdy (2002) reported that executive functioning abilities can be differentially impaired in individuals with aphasia and that understanding both cognitive and linguistic deficits will aid in predicting recovery and planning an intervention. Poor executive functioning abilities have been linked to poor functional recovery after stroke (Leśniak, Bak, Czepiel, Seniów, & Członkowska, 2008) and poor functional communication ability (Fridriksson, Nettles, Davis, Morrow, & Montgomery, 2006). Keil and Kasniak (2002) suggested that tests of executive functioning may aid in determining the presence of cognitive functioning in persons with aphasia; however, because of the heavy linguistic requirement they are often not appropriate for individuals with language disorders.

Finally, research has been aimed at predicting recovery from aphasia using language assessment results. Gialanella and colleagues (Gialanella, 2011; Gialanella, Bertolinelli, Lissi, & Promet, 2011) examined aphasia as both a predicting factor of outcome following stroke and as the object of prediction of outcome. They reported that the presence of aphasia is the most important predictor of social outcome in persons with aphasia, and that scores on the Aachen Aphasia Test (Huber, Poeck, & Willmes, 1984) were an important predictor of functional outcome. Difficulty in predicting aphasia outcome from assessment results was confirmed by Lazar, Speizer, Festa, Krakauer, and Marshall (2008) who speculated that individual variability had a powerful influence on recovery.

Psychosocial Models of Assessment

Two psychosocial models of aphasia have had a significant impact on aphasia assessment: Life-Participation Approach to Aphasia (LPAA, Chapey et al., 2008) and A-FROM (Kagan et al., 2008). LPAA reflects a philosophical shift in thinking about aphasia assessment and treatment that places persons with aphasia and individuals who touch their lives at the center of the model. It is a broad-based approach to management of aphasia that focuses on the consequences of aphasia. The authors note that assessment guided by LPAA would include ". . . determining relevant life participation needs and discovering competencies of clients" (Chapey et al., 2008, p. 280). A-FROM (Kagan et al., 2008) offers a model of assessment that is outcome based, reflecting WHO ICF (2001) principles. Two drivers for creation of this assessment approach are the recognition of the importance of advocacy for persons with aphasia and an assessment of functional communication and quality of communication life in a rigorous and scientifically sound manner. As these models, particularly the A-FROM, radiate throughout clinical practice they will influence not only test selection but also the breadth of assessment to include people and events beyond the individual with aphasia.

Psychosocial models of assessment also include recognition of the role and influence of family members and caregivers. The Communicative Effectiveness Index (CETI, Lomas et al., 1989) is an early example of an organized assessment of caregiver perceptions of the communicative abilities of a family member with aphasia. Understanding family members' reactions to aphasia and the ability to participate in treatment is part of assessment within a psychosocial model. Future research efforts in aphasia assessment should hone survey and interview methods, in particular as they examine convergence and divergence of opinion about living with aphasia between individuals with aphasia and their caregivers.

Telehealth

An exciting frontier in aphasia assessment is telehealth. A cursory search on the ASHA website and other search engines produces multiple articles describing approaches to telehealth. The application of telehealth to aphasia assessment parallels the emergence of technological sophistication and, notably, in 2010 ASHA approved a Special Interest Group devoted to the study of telehealth. An early report by Vaughn (1976) described successful remote delivery of aphasia treatment via telephone. Wertz et al. (1992) compared three methods of assessing neurogenic communication disorders in persons living in remote areas: face-to-face, closed-circuit television, and computer-controlled video laserdisc via telephone. They found similar results for outcome measures in all three conditions, suggesting the viability of remote assessment. Reflecting the rapid evolution of technology and the Internet, Mashima and Doarn (2008) reviewed the applications of technology for communication problems; they found several successful endeavors and a pressing need to develop more. Theodoros, Hill, Russell, Ward, and Wootton (2008) reported results of assessing aphasia using an Internet video-conferencing system.

In comparison to a traditional face-to-face assessment, Theodoros et al. (2008) reported good reliability and validity for this method of assessment as well as participant satisfaction.

Virtual reality is another avenue available for adaptation to aphasia assessment. In a survey of speech–language pathologists, Garcia, Rebolledo, Metth, and Lefebvre (2007) reported agreement that virtual reality might be used in assessment to represent daily life in order to systematically assess the impact of environmental factors on functional communication manner.

Telehealth and the Internet pose creative and patient-friendly methods of assessment, particularly for individuals living in remote settings. However, challenges remain such as installing and maintaining electronic video-conferencing systems with sufficient bandwidth, ensuring reliable response recording, and addressing reservations from clinicians and individuals with aphasia who lack technical proficiency. Nonetheless telehealth will continue to be an important and developing method of aphasia assessment.

Conclusions

Aphasia assessment continues to evolve as an art and science. Although numerous tests and protocols exist, with more appearing regularly, the onus for completing quality assessment rests with the clinician. Knowledge in areas such as test theory, statistical reliability and validity, and standard error of measurement is critical, and complements disorder-based knowledge about specific tests or assessment procedures. Understanding the role of evidence-based practice in assessment will aid clinicians in making sound test selections. Selection of tests and protocols should reflect all parts of the evidence-based practice triangle, including the linguistic and cultural needs and preferences of the individual with aphasia and family members, the clinician's best judgment, current evidence from the literature, as well as demonstrated ecological validity (Marquardt & Gillam, 1999).

References

Aphasia Institute. (2010). *Assessment for Living with Aphasia Toolkit.* http://www.aphasia.ca/ala.html.

Avent, J.A., Glista, S., Wallace, S., Jackson, J., Nishioka, J., & Yip, W. (2005). Family information needs about aphasia. *Aphasiology*, 19, 365–375.

Azuar, C., Leger, A., Arbizu, C., Henry-Amar, F., Chomed-Guilaume, S., & Samson, Y. (2013). The Aphasia Rapid Test: An NIHSS-like aphasia test. *Journal of Neurology*, 260, 2110–2117.

Babbitt, E., & Cherney, L.R. (2010). Communication confidence in persons with aphasia. *Topics in Stroke Rehabilitation*, 17, 197–206.

Baines, K.A., Heeringa, H.M., & Martin, A.W. (1999). *Assessment of Language-Related Functional Activities*. Austin, TX: Pro-Ed.

Bak, T., & Hodges, J.R. (2003). Kissing and dancing—a test to distinguish the lexical and conceptual contributions to noun/verb and action/object dissociation. Preliminary results in patients with frontotemporal dementia. *Journal of Neurolinguistics*, 16, 169–181.

Baines, K.A., Heeringa, H.M., & Martin, A.W. (1999). *Assessment of Language-Related Functional Activities*. Austin TX: Pro- Ed.

Bandura. A. (1977). Self-efficacy: Toward a unifying theory of behavioral change. *Psychological Review*, 84, 191–215.

Basso, A. (2003). *Aphasia and its therapy*. New York: Oxford University Press.

Beeson, P.M., & Henry, M.L. (2008). Comprehension and production of written words. In R. Chapey (Ed.), *Language intervention strategies in aphasia and related neurogenic communication disorders* (5th ed., pp. 654–688). Baltimore: Lippincott Williams & Wilkins.

Benson, D.F., & Ardila, A. (1996). *Aphasia: A clinical perspective*. Oxford: Oxford University Press.

Benton, A.L. (1981). Aphasia: Historical perspectives. In M.T. Sarno (Ed.),. *Acquired aphasia*, 1–25. New York: Academic Press.

Benton, A.L., Hamsher, K., Rey, G.J., & Sivan, A.B. (1994). *Multilingual Aphasia Examination* (3rd ed.). New York: Oxford University Press.

Benton, A.L., & Joynt, R.J. (1960). Early descriptions of aphasia. *Archives of Neurology*, 3, 109–126.

Bishop, D.V.M. (2003). *Test for Reception of Grammar (TROG-2)* (2nd ed.). San Antonio, TX: Harcourt Assessment.

Blackstone, S., & Berg, M. (2003). *Social networks: A communication inventory for individuals with complex communication needs and their partners*. Monterey, CA: Augmentative Communication.

Blair, J.R., & Spreen, O. (1989). Predicting premorbid I.Q.: A revision of the National Adult Reading Test. *The Clinical Neuropsychologist*, 3, 129–136.

Blomert, L., Kean, M.L., Koster, C., & Schokker, J. (1994). Amsterdam-Nijmegen Everyday Language Test: Construction, reliability, and validity. *Aphasiology*, 8, 381–407.

Bond, C., Ware, J., & Young, A. (2011). *The effect of caregiver communication competence on quality of life of homebound patients*. Paper presented at the annual meeting of the International Communication Association, New York, NY. Retrieved April 12, 2011 from http://www.allacademic.com/meta/p15191_index.html.

Bossuyt, P.M., Reitsma, J.B., Bruns, D.E., Gatsonis, C.A., Glasziou, P.P., Irwig, L.M., et al. for the STARD Group. (2003). Toward complete and accurate reporting of studies of diagnostic accuracy: The STARD initiative. *Annals of Internal Medicine*, 138, 40–45.

Bowers, L., Huisingh, R., LoGuidice, C., & Orman, J. (2005). *The Word Test -2: Adolescent*. Austin, TX: Pro-Ed.

Boysen, A., & Wertz, R.T. (1996). Clinical costs in aphasia treatment: How much is a word worth? *Clinical Aphasiology*, 24, 207–213.

Brain Attack Coalition. (2014). Stroke Scales. Retrieved May 6, 2014 from http://www.stroke-site.org/stroke_scales/stroke_scales.html.

Brookshire, R.H. (2003). *Introduction to neurogenic communication disorders* (6th ed.). St. Louis: Mosby.

Brookshire, R.H., & Nicholas, L.E. (1993). A system for quantifying the informativeness and efficiency of the connected speech of adults with aphasia. *Journal of Speech and Hearing Research*, 36, 338–350.

Brookshire, R.H., & Nicholas, L.E. (1997). *Discourse Comprehension Test*. Minneapolis: BRK.

Brown, V.L., Hammill, D.D., & Wiederholt, J.L. (1995). *Test of Reading Comprehension* (3rd. ed.). Austin, TX: Pro-Ed.

Chapey, R., Duchan, J.D., Elman, R.J., Garcia, L.J., Kagan, A., Lyon, J.G., et al. (2008). Life-participation approach to aphasia: A statement of values for the future. In R. Chapey (Ed.), *Language intervention strategies in aphasia and related neurogenic communication disorders* (5th ed., pp. 279–289). Baltimore: Lippincott Williams & Wilkins.

Cherney, L.R., Coelho, C.A., & Shadden, B.B. (1998). *Analyzing discourse in communicatively impaired adults*. Gaithersburg, MA: Aspen Publishers.

Cocchini, G., Gregg, N., Beschin, N., Dean, M., & Della Sala, S. (2010). VATA-L: Visual-analogue test assessing anosognosia for language impairment. *The Clinical Neuropsychologist*, 24, 1379–1399.

Crary, M. A., & Gonzalez Rothi, L.J. (1989). Predicting the Western Aphasia Battery Aphasia Quotient. *Journal of Speech, Language and Hearing Research*, 54, 163–166.

Crary, M. A., Haak, N.J., & Malinsky, A.E. (1989). Preliminary psychometric evaluation of an acute aphasia screening protocol. *Aphasiology*, 3, *611–618*.

Cruice, M., Worrall, L., Hickson, L., & Murison, R. (2003). Finding a focus for quality of life with aphasia: Social and emotional health, and psychological well-being. *Aphasiology*, 17, 333–353.

Cunningham, R., Farrow, V., Davies, C., & Lincoln, N. (1995). Reliability of the assessment of communicative effectiveness in severe aphasia. *European Journal of Disorders of Communication*, 30, 1–16.

Danek, A., Gade, M., Lunardelli, A., & Rumiati, R. (2013). Tomato and Tuna: A test for language-free assessment of action understanding. *Cognitive Behavioral Neurology*, 26, 208–217.

Del Toro, C.M., Bislick, L.P., Comer, M., Velozo, C., Romero, S., Gonzalez Rothi, L.J., et al. (2011). Development of a short form of the Boston Naming Test for individuals with aphasia. *Journal of Speech, Language and Hearing Research*, 54, 1089–1100.

DeRenzi, E., & Ferrari, C. (1978). The Reporter's Test: A sensitive test to detect expressive disturbances in aphasics. *Cortex*, 14, 279–293.

Doesborgh, S.J.C., van de Sandt-Koenderman, W.M.E., Dippel, D.W.J., van Harskamp, F., Koudstaal, P.J., & Visch-Brink, E.G. (2003). Linguistic deficits in the acute phase of stroke. *Journal of Neurology*, 250, 977–982.

Dollaghan, C.A. (2007). *The handbook of evidence-based practice in communication disorders*. Baltimore: Brookes.

Douglas, J.M., O'Flaherty, C.A., & Snow, P.A. (2000). Measuring perception of communication ability: The development and evaluation of the LaTrobe Communication Questionnaire. *Aphasiology*, 14, 251–268.

Doyle, P.J. (2002). Measuring health outcomes in stroke survivors. *Archives of Physical Medicine and Rehabilitation*, 83(Suppl. 2), S39–S43.

Doyle, P., McNeil, M., Hula, W., & Mikolic, J. (2003). The Burden of Stroke Scale (BOSS): Validating patient-reported communication difficulty and associated psychological distress in stroke survivors. *Aphasiology*, 17, 291–304.

Druks, J., & Masterson, J. (2000). *An Object and Action Naming Battery*. London: Psychology Press.

Duncan, P.W., Wallace, D., Lai, S.M., Johnson, D., Embretson, S., & Laster, L.J. (1999). The Stroke Impact Scale Version 2.0: Evaluation of reliability, validity, and sensitivity to change. *Stroke*, 30, 2131–2140.

Dunn, A.B. (2004). Influence of perceived self-efficacy on treatment outcomes for aphasia. *Theses and Dissertations*. Paper 1020. http://scholarcommons.usf.edu/etd/1020.

Dunn, L.M., & Dunn, D.M. (2007). *Peabody Picture Vocabulary Test*, (PPVT™-4). San Antonio, TX: Pearson.

Eadie, T., Yorkston, K., Klasner, E., Dudgeon, B., Deitz, J., Bayloe, C., Miller, R., & Amtmann, D. (2006). Measuring communication participation: A review of self-report instruments in speech-language pathology. *American Journal of Speech-Language Pathology*, 15, 307–320.

Eisenson, J. (1954). *Examining for aphasia*. New York: Psychological Corporation.

Eisenson, J. (1973). *Adult aphasia: Assessment and treatment*. Englewood Cliffs, NJ: Prentice-Hall, Inc.

Eisenson, J., & LaPointe, L.L. (2008). *Examining for Aphasia* (4th ed.). Austin, TX: Pro-Ed.

Eling, P. (1994). *Reader in the history of aphasia*. Philadelphia: Johns Benjamin Publishing Company.

Ellis, C., Lindrooth, R.C., & Horner, J. (2014). Retrospective cost-effectiveness analysis of treatments for aphasia: An approach using experimental data. *American Journal of Speech-Language Pathology*, 23, 1–10.

Enderby, P., Wood, V., & Wade, D. (2006). *Frenchay Aphasia Screening Test* (2nd ed.). Hoboken, NJ: John Wiley & Sons.

Enderby, P., Wood, V., Wade, D., & Hewer, R. (1987). The Frenchay Aphasia Screening Test: A short, simple test appropriate for non-specialists. *International Journal of Rehabilitation Medicine*, 8, 166–170.

Fastenau, P.S., Denburg, N.L., & Mauer, B.A. (1998). Parallel short forms for the Boston Naming Test: Psychometric properties and norms for older adults. *Journal of Clinical and Experimental Neuropsychology*, 20, 828–834.

Fitch-West, J., & Sands, E.S. (1998). *Bedside Evaluation Screening Test (BEST-2)*. Austin, TX: Pro-Ed.

Flamand-Roze, C., Fallissard, B., Roze, E., Maintigneux, L., Beziz, J., Chacon, A., Join-Lambert, C., Adams, D., & Denier, C. (2011). Validation of a new language screening tool for patients with acute stroke: The Language Screening Test (LAST). *Stroke*, 42, 1224–1229.

Franklin, S., Turner, J.E., & Ellis, A.W. (1992). *ADA Comprehension Battery*. London: Action for Dysphasic Adults.

Frattali, C., Thompson, C.K., Holland, A.L., Wohl, C.B., & Ferketic, M.M. (1995). *The Functional Assessment of Communication Skills for Adults (ASHA-FACS)*. Rockville, MD: American Speech-Language-Hearing Association.

Freed, D. (2009). A short history of the Veterans Administration's influence on aphasia assessment tools. *Aphasiology*, 23, 1146–1157.

Fridriksson, J., Baker, J.M., & Richardson, J.D. (2010). What can neuroimaging tell us about aphasia? *The ASHA Leader*, July, 6.

Fridriksson, J., Bonilha, L., Baker, J.M., Moser, D., & Rorden, C. (2010). Activity in preserved left hemisphere regions predicts anomia severity in aphasia. *Cerebral Cortex*, 20, 1013–1019.

Fridriksson, J., Nettles, C., Davis, M., Morrow, L., & Montgomery, A. (2006). Functional communication and executive function in aphasia. *Clinical Linguistics and Phonetics*, 20, 401–410.

Garcia, L.J., Rebolledo, M., Metth, L., & Lefebvre, R. (2007). The potential of virtual reality to assess functional communication in aphasia. *Topics in Language Disorders*, 27, 272–288.

Garrett, K.L., & Lasker, J. (2005). *Multimodal communication screening task for persons with aphasia*. Lincoln, NE: AAC Lab.

Gerber, S., & Gurland, G.B. (1989). Applied pragmatics in the assessment of aphasia. *Seminars in Speech and Language*, 10, 270–281.

German, D. (1989). *Test of Adolescent/Adult Word Finding*. Austin, TX: Pro-Ed.

Gialanella, B. (2011). Aphasia assessment and functional outcome prediction in patients with aphasia after stroke. *Journal of Neurology*, 258, 343–349.

Gialanella, B., Bertolinelli, M., Lissi, M., & Promet, P. (2011). Predicting outcome after stroke: The role of aphasia. *Disability and Rehabilitation*, 33, 122–129.

Glueckauf, R., Blonder, L., Ecklund-Johnson, E., Maher, L., Crosson, B., & Gonzalez Rothi, L. (2003). Functional outcome questionnaire for aphasia: Overview and preliminary psychometric evaluation. *NeuroRehabilitation*, 18, 281–290.

Goodglass, H. (1993). *Understanding aphasia*. New York: Academic Press.

Goodglass, H., & Kaplan, E. (1972). *Boston Diagnostic Aphasia Examination* (2nd ed.). Philadelphia: Lea & Febiger.

Goodglass, H., Kaplan, E., & Baressi, B. (2001). *Boston Diagnostic Aphasia Examination (BDAE-3)*. Baltimore: Lippincott Williams & Wilkins.

Goodman, R.A., & Caramazza, A. (1986a). *The Johns Hopkins University Dysgraphia Battery*. Baltimore, MD: The Johns Hopkins University.

Goodman, R.A., & Caramazza, A. (1986b). *The Johns Hopkins University Dyslexia Battery*. Baltimore, MD: The Johns Hopkins University.

Grill, J.J., & Kirwin, M.M. (1990). *Written language assessment*. Novato, CA: Academic Therapy.

Gurland, G., Chwat, S.E., & Wollner, S.G. (1982). Establishing a communication profile in adult aphasia: Analysis of communicative acts and conversation sequences. *Clinical Aphasiology*, 12, 18–27.

Hammill, D.D., Brown, V.L., Larsen, S., & Wiederholt, J.L. (2007). *Test of Adolescent and Adult Language (TOAL-4)*. San Antonio, TX: Pearson.

Head, H. (1926). *Aphasia and kindred disorders of speech*. Cambridge: Cambridge University Press.

Heilman, K.M. (2006). Aphasia and the diagram makers revisited: An update of information processing models. *Journal of Clinical Neurology*, 2,149–162.

Helm-Estabrooks, N. (1991). *Test of Oral and Limb Apraxia*. Austin, TX: Pro-Ed.

Helm-Estabrooks, N. (1992). *Aphasia Diagnostic Profiles*. Austin, TX: Pro-Ed.

Helm-Estabrooks, N., Ramsberger, G., Morgan, A.R., & Nicholas, M. (1989). *Boston Assessment of Severe Aphasia*. Chicago: Riverside.

Hilari, K., Byng, S., Lamping, D.L., & Smith, S.C. (2003). Stroke and aphasia quality of life scale-39 (SAQOL-39): Evaluation of acceptability, reliability, and validity. *Stroke*, 34, 1944–1950.

Hilari, K., Owen, S., & Farrelly, S. (2007). Proxy and self-report agreement on the Stroke and Aphasia Quality of Life

Scale (SAQOL-39). *Journal of Neurology, Neurosurgery and Psychiatry*, 78, 1072–1075.

Hillis, A.E. (2007). Aphasia: Progress in the last quarter of a century. *Neurology*, 69, 200–213.

Hillis, A.E., & Newhart, M. (2008). Cognitive neuropsychological approaches of treatment of language disorders. In R. Chapey (Ed.), *Language intervention strategies in aphasia and related neurogenic communication disorders* (5th ed., pp. 595–606). Baltimore: Lippincott Williams & Wilkins.

Hinckley, J., & Nash, C. (2007). Cognitive assessment and aphasia severity. *Brain and Language*, 103, 195–196.

Holland, A.L. (1980). *Communicative Activities of Daily Living*. Baltimore: University Park Press.

Holland, A.L., Frattali, C., & Fromm, D. (1999). *Communicative Activities of Daily Living-2*. Austin: Pro-Ed.

Houghton, P., Pettit, J.M., & Towey, M.P. (1982). Measuring communication competence in global aphasia. *Clinical Aphasiology*, 12, 28–39.

Howard, D., & Patterson, K.E. (1992). *Pyramids and Palm Trees*. Bury St. Edmonds: Thames Valley Test Company.

Huber, W., Poeck, K., & Willmes, K. (1984). The Aachen Aphasia Test. *Advances in Neurology*, 42, 291–303.

Hux, K., Wallace, S., Evans, K., & Snell, J. (2008). Performing "cookie theft" content analyses to delineate cognitive-communication impairments. *Journal of Medical Speech-Language Pathology* 16, 83–102.

Jacyna, L. (2008). *Medicine and modernism: A biography of Sir Henry Head*. London: Pickering & Chatto.

Jenkins, J.J., Jimenez-Pabon, E., Shaw, R.E., & Sefer, J.W. (1975). *Schuell's aphasia in adults* (2nd ed.). New York: Harper & Row.

Kagan, A., Simmons-Mackie, N., Rowland, A., Huijbregt, M., Shumway, E., McEwen, S., et al. (2008). Counting what counts: A framework for capturing real-life outcomes of aphasia. *Aphasiology*, 22, 258–280.

Kaplan, E., Goodglass, H., & Weintraub, S. (2001). *Boston Naming Test*. Baltimore: Lippincott Williams & Wilkins.

Kaufman, A.S., & Kaufman, N.L. (1994). *Kaufman Functional Academic Skills Test*. San Antonio, TX: Pearson.

Kay, J., Lesser, R., & Coltheart, M. (1992). *PALPA: Psycholinguistic Assessments of Language Processing in Aphasia*. London: Lawrence Erlbaum Associates.

Keil, K., & Kasniak, A.W. (2002). Examining executive function in individuals with brain injury: A review. *Aphasiology*, 16, 305–335.

Kerr, C. (1995). Dysnomia following traumatic brain injury: An information processing approach to assessment. *Brain Injury*, 9, 777–796.

Kertesz, A. (1977). *Western Aphasia Battery*. San Antonio: Psychological Corporation.

Kertesz, A. (1979). *Aphasia and associated disorders: Taxonomy, localization, and recovery*. New York: Grune & Stratton.

Kertesz, A. (2007). *Western Aphasia Battery–Revised*. San Antonio: Psychological Corporation.

Klee, T. (2008). Considerations for appraising diagnostic studies of communication disorders. *Evidence-Based Communication Assessment and Intervention*, 2, 34–45.

Koul, R. (2007). Clinicians must take into account the validity, reliability, sensitivity, and practical utility of aphasia screening assessment tools before using them on their patients. *Evidence Based Communication Assessment and Intervention*, 4, 162–163.

LaPointe, L.L., & Horner, J. (1998). *Reading Comprehension Battery for Aphasia* (2nd ed.). Austin, TX: Pro-Ed.

Lazar, R.M., Speizer, A.E., Festa, J.R., Krakauer, J.W., & Marshall, R.S. (2008). Variability in language recovery after first-time stroke. *Journal of Neurology, Neurosurgery and Psychiatry*, 79, 530–534.

Leśniak, M., Bak, T., Czepiel, W., Seniów, J., & Członkowska, A. (2008). Frequency and prognostic value of cognitive disorders in stroke patients. *Dementia and Geriatric Cognitive Disorders*, 26, 356–363.

Lomas, J., Pickard, L., Bester, S., Elbard, H., Finlayson, A., & Zoghaib, C. (1989). The Communicative Effectiveness Index: Development and psychometric evaluation of a functional communication measure for adult aphasia. *Journal of Speech and Hearing Disorders*, 54, 113–124.

Love, T., & Oster, E. (2002). On the categorization of aphasia typologies: The SOAP (a test of syntactic complexity). *Journal of Psycholinguistic Research*, 31, 503–529.

Luria, A.R. (1966). *Higher cortical functions in man*. New York: Basic Books.

Marquardt, T.P., & Gillam, R.B. (1999). Assessment in communication disorders: Some observations on current issues. *Language Testing*, 16, 249–269.

Marshall, R.C., & Wright, H.H. (2007). Developing a clinician-friendly aphasia test. *American Journal of Speech-Language Pathology*, 16, 295–315.

Mashima, P.A., & Doarn, C.R. (2008). Overview of telehealth activities in speech-language pathology. *Telemedicine and e-Health*, 14, 1101–1117.

McDonald, S., & Pearce, S. (1995). The 'dice' game: A new test of pragmatic language skills after closed-head injury. *Brain Injury*, 9, 255–271.

McNeil, M.M., & Prescott, T.E. (1978). *Revised Token Test*. Austin, TX: Pro-Ed.

Miller, N., Willmes, K., & De Bleser, R. (2000). The psychometric properties of the English language version of the Aachen Aphasia Test (EAAT). *Aphasiology*, 14, 683–722.

Mitchum, C.C., & Berndt, R.S. (2008). Comprehension and production of sentences. In R. Chapey (Ed.), *Language intervention strategies in aphasia and related neurogenic communication disorders* (5th ed., pp. 632–653). Baltimore: Lippincott Williams & Wilkins.

Murray, L.L., & Clark H. M. (2006). *Neurogenic disorders of language: Theory driven clinical practice*. Clifton Park, NJ: Thompson Delmar Learning.

N-CEP (2014). Retrieved May 6, 2014 from http://www.asha.org/members/ebp/EBSRs.htm.

NIH Stroke Scale. (2003). Retrieved May 6, 2014 from http://www.ninds.nih.gov/doctors/NIH_Stroke_Scale.pdf.

Obler, L.K., & Albert, M.L. (2009). *The Action Naming Test*. http://www.bu.edu/lab/action-naming-test/.

Odekar, A., & Hallowell, B. (2005). Comparison of alternatives to multidimensional scoring in the assessment of language comprehension in aphasia. *American Journal of Speech-Language Pathology*, 14, 337–345.

O'Halloran, R., Worrall, L., Toffolo, D., Code, C., & Hickson, L. (2004). *IFCI: Inpatient functional communication interview*. Bicester, UK: Speechmark.

Paradis, M., & Libben, G. (1987). *The assessment of bilingual aphasia*. Mahwah, NJ: LEA; and http://www.mcgill.ca/linguistics/research/bat/.

Patterson, J.P., & Chapey, R. (2008). Assessment of language disorders in aphasia. In R. Chapey (Ed.), *Language intervention strategies in aphasia and related adult neurogenic communication disorders* (5th ed., pp. 64–160). Philadelphia: Lippincott Williams & Wilkins.

Paul, D.R., Frattali, C.M., Holland, A.L., Thompson, C.K., Caperton, C.J., & Slater, S.C. (2005). *Quality of Communication Life Scale (ASHA-QCL)*. Rockville, MD: American Speech-Language-Hearing Association.

Payne, J.C. (1994). *Communication Profile: A Functional Skills Measure*. San Antonio, TX: Communication Skill Builders.

Penn, C. (1988). The profiling of syntax and pragmatics in aphasia. *Clinical Linguistics and Phonetics*, 2, 179–207.

Porch, B.E. (1967). *Porch Index of Communicative Ability*. Palo Alto, CA: Consulting Psychologists Press.

Porch, B.E. (2001). *Porch Index of Communicative Ability*. Albuquerque, NM: Pica Programs.

Porch, B.E. (2008). Treatment of aphasia subsequent to the Porch Index of Communicative Ability (PICA). In R. Chapey (Ed.), *Language intervention strategies in aphasia and related adult neurogenic communication disorders* (5th ed., pp. 800–813). Philadelphia: Lippincott Williams & Wilkins.

Prutting, C., & Kirchner, D. (1987). Applied pragmatics. In T. Gallagher & C. Prutting (Eds.), *Pragmatic assessment and intervention in language* (pp. 29–64). San Diego: College Park Press.

Purdy, M. (2002). Executive function ability in persons with aphasia. *Aphasiology*, 16, 549–557.

Raymer, A.M., & Rothi, L.J.G. (2008). Impairments of word comprehension and production. In R. Chapey (Ed.), *Language intervention strategies in aphasia and related neurogenic communication disorders* (5th ed., pp. 607–631). Baltimore: Lippincott Williams & Wilkins.

Raymer, A.M., Maher, L.M., Greenwald, M.L., Morris, M., Rothi, L.J.G., & Heilman, K.M. (1990). The Florida Semantics Battery (Unpublished). Stimuli appear in Raymer, A.M., & Rothi, L.J.G. (2008). Impairments of word comprehension and production. In R. Chapey (Ed.), *Language intervention strategies in aphasia and related neurogenic communication disorders* (5th ed., pp. 630–631). Baltimore: Lippincott Williams & Wilkins.

Roach, A., Schwartz, M.F., Martin, N., Grewal, R.S., & Brecher, A. (1996). The Philadelphia Naming Test: Scoring and rationale. *Clinical Aphasiology*, 24, 121–133. Also available at http://www.ncrrn.org/assessment/pnt/.

Roth, H.L., & Heilman, K.M. (2002). Aphasia: A historical perspective. In S.E. Nadeau, L.J.G. Rothi, & B. Crosson (Eds.), *Aphasia and language: Theory to practice* (pp. 3–28). New York: The Guilford Press.

Rothi, L.J.G., Raymer, A.M., & Heilman, K.M. (1997). Limb praxis assessment. In L.J.G. Rothi & K.M. Heilman (Eds.), *Apraxia: The neuropsychology of action* (pp. 61–73). Hove, UK: Psychology Press.

Ruff, R.M., Light, R.H., Parker, S.B., & Levin, H.S. (1996). Benton Controlled Oral Word Association Test: Reliability and updated norms. *Archives of Neuropsychology*, 11, 329–338.

Sales, A., Smith, J., Curran, G., & Kochevar, L. (2006). Models, strategies, and tools: Theory in implementing evidence-based findings into health care practice. *Journal of General Internal Medicine*, 21(Suppl 2), S43–49.

Salter, K., Bhogal, S.K., Foley, N., Jutai, J., & Teasell, R. (2007). The assessment of poststroke depression. *Topics in Stroke Rehabilitation*, 14, 1–24.

Salter, K., Jutai, J., Foley, N., Hellings, C., & Teasel, R. (2006). Identification of aphasia post stroke: A review of screening tests. *Brain Injury*, 2, 559–568.

Sarno, M.T. (1969). *The Functional Communication Profile*: Manual of directions. New York: Institute of Rehabilitation Medicine, New York University Medical Center.

Sarno, M.T., & Höök, O. (1980). *Aphasia: Assessment and treatment*. New York: Masson Publishing USA, Inc.

Schuell, H.M. (1965). *Minnesota Test for Differential Diagnosis of Aphasia*. Minneapolis: University of Minnesota Press.

Schwartz, R.L., Nadeau, S.E., Crosson, B., Rothi, L.J.G., & Heilman, K.M. (1996). *Florida Action Recall Test*. Unpublished psychological test. University of Florida, Gainesville.

Searle, J.R. (1969). *Speech acts*. Cambridge: Cambridge University Press.

Shewan, C.M. (1979). *Auditory Comprehension Test for Sentences*. Chicago: Biolinguistics Clinical Institutes.

Shewan, C.M. (1988). The Shewan spontaneous language analysis (SSLA) system for aphasic adults: Description, reliability, and validity. *Journal of Communication Disorders*, 21, 103–138.

Simmons-Mackie, N., & Damico, J. (1996). Accounting for handicaps in aphasia: Communicative assessment from an authentic social perspective. *Disability and Rehabilitation*, 18, 804–820.

Spellacy, F.J., & Spreen, O. (1969). A short form of the Token Test. *Cortex*, 5, 391–397.

Spreen, O., & Benton, A.L. (1969). *Neurosensory Centre Comprehensive Examination for Aphasia*. Victoria, BC: University of Victoria Neuropsychology Laboratory.

Spreen, O., & Risser, A.H. (2003). *Assessment of aphasia*. New York: Oxford University Press.

Spreen, O., & Strauss, E. (1998). *Neurosensory Center Comprehensive Examination for Aphasia*. Victoria, BC: University of Victoria Neuropsychology Laboratory.

Standards for the Reporting of Diagnostic Accuracy Studies (STARD). (2008). Retrieved April 2, 2011 from http://www.stard-statement.org/.

Stern, R., Arruda, J.E., Hooper, C.R., Wolfner, G.D., & Morey, C.E. (1997). Visual analog mood scales to measure internal mood state in neurologically impaired patients: Description and initial validation studies. *Aphasiology*, 11, 40–59.

Stroke Impact Scale. (2010). Retrieved May 6, 2014 from http://www.chrp.org/pdf/HSR082103_SIS_Handout.pdf.

Stroke Trials Registry. (2014). Retrieved from The Internet Stroke Center at Washington University. http://www.stroke-center.org/trials/scales/scales-overview.htm#h.

Swinburn, K., Porter, G., & Howard, D. (2005). *The Comprehensive Aphasia Test*. Hove, UK: Psychology Press.

Swindell, C.S., Pashek, G.V., & Holland, A.L. (1982). A questionnaire for surveying personal and communicative style. *Clinical Aphasiology*, 12, 50–63.

Syder, D., Body, R., Parker, M., & Boddy, M. (1993). *Sheffield Screening Test for Acquired Language Disorders*. Windsor: NFER-NELSON.

Tanner, D., & Culbertson, W. (1999). *Quick Assessment for Aphasia*. Oceanside, CA: Academic Communication Associates.

Tesak, J., & Code, C.C. (2008). *Milestones in the history of aphasia: Theories and protagonists*. Hove, UK: Psychology Press.

Theodoros, D., Hill, A., Russell, T., Ward, E., & Wootton, R. (2008). Assessing acquired language disorders in adults via the internet. *Telemedicine and e-Health*, 14, 552–559.

van der Meulen, T., van de Sandt-Koenderman, W.M.E., Duivenvoorden, H.J., & Ribbers, G.M. (2010). Measuring verbal and non-verbal communication in aphasia: Reliability, validity, and sensitivity to change of the Scenario Test. *International Journal of Language & Communication Disorders*, 45, 424–435.

Van Heutgen, C.M., Dekker, J., & Deelman, B.J. (1999). A diagnostic test for apraxia with stroke patients: Internal consistency and diagnostic value. *The Clinical Neuropsychologist*, 13, 182–192.

Vaughn, G.R. (1976). Tele-communicology: Health care delivery system for persons with communicative disorders. *Asha*, 18, 13–17.

Walker, G.M., & Schwartz, M.F. (2012). Short-Form Philadelphia Naming Test: Rationale and empirical evaluation. *American Journal of Speech-Language Pathology*, 21, S140–S153.

Wallace, G., & Hammill, D.D. (2002). *Comprehensive Receptive and Expressive Vocabulary Test—Adult* (2nd ed.). Austin, TX: Pro-Ed.

Wechsler, D. (2001). *Wechsler Test of Adult Reading*. San Antonio, TX: Pearson.

Weisenberg, T., & McBride, K. (1935). *Aphasia: A clinical and psychological study*. New York: Commonwealth Fund.

Wepman, J.M., & Jones, L.V. (1961). *The Language Modalities Test for Aphasia*. Chicago: Education-Industry Service, University of Chicago.

Wertz, R.T., Deal, J.L., & Robinson, A. (1984). Classifying the aphasias: A comparison of the Boston Diagnostic Aphasia Examination and the Western Aphasia Battery. *Clinical Aphasiology*, 14, 40–47.

Wertz, R.T., Dronkers, N.F., Bernstein-Ellis, E., Sterling, L.K., Shubitowski, Y., Elman, R., et al. (1992). Potential of telephonic and television technology for appraising and diagnosing neurogenic communication disorders in remote settings. *Aphasiology*, 6, 195–202.

Whiting, P.F., Weswood, M.E., Rutjes, A.W.S., Reitsma, J.B., Bossuyt, P.N.M., & Kleijnen, J. (2006). Evaluation of QUADAS, a tool for the quality assessment of diagnostic accuracy studies. *BMC Medical Research Methodology*, 6, 9.

Whitworth, A., Webster, J., & Howard, D. (2005). *A cognitive neuropsychological approach to assessment and intervention in aphasia*. New York: Psychology Press.

Whurr, R. (2011). *The Aphasia Screening Test* (3rd. ed.). San Diego: Singular.

Wiederholt, J.L., & Bryant, B.R. (2001). *Gray Oral Reading Tests* (4th ed.). Austin, TX: Pro-Ed.

Williams, C., Thwaites, A., Buttery, P., Geertzen, J., Randall, B., Shafto, M., et al. (2010). The Cambridge cookie-theft corpus: A corpus of directed and spontaneous speech of brain-damaged patients and healthy individuals. *Language Resources and Evaluation Proceedings of the Conference* (pp. 2824–2830).

Wirz, S., Skinner, C., & Dean, E. (1990). *Revised Edinburgh Functional Communication Profile*. Tucson, AZ: Communication Skill Builders.

World Health Organization. (1980). *International Classification of Impairments, Disabilities, and Handicaps: A manual of classification relating to the consequences of disease*. Geneva.

World Health Organization. (2001a). *International Classification of Functioning, Disability and Health (ICF)*. Geneva.

World Health Organization. (2001b). *WHOQOL: Measuring Quality of life*. Geneva.

Worrall, L. (1992). Functional communication assessment: An Australian perspective. *Aphasiology*, 6, 105–110.

Worrall, L. (1999). *Functional communication therapy planner*. Bicester, England: Speechmark.

Worster-Drought, C., & Allen, I.M. (1929). Congenital auditory imperceptions: (Word-deafness): Investigation of a case by Head's method. *Journal of Neurology and Psychopathology*, 9, 289–319.

Yesavage, J.A., Brink, T.L., Rose, T.L., Lunn, O., Huang, V., Adey, M., et al. (1983). Development and validation of a geriatric depression screening scale: A preliminary report. *Journal of Psychiatric Research*, 17, 37–49. Also available online and Android application from http://www.stanford.edu/~yesavage/GDS.html.

Yorkston, K.M., & Beukelman, D.R. (1980). An analysis of connected speech samples of aphasic and normal speakers. *Journal of Speech and Hearing Disorders*, 45, 27–36.

PART 2

Aphasia Syndromes

Wernicke's Aphasia: Auditory Processing and Comprehension

Margaret L. Greenwald

Abstract

This chapter includes a discussion of the symptoms of Wernicke's aphasia, including impaired auditory comprehension and neologistic verbal expression. Anosognosia, impaired attention, and impaired self-monitoring are discussed as they relate to Wernicke's aphasia. Current evidence of the neuroanatomical correlates of Wernicke's aphasia and the role of Wernicke's area is presented from a variety of experimental perspectives. Theoretical approaches to understanding impaired auditory processing in Wernicke's aphasia are discussed in relation to perception, recognition, and comprehension of speech. Methods for the assessment and interpretation of receptive and expressive language in Wernicke's aphasia and jargon aphasia are described within the context of a cognitive model depicting multiple input modalities and output modes of language. Finally, current methods for the treatment and management of Wernicke's aphasia are reviewed, with an emphasis on evidence-based practice.

Key Words: Wernicke's aphasia, Auditory processing, Comprehension, Neologistic, Jargon, Anosognosia, Wernicke's area, Aphasia assessment, Aphasia treatment

Introduction

Among the aphasia syndromes, the onset of Wernicke's aphasia may be one of the most striking and potentially frightening for the stroke survivor, family, and friends alike. Though typically able to walk and move normally, and to produce speech with normal rate and articulation, the person with sudden onset of Wernicke's aphasia has great difficulty understanding what others are saying and produces speech that is largely nonsensical. It is not uncommon for people with Wernicke's aphasia to seem initially unaware or unable to explain the source of their failure to communicate their ideas and needs. Healthcare professionals and others who are not familiar with Wernicke's aphasia may mistake these communication symptoms as reflecting a psychiatric disorder. Any means of successfully communicating with the individual with Wernicke's aphasia must be identified as quickly as possible. In addition to fostering communication, the clinicians working with these individuals must be advocates

and educators, and must address the counseling needs of the patient and loved ones presented with this devastating change in communication.

This chapter will include a discussion of the symptoms of Wernicke's aphasia and associated cognitive impairments. Current neuroanatomical and cognitive theories of Wernicke's aphasia and methods of its assessment and treatment are also included.

Syndrome Description and Unique Characteristics

Wernicke's aphasia was first described in 1874 by the German neuropsychiatrist Wernicke (Eggert, 1977), who called it sensory aphasia. The major features reported for this disorder were fluent but impaired speech, poor comprehension of spoken language, and impaired reading and writing. As described further below, the most frequent lesion associated with Wernicke's aphasia was in the posterior portion of the superior temporal gyrus of the left hemisphere, often called "Wernicke's area." This left hemisphere damage occurs in right-handed individuals, although a few cases of crossed Wernicke's aphasia have been reported as a result of right hemisphere damage in a right-handed individual (Sakurai et al., 1992; Seckin, Yigitkanli, Kapucu, & Bavbek, 2009). Wernicke's aphasia can be chronic, but can also have a transient course as a result of transient ischemic attack (TIA), seizure (Sahaya, Dhand, Goyal, Soni, & Sahota, 2010), or migraine (Mishra, Rossetti, Ménétrey, & Carota, 2009).

The combination of language symptoms that differentiates Wernicke's aphasia from other aphasia syndromes is fluent speech, poor auditory comprehension, poor repetition, and poor naming ability. The fluent speech of Wernicke's aphasia is characterized by easy articulation, normal rate, empty content, and numerous verbal paraphasias (i.e., verbal errors). The individual does not appear to be aware of the inadequacy of the speech output and may continue to speak rapidly despite the errors (Goodglass, Kaplan, & Barresi, 2001), which reflects poor self-monitoring. Individuals with Wernicke's aphasia have been described as hyperfluent, sometimes displaying seemingly incoherent talkativeness (i.e., logorrhea); however, Howes (1964) and Kerschensteiner, Poeck, and Brunner (1972) found that few if any individuals with aphasia had a speaking rate that was hyperfluent.

Individuals with Wernicke's aphasia represent approximately 14.5–16% of all individuals with aphasia in the acute stage (Godefroy, Dubois, Debachy, Leclerc, & Kreisler, 2002; Kertesz, 1993; Pedersen, Vinter, & Olsen, 2004; Yang, Zhao, Wang, Chen, & Zhang, 2008). At 1 year postonset, the incidence of Wernicke's aphasia is approximately 5% among those who had been diagnosed with aphasia in the acute stage and 8% of all those with continuing aphasia (Pedersen et al., 2004).

Laska, Hellblom, Murray, Kahan, and Von Arbin (2001) reported a higher incidence of Wernicke's aphasia (25%) among individuals with aphasia in the acute stage, noting that this might reflect the older age of their study participants and that older individuals may be more prone to posterior lesions and resulting comprehension difficulties (e.g., Obler, Albert, Goodglass, & Benson, 1978). In an 18-month follow-up, approximately 10% of these individuals with aphasia had the Wernicke's subtype. There was a high rate of recovery and evolution in the Wernicke's aphasia group.

In a prospective, longitudinal study of 75 individuals with a first-ever stroke resulting in aphasia,

Bakheit, Shaw, Carrington, and Griffiths (2007) examined the rate and extent of improvement from the different aphasia subtypes in the first year poststroke. When progress was compared at 4, 8, 12, and 24 weeks postonset, individuals with Wernicke's aphasia were found to make significantly less improvement than did individuals with Broca's aphasia. Those with Wernicke's aphasia had a significantly greater improvement than those with conduction or anomic aphasia at weeks 12 and 24, but less improvement than individuals with global aphasia at 24 weeks postonset.

The evolution of Wernicke's aphasia toward other forms of aphasia is desirable, most particularly the improvement of auditory comprehension. Wernicke's aphasia does not evolve into a nonfluent type (Godefroy et al., 2002; Pashek & Holland, 1988); therefore, evolution to a different aphasia subtype would reflect improvement in repetition and/or auditory comprehension. Although naming performance may improve, this alone would not result in a change of aphasia classification. Improved repetition would yield transcortical sensory aphasia, improvement in auditory comprehension would lead to conduction aphasia, and improvement in both repetition and auditory comprehension would result in anomic aphasia. Laska et al. (2001) found that at 18 months postonset Wernicke's aphasia most often had evolved to conduction aphasia (38%).

Healthcare professionals counseling family members of individuals with Wernicke's aphasia can advise them that an increase in frustration during speech may be noted as the auditory comprehension begins to improve, in that the individuals with aphasia may begin to detect the errors in their own speech and attempt to correct them. Improved auditory comprehension will allow these persons to understand better what other people are saying, but as discussed below, it does not always result in improved error detection or self-monitoring (e.g., Maher, Rothi, & Heilman, 1994).

Verbal output in Wernicke's aphasia is marked by a variety of paraphasias, including semantic paraphasias (i.e., real word errors related in meaning to the target, such as "boy" for woman), unrelated verbal paraphasias (i.e., real words unrelated to the target, such as "handle" for floor), verbal–phonological paraphasias (i.e., real words related phonologically but not semantically to the target, such as "trouble" for table), literal paraphasias (i.e., nonwords related phonologically to the presumed target, such as "tsair" for chair), and neologisms (i.e., nonwords that are unrelated to the target, such as "stilum" for "rabbit") (Nicholas, Obler, Albert, & Helm-Estabrooks, 1985).

Those individuals with Wernicke's aphasia who produce a large proportion of neologisms in their verbal output are often said to have "jargon aphasia" (e.g., Butterworth, 1979). Three types of jargon have been described (Rohrer et al., 2009): semantic jargon (real words conveying little or no meaning for the context), phonemic or phonological jargon (real words or nonwords that are phonemically related to what the individual may be attempting to say), and neologistic jargon (nonwords that are not phonemically related to the presumed target words) (Alajouanine, 1956). This distinction between phonologically related neologisms and unrelated neologisms has been made by some authors (e.g., Buckingham, 1987; Schwartz, Saffran, Bloch, & Dell, 1994), whereas others have used the term neologism to refer to any nonword response (e.g., Miller & Ellis, 1987). The neologisms may contain perseverated phonemes from neologisms the individual has recently produced (Moses, Nickels, & Sheard, 2004).

Comparing the "empty speech" of individuals with Wernicke's aphasia to anomic aphasia or Alzheimer's disease and the speech of healthy control subjects, Nicholas et al. (1985) found that the empty speech of Wernicke's aphasia was the least informative of the four groups, with the least content and the most empty speech measures. The production of neologisms was found to be crucial in distinguishing the individuals with Wernicke's aphasia from the other groups.

Within the clinical diagnosis of Wernicke's aphasia, there is variability across individuals, not only in the severity of the various language impairments, but also in the pattern of speech errors (e.g., Ardila, 2010; Kurowski, Blumstein, Palumbo, Waldstein, & Burton, 2007). Other cognitive disturbances that accompany Wernicke's aphasia also differ across individuals. Three types of cognitive disturbances that have been associated with Wernicke's aphasia are anosognosia (poor error awareness), impaired attention, and poor self-monitoring. These disturbances, described below, may be related to one another.

Associated Cognitive Deficits

ANOSOGNOSIA

Individuals with Wernicke's aphasia tend to have anosognosia (Babinski, 1914), though the degree of unawareness can vary. As summarized by Orfei et al. (2007), anosognosia is impaired recognition of the presence or severity of sensory, perceptual, motor, affective, or cognitive deficits by a person with brain dysfunction. Anosognosia has been studied primarily in individuals with stroke and hemiplegia, but can also be observed with other disorders such as hemianopia or aphasia (e.g., Heilman, Barrett, & Adair, 1998). Unawareness of motor impairment extends to a lack of awareness of resulting changes in functional motor skill (Kortte & Hillis, 2011).

Anosognosia may be related to impaired attention. Shuren, Smith-Hammond, Maher, Rothi, and Heilman (1995) described an individual with jargon aphasia and good auditory comprehension who was unaware of his own speech errors when he both listened and spoke simultaneously. His unawareness of his own speech errors was attributed to reduced attentional capacity for simultaneous linguistic tasks, because he was able to detect his own errors when he listened to a recording of his speech, but not when he listened and spoke simultaneously. As noted by Heilman et al. (1998), a single explanation might not account for the varieties of anosognosia. For example, they noted that anosognosia for aphasia seems to be dissociable from anosognosia for hemiplegia, suggesting that modular systems mediate awareness.

IMPAIRED ATTENTION

Allocation of attention between competing tasks appears to be difficult for individuals with aphasia as compared to healthy control subjects (e.g., King & Hux, 1996; Murray, Holland, & Beeson, 1997). Helm-Estabrooks (2011) recently summarized evidence that impaired attention may account for some of the problems in understanding spoken language displayed by individuals with aphasia. These problems are described as reflecting impaired attentional capacity, deployment, and allocation during the performance of a given linguistic task (e.g., Hula & McNeil, 2008). One line of evidence for this hypothesis is that the performance of an individual with aphasia will vary for specific test items across repeated administrations of the same test, possibly reflecting fluctuations in attention.

Others have argued (e.g., Shuster, 2005) that the explanation of impaired attentional capacity is insufficient to account for the linguistic deficits of aphasia. One factor used to support this viewpoint is that individuals with many types of brain damage (e.g., right hemisphere damage) have limited cognitive resources and yet do not display the linguistic deficits of aphasia. In a study of attention and aphasia, Korda and Douglas (1997) found that although individuals with aphasia demonstrated impaired attentional capacity, there was no significant relationship between severity of auditory comprehension deficits and attentional capacity, at least for the tasks they administered.

According to Wiener, Connor, and Obler (2004), impaired inhibition may underlie at least part of the attentional impairment in Wernicke's aphasia. In the classic Stroop (1935) color–word test, healthy volunteers demonstrated longer reaction times in naming the ink colors of words printed in incongruent colors (e.g., the word "BLUE" printed in red ink) as compared to naming the ink colors of solid color squares. Weiner et al. (2004) found that the severity of auditory comprehension deficit in Wernicke's aphasia was positively correlated with the magnitude of the Stroop interference effect. They interpreted this as evidence that impaired inhibition would affect resource allocation in Wernicke's aphasia, causing impaired suppression of distracting, automatically evoked information during lexical–semantic selection in language processing.

IMPAIRED SELF-MONITORING

Improved auditory comprehension in aphasia does not necessarily result in improvement to error detection and self-monitoring. Zheng, Munhall, and Johnsrude (2010) recently noted that the nature of the link between speech perception and speech motor production and its cognitive and neural organization are not well understood. Anosognosia and/or inattention may be related to difficulties in self-monitoring of speech in aphasia. For example, awareness of speech errors would be a prerequisite to attempts at self-correction (typically absent in Wernicke's aphasia), and inattention may be a factor in anosognosia in some individuals. Theories of self-monitoring of speech differ according to whether they can account for the concurrent speech comprehension disorders observed in some individuals with aphasia, and also in a number of other factors related to consciousness, volition, and control, the number of monitoring channels, and their speed, flexibility, and capacity (Postma, 2000).

There are a number of current theories of how self-monitoring is achieved. First, the perceptual loop theory (Levelt, 1983, 1989) remains influential. In this approach, there is a central, conscious monitor that analyzes the accuracy of ongoing speech. The same speech comprehension system that is used to understand the speech of others is also used to monitor speech production. Monitoring of inner and outer speech is accomplished through this self-comprehension. Second, the theory of production-based monitoring (e.g., Schlenk, Huber, & Willmes, 1987) includes multiple, autonomous monitors that might be tuned to different aspects of speech motor execution, such as efferent, tactile, and proprioceptive feedback (Postma, 2000). Third, in "node structure theory" (MacKay, 1987, 1992), awareness of speech errors arises naturally from activation patterns within the node system of speech production. A node is a unit that can be used in building representations at different levels of language processing; for example, a node can be a concept, word, morpheme, phoneme, or phonemic feature. When there is prolonged activation of uncommitted nodes (i.e., elements not forming a word), an error may be detected. In node theory, semantic, lexical, and phonological nodes are shared by perception and production. As described by Nickels and Howard (1995), it is difficult to reconcile node structure theory with clinical evidence that central deficits in auditory comprehension do not always correlate with naming errors.

Of the three theories described above, the perception-based monitor theory has been supported by Nickels and Howard (1995), Postma (2000), and Slevc and Ferriera (2006). However, clinical observations that reduced language comprehension abilities do not always correlate with defective self-repair (e.g., Maher et al., 1994; Marshall, Rappaport, & Garcia-Bunuel, 1985) are problematic for the perception theory, which predicts that reduced language comprehension will always be associated with impaired self-repair. This is not a problem for the production-based theory of monitoring, in which comprehension and repair during production vary independently (Postma, 2000). Based on this, Postma argued for a central, perception-based monitor that is potentially augmented to include additional automatic, production-based devices for error detection. Nickels and Howard (1995) supported a combination of the perception-based theory and the production-based theory, which would allow individuals with aphasia to abandon perception-based monitoring for strategic reasons under special circumstances and to rely on the more automatic production monitoring.

As discussed above, attentional impairment may be related to impaired self-monitoring of speech. There is evidence of capacity restrictions on error detection and correction (e.g., Oomen & Postma, 2002). These capacity restrictions have been interpreted as evidence for a centrally regulated, controlled process of speech monitoring that is consistent with the perceptual loop theory (Postma, 2000).

However, as noted by Slevc and Ferriera (2006), it is necessary to propose an inner speech monitor only if the model of speech production prohibits feedback (e.g., Levelt, Roelofs, & Meyer, 1999). These authors summarized evidence that speech production errors that are both semantically and phonologically similar to the target (i.e., mixed errors such as "rat" for the target word cat) are more common than would be predicted by chance (e.g., Dell & Reich, 1981; Martin, Gagnon, Schwartz, Dell, & Saffran, 1996), possibly because the errors are more difficult for the speech monitor to detect. Also, real words are more likely to result from phonological speech errors than nonwords (the "lexical bias effect"; Baars, Motley, & MacKay, 1975). In speech production models that allow feedback from phonological to lexical levels (e.g., Dell, 1986; Dell & Reich, 1981; Rapp & Goldrick, 2000), these effects may be explained by feedback rather than by the working of a central speech monitor (Humphreys, 2002), although there is also evidence for strategic effects on lexical bias (Hartsuiker, Pickering, & De Jong, 2005).

Speech monitoring theories in general have been criticized for not being constrained enough to generate testable hypotheses (e.g., Dell & Reich, 1981; Goldrick & Rapp, 2002; Martin, Weisberg, & Saffran, 1989). As noted above, the sensitivity of the monitor may vary depending on attention or strategy. Speakers may not always monitor all dimensions of their speech, and it is not clear what elements of speech are monitored, when they are monitored, and how production relates to this monitoring (Slevc & Ferreira, 2006).

Clinical observations of individuals with aphasia will continue to be important in increasing our understanding of how comprehension relates to self-monitoring. Of particular interest will be individuals with good comprehension ability but poor monitoring skills (e.g., Maher et al., 1994), or the reverse pattern of good monitoring but poor comprehension (e.g., Marshall et al., 1985). The more typical pattern reported in Wernicke's aphasia, however, is that poor auditory comprehension and poor self-monitoring of speech errors coexist.

Neuroanatomical Correlates of Wernicke's Aphasia

Wernicke (1874) described the first temporal gyrus on the left as a sensory region and the center of acoustic images. Kertesz and Benson (1970) found that persisting jargon aphasia had to involve both the left superior posterior temporal gyrus and the supramarginal gyrus, and poor recovery from Wernicke's aphasia has been associated with damage to the left superior temporal lobe and the supramarginal and angular gyri (Kertesz, Lau, & Polk, 1993). Increased blood flow in the left frontal lobe and the right perisylvian region was observed in six individuals who recovered from Wernicke's aphasia after destruction to the left perisylvian region (Weiller et al., 1995). Technological advances in recent years have allowed for more discrete analyses of the brain pathology underlying Wernicke's aphasia and its patterns of evolution or recovery. Wernicke's area appears to be part of a network of language regions, but the role of Wernicke's area in comprehension and naming is not entirely clear.

Hypoperfusion Studies

In acute stroke, regions of low blood flow surrounding structural damage may contribute to language deficits in aphasia (e.g., Hillis et al., 2002). These regions may be reperfused with treatment such as medication to raise blood pressure (Hillis, Kane et al., 2001). Reperfusion that occurs simultaneously with improved language function has been interpreted as evidence that the reperfused brain area normally supports that language function (Hillis, Barker, Beauchamp, Gordon, & Wityk, 2000).

Hillis et al. (2006) described several advantages of studying brain–behavior relationships by using measures of perfusion such as diffusion-weighted imaging (DWI) and magnetic resonance perfusion imaging (MRPI) over traditional lesion analysis. For example, they noted that if a behavioral deficit recovers with reperfusion, then the possibility that it was a premorbid deficit can be ruled out and that recovery only with reperfusion cannot be attributed to the reorganization of brain–behavior relationships.

The severity of hypoperfusion of Wernicke's area has been shown to relate linearly to the severity of word comprehension impairment (Hillis, Wityk et al., 2001), and reperfusion of Wernicke's area has been associated with improved comprehension in acute stroke (Hillis, Barker et al., 2001; Hillis et al., 2002). This evidence has been interpreted as supporting the critical role of Wernicke's area [Brodmann's Area (BA) 22] in word comprehension. As noted by Hillis, Wityk et al. (2001), BA 22 appears to be essential for linking the learned pronunciation of words to semantic information, and auditory input must first be processed in BA 22 before this link can be made (Selnes, Knopman, Niccum, & Rubens, 1985).

The naming deficits associated with Wernicke's aphasia have also been examined using hypoperfusion studies. Areas of hypoperfusion and structural damage were identified in a group of stroke survivors who then received reperfusion treatment immediately after stroke (Hillis et al., 2006). Comparison of verbal picture naming performance before and after restored blood flow showed that a network of brain regions supported the acute improvement in picture naming, including the left posterior middle temporal/fusiform gyrus, Broca's area, and/or Wernicke's area.

Diffusion Tensor Imaging Tractography Studies

Diffusion tensor imaging (DTI) in combination with tractography allows for noninvasive reconstruction and visualization of continuous white matter pathways in the brains of living humans (Catani & Mesalum, 2008). Wernicke's area in the left posterior superior temporal gyrus is generally thought to be connected to Broca's area via the arcuate fasciculus, first identified by Von Monakow (Geschwind, 1967). The complexity of the arcuate fasciculus has been specified recently with tractography studies (Catani & ffytche, 2005). It appears that Wernicke's and Broca's areas are connected via a long direct segment of the arcuate fasciculus, and that there is also an indirect pathway made up of two segments: an anterior segment connecting Broca's area to the inferior parietal lobule, and a posterior segment connecting the inferior parietal lobule with Wernicke's area (Catani & Mesalum, 2008). The arcuate fasciculus also appears to connect to part of the middle and precentral frontal gyrus and the posterior middle temporal gyrus, areas outside the traditional limits of Broca's and Wernicke's areas (Catani & ffytche, 2005).

Ventral fiber tracts link the left perisylvian language region with the medial, inferior, and anterior temporal cortices, areas that classically were not considered part of the language network, but that some researchers now consider as crucial to semantic processing (Catani & Mesalum, 2008). These ventral tracts include the inferior longitudinal fasciculus (linking the occipital areas to the temporal lobe) (Catani, Jones, Donato, & ffytche, 2003), the uncinate fasciculus (linking the anterior temporal lobe to the orbitofrontal area including the inferior frontal gyrus) (Catani, Howard, Pajevic, & Jones,

2002), and the inferior fronto-occipital fasciculus (possibly the only direct link between the occipital cortex and frontal cortex) (Catani, 2007). These ventral pathways posteriorly connect Wernicke's area to the lateral temporooccipital cortex and anteriorly connect Broca's area with the lateral orbitofrontal cortex (Catani & Mesalum, 2008).

Lesion Analysis Studies

The left posterior superior temporal gyrus has been viewed as crucial to linking spoken words to meaning and to naming in a variety of chronic lesion studies over the years (e.g., Hart & Gordon, 1990). However, more recently Dronkers, Wilkins, Van Valin, Redfern, and Jaeger (2004) did not find that left posterior superior temporal lobe damage was associated with significant comprehension deficits. They examined brain regions involved in auditory sentence comprehension using voxel-based lesion-symptom mapping analysis (VLSM, Bates et al., 2003) in chronic aphasia. A network of brain regions was associated with comprehension deficits in this study, as confirmed by a subsequent lesion analysis study including DTI tractography and resting-state functional magnetic resonance imaging (fMRI) (Turken & Dronkers, 2011). These brain regions were the left middle temporal gyrus and underlying white matter, the anterior superior temporal gyrus, a region including parts of the posterior superior temporal sulcus and angular gyrus, the orbital part of the inferior frontal gyrus, and the middle frontal gyrus. These regions supporting sentence comprehension involved both cortical hemispheres but primarily the left hemisphere, and were supported by numerous white matter pathways connecting temporal, parietal, and frontal association cortices. The role of the middle temporal gyrus (MTG) and an extensive connectivity pattern underlying the MTG was particularly noted by Turken and Dronkers (2011) as of interest given the severe and persisting single-word comprehension deficits resulting from damage to the MTG. Other brain regions in the network were thought to make higher-level contributions to sentence comprehension, such as morphological or syntactic comprehension, working memory, and general cognitive control during more difficult sentence comprehension tasks.

Damage to Wernicke's area was not found to be associated with semantic naming deficits in another recent voxel-based lesion analyses using VLSM to study chronic aphasia (Walker et al., 2011). Given the evidence from hypoperfusion studies, reported earlier, Walker et al. predicted that damage to the left posterior superior temporal lobe would be associated with semantic naming errors. Although they recalibrated their definition of semantic errors to closely align with previous studies of naming errors, they still found that lesions in Wernicke's area were not related to semantic error scores. Walker et al. (2011) did find, however, that the production of semantic naming errors (independent of semantic comprehension) was strongly associated with lesions in the left anterior temporal lobe, in the mid- to anterior MTG region, and not with BA 22, including Wernicke's area.

Discrepancies across studies of the anatomy of aphasia may be the result of methodological issues according to Kreisler et al. (2000). These authors used structural MRI brain analyses to localize regions of interest associated with the aphasia subtypes. Among their conclusions was that impaired auditory comprehension depended on the presence of posterior lesions of the temporal gyri. These analyses were reported as classifying 82% of individuals with impaired auditory comprehension. Yang et al. (2008) also used structural MRI analyses to study the neuroanatomical regions associated with aphasia. They found that 44 of 48 (95.8%) individuals with Wernicke's aphasia had damage in the left posterior superior temporal gyrus. In both of these studies, the results were interpreted as evidence in favor of the classical view of lesion localization in Wernicke's aphasia.

Functional Imaging Studies

Evidence that Wernicke's area is involved in semantic processing during comprehension and naming has been demonstrated by functional imaging studies, including fMRI and positron emission tomography (PET). In a review of these activation studies, Kuest and Karbe (2002) concluded that they agree with the classic model of language organization in which Wernicke's and Broca's areas are the crucial regions of speech processing. However, they noted that the activation studies also provide evidence that there is a widespread cortical network relevant for speech and language.

In a PET study, Wise et al. (2001) found that within the left superior temporal cortex posterior to the primary auditory cortex there were anatomically separable, functional subsystems specialized for perceiving external speech, one's own voice, word retrieval from memory, and transient processing of internally generated or rehearsed phonetic sequences. Other functional imaging studies

described distributed patterns of activation in comprehension and lexical–semantic language tasks (e.g., Binder, Desai, Graves, & Conant, 2009).

In another PET study of chronic aphasia, Warren, Crinion, Lambon Ralph, and Wise (2009) found that impaired single word and sentence comprehension was associated with the amount of damage to left–right anterolateral superior temporal cortical connectivity as well as local activity in the anterolateral superior temporal cortex (STC). They noted that the exact role of the left anterolateral STC in comprehension is debated but that it appears to be an interface between speech–sound representations and word meaning for single words but particularly for connected speech. They suggested that functional connectivity between left and right hemisphere anterolateral STC is a marker of speech comprehension outcome after stroke.

Zaehle, Geiser, Alter, Jancke, and Meyer (2008) used event-related fMRI to examine brain areas activated when healthy volunteers discriminated verbal and nonverbal auditory stimuli. When the discrimination required differentiation of subtle temporal acoustic features, activation was in the posterior part of the left inferior frontal gyrus and the parietal operculum. However, when the discrimination required differentiation based on changes in the frequency content, bilateral activation was observed in the middle temporal gyrus and the superior temporal sulcus. In another fMRI study of speech perception, Zheng et al. (2010) observed bilateral activation in the superior temporal gyrus region during speech production when auditory feedback did not match the predicted outcome of speaking, possibly reflecting a self-monitoring or feedback system linking speech perception and production.

Crinion and Price (2005) investigated the role of the right hemisphere in recovery of auditory comprehension following left hemisphere stroke using fMRI comparing healthy volunteers to individuals with left hemisphere stroke and aphasia. They found that for all of the left hemisphere-damaged participants, the right lateral superior temporal regions, anterior to the primary auditory cortex, were activated during auditory sentence comprehension. Also, when the stroke had spared the left temporal cortex, good auditory sentence comprehension performance was correlated with activation in the left posterior superior temporal cortex (Wernicke's area).

Recent studies by Blumstein and colleagues (e.g., Blumstein, 2011; Righi, Blumstein, Mertus, & Worden, 2009; Yee, Blumstein, & Sedivy, 2008) using eye-tracking and fMRI found that lesions extending into the left posterior superior temporal gyrus related to increased competition among lexical competitors in Wernicke's aphasia (Righi et al., 2009). More generally, the role of Wernicke's area in language was supported by earlier studies in which direct cortical stimulation of Wernicke's area was found to interfere with naming (Ojemann, 1994) and word meaning (Lesser et al., 1986).

Converging evidence across methodologies suggests that Wernicke's area is part of a network of brain regions that supports speech comprehension and naming in adults. However, the precise role of Wernicke's area in language function is still being specified.

Cognitive Neuropsychological Underpinnings

The difficulties in auditory comprehension associated with Wernicke's aphasia can arise from damage to one or more cognitive components involved in speech perception, recognition, and/or comprehension. Auditory comprehension is impaired at the single word level and for ongoing speech.

Perception and Recognition

Normal perception of the speech signal will support subsequent recognition of the stimulus as familiar. Since the 1950s, the focus of much research in perception of single words has been on how phonemes are identified and extracted from the speech signal, whereas recently much speech perception research has focused on how words are segmented and recognized in ongoing speech (see Jusczyk & Luce, 2002, for a review). According to Jusczyk and Luce (2002), phonetic, prosodic, lexical, and phonotactic information may all be used to help the listener to segment the words from ongoing speech.

Many fundamental questions in speech perception are still debated, such as the nature of the basic perceptual unit. Also, there is no consensus as to whether there is specialized perception for speech. As described by Jusczyk and Luce (2002), evidence that there are different modes of perceiving speech versus nonspeech auditory stimuli is provided by studies of sine-wave speech. Listeners process auditory input differently depending upon their expectations (i.e., whether they are told that the sine-wave stimuli are poor quality synthetic speech or nonspeech beeps and tones). Dissociations in performance for speech and nonspeech sounds have been reported in neurologically impaired individuals with forms of auditory agnosia who have preserved perception of environmental sounds and music in the context of impaired speech perception (Coslett, Brashear, & Heilman, 1984), or who have preserved speech comprehension in the context of impaired comprehension of nonspeech sounds (Saygin, Leech, & Dick, 2010). Music perception can dissociate from environmental sounds as well (Griffiths et al., 1997). There is ongoing debate as to how to account for these dissociations in performance across speech and nonspeech tasks (e.g., Slevc, Martin, Hamilton, & Joanisse, 2011).

Nearly all current theories of spoken word recognition involve processes of activation and competition; the speech signal activates multiple word candidates from memory, and competition occurs among the word candidates leading to the selection of the target word (e.g., McQueen & Cutler, 2001). However, the exact mechanisms of activation and competition differ across proposed cognitive models (Jusczyk & Luce, 2002). For example, versions of the influential Cohort Theory (Marslen-Wilson & Welsh, 1978) do not include lateral inhibition among lexical competitors, which would allow word units to suppress activation of their competitors during the recognition process. Lateral inhibition is an important feature of the Trace model (McClelland & Elman, 1986) and others, including the PARSYN model (Luce, Goldinger, Auer, & Vitevitch, 2000).

Activation of lexical representations that will compete for recognition has been viewed as constrained activation or radical activation. In constrained activation models, only parts of the speech input (such as word beginnings in Cohort Theory) are thought to influence activation of word forms. Models such as Trace and PARSYN include radical activation, in which any word form that is consistent with the speech signal will receive some degree of activation at any point in the flow of speech. Jusczyk and Luce (2002) note that the research overall supports the radical activation view of spoken word recognition. However, they argue that Cohort Theory should not be rejected completely because there is strong evidence for a definite left-to-right bias in spoken word recognition (but unlike Cohort Theory this activation is not limited to word beginnings).

Although the focus of much word recognition research has been on word identification, evidence suggests that listeners are able to remember specific acoustic and phonetic information about speech. In ongoing speech, segmenting is affected by changes in speaking rate or voice (e.g., Goldinger, 1996). At the single word level, speech perception is affected by variations in speaking rate in that changes in speech contrasts occur in identification of phonemes (Jusczyk & Luce, 2002). Thus, although lexical codes activated during speech recognition have often been assumed to be abstract phonological codes, there is evidence that temporal and contextual detail encoded in the speech signal is also stored in memory.

Comprehension

Recognition of the spoken word implies that the stimulus is known to be familiar; it does not imply that the meaning of the stimulus is understood. Comprehension of meaning does not occur until the corresponding semantic memory features are activated. For example, after recognition of the word "cow" as familiar, access to its unique combination of corresponding semantic features (e.g., animal, large, farm, gives milk, makes "moo" sound) would distinguish its meaning from other concepts within semantic memory.

The time course of spoken word recognition and comprehension is not clear. Apfelbaum, Blumstein, and McMurray (2011) addressed the possibility that these processes could occur either simultaneously or sequentially. That is, meaning could build simultaneously with lexical activation in a continuous cascade, or alternatively only after lexical activation is complete in a modular system. They found that the magnitude of semantic access is affected by the size of a word's phonological neighborhood (i.e., the number of lexical competitors differing in one phoneme from the target word) such that words with more competition had decreased semantic access. This finding that phonological competition affects semantic access supports the cascading model of word recognition and comprehension, rather than the modular, sequential approach.

A Cognitive Model of Receptive and Expressive Language

A schematic of general processes involved in comprehension and production of single-word language and cognitive processing is presented in Figure 4.1. Separable processes support perception and recognition of various input modalities of sensory stimuli, but these stimuli are often believed to activate meaning within the same semantic memory system (Chialant, Costa, & Caramazza, 2002; Hillis, Rapp, Romani, & Caramazza, 1990; but see

Allport, 1985, and Shallice, 1988, for alternative views). Perception and/or recognition can be differentially impaired across input modalities, disrupting one class of stimuli (e.g., spoken words) while others are spared (e.g., written words or viewed objects). Even when recognition is intact, comprehension can be impaired for one type of stimulus (e.g., spoken words) while remaining intact for other stimulus modalities.

The separability of the language functions depicted in Figure 4.1 is also supported by evidence from comprehension and naming errors in aphasia. For example, some individuals with aphasia produce many semantically related errors in oral naming (e.g., saying "chair" for table) but do not produce these errors in written naming, whereas other individuals display the opposite pattern. This double dissociation in performance across individuals has been interpreted as evidence that verbal (i.e., phonological) and written (i.e., orthographic) language representations are supported by independent cognitive and neural mechanisms (e.g., Hillis, Boatman, Hart, & Gordon, 1999).

As depicted in Figure 4.1, each output mode for expression requires activation of an abstract output form that is stored in memory. The characteristics of this abstract output form vary across output modes (e.g., gestures, spoken words, written words). For verbal output, this is abstract lexical–phonological information that supports verbal production of whole words. (Figure 4.1 does not include the sublexical grapheme-to-phoneme processes that allow oral reading of written novel words or nonwords, which by definition are not stored in lexical memory.)

In normal verbal naming or spontaneous speech, the semantic features of the concept to be expressed are activated within semantic memory. Each semantic feature would subsequently lead to activation of multiple word candidates within lexical phonology, including the target word and phonologically related competitors (e.g., Rapp & Goldrick, 2000). Of these candidates, the word form that is the best fit with the complete semantic feature information would be selected. In current cognitive models of single-word verbal production, activation of the lexical–phonological form is often described as including a whole-word phonological level as well as a subword level of phonological information (e.g., Slevc & Ferreira, 2006). Subword phonological information would be activated from the selected word and from its competitors in cascade fashion, eventually leading to the correct selection of those

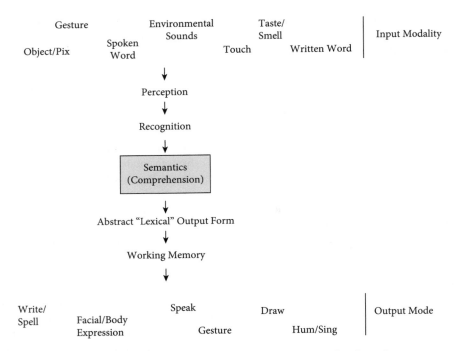

Figure 4.1 A schematic of cognitive processes involved in comprehension and production of single words.

subword units needed for correct articulation (e.g., Hillis et al., 1999).

The cognitive model in Figure 4.1 is a useful framework for interpreting deficits in comprehension and verbal expression in Wernicke's aphasia. Current theories of semantic memory and forms of semantic memory impairment are described by Reilly and Martin in detail in Chapter 6 of this volume. Also, further discussion of cognitive processes involved in verbal naming and its disorders is included in Chapter 7 by Harnish.

Impaired Auditory Comprehension in Wernicke's Aphasia

Disturbances to comprehension in Wernicke's aphasia could arise at any stage of speech perception, recognition, and/or comprehension. "Auditory agnosia" (Freud, 1891) refers to a disorder of auditory recognition with spared hearing, and can affect recognition of one type of auditory stimulus or all auditory stimuli. "Pure word deafness" is an agnosia specific to verbal sounds, resulting from disruption within auditory perception and/or recognition. However, two subtypes of pure word deafness have been suggested, a prephonemic (apperceptive) type in which verbal and nonverbal sound perception is impaired (associated with bitemporal lesions), and a deficit in perception of

verbal sounds only (associated with left unilateral lesions) (Auerbach, Allard, Naeser, Alexander, & Albert, 1982). "Word meaning deafness" is a different type of auditory agnosia in which meaning cannot be attached to spoken words, although the spoken words have been perceived and recognized. Word meaning deafness can also be called a modality-specific semantic access disorder, in that semantic memory cannot be activated from the spoken word but can be activated via other input modalities. In some cases, the full syndrome of Wernicke's aphasia has been reported to evolve to auditory agnosia (Slevc et al., 2011).

Some individuals with Wernicke's aphasia may have problems at the perceptual level in isolating or classifying phonemes. An early perceptual deficit in rapid temporal processing has also been proposed to underlie pure word deafness. Stefanatos, Gershkoff, and Madigan (2005) described an individual with a unilateral left superior temporal lobe infarct and pure word deafness who had difficulty processing transitional spectrotemporal cues from speech and nonspeech sounds. This person was impaired in distinguishing voicing onset and brief format frequency transitions, and could not differentiate stop consonant–vowel syllables in speech discrimination tasks. Additional testing showed that there was no general deficit in auditory temporal resolution that could account for the speech analysis difficulties. Stefanatos et al. (2005) concluded that this person's pure word deafness resulted from left hemisphere damage to auditory analysis of rapid spectrotemporal changes in sound frequency.

Slevc et al. (2011) recently argued that impaired perception of rapid temporal changes could be only a partial explanation of speech perception deficit in another individual with pure word deafness. Although Patient N.L. did demonstrate difficulty discriminating speech stimuli differing in rapid temporal features, he also performed poorly in some other speech discrimination tasks that did not require perception of rapid temporal features. Overall, it is not clear how much perceptual deficits in general can be linked to auditory comprehension impairments in Wernicke's aphasia, because some studies have not found a convincing association between perceptual ability and speech comprehension (e.g., Csépe, Osman-Sági, Molnár, & Gósy, 2001; Miceli, Gainotti, Caltagirone, & Masullo, 1980).

Individuals with Wernicke's aphasia may have impaired suppression of word candidates once they are activated during auditory word recognition. Janse (2006) measured the speed and accuracy of the ability to decide if a spoken stimulus was a real word or not (i.e., lexical decision) when it was preceded by a prime word that was either unrelated to the target as compared to phonologically related to the target word-initial positions. The phonologically related primes had a facilitatory effect on lexical decision for the individuals with Wernicke's aphasia, in contrast to the inhibitory effect of these primes among healthy volunteer participants. This greater speed in lexical decision for target stimuli following the phonologically related primes suggested that even when the prime has been recognized, other phonologically related stimuli that have been coactivated remain above resting level and are not deactivated normally in Wernicke's aphasia.

These results complement those of Wiener et al. (2004) who found that the severity of auditory comprehension deficit in Wernicke's aphasia was positively correlated with the magnitude of the Stroop interference effect. The Stroop interference effect, which reflects poor ability to ignore a distracting stimulus, was significantly greater in participants with Wernicke's aphasia as compared to age-matched healthy volunteers, and could not be accounted for by general slowing. Weiner and colleagues suggested that impaired inhibition would underlie impaired suppression of word candidates during lexical–semantic selection processes in Wernicke's aphasia.

In a study of eye-tracking, Yee et al. (2008) found that individuals with Wernicke's aphasia fixated significantly more often on distractor words that were phonologically similar to target words in word-initial positions than on unrelated distractors. These effects of the phonological competitor words were larger in the Wernicke's aphasia group than in the age-matched healthy volunteers. Based on these results, Yee and colleagues (2008) suggested that deactivation of word candidates is delayed in Wernicke's aphasia.

Mirman, Yee, Blumstein, and Magnuson (2011) recently argued that impaired deactivation of lexical-semantic information contributes to impaired auditory comprehension in Wernicke's aphasia. They used eye-tracking to compare fixation time during a spoken word-to-picture matching task in which the target picture was presented with three distractor pictures. Fixation times on picture choices were compared for rhyming distractors (e.g., parrot–carrot) versus distractors that were phonologically similar to targets in word initial positions (i.e., cohorts such as beaker–beetle). They found that the cohort distractors led to more competition as reflected in longer fixation times on the cohort pictures in individuals with Wernicke's aphasia as compared to age-matched healthy volunteers. Conversely, individuals with Broca's aphasia exhibited greater competition from the rhyme distractors compared to the Wernicke's aphasia participants or age-matched healthy volunteers. Also, a negative correlation was observed in that those individuals with aphasia who showed stronger cohort competition also showed weaker effects of rhyme competition and vice versa. They also reanalyzed data from Yee et al. (2008) and confirmed larger cohort competition effects in individuals with Wernicke's aphasia.

Mirman et al. (2011) simulated several computational models to see how the models could account for these results, and found that increased cohort competition could result from slow deactivation of lexical competitors. However, they also found that a different model simulating impaired selection among competing word alternatives could account for the performance of both the Wernicke's aphasia and Broca's aphasia groups, and also could account for the negative correlation observed within individual participants. On the basis of parsimony, Mirman et al. (2011) hypothesized that this latter simulation model could best account for their results, and also hypothesized that anterior and posterior brain regions may interact in a dynamic balance of activation and inhibition during auditory word recognition. They also noted that there is some support from brain imaging studies that activation of word meaning may be supported by posterior temporal brain regions whereas response selection may be mediated by prefrontal brain regions (e.g., Noppeney, Phillips, & Price, 2004).

In the classic description of Wernicke's aphasia, impaired auditory comprehension is accompanied by impaired reading and writing. The most parsimonious explanation of this pattern of impaired verbal and written comprehension with impaired verbal and written expression is a common source of disruption within semantic memory. It is possible that the semantic information has been lost or damaged, or the language symptoms could arise from impaired activation of lexical–semantic information (Blumstein & Milberg, 2000). In either case, impaired performance across receptive and expressive language tasks suggests that a primary source of language disturbance in Wernicke's aphasia is impaired semantic memory.

However, the auditory–verbal deficits characteristic of Wernicke's aphasia can be accompanied by intact reading and writing. Hillis and colleagues (1999) described Patient J.B.N., an individual with jargon aphasia for whom auditory comprehension was far worse than comprehension of written words, despite intact auditory perception. Verbal expression was marked by phonemic paraphasias and neologisms, and was much more disturbed than written expression. Repetition was very poor, but she could repeat simple consonant–vowel syllables such as "tay." In this case, semantic memory was intact, as measured across tasks such as reading comprehension and written naming of pictures. Comprehension of spoken words was poor, and she frequently accepted a phonologically related word as the correct verbal name for a picture in a word/picture verification task. Hillis and colleagues (1999) interpreted this individual's auditory comprehension impairment as reflecting an inability to associate subword-level phonological representations (i.e., phonemes, or syllables such as "tay") to the word level lexical phonological representations such as "table" during auditory word recognition. This disruption led to poor performance in deciding if a spoken word was a familiar real word or not (i.e., lexical decision) and to poor auditory comprehension.

Verbal Expression Deficits in Wernicke's Aphasia

As alluded to previously, verbal expression in Wernicke's aphasia is largely empty, marked by neologisms, paraphasias, and perseverations. Janse (2006) has suggested that problems in inhibition may affect production as well as comprehension in Wernicke's aphasia. Shindler, Caplan, and Hier (1984) suggested that the frequent perseverations in Wernicke's aphasia may relate to poor self-monitoring of speech. Others have suggested that perseverations reflect difficulty overriding a recently activated response that is persisting in activity beyond the normal time course (e.g., Cohen & Dehaene, 1998). Thus, if there is a problem in deactivation of previously activated word competitors, as discussed above in relation to auditory comprehension, this deactivation deficit could also affect verbal production in Wernicke's aphasia. Mirman et al. (2011) suggested that the fluent but empty speech in Wernicke's aphasia may result from too many words being selected during production.

Phonemic paraphasias and neologisms may result in verbal production when the associations between the whole word and subword levels of phonology are disrupted, as argued by Hillis et al. (1999) in relation to Patient J.B.N. They hypothesized that this disruption caused nontarget subword units to be activated and combined, resulting in phonemic paraphasias or neologisms. They also hypothesized that this disruption to word and subword phonological representations was the result of impaired connections between the posterior superior temporal gyrus in dorsal Brodmann's Area 22 and more ventral parts of Area 22. They suggested that dorsal Area 22 supports subword phonological processing and that ventral portions of Area 22 support processing of spoken word forms.

Verbal Working Memory in Wernicke's Aphasia

The schematic of cognitive–linguistic processes in Figure 4.1 includes working memory (i.e., immediate short-term memory) as a component wherein abstract forms for production are held temporarily prior to expression. For spoken language production, the type of information held in working memory is phonological information. As in Figure 4.1, this process by which verbal information is held in short-term memory is often depicted as a separate cognitive component that can be affected separately from lexical processing by brain damage. However, short-term memory has also been described as inextricable from lexical processing in that activation of lexical–phonological information involves maintaining that information over time (i.e., a form of short-term memory) (e.g., Martin & Gupta, 2004).

Individuals with Wernicke's aphasia, like those with other types of aphasia, perform poorly in some tasks of auditory–verbal short-term memory (e.g., repeating lists of digits in the digit span task). However, Martin and Ayala (2004) found that the specific type of span task used to measure short-term memory results in variations in performance across individuals with varying degrees of disruption to lexical–semantic or phonological processes. They argued that verbal short-term memory is not a unitary capacity and cannot be measured separately from lexical processing.

Impaired verbal short-term memory may affect both expression and comprehension of spoken words in Wernicke's aphasia. An abnormally rapid decay of phonological information during verbal naming would result in errors such as phoneme or syllable omissions and substitutions (e.g., Dell, Martin, & Schwartz, 2007). It has also been suggested that on the input side, auditory word recognition could be disrupted as a result of impaired auditory verbal short-term memory (Janse, 2006). As discussed above, it may be that impaired activation or deactivation during auditory word recognition may contribute to impaired auditory comprehension in some individuals with Wernicke's aphasia. Janse (2006) suggested that verbal short-term memory may be critical for stabilizing the process of auditory word recognition.

Beyond the single word level, there is evidence that semantic short-term memory impairment may interfere with auditory sentence comprehension (e.g., Martin & He, 2004). However, the basis of impaired sentence comprehension in Wernicke's aphasia is not clear, as described below.

Impaired Sentence Processing in Wernicke's Aphasia

Impaired comprehension of closed class words and bound grammatical morphemes contributes to impaired sentence comprehension in Wernicke's aphasia (Dick et al., 2001). In matching spoken sentences to pictures, individuals with Wernicke's aphasia make errors given semantically reversible sentences, and they also have difficulty making grammaticality judgments (see Saffran, 2001, for a review). Saffran noted that individuals with semantic dementia have impaired word comprehension but do not have difficulty in understanding semantically reversible sentences or making grammaticality judgments, suggesting that poor word comprehension alone cannot account for poor performance by individuals with Wernicke's aphasia on these tasks. Saffran (2001) suggested that individuals with Wernicke's aphasia appear to have an additional deficit in sentence processing, but that it is not clear whether this reflects limitations in syntax, impaired short-term memory, or both.

In sentence production, the grammatical abilities of individuals with Wernicke's aphasia may appear to be relatively intact in English. However, Dick et al. (2001) argued that in languages with structures that permit more morpheme substitution errors to emerge, the individuals with Wernicke's aphasia were noted to have a tendency to produce these grammatical substitution errors.

Assessment

During language screening, it may be readily apparent that an individual has Wernicke's aphasia in that verbal expression is fluent but relatively meaningless, and auditory comprehension and repetition are poor. Tests such as the *Boston Diagnostic Aphasia Examination* (BDAE; Goodglass et al., 2001) or the *Western Aphasia Battery-Revised* (WAB-R; Kertesz, 2007), among other tests, measure spontaneous speech, auditory word recognition, and verbal repetition, and also allow identification of impaired naming, reading, and writing. Figure 4.1 is a useful framework to guide in the diagnosis of the more specific source of language impairment within individuals diagnosed with Wernicke's aphasia.

Is Semantic Memory Impaired?

Poor comprehension across input modalities (e.g., spoken words, pictures, written words, observed gestures) likely reflects impairment to semantic memory. Disruption to semantic memory will also interfere with expression across output modes. Performance in understanding spoken stimuli as compared to other stimuli can be assessed using the tasks listed in Table 4.1. For all of these tasks, it is assumed that hearing and visual acuity are within normal limits. Individuals with semantic memory impairment will perform poorly on tasks requiring detailed knowledge of semantic features, but may be able to perform well on tasks designed to measure only general semantic knowledge. Milder forms of semantic memory impairment can be missed if more difficult semantic tasks are not administered.

Table 4.1 Selected Tasks for Assessment and Treatment of Auditory Comprehension

Cognitive Component Targeted	Task	Assessment	Treatment
Auditory perception	Same/different judgments of phonemes, syllables, nonwords or words	X	X
	Auditory segmentation	X	X
Auditory word recognition	Auditory lexical decision	X	
Auditory word	Match spoken word to picture, written word, or gesture	X	X
	Semantic decision	X	X
	Spoken word verification	X	X
	Semantic associate matching	X	X
	Synonym judgment	X	X
	Match spoken definition to picture or written word	X	X
	Gesture to command	X	X
	Semantic feature analysis		X
Alternate input modalities	Sort picture or written words	X	X
	Written word–picture matching	X	X
	Written word–picture verification	X	X
	Match gesture to picture or written word	X	X
	Semantic decision (picture or written words)	X	X
	Synonym judgments (written words)	X	X

(Comprehension spans the rows from Auditory word recognition through Alternate input modalities.)

To ensure the integrity of visual processing when testing individuals with suspected Wernicke's aphasia, it can be useful to perform a simple object identity matching task, in which three objects are presented, two of which are identical. Accurate selection of the identical objects suggests that the visual percept is intact even if the person fails subsequent tasks of visual comprehension that are more difficult. (It should be noted that a person with visual recognition impairment may perform poorly in this task, but could have better comprehension through a nonvisual input modality such as spoken words.)

A variety of tasks can be administered in the assessment of semantic processing. In sorting tasks, a set of picture cards or written word cards is given to the individual to sort into two semantic categories. The difficulty can vary by sorting semantically distant (e.g., food versus transportation) or semantically close (e.g., food versus drinks) categories (Grayson, Hilton, & Franklin, 1997).

In a semantic decision task, the individual is presented with a semantic category (e.g., "animals") and is then asked to indicate whether each spoken word (e.g., "camel") is in that category. The difficulty of this task can be modified depending on the specificity of the semantic category and the similarity of the distractors (e.g., easy: category = animals, distractors = office supplies; hard: category = winter clothing, distractors = summer clothing).

In cross-modality matching tasks, the examiner presents two types of stimuli simultaneously (e.g., spoken word–picture; picture–written word; spoken word–written word, gesture–picture, gesture–written word) and the participant is expected to correctly match one to the other. The difficulty of cross-modality matching can be increased systematically along two dimensions: (1) array size and (2) the similarity of distractors to the target. The task is made easier by reducing the number of choices and by reducing the similarity of the distractor to the target. For example, in an easy version of spoken word–picture matching, the individual could be presented with the spoken word "horse" and a picture of a horse and a pencil (unrelated distractor). In a difficult version of this task, the individual could be presented with the spoken word "horse" and five pictures: a horse, three distractor pictures that are related to horse, and an unrelated distractor. Distractors that are semantically related to the target "horse" (e.g., dog or cow) require detailed semantic knowledge to distinguish from the target. An individual who obtains only general semantic information from the spoken word may incorrectly match "horse" to one of these semantically related distractors. An individual with difficulty in recognizing spoken words may incorrectly select a phonologically related distractor (e.g., horn for the target "horse"). Some individuals with impaired auditory comprehension may make both of these types of errors, or may be so impaired that they respond randomly, even selecting unrelated distractors. One commercially available subtest of auditory word–picture matching is in the *Psycholinguistic Assessments of Language Processing in Aphasia* (PALPA; Kay, Lesser, & Coltheart, 1992).

Cross-modality matching tasks can be made particularly difficult by asking the individual to match to a semantic associate of the target. In spoken word–picture matching, for example, the spoken word "horse" would be presented with a choice of pictures including a semantic associate of the target (e.g., saddle) and distractor pictures. Available tests to assess semantic associate matching include the *Pyramids and Palm Trees Test* (Howard & Patterson, 1992).

Alternative to matching is a verification task using any combination of stimuli from two input modalities. For example, the individual could be presented with one spoken word and one picture, and is to respond "yes" or "no" to indicate whether the spoken word and the picture match. Performance on this task can be influenced by the types of distractors used. For example, an individual with semantic impairment will have difficulty rejecting distractors that are semantically related to the target (e.g., a picture of a dog presented with the spoken word "horse"). As administered by Hillis et al. (1999), each target item was presented three times: once with the correct name, once with a phonologically related distractor, and once with a semantically similar distractor. Participants were given credit for understanding the target only if they correctly verified its correct match and also correctly rejected it when it was incorrectly matched. This verification task has been found to be more sensitive to comprehension impairment (i.e., more difficult) than the word–picture matching task (e.g., Greenwald & Berndt, 1999; Breese & Hillis, 2004). This may reflect the effect of uncertainty in the verification task as compared to the word–picture matching task, in which individuals who are uncertain of the correct response can be successful when encouraged to guess in pointing to a picture.

In the synonym judgments task, two spoken words are presented (e.g., "start" and "beginning") and the participant is to respond "yes" or "no" to indicate whether or not the two words mean nearly the same thing. An alternate version of this comprehension task includes two written word stimuli instead of spoken words. From either spoken or written stimuli (e.g., PALPA; Kay et al., 1992), this is a difficult semantic task in that accurate synonym judgments require specific semantic knowledge.

In the matching to auditory definitions task, a spoken definition is presented and the participant matches the definition to a choice of pictures or written words. Comprehension of the definition requires specific semantic knowledge, and this task is also demanding of verbal working memory. Oral naming can also be used to measure the individual's comprehension of the definition; however, in this case poor performance could reflect either poor comprehension or simply poor naming ability.

An individual with impaired auditory comprehension but good comprehension via a different input modality (e.g., written words, gestures, or pictures) does not have semantic memory impairment. In this case, the impaired auditory comprehension results from a deficit in auditory perception or recognition, or from impaired access to semantic memory from the spoken word.

Is Auditory Word Recognition Impaired?

The task of auditory lexical decision is used to assess recognition of spoken words. The participant is presented with one spoken word or nonword and is expected to indicate "yes" or "no" as to whether the stimulus is a real word. The difficulty of this task can be modified depending upon the structure of the nonword stimuli and also the word frequency of the word stimuli. That is, nonwords such as "pgaf" do not sound like plausible English words and therefore are easier to reject than nonwords that contain very common English phoneme combinations (e.g., praf). Word stimuli that are more common in the English language (i.e., high frequency words) are easier to accept as real words than low frequency words.

Phonological errors in tasks of auditory word comprehension suggest impairment in auditory word recognition. For example, as described above, an individual who incorrectly matches the spoken word "horse" to a picture of a horn may have difficulty in auditory word recognition. A phonologically related error of this type indicates that auditory word recognition processes are insufficient to specify fully the correct lexical–phonological information.

Is Semantic Access from Spoken Words Impaired?

The assessments of semantic memory and of auditory word recognition, described above, will yield information about semantic access from the spoken word. If semantic memory is not impaired (as indicated by good performance in difficult semantic memory tasks from at least one input modality) and auditory word recognition is not impaired (as indicated by good performance in the auditory lexical decision task), then poor auditory comprehension reflects a disturbance in semantic access from spoken words. In the context of Figure 4.1, the locus of impairment is between the recognition level and the semantic level and results in an inability to associate meaning with the spoken word. As described above, this pattern is also called word meaning deafness.

Is Auditory Perception Impaired?

An individual can have poor auditory word recognition (as indicated by poor performance in the auditory lexical decision task described above) and still have intact auditory perception. However, the problem with auditory word recognition could result from an earlier disruption to auditory perception. A variety of tasks have been used to assess auditory perception of speech or nonspeech sounds, such as a discrimination task in which the individual is asked to respond "yes" or "no" as to whether or not two spoken stimuli are the same or different. The stimuli can be words (e.g., bat–pat) or nonwords (e.g., tay–tah). A repetition form of this task can also be administered in which the individual is asked to repeat the word or nonword stimulus, but poor performance in this case is more difficult to interpret because it could reflect poor auditory discrimination or poor verbal production.

Assessment of Expression across Tasks

Verbal expression in Wernicke's aphasia typically is similarly impaired across tasks such as spontaneous speech, picture description, and picture naming.

Whereas these abilities are commonly assessed in most aphasia batteries, testing of alternative modes of expression may not be included. When semantic memory is impaired, expression through all of the output modalities depicted in Figure 4.1 will be affected. (Sublexical reading and spelling routes are not depicted in Figure 4.1 and may allow regularly spelled words to be read or spelled despite semantic impairment.)

Impaired verbal expression in Wernicke's aphasia reflects disruption to lexical–phonological forms for output, as described above. This disruption will be reflected in poor performance across verbal expression tasks, and can also be detected using a rhyme judgment task. In this task, the person is presented with two written words or pictures and asked to respond "yes" or "no" to indicate if the two words rhyme or not. A difficulty in administering the rhyme judgment task to an individual with Wernicke's aphasia is that the person may not understand the task instructions.

Assessment of other output modes of expression (e.g., writing/spelling, drawing, facial/body expression, humming/singing, gesturing) involves determining whether the response conveys the correct meaning, and also whether there is a production impairment distorting the response. For example, an individual may produce a recognizable gesture to convey "eating," although the gesture may be distorted in timing, sequencing, or spatial organization (e.g., Rothi, Ochipa, & Heilman, 1991). Severe production impairment (e.g., severe ideomotor limb apraxia) will interfere with the expression of meaning and may require direct treatment.

Assessment of Functional and Social Communication

Determining areas of communication strength in the individual with Wernicke's aphasia requires a broader assessment approach than the tasks and standardized tests described above. As described by Marshall (2008), the individual with Wernicke's aphasia may demonstrate better functional communication when the language assessment includes stimuli that are personalized to the individual, and when the individual is engaged in the interview through this personalized approach. Observations of the person attempting to communicate in natural situations may provide valuable information about what strategies work best. There are a variety of direct and indirect means available for measuring functional communication as reviewed by Patterson in Chapter 3, including the *Communication Abilities in Daily Living* (CADL-2; Holland, Frattali, & Fromm, 1999) and the *Communicative Effectiveness Index* (CETI; Lomas et al., 1989).

Treatment

The overall goal of aphasia rehabilitation is to assist each individual in achieving the highest level of functional and social communication possible given his or her degree and type of impairment. Individuals with recent onset of Wernicke's aphasia may be discharged from the hospital rapidly because of intact sensory and motor abilities. The rehabilitation clinician must educate and counsel the other healthcare professionals, patient, and family about Wernicke's aphasia, and identify effective communication strategies. As time allows, treatment encompassing both restitutive and substitutive approaches can be implemented (Rothi, 1995; Raymer & Rothi, 2008). The goal of a restitutive treatment approach is to restore cognitive–linguistic processes that are impaired. The goal of a substitutive approach is to encourage the use of other cognitive–linguistic processes that are intact and could circumvent or facilitate the impaired language functions.

Counseling the person with recent onset of Wernicke's aphasia is a challenge because the person has poor comprehension and yet is in great need of information and reassurance. The rehabilitation clinician can attempt to convey information using multiple input modalities, such as short, simple verbal information combined with pictures, written words, or gestures. In trying to understand what has happened and the prognosis for recovery, the patient may depend heavily on information to be gained from the clinician's eye contact, facial expressions, speech prosody, and body language.

Counseling the patient's family or significant others may include providing information about aphasia evolution, the goals of aphasia rehabilitation, and training of communication partners. Because the person with Wernicke's aphasia is able to walk and to perform activities of daily living, and may not convey his or her lack of understanding during conversational attempts, others may not believe that the person has impaired comprehension. This can cause misunderstandings among family members when the patient does not react appropriately to their requests or concerns. Some family members can be included in treatment sessions to observe the patient's level of performance and to receive training in specific communication strategies as modeled by the clinician. There is evidence that training of family members or volunteers as conversational partners

can be effective in improving communicative interactions in aphasia, although more detailed measurement of these effects in individuals with Wernicke's aphasia is needed (Turner & Whitworth, 2006).

To meet the needs of an individual whose Wernicke's aphasia may be evolving rapidly in the early days and weeks postonset, treatment goals and activities must be flexible (Table 4.1). In Wernicke's aphasia, the clinician may cue the patient to stop talking so much if the fluent, empty output appears to be interfering with communicative interactions. In this case, nonverbal expression (e.g., gesturing; pointing to pictures) may be encouraged as a more successful way for the patient to express basic wants and needs, and may reduce frustration. However, Marshall (2008) has argued that an alternative approach (Martin, 1981) in which the patient is encouraged to use verbal expression is more beneficial in the early stage postonset. In Marshall's (2008) context-based approach to management of Wernicke's aphasia, whatever verbal communicative competence the patient does have available is highlighted in natural communicative contexts involving the patient's personal interests or concerns.

As a group, individuals with aphasia have slower processing speed than healthy volunteers and longer reaction times with increased processing load for both verbal and spatial material (Korda & Douglas, 1997). Although not every individual with aphasia has slow processing speed, this suggests that in general reducing the rate and amount of information conveyed to the person with aphasia can improve comprehension and response time. Increased auditory comprehension has been observed in aphasia when the rate of speech presented is slowed (Pashek & Brookshire, 1982).

Treatment of Auditory Comprehension Impairments

Impaired auditory comprehension can arise from a number of deficit patterns that may affect perception, recognition, and/or semantic activation. The type and severity of comprehension deficit in the individual will determine the specific stimuli and tasks used in treatment. Task instructions may be difficult to convey to an individual with impaired comprehension, and pairing gesture and modeling with simple instructions is beneficial.

RESTITUTIVE APPROACHES

As noted above, Wernicke's aphasia often evolves to conduction aphasia or to anomic aphasia, both reflecting improvement in auditory comprehension.

There is evidence that direct behavioral intervention can facilitate this restoration of comprehension abilities.

Several studies have documented improvement of speech perception abilities in individuals with perceptual impairments affecting auditory comprehension. Computerized training of phoneme discrimination and phoneme recognition was found to improve auditory comprehension in an individual with pure word deafness (Tessier, Weill-Chounlamountry, Michelot, & Pradat-Diehl, 2007). In an attempt to facilitate auditory comprehension in another individual with pure word deafness, Slevc et al. (2011) administered an intensive treatment of rapid temporal processing using the Fast ForWord program (Scientific Learning Corporation). After 43 sessions over 2.5 months, discrimination of rapid temporal differences in nonspeech sounds improved, but not in speech sounds. They concluded that this program was not effective for treatment of impaired speech perception in pure word deafness.

Auditory segmentation training led to improved auditory comprehension in an individual with Wernicke's aphasia (Jones, 1989). Despite an initial phase of treatment designed to improve expressive language, there was little change noted in this person's auditory analysis abilities until they were specifically targeted in therapy. Likewise, auditory processing improved following direct treatment in an individual with impaired auditory comprehension arising from impaired auditory perception (Morris, Franklin, Ellis, Turner, & Bailey, 1996). The auditory treatment included both perceptual tasks (e.g., phoneme discrimination; syllable discrimination) and comprehension tasks (e.g., matching spoken words to pictures or written words; spoken word verification). Lip-reading (a substitutive strategy) was encouraged. Two treatment sessions per week for 6 weeks resulted in significant improvement that was specific to auditory processing tasks rather than nonauditory tasks, suggesting that the improvement was secondary to treatment.

Three types of auditory comprehension tasks were used in three separate treatment phases in an attempt to facilitate auditory comprehension in an individual with jargon aphasia (Grayson et al., 1997). This individual had a severe semantic impairment and also had a deficit in auditory processing. Phase one of treatment was focused on semantic tasks (matching objects or pictures to a spoken or written word; sorting pictures by semantic category; semantic associate matching) with the goal of improving semantic processing. In word–picture matching, initially only two choices were provided: the target picture and one unrelated distractor. As the client improved, task difficulty was increased systematically by increasing the array size (to maximum of six) and the similarity of the distractors to the target. In the sorting task, difficulty was modified by increasing the semantic relatedness of the groups to be sorted (e.g., food versus drink), adding more groups (e.g., sorting transportation pictures into air/road/sea categories), or presenting the words verbally with no picture. One hour of treatment 5 days a week for 4 weeks resulted in significantly improved accuracy in written word–picture matching and fewer selections of the unrelated distractor in matching either written words or spoken words to pictures (i.e., errors became more closely related to the target). No general language improvement was observed, suggesting that these changes were due to the semantic treatment.

In Phase two treatment (Grayson et al., 1997), semantic treatment continued but an auditory training task was added involving spoken word to picture matching with rhyming word distractors (e.g., pictures of deer, beer, tear). The participant was encouraged to lip read (a substitutive strategy). After 3 weeks of training three times a week for 15-minute sessions, significant improvement was seen in auditory discrimination of minimal pairs and in auditory comprehension as measured by spoken word–picture matching (which had not improved significantly until Phase two auditory training). Phase three treatment was focused on increasing comprehension beyond single words. Treatment tasks (pointing to lists of spoken words in a sequence and spoken sentence–picture matching) resulted in significant improvement in sentence comprehension.

Musso et al. (1999) studied the effects of brief, intense auditory comprehension training involving verbal matching or verbal decision tasks in four individuals with Wernicke's aphasia. Eleven brief sessions resulted in improved auditory comprehension as measured by a shortened version of the *Token Test* (De Renzi & Vignolo, 1962) and in increased activation of the left precuneus and the right posterior portion of the superior temporal gyrus as measured by PET scan.

Francis, Clark, and Humphreys (2003) found that errorless learning training to improve attention and working memory resulted in improved language comprehension in an individual with receptive aphasia. Attention is thought to support speech perception and comprehension (e.g., Hugdahl, Bodner, Weiss, & Benke, 2003), although its role is not well understood. Barker-Collo et al. (2009) found that attention impairments a month after stroke can be improved through 4 weeks of Attention Process Training (APT; Sohlberg & Mateer, 1987). Helm-Estabrooks (2011) emphasized the role of attention in receptive language deficits in aphasia, and has argued for attention training as a cognitive approach to remediation of impaired auditory comprehension. Helm-Estabrooks and Albert (2004) described a cognitive approach to treating impaired auditory comprehension in aphasia that incorporates stimuli from the Cognitive Linguistic Task Book (CLTB; Helm-Estabrooks, 1995) into tasks of attention, concentration, visual memory, counting, number facts, judgments and estimations, visuoperception and construction, and semantic/conceptual knowledge. Three individuals with aphasia, including one with Wernicke's aphasia, demonstrated significant improvement in auditory comprehension following this CLTB treatment. One case study is described in more detail by Helm-Estabrooks and Holland (1998).

Persons with Wernicke's aphasia have been included among larger groups of participants in some aphasia treatment studies, but the extent to which the individuals with Wernicke's aphasia improved is unclear. For example, in a placebo-controlled study, Walker-Batson et al. (2001) found that the rate of auditory comprehension recovery increased when amphetamines were used as an adjunct to 10 1-hour sessions of speech–language therapy over 5 weeks. The 21 participants included five individuals with Wernicke's aphasia (one received amphetamines and four received placebo), but the outcome for the Wernicke's participants alone was not reported. A different treatment study included four individuals with Wernicke's aphasia among a total of 28 individuals with chronic aphasia (Meinzer et al., 2004). The participants with Wernicke's aphasia received 30 hours (3 hours a day for 10 days) of constraint-induced therapy involving verbal production tasks and a restraint on alternative, nonverbal communication. The average test scores of the group of 28 individuals on the *Token Test* significantly improved, indicating improved auditory comprehension. However, the specific language scores for the four participants with Wernicke's aphasia were not reported. It is not possible to determine how well the Wernicke's patients

actually improved in this context, but this warrants more careful examination.

Computerized training of semantic tasks resulted in improved auditory comprehension in two individuals with semantic impairment (Raymer, Kohen, & Saffell, 2006). Training involved matching a spoken or written word to a picture when presented with the target picture and semantic distractors. Because many individuals with Wernicke's aphasia have semantic impairment, we can speculate that a similar form of computerized auditory training may be appropriate for individuals with Wernicke's aphasia. However, this computerized treatment approach has not been directly tested in Wernicke's aphasia.

SUBSTITUTIVE APPROACHES

Treatments for impaired auditory comprehension have included a variety of input modalities to supplement or replace the auditory speech channel. Lip-reading has been a component of successful treatments for auditory comprehension (Grayson et al., 1997; Morris et al., 1996), but has not always provided an advantage (Maneta, Marshall, & Lindsay, 2001). Written word input has been used in a number of treatment studies as a means of facilitating semantic processing (e.g., Francis, Riddoch, & Humphreys, 2001; Hough, 1993). In the treatment of pure word deafness, Tessier et al. (2007) used systematic visual cues that were gradually delayed and suppressed.

Treatment of Impaired Verbal Expression
RESTITUTIVE APPROACHES

In Wernicke's aphasia, neologisms and paraphasias in speech production may result from disrupted associations between the whole word and subword levels of output phonology, and/or insufficient activation of output phonology via semantics. Treatment focused on strengthening semantics has been used to treat verbal expression in Wernicke's aphasia, with the rationale that this would lead to stronger activation of phonology via semantics (Jones, 1989). Selected semantic-based treatment tasks are described above in relation to treating auditory comprehension impairments.

An additional approach to facilitating semantic processing is semantic feature analysis (SFA; Ylvisaker & Szekeres, 1985). The participant is asked to generate the semantic features of a target concept, particularly features that distinguish it from similar concepts. The treatment rationale is that (1) this will facilitate associations between the target semantic features and their corresponding phonological word forms in output phonology, and (2) the phonological word form that best fits all of the semantic features would receive the most activation and would be selected for output. Boyle (2010) reviewed seven treatment studies using SFA or variations of SFA to treat word retrieval deficits in aphasia. She noted that not all treatment studies using this general approach have required the participants to generate the semantic features, but that most participants improved in verbal naming even if treatment involved analyzing semantic features generated by others rather than the patient generating them.

An individual with Wernicke's aphasia characterized by deficits in auditory word recognition and in semantic processing was provided with semantic feature analysis treatment for anomia (Boyle, 2004). The treatment schedule was three 75-minute sessions per week for 4 weeks (Phase 1), followed by a 4-week break, and then another 12 sessions (Phase 2). Improved verbal picture naming for trained and untrained items was observed. Five discourse elicitation tasks were also used to evaluate the effects of treatment on more typical speaking contexts. Although the number of correct information units (CIUs) in discourse increased, the percentage of CIUs in discourse did not change significantly, nor did the response time during word retrieval.

In a treatment study of oral naming of nouns and verbs, two individuals with Wernicke's aphasia were provided training in producing a gesture along with a verbal name (Raymer et al., 2006). Noun naming did not improve for either of the participants with Wernicke's aphasia, but one of them did demonstrate significantly improved oral naming of trained verbs following treatment. One of these individuals also showed an increase in spontaneous use of gestures after treatment.

SUBSTITUTIVE APPROACHES

As described above, there are two basic approaches to the management of verbal expression deficits in individuals with Wernicke's aphasia: encouraging reliance on speech output (Marshall, 2008) or discouraging verbal output in favor of alternative modes of expression. Substitutive treatments for impaired speech can include any of the output modes in Figure 4.1, as well as the use of augmentative and alternative communication (AAC) devices. For example, the clinician may provide paper and pencil and encourage the patient to attempt drawing, or may assist the patient in learning to use a picture pointing board or similar electronic device. Some individuals with Wernicke's aphasia may spontaneously express semantic concepts nonverbally; for example, when unable to name a picture of cake, the person might hum "Happy Birthday," pretend to blow out a candle, or smile and say "yum." The clinician can encourage these means of substituting for impaired naming (e.g., melodies, body language, and gestures).

Expression via multiple output modes is encouraged through the therapy program Promoting Aphasics' Communicative Effectiveness (PACE; Davis & Wilcox, 1985). In this conversational training program, the clinician and the client take equal turns in sending or receiving new messages contained on selected cards. The benefit of using games in aphasia treatment has been described by Marshall (2008) and others as a way of incorporating receptive and expressive language goals into naturalistic, social contexts. A modified version of the PACE program can be used as a guessing game for family members to play with the individual who has aphasia. The patient and family member can take turns selecting a card from a small set of pictures and then using any expressive mode they wish to convey the picture on the card. The receiver of the message can indicate a guess by pointing to a set of options. This simple game can provide a familiar context for patient and family communication after stroke, such as playing a game with a grandchild. Treatment methods to promote use of gesture and overall communicative effectiveness may be effective for Wernicke's aphasia; however, the use of these methods in Wernicke's aphasia has not been specifically reported and warrants further study.

Written language was used as a substitutive mode of expression in the treatment of six individuals with jargon aphasia (Robson, Marshall, Chiat, & Pring, 2001). Initially, written production was targeted through tasks of copying, word completion, and written picture naming. This resulted in improved written naming but little change in the ability to use written words to convey functional messages. Therefore, three of the participants received additional treatment that involved communicating written messages to a partner. Functional use of writing then improved across a variety of communicative contexts.

Conclusions

The symptoms of Wernicke's aphasia and the associated cognitive deficits of anosognosia, impaired attention, and impaired self-monitoring have been reviewed in this chapter. The neuroanatomical substrates of Wernicke's aphasia were discussed in the context of advanced technological methodologies. Current cognitive–linguistic theories of Wernicke's aphasia were examined, particularly impaired auditory processing resulting from deficits in speech perception, recognition, and comprehension. Finally, the chapter included a review of methods for the assessment and treatment of Wernicke's aphasia.

Further research is needed to explore the following questions related to Wernicke's aphasia: (1) What communication strategies employed by individuals with Wernicke's aphasia are effective in improving functional communication? (2) In a group of individuals with varying degrees of severity of Wernicke's aphasia, do comprehension and expression deficits reflect impaired deactivation of lexical items? (3) In the context of new computational models of language, how does the pattern of Wernicke's aphasia relate to impairments in conceptual knowledge, short-term memory, and attention?

References

Alajouanine, T. (1956). Verbal realization in aphasia. *Brain*, *79*, 1–28.

Allport, D.A. (1985). Distributed memory, modular subsystems and dysphasia. In S. Newman & R. Epstein (Eds.), *Current perspectives in dysphasia* (pp. 32–60). Edinburgh: Churchill Livingstone.

Apfelbaum, K.S., Blumstein, S.E., & McMurray, B. (2011). Semantic priming is affected by real-time phonological competition: Evidence for continuous cascading systems. *Psychonomics Bulletin Review*, *18*, 141–149.

Ardila, A. (2010). A proposed reinterpretation and reclassification of aphasic syndromes. *Aphasiology*, *24*, 363–394.

Auerbach, S.H., Allard, T., Naeser, M., Alexander, M.P., & Albert, M.L. (1982). Pure word deafness. Analysis of a case with bilateral lesions and a defect at the prephonemic level. *Brain*, *105*, 271–300.

Baars, B.J., Motley, M.T., & MacKay, D.G. (1975). Output editing for lexical status in artificially elicited slips of the tongue. *Journal of Verbal Learning and Verbal Behavior*, *14*, 382–391.

Babinski, J. (1914). Contribution a l'etude de troubles mentaux dans l'hemiplegie organique cerebrale. *Revue Neurologie*, *27*, 845–847.

Bakheit, A.M., Shaw, S., Carrington, S., & Griffiths, S. (2007). The rate and extent of improvement with therapy from the different types of aphasia in the first year after stroke. *Clinical Rehabilitation*, *21*, 941–949.

Barker-Collo, S.L., Feigin, V.L., Lawes, C.M., Parag, V., Senior, H., & Rodgers, A. (2009). Reducing attention deficits after stroke using attention process training: A randomised controlled trial. *Stroke*, *40*, 3293–3298.

Bates, E., Wilson, S.M., Saygin, A.P., Dick, F., Sereno, M.I., Knight, R.T., & Dronkers, N.F. (2003). Voxel-based lesion-symptom mapping. *Nature Neuroscience, 6*, 448–450.

Binder, J.R., Desai, R.H., Graves, W.W., & Conant, L.L. (2009). Where is the semantic system? A critical review and meta-analysis of 120 functional neuroimaging studies. *Cerebral Cortex*, *19*, 2767–2796.

Blumstein, S.E. (2011). Neural systems underlying lexical competition in auditory word recognition and spoken word production: Evidence from aphasia and functional neuroimaging. In G. Gaskell & P. Zwitserlood (Eds.), *Lexical representation: A multidisciplinary approach* (pp. 123–148). New York: De Gruyter Mouton.

Blumstein, S.E., & Milberg, W.P. (2000). Language deficits in Broca's and Wernicke's aphasia: A singular impairment. In Y. Grodzinsky, L. Shapiro, & D. Swinney (Eds.), *Language and the brain: Representation and processing* (pp. 167–183). New York: Academic Press.

Boyle, M. (2004). Semantic feature analysis treatment for anomia in two fluent aphasia syndromes. *American Journal of Speech Language Pathology*, *13*, 236–249.

Boyle, M. (2010). Semantic feature analysis treatment for aphasic word retrieval impairments: What's in a name? *Topics in Stroke Rehabilitation*, *17*, 411–422.

Breese, E.L., & Hillis, A.E. (2004). Auditory comprehension: Is multiple choice really good enough? *Brain and Language*, *89*, 3–8.

Buckingham, H.W. (1987). Phonemic paraphasias and psycholinguistic production models for neologistic jargon. *Aphasiology*, *1*, 381–400.

Butterworth, B. (1979). Hesitation and the production of verbal paraphasias and neologisms in jargon aphasia. *Brain and Language*, *18*, 133–161.

Catani, M. (2007). From hodology to function. *Brain*, *130*, 602–605.

Catani, M., & ffytche, D.H. (2005). The rises and falls of disconnection syndromes. *Brain*, *128*, 2224–2239.

Catani, M., Howard, R.J., Pajevic, S., & Jones, D.K. (2002). Virtual in vivo interactive dissection of white matter fasciculi in the human brain. *Neuroimage*, *17*, 77–94.

Catani, M., Jones, D.K., Donato, R., & ffytche, D.H. (2003). Occipito-temporal connections in the human brain. *Brain*, *126*, 2093–2107.

Catani, M., & Mesalum, M. (2008). The arcuate fasciculus and the disconnection theme in language and aphasia: History and current state. *Cortex*, *44*, 953–961.

Chialant, D., Costa, A., & Caramazza, A. (2002). Models of naming. In A.E. Hillis (Ed.), *The handbook of adult language disorders* (pp. 123–142). New York: Psychology Press.

Cohen, L., & Dehaene, S. (1998). Competition between past and present: Assessment and interpretation of verbal perseverations. *Brain*, *121*, 1641–1659.

Coslett, H.B., Brashear, H.R., & Heilman, K.M. (1984). Pure word deafness after bilateral primary auditory cortex infarcts. *Neurology*, *34*, 347–352.

Crinion, J., & Price, C.J. (2005). Right anterior superior temporal activation predicts auditory sentence comprehension following aphasic stroke. *Brain*, *128*, 2858–2871.

Csépe, V., Osman-Sági, J., Molnár, M., & Gósy, M. (2001). Impaired speech perception in aphasic patients: Event-related potential and neuropsychological assessment. *Neuropsychologia*, *39*, 1194–1208.

Davis, G.A., & Wilcox, M.J. (1985). *Adult aphasia rehabilitation: Applied pragmatics*. San Diego: Singular.

Dell, G.S. (1986). A spreading-activation theory of retrieval in sentence production. *Psychological Review*, *93*, 283–321.

Dell, G.S., Martin, N., & Schwartz, M.F. (2007). A case-series test of the interactive two-step model of lexical access: Predicting word repetition from picture naming. *Journal of Memory and Language, 56*, 490–520.

Dell, G.S., & Reich, P.A. (1981). Stages in sentence production: An analysis of speech error data. *Journal of Verbal Learning and Verbal Behavior, 20*, 611–629.

De Renzi, E., & Vignolo, L. (1962). The Token Test: A sensitive test to detect receptive disturbances in aphasics. *Brain, 85*, 665–678.

Dick, F., Bates, E., Wulfeck, B., Utman, J.A., Dronkers, N., & Gernsbacher, M.A. (2001). Language deficits, localization, and grammar: Evidence for a distributive model of language breakdown in aphasic patients and neurologically intact individuals. *Psychological Review, 108*, 759–788.

Dronkers, N.F., Wilkins, D.P., Van Valin, R.D., Redfern, B.B., & Jaeger, J.J. (2004). Lesion analysis of the brain areas involved in language comprehension. *Cognition, 92*, 145–177.

Eggert, G.H. (1977). *Wernicke's works on aphasia: A sourcebook and review.* The Hague: Mouton Publishers.

Fast ForWord Language. Scientific Learning Corporation, Oakland, CA.

Francis, D.R., Clark, N., & Humphreys, G.W. (2003). The treatment of an auditory working memory deficit and the implications for sentence comprehension abilities in mild "receptive" aphasia. *Aphasiology, 17*, 723–750.

Francis, D.R., Riddoch, M.J., & Humphreys, G.W. (2001). Cognitive rehabilitation of word meaning deafness. *Aphasiology, 15*, 749–766.

Freud, S. (1891). *On aphasia.* New York: International University Press, Inc.

Geschwind, N. (1967). Wernicke's contributions to the study of aphasia. *Cortex, 3*, 449–463.

Godefroy, O., Dubois, C., Debachy, B., Leclerc, M., & Kreisler, A. (2002). Vascular aphasias: Main characteristics of patients hospitalized in acute stroke units. *Stroke, 33*, 702–705.

Goldinger, S.D. (1996). Words and voices: Episodic traces in spoken word identification and recognition memory. *Journal of Experimental Psychology: Learning, Memory and Cognition, 22*, 1166–1183.

Goldrick, M., & Rapp, B. (2002). A restricted interaction account (RIA) of spoken word production: The best of both worlds. *Aphasiology, 16*, 20–55.

Goodglass, H., Kaplan, E., & Barresi, B. (2001). *Boston Diagnostic Aphasia Examination* (3rd ed.). Hagerstown, MD: Lippincott Williams & Wilkins.

Grayson, E., Hilton, R., & Franklin, S. (1997). Early intervention in a case of jargon aphasia: Efficacy of language comprehension therapy. *European Journal of Disorders of Communication, 32*, 257–276.

Greenwald, M.L., & Berndt, R.S. (1999). Impairment of abstract letter order knowledge: Severe alexia in a mildly aphasic patient. *Cognitive Neuropsychology, 16*, 513–556.

Griffiths, T.D., Bates, D., Rees, A., Witton, C., Gholkar, A., & Green, G.G. (1997). Sound movement detection deficit due to a brainstem lesion. *Journal of Neurology, Neurosurgery, and Psychiatry, 62*, 522–526.

Hart, J., & Gordon, B. (1990). Delineation of single-word semantic comprehension deficits in aphasia, with anatomical correlation. *Annals of Neurology, 27*, 226–231.

Hartsuiker, R.J., Pickering, M.J., & De Jong, N.H. (2005). Semantic and phonological context effects in speech error repair. *Journal of Experimental Psychology: Learning, Memory, & Cognition, 31*, 921–932.

Heilman, K.M., Barrett, A.M., & Adair, J.C. (1998). Possible mechanisms of anosognosia: A defect in self-awareness. *Philosophical Transactions of the Royal Society of London, 353*, 1903–1909.

Helm-Estabrooks, N. (1995). *Cognitive linguistic task book.* Sandwich, MA: Cape Cod Institute for Communication Disorders.

Helm-Estabrooks, N. (2011). Treating attention to improve auditory comprehension deficits associated with aphasia. *Perspectives on Neurophysiology and Neurogenic Speech and Language Disorders, 21*, 64–71.

Helm-Estabrooks, N., & Albert, M.L. (2004). *Manual of aphasia and aphasia therapy* (2nd ed.). Austin, TX: PRO-ED.

Helm-Estabrooks, N., & Holland, A.L. (1998). *Approaches to the treatment of aphasia.* San Diego, CA: Singular.

Hillis, A.E., Barker, P., Beauchamp, N.J., Gordon, B., & Wityk, R.J. (2000). MR perfusion imaging reveals regions of hypoperfusion associated with aphasia and neglect. *Neurology, 55*, 782–788.

Hillis, A.E., Barker, P., Beauchamp, N., Winters, B., Mirski, M., & Wityk, R. (2001). Restoring blood pressure reperfused Wernicke's area and improved language. *Neurology, 56*, 670–672.

Hillis, A.E., Boatman, D., Hart, J., & Gordon, B. (1999). Making sense out of jargon: A neurolinguistic and computational account of jargon aphasia. *Neurology, 53*, 1813–1824.

Hillis, A.E., Kane, A., Tuffiash, E., Ulatowski, J.A., Barker, P.B., Beauchamp, N.J., et al. (2001). Reperfusion of specific brain regions by raising blood pressure restores selective language functions in subacute stroke. *Brain and Language, 79*, 495–510.

Hillis, A.E., Kleinman, J.T., Newhart, M., Heidler-Gary, J., Gottesman, R., Barker, P.B., et al. (2006). Restoring cerebral blood flow reveals neural regions critical for naming. *Journal of Neuroscience, 26*, 8069–8073.

Hillis, A., Rapp, B., Romani, C., & Caramazza, A. (1990). Selective impairment of semantics in lexical processing. *Cognitive Neuropsychology, 7*, 191–243.

Hillis, A.E., Wityk, R.J., Barker, P.B., Beauchamp, N.J., Gailloud, P., Murphy, K., Cooper, O., & Metter, E.J. (2002). Subcortical aphasia and neglect in acute stroke: The role of cortical hypoperfusion. *Brain, 125*, 1094-1104.

Hillis, A.E., Wityk, R.J., Tuffiash, E., Beauchamp, N.J., Jacobs, M.A., Barker, P.B., et al. (2001). Hypoperfusion of Wernicke's area predicts severity of semantic deficit in acute stroke. *Annals of Neurology, 50*, 561–566.

Holland, A.L., Frattali, C., & Fromm, D. (1999). *Communication Abilities of Daily Living* (2nd ed.). Austin, TX: PRO-ED.

Hough, M.S. (1993). Treatment of Wernicke's aphasia with jargon: A case study. *Journal of Communication Disorders, 26*, 101–111.

Howard, D., & Patterson, K.E. (1992). *The Pyramids and Palm Trees Test.* Bury St. Edmunds: Thames Valley Test Corporation.

Howes, D. (1964). Application of word-frequency concept to aphasia. In A.V.S. de Reuch & M. O'Conner (Eds.), *Disorders of language* (pp. 47–62). London: Churchill.

Hugdahl, K., Bodner, T., Weiss, E., & Benke, T. (2003). Dichotic listening performance and frontal lobe function. *Cognitive Brain Research, 16*, 58–65.

Hula, W.D., & McNeil, M.R. (2008). Models of attention and dual task performance as explanatory concepts in aphasia. *Seminars in Speech and Language, 29*, 169–187.

Humphreys, K.R. (2002). Lexical bias in speech errors. Unpublished doctoral dissertation, University of Illinois, Urbana-Champaign.

Janse, E. (2006). Lexical competition effects in aphasia: Deactivation of lexical candidates in spoken word processing. *Brain and Language, 97*, 1–11.

Jones, E.V. (1989). A year in the life of EVJ and PC. *Proceedings of the Summer Conference of the British Aphasiology Society.* London: University of London Printing Services.

Jusczyk, P.W., & Luce, P.A. (2002). Speech perception and spoken word recognition: Past and present. *Ear and Hearing, 23*, 2–40.

Kay, J., Lesser, R., & Coltheart, M. (1992). *PALPA: Psycholinguistic Assessments of Language Processing in Aphasia.* East Sussex, England: Lawrence Erlbaum.

Kerschensteiner, M., Poeck, K., & Brunner, E. (1972). The fluency-nonfluency dimension in the classification of aphasic speech. *Cortex, 8*, 233–247.

Kertesz, A. (1993). Clinical forms of aphasia. *Acta Neurochirurgica, 56*, 52–58.

Kertesz, A. (2007). *The Western Aphasia Battery-Revised.* San Antonio, TX: Harcourt Publishers.

Kertesz, A., & Benson, F. (1970). Neologistic jargon—a clinico-pathological study. *Cortex, 6*, 362–386.

Kertesz A., Lau W.K., & Polk M. (1993). The structural determinants of recovery in Wernicke's aphasia. *Brain and Language, 44*, 153–164.

King, J., & Hux, K. (1996). Attention allocation in adults with and without aphasia: Performance on linguistic and nonlinguistic tasks. *Journal of Medical Speech-Language Pathology, 4*, 245–256.

Korda, R., & Douglas, J. (1997). Attention deficits in stroke patients with aphasia. *Journal of Clinical and Experimental Neuropsychology, 19*, 525–542.

Kortte, K.B., & Hillis, A.E. (2011). Recent trends in rehabilitation interventions for visual neglect and anosognosia for hemiplegia following right hemisphere stroke. *Future Neurology, 6*, 33–43.

Kreisler, A., Godefroy, O., Delmaire, C., Debachy, B., Leclercq, M., Pruvo, J.P., et al. (2000). The anatomy of aphasia revisited. *Neurology, 54*, 1117–1123.

Kuest, J., & Karbe, H. (2002). Cortical activation studies in aphasia. *Current Neurology and Neuroscience Reports, 6*, 511–515.

Kurowski, K.M., Blumstein, S.E., Palumbo, C.L., Waldstein, R.S., & Burton, M.W. (2007). Nasal consonant production in Broca's and Wernicke's aphasics: Speech deficits and neuroanatomical correlates. *Brain and Language, 100*, 262–275.

Laska, A.C., Hellblom, A., Murray, V., Kahan, T., & Von Arbin, M. (2001). Aphasia in acute stroke and relation to outcome. *Journal of Internal Medicine, 249*, 413–422.

Lesser, R.P., Luders, H., Morris, H.H., Dinner, D.S., Klem, G., Hahn, J., et al. (1986). Electrical stimulation of Wernicke's area interferes with comprehension. *Neurology, 36*, 548–663.

Levelt, W.J.M. (1983). Monitoring and self-repair in speech. *Cognition, 14*, 41–104.

Levelt, W.J.M. (1989). *Speaking: From intention to articulation.* Cambridge, MA: MIT Press.

Levelt, W.J.M., Roelofs, A., & Meyer, A.S. (1999). A theory of lexical access in speech production. *Behavioral & Brain Sciences, 22*, 1–75.

Lomas, J., Picard, L., Bester, S., Elbard, H., Finlayson, A., & Zoghaib, C. (1989). The Communicative Effectiveness Index: Development and psychometric evaluation of a functional communication measure for adult aphasia. *Journal of Speech and Hearing Disorders, 54*, 113–124.

Luce, P.A., Goldinger, S.D., Auer, E.T., & Vitevitch, M.S. (2000). Phonetic priming, neighborhood activation, and PARSYN. *Perception and Psychophysics, 62*, 615–625.

MacKay, D.G. (1987). *The organization of perception and action: A theory for language and other cognitive skills.* New York: Springer.

MacKay, D.G. (1992). Awareness and error detection: New theories and research paradigms. *Consciousness and Cognition, 1*, 199–225.

Maher, L.M, Rothi, L.J., & Heilman, K.M. (1994). Lack of error awareness in an aphasic patient with relatively preserved auditory comprehension. *Brain and Language, 46*, 402–418.

Maneta, A., Marshall, J., & Lindsay, J. (2001). Direct and indirect therapy for word sound deafness. *International Journal of Language and Communication Disorders, 36*, 91–106.

Marshall, R.C. (2008). Early management of Wernicke's aphasia: A context-based approach. In R. Chapey (Ed.), *Language intervention strategies in aphasia and related neurogenic communication disorders* (5th ed., pp. 507–529). Philadelphia: Lippincott Williams & Wilkins.

Marshall, R.C., Rappaport, B.Z., & Garcia-Bunuel, L. (1985). Self-monitoring behavior in a case of severe auditory agnosia with aphasia. *Brain & Language, 24*, 297–313.

Marslen-Wilson, W.D., & Welsh, A. (1978). Processing interactions and lexical access during word recognition in continuous speech. *Cognitive Psychology, 10*, 29–63.

Martin, A.D. (1981). Therapy with the jargonaphasic. In J. Brown (Ed.), *Jargonaphasia* (pp. 305–326). New York: Academic Press.

Martin, N., & Ayala, J. (2004). Measurements of auditory-verbal STM span in aphasia: Effects of item, task, and lexical impairment. *Brain and Language, 89*, 464–483.

Martin, N., Gagnon, D.A., Schwartz, M.F., Dell, G.S., & Saffran, E.M. (1996). Phonological facilitation of semantic errors in normal and aphasic speakers. *Language & Cognitive Processes, 11*, 257–282.

Martin, N., & Gupta, P. (2004). Exploring the relationship between word processing and verbal short-term memory: Evidence from associations and dissociations. *Cognitive Neuropsychology, 21*, 213–228.

Martin, N., Weisberg, R.W., & Saffran, E.M. (1989). Variables influencing the occurrence of naming errors: Implications for models of lexical retrieval. *Journal of Memory & Language, 28*, 462–485.

Martin, R.C., & He, T. (2004). Semantic short-term memory and its role in sentence processing: A replication. *Brain and Language, 89*, 76–82.

McClelland, J.L., & Elman, J.L. (1986). The TRACE model of speech perception. *Cognitive Psychology, 18*, 1–86.

McQueen, J.M., & Cutler, A. (2001). Spoken word access processes: An introduction. *Language and Cognitive Processes, 16*, 469–490.

Meinzer, M., Elbert, T., Wienbruch, C., Djundja, D., Barthel, G., & Rockstroh, B. (2004). Intensive language training enhances brain plasticity in chronic aphasia. *BMC Biology, 2*, 20–29.

Miceli, G., Gainotti, G., Caltagirone, C., & Masullo, C. (1980). Some aspects of phonological impairment in aphasia. *Brain and Language, 11*, 159–169.

Miller, D., & Ellis, A.W. (1987). Speech and writing errors in "neologistic jargon aphasia:" A lexical activation hypothesis. In M. Coltheart, G. Sartori, & R. Job (Eds.), *The cognitive neuropsychology of language* (pp. 253–271). Hove: Lawrence Erlbaum Associates.

Mirman, D., Yee, E., Blumstein, S.E., & Magnuson, J.S. (2011). Theories of spoken word recognition deficits in aphasia: Evidence from eye-tracking and computational modeling. *Brain and Language*, *117*, 53–68.

Mishra, N.K., Rossetti, A.O., Ménétrey, A., & Carota, A. (2009). Recurrent Wernicke's aphasia: Migraine and not stroke! *Headache*, *49*, 765–768.

Morris, J., Franklin, S., Ellis, A.W., Turner, J.E., & Bailey, P.J. (1996). Remediating a speech perception deficit in an aphasic patient. *Aphasiology*, *10*, 137–158.

Moses, M.S., Nickels, L.A., & Sheard, C. (2004). Disentangling the web: Neologistic perseverative errors in jargon aphasia. *Neurocase*, *10*, 452–461.

Murray, L., Holland, A., & Beeson, P. (1997). Auditory processing in individuals with mild aphasia: A study of resource allocation. *Journal of Speech, Language, Hearing Research*, *40*, 792–808.

Musso, M., Weiller, C., Kiebel, S., Muller, S., Bulau, P., & Rijntjes, M. (1999). Training-induced brain plasticity in aphasia. *Brain*, *122*, 1781–1790.

Nicholas, M., Obler, L.K., Albert, M.L., & Helm-Estabrooks, N. (1985). Empty speech in Alzheimer's disease and fluent aphasia. *Journal of Speech and Hearing Research*, *28*, 405–410.

Nickels, L., & Howard, D. (1995). Phonological errors in aphasic naming: Comprehension, monitoring and lexicality. *Cortex*, *31*, 209–237.

Noppeney, U., Phillips, J., & Price, C. (2004). The neural areas that control the retrieval and selection of semantics. *Neuropsychologia*, *42*, 1269–1280.

Obler, L.K., Albert, M.L., Goodglass, H., & Benson, F.D. (1978). Aphasia type and aging. *Brain and Language*, *6*, 318–322.

Ojemann, G.A. (1994). *Cortical stimulation and recording in language*. London: Academic Press.

Oomen, C.C.E., & Postma, A. (2002). Limitations in processing resources and speech monitoring. *Language & Cognitive Processes*, *17*, 163–184.

Orfei, M.D., Robinson, R.G., Prigatano, G.P., Starkstein, S., Rusch, N., Bria, P., et al. (2007). Anosognosia for hemiplegia after stroke is a multifaceted phenomenon: A systematic review of the literature. *Brain*, *130*, 3075–3090.

Pashek, G.V., & Brookshire, R.H. (1982). Effects of rate of speech and linguistic stress on auditory paragraph comprehension of aphasic individuals. *Journal of Speech and Hearing Research*, *25*, 377–383.

Pashek, G.V., & Holland, A.L. (1988). Evolution of aphasia in the first year post-onset. *Cortex*, *24*, 411–423.

Pedersen, P.M., Vinter, K., & Olsen, T.S. (2004). Aphasia after stroke: Type, severity and prognosis. The Copenhagen aphasia study. *Cerebrovascular Disorders*, *17*, 35–43.

Postma, A. (2000). Detection of errors during speech production: A review of speech monitoring models. *Cognition*, *77*, 97–131.

Rapp, B., & Goldrick, M. (2000). Discreteness and interactivity in spoken word production. *Psychological Review*, *107*, 460–499.

Raymer, A., Kohen, F., & Saffell, D. (2006). Computerised training for impairments for word comprehension and retrieval in aphasia. *Aphasiology*, *20*, 257–268.

Raymer, A.M., & Rothi, L.J.G. (2008). Impairments of word comprehension and production. In R. Chapey (Ed.), *Language intervention strategies in aphasia and related neurogenic communication disorders* (5th ed., pp. 607–631). Baltimore: Lippincott Williams & Wilkins.

Raymer, A.M., Singletary, F., Rodriguez, A., Ciampitti, M., Heilman, K.M., & Rothi, L.J.G. (2006). Effects of gesture + verbal treatment for noun and verb retrieval in aphasia. *Journal of the International Neuropsychological Society*, *12*, 867–882.

Righi, G., Blumstein, S.E., Mertus, J., & Worden, M.S. (2009). Neural systems underlying lexical competition: An eye tracking and fMRI study. *Journal of Cognitive Neuroscience*, *22*, 213–224.

Robson, J., Marshall, J., Chiat, S., & Pring, T. (2001). Enhancing communication in jargon aphasia: A small group study of writing therapy. *International Journal of Language and Communication Disorders*, *36*, 471–488.

Rohrer, J.D., Warren, J.D., Modat, M., Ridgway, G.R., Douiri, A., Rossor, M.N., et al. (2009). Patterns of cortical thinning in the language variants of frontotemporal lobar degeneration. *Neurology*, *72*, 1562–1569.

Rothi, L.J.G. (1995). Behavioral compensation in the case of treatment of acquired language disorders resulting from brain damage. In R.A. Dixon & L. Mackman (Eds.), *Compensating for psychological deficits and declines: Managing losses and promoting gains* (pp. 219–230). Mahwah, NJ: Lawrence Erlbaum.

Rothi, L.J.G., Ochipa, C., & Heilman, K M. (1991). A cognitive neuropsychological model of limb praxis. *Cognitive Neuropsychology*, *8*, 443–458.

Saffran, E.M. (2001). Effects of language impairment on sentence comprehension. In R.S. Berndt (Ed.), *The handbook of neuropsychology* (2nd ed., Vol. 3, pp. 157–171). Amsterdam: Elsevier.

Sahaya, K., Dhand, U.K., Goyal, M.K., Soni, C.R., & Sahota, P.K. (2010). Recurrent epileptic Wernicke aphasia. *Journal of the Neurological Sciences*, *291*, 98–99.

Sakurai, Y., Kurisaki, H., Takeda, K., Iwata, M., Bandoh, M., Watanabe, T., et al. (1992). Japanese crossed Wernicke's aphasia. *Neurology*, *42*, 144–148.

Saygin, A.P., Leech, R., & Dick, F. (2010). Nonverbal auditory agnosia with lesion to Wernicke's area. *Neuropsychologia*, *48*, 107–113.

Schlenk, K.J., Huber, W., & Willmes, K. (1987). "Prepairs" and repairs: Different monitoring functions in aphasic language production. *Brain and Language*, *30*, 226–244.

Schwartz, M.F., Saffran, E.M., Bloch, D.E., & Dell, G.S. (1994). Disordered speech production in aphasic and normal speakers. *Brain and Language*, *47*, 52–88.

Seckin, H., Yigitkanli, K., Kapucu, O., & Bavbek, M. (2009). Crossed Wernicke's aphasia after aneurysmal subarachnoid hemorrhage: A case report. *Turkish Neurosurgery*, *19*, 77–81.

Selnes, O.A., Knopman, D.S., Niccum, N., & Rubens, A.B. (1985). The critical role of Wernicke's area in sentence repetition. *Annals of Neurology*, *17*, 549–557.

Shallice, T. (1988). *From neuropsychology to mental structure*. Cambridge: Cambridge University Press.

Shindler, A.G., Caplan, L.R., & Hier, D.B. (1984). Intrusions and perseverations. *Brain and Language*, *23*, 148–158.

Shuren, J.E., Smith-Hammond, C., Maher, L.M., Rothi, L.J.G., & Heilman, K.M. (1995). Attention and anosognosia: The case of a jargonaphasic patient with unawareness of language deficit. *Neurology*, *45*, 376–378.

Shuster, L.I. (2005, March 01). Aphasia theories and treatment. *The ASHA Leader*.

Slevc, L.R., & Ferriera, V.S. (2006). Halting in single word production: A test of the perceptual loop theory of speech monitoring. *Journal of Memory and Language, 54*, 515–540.

Slevc, L.R., Martin, R.C., Hamilton, A.C., & Joanisse, M.F. (2011). Speech perception, rapid temporal processing, and the left hemisphere: A case study of unilateral pure word deafness. *Neuropsychologia, 49*, 216–230.

Sohlberg M., & Mateer, C.A. (1987). Effectiveness of an attention-training program. *Journal of Clinical and Experimental Neuropsychology, 9*, 117–130.

Stefanatos, G.A., Gershkoff, A., & Madigan, S. (2005). On pure word deafness, temporal processing, and the left hemisphere. *Journal of the International Neuropsychological Society, 11*, 456–470.

Stroop, J.R. (1935). Studies of interference in serial verbal reactions. *Journal of Experimental Psychology, 18*, 643–662.

Tessier, C., Weill-Chounlamountry, A., Michelot, N., & Pradat-Diehl, D. (2007). Rehabilitation of word deafness due to auditory analysis disorder. *Brain Injury, 21*, 1165–1174.

Turken, A.U., & Dronkers, N.F. (2011). The neural architecture of the language comprehension network: Converging evidence from lesion and connectivity analyses. *Frontiers in Systems Neuroscience, 5*, 1–20.

Turner, S., & Whitworth, A. (2006). Conversational partner training programmes in aphasia: A review of key themes and participants' roles. *Aphasiology, 20*, 483–510.

Walker, G.M., Schwartz, M.F., Kimberg, D.Y., Faseyitan, O., Brecher, A., Dell, G.S., et al. (2011). Support for anterior temporal involvement in semantic error production in aphasia: New evidence from VLSM. *Brain & Language, 117*, 110–122.

Walker-Batson, D., Curtis, S., Natarajan, R., Ford, J., Dronkers, N., Salmeron, E., et al. (2001). A double-blind, placebo-controlled study of the use of amphetamine in the treatment of aphasia. *Stroke, 32*, 2093–2098.

Warren, J., Crinion, J.T., Lambon Ralph, M.A., & Wise, R. J. (2009). Anterior temporal lobe connectivity correlates with functional outcome after aphasic stroke. *Brain, 132*, 3428–3442.

Weiller, C., Isensee, C., Rijntjes, M., Huber, W., Muller, S., Bier, D., et al. (1995). Recovery from Wernicke's aphasia: A positron emission tomographic study. *Annals of Neurology, 37*, 723–732.

Wernicke, C. (1874). Der aphasische symptomencomplex. Ein psychologische studie auf anatomischer basis. Breslau: Cohn & Weigert.

Wiener, D.A., Connor, L.T., & Obler, L.K. (2004). Inhibition and auditory comprehension in Wernicke's aphasia. *Aphasiology, 18*, 599–609.

Wise, R.J., Scott, S.K., Blank, S.C., Mummery, C.J., Murphy, K., & Warburton, E.A. (2001). Separate neural subsystems within "Wernicke's area." *Brain, 124*, 83–95.

Yang, Z.H., Zhao, X.Q., Wang, C.X., Chen, H.Y., & Zhang, Y.M. (2008). Neuroanatomic correlation of the post-stroke aphasias studied with imaging. *Neurological Research, 30*, 356–360.

Yee, E., Blumstein, S.E., & Sedivy, J.C. (2008). Lexical–semantic activation in Broca's and Wernicke's aphasia: Evidence from eye movements. *Journal of Cognitive Neuroscience, 20*, 592–612.

Ylvisaker, M., & Szekeres, S. (1985). Cognitive-language intervention with brain-injured adolescents and adults. Paper presented at the Annual Convention of the Illinois Speech-Language-Hearing Association, Chicago, Illinois.

Zaehle, T., Geiser, E., Alter, K, Jancke, L., & Meyer, M. (2008). Segmental processing in the human auditory dorsal stream. *Brain Research, 1220*, 179–190.

Zheng, Z.Z., Munhall, K.G., & Johnsrude, I.S. (2010). Functional overlap between regions involved in speech perception and in monitoring one's own voice during speech production. *Journal of Cognitive Neuroscience, 22*, 1770–1781.

Conduction Aphasia: Impaired Phonological Processing

Carolyn E. Wilshire

Abstract

Conduction aphasia is a syndrome characterized by impaired repetition in the context of relatively preserved auditory comprehension and fluent speech. The classical conceptualization of conduction aphasia as a disconnection syndrome has been undermined in recent years. Nevertheless, this diagnosis delineates a small subset of individuals with aphasia who have many common cognitive and anatomical characteristics. Conduction aphasia is associated with damage to a relatively narrow and well-defined group of left hemisphere brain structures, which may include the posterior superior temporal lobe, the inferior parietal lobe, and the insula. According to current cognitive neuropsychological frameworks, an impairment in phonological planning for speech production is the common underlying cognitive dysfunction in the majority of cases, which may sometimes be accompanied by an analogous impairment in receptive phonology. Other common features, such as sentence repetition problems and reduced short-term memory span, may be a secondary consequence of the primary phonological impairment. Current approaches to the treatment of conduction aphasia target the underlying impairment in phonological planning. It is argued that the diagnosis of conduction aphasia can be a useful first step toward understanding a person's language difficulties and planning effective treatment interventions.

Key Words: Conduction aphasia, Phonological output, Phonemic paraphasias, Short-term memory

Introduction

In 1874, neurologist Carl Wernicke described an aphasic condition in which individuals were able to speak fluently and articulate normally, but sometimes struggled to find the words they needed to express themselves, often making multiple attempts at each word (see Wernicke, 1977, for an English translation of Wernicke's work by Eggert). In stark contrast to those with Wernicke's aphasia, these individuals had no apparent difficulty understanding spoken language. For example, Wernicke described the case of Beckman, a 64-year-old pharmacist, as follows:

> He might speak fluently in conversation for some time, then suddenly come upon a word and hesitate, remaining hanging for a time, struggle to find the word, but each attempt was inappropriate. He

repeatedly corrected himself, but the harder he tried, the more frustrating the situation became … (From the English translation in Wernicke, 1977, p. 126)

Wernicke reasoned that this pattern of performance is precisely what would be expected if there were a partial or total disconnection between Broca's and Wernicke's areas. Such a lesion would impede the efficient transmission of information from the auditory "word store," located in Wernicke's area, to the motor speech center in Broca's area, so that word form information was not always consistently available (Wernicke, 1977, p. 130). In line with this disconnection hypothesis, Wernicke named the disorder *Conduction aphasia* (or to be more precise, its German equivalent, *Leitungsaphasie:* Wernicke, 1874; see also Henderson, 1992, for a more extensive history of conduction aphasia). Subsequent researchers, such as Lichtheim (1885), further pre-dicted that individuals with this disorder might have particular difficulty repeating spoken words or sentences, because this skill would rely heavily on the ability to transmit information efficiently from auditory to motor speech areas. Lichtheim (1885) was able to confirm this prediction in several cases that were similar in many respects to those of Wernicke. Later researchers, such as Geschwind (1965), further suggested that the hypothesized "disconnection" in conduction aphasia might arise as a result of damage to the *arcuate fasciculus*, a bundle of white matter fibers that connects Wernicke's and Broca's areas, which runs through the white matter beneath the supramarginal gyrus.

This history highlights one important feature of conduction aphasia that sets it apart from the other major aphasia syndromes: conduction aphasia earned its status not so much because its features were dramatically different from those of other syndromes, but rather because of its theoretical significance to aphasiologists at the time of it being the result of a disconnection. The idea of a "disconnection syndrome" emerged quite naturally from the neurally based language models of the nineteenth century, and so it is perhaps not surprising that researchers sought support for its existence. The current usefulness of the concept of disconnection lies in its selectivity; the defining characteristics of conduction aphasia delineate quite a small subset of cases involving patients with many common cognitive and anatomical characteristics. This diagnosis can therefore be a useful first step toward understanding the person's language difficulties and planning treatment interventions.

Syndrome Description and Characteristics

There are three primary diagnostic criteria for conduction aphasia. The first is poor word and/or sentence repetition. In both the Boston Aphasia Diagnostic Assessment (BDAE, 3rd ed.; Goodglass, Kaplan, & Barresi, 2001) and the Western Aphasia Battery (WAB-R; Kertesz, 2007), conduction aphasia is identified by a marked difficulty in sentence and word repetition. The repetition disorder is the primary feature that distinguishes conduction aphasia from (fluent) anomic aphasia, in which the range of acceptable repetition scores is higher. The second criterion for a diagnosis of conduction aphasia is relatively spared comprehension of auditorily presented words and sentences. In general, the profile for conduction aphasia significantly overlaps that of mild Wernicke's aphasia except on auditory

comprehension measures, in which the range of acceptable scores for conduction aphasia is considerably higher. The third criterion is relatively fluent speech. Although some hesitancy or distortion may be evident on troublesome words, and there may be frequent pauses due to word-finding difficulties, overall scores on measures of articulatory fluency and phrase length should be consistently higher than those associated with Broca's or other nonfluent forms of aphasia. These three key characteristics of conduction aphasia are universal to all cases simply by definition alone.

There are two points to note about the defining features of conduction aphasia. The first is that they are based as much on exclusionary criteria as they are on inclusionary criteria. The requirements for well-preserved auditory comprehension *and* fluent speech eliminate a large number of potential cases, particularly in the acute phase, making the diagnosis quite narrow. The second point to note is that the distinction between conduction aphasia and Wernicke's aphasia is more quantitative than qualitative. In current assessment tools, the relevant measure of auditory comprehension is usually an aggregate score based on a range of word and sentence comprehension tasks, and there is generally a predefined cut-off score that separates conduction aphasia from Wernicke's aphasia. In reality, however, the auditory comprehension scores of individuals with Wernicke's aphasia and conduction aphasia do not form two neatly separated clusters, but rather lie on a continuum. Cases of conduction aphasia that score near the cut-off are sometimes described as "Borderline conduction aphasia" or "Wernicke conduction aphasia" (e.g., Goodglass, 1992). It has been suggested that these cases may be anatomically and/or cognitively distinct. We consider the issue of variability within conduction aphasia in more detail below.

The most common etiology of conduction aphasia is an ischemic infarct affecting the posterior territory of the left middle cerebral artery; less common causes are subarachnoid hemorrhage, intracerebral hematoma, lacunar infarct, and tumor resection (Bartha & Benke, 2003; Wilshire, 2002). In the acute phase, the incidence of conduction aphasia appears to be quite low compared to other aphasia syndromes (Bartha & Benke, 2003), perhaps because only a small proportion of such cases has sufficiently good comprehension and is sufficiently fluent to meet the diagnosis. In chronic aphasia, the incidence of conduction aphasia may be higher, as it usually includes some individuals originally diagnosed with Wernicke's aphasia acutely, whose auditory comprehension has since improved (sometimes called "recovered Wernicke's"). Most studies of conduction aphasia have focused on chronic cases. Consequently, the research summarized in this chapter focuses primarily on the chronic form of the disorder (except where otherwise noted).

Conduction Aphasia: Other Common Features

SPOKEN LANGUAGE PRODUCTION

Aside from its defining features, the single most universal characteristic of conduction aphasia is the production of *phonemic paraphasias* (phonological errors; e.g., "totato" for tomato) not just in repetition, but in all tasks requiring spoken output. As the examples in Table 5.1 illustrate, these phonemic paraphasias are often very similar to the intended word, but with one or more phonemes missing or others substituted in their place (Béland, Caplan, & Nespoulous, 1990; Kohn, 1984; Kohn & Smith, 1991; Laganaro & Zimmerman, 2010; Pate, Saffran, & Martin, 1987; Shallice, Rumiati, & Zadini, 2000; Wilshire & McCarthy, 1996; Wilshire, 2002). Other types of errors may also be produced, including formal paraphasias (phonologically related real word substitutions; e.g., saddle → "*sandal*"; mushroom → "*marshmallow*"), interrupted, incomplete attempts (e.g., "fl-"), and occasionally, semantic errors (e.g., camel → "horse"). However, phonemic paraphasias are the predominant error type. Another almost universal characteristic of conduction aphasia is a sensitivity to word length; longer words almost invariably elicit more errors than shorter ones on all kinds of speech production tasks (e.g., Caplan, Vanier, & Baker, 1986; Caramazza, Papagno, & Ruml, 2000; Franklin, Buerk, & Howard, 2002; Kohn, 1989; Kohn & Smith, 1990, 1991, 1995; Laganaro & Zimmerman, 2010; McCarthy & Warrington, 1984; Pate et al., 1987; Shallice et al., 2000; Wilshire & McCarthy, 1996). Many individuals also demonstrate word frequency effects, producing significantly more errors on rare than on more common words, even when word length is controlled (e.g., Shallice et al., 2000; cases EF, EL, and GM: Wilshire, 2002). However, not all individuals show this effect (e.g., Pate et al., 1987; Wilshire & McCarthy, 1996; case ED: Wilshire, 2002).

Individuals with conduction aphasia are usually very aware of their errors. Indeed, they often attempt to correct them, sometimes repeatedly, producing strings of successive phonological approximations to the target. This behavior is known as

Conduite d'Approche (Joanette, Keller, & Lecours, 1980; Laganaro & Zimmerman, 2010; Wilshire & McCarthy, 1996). These attempts may sometimes, but not always, end in success. For example, when shown a picture of a turtle, case GL reported by Wilshire and Saffran (2005) responded, "*um.. tor-net, no that's not right.. t-.. turry-.. no.. turkey.. no .... oh gosh.. tur-.. turk-.... turking.. that's wrong what's the end part?.. um.. I can't remember ....*" When shown a picture of garlic, she responded, "*garf ... garsit ... gar ... har ... garlict ... garlic!*"

In general, speech errors in conduction aphasia are most evident on constrained word production tasks such as picture naming (Table 5.1) and word repetition, especially if these tasks include a number of longer words. Interestingly, and contrary to the classical disconnection account, most individuals actually perform more poorly in picture naming than in word repetition, at least when the same kinds of materials are used in both tasks (e.g., Caplan et al., 1986; Franklin et al., 2002; Kohn, 1989; Kohn & Smith, 1991; Laganaro & Zimmerman, 2010; Pate et al., 1987; Wilshire & McCarthy, 1996; cases EL, EF, GL, ED, and GM: Wilshire, 2002). However, not all cases exhibit this pattern, a point we return to below. In connected speech, errors may occur much less frequently than they do in constrained tasks. Indeed, as the speech samples in Table 5.2 illustrate, most individuals with conduction aphasia are capable of producing long runs of well-articulated speech, sometimes spanning several utterances, before they encounter a troublesome word.

The phonemic paraphasias observed in conduction aphasia sometimes appear similar to the verbal apraxic errors observed in Broca's aphasia. However, they have several distinctive qualities. First, the errors do not create forms that are necessarily easier to articulate. Many errors are actually more complex from an articulatory point of view than their intended targets. For example, individuals may insert a complex consonant cluster into their error even when none was required, or may substitute a voiced for an unvoiced consonant, even though the former requires more precise articulatory–motor coordination (Nespoulous, Joanette, Béland, Caplan, & Lecours, 1984; Nespoulous, Joanette, Ska, Caplan, & Lecours, 1987; Romani, Olson, Semenza, & Granà, 2002; Romani & Galluzzi, 2005; see also Franklin et al., 2002; Romani, Galluzzi, Bureca, & Olson, 2011). Second, aside from the phonemic paraphasias and other errors, speech in conduction aphasia is usually articulated without effort, and sounds undistorted to the listener. Indeed, as

Table 5.1 Examples of Phonemic Paraphasic Errors Produced in Picture Naming

Case	Examples
EG	anchor → "*angkwen*"; Eskimo → "*elephone*"; ghost → "*gofe*"
ES	dice → "*drice*"; turkey → "*turchey*"; volcano → "*vengka*"
JG	belt → "*ben*"; chimney → "*chimley*"; volcano → "*vengkawna*"
CW	bench → "*brench*"; Eskimo → "*eskierio*"; fish → "*fritch*"
HB	elephant → "*elemus*"; Eskimo → "*haskemu*"; train → "*treel*"
LH	Eskimo → "*Esko*"; necklace → "*narksla*"; spider → "*snider*"
EF	calendar → "*caldenden*"; moustache → "*mustaush*"; pencil → "*prencil*"
MA	ambulance → "*umbelen*"; dice → "*dase*"; pirate → "*parget*"
JL	broom → "*broofs*"; pineapple → "*canapple*"; scarf → "*scorf*"
EL	ostrich → "*orswatch*"; plug → "*slug*"; anchor → "*kanger*"
ED	acorn → "*ocrorn*"; Eskimo → "*isekemay*"; wheelbarrow → "*liberel*"
GM	chimney → "*chummel*"; helmet → "*helen*"; pineapple → "*penanel*"

Note: Examples from 12 speakers of U.S. English with a diagnosis of conduction aphasia on the BDAE (from Wilshire, 2002). These errors represent the person's first complete (uninterrupted) attempt at each item.

noted above, there may be long runs of well-paced, well-articulated speech, sometimes spanning several utterances. Third, individuals with conduction aphasia often produce types of errors in writing similar to the ones they produce in speech (e.g., rhinoceros → "*rhinorius*"; rectangle → "*rectalge*": Wilshire & McCarthy, 1996; see also Gandour, Dardarananda, & Holasuit, 1991; Shallice et al., 2000). This observation suggests that the primary difficulty lies not in articulatory programming per se, but rather in a more abstract process that is common to both spoken and written production.

The features of conduction aphasia we have discussed so far strongly suggest an impairment

Table 5.2 Descriptions of the Cookie Theft Picture from the BDAE by Two Individuals Diagnosed with Conduction Aphasia

Case VM (Goodglass, Kaplan, & Barresi, 2001):

"Well, there's a boy on a <u>stoor</u>.... <u>stoor</u> .... <u>stoor</u>.. <u>sstor</u>, s-, that's just about ready to <u>fod</u> . . <u>fall</u> . . He's getting cookies from a <u>car</u> . . . jar, and giving some to his sister. His mother doesn't even care anything. She's doesn't know what's going on. She's <u>wah</u> . . <u>wah</u> . . she's walking . . . she's <u>tr</u>. drying some dishes and, uh, the . . . She's letting the <u>wad</u> . . . water run over the sh . . . sh . . <u>shtree</u> on the . . on the floor. He's ge . . . She doesn't care and she's looking through. She doesn't even looking out of the window to see the . . . um . . . the other part of the house . . . and <u>bu-</u> . . . busses (tgt: bushes) and lawn. That's about it."

Case ED (Wilshire, 2002):

"She's . . . . she's gonna fall the s- . . . . the s- . . . <u>sto-</u> ah . . . <u>stoke</u>.. I say, not the <u>stoke</u> . . . the <u>stoke's</u> over here . . . that's a, um. . . . . that's a boy and a girl . . . . he's getting in a . . . . cookies. . . . . . . she's gonna eat one . . . he's gonna fall off the . . . stool . . . Mommy's there, watching 'er . . . ah- . . . . the mother's watching . . . . the water's running out o' here. . . . . . . she's washing, ah dryin' the . . . . cups . . . . wha' else is on there . . . /<u>wor</u>/, wall . . . ."

in speech planning at the phonological level. The high incidence of phonemic paraphasias and other phonologically related errors, the tendency to produce successive phonological approximations to the target, and the strong influence of word length on errors all appear to point toward an impairment in retrieval and/or processing of phonological information for speech production. Indeed, as we will see below, this view forms the cornerstone of most contemporary theoretical accounts of conduction aphasia. One further feature of conduction aphasia that is also consistent with a phonological planning impairment is that individuals tend to perform extremely poorly on tasks that require the production of nonsense words (reading or repeating strings such as "*splent*" and "*teg*"; Bub, Black, Howell, & Kertesz, 1987; Caplan et al., 1986; Jacquemot, Dupoux, & Bachoud-Lévi, 2007; Kohn, 1989; Shallice et al., 2000; Wilshire, 2002; Wilshire & McCarthy, 1996). Because nonsense words have no corresponding lexical or semantic representations, these kinds of materials might be expected to tax phonological encoding processes particularly heavily.

MULTIPLE-WORD AND SENTENCE REPETITION

So far, we have considered a number of features of conduction aphasia that reveal themselves most strongly in tasks of single-word production. However, some other characteristics of conduction aphasia do not become evident until we move beyond single words. One such characteristic is poor repetition of spoken sentences and other types of word sequences. On most current assessments, the repetition score used to arrive at a diagnosis of conduction aphasia reflects the person's combined scores on tasks of both word *and* sentence repetition, and in fact, many individuals with conduction aphasia reveal significant impairments only in sentence repetition tasks. On these tasks, individuals may paraphrase the original sentence by substituting words with similar meanings (e.g., "*The residence was located in a peaceful neighborhood*" → "The residence was situated in a quiet district"; Saffran & Marin, 1975; see also Baldo, Klostermann, & Dronkers, 2008; Butterworth, Campbell, & Howard, 1986). This error pattern contrasts markedly with that observed in single-word tasks, where phonological, rather than semantic errors are the primary error type. Specifically, it suggests that individuals with conduction aphasia are able to understand and retain the semantic

"gist" of the sentence, but lose information about the specific word content. Indeed, sentences or phrases that cannot be successfully paraphrased, such as idiomatic phrases (e.g., "no ifs, ands, or buts"), are often particularly problematic for these individuals (McCarthy & Warrington, 1984), and have even sometimes been used as a diagnostic tool (e.g., Goodglass, 1992).

Other tasks that involve the retention of verbatim information over short intervals are also difficult for individuals with conduction aphasia. For example, on auditory span tasks, in which a sequence of random digits or other words must be repeated back in its original order, these individuals usually score significantly below the normal range, or at the very least in the low normal range (Bartha & Benke, 2003; Friedmann & Gvion, 2003; Heilman, Scholes, & Watson, 1976; Sakurai et al., 1998). Similar to sentence repetition, their errors on this type of task are mostly omissions or substitutions of whole words rather than phonological errors. These features of the conduction aphasia profile, considered together, suggest that a verbal short-term memory impairment may also be a central feature of the disorder.

CALCULATION AND NUMBER PROCESSING

Another common feature of conduction aphasia is a marked impairment on tests of simple arithmetic (Baldo & Dronkers, 2007; Bartha & Benke, 2003; Sakurai et al., 1998). This difficulty may be linked to the verbal short-term memory deficit. It has been suggested that the ability to retain verbal information over short intervals may be particularly crucial when performing numerical calculations (Hitch, 1978; Logie, Gilhooly, & Wynn, 1994; Noël, Désert, Aubrun, & Seron, 2001). Also, more anecdotally, many individuals with conduction aphasia complain of general difficulties with numbers, which may include dialing new phone numbers, understanding/repeating/writing complex numerals (e.g., 726), managing change when shopping, and/or telling the time. All of these tasks would appear to place heavy demands on processes that maintain verbatim information over short intervals, and may therefore also be connected with the verbal short-term memory impairment.

SPOKEN LANGUAGE COMPREHENSION

One of the primary defining characteristics of conduction aphasia is relatively well-preserved auditory comprehension. By definition, individuals with conduction aphasia tend to perform quite well on the kinds of comprehension tasks that are used in standard assessments, for example, selecting a picture to match a given word from among a group of semantically related alternatives, responding to simple commands and questions, or extracting meaning from simple short stories. However, more detailed analysis suggests that certain types of spoken language processing skills may not be entirely normal. First, some individuals with conduction aphasia have difficulty with auditory tasks that require fine-grained phonological analysis of the material, for example, discriminating words or nonwords that differ by only one phoneme (e.g., "cat" vs. "cap"), identifying nonsense words that are phonologically similar to real words (e.g., "stadent"), or selecting a picture match for a word when the alternatives are phonologically similar (e.g., "comb," "cone," and "coat"; see, for example, case EA: Friedrich, Glenn, & Marin, 1984; cases GL and ED: Wilshire, 2002). These difficulties suggest that at least in some cases, the phonological impairment has an impact on input phonological processing as well as phonological planning for output. However, as we discuss further below, the extent of these phonological difficulties varies considerably from case to case, with some individuals exhibiting almost no detectable impairment and others exhibiting more extensive difficulties. Of course, very severe impairments in these skills are unlikely to occur, because these would have an impact even on standard assessments of comprehension, and consequently, the diagnostic criteria for conduction aphasia would never be met.

Another type of comprehension difficulty observed in conduction aphasia involves understanding long, multiclausal sentences whose meaning can be established only through the analysis of syntactic structure (e.g., Goodglass et al., 1972; Heilman et al., 1976). For example, Heilman et al. (1976) examined sentence comprehension in a group of individuals with conduction aphasia on a sentence–picture matching task. When the sentences consisted of only one clause, these individuals showed minimal impairment (e.g., "*The man is hitting the girl*," "*The man is being hit by the girl*"). However, on two-clause sentences, they performed little above chance ("*The girl holding the flower is hitting the man*"). The number of clauses in the sentence appeared to be the most crucial determinant of performance, not its particular syntactic form. This pattern is again suggestive of some sort of processing capacity limitation, and it has frequently been linked to the impairment in verbal short-term memory. However, again, this difficulty is much more prominent in some cases than in others.

READING AND WRITING

We have already noted that individuals with conduction aphasia often produce errors in written production that are similar to the ones they produce in spoken language production. These written errors are also sensitive to some of the same variables. For example, in written production of single words, individuals with conduction aphasia tend to produce more errors on longer than on shorter words (e.g., Shallice et al., 2000).

Similar parallels are observed in single-word reading. For example, tasks of oral reading tend to elicit errors that are similar in quality to those observed in other spoken word production tasks (e.g., Friedman & Kohn, 1990; Wilshire & McCarthy, 1996). Again, these errors tend to be more common on longer than on shorter words, and are particularly abundant when the material consists of nonsense words (e.g., "*splent*," "*paff*"). This pattern of performance in which nonword reading is disproportionately impaired is referred to in the reading literature as *phonological dyslexia*. However, some individuals also show weak effects of spelling sound regularity/consistency. For example, they may read regular words such as "*smog*" or "*barge*" more accurately than highly irregular/inconsistent words such as "*yacht*" or "*sieve*" (e.g., Caplan & Waters, 1995; case RAN: McCarthy & Warrington, 1984; Wilshire & McCarthy, 1996). In these cases, words whose spelling provides reliable information about their phonological form appear to have an advantage, at least when it comes to production. This pattern would seem to suggest that at least some individuals are able to utilize the written orthography of the word to support phonological encoding.

VARIABLE FEATURES OF CONDUCTION APHASIA

One source of variation that has been noted among individuals with conduction aphasia is in their performance on single-word relative to multiple-word tasks. Some individuals with conduction aphasia make many phonological errors in single-word production tasks, but still perform at near normal levels in multiple-word tasks such as sentence repetition and digit span (e.g., case SC: Bartha & Benke, 2003; case JGo: Martin & Ayala, 2004; case DK: Friedmann & Gvion, 2007; Shallice et al., 2000). Others show very little impairment in single-word tasks, but quite

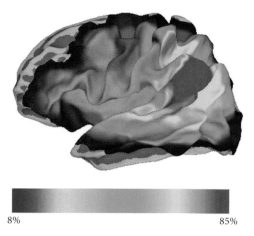

8%   85%

Figure 5.1 Regions of maximal lesion overlap in a sample of 14 individuals diagnosed with conduction aphasia.
Figure reproduced with permission from Buchsbaum, Baldo, D'Esposito, Dronkers, Okada, and Hickok (2011).

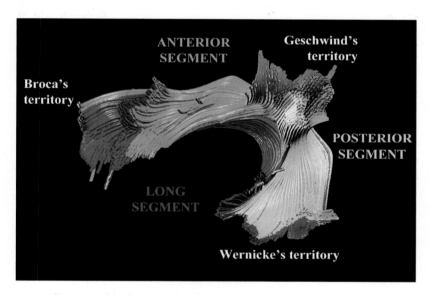

Figure 5.3 Diagrammatic illustration of the three major bundles of white matter fibers identified by Catani, Jones, and ffytche (2005). The bundle of long fibers shown in red connects Broca's and Wernicke's areas directly, and corresponds to classical descriptions of the arcuate fasciculus. The bundles of shorter fibers in green and yellow represent the indirect pathway identified by Catani and colleagues. The bundle in yellow connects the posterior superior temporal lobe to the inferior parietal region (labeled "Geschwind's territory" in the figure) and the bundle in green connects the inferior parietal region directly to anterior regions, including the precentral gyrus.
Figure reproduced with permission from Catani, Jones, and ffytche (2005).

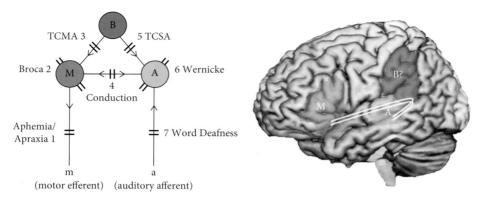

Figure 6.3 Depiction of the Wernicke–Lichtheim–Geschwind model and superposition on the human brain.
Note: Abbreviations retained from Lichtheim's original schema include the following: M (Motor Center corresponding to Broca's area); B (Concept Center corresponding to what Geschwind and others loosely localized to the supramarginal and angular gyri); A (Auditory Word Form Center localized to Wernicke's area); a (auditory afferent pathway marking input to the language network); m (motor speech peripheral musculature, efferent output pathway). The model predicts the presence of seven distinct classical aphasia subtypes, numbered sequentially above and described as follows. (1) Damage to m → M compromises the transmission of high-level motor programs to the speech musculature resulting in a primary articulatory disorder; (2) damage to M produces the classic profile of Broca's aphasia; (3) damage to the B → M pathway disconnects the putative concept and motor planning centers, resulting in the profile of transcortical motor aphasia (TCMA); (4) damage to the major tract (i.e., arcuate fasiculus) joining Broca's and Wernicke's areas impairs bidirectional communication between A ↔ M resulting in conduction aphasia; (5) damage to the pathway joining the putative concept center (B) with the center for auditory word forms (A) results in the disconnection of words from concepts that is the classic hallmark of TCSA; (6) damage to A produces Wernicke's Aphasia; (7) damage to the a→A pathway produces pure word deafness.

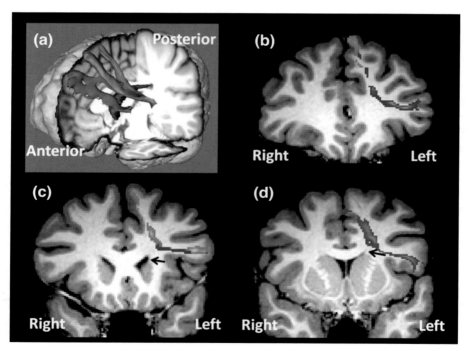

Figure 10.1 Fiber pathways between the medial frontal cortex and Broca's area. Fiber pathways between the medial frontal cortices and Broca's area were traced with probabilistic tractography using FSL in a neurologically normal participant from Ford et al. (2010). These images were created specifically for this chapter to demonstrate the relationship between the fiber pathways and other subcortical and cortical structures. **(a)** Fiber pathways between Broca's area and Brodmann's area 9 (blue), Brodmann's area 8 (orange), and pre-SMA (green) are shown in relation to the position of the left caudate nucleus (red). A block consisting of the frontal and superior temporal lobes has been "cut away" so that the course of the pathways between medial frontal cortices and Broca's area can be clearly seen. **(b)** A relatively anterior coronal section demonstrates the fiber pathway between Brodmann's area 9 and Broca's area as it courses inferiorly, laterally, and somewhat posteriorly toward Broca's area. Orange represents fibers from Brodmann's area 8. **(c)** A coronal section posterior to **(b)** shows fibers from Brodmann's area 8 to Broca's area in orange; blue represents some overlap with fibers from Brodmann's area 9. The black arrow shows the approximate position of the subcallosal fasciculus. Fibers course over the insula to approach Broca's area. **(d)** Green represents fibers from pre-SMA to Broca's area in this coronal section posterior to **(c)**. The black arrow shows the approximate position of the subcallosal fasciculus. Note how closely the pathway from pre-SMA to Broca's area passes to the subcallosal fasciculus at this point. Fibers course over the insula to approach Broca's area. (See color insert)

severe difficulties on multiple-word tasks (e.g., case JB: Shallice & Butterworth, 1977; case PV: Basso, Spinnler, Vallar, & Zanobio, 1982; case TB: Baddeley, Vallar, & Wilson, 1987). Such differences have led to the proposal that there may be two distinct cognitive impairments contributing to the conduction aphasia profile (Shallice & Warrington, 1977; see also Caplan et al., 1986). The first affects phonological encoding, and results in the production of phonemic paraphasias in single-word tasks and in spontaneous speech. The second affects verbal short-term memory, and results in poor performance on sentence repetition and span tasks. Shallice and Warrington (1977) suggested that these two cognitive impairments were functionally unrelated, but often cooccurred in individuals with conduction aphasia due to the anatomical proximity of the brain regions implicated in each. They suggested the term "Reproduction conduction aphasia" for those cases in which the phonological encoding impairment dominates and "Repetition conduction aphasia" for those in which the short-term memory impairment dominates. However, more recent case series suggest that pure dissociations involving these two functions may be extremely rare, particularly when more sensitive diagnostic tests are used; also, when they do occur, they are generally confined to cases in which there is only a very mild impairment in the affected domain (see especially Martin & Saffran, 1997). So the evidence for the independence of these two functions is weak. Furthermore, many current theories consider verbal short-term memory to be an emergent property of the phonological processing system itself (e.g., Martin & Ayala, 2004; Martin & Gupta, 2004; Martin & Saffran, 1997). So current frameworks no longer make a functional distinction between phonological processing and verbal short-term memory.

Nevertheless, leaving aside the issue of verbal short-term memory for the moment, individuals with conduction aphasia may also show considerable variability even when we consider only single-word tasks. As noted earlier, most people with documented cases of conduction aphasia perform more accurately in word repetition than they do in naming tasks. These individuals seem to be able to make use of the auditory stimulus to support phonological encoding of the word. Indeed, as we might expect, individuals with this profile generally exhibit well-preserved auditory–phonological skills, performing well on tasks such as discriminating between phonologically similar words (see especially Laganaro & Zimmerman, 2010; cases

EL and EF: Wilshire, 2002; Wilshire & McCarthy, 1996). However, a few individuals show the converse pattern, performing more poorly in repetition than in naming (e.g., Ablinger, Abel, & Huber, 2008; Corsten, Mende, Cholewa, & Huber, 2007; case RAN: McCarthy & Warrington, 1984; Sidiropoulos, Ackermann, Wannke, & Hertrich, 2010; Wilshire & Fisher, 2004). These individuals also tend to score poorly on purely auditory tasks such as discriminating between phonologically similar words, sometimes earning them a diagnosis of "Borderline Wernicke's-conduction aphasia" (e.g., Wilshire & Fisher, 2004; Martin, Breedin, & Damian, 1999). This profile suggests a form of phonological deficit that impacts both production *and* comprehension. It appears closely related to "deep dysphasia," a more severe repetition disorder seen in some cases of Wernicke's aphasia in which semantic (e.g., *dinosaur* → "horse") as well as phonological errors are produced, and in which auditory comprehension is also severely impaired (Howard & Franklin, 1988; Katz & Goodglass, 1990; Martin, Dell, Saffran, & Schwartz, 1994; Michel & Andreewsky, 1983). It is possible that those individuals with conduction aphasia suffer from the same underlying cognitive impairment, only in milder form.

Neuroanatomical Correlates of Conduction Aphasia

The classical anatomical explanation for conduction aphasia is that it is due to a disconnection between Wernicke's and Broca's areas. Geschwind (1965) and several researchers following him proposed that the structure critically implicated in conduction aphasia is the *arcuate fasciculus*, a bundle of white matter fibers that runs between Wernicke's and Broca's areas. However, although the arcuate fasciculus is clearly damaged in some individuals with conduction aphasia (e.g., Geldmacher, Quigg, & Elias, 2007; Tanabe et al., 1987; Yamada et al., 2007), others have cortical damage that does not substantially encroach upon the underlying white matter (Anderson et al., 1999; Dronkers, 2000; Quigg, Geldmacher, & Elias, 2006). Indeed, one group study involving 32 patients with fluent aphasia found that the most consistent predictor of persistent repetition impairment (beyond the first few months) was not damage to the arcuate fasciculus, but rather to Wernicke's area itself (Selnes, Knopman, Niccum, & Rubens, 1985). Damage that spared Wernicke's area tended to result in a more transient repetition impairment, which resolved within the first 6 months. Furthermore, not all individuals with damage to the arcuate fasciculus necessarily exhibit conduction aphasia (Dronkers, Redfern, & Shapiro, 1993; Selnes, van Zijl, Barker, Hillis, & Mori, 2002; Shuren et al., 1995; Whittle & Fraser, 1991). For example, when the arcuate fasciculus is completely severed, a common consequence is a severe form of Broca's aphasia, characterized by extremely limited speech and recurring utterances (Dronkers et al., 1993).

Detailed clinicoanatomical case studies now indicate that a range of cortical and/or subcortical structures may be implicated in conduction aphasia. Damasio and Damasio (1980) examined the computed tomography (CT) or magnetic resonance imaging (MRI) scans of six individuals with conduction aphasia and found that in five of the six, there was damage to the left insula, the posterior superior temporal gyrus (in the region of Wernicke's area), and the left supramarginal gyrus.[1] In all six cases, the damage extended into the underlying white matter (see also Caplan et al., 1986; Jacquemot et al., 2007; Shallice et al., 2000, for cases with a similar lesion distribution). The arcuate fasciculus was implicated to some extent in most, but not all, cases. The frequent involvement of Wernicke's area was particularly noteworthy. Damasio and Damasio (1980) suggested that the syndrome of Wernicke's aphasia may differ from conduction aphasia only in that it requires more extensive damage to the posterior extent of Wernicke's area, as well as to adjacent regions such as the angular gyrus and/or posterior middle temporal gyrus. The finding of significant insular involvement was also unexpected. Recent large group studies have suggested that damage to this region may be responsible for the apraxia of speech observed in many cases of nonfluent Broca's-type aphasia (Dronkers et al., 1993). If so, then its involvement in conduction aphasia may vary depending upon how strictly the fluency criteria are applied in the diagnosis of conduction aphasia. One unusual aspect of the selection criteria for the Damasio and Damasio (1980) study was that the participants had to exhibit normal to near-normal digit span. Since poor digit span is such a ubiquitous feature of conduction aphasia, this sample may have been somewhat atypical. Recent evidence suggests that inferior parietal structures may be particularly crucial for verbal short-term memory (Baldo & Dronkers, 2006), and if so, then Damasio and Damasio's selection criteria may have effectively excluded many cases with more extensive inferior parietal damage.

Palumbo, Alexander, and Naeser (1992) examined a sample of nine individuals diagnosed with conduction aphasia using more standard assessments. On CT scans, all nine showed evidence of damage to the left inferior parietal lobe—in particular, the supramarginal gyrus. Seven out of the nine individuals also had accompanying partial damage to the left insula, and four had accompanying partial damage to Wernicke's area. In the majority of the cases, the lesion extended into the underlying white matter. Interestingly, at least two of the individuals with accompanying damage to Wernicke's area also scored substantially more poorly than the rest of the sample on standard assessments of auditory comprehension, and in fact, one was diagnosed with "borderline Wernicke's-conduction aphasia." Also, the observation of significant insular involvement supports Damasio and Damasio's (1980) earlier finding and suggests that this region may play an important role not only in articulatory–motor planning, but also in prearticulatory phonological processing.

Two other large sample studies provide evidence that converges with these earlier studies, particularly with respect to the importance of posterior–superior temporal and inferior parietal structures. Axer, Gräfin von Keyserlingk, Berks, and Graf von Keyserlingk (2001) examined the CT scans of 15 individuals with clinically diagnosed conduction aphasia. All of them had a significant impairment in single-word repetition. The regions of highest lesion overlap in this group were the posterior superior temporal gyrus and the supramarginal gyrus/ parietal operculum. In the Axer et al. (2001) sample, the arcuate fasciculus was significantly damaged in only 7 out of 15 cases. Also, more recently, Baldo, Buchsbaum, and colleagues (Baldo et al., 2008; Buchsbaum et al., 2011) performed a lesion overlap analysis of 14 cases of conduction aphasia diagnosed on standard assessments, and found that the regions of maximal overlap were the superior temporal gyrus and inferior parietal cortex. However, lesions also extended more anteriorly in some cases. Their results are illustrated diagrammatically in Figure 5.1.

These lesion studies highlight two important points. First, at least three distinct regions of the left hemisphere appear to be implicated in conduction aphasia: the superior posterior temporal lobe, the inferior parietal lobe/supramarginal gyrus, and the insula. Second, there is considerable individual variation from case to case. This is perhaps not unexpected, given the variability observed in the behavioral profile of conduction aphasia. If the clinical features of conduction aphasia reflect more than

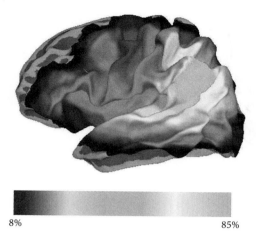

8%   85%

Figure 5.1 Regions of maximal lesion overlap in a sample of 14 individuals diagnosed with conduction aphasia. (See color insert). Figure reproduced with permission from Buchsbaum, Baldo, D'Esposito, Dronkers, Okada, and Hickok (2011).

one type of cognitive impairment, then it would not be at all surprising to find that they are also associated with more than one brain structure.

Axer et al. (2001) addressed the issue of anatomical–functional heterogeneity directly by comparing two major subgroups of conduction aphasia cases. In the "suprasylvian" subgroup, the damage was largely restricted to the inferior parietal lobule/supramarginal gyrus, as illustrated in panel a of Figure 5.2. In the "infrasylvian" group, the damage was largely restricted to the superior temporal lobe (around the region of Wernicke's area), as illustrated in panel b of Figure 5.2. Those in the suprasylvian group tended to score better on most of the diagnostic language tests than the infrasylvian group; the only notable difference in the opposite direction was that the suprasylvian group tended to produce more phonemic paraphasias in their spontaneous speech. The infrasylvian group tended to perform more poorly on all tasks, but the most marked differences were in repetition tasks, where their scores did not overlap those of the suprasylvian group. These findings suggest that superior posterior temporal damage may be strongly implicated in that variant of conduction aphasia characterized by disproportionately impaired repetition. In contrast, supramarginal gyrus and/or insula damage may be implicated in that variant characterized by across-the-board difficulties in all tasks involving word production.

This lesion evidence points toward a possible circuit of left hemisphere structures that is crucial for phonological processing, which includes the posterior superior temporal gyrus, the supramarginal gyrus, and the insula. Each of these structures

appears to contribute in different ways. The posterior superior temporal gyrus appears to play a critical role in both phonological perception and production. In contrast, the role of the inferior parietal lobe and the insula appears to be largely restricted to phonological processing for production. These regions may possibly play a role in the construction of a phonological plan for production and/or its transmission to more anterior sites involved in articulatory planning. The inferior parietal lobe also seems to play a crucial role in tasks that make heavy demands on phonological maintenance, perhaps as part of a larger phonological processing circuit (Turken et al., 2008; see also Baldo & Dronkers, 2006).

Some support for this circuit hypothesis comes from recent studies of white matter tracts using diffusion tensor imaging, a functional MRI (fMRI) technique that allows researchers to examine the direction of flow of water molecules within brain tissue. Regions in which the flow is highly directional are suggestive of the presence of long white matter fibers. Using this method, Catani, Jones, and ffytche (2005) identified at least three major bundles of white matter fibers connecting the posterior superior temporal gyrus with anterior regions, including Broca's area and also parts of the precentral gyrus (Figure 5.3). The first bundle of fibers connected these two sets of regions directly, and ran dorsally beneath the inferior parietal lobe, terminating mainly in the region of Broca's area. This bundle would appear to correspond to the arcuate fasciculus. However, Catani and colleagues (2005) also identified two further bundles of shorter tracts: one that connected the posterior superior temporal lobe to the inferior parietal lobe, and another that connected the inferior parietal lobe directly to anterior regions, including the precentral gyrus (see also Bernal & Altman, 2010).

Diffusion tensor imaging does not provide information about the direction of flow of neural signals; however, some recent electrophysiological studies suggest that neural transmission within these fibers may be bidirectional, at least for the longer ones (Matsumoto et al., 2007). One possibility is that these longer pathways connecting the superior temporal gyrus to anterior areas create a very direct and efficient circuit that sustains phonological information long enough to support immediate spoken word recognition and repetition, and also monitoring of phonological output more generally (see Buchsbaum et al., 2011, for an expansion of this idea). This would explain the catastrophic effects of superior temporal damage on all tasks that rely on accurate phonological input and/or output

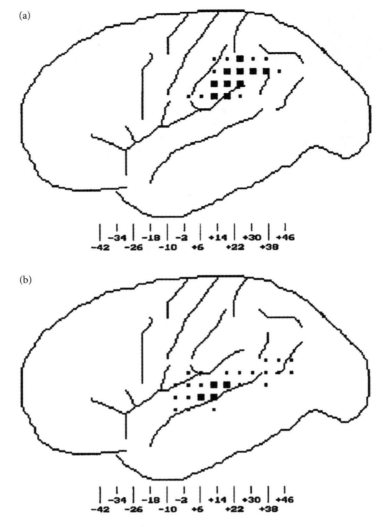

Figure 5.2 Regions of at least 60% lesion overlap in Axer and colleagues' (2001) pure suprasylvian subgroup (a) and pure infrasylvian subgroup (b).
Figures reproduced with permission from Axer, von Keyserlingk, Berks, and von Keyserlingk (2001).

processing. In contrast, the shorter pathways that converge on the left inferior parietal lobe play a supportive role that becomes crucial when there are high demands of phonological planning and/or maintenance, for example, when the speaker needs to plan a long phonological sequence and/or maintain it in memory. This would explain the particularly strong association between parietal damage and the production of phonemic paraphasias on longer words.

Cognitive Neuropsychological Underpinnings
Theoretical Accounts of the Speech Production Deficit in Conduction Aphasia

It is now widely accepted that the primary speech impairment in individuals with conduction aphasia involves some aspect of phonological planning for production. Nevertheless, there are different explanations as to its precise nature. These fall into two broad classes. "Lexical" explanations propose that individuals with conduction aphasia have difficulty retrieving information from the mental lexicon about the phonological forms of words. "Postlexical" explanations, on the other hand, propose that there is an impairment to one or more of the processes that convert this stored phonological information into a fully specified phonological representation of the planned utterance.

"Lexical" explanations attribute the phonological errors observed in conduction aphasia to a difficulty in retrieving information from the mental lexicon about the phonological composition

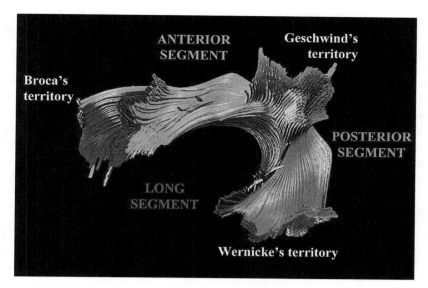

Figure 5.3 Diagrammatic illustration of the three major bundles of white matter fibers identified by Catani, Jones, and ffytche (2005). The bundle of long fibers shown in red connects Broca's and Wernicke's areas directly, and corresponds to classical descriptions of the arcuate fasciculus. The bundles of shorter fibers in green and yellow represent the indirect pathway identified by Catani and colleagues. The bundle in yellow connects the posterior superior temporal lobe to the inferior parietal region (labeled "Geschwind's territory" in the figure) and the bundle in green connects the inferior parietal region directly to anterior regions, including the precentral gyrus. (See color insert).
Figure reproduced with permission from Catani, Jones, and ffytche (2005).

of words (e.g., Goldrick & Rapp, 2007, and references therein; Schwartz, Wilshire, Gagnon, & Polansky, 2004; Wilshire, 2002). As a result, sometimes only partial phonological information can be accessed about the word, and the rest is either omitted or replaced by other phonemes that are activated at that time. These errors therefore constitute mild examples of the same phonological problem that gives rise to the more severe phonological errors and neologisms observed in Wernicke's aphasia. One feature of conduction aphasia that would seem to suggest an impairment in lexical–phonological retrieval is the observation that many individuals perform considerably more poorly in tasks of picture naming that require spontaneous retrieval of the word's phonology than in word repetition, in which an auditory model of the target word is provided. Also, more anecdotally, some individuals with conduction aphasia make comments during their naming efforts that suggest an inability to access word phonology. An example of this kind of behavior comes from case GL, described earlier, whose responses contained comments such as *"what's the end part? . . . I can't remember"* (Wilshire & Saffran, 2005). Further support for a lexical–phonological retrieval account comes from the marked effects of word frequency observed in some cases. It has been

suggested that the phonemes of common words may be retrieved more rapidly and efficiently than those of less common words, so consequently, they may be more resistant to retrieval failures in impaired individuals (e.g., Levelt, Roelofs, & Meyer, 1999; for a discussion see Kittredge, Dell, Verkuilen, & Schwartz, 2008).

Finally, some recent case studies of conduction aphasia have also reported effects of *phonological neighborhood density*. Words that have many closely phonologically related neighbors are produced more accurately than those with few such neighbors, even when controlling for other factors, such as word length and frequency (Goldrick & Rapp, 2007; Laganaro & Zimmerman, 2010; Goldrick, Folk, & Rapp, 2010; Middleton & Schwartz, 2010). According to some theories, words that are phonologically similar to the desired word also become partially activated during the process of word production, and so too do their constituent phonemes. Consequently, any phonemes that are shared between the target and these neighbors will receive an additional boost to their activation, improving the likelihood of correct phonological retrieval (see especially Dell & Gordon, 2003). Again, this sensitivity to factors that influence ease of retrieval is suggestive of a difficulty accessing lexical–phonological information.

In contrast to this lexical account, "postlexical" explanations propose that the primary underlying impairment in conduction aphasia involves a later stage of phonological processing, one that applies after the relevant phonological information has been retrieved from the lexicon. According to some theories, phonological information retrieved from the lexicon may be temporarily held in a specialized phonological buffer until it is ready to be sent to the articulators (Bub et al., 1987; Shallice et al., 2000). It has been suggested that some individuals with conduction aphasia may have an impairment affecting this buffer, so that they are unable to effectively maintain phonological information. Consequently, when the person comes to produce the planned utterance, some phonemes are omitted and/or replaced with incorrect ones. Other theories of spoken language production postulate that the phonological information retrieved from the lexicon undergoes some further, more active processing before it is sent on for articulatory–motor planning. Some suggest that the phonological information retrieved for each of the words planned for the utterance needs to be combined and resyllabified to create more integrated "phonological phrases" (Levelt et al., 1999). Other theories suggest that the retrieved phonological information may be highly underspecified, and may need to undergo some further fleshing out to produce a featurally complete form ready for articulatory–motor programming (Béland et al., 1990; Caplan et al., 1986; Kohn & Smith 1994). The pattern of performance seen in many cases of conduction aphasia would appear consistent with an impairment to any one of these "postlexical" processes. Common features of conduction aphasia, such as the powerful effects of word length and the qualitative similarities in errors across different tasks (e.g., naming, reading, and repetition), would certainly appear consistent with this kind of account. The effects of word length would arise because longer words would tax these impaired postlexical systems more than shorter ones. Also, the similarity in errors across different types of word production tasks would seem consistent with a difficulty at a relatively late stage of phonological processing, one that applies to all phonological material, regardless of how it was obtained. In addition, a postlexical account seems well placed to explain those phonemic paraphasias in which one or more phonemes are moved or exchanged, that is, where the correct phonological information seems to have been retrieved, but has become misordered during some subsequent process (e.g., Laganaro & Zimmerman, 2010).

Of course, these "lexical" and "postlexical" accounts of the speech production deficit in conduction aphasia are not mutually exclusive. The critical impairment may vary from case to case. Indeed, it has been proposed that some individuals may suffer from a "postlexical" impairment, whereas others have a "lexical" impairment (Goldrick & Rapp, 2007; Kohn & Smith, 1994; Laganaro & Zimmerman, 2010). Studies that have contrasted patterns of performance across different cases provide some support for this view. For example, Goldrick and Rapp (2007) described two people, both of whom produced phonemic paraphasias, but whose speech profile differed in a number of important ways. The first case, CSS, showed effects of word frequency and also neighborhood density. CSS also performed considerably more poorly in picture naming than in spoken word repetition, suggesting that he was particularly disadvantaged on tasks that can be accomplished only by retrieving lexically stored information. In contrast, case BON demonstrated no effects of frequency or neighborhood density, and performed similarly in picture naming and word repetition, suggesting an impairment to a stage of processing that operates after lexical retrieval is complete. Laganaro and Zimmerman (2010) further suggested that "lexical" and "postlexical" impairments may also produce qualitatively different types of phonological errors: a postlexical impairment may give rise to more phoneme movement errors, such as phoneme anticipations, perseverations, or exchanges. They report two individuals who differ in the proportions of phoneme movement errors they produce, suggesting a possible difference in the functional origin of the errors in each case.

However, not all researchers agree that two different functional impairments are necessary to explain the speech production deficit in conduction aphasia. Some have argued that all such errors may arise as a result of a single type of impairment, one that affects lexical–phonological retrieval. Within interactive–activation frameworks, the probability of successfully activating all the phonemes of a given word will depend upon both its frequency *and* its length (the relative prominence of these two variables may depend upon the overall severity of the impairment). Also, a failure to retrieve one or more phonemes can potentially give rise to phoneme movement errors as well as omissions and substitutions. If a particular phoneme of the target word does not become sufficiently activated to be selected for production, the next most highly activated phoneme may be selected in its place. This might commonly be a phoneme that is activated because it is planned for production elsewhere in the word or utterance (Schwartz et al., 2004, Wilshire, 2002). So within this framework, both movement and nonmovement errors could potentially arise from a single common impairment. Individual differences in performance across tasks would be said to reflect the overall severity of the phonological impairment and/or the degree of impairment to other contributing processes, such as those involved in auditory–phonological processing. The latter in particular may be responsible for differences in performance on tasks that involve auditory input, such as repetition, and those that do not, such as picture naming.

This debate between single-origin and dual-origin accounts of phonological impairments is likely to continue in the literature for some time. Nonetheless, it does illustrate an important point, that the interpretation of the phonological encoding impairment in conduction aphasia is crucially dependent on the researcher's theoretical framework. Evidence that appears to support the idea of two different origins for phonological errors within one framework may appear entirely consistent with a single origin within another framework. Another issue highlighted by this debate is that it might not be possible to gain a full understanding of individual variability in phonological encoding until we can understand how the error patterns within and across tasks vary with the overall severity of the impairment and the extent of other accompanying impairments, such as those affecting auditory–phonological input processing.

Theoretical Accounts of Other Features of Conduction Aphasia

We noted above that although the key speech characteristics of conduction aphasia appear universal to almost all sufferers, other features may vary from case to case. As noted above, early theoretical accounts proposed that some of the variability among cases may be due to differences in the degree of accompanying impairment to verbal short-term memory (see especially Shallice & Warrington, 1977). However, recent models of verbal short-term memory propose a very tight relationship between very short-term memory and phonological processing, and in these types of frameworks it is no longer necessary to consider these functions as separate and independent. For example, Martin and Saffran (1997) proposed that verbal short-term memory is an emergent property of the network that represents

information about words and their phonemes. In normal spontaneous speech, activation is transmitted through this network, but decays quickly. However, the continuous upward and downward flow of activation between units in different layers of the network can "refresh" that activation, enabling representations to be maintained for longer periods (see also Martin & Ayala, 2004; Martin & Gupta, 2004). According to this theory, activation flowing to and from phonological representations plays a crucial role in verbal short-term memory, so much so that it is impossible to separate phonological processing and short-term memory. If this interpretation is correct, then a severe phonological processing deficit will always compromise verbal short-term memory capacity, at least to some extent. Any variation among cases may be better explained in other ways.

One other important source of variation among cases that was described above involves the extent of accompanying impairment to phonological *input* processing. Some individuals with conduction aphasia produce numerous phonological errors in spoken word production tasks, but have little difficulty with tasks that involve discriminating among phonologically similar spoken words. Others have considerable accompanying impairment in these kinds of input processing tasks. Furthermore, this variation cannot always be explained in terms of the overall severity of the phonological impairment (e.g., Wilshire, 2002).

Based on this and other evidence, some researchers have argued that phonological input and output processing might be supported by separate and distinct sets of processes and representations (e.g., Howard & Nickels, 2005; Jacquemot et al., 2007; Martin, Lesch, & Bartha, 1999). There are strong links between the two sets of representations that are crucial for supporting direct conversion between the two, such as is required for word and nonword repetition (and perhaps also for more conventional span tasks: see especially Jacquemot et al., 2007). This idea of a separate "direct" route between input and output phonological representations, which is particularly crucial for repetition, has been incorporated into a number of models of word processing, including interactive–activation models (e.g., Baron, Hanley, Dell, & Kay, 2008; see also Nozari, Kittredge, Dell, & Schwartz, 2010, and references therein, for supporting evidence from aphasia). Within this type of framework, phonological input and output representations/processes can each become selectively impaired, but the two types of impairment can sometimes cooccur in individuals with conduction aphasia.

An alternative account that proposes an even closer relationship between phonological input and output processing is that both types of tasks activate a single common set of phonological representations (Martin et al., 1994; see also Martin et al., 1999; Wilshire & Fisher, 2004). According to these proposals, if there is an impairment affecting the strength of lexical–phonological connections, this will have a disproportionate impact on tasks requiring spoken output. This is because tasks involving spoken output require one-to-many mapping of words to sounds, and therefore offer a greater opportunity for error than input processing tasks, in which the mapping is many-to-one (at least in tasks involving familiar words). However, if the impairment has an impact on the phonological representations themselves, rendering activation patterns within these representations noisy or unstable, phonological information may not be sustained long enough for effective processing of the task at hand. Such an impairment will impact heavily on phonological input processes as well as output processes, particularly if the input also requires the temporary maintenance of the phonological information, for example, if it involves comparing two successively presented words (as in phoneme discrimination tasks) or converting it into a sequence of articulatory commands for subsequent reproduction (see especially N. Martin et al., 1994; R.C. Martin et al., 1999; Wilshire & Fisher, 2004). The idea that individuals with conduction aphasia may have qualitatively different types of impairments to phonological processing, one involving weakened lexical–phonological connections and the other involving instability of activation of phonological representations, could therefore offer an alternative explanation as to why some exhibit marked phonological input as well as output processing deficits, whereas others do not.

Assessment of Conduction Aphasia

In standard aphasia assessments such as the BDAE (Goodglass et al., 2001) and the WAB-R (Kertesz, 2007), the defining criteria for conduction aphasia are very similar. In both assessments, conduction aphasia is identified by difficulty in word and sentence repetition in the context of fluent speech and relatively well-preserved auditory comprehension. More informally, an experienced clinician can often recognize a typical case of conduction aphasia through its characteristic speech features alone, which include runs of relatively fluent speech, punctuated by occasional phonemic paraphasias, and an accompanying awareness of those errors, usually demonstrated though frequent attempts at self-correction.

It has been argued above that the usefulness of the diagnosis of conduction aphasia stems from its narrowness. This diagnostic classification applies to only a small proportion of individuals with aphasia, and these individuals share many similarities in their communication difficulties as well as in their underlying cognitive and neural deficits. When viewed from this perspective, then, the classification of conduction aphasia will be most useful to the clinician if it is applied conservatively. One potential source of difficulty in the diagnosis of conduction aphasia concerns the requirement for fluent speech. Many individuals with conduction aphasia are not "fluent" to the same extent as those with Wernicke's aphasia. Speech may be broken by word finding pauses and there may be hesitations, or perhaps even multiple false starts on difficult words, giving the speech a stammering quality. However, the critical distinction between Broca's and conduction aphasia concerns the quality of the speech in the runs *between* errors and also the length of those runs. In conduction aphasia, speech in those runs sounds normally articulated to the listener. The premorbid qualities of the person's speech, such as their regional accent or other particular vocal qualities, should still be clearly evident.

Another potential challenge in the diagnosis of conduction aphasia is distinguishing this disorder from less severe forms of Wernicke's aphasia. Standard assessments can be particularly useful here, providing the examiner with a precise cut-off score for comprehension that distinguishes conduction aphasia from Wernicke's aphasia. However, it is important to recognize that this distinction may be more artificial than real, and that comprehension scores for individuals with fluent aphasia are more likely to lie on a continuum than to be organized into two separate and distinct clusters corresponding to conduction aphasia and Wernicke's aphasia, respectively. Again, the diagnosis should be considered a starting point only, which can guide further, more detailed testing of specific psycholinguistic functions.

One final issue that arises in assessment concerns the classification of "recovered" cases, that is, cases involving individuals initially diagnosed with Wernicke's aphasia who recover sufficiently to fit the profile of conduction aphasia on subsequent testing.

Some researchers and clinicians argue that these "recovered" Wernicke's cases should be considered as a distinct category, because they may have some unique features. However, there has been little systematic research as to how these individuals actually differ from other cases of conduction aphasia, either functionally or anatomically. At present, a better approach may be to use the diagnosis of conduction aphasia as a starting point, and to note any unusual characteristics of the case, without regard to any earlier diagnosis.

Treatment of Conduction Aphasia

Conduction aphasia is a relatively mild and selective form of aphasia, in which only one or two key language functions appear to be impaired. Perhaps for this reason, most approaches to the rehabilitation of conduction aphasia focus on restoring the impaired function(s) rather than on teaching ways to compensate through the use of preserved skills. In the case of conduction aphasia, the focus of treatment is usually on improving spoken language production, usually with a focus on particularly troublesome words. In an early attempt to treat the speech production deficit in conduction aphasia, Cubelli, Foresti, and Consolini (1988) designed a series of exercises intended to encourage their conduction aphasia participants to focus more attention on the *forms* of words and sentences. To achieve this, they made heavy use of written word stimuli, taking advantage of the less transient nature of written orthography when compared to auditory stimuli. Those exercises that were focused on the forms of words required participants to select a written word form to match a given picture, and subsequently to construct its written name themselves using cards containing individual letters or letter sequences. Cubelli et al. (1988) provided this treatment to three individuals with conduction aphasia and were able to demonstrate significant improvement in all three on a range of psycholinguistic tests. However, because all individuals were treated within the first few months following their initial illness, it was not possible to tease apart the effects of the treatment from those that may be attributable to spontaneous recovery.

A number of more recent treatment studies have provided more conclusive evidence of treatment-specific gains. Many of these have used treatments that focus on repeated practice with difficult or troublesome words. In these approaches, phonological or written cues are initially used to help facilitate correct production of the word, and

then these cues are systematically reduced until the word can be successfully produced without support. The word is then practiced repeatedly. The cues provided may include rhyming words (e.g., for *parrot*, "rhymes with *carrot*"), the first phoneme or syllable of the word (e.g., "p" or "pa-"), some or all of the word's letters, or even a series of taps to indicate the number of syllables in the word (Biedermann, Blanken, & Nickels, 2002; DeDe, Parris, & Waters, 2003; Raymer, Thompson, Jacobs, & le Grand, 1993; Wambaugh, 2003; Wambaugh et al., 2001).

This type of approach has been shown to be effective at improving production of the treated items in a number of individuals with phonological impairments of the kind observed in conduction aphasia (case GC: Raymer et al., 1993; Speaker 3: Wambaugh et al., 2001; Greenwood, Grassly, Hickin, & Best, 2010), with the gains maintained over short follow-up periods (4 to 6 weeks). Also, in at least two cases, some generalization to untrained items was observed, which is perhaps surprising given the word-focused nature of these treatments (Raymer et al., 1993; Greenwood et al., 2010). In one study, in which the participant was given practice with the trained words both in isolation and in connected speech, the authors were also able to document improvements in the participants' spontaneous speech following treatment (Greenwood et al., 2010).

This kind of supported naming practice is usually postulated to work by strengthening connections between lexical items and their phonemes. It is hypothesized that these connections are strengthened each time the word is successfully produced (this is sometimes referred to as the *repetition priming effect*: see especially Renvall, Laine, & Martin, 2007). The phonological/orthographic supports improve the efficiency of the treatment by increasing the incidence of successful productions of each word. Given its emphasis on word-specific strengthening, this sort of treatment may be best suited to those individuals in whom the primary difficulty appears to involve retrieving phonological information from the lexicon (see especially Greenwood et al., 2010; Nickels, 2002).

A different approach that may operate in a similar way is Martin and colleagues' contextual priming technique, in which words are presented auditorily, in semantically related, phonologically related, or unrelated sets, and the participant practices repeating them (Renvall et al., 2007; Cornelissen et al., 2003; Laine & Martin, 1996; Martin, Fink, &

Laine, 2004; Martin, Fink, Laine, & Ayala, 2004; Martin & Laine, 2000; Renvall, Laine, Laakso, & Martin, 2003). The rationale underlying this approach is that the repeated practice strengthens the relevant damaged connections (the repetition priming effect). The relatedness groupings work in a similar way to phonological cues by temporarily facilitating access to the correct word, so that practice can be maximized. However, they do so implicitly, rather than explicitly, by taking advantage of the manner in which activation spreads among items that are related either semantically or phonologically. This technique has been successfully used to treat a number of individuals with conduction aphasia-like phonological impairments, leading to improvements on the treated items (case LP: Martin, Fink, Laine, & Ayala, 2004; case JP: Renvall et al., 2007; case YK: Renvall et al., 2003; and case HH: Cornelissen et al., 2003), and in one case some generalization to untrained items (case YK: Renvall et al., 2003). Curiously, the benefits reported in most of the studies are not tied to a particular type of grouping; semantically grouped as well as phonologically grouped sets appear to be similarly beneficial for individuals with phonological encoding impairments.

One study that was able to report more selective effects using a similar type of approach was that of Fisher, Wilshire, and Ponsford (2009) who treated a single individual with a mild impairment in phonological encoding (originally diagnosed with conduction aphasia, but exhibiting only a mild residual phonological impairment at the time of treatment). In this study, the task used in training was picture naming, and items were grouped into phonologically related and unrelated triplets. For this mild case, naming of the trained items improved significantly, and moreover, gains were significantly faster for the words trained within phonologically related triplets than those in unrelated triplets. Significant generalization to untreated items was also observed and was maintained at 3 months posttherapy. Fisher and colleagues (2009) suggested that in addition to repeated practice with the words themselves, one of the mechanisms underlying improvement in their case may have been a type of error-driven correction. The phonologically related triplets may have initially induced phonological confusions among items, which may have stimulated a self-correction and checking process that further strengthened the relevant connections. Renvall and colleagues (2007) also suggested that a similar mechanism may be at play in other forms of contextual priming.

Another example of an approach that has utilized phonologically similar word sets is that of Corsten et al. (2007), who report treatment of a single case of conduction aphasia with disproportionately impaired repetition and poor auditory–phonological decoding skills. Their treatment method utilized quadruples of words and nonwords whose members differed from one another by only a single phoneme or cluster at either onset or coda position. The training sets included nonwords as well as real words, under the reasoning that training with real words may be maximally effective at treating impairments in lexical–phonological retrieval, whereas training with nonwords may be more effective in treating postlexical phonological impairments (both at input and output level). The training included tasks of auditory discrimination as well as reproduction, in order to target both input and output difficulties. In the treatment, the participants were first presented with spoken word/nonword pairs drawn from the same quadruple, and asked to judge whether they were the same or different. Then they were given single spoken word/nonwords and were asked to select their corresponding written form from among the four possible ones from that quadruple. The training concluded with a reproduction phase in which the four items in each quadruple were presented both visually and auditorily and the participant had to read/repeat them, first starting with one word at a time, then increasing to two, three, and all four words at once. The treatment effects were very specific, and significant benefits were observed only for quadruples (both words and nonwords) in which the members differed in their coda consonant. There was generalization to tasks of repetition (both words and nonwords), rhyme judgments (words, and marginally for nonwords), and picture naming. This study provides some converging evidence that the most effective types of contextual manipulations to include in training are those that involve phonological relatedness, perhaps most particularly those in which words in the same set share similar beginnings and differ only at later positions.

Another rather different approach to treating the phonological production difficulties in conduction aphasia focuses not on specific, troublesome words, but rather on training more general skills and strategies that may help to overcome "blocks" and/or facilitate successful self-correction. The reasoning behind these approaches is that because they train general strategies rather than specific words, they may have the potential to elicit greater generalization to untrained items. One approach that has proven successful with a number of individuals with aphasia, including some with conduction aphasia, involves training individuals to develop their own cues to facilitate naming (e.g., Lowell, Beeson, & Holland, 1995; Marshall & Freed, 2006). In this approach, participants are encouraged to create their own cue for a troublesome word that will help them retrieve it. For example, they might be encouraged to think of another related word (e.g., for *potatoes*, perhaps *chips*) or a phrase incorporating the word (e.g., *mashed potatoes*), or to say to themselves the word's first phoneme, or even to visualize its written form. Then the participant is given practice pairing the cue with the target word. If the participant finds this strategy helpful, he or she may then apply it regularly during speech. In this type of treatment, the participant takes an active role in selecting the appropriate cue, a feature that may arguably encourage longer-lasting effects. Lowell et al. (1995) treated two individuals with conduction aphasia using a self-cueing approach that focused on semantic cues. One of these individuals improved significantly on the trained words, and there was some evidence of generalization to untrained words. There is also some evidence to suggest that self-cueing training that focuses specifically on phonological cues may be beneficial, particularly for individuals with severe phonological impairments (Robson, Marshall, Pring, & Chiat, 1998). However, this type of technique is yet to be extended to the types of milder phonological impairments observed in conduction aphasia.

Another general skills training strategy that has been applied to individuals with conduction aphasia involves training participants to monitor and correct their own errors. Again, this is a strategy that, if successful, can be applied by the participant to untrained words. Also, unlike many of the other treatments so far described, it does not assume difficulty with lexical–phonological retrieval, but rather remains neutral as to the possible origin of the difficulty, and focuses entirely on self-correction. It is therefore suitable for individuals with a postlexical phonological impairment, in which techniques oriented toward restrengthening of specific lexical–phonological connections may be less appropriate (see Howard, 2000, for a discussion). Franklin et al. (2002) treated an individual with conduction aphasia who produced numerous phonemic paraphasias by training his error monitoring and self-correction abilities. The treatment first trained the participant to analyze the phonological composition of spoken

words and then to detect deliberate phonological errors in such words (for example, omitted or substituted phonemes). The participant was then trained to listen to his or her own recorded speech and to evaluate its correctness, then finally to do this in real time, following his or her own attempt(s) at a difficult word. This treatment not only improved the participant's naming of the trained words, but also generalized to untrained words and even to connected speech. However, a later study by Waldron, Whitworth, and Howard (2011) used this technique with three people whose profiles were consistent with conduction aphasia, and although all three improved on the trained items, none showed generalization to other items. The authors suggested that monitoring therapy might produce generalizable benefits only in individuals with a genuine postlexical phonological impairment; those with an impairment that affects mapping from words to their phonemes may show specific benefits as a result of practice with the treatment words, but these may be restricted to the actual words upon which they are trained.

Conclusions

The existence of conduction aphasia as a distinct syndrome is a result of historical factors. The syndrome emerged within the context of nineteenth-century neurolinguistic frameworks, which emphasized key "centers" of language processing and the pathways that connect them. Current research has discredited the original neural and functional interpretation of this syndrome. The view that has emerged in its place is that the label *conduction aphasia* defines a cluster of functionally and anatomically related deficits that share phonological processing as their common theme. Indeed, recently the usefulness of a syndrome-based classification more generally has been questioned, and instead analysis of language impairments into their cognitive components, without reference to classical syndromes, has been advocated. This alternative, *cognitive neuropsychological* approach has much to recommend it, not only in drawing our attention to some of the outmoded assumptions underlying classical symptom-based approaches, but also in providing us with new ways to understand the variability within different syndrome classifications. However, such an approach has the disadvantage that it treats each cognitive function as separate and independent. The descriptions it offers of individual cases are therefore often complex and unwieldy. Also, and perhaps even more importantly, these frameworks may overemphasize functional independence, and fail to consider common associations observed between different features, some of which may indicate important functional relationships between different skills. By considering commonly cooccurring patterns of impairment such as are observed within the syndrome of conduction aphasia, it is possible to obtain a more integrated picture of the person's language functioning. If syndrome labels such as conduction aphasia are used with a full awareness of their limits, and of the way they are constrained by the defining criteria themselves, they can provide a useful means of capturing the gestalt of features shown by a particular individual.

Note

1. The remaining case had clear damage to the insula and the primary auditory cortex, but due to the space-occupying nature of the lesion, damage to other adjacent areas could not be ruled out.

References

Ablinger, I., Abel, S., & Huber, W. (2008). Deep dysphasia as a phonetic input deficit: Evidence from a single case. *Aphasiology*, 22, 537–556.

Anderson, J.M., Gilmore, R., Roper, S., Crosson, B., Bauer, R.M., Nadeau, S., Beversdorf, D.Q., Cibula, J., Rogish, M., Kortencamp, S., Hughes, J.D., Rothi, L.J.G., & Heilman, K.M. (1999). Conduction aphasia and the arcuate fasciculus: A reexamination of the Wernicke-Geschwind model. *Brain and Language*, 70(1), 1–12.

Axer, H., von Keyserlingk, A.G., Berks, G., & von Keyserlingk, D.G. (2001). Supra- and infrasylvian conduction aphasia. *Brain and Language*, 76(3), 317–331.

Baddeley, A.D., Vallar, G., & Wilson, B. (1987). Sentence comprehension and phonological memory: Some neuropsychological evidence. In M. Coltheart (Ed.), *Attention and performance XII: The psychology of reading* (pp. 509–529). London: Lawrence Erlbaum Associates.

Baldo, J.V., & Dronkers, N.F. (2006). The role of inferior parietal and inferior frontal cortex in working memory. *Neuropsychology*, 20(5), 529–538.

Baldo, J., & Dronkers, N. (2007). Neural correlates of arithmetic and language comprehension: A common substrate? *Neuropsychologia*, 45, 229–235.

Baldo, J.V., Klostermann, E.C., & Dronkers, N.F. (2008). It's either a cook or a baker: Patients with conduction aphasia get the gist but lose the trace. *Brain and Language*, 105, 134–140.

Baron, R., Hanley, J.R., Dell. G., & Kay, J.M. (2008). Testing single and dual route computational models of auditory repetition with new data from six aphasic patients. *Aphasiology*, 22, 62–76.

Bartha, L., & Benke, T. (2003). Acute conduction aphasia: An analysis of 20 cases. *Brain and Language*, 85(1), 93–108.

Basso, A. Spinnler, H., Vallar, G., & Zanobio, E. (1982). Left hemisphere damage and selected impairment of auditory verbal short-term memory: A case study. *Neuropsychologia*, 20, 263–274.

Béland, R., Caplan, D., & Nespoulous, J-L. (1990). The role of abstract phonological representations in word production: Evidence from phonemic paraphasias. *Journal of Neurolinguistics*, 5, 125–164.

Bernal, B., & Altman, N.A. (2010). The connectivity of the superior longitudinal fasciculus: A tractography DTI study. *Magnetic Resonance Imaging*, 28, 217–225.

Biedermann, B., Blanken, G., & Nickels, L.A. (2002). The representation of homophones: Evidence from remediation. *Aphasiology*, 16, 935–980.

Bub, D., Black, S., Howell, J., & Kertesz, A. (1987). Damage to input and output buffers—What's a lexicality effect doing in a place like that? In E. Keller & M. Gopnik (Eds.), *Motor and sensory processes of language* (pp. 79–110). Hillsdale, NJ: Erlbaum.

Buchsbaum, B.R., Baldo, J., D'Esposito, M., Dronkers, N., Okada, K., & Hickok, G. (2011). Conduction aphasia, sensory-motor integration and phonological short-term memory—An aggregate analysis of lesion and fMRI data. *Brain and Language*, 119(3), 119–128.

Butterworth, B., Campbell, R., & Howard, D. (1986). The uses of short-term memory: A case study. *Quarterly Journal of Experimental Psychology A*, 38(4), 705–737.

Caplan, D., Vanier, M., & Baker, C. (1986). A case study of reproduction conduction aphasia. I: Word production. *Cognitive Neuropsychology*, 3, 99–128.

Caplan, D., & Waters, G.S. (1995). Aphasic disorders of syntactic comprehension and working memory capacity. *Cognitive Neuropsychology*, 12, 637–650.

Caramazza, A., Papagno, C., & Ruml, W. (2000). The selective impairment of phonological processing in speech production. *Brain and Language*, 75, 428–450.

Catani, M., Jones, D.K., & ffytche, D.H. (2005). Perisylvian language networks of the human brain. *Annals of Neurology*, 57, 8–16.

Cornelissen, K., Laine, M., Tarkiainen, A., Jarvensivu, T., Martin, N., & Salmelin, R. (2003). Adult brain plasticity elicited by anomia treatment. *Journal of Cognitive Neuroscience*, 15, 444–461.

Corsten, S., Mende, M., Cholewa, J., & Huber, W. (2007). Treatment of input and output phonology in aphasia: A single case study. *Aphasiology*, 21(6–8), 587–603.

Cubelli, R., Foresti, A., & Consolini, T. (1988). Reeducation strategies in conduction aphasia. *Journal of Communication Disorders*, 21, 239–249.

Damasio, H., & Damasio, A.R. (1980). The anatomical basis of conduction aphasia. *Brain*, 103, 337–350.

DeDe, G., Parris, D., & Waters, G. (2003). Teaching self-cues: A treatment approach for verbal naming. *Aphasiology*, 17, 465–480.

Dell, G.S., & Gordon, J.K. (2003). Neighbors in the lexicon: Friends or foes? In N.O. Schiller & A.S. Meyer (Eds.), *Phonetics and phonology in language comprehension and production: Differences and similarities* (pp. 9–37). New York: Mouton.

Dronkers, N.F. (2000). The pursuit of brain–language relationships. *Brain and Language*, 71, 59–61.

Dronkers, N.F., Redfern, B., & Shapiro, J.K. (1993). Neuroanatomic correlates of production deficits in severe Broca's aphasia. *Journal of Clinical and Experimental Neuropsychology*, 15(1), 59–60.

Fisher, C.A., Wilshire, C.E., & Ponsford, J.L. (2009). Word discrimination therapy: A new technique for the treatment of a phonologically based word-finding impairment. *Aphasiology*, 23(6), 676–693

Franklin, S., Buerk, F., & Howard, D. (2002). Generalised improvement in speech production for a subject with reproduction conduction aphasia. *Aphasiology*, 16(10–11), 1087–1114.

Friedman, R.B., & Kohn, S.E. (1990). Impaired activation of the phonological lexicon: Effects upon oral reading. *Brain and Language*, 38, 278–297.

Friedmann, N., & Gvion, A. (2003). Sentence comprehension and working memory limitation: A dissociation between semantic and phonological encoding. *Brain and Language*, 86, 23–39.

Friedmann, N., & Gvion, A. (2007). As far as individuals with conduction aphasia understood these sentences were ungrammatical: Garden path in conduction aphasia. *Aphasiology*, 21, 570–586.

Friedrich, F.J., Glenn, C.G., & Marin, O.S. (1984). Interruption of phonological coding in conduction aphasia. *Brain and Language*, 22(2), 266–291.

Gandour J., Dardarananda, R., & Holasuit S. (1991). Nature of spelling errors in a Thai conduction aphasic. *Brain and Language*, 41(1), 96–119.

Geldmacher, D.S., Quigg, M., & Elias, W.J. (2007). MR tractography depicting damage to the arcuate fasciculus in a patient with conduction aphasia. *Neurology*, 69(3), 321–322.

Geschwind, N. (1965). Disconnection syndromes in animals and man. *Brain*, 88, 585–644.

Goldrick, M., Folk, J.R., & Rapp, B. (2010). Mrs. Malaprop's neighborhood: Using word errors to reveal neighborhood structure. *Journal of Memory and Language*, 62(2), 113–134.

Goldrick, M., & Rapp, B. (2007). Lexical and post-lexical phonological representations in spoken production. *Cognition*, 102, 219–260.

Goodglass, H. (1992). Diagnosis of conduction aphasia. In S.E Kohn (Ed.), *Conduction aphasia* (pp. 39–49). Hillsdale, NJ: Erlbaum.

Goodglass, H., Blumstein, S.E., Gleason, J.B., Hyde, M.R., Green, E., & Statlender, S. (1972). Some linguistic structures in the speech of a Broca's aphasic. *Brain and Language*, 7, 201–209.

Goodglass, H., Kaplan, E., & Barresi, B. (2001). *The Boston diagnostic aphasia examination* (3rd ed.). Philadelphia: Lippincott Williams & Wilkins.

Greenwood, A., Grassly, J., Hickin, J., & Best, W. (2010). Phonological and orthographic cueing therapy: A case of generalised improvement. *Aphasiology*, 24(9), 991–1016.

Heilman, K.M., Scholes, R., & Watson, R.T. (1976). Defects of immediate memory in Broca's and conduction aphasia. *Brain and Language*, 3(2), 201–208

Henderson, V. (1992). Early concepts of conduction aphasia. In S. Kohn (Ed.), *Conduction aphasia* (pp. 22–38). Hillsdale, NJ: Erlbaum.

Hitch, G.J. (1978) The role of short-term working memory in mental arithmetic. *Cognitive Psychology*, 10(3), 302–323.

Howard, D. (2000). Cognitive neuropsychology and aphasia therapy: The case of word retrieval. In I. Papathanasiou (Ed.), *Acquired neurogenic communication disorders: A clinical perspective* (pp. 76–99). Oxford, UK: Blackwell.

Howard, D., & Franklin, S. (1988). *Missing the meaning?: A cognitive neuropsychological study of the processing of words by an aphasic patient*. Cambridge, MA: MIT Press.

Howard, D., & Nickels, L.A. (2005). Separating input and output phonology: Semantic, phonological and orthographic effects in short term memory impairment. *Cognitive Neuropsychology*, 22, 42–77.

Jacquemot, C., Dupoux, E., & Bachoud-Lévi, A.-C. (2007). Breaking the mirror: Asymmetrical disconnection between the phonological input and output codes. *Cognitive Neuropsychology*, 24(1), 3–22.

Joanette, Y., Keller, E., & Lecours, A.R. (1980). Sequences of phonemic approximations in aphasia. *Brain and Language*, 11, 30–44.

Katz, R. B., & Goodglass, H. (1990). Deep dysphasia: Analysis of a rare form of repetition disorder. *Brain and Language*, 39, 153–185.

Kertesz, A. (2007). *The Western Aphasia Battery-Revised*. San Antonio, TX: Harcourt Assessments.

Kittredge, A.K., Dell, G.S., Verkuilen, J., & Schwartz, M.F. (2008). Where is the effect of lexical frequency in word production? Insights from aphasic picture naming errors. *Cognitive Neuropsychology*, 25(4), 463–492.

Kohn, S.E. (1984). The nature of the phonological disorder in conduction aphasia. *Brain and Language*, 23, 97–115.

Kohn, S.E. (1989). The nature of the phonemic string deficit in conduction aphasia. *Aphasiology*, 3, 209–239.

Kohn, S.E., & Smith, K.L. (1990). Between-word speech errors in conduction aphasia. *Cognitive Neuropsychology*, 7, 133–156.

Kohn, S.E., & Smith, K.L. (1994). Distinctions between two phonological lexicons. *Applied Psycholinguistics*, 15, 75-95.

Kohn, S.E., & Smith, K.L. (1991). The relationship between oral spelling and phonological breakdown in conduction aphasia. *Cortex*, 27, 631–639.

Kohn, S.E., & Smith, K.L. (1995). Serial effects in phonemic planning during word production. *Aphasiology*, 9, 209–222.

Laganaro, M., & Zimmerman, C. (2010). Origin of phoneme substitution and phoneme movement errors in aphasia. *Language and Cognitive Processes*, 25(1), 1–37.

Laine, M., & Martin, N. (1996). Lexical retrieval deficit in picture naming: Implications for word production models. *Brain and Language*, 53, 283–314.

Levelt, W.J.M., Roelofs, A., & Meyer, A.S. (1999). A theory of lexical access in speech production. *Behavioral and Brain Sciences*, 22, 1–75.

Lichtheim, L. (1885). On aphasia. *Brain*, 7, 433–484.

Logie, R.H., Gilhooly, K.J., & Wynn, V. (1994). Counting on working memory in arithmetic problem solving. *Memory and Cognition*, 22, 395–410.

Lowell, S., Beeson, P.M., & Holland, A.L. (1995). The efficiency of a semantic cueing procedure on naming performance of adults with aphasia. *American Journal of Speech-Language Pathology*, 4(4), 109–114.

Marshall, R.C., & Freed, D.B. (2006). The personalized cueing method: From the laboratory to the clinic. *American Journal of Speech-Language Pathology*, 15(2), 103–112.

Martin, N., & Ayala, J. (2004). Measurements of auditory-verbal STM span in aphasia: Effects of item, task, and lexical impairment. *Brain and Language*, 89(3), 464–483.

Martin, N., Dell, G.S,. Saffran, E.M., & Schwartz, M.F. (1994). Origins of paraphasias in deep dysphasia: Testing the consequences of a decay impairment to an interactive spreading activation model of lexical retrieval. *Brain and Language*, 47, 609–660.

Martin, N., Fink, R., & Laine, M. (2004). Treatment of word retrieval deficits with contextual priming. *Aphasiology*, 18, 457–471.

Martin, N., Fink, R., Laine, M., & Ayala, J. (2004). Immediate and short-term effects of contextual priming on word retrieval in aphasia. *Aphasiology*, 18, 867–898.

Martin, N., & Gupta, P. (2004). Exploring the relationship between word processing and verbal short term memory: Evidence from association and dissociation. *Cognitive Neuropsychology*, 21(2–4), 213–228.

Martin, N., & Laine, M. (2000). Effects of contextual priming on impaired word retrieval. *Aphasiology*, 14, 53–70.

Martin, N., & Saffran, E. M. (1997). Language and auditory-verbal short-term memory impairments: Evidence for common underlying processes. *Cognitive Neuropsychology*, 14, 641–682.

Martin, R.C., Breedin, S.D., & Damian, M.F. (1999). The relation of phoneme discrimination, lexical access, and short-term memory: A case study and interactive activation account. *Brain and Language*, 70, 437–482.

Martin, R.C., Lesch, M.F., & Bartha, M.C. (1999). Independence of input and output phonology in short-term memory and word processing. *Journal of Memory and Language*, 41, 3–29.

Matsumoto, R., Nair, D.R., LaPresto, E., Bingaman, W., Shibasaki, H., & Luders, H.O. (2007). Functional connectivity in human cortical motor system: A cortico-cortical evoked potential study. *Brain*, 130, 181–197.

McCarthy, R.A., & Warrington, E.K. (1984). A two-route model of speech production. *Brain*, 107, 463–485.

Michel, F., & Andreewsky, E. (1983). Deep dysphasia: An analog of deep dyslexia in the auditory modality. *Brain and Language*, 18, 212–223.

Middleton, E.L., & Schwartz, M.F. (2010). Density pervades: An analysis of phonological neighbourhood density effects in aphasic speakers with different types of naming impairment. *Cognitive Neuropsychology*, 27(5), 401–427.

Nespoulous, J-L., Joanette, Y., Béland, R., Caplan, D., & Lecours, A.R. (1984). Phonological disturbance in aphasia: Is there a "markedness effect" in aphasic phonemic errors? In F.C. Rose (Ed.), *Advances in neurology, Vol. 42: Progress in Aphasiology* (pp. 203–214). London: Raven Press.

Nespoulous, J-L., Joanette, Y., Ska, B., Caplan, J.D., & Lecours, A-R. (1987). Production deficits in Broca's and conduction aphasia: Repetition versus reading. In E. Keller & M. Gopnik (Eds.), *Motor and sensory processes of language. Neuropsychology and neurolinguistics* (pp. 53–81). Hillsdale, NJ: Erlbaum.

Nickels, L. (2002). Improving word finding: Practice makes (closer to) perfect? *Aphasiology*, 16, 1047–1060.

Noël, M-P., Désert, M., Aubrun, A., & Seron, X. (2001). Involvement of short-term memory in complex mental calculation. *Memory and Cognition*, 29, 34–42.

Nozari, N., Kittredge, A.K., Dell, G.S., & Schwartz, M.F. (2010). Naming and repetition in aphasia: Steps, routes, and frequency effects. *Journal of Memory and Language*, 63, 541–559.

Palumbo, C.L., Alexander, M.P., & Naeser, M.A. (1992). CT scan lesion sites associated with conduction aphasia. In S.E. Kohn (Ed.), *Conduction aphasia* (pp. 51–75). Hillsdale, NJ: Erlbaum.

Pate, D.S., Saffran, E.M., & Martin, N. (1987). Specifying the nature of the production impairment in a conduction aphasic: A case study. *Language and Cognitive Processes*, 2, 43–84.

Quigg, M., Geldmacher, D.S., & Elias, W.J. (2006). Conduction aphasia as a function of the dominant posterior perisylvian cortex. Report of two cases. *Journal of Neurosurgery*, 104(5), 845–848.

Raymer, A.M., Thompson, C.K., Jacobs, B., & le Grand, H.R. (1993). Phonological treatment of naming deficits in aphasia: Model-based generalization analysis. *Aphasiology*, 7, 27–53.

Renvall, K., Laine, M., Laakso, M., & Martin, N. (2003). Anomia treatment with contextual priming: A case study. *Aphasiology*, 17, 305–328.

Renvall, K., Laine, M., & Martin, N. (2007). Treatment of anomia with contextual priming: Exploration of a modified procedure with additional semantic and phonological tasks. *Aphasiology*, 21(5), 499–527.

Robson, J., Marshall, J., Pring, T., & Chiat, S. (1998). Phonological naming therapy in jargon aphasia: Positive but paradoxical effects. *Journal of the International Neuropsychological Society*, 4, 675–686.

Romani, C., & Galluzzi, C. (2005). Effects of syllabic complexity in predicting accuracy of repetition and direction of errors in patients with articulatory and phonological difficulties. *Cognitive Neuropsychology*, 22(7), 817–850.

Romani, C., Galluzzi, C., Bureca, I., & Olson, A. (2011). Effects of syllable structure in aphasic errors: Implications for a new model of speech production. *Cognitive Psychology*, 62(2), 151–192.

Romani, C., Olson, A., Semenza, C., & Granà, A. (2002). Patterns of phonological errors as a function of a phonological versus an articulatory locus of impairment. *Cortex*, 38(4), 541–567.

Saffran, E.M., & Marin, O.S.M. (1975). Immediate memory for word lists and sentences in a patient with a deficient auditory short-term memory. *Brain and Language*, 2, 420–433.

Sakurai, Y., Takeuchi, S., Kojima, E., Yazawa, I., Murayama, S., Kaga, K., Momose, T., Nakase, H., Sakuta, M., & Kanazawa, I. (1998). Mechanism of short-term memory and repetition in conduction aphasia and related cognitive disorders: A neuropsychological, audiological and neuroimaging study. *Journal of the Neurological Sciences*, 154(2), 182–193

Schwartz, M.F., Wilshire, C.E., Gagnon, D.A., & Polansky, M. (2004). The origins of nonword phonological errors in aphasics' picture naming. *Cognitive Neuropsychology*, 21, 159–186.

Selnes, O.A., Knopman, D.S., Niccum, N., & Rubens, A.B. (1985). The critical role of Wernicke's area in sentence repetition. *Annals of Neurology*, 17(6), 549–557.

Selnes, O.A., van Zijl, P., Barker, P.B., Hillis, A.E., & Mori, S. (2002). MR diffusion tensor imaging documented arcuate fasciculus lesion in a patient with normal repetition performance. *Aphasiology*, 16, 897–902.

Shallice, T., & Butterworth, B. (1977). Short term memory impairment and spontaneous speech. *Neuropsychologia*, 15, 729–735.

Shallice, T., Rumiati, R.I., & Zadini, A. (2000). The selective impairment of the phonological output buffer. *Cognitive Neuropsychology*, 17, 517–546.

Shallice, T., & Warrington, E. (1977). Auditory–verbal short-term memory impairment and conduction aphasia. *Brain and Language*, 4, 479–491.

Shuren, J.E., Schefft, B.K., Yeh, H.S., Privitera, M.D., Cahill, W.T., & Houston, W. (1995). Repetition and the arcuate fasciculus. *Journal of Neurology*, 242(9), 596–598.

Sidiropoulos, K., Ackermann, H., Wannke, M., & Hertrich, I. (2010). Temporal processing capabilities in repetition conduction aphasia. *Brain and Cognition*, 73(3), 194–202.

Tanabe, H., Sawada, T., Inoue, N., Ogawa, M., Kuriyama, Y., & Shiraishi, J. (1987). Conduction aphasia and arcuate fasciculus. *Acta Neurologica Scandinavica*, 76(6), 422–427.

Turken, A., Whitfield-Gabrieli, S., Bammer, R., Baldo, J., Dronkers, N., & Gabrieli, J. (2008). Cognitive processing speed and the structure of white matter pathways: Convergent evidence from normal variation and lesion studies. *NeuroImage*, 42(2), 1032–1044.

Waldron, H., Whitworth, A., & Howard, D. (2011). Therapy for phonological assembly difficulties: A case series. *Aphasiology*, 25(4), 434–455.

Wambaugh, J.L. (2003). A comparison of the relative effects of phonologic and semantic cueing treatments. *Aphasiology*, 17, 433–441.

Wambaugh, J.L., Linebaugh, C.W., Doyle, P.J., Martinez, A.L., Kalinyak-Fliszar, M., & Spencer, K. (2001). Effects of two cueing treatments on lexical retrieval in aphasic speakers with different levels of deficit. *Aphasiology*, 15, 933–950.

Wernicke, C. (1874). *Der aphasiche Symptomenkomplex.* Breslau: Cohn and Weigert.

Wernicke, C. (1977). The aphasia symptom complex: A psychological study on an anatomic basis. In G.H. Eggert (Trans.), *Wernicke's works on aphasia: A sourcebook and review.* The Hague: Mouton.

Whittle, I. R., & Fraser, D. E. (1991). Resolution of fluent dysphasia following excision of metastatic carcinoma from the arcuate fasciculus. *British Journal of Neurosurgery*, 5(6), 647–649.

Wilshire, C. E. (2002). Where do aphasic phonological errors come from? Evidence from phoneme movement errors in picture naming. *Aphasiology*, 16, 169–197.

Wilshire, C.E., & Fisher, C.A. (2004). "Phonological" dysphasia: A cross-modal phonological impairment affecting repetition, production, and comprehension. *Cognitive Neuropsychology*, 21(2–4), 187–210.

Wilshire, C.E., & McCarthy, R.A. (1996). Experimental investigations of an impairment in phonological encoding. *Cognitive Neuropsychology*, 13, 1059–1098

Wilshire, C.E., & Saffran. E.M. (2005). Contrasting effects of phonological priming in aphasic word production. *Cognition*, 95, 31–71.

Yamada, K., Nagakane, Y., Mizuno, T., Hosomi, A., Nakagawa, M., & Nishimura, T. (2007). MR tractography depicting damage to the arcuate fasciculus in a patient with conduction aphasia. *Neurology*, 68, 789.

Semantic Processing in Transcortical Sensory Aphasia

Jamie Reilly *and* Nadine Martin

Abstract

Transcortical sensory aphasia (TCSA) has historically been regarded as a disconnection syndrome characterized by impaired access between words and otherwise intact core object knowledge. Yet, an extensive body of research has also demonstrated a range of associated nonverbal semantic deficits in TCSA, suggestive of a multimodal semantic impairment that transcends representational modality (i.e., language). Here we delineate the semantic impairment incurred in TCSA within a neurologically constrained model of semantic memory premised upon dynamic interactivity between stored knowledge (e.g., semantic features) and integrative processes that serve to bind this knowledge into cohesive object representations. We discuss practical implications for clinical aphasiology and outline considerations for the broader fields of cognitive neuropsychology and neurolinguistics.

Key Words: Aphasia, Semantic memory, Transcortical sensory aphasia, Disconnection syndrome, Language disorder

Introduction

In a 1992 review of aphasia for the *New England Journal of Medicine*, Antonio Damasio remarked that since the latter half of the nineteenth century, "little new has been uncovered regarding the transcortical aphasias" (p. 535). The same cannot be said for today's view of the unique neurological disorder known as transcortical sensory aphasia (TCSA). During the past decade, there has been a great resurgence of interest in TCSA and its associated semantic impairment. TCSA has since emerged as a controversial lesion model for parsing the organization of word and object knowledge, and much of this controversy is derived from recent studies that have revealed cracks in the assumption that the semantic impairment in TCSA, and more broadly in classical cortical aphasias, reflects a pure disconnection syndrome (Baldo et al., 2005; Bay, 1962; Caramazza, Berndt, & Brownell, 1982; Chertkow, Bub, Deaudon, & Whitehead, 1997; De Renzi, Faglioni, Scotti, & Spinnler, 1972; Gardner et al., 2012; Hamsher, 1998; Jefferies & Lambon Ralph, 2006;

Noonan, Jefferies, Eshana, Garrard, & Lambon Ralph, 2013; Sandberg, Sebastian, & Kiran, 2012; Vallila-Rohter & Kiran, 2013).

Many neurolinguistic models hold in common the assumption that TCSA reflects a disruption in mapping between arbitrary symbols (i.e., words) and their associated object concepts (Lichtheim, 1885; Wernicke, 1874). An aphasiologist steeped in the associationist tradition expects to observe deficits in naming and auditory comprehension in TCSA. However, the associationist also operates under the assumption that this linguistic impairment masks intact object knowledge and that such knowledge can often be accessed through alternative representational modalities (e.g., tactile handling, odor, visual presentation) (for theory regarding the visual modality as providing "privileged access" to the semantic system see Caramazza & Shelton, 1998). For a concrete example of this linguistic access assumption, consider the situation in which an *apple* is placed into the hand of an individual with TCSA. Almost all aphasia models generate the prediction that the person will spontaneously demonstrate his or her preserved knowledge by appropriately taking a bite out of the apple rather than throwing it like a baseball. Moreover, this access assumption also forms the basis for many multimodal treatment strategies and semantic cueing hierarchies for aphasias such as TCSA that incur a primary semantic component (i.e., collectively referred to as semantic aphasia) (Boyle, 2004; Head, 1926; Hoffman, Jefferies, Ehsan, Hopper, & Lambon Ralph, 2009).

Over the past decade, the tenability of the linguistic access assumption has slowly been eroded by a growing body of literature demonstrating that individuals with TCSA also present with a range of nonverbal semantic impairments. People with various forms of poststroke semantic aphasia have been reported to experience paradoxic dissociations in tasks not commonly viewed as heavily language mediated. For example, De Renzi and colleagues (1972) reported impairment among persons with aphasia in reliably choosing an appropriate colored pencil to fill in the dominant color in a series of line drawings depicting common objects (e.g., selecting "yellow" to fill the boundaries of a banana). A variety of other studies have reported impairments in TCSA on tasks that measure semantic association and categorization abilities for pictures (Martin, Schwartz, & Kohen, 2006; Noonan, Jefferies, Corbett, & Lambon Ralph, 2010). Semantic aphasias such as TCSA have also been associated with paradoxic impairment on a variety of other nonlinguistic tasks such as pantomiming the gestures of actions, using tools appropriately, discriminating between real and artificial environmental sounds, and matching environmental sounds to referents.

Some have argued that many experimental tasks used to elicit nonverbal semantic deficits in TCSA are confounded by numerous factors such as verbally mediated instructions and high executive demands, a factor we will soon revisit. This thorny point is not meant to obscure our central premise but instead to highlight our hypothesis that the dominant semantic impairment in TCSA has roots that transcend language. In this chapter we will make our case for this claim of a supralinguistic impairment within the constraints of a model of semantic memory that we have recently advanced through work in other semantically impaired populations (Reilly, Cross, Troiani, & Grossman, 2007; Reilly & Peelle, 2008; Reilly, Peelle, Antonucci, & Grossman, 2011; Reilly, Rodriguez, Peelle, & Grossman, 2011; Reilly et al., 2012). It is important to acknowledge that this model-driven approach represents one view among many potential alternatives and also offers a point of divergence from many previous descriptions of the disorder (e.g., Wernicke–Lichtheim model). Disclaimers aside, we turn now to a description of semantic memory and our guiding theoretical framework.

Semantic Memory: The What and Where of It

Semantic memory encompasses knowledge of object and word meaning, including encyclopedic facts and general world knowledge (Saffran, Schwartz, Umiltà, & Moscovitch, 1994; Tulving, 1972). As might be predicted, the integrity of semantic memory is essential for negotiating many of our most fundamental interactions with the world. Thus, impairment in either access to object representations or degradation of the object representations themselves will typically compromise many global aspects of daily functioning (e.g., following a recipe, interpreting a road sign), including basic language expression and comprehension (Warrington, 1975).

The formal distinction between episodic and semantic memory is often attributed to cognitive psychologist Endel Tulving (1972). By Tulving's episodic–semantic dichotomy, episodic memory is constrained to a specific temporal and environmental context linked to a singular event (e.g., source detail about when I was lost at the mall) or exemplar (e.g., my dog, Felix). In contrast, semantic memory consists of a form of decontextualized knowledge that has been generated often over long periods of time by forming "central tendencies" (e.g., dogs, mammals, tools) upon our exposure to many exemplars (see also Moscovitch, Nadel, Winocur, Gilboa, & Rosenbaum, 2006; Murphy, 2002). Since the early 1970s, our understanding of semantic memory as a dissociable system (or systems) has undergone a rapid evolution that has been fueled by a vast body of parallel empirical work from aphasiology, neuropsychology, functional neuroimaging, and behavioral paradigms (e.g., psycholinguistic investigations of semantic priming). Paradoxically, with the advent of new and sophisticated imaging and cortical stimulation technologies, the field has seen even further divergence. Today, there exist several entrenched and also diametrically oppositional theories of semantic organization within the human brain (Antonucci & Reilly, 2008; Binder, Desai, Graves, & Conant, 2009; Patterson, Nestor, & Rogers, 2007).

It has long been theorized that object knowledge is represented within the human brain by a process of decomposition whereby objects are initially torn apart and then reconstructed ad hoc. For example, a

Labrador Retriever has a set of distinct visual, odor, auditory, and tactile properties in addition to a range of affective and encyclopedic associations. In addition, object knowledge is mediated by representational modality (e.g., verbally learned versus visually observed) (see Dual Coding Theory as a multiple semantic systems hypothesis in Paivio, 1985, 1991, 1995). Many cognitive neuroscientists believe that these disparate bits of information about objects are stored in long-term memory across a widely distributed network of neuroanatomically remote brain regions. Moreover, theories of semantic memory that have strong sensorimotor grounding emphasize the idea that semantic features are stored either within or proximal to brain structures that are also engaged during the actual processes of sensation, perception, and motor execution (Barsalou, Simmons, Barbey, & Wilson, 2003; Gallese & Lakoff, 2005; Martin, 2007a, 2007b).

Wernicke and several prominent contemporaries, including Freud and Lissauer, proposed various iterations of fully distributed models of conceptual knowledge (Eggert, 1977; Freud, 1891; Gage & Hickok, 2005; Lissauer, 1890/1988; Wernicke, 1874), an overarching approach to memory organization that has both endured and evolved into one of the dominant theories of semantic representation today. Wernicke and others (e.g., Lichtheim) also held that the putative concept center or "semantic field" (i.e., *Begriffsfeld* in the original German) was so diffusively distributed as to be almost undifferentiated cortically (see also later

theories of equipotentiality and mass action propounded by Lashley, 1948). The consensus within cognitive neuropsychology today is that the supporting architecture of semantic memory, although highly distributed, does have both specificity and localization. Nevertheless, extant theories of semantic memory still radically differ with respect to just how "distributed" they view knowledge representation (Reilly et al., 2014).

A fully distributed view holds that knowledge is maintained across many different parts of the brain without the necessity for a central organizing structure (i.e., a binding site or convergence zone). In the parlance of neural network modeling, our knowledge of objects reflects an autoassociative pattern of activation across multiregional cell assemblies. As complex as this statement sounds, we can reframe it within the simple Hebbian maxim that as clusters of neurons repeatedly fire together, they soon wire together. This means that patterns of neural coactivation (i.e., simultaneous activity) that are potentiated through repeated experience (e.g., seeing many different dogs) ultimately serve to ground a basic object concept as a distributed activation pattern (Gage & Hickok, 2005; Pulvermüller, 1999, 2001). Importantly, this fully distributed theory makes the explicit prediction that there is no single brain region dedicated to the binding and representation of semantic memory. Therefore, this view also predicts that only the most diffuse and catastrophic brain injury would be sufficient to produce a global impairment of semantic memory. Figure 6.1 depicts

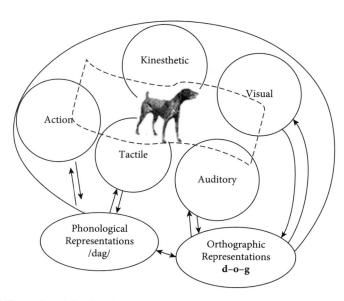

Figure 6.1 Schematic of Allport's (1985) distributed semantic memory model.

a schematic of the fully distributed theory of semantic feature representation and connectivity with the language system advanced by Allport (1985).

One of the greatest challenges for a fully distributed model of semantic memory is ambiguity with respect to its mechanism of semantic binding. That is, it is unclear how the brain can pull together and interpret a plethora of data into cohesive object representations with such remarkable speed and accuracy in the absence of a dedicated "center." This fundamental question, known as the *binding problem*, remains highly charged across neuroscience, consciousness research, and the philosophy of mind (Kandel, 2006; McNorgan, Reid, & McRae, 2011).

The polar alternative to a fully distributed model of semantic organization holds that human conceptual knowledge is organized in an entirely abstract, propositional manner that does not rigidly honor an object's sensorimotor properties (Fodor, 2000). That is, modality neutral regions of the human cortex pull from primary sensory regions and bind features into higher level conceptual representations. An important distinction with respect to this class of theory is that object concepts (e.g., Labrador Retriever) are far more complex than the simple sum of their distributed parts (e.g., color, odor, sound). This class of theories has collectively been described as *amodal* or *supramodal* with respect to a necessary role of grounding semantic features across regions of the cortex that are critical for sensorimotor processing, perceptual simulation, and mental imagery.

One of the primary criticisms of early amodal semantics theories is that mapping a construct such as "amodality" to the brain is opaque. In contrast, fully distributed models of semantic organization make the explicit and testable assumption that knowledge of a specific feature is organized within or near the brain structure that is dedicated to the actual perception of that feature. For example, functional imaging studies have demonstrated that when participants are asked to imagine the color of a tomato, they engage anterior projections of the visual cortex that are also engaged when seeing a tomato (Chao, Haxby, & Martin, 1999; Chao & Martin, 1999). Thus, many distributed theories predict that the "redness" feature of a tomato lives in the inferior temporal lobe. From a hypothesis testing standpoint, distributed theories offer a remarkable advantage relative to early amodal semantics theories that tended to be unapologetically mute on the following questions: (1) What exactly is an abstract propositional representation of an object

concept? and (2) Where are these putative abstract representations housed within the human brain?

Contemporary amodal semantic theories have undergone a radical evolution in terms of their capacity to map onto brain structure. Much of this neurological foundation can be attributed to a highly influential theory known as the *convergence zone framework* proposed by Damasio, Tranel, and colleagues (Damasio & Damasio, 1994; Tranel, Grabowski, Lyon, & Damasio, 2005). These authors have advanced the hypothesis that distributed semantic feature knowledge gradually converges upon regions of the brain that are dedicated to polymodal feature binding (e.g., barking + musky odor = dog). Neurally encoded information streams efferently from the various receptive fields of topographically organized sensory regions (e.g., retinotopic organization within the primary visual cortex) toward the various sensory association areas. An important part of this process is that as featural information streams away from the primary sensory areas and into polymodal convergence zones, such information grows incrementally less literal and more abstracted (for rejection of this view in toto see Gallese & Lakoff, 2005).

Single cell recording and functional imaging data provide compelling evidence for a variety of convergence zones in the human brain (Beauchamp, 2005; Beauchamp, Argall, Bodurka, Duyn, & Martin, 2004; Binder et al., 2009; Fuster, Bodner, & Kroger, 2000; Taylor, Moss, Stamatakis, & Tyler, 2006). In an extensive meta-analysis of functional neuroimaging studies of semantic processing, Binder and colleagues (2009) reported that one of the most consistently activated polymodal convergence zones is the angular gyrus and adjacent regions of the temporoparietal junction (TPJ). As we will soon discuss, this finding has critical relevance because the TPJ is also a canonical site of lesion for TCSA (Damasio, 1998, 2001).

Convergence zone theories hold in common the assumption that particular regions of the brain are essential for the integrity of semantic memory. That is, unlike the redundancy offered by a fully distributed organization of object knowledge, this framework predicts that focal damage to a convergence zone will produce a global impairment in semantic knowledge that transcends access-related factors such as representational modality (e.g., writing or speech) or sensory domain (e.g., odor, visual form, environmental sound). Elizabeth Warrington (1975) was perhaps the first to show that such a selective impairment of semantic memory, although rare, is indeed possible in a disorder later termed *semantic dementia*.

Today's dominant model of semantic memory (i.e., the Hub & Spoke Model) is largely fueled by the unique phenotype and corresponding distribution of brain morphology in semantic dementia, the temporal lobe variant of frontotemporal degeneration, whose ubiquitous semantic impairment has been linked to bilateral dysfunction within the anterolateral temporal lobes (Gorno-Tempini et al., 2011; Jefferies & Lambon Ralph, 2006; Lambon Ralph, Cipolotti, Manes, & Patterson, 2011; Lambon Ralph, Graham, Ellis, & Hodges, 1998; Lambon Ralph, Lowe, & Rogers, 2007; Lambon Ralph & Patterson, 2008). The Hub & Spoke Model holds that ventral and anterolateral portions of the temporal lobes (i.e., temporal poles) act as massive convergence zones wherein modality-specific knowledge is bound and differentiated into an amodal form (Lambon Ralph et al., 2011; Lambon Ralph, Sage, Jones, & Mayberry, 2010; Patterson et al., 2007; Rogers et al., 2004, 2006). The function of this putative "hub" is to organize the distributed bits of knowledge that radiate inward from a series of "spokes" that constitute modality-specific regions of the cortex. Proponents of the Hub & Spoke Model have argued that the temporal poles are anatomically well-suited to this purpose due to both their centrality and underlying functional connectivity (i.e., massive interconnections to the medial temporal and frontal lobes in addition to direct relays to primary sensory areas).

Hub & Spoke Model proponents have described semantic memory as an amodal and dynamic system whose effectiveness relies on a precise orchestration between stored knowledge and cognitive control mechanisms (i.e., semantic control) that operate on such knowledge (Coccia, Bartolini, Luzzi, Provinciali, & Lambon Ralph, 2004).[1] In our own work, we have outlined a similar dichotomy between the content of stored representations (i.e., *content*) and the range of functions (i.e., *process*) that are crucial for acting upon knowledge and constructing meaning (Grossman, Koenig, Troiani, Work, & Moore, 2007; Koenig & Grossman, 2007; Koenig, Smith, & Grossman, 2010; Peelle, Troiani, & Grossman, 2009; Reilly et al., 2011, 2014). Thus far, our discussion has focused on the organization of semantic content. It is our central premise, however, that many of the semantic difficulties in TCSA have a basis within *process*. Thus, we shift our discussion to the role of process in semantic memory.

Process in Semantic Memory

Much of our daily functioning demands rapid object recognition and flexible use of our vast repertoire of semantic knowledge. By no means is this a passive process. We construct our own understanding of the world through long-term experience and assimilate a great deal of incoming perceptual and semantic detail with previous knowledge. Much of our online semantic processing is conducted so quickly that we must employ efficient cognitive shortcuts in the form of active organizing principles. For example, it has long been believed that object knowledge is organized in a hierarchical manner such that specific exemplars (e.g., Labrador Retriever) are nested within successively broader category distinctions (e.g., dog, animal, thing) (Rosch, 1973). We derive a rapid understanding of word and object identity (e.g., a tiny unfamiliar dog) by assigning tentative category membership through an active evaluative process comparing "goodness of fit" (i.e., typicality) and updating the tenability of this initial guess as incoming data arrive (e.g., the tiny "dog" unexpectedly meows) (Sandberg et al., 2012). Clearly these semantic processing heuristics are resource demanding. Yet, we are just beginning to understand the unique and often idiosyncratic role played by process in assigning structure to semantic knowledge.

One unanswered question in cognitive neuropsychology is whether a dedicated executive semantic system exists or whether human conceptual knowledge is mitigated by a "domain-general" executive process that supports more global cognitive functions. Randi Martin and others have argued for the existence of a semantic short-term memory (STM) store, which is one component of a multistore verbal STM model along with lexical and phonological STM stores (Martin, 2009; Martin, Shelton, & Yaffee, 1994). According to Saffran (1990) these levels of short-term storage are extensions of the levels of word representation (e.g., phonological, lexical) postulated in interactive activation models of word processing (Dell, 1986; Dell & O'Seaghdha, 1992; Dell, Schwartz, Martin, Saffran, & Gagnon, 1997; Foygel & Dell, 2000). The common factor that defines this extension is the maintenance of activated word representations during language processing. The process of activating and maintaining activation of semantic, lexical, and phonological representations of words is time dependent whether the language system is generating a single word or multiple words. This implicates some sort of short-term memory process as integral to word processing. As noted earlier, "process" differs from content in that it operates over content. In this model, maintenance of activation is one of those operations, but others have also been implicated (e.g., strength of activation, inhibition of other competing activated representations, and response selection).

It is worth noting an important distinction made in many models of word processing between conceptual semantic and word-specific (sometimes called verbal) semantic processing. In the word processing models of Dell and colleagues, for example, word-specific semantic features are distinguished from a conceptual semantic level of representation from which they are generated (Dell et al., 1997). It is the word-specific semantic features that subsequently activate associated words in the lexicon, which in turn connect with phonemes that comprise those words. As in multistore models of verbal STM, some have postulated an extension of lexical–semantic representations toward encompassing a wider domain-neutral conceptual STM (e.g., words, pictures, environmental sounds). Potter (1993), for example, hypothesized the existence of a very short-term conceptual memory dedicated to knowledge representation. This lexical versus conceptual processing distinction is of particular importance when considering the established view that TCSA reflects a focal breakdown in accessing lexical representations. If we consider the existence of a short-term conceptual store, it is conceivable that reports of impaired object knowledge in TCSA may actually be related to an impaired conceptual STM that subserves both lexical and nonlexical aspects of semantic memory in a blanket fashion.

Potter's (1976, 1993) work on conceptual STM focuses primarily on its role in enabling consolidation of fleeting conceptual events evoked by perceptual experience into long-term memory. She proposed a model detailing the relation between a modality-independent conceptual STM in relation to a conventional working memory model (Baddeley, 1986) whereby a verbal sentence is perceived and processed by the phonological STM system with its articulatory system but simultaneously is processed by conceptual STM in which the conceptual aspects of the utterance are briefly activated in this short-term store and are integrated with long-term memory. This model schematic is reflected in Figure 6.2a.

Potter's (1993) original model did not specify a mechanism by which conceptual STM interacts further with language comprehension or production systems. Neither does it presuppose a mechanism of mapping components onto the human brain. However, if we consider a typical word production model such as Dell's (1986) interactive activation model (Figure 6.2b), it is possible to extrapolate some semantic components from Potter's model. The semantic feature network, for example, may be equated with Potter's conceptual STM. Semantic features of words to be spoken are briefly activated as they initiate a spread of activation through the word production system. They are the first to be activated in production and the last to be activated in repetition or comprehension of auditory input. The conceptual "cloud" that is often depicted above this semantic feature system may be equated with long-term memory in Potter's model. It seems likely that disparate terminology has made it difficult to think about Potter's conceptual STM and Dell's semantic feature system similarly, but when focusing on descriptions of their functions, the overlap is more apparent.

The contribution of a conceptual STM to the execution of nonverbal semantic tasks is crucial to consider. The selective impairment of semantic STM is one potential factor among a constellation of other dysexecutive impairments that have been argued to qualitatively distinguish the semantic impairment in TCSA from that evident in semantic dementia (Corbett, Jefferies, Ehsan, & Lambon Ralph, 2009; Corbett, Jefferies, & Lambon Ralph, 2011; Jefferies & Lambon Ralph, 2006; Noonan et al., 2010). Proponents of the Hub & Spoke Model have referred to the range of executive functions that supports semantic processing collectively under the rubric of *semantic control*. Hub & Spoke proponents have also argued that brain damage in TCSA compromises a diverse range of cognitive control mechanisms, resulting in deregulation of semantic memory.

Hub & Spoke proponents have hypothesized that semantic control constitutes a subdomain of generalized executive functioning (EF) (Hoffman et al., 2009). That is, semantic control draws on the same executive resource pool that is also dedicated to various other EF demands. As such, *semantic control* is vulnerable to many of the same criticisms that have been lodged against EF regarding limited construct specificity. Consider, for example, the wide range of EF abilities that contributes to our online construction of meaning, of which only a small subset includes (1) inhibitory control and suppression of plausible competitors, (2) attentional vigilance,

(a) Very short term conceptual memory model (Potter)

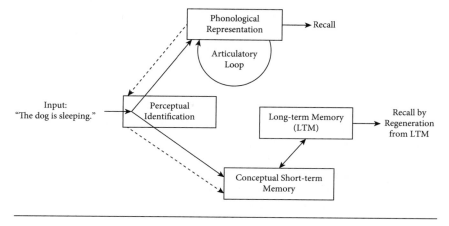

(b) Interactive activation model of word processing (Dell)

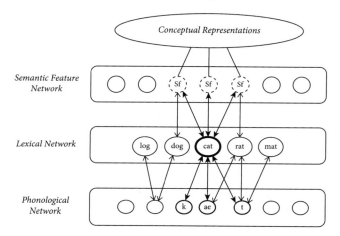

Figure 6.2 Depictions of (a) Potter's (1993) model of conceptual short-term memory (STM) and (b) Dell and colleagues' interactive activation model of word processing.

Note: In Figure 6.2a, auditory input (e.g., a spoken sentence) is perceived and simultaneously processed through phonological STM and also conceptual STM. It can be recalled verbatim via the phonological STM (with rehearsal support via the articulatory loop) and can also be recalled by regeneration via the interaction of conceptual STM and LTM. Figure 6.2b depicts Dell's interactive spreading activation model (e.g., Dell & O'Seaghdha, 1992). Word production begins the activation spreading from conceptual knowledge to specific semantic features of a concept (e.g., tactile, visual, auditory features), which in turn activates the target word form in the lexicon and to a lesser extent other word forms that share some of those features. Activation from the word forms spreads again to the phonemes that comprise the activated word forms. The model is "interactive" because the activation spreading forward through each stage of linguistic representation sends feedback to the previous stage. This interactivity continues until a word form is selected for production. In a second stage (not depicted), the selected lexical form is phonologically encoded and eventually articulated.

(3) selective attention, (4) error and anomaly detection, (5) hierarchical semantic categorization, (6) working memory updating ability, (7) cognitive flexibility and task switching, (8) response selection, (9) lexical retrieval, (10) filtering irrelevant or nondiagnostic detail, (11) self-monitoring and arousal, (12) sustained attention, and (13) divided attention and mitigation of dual task interference.

We have identified at least 13 distinct executive components, many of which are believed to be both neurologically and behaviorally dissociable. We see ample evidence for dissociable components of EF within clinical aphasiology. For example, a bilingual adult's ability to flexibly switch between languages (i.e., code switching) is sometimes compromised by damage to portions of the basal ganglia (e.g., left caudate nucleus) that are also engaged during more general EF-related switching behaviors (e.g., switching during verbal fluency, changing the subject during conversation) (Crinion et al., 2006). In contrast, individuals with damage to more lateral aspects of the frontal cortex (e.g., the left inferior frontal gyrus) tend to show a different pattern of executive impairment that is characterized by strong proactive interference effects and a weakened ability to inhibit competing alternatives (Barde, Schwartz, Chrysikou, & Thompson-Schill, 2009; Schnur, Schwartz, Brecher, & Hodgson, 2006; Schnur et al., 2009). Thus, the emerging picture of EF is that of an umbrella construct that unites numerous subcomponents, and we can readily imagine how a selective "lesion" to any single one of these subcomponents of EF might perturb online semantic processing. Yet, there is a paradox with respect to the relation between EF dysfunction and semantic impairment. That is, many studies have reported either null or weak correlations between measures of EF and semantic abilities (Fine, Delis, Paul, & Filoteo, 2011; Gongvatana, Woods, Taylor, Vigil, & Grant, 2007; Laisney et al., 2009). We see evidence for this null relation in both healthy and neuropsychologically impaired populations. If indeed semantic memory loads on a domain-general EF, then healthy normal adults should also show dual task costs (i.e., interference) when juggling almost any other resource-demanding task. Yet, our ability to process basic conceptual knowledge is not radically impacted by concurrent attentional demands. Moreover, a number of neurological disorders present with prominent dysexecutive impairment, including traumatic brain injury, frontal variant of frontotemporal dementia, HIV dementia complex, and nondemented Parkinson's disease. Yet, these patients do not typically experience the profound severity of multimodal semantic impairment seen in semantic dementia or TCSA (Reilly et al., 2011).

In summary, much remains unclear about the role of process in semantic memory and whether there exists a dedicated module to conceptual STM (e.g., Potter, 1993). However, we have identified several reasons why a domain-general EF impairment might fail to drive the semantic impairment in TCSA.

A Hybrid Model of Semantic Memory: Multiple Convergence Zones with Sparse Representation

We recently proposed a model of semantic organization that integrates many of the relative merits of amodal and modality-specific theories of knowledge representation (Reilly, Antonucci, Peelle, & Grossman, 2011; Reilly & Peelle, 2008; Reilly et al., 2011). We turn now to a description of the cognitive and neural substrates of this particular theory, starting from the premise that semantic organization is highly distributed but also relies on a series of convergence zones. Thus, we are aligned with approaches to the architecture of semantic memory that are best described as hybrid in nature (Hart et al., 2007; Hart & Kraut, 2007). However, we diverge from extant hybrid theories in (1) how we view the nature of the semantic representation within convergence zones and (2) which convergence zones we view as being essential for semantic memory.

We hypothesize that within convergence zones, object knowledge is stripped of its original sensorimotor salience and is maintained in a sparse form (Reilly et al., 2012, 2014). A sparse representation can be conceived as analogous to the way that the brain stores details about episodic memories. That is, memory does not behave in a photorealistic manner but instead much nonessential source detail is filtered. For example, when we recall details of a specific salient event (e.g., the time we were lost at a mall), details such as what we were wearing at the time are more vulnerable to forgetting and/or distortion than more salient diagnostic details. Sparse representations, therefore, reflect the aggregate of many modality-specific semantic features.

In this sparse representation approach, we have emphasized the role of reciprocal activation between convergence zones and distributed features. That is, as task demands dictate, we must perceptually enrich a sparse representation by indexing modality-specific brain regions of the cortex. Thus, object knowledge is reconstructed on line through a process of perceptual simulation or enactment (Barsalou, 2008; Kosslyn, 2005; Kosslyn, Ganis, & Thompson, 2001). We hypothesize that these imagery and mental simulation processes are mediated by a modular semantic working memory system that is at least partially dissociable from that of the neural system that supports more general EF (Martin, Dell, Saffran, & Schwartz, 1994; Martin & Saffran, 1990; Martin et al., 1994; Poldrack et al., 1999; Thompson-Schill, D'Esposito, Aguirre, & Farah, 1997). This interactive system is perhaps best illustrated by a real-world example. Consider the following:

1. Is a Labrador Retriever *friendlier than* a German Shepherd?

2. Is a Labrador Retriever *larger than* a German Shepherd?

3. Does a Labrador Retriever *bark louder than* a German Shepherd?

4. Does a Labrador Retriever *smell muskier than* a German Shepherd?

These are simple questions that might be encountered any time. Yet, they tap very different aspects of conceptual knowledge, including affective associations (e.g., *friendlier than*), relative size (e.g., *larger than*), environmental sound (e.g., *louder than*), and olfaction (e.g., *smell muskier than*). We hypothesize that each of these questions forces the reader to ultimately converge upon a common, sparse representation for Labrador Retrievers and German Shepherds. However, convergence upon a common representation is only half of the battle; we must also index various modality-specific regions in order to successfully evaluate the given proposition (see also Kellenbach, Brett, & Patterson, 2001). That is, to make a relative size judgment in the absence of a visual stimulus (i.e., assuming neither dog is physically present while you read this), we must invoke visual imagery and spatial working memory. This specific task demand, therefore, calls for communication between a sparse representation and a concrete set of visual features stored primarily in the visual association cortex. Importantly, we hypothesize that this communication between convergence zones and modality-specific regions of the cortex is both reciprocal (i.e., two-way) and cognitive resource demanding.

We offer the following analogy for understanding this multiple component approach to semantic memory. Consider being tasked with completing a research project that requires visiting the stacks of a massive reference library. Successful retrieval is contingent upon both a comprehensive inventory of books (semantic features) in tandem with a skilled librarian or search engine. Thus, in semantic memory there is an inextricable link between the content of stored knowledge and processes that operate upon such knowledge. *Process* includes resources that are dedicated to response selection, inhibitory control of competing alternatives, semantic categorization, error and novelty detection, vigilance, sustained attention, and semantic working memory. *Content* encompasses our vast array of knowledge about the features of objects, including sensorimotor properties (e.g., color, form) as well as abstract lexical associations and verbally learned encyclopedic facts. As the discussion of TCSA unfolds, we interpret semantic impairment within the context of this overarching, multiple component model of semantic memory.

A Brief History of Transcortical Sensory Aphasia

Although an extensive historical treatise is beyond the scope of this review, we must first contextualize the evolution of our understanding of TCSA within the zeitgeist under which the syndrome was conceived. TCSA emerged as a unique syndrome at a pivotal point during the classical period of aphasiology of the nineteenth century. One of the major lower branches of an expanding tree structure of aphasia was propounded by Paul Broca (1865) who linked the seat of articulate language to the third frontal convolution of the left hemisphere [for parallel work see Marc Dax as reviewed in Buckingham (2006), and for a critique of the logic of language localization see Luria (1974)]. Broca is also renowned for establishing a distinction between classes of aphasia marked by deficits in fluent articulatory production (i.e., aphemia) or abstract symbol manipulation. Broca's localization of a fluent–nonfluent aphasia distinction using the lesion model approach set the stage for a rapid series of advances.

The next major bifurcation in a rapidly evolving aphasia tree structure resulted from Carl Wernicke's (1874) monograph, *Der Aphasiche Symptomcomplex: Eine Psychologische Studie auf Anatomischer Basis*. In this work, Wernicke proposed the concept of a sensory aphasia, characterized by impaired auditory comprehension in the context of generally fluent but often highly paraphasic expressive language production (Berthier, 1999a, 1999b, 1999c; Eggert, 1977; Wernicke, 1874). Using the mortem lesion correlation approach, Wernicke linked the neural substrate of sensory aphasia (now called Wernicke's Aphasia) to middle and posterior portions of the superior and middle temporal gyri, regions now collectively referred to as Wernicke's area. Wernicke's localization of sensory aphasia in tandem with Broca's earlier localization of motor aphasia offered a substantive leap forward in our understanding of the instantiation of language within the human brain. Yet, his contribution went far beyond the localization of sensory aphasia. Neuroscience owes Wernicke such a great debt because he pioneered a formal computational mechanism for mapping the various components of language onto the human brain. From a philosophy of science standpoint,

Wernicke's proposal was revolutionary in that it afforded systems level hypothesis testing on a grand scale.

TCSA originally emerged out of the early connectionist models proposed by Wernicke, Lichtheim, and other prominent contemporaries (e.g., Kussmaul) (Roth & Heilman, 2000). The clear power of these models is that they could derive aphasia subtypes based on a fixed taxonomy. Thus the connectionist modeling approach offered a new and highly deductive way of generating a set of concrete predictions about specific behavior(s) related to focal brain injuries. Put simply, it was now possible to "lesion" a computational model and look for confirmatory evidence from individuals with brain damage in contrast to the extraordinary limitations imposed by the inductive approach of observing behavior and attempting to derive a unified theory of brain (for a bitter dissent see Berthier, 1999b; Head, 1926; Luria, 1974).

Importantly, many of the early connectionist models that originally gave rise to the syndrome of TCSA incorporated an assumption that portended the concept of a *disconnection syndrome*, later formalized by Dejerine (1891) and Geschwind (1965). Namely, many of the connectionist models offered contingencies for lesions to either impact a dedicated language center (e.g., Broca's or Wernicke's area) or the major fiber tracts that join these centers.

Goldstein (1948) offered the formal nomenclature for this *cortical–transcortical* distinction as a means for discriminating classes of aphasia characterized by either the former (e.g., cortical) or the latter (transcortical) type of damage. Consequently, within the classical aphasia taxonomy, TCSA was conceived very much like a disconnection syndrome despite the fact the formal terminology for such a syndrome had not yet been proposed. Figure 6.3 illustrates how a hypothetical lesion to the combined Wernicke–Lichtheim–Geschwind connectionist model would produce the unique behavioral profile of TCSA in addition to seven other aphasia subtypes.

In summary, as its name implies, TCSA reflects the historical confluence of two overarching dichotomies: (1) cortical–transcortical and (2) sensory–motor. The term *transcortical* itself invokes the Latin prefix *trans-* (meaning across), thus denoting an aphasia syndrome that results from disrupted communication *across* dedicated language centers (i.e., a disconnection syndrome). The second half of the name TCSA denotes primary impairment to afferent *sensory* rather than efferent motor functions. Since its inception, TCSA has evolved in terms of specificity, and many formal aphasia batteries today include TCSA among their diagnostic classifications (Goodglass, Kaplan, & Barresi, 2001; Kertesz, 2007).

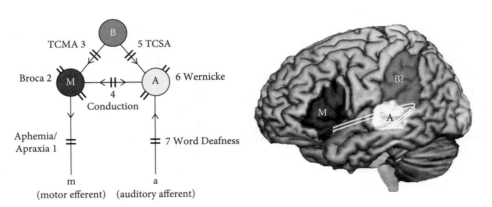

Figure 6.3 Depiction of the Wernicke–Lichtheim–Geschwind model and superposition on the human brain. (See color insert). *Note:* Abbreviations retained from Lichtheim's original schema include the following: M (Motor Center corresponding to Broca's area); B (Concept Center corresponding to what Geschwind and others loosely localized to the supramarginal and angular gyri); A (Auditory Word Form Center localized to Wernicke's area); a (auditory afferent pathway marking input to the language network); m (motor speech peripheral musculature, efferent output pathway). The model predicts the presence of seven distinct classical aphasia subtypes, numbered sequentially above and described as follows. (1) Damage to m → M compromises the transmission of high-level motor programs to the speech musculature resulting in a primary articulatory disorder; (2) damage to M produces the classic profile of Broca's aphasia; (3) damage to the B → M pathway disconnects the putative concept and motor planning centers, resulting in the profile of transcortical motor aphasia (TCMA); (4) damage to the major tract (i.e., arcuate fasciculus) joining Broca's and Wernicke's areas impairs bidirectional communication between A ↔ M resulting in conduction aphasia; (5) damage to the pathway joining the putative concept center (B) with the center for auditory word forms (A) results in the disconnection of words from concepts that is the classic hallmark of TCSA; (6) damage to A produces Wernicke's Aphasia; (7) damage to the a→A pathway produces pure word deafness.

Clinical Criteria for Transcortical Sensory Aphasia

TCSA is characterized by severe deficits in auditory comprehension and language production in the context of preserved repetition ability (Goodglass et al., 2001; Kertesz, 2007). Within the schema of the Boston Diagnostic Examination of Aphasia (BDAE), TCSA is marked by well-articulated speech with appropriate prosodic contours and melodic line. However, the output of spontaneous language production is peppered by a combination of irrelevant semantic paraphasias (i.e., real word substitution errors) and neologisms (i.e., nonword errors). Naming and spontaneous narrative speech production in TCSA are often profoundly impaired, and these individuals typically experience comparable impairment for reading and writing (i.e., alexia and agraphia) (but for a unique subtype of TCSA without disturbance in these domains see Heilman, Rothi, McFarling, & Rottmann, 1981).

One remarkable feature that distinguishes TCSA from Wernicke's Aphasia is its associated pattern of preserved auditory repetition. That is, individuals with TCSA often show accurate repetition ability for both words and nonwords. Moreover, echophenomena (e.g., echolalia) are commonly reported in TCSA, as is the selective preservation of islands of rote memorized material such as prayers and songs (Berthier, 1999a; Goodglass, 1993; Goodglass et al., 2001). Patients with TCSA often talk excessively (i.e., logorrhea) and show "press of speech," a phenomenon characterized by speaking over others with great pressure and at a rapid rate. Moreover, these characteristics are usually amplified by anosognosia and poor self-monitoring abilities. In Henry Head's (1926, pp. 257–260) description of this phenomenon he remarked, "These patients tend to talk rapidly as if afraid of forgetting what they wanted to say; at times this actually occurs and the conversation tails away aimlessly" [as noted by Berthier (1999b)]. Head's comment has special relevance for the hypothesis we will soon attempt to advance, namely, that aspects of the cognitive–linguistic impairment in TCSA result from the impact of amnestic and/or dysexecutive impairments on the maintenance of a memory trace, regardless of the representational modality of the particular trace (e.g., language or nonverbal).

Despite remarkably preserved repetition ability, there is strong evidence to suggest that much of what an individual with TCSA repeats is not understood. Experimental evidence for this claim is derived from several sources, including both receptive and expressive language tasks. For example, individuals with TCSA typically fail to self-correct semantic anomalies when repeating sentences, but do in fact show sensitivity to and will tend to spontaneously correct grammatical violations (Berthier et al., 1991; Cimino-Knight, Hollingsworth, & Gonzalez Rothi, 2005; Martin, Saffran, & Pate, 1984). In addition to these unique patterns of self-correction in TCSA, repetition accuracy is often relatively immune to the manipulation of lexical–semantic variables such as word concreteness, imageability, frequency, age of acquisition, or even lexicality (i.e., whether the target item is a real word or nonword), whereas these individuals continue to show normal effects of word length and other phonological variables (Martin & Saffran, 1990).

In terms of classic dual route models of reading and repetition, we might account for TCSA repetition in terms of phonology as a dominant encoding strategy. That is, in the context of an impaired semantic contribution to recall, individuals with TCSA tend to quickly parrot information back to their interlocutor through an exclusive reliance upon form. Moreover, when memory span is taxed by presenting many items, individuals with TCSA often revert to a pattern of recall that is characterized by rapid forgetting of earlier presented items (i.e., lack of primacy effects) in the context of more accurate recall of the most recently presented items (i.e., recency effects), further suggestive of a pervasive lack of semantic support for recall (Martin & Saffran, 1990) and a reliance on activated phonological representations to repeat.

The Puzzling Neurology of Transcortical Sensory Aphasia: Site(s) of Lesion

TCSA is a prominent aphasia subtype in terms of its theoretical relevance. However, in the daily course of clinical practice, pure TCSA is a relatively rare phenomenon. In a large and well-characterized aphasia sample, Berthier and colleagues (1991) reported a prevalence of approximately 18% for all of the transcortical aphasias combined (i.e., motor, sensory, and mixed) and noted that this estimate is convergent with other aphasia classification studies (e.g., Kertesz, 1982). The relative infrequency of TCSA can be attributed to its somewhat atypical lesion distribution. That is, although numerous neurological disorders can produce TCSA (e.g., neoplasm, Alzheimer's disease), stroke is the most common reported cause.

The most common site of vascular occlusion in stroke is the middle cerebral artery (MCA), which perfuses the basal ganglia and much of the perisylvian cortex (i.e., Broca's area, inferior precentral gyrus, Heschl's gyrus, Wernicke's area) (Berthier, 1999a, 1999b, 1999c). As such, left MCA stroke commonly produces the classical perisylvian aphasia subtypes. However, in its chronic form TCSA is classified as an extrasylvian syndrome, unique for its preservation of the classical perisylvian language regions. Damasio (1998) noted that the one of the most distinctive neuropathological features of TCSA is that it is rarely induced by a lesion that obliterates the whole of Wernicke's area but instead typically affects more rostral structures such as the temporoparietal junction. Today the most common reported site of lesion for chronic TCSA is the TPJ, whose gross anatomy is illustrated in Figure 6.4 (Alexander, Hiltbrunner, & Fischer, 1989; Berthier, 1999a, 1999b, 1999c; Boatman et al., 2000; Damasio, 1998; Nadeau, Gonzalez Rothi, & Crosson, 2000; Otsuki et al., 1998; Sarno, 1998).

TCSA most commonly results from damage to the supramarginal and angular gyri and the posterior terminating portion of the superior temporal gyrus, areas sometimes classified as "watershed" regions in terms of their distal proximity to the major arterial vasculature supplying the cortex (Damasio, 1998; Geschwind, Quadfasel, & Segarra, 1968; Goodglass et al., 2001; Roth & Heilman, 2000). Often the TPJ is impacted by extensive left hemisphere strokes whose associated global aphasia during the acute stage resolves only later into the more chronic form of TCSA. In most cases of acute stroke, however, TCSA tends to manifest in a transient form. Although the TPJ is the most commonly reported site of the lesion, TCSA also emerges from lesions to other temporal lobe regions. Boatman et al. (2000), for example, reported eliciting the auditory profile of TCSA through direct cortical stimulation of the middle temporal gyrus among a group of patients undergoing presurgical cortical mapping for intractable epilepsy. Alexander et al. (1989) and Berthier et al. (1991) both reported cases of TCSA that occurred in the context of posterior cerebral artery (PCA) strokes that impacted more ventral and posterior temporooccipital regions just superior to the inferior temporal gyrus (i.e., visual association cortex) (see also Chertkow et al., 1997). A variety of other lesion correlation studies have implicated more anterior frontal and mesial structures, including the left prefrontal cortex (Berthier, 1991, 1999a, 1999b, 1999c; Cimino-Knight et al., 2005; Otsuki et al., 1998; Zahn et al., 2002), left basal ganglia (Crosson, 1992; Yamadori, Ohira, Seriu, & Ogura, 1984), and portions of the left midbrain (i.e., thalamus) (Alexander et al., 1989; Cappa & Vignolo, 1979; McFarling, Rothi, & Heilman, 1982).

Anatomical variability underlying TCSA creates a paradox that at first glance thwarts any principled attempt at localization. How is it possible that damage to a range of distant brain structures can produce an identical TCSA phenotype?[2] Perhaps the

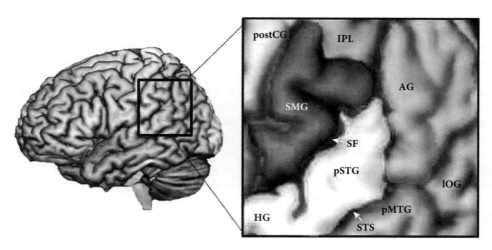

Figure 6.4 Gross anatomy of the temporoparietal junction (TPJ). *Note*: Landmarks and abbreviations were adapted from the neuroanatomical atlas of Hanna Damasio (2005) superimposed upon a lateral rendering of a single subject from the ch2better.nii brain template from MRIcron (Rorden, 2007). Anatomical abbreviations: **AG** = Angular Gyrus; **HG** = Heschl's Gyrus; **IPL** = Inferior Parietal Lobule; **LOG** = Lateral Occipital Gyrus; **postCG** = Post Central Gyrus; **pMTG** = Posterior Middle Temporal Gyrus; **pSTG** = Posterior Superior Temporal Gyrus; **SF** = Sylvian Fissure; **SMG** = Supramarginal Gyrus; **STS** = Superior Temporal Sulcus.

best hope for an answer to this anatomical riddle lies within network hypotheses. That is, TCSA results from damage to one or more components of a distributed but highly functionally connected network dedicated to a specific cognitive function (e.g., sensorimotor feature representation, executive functioning). Using such systems-level logic, Alexander and colleagues (1989) hypothesized that TCSA reflects damage to a distributed network dedicated to feature representation in semantic memory, a controversial claim that we will soon revisit.

Proponents of the Hub & Spoke Model have recently offered perhaps the most cogent solution to the riddle of brain–behavior localization in TCSA, arguing that the TPJ and the prefrontal cortex (PFC) constitute two highly interactive components of the cortical network supporting EF and semantic control (see the earlier discussion of process in semantic memory). Accordingly, damage to either a frontal or temporoparietal distribution might produce a similar profile of dysexecutive impairment that deregulates semantic memory.

Semantic Impairment in Transcortical Sensory Aphasia: Lexical and Beyond

The question of whether TCSA impacts semantic memory and other global aspects of cognition and intelligence remains highly controversial. At the heart of this debate lies one of the most fundamental questions about the relationship between language and consciousness. That is, do we think in words, or does language simply act as a blanket upon which abstract propositional thought is draped? The Roman emperor and stoic philosopher Marcus Aurelius (AD 121–180) remarked, "Your life is an expression of all your thoughts." If we were to agree with Aurelius, we must pursue the conclusion to its logical end and assume that TCSA fundamentally compromises abstract thought. Although this was indeed the position espoused by a number of highly influential figures such as Hughlings Jackson (1878), Luria (1974), and Goldstein (1948), it represents a departure from the mainstream position that TCSA reflects an immutable divorce between language and thought.

Today's dominant view holds that the semantic impairment in TCSA qualitatively differs in many respects from that of semantic dementia or Alzheimer's disease. Jefferies and Lambon Ralph (2006) conducted the first case study formally pitting TCSA against semantic dementia, concluding that the verbal semantic impairment in TCSA is marked by the following distinct characteristics[3]:

1. *Insensitivity to word frequency/familiarity*: Individuals with TCSA tend to manifest similar degrees of impairment for low-frequency relative to high-frequency words; for example, an individual with TCSA might experience an equal likelihood of erring on *pterodactyl* versus *alligator*. As a result, individuals with TCSA often show similar patterns of impairment across split halves of naming tests that are graded in difficulty by familiarity or frequency [e.g., Boston Naming Test/BNT (Kaplan, Goodglass, & Weintraub, 2001)].

2. *Response inconsistency and poor inter-item correlations*: Individuals with TCSA tend to show high variability in their response accuracy both across and within sessions. For example, test–retest consistency with respect to item-level accuracy tends to be weak in TCSA. In contrast, patients with semantic dementia or Alzheimer's disease tend to show a strong pattern of consistency in their anomia across repeated trials, as well as a strong correlation between "naming and knowing" that manifests as reduced semantic knowledge for items they cannot name (Hodges, 2003; Hodges, Graham, & Patterson, 1995; Hodges & Patterson, 1995; Hodges, Salmon, & Butters, 1992; Lambon Ralph et al., 1998; Lambon Ralph, Graham, Patterson, & Hodges, 1999). In TCSA, this correlation between successful naming and the quality of underlying semantic knowledge is thought to be weak. Such inconsistency is also apparent when contrasting performance in verbal versus nonverbal tests of semantic knowledge, whereas a patient with semantic dementia typically shows comparable performance across different representational formats (Reilly et al., 2011; Reilly & Peelle, 2008).

3. *Receptivity to cueing and priming*: Individuals with TCSA often remain receptive and stimulable to cueing. For example, this is evident in progressively gating the phonemes of a target word (e.g., d, da, dak . . .), incrementally providing semantic detail (e.g., the person who you see at the hospital when you are sick), or asking the person to complete a cloze fragment (e.g., When you are sick you see a . . .). The benefit of cueing suggests that these individuals experience difficulties that can be ameliorated by increasing the salience of the target item or otherwise shifting task demands.

4. *Associative naming errors*: Individuals with TCSA tend to produce many associative naming errors in spontaneous speech (e.g., scissors → paper), whereas this pattern is less common in

semantic dementia in which category coordinate (e.g., cat → dog) or superordinate (e.g., cat → animal) naming errors predominate.

In addition to a prominent language disturbance, TCSA is also associated with a range of nonverbal semantic impairments. A sampling of these deficits, summarized in Table 6.1, includes difficulties in categorization of picture stimuli, matching pictures of gestures to tools, matching environmental sounds to pictures, and detecting absurdities in pictures. In addition, a range of naturalistic action deficits has also been reported in aphasia, including the inability to pantomime gestures or use objects appropriately. Finally, others have reported even more paradoxic deficits in aphasia such as matching color to global visual form (e.g., coloring a banana yellow) and categorical visual perception of the cup–bowl distinction.

The presence of a multimodal (verbal + nonverbal) semantic impairment in TCSA suggests the disturbance of a latent factor that affects both language and cognition (see also Jackson, 1878). We might argue that such nonverbal semantic impairments offer the proverbial "slam dunk" against the Wernicke–Lichtheim–Geschwind account of TCSA as a language disconnection syndrome. Yet, it has been argued that many of the tasks used to elicit nonverbal semantic impairment in aphasia lack ecological validity and are highly confounded by task demands (e.g., high EF demands and verbally mediated instructions). Further complicating matters is the fact that many studies that have reported nonverbal conceptual impairment have categorized individuals not in terms of a specific syndrome (e.g., TCSA) but by broader distinctions such as fluent-or-nonfluent, anterior-or-posterior, or dominant semantic-or-phonological impairment, thus limiting inference both across and within studies (for treatment of this quandary see Chertkow et al., 1997).

Heterogeneity introduced by variable sites of lesion and TCSA subtypes lends further murkiness. This is especially apparent when considering studies that have collapsed the profiles of patients with posterior relative to middle cerebral artery strokes. That is, PCA and massive MCA strokes can both produce TCSA-like symptoms in the context of damage to the posterior, inferior temporal, and temporooccipital cortex (BA 37). However, these regions of the brain that comprise the visual association cortex are more commonly implicated in the semantic impairments seen in semantic dementia and Alzheimer's

disease (Grossman et al., 2004; Mummery et al., 2000; Rosen et al., 2002). Some have argued accordingly that the extent of damage along the dorsoventral axis of the brain is strongly predictive of the severity of nonverbal semantic impairment (i.e., ventral = worse) (Antonucci, Beeson, Labiner, & Rapcsak, 2007; Antonucci, Beeson, & Rapcsak, 2004; Chertkow et al., 1997). Chertkow and colleagues (1997), for example, found that individuals with fluent aphasia clustered into two groups with respect to verbal–nonverbal impairment. Those with damage to the TPJ (the dorsal group) showed an isolated verbal comprehension deficit with preserved performance on a picture variation of the same task (i.e., matching a picture of a lemon to a teacup or coffee mug). In contrast, individuals with posterior and inferior temporal lobe damage (the ventral group) showed comparable impairment for both words and pictures (but see Jefferies & Lambon Ralph, 2006).

In summary, a gestalt of TCSA is emerging that paints the syndrome as only truly "semantic" (i.e., satisfies criteria for multimodal storage impairment) in the context of an inferior and posterior distribution of temporal lobe damage. On a related note, Berthier (1999b) has described semantic dementia as a form of TCSA due to its profile of preserved repetition and impaired comprehension. Although semantic dementia does technically satisfy broad criteria for TCSA, its designation as a form of TCSA has not met with widespread acceptance. Rather, many emphasize that the canonical profile of TCSA results from a more superior distribution of TPJ and/or frontal subcortical involvement and that TCSA exclusively represents a form of stroke aphasia (Corbett et al., 2011; Geschwind, 1965; Geschwind et al., 1968; Hoffman et al., 2009; Noonan et al., 2010). Thus, most argue that TCSA and semantic dementia offer orthogonal semantic impairments that are subject to comparison but not combination/collapsing.

For the sake of argument, let us suspend disbelief for a moment and ignore the frontal, midbrain, and inferior temporal lobe manifestations of TCSA and assume that the TPJ is the primary site of lesion for TCSA. This assumption might at the very least yield a logical starting point for delineating the semantic impairment in TCSA. Yet, this reductionist approach of focusing on the TPJ is riddled with problems in that damage to the inferior parietal lobe, in addition to causing aphasia, is also commonly associated with a constellation of

Table 6.1 A Sample of Studies Reporting Nonverbal Semantic Impairment in Nonprogressive Manifestations of Aphasia (e.g., Stroke, Focal Neurological Insult)

Impaired Nonverbal Domain	References
Semantic association ability for pictures • Picture Subtest: Pyramids and Palm Trees Test (3-choice) • Picture Subtest: Camels & Cactus Test (4-choice) • Judging best fit for picture triads (e.g., lemon: coffee pot or teapot)	Martin et al. (2006) [†]Jefferies and Lambon Ralph (2006) Chertkow et al. (1997)
Categorization/category sorting of pictures • Sorting pictures by intersections of different perceptual features (e.g., canary = yellow + bird)	Gainotti et al. (1986)
Nonverbal abstract problem solving and EF • Raven's Progressive Matrices Test • Wisconsin Card Sorting Test	Baldo et al. (2005) Hoffman et al. (2009)
Naturalistic action deficits • Matching pictures along a common dimension of action, function, or use (e.g., <twisting> corkscrew-to-screwdriver; <cutting> knife-to-scissors; <canonical recipient of an action> hammer-to-nail) • Spontaneous manipulation ability for actual tools during tactile handling [e.g., scissors → grasp, movement, and orientation] • Comprehension, pantomime, and matching of symbolic gestures to pictures (e.g., gestured guitar playing match to guitar)	[†]Corbett et al. (2009) [†]Corbett et al. (2009) Gainotti and Lemmo (1976)
Matching color to global visual form via spontaneous drawing • Coloring line drawings of common objects	De Renzi et al. (1972)
Figure drawing deficits • Figure reproduction upon delay • Reduced specificity/omission of features among freehand line drawings of natural objects	Gainotti (1983) Grossman (1993)
Higher level visual deficits in the absence of a frank apperceptive agnosia • Cup/Bowl Categorical Perception: As a cup flattens and its diameter simultaneously expands, a critical threshold is reached at which most people perceive it as a bowl (Labov, 1973). This study reported a threshold shift in aphasia.	Caramazza et al. (1982)
Detection of "absurdities" in pictures via gesture/pointing	Bay (1962)
Environmental sound perception • Matching common environmental sounds to their respective picture referents via pointing	[†]Jefferies and Lambon Ralph (2006) Vignolo (1982) Saygin et al. (2003)

Note: [†]Signifies that the particular study isolated TCSA; Pyramids and Palm Trees Test (Howard & Patterson, 1992); Camels & Cactus Test (Bozeat, Lambon Ralph, Patterson, Garrard, & Hodges, 2000); Raven's Coloured Progressive Matrices Test (Raven, 1962); Wisconsin Card Sorting Test (Heaton, Chelune, Talley, Kay, & Curtis, 1993).

nonlinguistic impairments that impacts semantic memory (or at least tests thereof). Parietal dysfunction commonly produces difficulties in constructional praxis, spatial working memory, and the four classic symptoms of Gerstmann's syndrome (i.e., dyscalculia, finger agnosia, dysgraphia, and right–left directional confusion) (Gold, Adair, Jacobs, & Heilman, 1995). We can imagine how a combination of aphasia and Gerstmann's syndrome can potentially interact to degrade performance on a variety of cognitive measures that assess both verbal and nonverbal semantic knowledge (and more general fluid intelligence) (Hamsher, 1998). Such effects were apparent in early work correlating TPJ damage with poor performance on the Army General Classification Test (AGCT), a measure of purported general intelligence whose three components include vocabulary, arithmetical reasoning, and block counting (Weinstein & Teuber, 1957).

Summary of Semantic Impairment in Transcortical Sensory Aphasia

We have conveyed a picture of great complexity with respect to semantic impairment in TCSA. Yet, we have also highlighted some recurrent themes and offered an interpretative theoretical framework. To reiterate, this hybrid theory of semantic memory is premised upon multiple convergence zones and sparse representation (see the earlier discussion). Within the context of this model, we view TCSA as a primary impairment of semantic *process*. Neurological damage to either a high level semantic convergence zone within the TPJ (e.g., angular gyrus) or a lower level sensory convergence zone within the midbrain (e.g., thalamus) compromises the ability to integrate and effectively package distributed feature knowledge into cohesive wholes. Importantly, this loss of semantic convergence is likely to impact both online perception and remote reconstructive processes (i.e., perceptual enactment and mental imagery) that are critical for enriching object knowledge.

As aphasiologists, in our daily clinical practice we do not often associate frank semantic errors such as pouring bleach into our spaghetti sauce as representative of TCSA. Yet, such errors are commonplace in semantic dementia and Alzheimer's disease (Bozeat et al., 2003; Bozeat, Ralph, Patterson, & Hodges, 2002; Coccia et al., 2004; Funnell, 2001; Hodges, Bozeat, Lambon Ralph, Patterson, & Spatt, 2000; Patterson, 2007; Pulvermuller et al., 2009). One potential explanation for this aphasia–dementia discrepancy involves redundancy in the organization of convergence zones across the human brain. That is, a number of potential semantic convergence zones have been identified bilaterally across the cortex (e.g., temporopolar cortex, superior temporal sulcus, middle temporal gyrus, perirhinal cortex) (Binder et al., 2009; Damasio & Damasio, 1994; Damasio, Grabowski, Tranel, Hichwa, & Damasio, 1996; Davies, Graham, Xuereb, Williams, & Hodges, 2004; Ding, Van Hoesen, Cassell, & Poremba, 2009; Turken & Dronkers, 2011). It has also been hypothesized that semantic convergence occurs in a series of successive hierarchical steps, beginning with lower order sensory conjunctions ascending to higher order perceptual and linguistic crossmodal integration processes (see also conceptual structure

account and related work by Bussey & Saksida, 2002; Tyler & Moss, 2001; Tyler, Moss, Durrant-Peatfield, & Levy, 2000). The TPJ in general and the angular gyrus in particular have been identified as sites of higher order semantic convergence (Binder et al., 2009; Ramachandran & Hubbard, 2001). Yet, the TPJ does not appear to be the only site of semantic convergence in the human brain, nor does it appear to be the most critical relative to more inferior temporal lobe regions compromised in semantic dementia.

When comparing the semantic impairment in TCSA to that of semantic dementia or Alzheimer's disease there are additional considerations. The most common brain injury that produces TCSA is stroke, and with rare exceptions, manifests as unilateral brain injury. Thus, individuals who incur TCSA in the context of a left hemisphere TPJ infarct typically retain their right hemisphere TPJ homologue. This affords the possibility of a right hemisphere contribution to semantic memory in addition to the possibility of poststroke functional reorganization (see also Berthier, 2001). In addition, the nature of stroke is also such that beyond the acute stage, cognition is typically either static or improving. The same cannot be said for neurocognitive disorders such as semantic dementia and Alzheimer's disease that both manifest in a progressive and bilateral form (Galton et al., 2001; Hodges et al., 1992; Lambon Ralph et al., 2011).

It is undeniable that some aspects of the semantic impairment in TCSA are related to executive resource limitations. However, the nature of the executive resource pool remains a question of intense debate. One possibility espoused by Hub & Spoke Model proponents is that the semantic impairment in TCSA is driven by a subset of domain-neutral EF capabilities (Hoffman et al., 2009; Hoffman, Jefferies, Ehsan, Jones, & Lambon Ralph, 2012; Hoffman, Jefferies, & Lambon Ralph, 2011; Jefferies & Lambon Ralph, 2006; Noonan et al., 2010). An alternative view holds that semantic memory is subserved by a modular and at least partially dissociable semantic working memory system from that of general EF (Martin & Saffran, 1990, 1992, 1997). This hypothesis is supported by the presence of weak or null correlations between impaired EF and semantic processing in many neuropsychologically impaired populations (e.g., traumatic brain injury, Parkinson's disease) (but see Baldo et al., 2005), as well as the absence of prominent dual-task EF-semantic costs in healthy normal adults.

We have offered a point of departure from the classical disconnection account of TCSA and posed the alternative hypothesis that many associated difficulties in TCSA are rooted in semantic process. The contention that a latent, supralinguistic cognitive impairment lurks quietly within TCSA is by no means new (Goldstein, 1948; Head, 1926; Jackson, 1878; Luria, 1974). Yet, the specific mechanism of impairment that we have proposed here (i.e., multiple convergence zone + sparse representation) is in many respects novel. Although any incipient theory should be met with a healthy dose of skepticism, there are many reasons to consider a semantic process-based approach to TCSA. This perspective has the potential to elucidate our theoretical understanding of language and conceptual organization while also offering practical and innovative considerations for language rehabilitation.

Clinical Implications

In its chronic form, TCSA is a rare but severe and highly debilitating form of aphasia that is often resistant to behavioral treatment. Standard therapies for semantically based language disorders such as TCSA tend to focus heavily on retraining semantic features and semantic category structure. Semantic feature analysis (SFA) is a prime example of a feature-based therapy that operates through a paired associate learning approach wherein individuals with aphasia repeatedly generate multimodal semantic features in an effort to link conceptual salience with an object's name (Antonucci, 2009; Boyle, 2004). Another popular approach to semantic treatment (i.e., typicality) involves capitalizing on the nature of semantic category structure through training atypical exemplars (e.g., *penguin*) with the goal of reestablishing cohesion, breadth, and central tendencies/prototypes (e.g., *robins*) within weakened semantic networks (Kiran & Thompson, 2003).

SFA and typicality treatments are heavily driven by semantic content. Although the purpose of these therapies may be to strengthen connections within a network of semantic content, they do this by manipulating content of treatment tasks. We have argued for a process account of TCSA that involves poor feature binding and retrieval. An approach to language treatment that shifts the focus from semantic content to process offers unique direction for aphasia therapy. That is, semantic impairment in TCSA might paradoxically be ameliorated by selective training on an EF component such as inhibitory control, or a perceptual process such as audiovisual crossmodal integration (e.g., pairing tones with colors or environmental sounds with images). One possible solution is to forego treatment specificity and employ a "kitchen sink" approach that simultaneously addresses many general domains of EF, whereas a more principled alternative might involve isolating and rehabilitating one or more specific component(s) of EF (e.g., inhibitory control but not sustained attention). Both of these EF-driven approaches pose individual strengths but also share a common pitfall. That is, if semantic memory is subserved by its own modular processing system, we would predict a minimal therapeutic benefit from training general EF. This remains an important unanswered empirical question with respect to structuring semantic treatments for both TCSA and many other forms of semantic aphasia.

A third approach that could potentially address semantic process impairments is to manipulate executive function demands in the context of treatment tasks. We have recently employed such an approach toward treatment of a person with conduction aphasia (Kalinyak-Fliszar, Kohen, & Martin, 2011) and two others, one with Wernicke's Aphasia (Martin, Kohen, McCluskey, Kalinyak-Fliszar, & Gruberg, 2009) and one with anomia (Kalinyak-Fliszar, Kohen, & Martin, 2011). In each of these cases, the treatment task was repetition of words or nonwords under three conditions that gradually increased the memory and executive function load of the task: immediate repetition, repetition after 5 seconds, and repetition after naming aloud numbers on a screen for 5 seconds. The second condition increased memory load on simple repetition and the third condition increased STM and executive load. It is the claim of Martin and colleagues that this treatment stimulates fundamental processes that drive access to and maintain activation of semantic and phonological representations of words. Consistent with this hypothesis, they observed in all three cases improvement on the training task (repetition) as well as improvement on other language tasks (e.g., phoneme discrimination, rhyming, verbal span tasks). To use this treatment approach in cases of TCSA, the treatment task would have to be changed to a task that stimulates pathways between lexical and semantic representations (input and output). For example, to promote comprehension of words, word-to-picture matching tasks could be used and STM and executive loads could be manipulated as described for repetition. Whether this treatment would be effective with TCSA remains to be seen. However, the preliminary success of these few treatments that incorporate STM/executive load on other aphasias is promising.

Concluding Remarks

TCSA has recently provided both a compelling and controversial lesion model for parsing the structure of semantic memory. Moreover, many theories of semantic organization now incorporate active processing components and recognize that semantic memory is a dynamic system. It is now apparent that we must reconsider Damasio's (1992) claim that little new has been uncovered regarding TCSA. Yet, it is also clear that much remains to be learned about the nature of this unique disorder and ways to address the considerable disability posed for these individuals with TCSA.

Acknowledgments

Supported by U.S. Public Health Service Grants K23 DC010197 (J.R.), R01 DC013063 (J.R.), R21 DC008782 (N.M.), and R01 DC001927 (N.M.).

Notes

1. When referring to *Proponents of the Hub & Spoke Model*, we are collectively describing the combined efforts of a highly talented group of affiliated scientists, including Karalyn Patterson, Matthew Lambon Ralph, Elizabeth Jefferies, Paul Hoffman, Timothy Rodgers, John Hodges, and their many collaborators.
2. This statement might not be entirely accurate. Many researchers have argued that sensitive testing can reveal distinct TCSA subtypes (Coslett, Roeltgen, Gonzalez Rothi, & Heilman, 1987; Heilman et al., 1981).
3. Warrington and Shallice have proposed formal criteria by which disorders of access versus storage could be discriminated (Shallice, 1988; Warrington & Crutch, 2004; Warrington & McCarthy, 1983). The criteria for a semantic access impairment are as follows: (1) preserved facilitative effects of priming and cueing; (2) response inconsistency across sessions; (3) insensitivity to word frequency; (4) facilitation from superordinate category exemplars; (5) sensitivity to rate of presentation (i.e., see discussions of semantic refractory access disorders). In contrast, the criteria for a semantic storage disorder include the following: (1) negligible priming and cueing effects; (2) consistency in task performance across repeated sessions; (3) sensitivity to word frequency and object familiarity; (4) retention of superordinate detail (e.g., "animal" but not "Labrador").

References

Alexander, M. P., Hiltbrunner, B., & Fischer, R. S. (1989). Distributed anatomy of transcortical sensory aphasia. *Archives of Neurology*, 46(8), 885–892.

Allport, D. A. (1985). Distributed memory, modular subsystems and dysphasia. In S. K. Newman & R. Epstein (Eds.), *Current perspectives in dysphasia* (pp. 207–244). Edinburgh: Churchill Livingstone.

Antonucci, S. M. (2009). Use of semantic feature analysis in group aphasia treatment. *Aphasiology*, 23(7–8), 854–866.

Antonucci, S. M., Beeson, P. M., Labiner, D. M., & Rapcsak, S. Z. (2007). Lexical retrieval and semantic knowledge in patients with left inferior temporal lobe lesions. *Aphasiology*, 22(3), 1–24.

Antonucci, S. M., Beeson, P. M., & Rapcsak, S. Z. (2004). Anomia in patients with left inferior temporal lobe lesions. *Aphasiology*, 18(5–7), 543–554.

Antonucci, S. M., & Reilly, J. (2008). Semantic memory and language: A primer. *Seminars in Speech and Language*, 29, 5–17.

Baddeley, A. D. (1986). *Working memory*. Oxford: Oxford University Press.

Baldo, J. V., Dronkers, N. F., Wilkins, D., Ludy, C., Raskin, P., & Kim, J. (2005). Is problem solving dependent on language? *Brain and Language*, 92(3), 240–250.

Barde, L. H. F., Schwartz, M. F., Chrysikou, E. G., & Thompson-Schill, S. L. (2009). Reduced short-term memory span in aphasia and susceptibility to interference: Contribution of material-specific maintenance deficits. *Neuropsychologia*, 48(4), 909–920.

Barsalou, L. W. (2008). Grounded cognition. *Annual Review of Psychology*, 59, 617–645.

Barsalou, L. W., Simmons, W. K., Barbey, A. K., & Wilson, C. D. (2003). Grounding conceptual knowledge in modality-specific systems. *Trends in Cognitive Sciences*, 7(2), 84–91.

Bay, E. (1962). Aphasia and non-verbal disorders of language. *Brain*, 85, 411–426.

Beauchamp, M. S. (2005). See me, hear me, touch me: Multisensory integration in lateral occipto-temporal cortex. *Current Opinion in Neurobiology*, 15, 145–153.

Beauchamp, M. S., Argall, B. D., Bodurka, J., Duyn, J. H., & Martin, A. (2004). Unraveling multisensory integration: Patchy organization within human STS multisensory cortex. *Nature Neuroscience*, 7(11), 1190–1192.

Berthier, M. L. (1999a). Echophenomenon, automatic speech, and prosody in transcortical aphasias. In M. L. Berthier (Ed.), *Transcortical aphasias* (pp. 151–178). East Sussex: Psychology Press, Ltd.

Berthier, M. L. (1999b). *Transcortical aphasias*. East Sussex, Hove England: Psychology Press/Taylor & Francis (UK).

Berthier, M. L. (1999c). Transcortical sensory aphasia. In M. L. Berthier (Ed.), *Transcortical aphasias* (pp. 75–91). East Sussex: Psychology Press, Ltd.

Berthier, M. L. (2001). Unexpected brain-language relationships in aphasia: Evidence from transcortical sensory aphasia associated with frontal lobe lesions. *Aphasiology*, 15(2), 99–130.

Berthier, M. L., Starkstein, S. E., Leiguarda, R., Ruiz, A., Mayberg, H. S., Wagner, H.,. . . Robinson, R. G. (1991). Transcortical aphasia. Importance of the nonspeech dominant hemisphere in language repetition. *Brain*, 114(3), 1409–1427.

Binder, J. R., Desai, R. H., Graves, W. W., & Conant, L. L. (2009). Where is the semantic system? A critical review and meta-analysis of 120 functional neuroimaging studies. *Cerebral Cortex*, 19(12), 2767–2796.

Boatman, D., Gordon, B., Hart, J., Selnes, O., Miglioretti, D., & Lenz, F. (2000). Transcortical sensory aphasia: Revisited and revised. *Brain*, 123(8), 1634–1642.

Boyle, M. (2004). Semantic feature analysis treatment for anomia in two fluent aphasia syndromes. *American Journal of Speech-Language Pathology*, 13(3), 236–249.

Bozeat, S., Lambon Ralph, M. A., Graham, K. S., Patterson, K., Wilkin, H., Rowland, J.,. . . Hodges, J. R. (2003). A duck with four legs: Investigating the structure of conceptual knowledge using picture drawing in semantic dementia. *Cognitive Neuropsychology*, 20(1), 27–47.

Bozeat, S., Lambon Ralph, M. A., Patterson, K., Garrard, P., & Hodges, J. R. (2000). Non-verbal semantic impairment in semantic dementia. *Neuropsychologia*, 38, 1207–1215.

Bozeat, S., Ralph, M. A., Patterson, K., & Hodges, J. R. (2002). The influence of personal familiarity and context on object use in semantic dementia. *Neurocase*, 8(1–2), 127–134.

Broca, P. (1865). Location of cerebral functions. Location of articulate language. *Bulletin of the Society of Anthropology (Paris)*, 4, 200–203.

Buckingham, H. W. (2006). The Marc Dax (1770–1837)/Paul Broca (1824–1880) controversy over priority in science: Left hemisphere specificity for seat of articulate language and for lesions that cause aphemia. *Clinical Linguistics & Phonetics*, 20(7–8), 613–619.

Bussey, T. J., & Saksida, L. M. (2002). The organization of visual object representations: A connectionist model of effects of lesions in perirhinal cortex. *European Journal of Neuroscience*, 15, 355–364.

Cappa, S. F., & Vignolo, L. A. (1979). "Transcortical" features of aphasia following left thalamic hemorrhage. *Cortex*, 15(1), 121–130.

Caramazza, A., Berndt, R. S., & Brownell, H. H. (1982). The semantic deficit hypothesis: Perceptual parsing and object classification by aphasic patients. *Brain and Language*, 15(1), 161–189.

Caramazza, A., & Shelton, J. R. (1998). Domain-specific knowledge systems in the brain: The animate-inanimate distinction. *Journal of Cognitive Neuroscience*, 10(1), 1–34.

Chao, L. L., Haxby, J. V., & Martin, A. (1999). Attribute-based neural substrates in temporal cortex for perceiving and knowing about objects. *Nature Neuroscience*, 2(10), 913–919.

Chao, L. L., & Martin, A. (1999). Cortical regions associated with perceiving, naming, and knowing about colors. *Journal of Cognitive Neuroscience*, 11(1), 25–35.

Chertkow, H., Bub, D., Deaudon, C., & Whitehead, V. (1997). On the status of object concepts in aphasia. *Brain and Language*, 58(2), 203–232.

Cimino-Knight, A. M., Hollingsworth, A. L., & Gonzalez Rothi, L. J. (2005). The Transcortical aphasias. In L. L. LaPointe (Ed.), *Aphasia and related neurogenic language disorders* (3rd ed., pp. 169–185). New York: Thieme New York.

Coccia, M., Bartolini, M., Luzzi, S., Provinciali, L., & Lambon Ralph, M. A. (2004). Semantic memory is an amodal, dynamic system: Evidence from the interaction of naming and object use in semantic dementia. *Cognitive Neuropsychology*, 21(5), 513–527.

Corbett, F., Jefferies, E., Ehsan, S., & Lambon Ralph, M. A. (2009). Different impairments of semantic cognition in semantic dementia and semantic aphasia: Evidence from the non-verbal domain. *Brain*, 132(9), 2593–2608.

Corbett, F., Jefferies, E., & Lambon Ralph, M. A. (2011). Deregulated semantic cognition follows prefrontal and temporo-parietal damage: Evidence from the impact of task constraint on nonverbal object use. *Journal of Cognitive Neuroscience*, 23(5), 1125–1135.

Coslett, H. B., Roeltgen, D. P., Gonzalez Rothi, L., & Heilman, K. M. (1987). Transcortical sensory aphasia: Evidence for subtypes. *Brain and Language*, 32(2), 362–378.

Crinion, J., Turner, R., Grogan, A., Hanakawa, T., Noppeney, U., Devlin, J. T.,. . . Price, C. J. (2006). Language control in the bilingual brain. *Science*, 312(5779), 1537–1540.

Crosson, B. (1992). *Subcortical functions in language and memory*. New York: Guilford Press.

Damasio, A. R. (1992). Aphasia. *New England Journal of Medicine*, 326(8), 531–539.

Damasio, A. R., & Damasio, H. (1994). Cortical systems for retrieval of concrete knowledge: The convergence zone framework. In C. Koch & J. L. Davis (Eds.), *Large-scale neuronal theories of the brain* (pp. 61–74). Cambridge, MA: MIT Press.

Damasio, H. (1998). Neuroanatomical correlates of the aphasias. In M. T. Sarno (Ed.), *Acquired aphasia* (3rd ed., pp. 43–70). San Diego, CA: Academic Press.

Damasio, H. (2001). Neural basis of language disorders. In R. Chapey (Ed.), *Language intervention strategies in aphasia and related neurogenic language disorders* (4th ed., pp. 18–36). Baltimore: Lippincott Williams & Wilkins.

Damasio, H. (2005). *Human brain anatomy in computerized images* (2nd ed.). New York: Oxford University Press.

Damasio, H., Grabowski, T. J., Tranel, D., Hichwa, R. D., & Damasio, A. R. (1996). A neural basis for lexical retrieval. *Nature*, 380, 499–505.

Davies, R. R., Graham, K. S., Xuereb, J. H., Williams, G. B., & Hodges, J. R. (2004). The human perirhinal cortex and semantic memory. *European Journal of Neuroscience*, 20(9), 2441–2446.

De Renzi, E., Faglioni, P., Scotti, G., & Spinnler, H. (1972). Impairment in associating colour to form, concomitant with aphasia. *Brain*, 95(2), 293–304.

Dejerine, J. (1891). Sur un cas de cecite verbale avec agraphie, suivie d'autopsie. *Memoires Societe Biologique*, 3, 197–201.

Dell, G. S. (1986). A spreading activation theory of retrieval in language production. *Psychological Review*, 93, 283–321.

Dell, G. S., & O'Seaghdha, P. G. (1992). Stages of lexical access in language production. *Cognition*, 42(1–3), 287–314.

Dell, G. S., Schwartz, M. F., Martin, N., Saffran, E. M., & Gagnon, D. A. (1997). Lexical access in aphasic and nonaphasic speakers. *Psychological Review*, 104(4), 801–838.

Ding, S. L., Van Hoesen, G. W., Cassell, M. D., & Poremba, A. (2009). Parcellation of human temporal polar cortex: A combined analysis of multiple cytoarchitectonic, chemoarchitectonic, and pathological markers. *Journal of Comparative Neurology*, 514(6), 595–623.

Eggert, G. H. (1977). *Wernicke's works on aphasia: A sourcebook and review* (Vol. 1). The Hague, Netherlands: Mouton.

Fine, E. M., Delis, D. C., Paul, B. M., & Filoteo, J. V. (2011). Reduced verbal fluency for proper names in nondemented patients with Parkinson's disease: A quantitative and qualitative analysis. *Journal of Clinical and Experimental Neuropsychology*, 33(2), 226–233.

Fodor, J. A. (2000). *The mind doesn't work that way: The scope and limits of computational psychology*. Cambridge, MA: MIT Press.

Foygel, D., & Dell, G. S. (2000). Models of impaired lexical access in speech production. *Journal of Memory and Language*, 43, 182–216.

Freud, S. (1891). *On aphasia* (E. Stengel, Trans.). New York: International University Press.

Funnell, E. (2001). Evidence for scripts in semantic dementia: Implications for theories of semantic memory. *Cognitive Neuropsychology*, 18(4), 323–341.

Fuster, J. M., Bodner, M., & Kroger, J. K. (2000). Cross-modal and cross-temporal association in neurons of frontal cortex. *Nature*, 405(6784), 347–351.

Gage, N., & Hickok, G. (2005). Multiregional cell assemblies, temporal binding and the representation of conceptual knowledge in cortex: A modern theory by a 'classical' neurologist, Carl Wernicke. *Cortex*, 41(6), 823–832.

Gainotti, G. (1983). Drawing objects from memory in aphasia. *Brain*, 106, 613–622.

Gainotti, G., Carlomagno, S., Craca, A., & Silveri, M. C. (1986). Disorders of classificatory activity in aphasia. *Brain and Language*, 28(2), 181–195.

Gainotti, G., & Lemmo, M. A. (1976). Comprehension of symbolic gestures in aphasia. *Brain and Language*, 3(3), 451–460.

Gallese, V., & Lakoff, G. (2005). The brain's concepts: The role of the sensory-motor system in conceptual knowledge. *Cognitive Neuropsychology*, 22(3), 455–479.

Galton, C. J., Patterson, K., Graham, K., Lambon Ralph, M. A., Williams, G., Antoun, N.,... Hodges, J. R. (2001). Differing patterns of temporal atrophy in Alzheimer's disease and semantic dementia. *Neurology*, 57(2), 216–225.

Gardner, H. E., Lambon Ralph, M. A., Dodds, N., Jones, T., Ehsan, S., & Jefferies, E. (2012). The differential contributions of pFC and temporo-parietal cortex to multimodal semantic control: Exploring refractory effects in semantic aphasia. *Journal of Cognitive Neuroscience*, 24(4), 778–793.

Geschwind, N. (1965). Disconnexion syndromes in animals and man. *Brain*, 88, 237–297.

Geschwind, N., Quadfasel, F., & Segarra, J. M. (1968). Isolation of the speech area. *Neuropsychologia*, 6(4), 327–340.

Gold, M., Adair, J. C., Jacobs, D. H., & Heilman, K. M. (1995). Right-left confusion in Gerstmann's syndrome: A model of body centered spatial orientation. *Cortex*, 31(2), 267–283.

Goldstein, K. (1948). *Language and language disturbances*. New York: Grune & Stratton.

Gongvatana, A., Woods, S. P., Taylor, M. J., Vigil, O., & Grant, I. (2007). Semantic clustering inefficiency in HIV-associated dementia. *Journal of Neuropsychiatry and Clinical Neuroscience*, 19(1), 36–42.

Goodglass, H. (1993). *Understanding aphasia*. San Diego, CA: Academic Press.

Goodglass, H., Kaplan, E., & Barresi, B. (2001). *The assessment of aphasia and related disorders* (3rd ed). Philadelphia: Lippincott Williams and Wilkins.

Gorno-Tempini, M. L., Hillis, A. E., Weintraub, S., Kertesz, A., Mendez, M., Cappa, S. F.,... Grossman, M. (2011). Classification of primary progressive aphasia and its variants. *Neurology*, 76, 1006–1014.

Grossman, M. (1993). Semantic and perceptual errors in aphasics' freehand category drawing. *Neuropsychology*, 7(1), 27–40.

Grossman, M., Koenig, P., Troiani, V., Work, M., & Moore, P. (2007). How necessary are the stripes of a tiger? Diagnostic and characteristic features in an fMRI study of word meaning. *Neuropsychologia*, 45, 1055–1064.

Grossman, M., McMillan, C., Moore, P., Ding, L., Glosser, G., Work, M., & Gee, J. (2004). What's in a name: Voxel-based morphometric analyses of MRI and naming difficulty in Alzheimer's disease, frontotemporal dementia and corticobasal degeneration. *Brain*, 127(3), 628–649.

Hamsher, K. (Ed.). (1998). *Intelligence and aphasia*. San Diego, CA: Academic Press.

Hart, J. J., Anand, R., Zoccoli, S., Maguire, M., Gamino, J., Tillman, G.,... Kraut, M. A. (2007). Neural substrates of semantic memory. *Journal of the International Neuropsychological Society*, 13(5), 865–880.

Hart, J. J., & Kraut, M. A. (2007). *Neural basis of semantic memory*. New York: Cambridge University Press.

Head, H. (1926). *Aphasia and kindred disorders of speech*. London: Cambridge University Press.

Heaton, R. K., Chelune, G. J., Talley, J. L., Kay, G. G., & Curtis, G. (1993). *Wisconsin card sorting test (WCST) manual revised and expanded*. Odessa, FL: Psychological Assessment Resources.

Heilman, K. M., Rothi, L., McFarling, D., & Rottmann, A. L. (1981). Transcortical sensory aphasia with relatively spared spontaneous speech and naming. *Archives of Neurology*, 38(4), 236–239.

Hodges, J. R. (2003). Semantic dementia: Disorder of semantic memory. In M. D'Esposito (Ed.), *Neurological foundations of cognitive neuroscience* (pp. 67–87). Cambridge, MA: MIT Press.

Hodges, J. R., Bozeat, S., Lambon Ralph, M. A., Patterson, K., & Spatt, J. (2000). The role of conceptual knowledge in object use: Evidence from semantic dementia. *Brain*, 123(9), 1913–1925.

Hodges, J. R., Graham, N., & Patterson, K. (1995). Charting the progression in semantic dementia: Implications for the organisation of semantic memory. *Memory*, 3, 463–495.

Hodges, J. R., & Patterson, K. (1995). Is semantic memory consistently impaired early in the course of Alzheimer's disease? Neuroanatomical and diagnostic implications. *Neuropsychologia*, 33(4), 441–459.

Hodges, J. R., Salmon, D. P., & Butters, N. (1992). Semantic memory impairment in Alzheimer's disease: Failure of access or degraded knowledge? *Neuropsychologia*, 30(4), 301–314.

Hoffman, P., Jefferies, E., Ehsan, S., Hopper, S., & Lambon Ralph, M. A. (2009). Selective short-term memory deficits arise from impaired domain-general semantic control mechanisms. *Journal of Experimental Psychology: Learning Memory and Cognition*, 35(1), 137–156.

Hoffman, P., Jefferies, E., Ehsan, S., Jones, J. E., & Lambon Ralph, M. A. (2012). How does linguistic knowledge contribute to STM? Contrasting effects of impaired semantic knowledge and executive control. *Aphasiology*, 24(3–4), 383–403.

Hoffman, P., Jefferies, E., & Lambon Ralph, M. A. (2011). Explaining semantic short-term memory deficits: Evidence for the critical role of semantic control. *Neuropsychologia*, 49(3), 368–381.

Howard, D., & Patterson, K. (1992). *The pyramids and palm trees test: A test of semantic access from words and pictures*. Bury St. Edmonds: Thames Valley Test Company.

Jackson, J. H. (1878). On affectations of speech from diseases of the brain. *Brain*, 1, 304–330.

Jefferies, E., & Lambon Ralph, M. A. (2006). Semantic impairment in stroke aphasia versus semantic dementia: A case-series comparison. *Brain*, 129(8), 2132–2147.

Kalinyak-Fliszar, M., Kohen, F. P., & Martin, N. (2011). Remediation of language processing in aphasia: Improving activation and maintenance of linguistic representations in (verbal) short-term memory. *Aphasiology*, 25(10), 1095–1131.

Kandel, E. (2006). *In search of memory*. New York: W.W. Norton and Company, Inc.

Kaplan, E., Goodglass, H., & Weintraub, S. (2001). *The Boston naming test*. Philadelphia: Lea & Febiger.

Kellenbach, M. L., Brett, M., & Patterson, K. (2001). Large, colorful, or noisy? Attribute—and modality-specific activations during retrieval of perceptual attribute knowledge. *Cognitive, Affective, and Behavioral Neuroscience*, 1(3), 207–221.

Kertesz, A. (1982). *The Western Aphasia Battery*. New York: Grune and Stratton.

Kertesz, A. (2007). *The Western Aphasia Battery Revised (WAB-R)*. New York: Pro-Ed.

Kiran, S., & Thompson, C. K. (2003). The role of semantic complexity in treatment of naming deficits: Training semantic categories in fluent aphasia by controlling exemplar typicality. *Journal of Speech, Language, and Hearing Research*, 46(3), 608–622.

Koenig, P., & Grossman, M. (2007). Process and content in semantic memory. In J. J. Hart & M. A. Kraut (Eds.), *Neural basis of semantic memory* (pp. 247–264). Cambridge: Cambridge University Press.

Koenig, P., Smith, E. E., & Grossman, M. (2010). Categorization of novel tools by patients with Alzheimer's disease: Category-specific content and process. *Neuropsychologia*, 48(7), 1877–1885.

Kosslyn, S. M. (2005). Mental images and the brain. *Cognitive Neuropsychology*, 22(3–4), 333–347.

Kosslyn, S. M., Ganis, G., & Thompson, V. A. (2001). Neural foundations of imagery. *Nature Reviews Neuroscience*, 2, 635–642.

Labov, W. (1973). The boundaries of words and their meanings. In C. J. N. Bailey & R. W. Shuy (Eds.), *New ways of analyzing variation in English* (pp. 340–373). Washington, D.C.: Georgetown University Press.

Laisney, M., Matuszewski, V., Mezenge, F., Belliard, S., de la Sayette, V., Eustache, F., & Desgranges, B. (2009). The underlying mechanisms of verbal fluency deficit in frontotemporal dementia and semantic dementia. *Journal of Neurology*, 256(7), 1083–1094.

Lambon Ralph, M. A., Cipolotti, L., Manes, F., & Patterson, K. (2011). Taking both sides: Do unilateral anterior temporal lobe lesions disrupt semantic memory? *Brain*, 133(11), 3243–3255.

Lambon Ralph, M. A., Graham, K. S., Ellis, A. W., & Hodges, J. R. (1998). Naming in semantic dementia–what matters? *Neuropsychologia*, 36(8), 775–784.

Lambon Ralph, M. A., Graham, K. S., Patterson, K., & Hodges, J. R. (1999). Is a picture worth a thousand words? Evidence from concept definitions by patients with semantic dementia. *Brain and Language*, 70(3), 309–335.

Lambon Ralph, M. A., Lowe, C., & Rogers, T. T. (2007). Neural basis of category-specific semantic deficits for living things: Evidence from semantic dementia, HSVE and a neural network model. *Brain*, 130(4), 1127–1137.

Lambon Ralph, M. A., & Patterson, K. (2008). Generalization and differentiation in semantic memory: Insights from semantic dementia. *Annals of the New York Academy of Science*, 1124, 61–76.

Lambon Ralph, M. A., Sage, K., Jones, R. W., & Mayberry, E. J. (2010). Coherent concepts are computed in the anterior temporal lobes. *Proceedings of the National Academy of Sciences of the United States of America*, 107(6), 2717–2722.

Lashley, K. S. (1948). Brain mechanisms and intelligence, 1929. In W. Dennis (Ed.), *Readings in the history of psychology* (pp. 557–570). East Norwalk, CT: Appleton-Century-Crofts.

Lichtheim, L. (1885). On aphasia. *Brain*, 7, 433–484.

Lissauer, H. (1890/1988). A case of visual agnosia with a contribution to theory. *Cognitive Neuropsychology*, 5(2), 157–192.

Luria, A. R. (1974). Towards the basic problems of neurolinguistics. *Brain and Language*, 1, 1–14.

Martin, A. (2007a). Neural foundations for conceptual representations: Evidence from functional brain imaging. In J. J. Hart & M. A. Kraut (Eds.), *Neural basis of semantic memory* (pp. 302–330). Cambridge, UK: Cambridge University Press.

Martin, A. (2007b). The representation of object concepts in the brain. *Annual Review of Psychology*, 58, 25–45.

Martin, N. (2009). The roles of semantic and phonological processing in short-term memory and learning: Evidence from aphasia. In A. S. Thorn & M. P. A. Page (Eds.), *Interactions between short-term and long-term memory in the verbal domain* (pp. 220–243). New York: Psychology Press.

Martin, N., Dell, G. S., Saffran, E. M., & Schwartz, M. F. (1994). Origins of paraphasias in deep dysphasia: Testing the consequences of a decay impairment to an interactive spreading activation model of lexical retrieval. *Brain and Language*, 47(4), 609–660.

Martin, N., Kohen, F. P., McCluskey, M., Kalinyak-Fliszar, M., & Gruberg, N. (May, 2009). *Treatment of a language activation maintenance deficit in Wernicke's Aphasia*. Paper presented at the Clinical Aphasiology Conference, Keystone, Colorado.

Martin, N., & Saffran, E. M. (1990). Repetition and verbal STM in transcortical sensory aphasia: A case study. *Brain and Language*, 39(2), 254–288.

Martin, N., & Saffran, E. M. (1992). A computational account of deep dysphasia: Evidence from a single case study. *Brain and Language*, 43(2), 240–274.

Martin, N., & Saffran, E. M. (1997). Language and auditory-verbal short-term memory impairments: Evidence for common underlying processes. *Cognitive Neuropsychology*, 14(5), 641–682.

Martin, N., Saffran, E. M., & Pate, D. S. (October, 1984). *Linguistic processes involved in repetition: A case study of a patient with transcortical sensory aphasia*. Paper presented at the Academy of Aphasia, Los Angeles.

Martin, N., Schwartz, M. F., & Kohen, F. P. (2006). Assessment of the ability to process semantic and phonological aspects of words in aphasia: A multi-measurement approach. *Aphasiology*, 20(2–4), 154–166.

Martin, R. C., Shelton, J. R., & Yaffee, L. S. (1994). Language processing and working memory: Neuropsychological evidence for separate phonological and semantic capacities. *Journal of Memory and Language*, 33(1), 83–111.

McFarling, D., Rothi, L. J., & Heilman, K. M. (1982). Transcortical aphasia from ischaemic infarcts of the thalamus: A report of two cases. *Journal of Neurology, Neurosurgery, & Psychiatry*, 45(2), 107–112.

McNorgan, C., Reid, J., & McRae, K. (2011). Integrating conceptual knowledge within and across representational modalities. *Cognition*, 118(2), 211–233.

Moscovitch, M., Nadel, L., Winocur, G., Gilboa, A., & Rosenbaum, R. S. (2006). The cognitive neuroscience of remote episodic, semantic and spatial memory. *Current Opinion in Neurobiology*, 16(2), 179–190.

Mummery, C. J., Patterson, K., Price, C. J., Ashburner, J., Frackowiak, R. S. J., & Hodges, J. R. (2000). A voxel-based morphometry study of semantic dementia: Relationship between temporal lobe atrophy and semantic memory. *Annals of Neurology*, 47, 36–45.

Murphy, G. L. (2002). *The big book of concepts*. Cambridge, MA: MIT Press.

Nadeau, S. E., Gonzalez Rothi, L. J., & Crosson, B. (2000). *Aphasia and language: Theory to practice*. New York: Guilford Press.

Noonan, K. A., Jefferies, E., Corbett, F., & Lambon Ralph, M. A. (2010). Elucidating the nature of deregulated semantic cognition in semantic aphasia: Evidence for the roles of prefrontal and temporo-parietal cortices. *Journal of Cognitive Neuroscience, 22*(7), 1597–1613.

Noonan, K. A., Jefferies, E., Eshana, S., Garrard, P., & Lambon Ralph, M. A. (2013). Demonstrating the qualitative differences between semantic aphasia and semantic dementia: A novel exploration of nonverbal semantic processing. *Behavioural Neurology, 26*(1–2), 7–20.

Otsuki, M., Soma, Y., Koyama, A., Yoshimura, N., Furukawa, H., & Tsuji, S. (1998). Transcortical sensory aphasia following left frontal infarction. *Journal of Neurology, 245*(2), 69–76.

Paivio, A. (1985). *Mental representations: A dual coding approach.* New York: Oxford University Press.

Paivio, A. (1991). Dual coding theory: Retrospect and current status. *Canadian Journal of Psychology, 45*(3), 255–287.

Paivio, A. (Ed.). (1995). *Imagery and memory* (Vol. XIV). Cambridge, MA: MIT Press.

Patterson, K. (2007). The reign of typicality in semantic memory. *Philosophical Transactions of the Royal Society of London B: Biological Sciences, 362*(1481), 813–821.

Patterson, K., Nestor, P. J., & Rogers, T. T. (2007). Where do you know what you know? The representation of semantic knowledge in the human brain. *Nature Reviews Neuroscience, 8*(12), 976–987.

Peelle, J. E., Troiani, V., & Grossman, M. (2009). Interaction between process and content in semantic memory: An fMRI study of noun feature knowledge. *Neuropsychologia, 47,* 995–1003.

Poldrack, R. A., Wagner, A. D., Prull, M. W., Desmond, J. E., Glover, G. H., & Gabrieli, J. D. E. (1999). Functional specialization for semantic and phonological processing in the left inferior frontal cortex. *Neuroimage, 10,* 15–35.

Potter, M. C. (1976). Short-term conceptual memory for pictures. *Journal of Experimental Psychology: Human Learning and Memory, 2,* 509–522.

Potter, M. C. (1993). Very short-term conceptual memory. *Memory and Cognition, 21,* 156–161.

Pulvermüller, F. (1999). Words in the brain's language. *Behavioral and Brain Sciences, 22,* 253–279.

Pulvermüller, F. (2001). Brain reflections of words and their meaning. *Trends in Cognitive Sciences, 5,* 517–524.

Pulvermüller, F., Cooper-Pye, E., Dine, C., Hauk, O., Nestor, P. J., & Patterson, K. (2009). The word processing deficit in semantic dementia: All categories are equal, but some categories are more equal than others. *Journal of Cognitive Neuroscience, 22*(9), 2027–2041.

Ramachandran, V. S., & Hubbard, E. M. (2001). Synaesthesia—a window into perception, thought and language. *Journal of Consciousness Studies, 8*(12), 3–34.

Raven, J. (1962). *Coloured progressive matrices.* New York: Psychological Corporation.

Reilly, J., Cross, K., Troiani, V., & Grossman, M. (2007). Single word semantic judgments in semantic dementia: Do phonology and grammatical class count? *Aphasiology, 21*(6/7/8), 558–569.

Reilly, J., Harnish, S., Garcia, A., Hung, J., Rodriguez, A. D., & Crosson, B. (2014). Lesion symptom mapping of manipulable object naming in nonfluent aphasia: Can a brain be both embodied and disembodied? *Cognitive Neuropsychology, 31*(4), 287–312.

Reilly, J., & Peelle, J. E. (2008). Effects of semantic impairment on language processing in semantic dementia. *Seminars in Speech and Language, 29,* 32–43.

Reilly, J., Peelle, J. E., Antonucci, S. M., & Grossman, M. (2011). Anomia as a marker of distinct semantic memory impairments in Alzheimer's disease and semantic dementia. *Neuropsychology, 25*(4), 413–426.

Reilly, J., Rodriguez, A., Peelle, J. E., & Grossman, M. (2011). Frontal lobe damage impairs process and content in semantic memory: Evidence from category specific effects in progressive nonfluent aphasia. *Cortex, 47,* 645–658.

Reilly, J., Troche, J., Paris, A., Park, H., Kalinyak-Fliszar, M., Antonucci, S. M., & Martin, N. (2012). Lexicality effects in word and nonword recall of semantic dementia and progressive nonfluent aphasia. *Aphasiology, 26*(3–4), 404–427.

Rogers, T. T., Hocking, J., Noppeney, U., Mechelli, A., Gorno-Tempini, M. L., Patterson, K., & Price, C. J. (2006). Anterior temporal cortex and semantic memory: Reconciling findings from neuropsychology and functional imaging. *Cognitive, Affective & Behavioral Neuroscience, 6*(3), 201–213.

Rogers, T. T., Lambon Ralph, M. A., Garrard, P., Bozeat, S., McClelland, J. L., Hodges, J. R., & Patterson, K. (2004). Structure and deterioration of semantic memory: A neuropsychological and computational investigation. *Psychological Review, 111*(1), 205–235.

Rorden, C. (2007). MRIcron (Version Beta 7). Retrieved from http://www.cabiatl.com/mricro/mricron/index.html.

Rosch, E. H. (1973). Natural categories. *Cognitive Psychology, 4*(3), 328–350.

Rosen, H. J., Gorno-Tempini, M. L., Goldman, W. P., Perry, R. J., Schuff, N., Weiner, M. W.,. . . Miller, B. L. (2002). Patterns of brain atrophy in frontotemporal dementia and semantic dementia. *Neurology, 58*(2), 198–208.

Roth, H. L., & Heilman, K. M. (2000). Aphasia: A historical perspective. In S. E. Nadeau, L. J. Gonzalez Rothi, & B. Crosson (Eds.), *Aphasia and language: Theory to practice* (pp. 3–28). New York: Guilford Press.

Saffran, E. M. (1990). Short-term memory impairment and language processing. In A. Caramazza (Ed.), *Cognitive neuropsychology and neurolinguistics: Advances in models of cognitive function and impairment* (pp. 137–168). Hillsdale, NJ: Lawrence Erlbaum Associates.

Saffran, E. M., Schwartz, M. F., Umiltà, C., & Moscovitch, M. (1994). *Of cabbages and things: Semantic memory from a neuropsychological perspective—A tutorial review.* Cambridge, MA: MIT Press.

Sandberg, C., Sebastian, R., & Kiran, S. (2012). Typicality mediates performance during category verification in both ad-hoc and well-defined categories. *Journal of Communication Disorders, 45*(2), 69–83.

Sarno, M. T. (1998). *Acquired aphasia* (3rd ed.). San Diego, CA: Academic Press.

Saygin, A. P., Dick, F., Wilson, S. M., Dronkers, N. F., & Bates, E. (2003). Neural resources for processing language and environmental sounds: Evidence from aphasia. *Brain, 126*(4), 928–945.

Schnur, T. T., Schwartz, M. F., Brecher, A., & Hodgson, C. (2006). Semantic interference during blocked-cyclic naming: Evidence from aphasia. *Journal of Memory and Language, 54*(2), 199–227.

Schnur, T. T., Schwartz, M. F., Kimberg, D. Y., Hirshorn, E., Coslett, H. B., & Thompson-Schill, S. L. (2009). Localizing interference during naming: Convergent neuroimaging and neuropsychological evidence for the function of Broca's area. *Proceedings of the National Academy of Sciences of the United States of America, 106*(1), 322–327.

Shallice, T. (1988). Specialisation within the semantic system. *Cognitive Neuropsychology, 5*(1), 133–142.

Taylor, K. I., Moss, H. E., Stamatakis, E. A., & Tyler, L. K. (2006). Binding crossmodal object features in perirhinal cortex. *Proceedings of the National Academy of Sciences of the United States of America, 103*(21), 8239–8244.

Thompson-Schill, S. L., D'Esposito, M., Aguirre, G. K., & Farah, M. J. (1997). Role of left inferior frontal cortex in retrieval of semantic knowledge: A re-evaluation. *Proceedings of the National Academy of Sciences of the United States of America, 94*, 14792–14797.

Tranel, D., Grabowski, T. J., Lyon, J., & Damasio, H. (2005). Naming the same entities from visual or from auditory stimulation engages similar regions of left inferotemporal cortices. *Journal of Cognitive Neuroscience, 17*(8), 1293–1305.

Tulving, E. (1972). Episodic and semantic memory. In E. Tulving & W. Donaldson (Eds.), *Organization of memory* (pp. 381–403). New York: Academic Press.

Turken, A. U., & Dronkers, N. F. (2011). The neural architecture of the language comprehension network: Converging evidence from lesion and connectivity analyses. *Frontiers in Systems Neuroscience, 5*, 1.

Tyler, L. K., & Moss, H. E. (2001). Towards a distributed account of conceptual knowledge. *Trends in Cognitive Sciences, 5*(6), 244–252.

Tyler, L. K., Moss, H. E., Durrant-Peatfield, M. R., & Levy, J. P. (2000). Conceptual structure and the structure of concepts: A distributed account of category-specific deficits. *Brain and Language, 75*(2), 195–231.

Vallila-Rohter, S., & Kiran, S. (2013). Non-linguistic learning and aphasia: Evidence from a paired associate and feedback-based task. *Neuropsychologia, 51*(1), 79–90.

Vignolo, L. A. (1982). Auditory agnosia. *Philosophical Transactions of the Royal Society of London B: Biological Sciences, 298*(1089), 49–57.

Warrington, E. K. (1975). The selective impairment of semantic memory. *Quarterly Journal of Experimental Psychology, 27*(4), 635–657.

Warrington, E. K., & Crutch, S. J. (2004). A circumscribed refractory access disorder: A verbal semantic impairment sparing visual semantics. *Cognitive Neuropsychology, 21*(2–4), 299–315.

Warrington, E. K., & McCarthy, R. A. (1983). Category specific access dysphasia. *Brain, 106*, 859–878.

Weinstein, S., & Teuber, H. L. (1957). Effects of penetrating brain injury on intelligence test scores. *Science, 125*(3256), 1036–1037.

Wernicke, C. (1874). *Der aphasische symptomemkomplex: Eine psychologische Studie auf anatomischer basis*. Breslau: Cohn und Weigert.

Yamadori, A., Ohira, T., Seriu, M., & Ogura, J. (1984). Transcortical sensory aphasia produced by lesions of the anterior basal ganglia area [Japanese translation]. *Brain and Nerve, 36*(3), 261–266.

Zahn, R., Huber, W., Drews, E., Specht, K., Kemeny, S., Reith, W., . . . Schwarz, M. (2002). Recovery of semantic word processing in transcortical sensory aphasia: A functional magnetic resonance imaging study. *Neurocase, 8*(5), 376–386.

Anomia and Anomic Aphasia: Implications for Lexical Processing

Stacy M. Harnish

Abstract

Anomia is a term that describes the inability to retrieve a desired word, and is the most common deficit present across different aphasia syndromes. Anomic aphasia is a specific aphasia syndrome characterized by a primary deficit of word retrieval with relatively spared performance in other language domains, such as auditory comprehension and sentence production. Damage to a number of cognitive and motor systems can produce errors in word retrieval tasks, only subsets of which are language deficits. In the cognitive and neuropsychological underpinnings section, we discuss the major processing steps that occur in lexical retrieval and outline how deficits at each of the stages may produce anomia. The neuroanatomical correlates section will include a review of lesion and neuroimaging studies of language processing to examine anomia and anomia recovery in the acute and chronic stages. The assessment section will highlight how discrepancies in performance between tasks contrasting output modes and input modalities may provide insight into the locus of impairment in anomia. Finally, the treatment section will outline some of the rehabilitation techniques for forms of anomia, and take a closer look at the evidence base for different aspects of treatment.

Key Words: Anomia, Anomic aphasia, Word retrieval, Lexical processing

Syndrome Description and Unique Characteristics

The term *anomia* refers to the inability to retrieve a desired word, typically in the course of conversational sentence production. Anomia is a very common symptom present across different aphasia syndromes. In contrast, *anomic aphasia* refers to a specific aphasia syndrome characterized by a primary deficit of word retrieval with relatively spared performance in other language domains, namely auditory comprehension and sentence production. Anomia across aphasia syndromes varies by the source of failure in a lexical system that is distributed across cortical regions, leading to varied types of errors when word retrieval processes fail. *Semantic anomia* is a syndrome thought to reflect damage to the semantic system. These individuals tend to experience difficulties in word retrieval that span lexical tasks that use different input modalities

(e.g., picture naming, naming to definition or to tactile information) and/or different output modes (e.g., oral, written, and gestural communication) (Rothi, Raymer, Maher, Greenwald, & Morris, 1991). They often demonstrate disturbances in auditory comprehension and reading comprehension, which both rely on the integrity of the semantic system. Moreover, the same items tend to be in error across different tasks (Shallice, 1988), and errors are often semantic in nature (Raymer et al., 1997) (e.g., "birthday" for present). If the semantic impairment is a result of a degenerative disease process, the word-finding difficulties may also progress in severity with time.

Classical *anomia or pure anomia* is a form of anomic aphasia thought to reflect a deficit to the lexical system without semantic or phonological impairment. To be characterized as classical anomia, a person must demonstrate intact auditory comprehension, relatively few if any phonological errors in picture naming, and the ability to read and repeat words as well as nonwords (Geschwind, 1967; Lambon Ralph, Sage, & Roberts, 2000). Importantly, conceptual information appears intact in these individuals, so the person can often choose the correct word among spoken choices and gesture the use of the word, provided there is no comorbid limb apraxia or paresis. Classical anomia can be thought of as a disconnection between intact semantic knowledge and phonological word forms, or a postsemantic, prephonological impairment (Lambon Ralph et al., 2000).

The time course of the onset of anomia depends on the underlying pathology. Anomia as a result of stroke or traumatic brain injury is more likely to occur suddenly, as opposed to the progressive decline that occurs with neurodegenerative diseases such as Alzheimer's disease (AD). The prognosis for progressive (e.g., semantic dementia, primary progressive aphasia [PPA]) versus static (e.g., stroke) etiologies of anomia inherently will be different due to the difference in the time course of the underlying neuropathologies, but treatment strategies have been shown to be helpful in anomia as a result of both stroke (Crosson, Fabrizio, et al., 2007; Edmonds, Nadeau, & Kiran, 2009; Fridriksson, Holland, Beeson, & Morrow, 2005; Fridriksson et al., 2007; Kendall et al., 2008; Raymer et al., 2012) and dementia (Cotelli, Manenti, Cappa, Zanetti, & Miniussi, 2008; Jokel, Rochon, & Anderson, 2010; Jokel, Rochon, & Leonard, 2002; Marcotte & Ansaldo, 2010; Ousset et al., 2002).

Neuroanatomical Correlates of Anomia in Acute and Chronic Stages

Damage to a variety of brain regions in the language network that assist with the lexical retrieval process can produce word retrieval deficits, including regions in the frontal, temporal, and parietal cortex, particularly in the left hemisphere (Mesulam, 2008). Brain scans taken during the acute stages following stroke have provided insight into which cortical regions play a major role in early aphasia onset and recovery. By contrasting a measure of structural damage (i.e., diffusion-weighted imaging, DWI) with a measure of decreased blood flow to specific brain regions (i.e., perfusion-weighted imaging, PWI) it is possible to investigate diffusion–perfusion mismatch (Hillis et al., 2006, 2008). This measurement indicates the amount of salvageable tissue or penumbra of the lesion after stroke, which can predict recovery from anomia in the acute stages. Hillis and colleagues (2008) found that for individuals with a greater than 20% difference between DWI and PWI in the left Brodmann Area (BA) 37 (i.e., the occipitotemporal area that encompasses caudal portions of the fusiform gyrus and inferior temporal gyrus) on the first day after stroke, the degree of diffusion–perfusion mismatch significantly predicted the degree of recovery in word retrieval abilities, as tested in a picture-naming task. The implication is that reperfusion of BA 37 is important for recovery of naming function (see Figure 7.1). Those individuals who do not show reperfusion in that area show poorer prognosis for anomia recovery than those who do show reperfusion.

Additional support for BA 37 as an important region in the network for word retrieval is found in studies that document anomia after damage to this region (Damasio, Grabowski, Tranel, Hichwa, & Damasio, 1996; Foundas, Daniels, & Vasterling, 1998; Raymer et al., 1997) and functional magnetic resonance imaging (fMRI) studies (Antonucci, Beeson, Labiner, & Rapcsak, 2008; Antonucci, Beeson, & Rapcsak, 2004). One such study presents an individual, H.H., with an acute focal lesion of BA 37 (Raymer et al., 1997). He presented with a collection of behavioral deficits consistent with damage when accessing the phonological output lexicon and in accessing orthographic representations by way of semantics, that is, disconnection between semantics and the phonological lexicon. This resulted in severely impaired confrontation naming and word-finding difficulties in conversation.

Brodmann Areas 44 (pars opercularis), 45 (pars triangularis), and 22 (superior temporal gyrus) are additional cortical regions that seem to be important for recovery of word retrieval function. Reperfusion of blood flow for each of these regions during the first few days after stroke was associated with the degree of picture-naming improvement (Hillis et al., 2006).

Subcortical structures in the basal ganglia also appear to play a role in the word retrieval process by assisting with the selection of a word among competitors (Crosson, McGregor, et al., 2007; Mink, 1996). Damage to basal ganglia themselves is unlikely to produce anomia if language regions receive adequate blood perfusion (Hillis et al., 2006), but basal ganglia lesions can exacerbate the deficit seen with hypoperfused primary language regions after injury, and possibly impact the reorganization of neural networks in individuals in

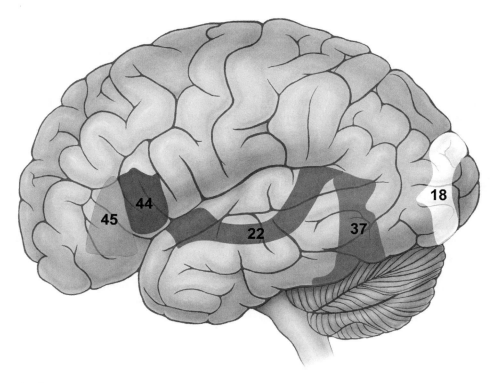

Figure 7.1 Brodmann areas 18, 22, 37, 44, and 45.

the chronic stages of aphasia as well (Parkinson, Raymer, Chang, Fitzgerald, & Crosson, 2009).

It has been suggested that right basal ganglia assist with inhibiting right frontal activity that serves as noise in the system during language production (Crosson et al., 2003). Thus, after a right basal ganglia lesion, right hemisphere frontal activity during a picture-naming task may indicate a disinhibitory response rather than compensatory "recruitment." In other words, right hemisphere frontal activation may be a maladaptive response instead of an indication of recovery. Similarly, it is thought that the left basal ganglia inhibit left frontal activity (Parkinson et al., 2009). After a stroke, this inhibition may be degraded or inefficient, resulting in interference with word retrieval. In sum, intact basal ganglia may help the brain with productive reorganization of language networks after stroke.

Right versus Left Hemisphere Language Processing in Aphasia

Lesion size and location appear to influence the neural recovery patterns for individuals with chronic anomia. Individuals with smaller lesions in the left hemisphere tend to show reengagement of the perilesional cortex associated with language recovery, whereas individuals with larger

left hemisphere lesions tend to show recruitment of right hemisphere homologues of language areas to complete language tasks (Crosson, McGregor, et al., 2007; Vitali et al., 2007, 2010). Although this is still an area of debate in the literature, individuals who are able to utilize left hemisphere areas are apt to show better overall recovery than individuals who rely on recruitment of right hemisphere structures (Breier et al., 2009; Fridriksson, 2010; Fridriksson, Bonilha, Baker, Moser, & Rorden, 2010).

There are several possible explanations for why persons with aphasia who utilize the left hemisphere show better recovery than those who use the right hemisphere. First, perilesional areas may serve better to support language functions because they may actually represent an expansion of the original cortical map. Fridriksson et al. (2010) found that in individuals with aphasia, BA 18 (lateral occipital lobe) modulated naming performance. This area is in proximity to BA 37, an important region for word retrieval in healthy people, and may have become part of the expanded cortical map for naming in individuals with BA 37 damage. Healthy participants also showed BA 18 activity, albeit much less than individuals with aphasia, which indicates that it is probably part of the network to support naming function in healthy persons, but does not become a primary region until injury to other regions requires that it take on a heavier processing load. Hence, the left hemisphere regions may be better equipped and more specialized for language functions if they played a supportive role prior to injury.

Another possible reason why left hemisphere activity tends to be associated with better anomia recovery is that the mere presence of perilesional activity means that the perilesional cortex is somewhat available. Individuals with smaller lesions in the language cortex may have sufficient available cortex in those regions to support language functions, whereas those with larger cortical lesions may have insufficient cortex available and therefore recruit the right hemisphere. Hence, the shift to the right hemisphere may be a result of a larger lesion producing more severe deficits, as well as less available language cortex in the left hemisphere to restore function.

These are likely not the only explanations for right hemisphere involvement in language after stroke. There also seem to be laterality effects in aging, in that older individuals tend to show positive fMRI activation in the right hemisphere for language (Meinzer et al., 2012) and motor tasks (McGregor et al., 2011), whereas younger people show negative fMRI activation in the right hemisphere. It has been hypothesized that older people have increased difficulty inhibiting the right hemisphere (Cabeza, 2002). Because many of the stroke participants in research studies are older, the interpretation of right hemisphere activity may not be as straightforward as a compensatory mechanism after stroke, but may also be due to age-related changes in laterality (Eyler, Sherzai, Kaup, & Jeste, 2011; Guidotti Breting, Tuminello, & Duke Han, 2012; Obler et al., 2010). Additional research is necessary to gain a more complete picture of these age-related changes and how they may influence recovery from stroke.

Left versus right hemisphere activation may also be related to accuracy of word retrieval. People making errors in picture-naming tasks appear to recruit a different network than people making successful attempts (Fridriksson, Baker, & Moser, 2009; Vitali et al., 2010). Among a group of 11 individuals with various profiles of aphasia, semantic paraphasias in naming produced fMRI activity in right hemisphere regions (e.g., middle occipital gyrus, cuneus, posterior inferior temporal gyrus) and phonemic paraphasias in naming produced fMRI activity in left hemisphere regions (e.g., left cuneus, precuneus, and posterior and inferior temporal

lobe), both of which were different from successful attempts at naming that tended to engage the right hemisphere (e.g., right hemisphere homologues of Broca's area, right precentral gyrus, and Wernicke's areas, right supplementary motor area, right supra-marginal gyrus, right middle and superior temporal lobe, and right temporal pole) (Fridriksson et al., 2009). These results indicate that across different profiles of aphasia, semantic and phonemic errors in naming attempts produced common activity in particular cortical regions. In addition, the right hemisphere language network that was used for correct attempts at picture naming for individuals with aphasia includes the same regions that were reported for control participants, indicating that these right hemisphere areas are a part of the "normal" language network.

After a left hemisphere lesion, the residual right hemisphere regions that belong to the normal language network may be relied upon to a much greater degree in individuals with anomia. Instead of serving a supporting role to the left hemisphere, the bulk of the language processing may now occur in these right hemisphere regions. One hypothesis posits that paraphasias in picture-naming attempts after stroke are a result of the less proficient right hemisphere completing the language task instead of the disrupted left hemisphere causing the error; however, there is no clear evidence to support this claim (Code, 1996). Given the results by Fridriksson et al. (2009) indicating that semantic and phonemic errors correspond to activity in different hemispheres, it seems more likely that both hemispheres are adjusting to a disrupted and noisy system.

There is some evidence that left hemisphere frontal activity interferes with the word retrieval process in individuals with aphasia. Suppression of left hemisphere frontal activity due to cathodal transcranial direct current stimulation (Monti et al., 2008), cathodal repetitive transcranial magnetic stimulation (Naeser et al., 2005), or large frontal lesions (Parkinson et al., 2009) improves picture naming in some individuals. One plausible explanation for this finding is that in individuals with aphasia, the left frontal cortex produces noise in the system because of the damaged network. Lesions or cathodal stimulation to this area suppress hyperactive inhibitory interneurons (Classen et al., 1997), which removes competing neural activity in the left frontal lobe and releases or disinhibits other regions that can then assist with taking over language function, including word retrieval (Monti et al., 2008).

Crosson and colleagues (Crosson, McGregor, et al., 2007; Crosson et al., 2009) demonstrated that therapeutic strategies can be used in treatment to target specific neural mechanisms to enhance aphasia recovery. As reviewed above, although left hemisphere perilesional activity has been associated with better gains in individuals with aphasia, there is evidence that in chronic moderate–severe aphasia, left frontal activity may hamper treatment response by creating "noise" in the system (Parkinson et al., 2009). Crosson and colleagues (Benjamin et al., 2014; Crosson et al., 2009) set out to target the right frontal lobe as a potential neural mechanism to support word retrieval recovery. Participants with left frontal lesions underwent a naming treatment that incorporated a left hand movement intended to activate intention mechanisms and shift activity to the right frontal lobe. Participants who improved with the treatment showed relateralization to the right frontal lobe. When compared to control participants undergoing the same naming treatment minus the left hand movement, a rightward shift in activity occurred only for the naming treatment with the hand movement. The control treatment did not produce this relateralization. As neuroimaging techniques continue to advance, so will the capacity to develop and test theoretically grounded anomia treatments that target specific neural mechanisms to enhance recovery.

Other cognitive and linguistic strategies, driven by therapeutic techniques, will also impact how the brain completes a linguistic task. Inferior frontal and inferior parietal regions have been shown to support recovery from anomia after phonological treatment (Cornelissen et al., 2003; Fridriksson, Morrow-Odom, Moser, Fridriksson, & Baylis, 2006; Leger et al., 2002; Vitali et al., 2007). Using structural equation modeling, a connectivity analysis of fMRI data, Vitali et al. (2010) found that for a single case study (S.A.), phonological training of picture naming resulted in bilateral activation of the inferior frontal gyrus, whereas naming of untrained items resulted in connectivity of a large number of regions mainly in the right hemisphere. One interpretation of these results is that the training instantiated a phonological cognitive strategy to successfully retrieve trained items using the bilateral inferior frontal gyrus. However, for untrained items this strategy was unsuccessful, and inefficient widespread right hemisphere activation may have represented a struggling system.

In sum, a wide network of brain regions appears to play active or supportive roles in word retrieval abilities. After stroke, acute reperfusion of BA 44, 45, and 22 assists with recovery of naming function (Hillis et al., 2006). Activity in BA 18 may be evidence of an expanded cortical map, as it lies in proximity to BA 37, a region that is a key part of the naming network in healthy individuals (Fridriksson et al., 2010). Lesion size and location, as well as severity of aphasia, appear to influence whether an individual utilizes primarily left or right hemisphere structures for word retrieval (Crosson, McGregor, et al., 2007; Vitali et al., 2007, 2010), but in general, people who are able to use left hemisphere structures tend to fare better (Breier et al., 2009; Fridriksson et al., 2010). The study of age-related changes in brain functioning, including lateralization for language (Meinzer et al., 2012), should be a consideration for aphasia treatment research, because many study participants are older. Finally, therapeutic techniques that target optimal brain activation patterns during naming for individuals with particular lesion characteristics (Benjamin et al., 2014) may provide a crucial link between technological advances in neuroimaging and growth in clinical service delivery for individuals with anomia.

Cognitive Neuropsychological Underpinnings of Anomia

Regardless of the theoretical model of "naming" to which we subscribe, there is general agreement that a collection of processes has to occur to produce the phonetic code that represents a name corresponding to a given concept: selecting the concept/meaning (i.e., semantic representation), mapping that representation onto a lexical entry or phonological code, and producing the articulatory movements that correspond to the desired lexical entry (i.e., phonetics) (see Figure 7.2). The relationship among these processes and how they interact directly or indirectly with one another are precisely what constitute the differences between these theoretical models of lexical retrieval. It is beyond the scope of this chapter to compare and contrast these models, but these processes will be discussed to describe the possible cognitive neuropsychological basis of word retrieval deficits in aphasia.

Semantic Anomia

After stroke, and commonly in some forms of dementia, word retrieval deficits can be due to the loss of core semantic knowledge or access to semantic knowledge, which is known as *semantic anomia*. There has been a longstanding debate in the literature about the nature of semantic impairment and

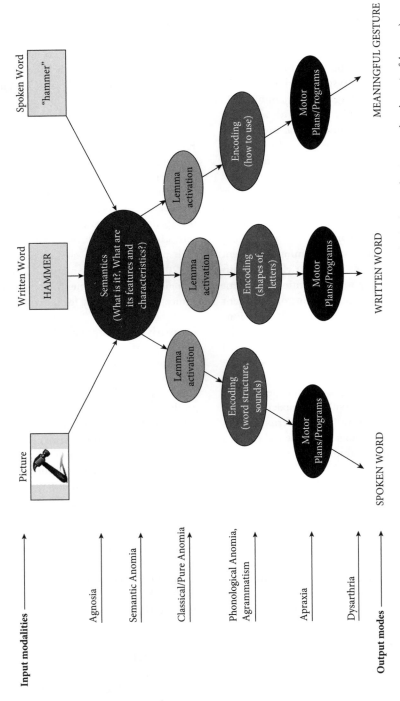

Figure 7.2 Relationship between input modalities (picture, written word, and spoken word) and output modes (spoken word, written word, and meaningful gesture).

whether the semantic representations themselves are degraded in the semantic memory store (Hodges, Patterson, Oxbury, & Funnell, 1992) or if access to intact representations is impaired (Warrington & McCarthy, 1983; Warrington & Shallice, 1979). Thompson and Jefferies (2013) outlined three ways in which semantic impairment may present. Following is an overview of these profiles of semantic impairment and a discussion of the implications for word retrieval with the caveat that these profiles are still under debate in the literature.

The first profile of semantic impairment is little or no damage to representations within the semantic storage, but impaired attentional control mechanisms that allow the individual to focus on relevant aspects of the concept (Jefferies & Lambon Ralph, 2006; Thompson & Jefferies, 2013). This pattern is seen in poststroke *semantic anomia*, whereby access to semantic knowledge is impaired causing difficulties with word retrieval despite intact or mostly intact semantic representations (as demonstrated by good performance on auditory comprehension tasks). It has been suggested that the integrity of semantic access is necessary for individuals with aphasia to learn new words (Gupta, Martin, Abbs, Schwartz, & Lipinski, 2006) and combine known words into new utterances (Martin & Saffran, 1999). Many studies investigating treatments for anomia target deficits in linking intact semantic representations to lexical word form (i.e., encoding of sounds and word structure) (Boyle & Coelho, 1995; Freed & Marshall, 1995).

Breakdown in the word retrieval process either in the connections between the semantic and lemma activation levels or at the semantic level itself may result in semantic paraphasias. *Semantic paraphasias* occur when the incorrect production is semantically related to the target. It is thought that either the individual is unsure of the semantic characteristics that distinguish the target from the inaccurate production of a semantically related item or he or she is unable to activate the target lemma to a greater extent than competing lemmas and therefore accesses a semantically related, but inaccurate lemma (Rapp & Goldrick, 2006). Semantic paraphasias may be classified according to the inaccurate word's relationship to the target, for example, coordinate errors (e.g., truck for car), subordinate errors (e.g., sedan for car) or superordinate errors (e.g., vehicle for car). Some paraphasic errors are semantically related associates of the target word (e.g., garage for car). Individuals with semantic impairment may demonstrate semantic paraphasias, but

the presence of semantic paraphasias does not necessarily imply semantic system damage (Maher & Raymer, 2004). Individuals may activate an incorrect lemma despite intact semantic representations (Hillis & Caramazza, 1995; Rothi et al., 1991).

Category-specific anomia is a specific type of semantic anomia characterized by the inability to name items in a particular category (e.g., colors, proper names) despite normal performance on other categories of words (Geschwind & Fusillo, 1966; Lucchelli & De Renzi, 1992; Oxbury, Oxbury, & Humphrey, 1969). There have also been examples of double dissociation between the ability to name living items versus nonliving items (Hillis & Caramazza, 1991; Warrington & McCarthy, 1994; Warrington & Shallice, 1984), which suggests that the neural processes required to identify these categories are organized differently in the brain (Chouinard & Goodale, 2010).

One theory of category-specific anomia states that as cortical regions that process and store semantic concepts are lost or degenerate, the ability to name items that depend on these regions will also deteriorate (Brambati et al., 2006). An alternate hypothesis is that because some neurodegenerative diseases such as AD show patchy neuropathology associated with anomia, the selective disruption of naming items in a particular semantic category is not due to specific cortical regions that store these concepts. Rather impaired performance is dependent on the semantic features of the items to be named. Items with semantic features that tend to cooccur (such as "has fur" and "has four legs") are more resilient to degradation than items with few correlated features (Gonnerman, Andersen, Devlin, Kempler, & Seidenberg, 1997). Thus, the selective disruption of a category is merely a result of the vulnerability of items in that semantic category because of few correlating feature pairs. According to this theory, living things have more intercorrelated features (Tyler & Moss, 2001) and therefore tend to be more resilient to damage. Despite reported cases in the literature, a meta-analysis (Capitani, Laiacona, Mahon, & Caramazza, 2003) concluded that evidence for the existence of cases of reliable category-specific anomia is weak.

The second profile of semantic impairment is degeneration of the representations in the semantic store resulting in a permanent loss of semantic knowledge (Hodges et al., 1992; Thompson & Jefferies, 2013; Warrington, 1975). This profile causes deficient processing across modalities and affects words, pictures, and object use, and is consistent with what occurs in *semantic dementia*. The person becomes unaware of the differences between items in a category (e.g., all round fruits become an apple) because semantic knowledge is lost or degraded. Similarly, when seeing a pair of scissors, for example, there may only be partial knowledge about what the object is, how it is used, where it is found, and what we call it.

The study of progressive forms of anomia, such as in PPA, allows us to investigate a progressive decline in naming abilities associated with cortical atrophy in specific brain regions over time in the same individual in order to better establish brain–behavior relationships. Neurodegenerative diseases are mostly confined to gray matter (Mesulam et al., 2009), as opposed to stroke, which often affects white matter as well. Investigations of the types of errors that individuals with semantic anomia produce, in combination with neuroimaging methods to identify areas of cortical dysfunction, lend insight into possible brain–behavior relationships in the lexical retrieval process. Along these lines, Budd et al. (2010) investigated the naming abilities of 50 individuals with poststroke aphasia and 55 individuals with PPA. Stroke participants were grouped according to one of five left hemisphere lesion locations [i.e., anterior middle cerebral artery (MCA), posterior MCA, mixed anterior and posterior MCA, posterior cerebral artery (PCA), or purely subcortical regions] and PPA participants were grouped according to the three variants (i.e., semantic, logopenic, and agrammatic PPA), which also corresponded to specific areas of cortical atrophy. They found that coordinate semantic errors (i.e., within category errors, such as "world map" for "globe") were present across all five locations of stroke and three subtypes of PPA, despite different locations of dysfunctional cortex. This is consistent with other research that has shown that coordinate errors can occur as a result of disruption in several processes involved in lexical retrieval (Cloutman et al., 2009; Hillis & Caramazza, 1995). The group of individuals with the semantic variant of PPA (i.e., semantic dementia), whose neuropathology shows atrophy, hypoperfusion, or hypometabolism in the anterior temporal lobes, had a distinct profile of naming errors in that they made more visual errors (e.g., snake for rope) and superordinate errors (e.g., animal for dog) than the other groups. These error types are consistent with the idea that core semantic knowledge is degraded in the semantic variant of PPA (Budd et al., 2010).

Individuals with all three variants of PPA may present with anomia; however, persons with the logopenic and agrammatic subtypes will often be able to identify a picture from among semantically related foils when the word is spoken, whereas those with the semantic subtype will have difficulty with this as the disease progresses (Mesulam et al., 2009). As individuals with the semantic variant of PPA decline, the semantic maps become nonspecific in that distinctions between members of a semantic category are no longer clear. In essence, the label is neither independently retrieved nor comprehended when spoken because the core understanding of the concept is degraded or lost.

The third profile of semantic impairment occurs when an individual is able to identify semantic information about an object in one modality (e.g., auditory), but is unable to identify semantic information about the object in another modality (e.g., visual). This is known as *modality-specific impairment*, and indicates that there are damaged connections between a sensory input (e.g., visual, auditory, or tactile) and the semantic storage system (Catani & ffytche, 2005).

As previously discussed, it has been suggested that semantic anomia may be due to difficulties *accessing* semantic representations, as opposed to actual *loss* of information (Warrington & McCarthy, 1983; Warrington & Shallice, 1979). The often inconsistent nature of word retrieval abilities seems to support this semantic access account. The idea is not black and white, but for the sake of simplicity, the position states that if a concept is completely lost, then a person should not be able to inconsistently bring it up during word retrieval tasks, as is often seen with aphasia. If someone can identify semantic information from one modality (e.g., visual), but not from another (e.g., auditory), then there is evidence that the entire concept is not lost, but that access to the concept from one modality is impaired (Bartels & Wallesch, 1996; Marangolo, Rinaldi, & Sabatini, 2004). For example, poor performance on picture or object naming and other semantic tasks that use visual objects or pictures (e.g., matching pictures that are related), but good performance on semantic tasks for words that are read or heard, may indicate an intact semantic representation, but degraded access to it via objects or pictures (Ellis & Young, 1996).

An example of modality-specific naming impairment comes from the classic neuropsychological case of Johann Voit, the German beer brewer who fell from a staircase and sustained a head injury in 1883 (Bartels & Wallesch, 1996). Voit demonstrated significant anomia, but was able to gradually write the names of objects, letter by letter. Once he was close to completing a written word, he was able to speak the name of the object. The graphomotor action of writing the word or making the motion of writing the word with his hand, foot, or tongue allowed him to speak the word. When his limbs were constrained and he was asked to stick out his tongue to avoid the cueing movements, he was unable to name objects or give information about the number of syllables or initial letter. It is thought that Voit demonstrated deficits in modality-specific semantic access, as he was unable to describe nonvisual sensory attributes of objects when the names were spoken to him. It has also been suggested that his deficits may have been due to degraded associations between different sensory aspects of objects as well as a rapid decay of perceptions. He may have learned that he was able to access semantic information from graphomotor actions and then started using these motions as a compensatory strategy. This case highlights how brain injury can selectively affect input modalities to the semantic system and emphasizes the importance of including naming tasks across different modalities in identifying the source of word retrieval impairment.

Another example of modality-specific naming impairment comes from a case study by Marangolo et al. (2004) that described an individual with anomia who had greater difficulty naming to definition than picture naming. When asked to focus on the perceptual features of an item that was described by drawing it, he retrieved the name based on visual attributes of his drawing. The authors hypothesized that this individual could access semantic knowledge by way of a visual structural description system. He could activate pictorial input in the visual structural description system directly from a spoken word, but it bypassed verbal semantics. The visual stimulus then allowed him to use his less impaired visual naming pathway to name the item.

In sum, semantic impairment may impact word retrieval in three ways. First, an individual with semantic anomia may have good knowledge of an item (i.e., the semantic representation is intact), but may be unable to retrieve the label for it because access to that representation is degraded. Second, a person with degraded representations within the semantic store will have difficulty with word retrieval because specific knowledge about the item is lost,

such that it becomes generic and nonspecific. An individual with semantic dementia may not be able to retrieve the word "stapler," for example, because he or she does not have the core knowledge of what the item is, how it is used, etc. . . . . Finally, semantic impairment may present itself in one modality while leaving another alone, indicating difficulty in accessing an intact semantic representation. An individual with modality-specific impairment may be able to identify an item visually, but not from auditory information, such as a definition.

Classical Anomia

Another locus of impairment in anomia is disruption in determining the label or grammatical features for an activated concept. This is sometimes referred to as lemma activation (Bock & Levelt, 1994; Caramazza, 1997; Dell, 1986; Levelt, 1992; Roelofs, 1992). A person with a selective deficit in this process may be able to provide conceptual information about an object, show how it is used, indicate where it can be found, and repeat the name, but will be unable to speak or write the name independently. Anomia that is a result of a deficit to the lexical system without semantic or phonological impairment is referred to as *classical* or *pure anomia*. Recall that classical anomia can be thought of as a disconnection between intact semantic knowledge and intact phonological word form knowledge (Damasio et al., 1996; Foundas et al., 1998; Raymer et al., 1997). Phonemic cueing can often assist with word retrieval in a person with classical anomia because it helps with the selection of a lemma or lexical word form among competitors.[1]

Phonological Anomia

Impaired phonological processing can also impact lexical retrieval. An individual who cannot select the phonemes for a given concept, insert phonemes into the correct position in a syllable, or maintain the phonemes in working memory before they are used will experience difficulty expressing that concept (Nickels, 2002) because downstream verbal execution processes rely on accurate information at the phonological level. If the semantic representation has been accessed, but difficulty activating the correct phonological entry during the phonological encoding stage occurs, then this may demonstrate phonemic paraphasias, or sound-based errors. Phonemic paraphasias include sound additions, subtractions, and distortions, as well as produced words that sound similar, rhyme, or share some of the same letters as the target word. Nickels

(2002) defined phonological impairment primarily by its symptoms: "the individual makes phonological errors in all tasks requiring speech output and these are more common on words with more phonemes" (p. 948). Moreover, there is some evidence that phonological neighborhood density, or the degree to which other words sound like a target word, plays a role in phonological error rates (Middleton & Schwartz, 2011).

Assessment of Anomia

We have established that the expression of a word or utterance depends on the integrity of a series of lexical processing steps. The ability to accurately retrieve and express a desired word may be disrupted by deficits in any one or more of these processes. It is not uncommon to read in clinical reports and research articles that a diagnosis of anomia was determined based on performance on one standardized language assessment, such as a picture-naming test. However, it is important to consider what the tasks in these assessments measure, and more specifically, which cognitive processes are vital to complete the tasks. First, I will briefly review published assessments for anomia. Then I will discuss some alternate ways to assess word retrieval that provide additional knowledge about potential disrupted and preserved stages in the naming process.

Published Assessments for Anomia

The Western Aphasia Battery-Revised (WAB-R) (Kertesz, 2007) assesses auditory comprehension, verbal fluency, and repetition to provide a measure of severity of overall language impairment and to classify aphasia type on the basis of performance in each of the areas. Based on this assessment, anomic aphasia is the least severe classification of aphasia subtype, characterized by minor to severe deficits in naming and word retrieval (0–9) in the context of normal (or minor impairments in) fluency, comprehension, and repetition. The naming portion of this assessment elicits responses for confrontation naming of objects and responses to questions. In addition, it assesses sentence completion and category member generation (animals). The WAB-R provides information about deficits in confrontation naming, as 60% of the naming score is based on confrontation naming, but it may not be sensitive enough to detect minor word retrieval deficits in conversation. Moreover, it does not indicate which stage in the naming process may be experiencing breakdown.

The Boston Naming Test (BNT) (Kaplan, Goodglass, & Weintraub, 2001) also serves as a measure of confrontation-naming abilities. It consists of 60 black and white line drawings of objects to name. If the person exhibits gross visual confusions (e.g., snake for pretzel), then the examiner may provide a semantic cue to redirect the person to the correct item that is to be named. Phonemic cues may also be provided in the event the person is unable to retrieve the object name in the allotted time, but a correct answer after a phonemic cue does not increase the total score for this test. It does, however, indicate to the examiner whether the person is stimulable based on phonemic cues, which may assist with diagnosis and treatment planning. An additional useful portion of the revised version of the BNT for distinguishing semantic as opposed to phonological-based anomia is the inclusion of a multiple choice picture/written word matching task that can be used after completing the naming task.

The Psycholinguistic Assessments of Language Processing in Aphasia (PALPA) (Kay, Lesser, & Coltheart, 1992) is an assessment tool that allows the clinician to choose from 60 subtests based on an individual's needs. The assessments are divided into four sections: Auditory Processing, Reading and Spelling, Picture and Word Semantics, and Sentence Comprehension. There are eight subtests of word and picture semantics that examine spoken and written word-to-picture matching, spoken and written synonym judgments, word semantic associations, spoken-to-written word matching, spoken and written picture naming, repetition, oral reading, and written spelling. Overall, the PALPA is designed to allow the clinician to develop hypotheses about the nature of the impairments in a given individual and choose subtests that assess those impairments. Strengths of the PALPA relevant to word retrieval assessment are that it systematically manipulates and controls for psycholinguistic variables, such as word frequency, number of syllables, imageability, and morphemic complexity.

The Northwestern Assessment of Verbs and Sentences (NAVS) (Thompson, 2011) is a relatively new assessment designed to examine the production and comprehension of action verbs as well as the production of verb argument structure in sentences and the comprehension and production of canonical and noncanonical sentences. The NAVS has five subtests: the Verb Naming Test, the Verb Comprehension Test, the Argument Structure

Production Test, the Sentence Production Priming Test, and the Sentence Comprehension Test.

Interpretation of Anomia Assessments

Accurate picture naming requires intact visual processing, from the integrity of the eye (e.g., cones and rods reacting to light) to basic visual and spatial abilities (e.g., perceiving shapes on a page). Impairment in these early visual processes could lead to the inability to produce the name of a picture, but these errors are not disruptions in word retrieval abilities. Similarly, some individuals perceive visual information correctly as demonstrated by the ability to copy a picture, and demonstrate intact knowledge about the meaning of objects by correctly identifying an object when provided with the definition, but are unable to name an item from visual information alone, due to the inability to link intact visual perception to an intact semantic representation. This is a visual perceptual impairment termed *associative agnosia*. Although visual agnosias are not language based, they result in poor performance on picture-naming assessments.

Similar examples of modality-specific impairments prior to semantic access can be found in the auditory modality. The inability to identify an item when given the definition due to hearing impairment or due to the inability to link speech to intact semantic representations, such as with word meaning deafness,[2] is not considered an anomic error. Language assessments that require a response to information presented in the auditory modality rely on the integrity of the hearing system and of linking auditory information to meaningful concepts in the semantic system. Hence, disruptions in auditory perception may impact performance on these assessments.

The most direct way to determine if someone has a modality-specific impairment in naming is to present stimuli in different modalities and look for discrepancies in performance. For example, to assess the naming of 10 items, the stimuli can be presented as pictures, written words, spoken words, and spoken definitions. Better performance on naming to definition than picture naming might indicate impairment in visual perception or accessing semantic information in the visual modality. Conversely, better performance on picture naming than naming to definition may indicate impairment in auditory perception or accessing semantic information in the auditory modality. If a person shows similar naming impairment across presentation modalities, then the clinician can rule out the likelihood of a primary perceptual impairment causing the naming deficit, or disrupting the access to semantic representations from a particular modality.

Plausible explanations for *similarly* impaired performance across input modalities are that the person has an impairment in (1) the semantic system, (2) the phonological encoding system, or (3) the motor speech system. To determine the most likely candidates for language disruption, the clinician can assess different output modes by asking the participant to speak the word, write the word, point to a picture of the word, or gesture the use of the word (Rothi et al., 1991). A person who is equally impaired in all input modalities and output modes may demonstrate core semantic impairment, whereby the concepts themselves are degraded.

In sum, the modality in which we present stimuli has the potential to impact performance on language assessments because of (1) perceptual impairments in a particular modality (e.g., vision, hearing), or (2) impairment in organizing perceptual information and linking the percept to meaningful concepts in the semantic system (e.g., visual or auditory agnosias). Presenting stimuli in multiple input modalities and eliciting responses in multiple output modes will result in better understanding of the locus of impairment in the word retrieval process.

Treatment

For more than 100 years, treatments for aphasia have focused on relearning lost functions via repeated practice. In 1898, Henry Charlton Bastian proposed that individuals with aphasia may be able to regain language functions by beginning to relearn individual sounds and eventually working up to words, phrases, and sentences (Finger, 1994). A few years later, Charles Mills published techniques to "re-educate" individuals with aphasia, which included repetition of real and meaningless syllables, reading aloud, copying and writing from dictation, phonetic methods, observation of articulatory movements using a mirror, and retraining in grammar (Finger, 1994). Despite the advances in neuroscience and technology over the past century, many of the same therapeutic strategies are used today in various treatments for communication disorders, including anomia.

One plausible strategy to developing theoretically based treatments for anomia is to determine at which level in cognitive processing breakdown occurs, and then to investigate how particular treatments affect activation of that process (e.g., semantics, word form lexicon, and/or phonology) (Martin, Fink, Renvall, & Laine, 2006). In fact, many treatment studies in the literature can be categorized according to the nature of the treatment task or the stage in the lexical retrieval process they target.[3] Even so, there is evidence that individuals with different profiles of anomia (e.g., distinct deficits and preserved abilities) are able to respond to similar treatments by taking from the therapy whichever strategies they need to address deficient areas (Hillis, 1998). In such a case, a combination treatment approach incorporating semantic and phonological cueing may provide sufficient stimulation at a number of stages in cognitive processing to improve naming in individuals with various deficits that ultimately lead to anomia (Nickels, 2002).

With information obtained by assessing word retrieval across modalities, it is possible to obtain a general idea of the deficient process(es) (e.g., semantic knowledge, lexical access, phonology), input modalities (e.g., visual, auditory), and output modes (e.g., oral, graphemic) that may be affected most in a given individual leading to word retrieval difficulties. This knowledge will help to determine which areas may benefit most from task-specific training. To capitalize on task-specific training and translate the skill to functional communication, the recommendation is to concurrently provide real-world experiences to link the training to a meaningful social context. These meaningful experiences in which the skill is practiced provide personal value in learning and an opportunity for social engagement. This is consistent with the World Health Organization (WHO, 2001) International Classification of Functioning, Disability and Health guidelines for treatment of an individual with a disability at the (1) impairment, (2) activity limitation, and (3) participation restriction levels. Treatment at the impairment level occurs by targeting the process, input, and output modality that most affects a person's word-finding deficits. Activity limitations posed by deficits in word retrieval can be targeted by concurrently using the skill in various communication activities (e.g., use of the word in conversation). To make the treatment meaningful, and take it from the language treatment session to life experiences, the skill should be used in real social contexts to target participation restriction. Ideally training at the impairment and the activity level continues throughout this social training to boost the process that needs enhancement. Concurrent use of the skill in meaningful situations is important to facilitate long-term maintenance.

Treatments for anomia attempt to promote (1) the use of the remaining neural systems to complete language processing via a restorative approach, or (2) compensation for the loss by use of technology, gesture (pantomimes), or another alternative modality (drawing, communication device). In the former approach to treatment, we attempt to reengage what is left of the neural system in order to create functional networks to produce language. Spontaneous and therapy-induced recovery occurs via "experience" or "use of the system." Repeated exposure to specific demands on the system, such as producing the names of objects or actions, is the impetus for changing the neural system. In other words, experience is the most potent modulator of neural adaptation. Multiple repetitions or exposures of an experience are needed to make lasting changes in the nervous system (Kleim & Jones, 2008; Nudo, 2011). If the deficit is so severe or the loss of neural tissue is so great that sufficient activation cannot be achieved to enhance restorative connections with experience, then there will be a decreased likelihood of *restoring* function, even with treatment. For these individuals, the use of compensatory strategies to communicate, such as alternative and augmentative communication (AAC) devices, may be the most beneficial clinically.

Semantic Treatments for Anomia

There is a large literature on theories of how the semantic system is organized in the brain and how it responds to illness or injury. In general, it is believed that when the semantic system is damaged, it becomes difficult for a concept or semantic representation to be distinguished from other competing representations. As described in the cognitive and neurological underpinnings section of this chapter, the semantic representations themselves become degraded or access to the representations is disturbed. In essence, categories of items become large and nonspecific (e.g., all four-legged animals are a dog). Therefore, treatments for anomia as a result of semantic impairment often use tasks and cueing strategies that focus on the meaning of the target and features that make up the target to assist with providing the details about the item that the system is either neglecting to process or does not know exists, such as distinguishing features or knowledge of how an object is used (Boyle, 2004; Boyle & Coelho, 1995; Coelho, McHugh, & Boyle, 2000; Hillis, 1998).

Semantically based treatment tasks include sorting pictures according to semantic categories (e.g., animals versus fruits), choosing the picture that does not belong in the category (e.g., cat, dog, horse, *bee*), answering yes/no questions about semantic features of a word (e.g., Does a dog meow?), and word–picture matching with semantically related distracters (e.g., target word: dog; choices: dog, cat, horse, cow). Some semantic treatments also include a verbal production component, such as describing features of an item or how the item is used (Boyle, 2004; Boyle & Coelho, 1995; Lowell, Beeson, & Holland, 1995). Studies have shown that in some individuals, word retrieval improves following semantic-based treatments (Boyle, 2010; Davis & Pring, 1991; Fink, Schwartz, Sobel, & Myers, 1997; Marshall, Pound, White-Thompson, & Pring, 1990; Marshall, Pring, & Chiat, 1998; Nickels & Best, 1996; Wambaugh, Mauszycki, Cameron, Wright, & Nessler, 2013). There is also evidence that semantic tasks can improve naming in individuals without semantic impairment (Nickels & Best, 1996). Therefore, Nickels (2002) suggests that in some cases, semantic treatments focusing on semantic properties of items may be thought of as teaching a semantic strategy rather than actually remediating the semantic system.

Semantic feature analysis is one treatment technique used to target semantic knowledge by asking a person with aphasia to name a picture and then describe the semantic attributes of the picture with prompts (e.g., category, location, function, associated object, use, visual characteristics) (Boyle, 2004, 2010; Boyle & Coelho, 1995; Coelho et al., 2000; Rider, Wright, Marshall, & Page, 2008; Wambaugh et al., 2013). According to the Hebbian learning principle (Hebb, 1949), repeated production of the labels and semantic features of the items results in strengthening of connections among features and labels, and consequently higher likelihood of retrieving the label during subsequent attempts. Another possibility is that semantic feature analysis instantiates a mediating/compensatory strategy for the individual with aphasia (Boyle, 2004; Wambaugh et al., 2013). Regardless of the mechanism, improvements in naming have been reported using Semantic Feature Analysis training (Boyle, 2004, 2010; Coelho et al., 2000; Wambaugh et al., 2013), and generalization to untreated items within the same semantic categories as treated items has been demonstrated in some individuals (Boyle, 2004).

The semantic system is engaged during language tasks, including word retrieval. Phonological and orthographic tasks probably always engage the semantic system because it is difficult to bypass conceptual understanding when we read or hear something, except potentially in instances of dementia, whereby representations in the semantic store are so degraded that reading and repetition occur via a grapheme-to-phoneme or phoneme-to-phoneme route (e.g., reading without understanding or repeating without understanding) (Ellis & Young, 1996). Hence whatever we do in treatment will likely engage the semantic system to some extent whether or not it is our intention to do so.

Phonological Treatments for Anomia

Therapies that are phonologically based attempt to strengthen connections between the semantic system and phonological representations (Maher & Raymer, 2004). Phonological treatments operate under the assumptions that better phonological sequence knowledge may (1) enhance an individual's lexical semantic knowledge, similar to what occurs in typical child language development (Kendall et al., 2008), or (2) improve phonological self-cueing (Vitali et al., 2010). They include tasks such as repetition, phonemic cueing hierarchies, syllable judgments, initial phoneme discrimination, phoneme counting, and rhyme judgment (van Hees, Angwin, McMahon, & Copland, 2013).

For phonological self-cueing to be successful, Bruce and Howard (1988) proposed that individuals must have access to the first letter of words they are unable to retrieve, be able to convert letters to sounds, and benefit from phonemic cueing. However, studies that show improvements with phonological self-cueing often indicate that participants demonstrate two of the three principles above: they are able to retrieve the first letter of words they are unable to name and they are stimulable to phonemic cues, but they are often unable to convert letters to sounds (Nickels, 2002). Nevertheless, long lasting effects of phonological treatments have been reported (Davis & Pring, 1991; Raymer, Thompson, Jacobs, & LeGrand, 1993; Rose, Douglas, & Matyas, 2002).

It is thought that there are sensory feedback mechanisms in place from the articulators that may enhance phonological processing (Tremblay, Shiller, & Ostry, 2003). Just as a child learns to produce words in part by learning how sounds feel when they are produced, enhancing awareness of sensory feedback may assist with phonological processing in individuals with aphasia who may have lost some of the information about how phonemes are produced (Kendall, Nadeau, et al., 2006; Kendall et al., 2008). In a healthy system, these sensory feedback mechanisms allow us to make small real time adjustments in articulation, and may over time assist with rewriting the programs and plans of how the phonemes are produced (i.e., motor speech processes) (Kendall, Rodriguez, Rosenbek, Conway, & Gonzalez Rothi, 2006) as well as the attributes of how the phonemes sound and in which lexical items they are used (i.e., phonological awareness) (Kendall et al., 2008).

Individuals with anomia often respond to various cues to retrieve the name of an object or action. The most common cueing techniques are semantic cueing (e.g., providing conceptual attributes associated with a word) and phonemic cueing (e.g., providing sound-based information, often the first phoneme of a word). Semantic and phonemic cueing may enhance activation of a semantic representation among competing representations by providing direct conceptual information in the case of the former and via feedback from the phonological system to the semantic system in the latter. Phonemic cueing may also assist in choosing a phonological code among competitors for a particular concept or may provide a model for motor planning for the execution of the speech sounds. The reasons the cues enhance performance depend on specific abilities, which can be different from person to person. Nevertheless, the cues seem to be able to target different stages in lexical retrieval, which makes them useful for a variety of anomia profiles.

Kendall and colleagues (2008) trained individuals with aphasia using a multimodal approach to discovery of phonemes. The treatment utilized auditory, visual, and tactile–kinesthetic cues to learn about how phonemes are produced at a basic level before progressing to words. They hypothesized that by acquiring sequences of phonemes during training, individuals with aphasia would be better able to generalize these sequences to other untrained words that contained the same sequences of phonemes. They also suggest that participants may enhance residual lexical semantic knowledge by strengthening connections between concepts and phonology. Indeed, after treatment, 8 out of 10 individuals showed evidence of improved naming abilities.

Locus of Impairment and Target for Therapy

Should treatment for anomia target the stage in naming at which breakdown occurs or processes that are relatively intact? Phonological treatments have been shown to improve naming in some individuals with semantic impairments (Drew & Thompson, 1999; Nickels & Best, 1996; Raymer et al., 1993; van Hees et al., 2013), potentially by strengthening representations at the phonological word form (Maher & Raymer, 2004) or the connections between the semantic system and the phonological word form (Martin et al., 2006), particularly if pictured stimuli that likely activate semantic processing are used (van Hees et al., 2013).

Van Hees et al. (2013) investigated the response to semantic feature analysis and phonological components analysis for improving naming abilities in eight people with aphasia to further elucidate the relationship between the locus of breakdown in word retrieval and their responses to treatment targeting different lexical stages, namely the semantic system and phonological encoding. They found that seven of eight participants showed improvements in naming after phonological components analysis, whereas four of eight participants showed improvements after semantic feature analysis. Moreover, they found that the semantic treatment was not beneficial for people with semantic deficits, but the phonological treatment was beneficial for most participants, regardless of the locus of breakdown. Possible explanations for this finding are that phonological components analysis better facilitated a strategy for self-cueing during naming or that phonological components analysis may have bypassed the impaired semantic system, whereby naming occurred via a direct nonsemantic route, although the existence of this route is controversial (van Hees et al., 2013).

Nickels (2002) suggests that semantic and phonological treatments do not actually isolate the semantic or phonological system because semantic treatments tend to also rely on phonology (i.e., speaking the name of the word), and phonological treatments tend to activate the semantic system automatically by virtue of treating a target word. Thus, they often activate both systems, albeit potentially to different degrees. Nevertheless, better understanding of the relationship between the stage of breakdown in word retrieval and treatment tasks that target different stages in the naming process may facilitate better customization of treatments in the future. To ensure that a treatment task is beneficial for a person with anomia, Nickels (2002) recommends short trials of a treatment to see if the person responds prior to beginning a course of treatment using that technique (Best, Herbert, Hickin, Osborne, & Howard, 2002; Rose et al., 2002).

In sum, clinicians often need to make an educated guess about which treatment approach will work best for a given client, sometimes based on that person's probable locus of impairment in the word retrieval process. In a clinical setting, it is unrealistic to expect that an exhaustive assessment will point to a specific treatment approach that will inevitably work for the individual with anomia. More likely, the clinician will use an approach that tends to yield treatment gains with a wide variety of profiles of anomia. At present, the best bets seem to be cueing hierarchies and multimodal treatments (Nickels, 2002) that allow multiple attempts at remediating the language system at different stages of processing so that each person can take away from the treatment what is most beneficial to his or her language.

Errorless versus Errorful Learning

In thinking about the application of errorful versus errorless learning to anomia rehabilitation, it is necessary to consider the utility of producing errors and whether these errors mean something to the cognitive system. Does perceptual feedback that an error was produced assist with changing performance? This seems to hold true with the healthy language system, as errors are often perceived by the speaker and corrected, but it may or may not be true with a disordered language system. When a person with a lexical retrieval deficit makes a lexical error, is the person able to use the knowledge about this error to improve performance or is the error reinforced? According to Hebbian learning principles (Hebb, 1949), connections are reinforced when neurons fire together. When a person with aphasia produces language errors, it is plausible that the connections between inaccurate associations are strengthened, thereby reinforcing the errors. Hence, via repeated exposure, the coupling between a semantic representation and either an inaccurate lexical entry or multiple inaccurate attempts may become strengthened such that inaccuracies and "noise" in the system prevent successful lexical retrieval. In an errorless learning treatment paradigm, opportunities for making errors are reduced in order to decrease the likelihood of reinforcing them via repeated unsuccessful attempts. A review of anomia treatment studies (Fillingham, Hodgson, Sage, & Lambon Ralph, 2003) that investigated (1) error-eliminating therapies, (2) error-reducing therapies (because true error elimination is difficult to implement in aphasia treatment), and (3) errorful learning therapies found no differences between immediate treatment effects, follow-up effects, and generalization between techniques. Subsequent studies that directly assessed differences between errorful and errorless treatment techniques (Conroy, Sage, & Ralph, 2009; Fillingham, Sage, & Lambon Ralph, 2006; Fillingham, Sage, & Ralph, 2005) also indicate that errorful and errorless therapy techniques were equally beneficial to participants who were responsive to treatment.

Whether errorful or errorless learning is more beneficial to individuals with anomia may depend on the degree to which their working memory, recall memory, and attention are intact, because the integrity of these skills may impact their ability to self-monitor and incorporate feedback (Fillingham et al., 2005). Oomen, Postma, and Kolk (2001) suggested that individuals with Broca's aphasia rely primarily on prearticulatory self-monitoring for detecting and repairing errors, as opposed to healthy controls who use both prearticulatory and postarticulatory self-monitoring. Possible explanations for this finding are that individuals with Broca's aphasia (1) better detect errors via a production-based monitor, as opposed to an auditory loop monitor, or (2) attempt to optimize their speech before articulation in an attempt to compensate for dysfluencies. Oomen et al. (2001) suggested that explicit training of postarticulatory self-monitoring via the auditory loop may be beneficial for these individuals to facilitate better speech fluency; however, additional research is necessary to substantiate this claim.

Classically, errorless learning paradigms were used as a treatment approach in amnestic disorders to capitalize on automaticity and procedural memory (Middleton & Schwartz, 2012). One reason the limited evidence on the application of errorless learning to individuals with anomia shows no clear advantage may be that prior to speaking the words, errors are reinforced simply by the internal word retrieval process. Hence, treatments that ask a participant to say the word only if he or she is confident that the word is correct may still be allowing ample opportunity for reinforcement of lexical retrieval errors. To truly capitalize on errorless learning, then, the participant must not be given the opportunity to independently retrieve a label (and potentially make errors), but rather listen to or repeat correct responses. There is limited evidence that a treatment approach without word retrieval demands can improve the word retrieval process (Conroy et al., 2009).

In sum, research to date indicates that there is no clear advantage to errorful or errorless treatment techniques for anomia (Conroy et al., 2009; Fillingham et al., 2005, 2006; McKissock & Ward, 2007). A person's ability to correct errorful productions may depend in part on his or her attention and working memory in order to monitor productions and self-correct (Fillingham et al., 2005). Individuals with Broca's aphasia seem to be less able to monitor productions after they have occurred, but do show some evidence of prearticulatory monitoring (Oomen et al., 2001).

Feedback versus No Feedback

Approximately 35 years ago, Brookshire and colleagues (Brookshire, Nicholas, Redmond, & Krueger, 1979) analyzed videotaped aphasia treatment sessions to determine if clinician behaviors or characteristics of the treatment task were related to the correctness of response of the individual with aphasia. They found patterns that suggested that indeed, some clinician behaviors were associated with errors by the person with aphasia. Specifically, people were more likely to make errors following explanation events, whereby the clinician explained or instructed on an upcoming task, which tended to occur at the beginning of a session or during a transition from one task to another. They also found that positive spoken or gestural feedback occurred after acceptable responses that followed unacceptable responses, suggesting that the unacceptable responses did not occur because of a lack of clinician feedback. Further analysis indicated that clinicians tended to repeat and elaborate after acceptable responses, but did not provide this type of feedback as often after unacceptable responses. In fact, when any clinician feedback was provided after unacceptable responses, it was more likely to be negative and contain corrections. Moreover, when the individual made an error, the clinician was likely to ask for the same response during the subsequent trial, which was often in error again. Although this research did not explicitly investigate word retrieval deficits, it does provide some evidence that the type of feedback may differentially impact performance on subsequent trials.

Feedback may not be necessary in language relearning for individuals with aphasia because it is not necessary in typical language development (Breitenstein, Kamping, Jansen, Schomacher, & Knecht, 2004). Breitenstein et al. (2004) were able to train one individual with chronic nonfluent aphasia and one individual with chronic fluent aphasia on an associative learning paradigm using pseudowords. Associative learning occurs when a stimulus is paired with an outcome (e.g., pseudoword and picture), and the learner begins to associate items based on repetition of their cooccurrence (Breitenstein et al., 2004; Vallila-Rohter & Kiran, 2013), as opposed to feedback-based learning that requires monitoring of feedback about performance to a goal. These two types of learning paradigms have different demands and depend on different brain regions, with feedback-based learning relying on corticostriatal loops and associative learning relying on medial temporal lobe memory systems (Poldrack et al., 2001). Breitenstein et al. (2004) found that both individuals demonstrated the ability to associate the pseudowords with pictures of real objects without explicit feedback. They were also able to pair the pseudoword with the correct word after completion of the training. The same paradigm found that healthy participants were able to associate the pseudowords with pictures in both a feedback and no feedback condition. The feedback group learned faster, but both groups demonstrated similar retention at 1 week, 1 month, and 2 months. Breitenstein et al. (2004) stated that therefore ". . . language acquisition in adults can be achieved through bottom-up processing of statistical properties, and [that] top-down processing through feedback is not required for successful word learning" (p. 454). In individuals with aphasia, feedback may contribute to the avoidance of speech via operant conditioning (Breitenstein et al., 2004). Thus, limiting top-down processing by eliminating feedback may assist with rehabilitating language in a bottom-up manner. Similar processing models that exclude feedback loops have been proposed for speech recognition, phonemic decisions, and language processing as well (Norris, McQueen, & Cutler, 2000).

One recent experimental strategy for limiting top-down, conscious processing of language during picture-naming treatment is masked repetition priming (Silkes, Dierkes, & Kendall, 2013; Silkes & Rogers, 2012), whereby a masked visual prime showing the object name is presented before the picture to be named. Preliminary evidence shows that this strategy has the potential to elicit changes in naming (Silkes et al., 2013). Further research is necessary to determine the degree to which implicit learning assists with word retrieval and production in individuals with aphasia.

Vallila-Rohter and Kiran (2013) investigated feedback and no-feedback instruction of nonlinguistic material via paired-associate versus feedback-based instruction in healthy individuals and individuals with aphasia. They found that healthy individuals were able to learn by both instruction types, but individuals with aphasia showed more variable performance. Interestingly, they found no significant difference between paired-associative and feedback-based learning in individuals with aphasia, even though the material was nonlinguistic. They demonstrated that new category learning that was nonlinguistic in nature was impaired in individuals with aphasia. Implications of this finding are that learning and memory systems may be impaired in individuals with aphasia, which may impact the ability to respond to treatment.

Currently, there is no clear advantage of treatments incorporating feedback over no feedback approaches. Just as someone with aphasia may or may not be able to incorporate knowledge of errors in learning based on working memory, recall memory, and attention, it is possible that the ability to incorporate feedback may rely on memory and attention systems as well.

Intensity of Treatment

Recently, studies on treatment for anomia and other language disorders have been investigating the potency of intensity or dosage on treatment outcomes (Bhogal, Teasell, & Speechley, 2003; Cherney, 2012; Cherney, Patterson, Raymer, Frymark, & Schooling, 2008; Cherney, Patterson, & Raymer, 2011; Harnish, Neils-Strunjas, Lamy, & Eliassen, 2008; Harnish et al., 2014; Ramsberger & Marie, 2007; Raymer, Kohen, & Saffell, 2006; Sage, Snell, & Lambon Ralph, 2011). The investigation of dosage is both theoretically and practically driven. From a practical standpoint, intensive treatment schedules tend to be more difficult to implement in a clinical setting due to insurance reimbursement rates, clinician availability, and patient fatigue. For this reason, investigations of dosage are necessary to determine the most efficient and cost-effective way of providing treatment to individuals with anomia. Theoretically, there is a critical number of repetitions of a behavior that is necessary in order to change cortical maps (Kleim et al., 2004; Kleim & Jones, 2008). Kleim et al. (2004) demonstrated in an animal model that despite behavioral gains on a skilled reaching task, cortical maps did not change until after several days of training, implying that lasting change requires many repetitions (Kleim & Jones, 2008) and perhaps continual practice. Animal research has shown that a skilled reaching task delivered 400 times per day elicited increases in the number of synapses in the motor cortex (Kleim et al., 2002),

whereas the same task delivered 60 times per day did not elicit these changes (Luke, Allred, & Jones, 2004). Intensive treatment schedules allow for a greater number of repetitions of a skill, resulting in an increased likelihood of changing cortical maps. Indeed, a recent systematic review of the intensity of aphasia treatment (Cherney et al., 2008) found that moderate evidence exists favoring more intensive treatment schedules on behavioral outcomes. Of the studies that specifically investigated the effects of intensity of treatment on word retrieval outcomes, Ramsberger and Marie (2007) and Raymer et al. (2006) reported similar results between intensive and nonintensive treatment, whereas Sage et al. (2011) reported more favorable outcomes with nonintensive treatment.

It has been proposed that in order to consider the effects of dosage on treatment outcomes for different aphasia treatments, it is necessary to have a systematic way of defining dosage (Baker, 2012; Cherney, 2012). More intense treatment could mean (1) a greater number of therapeutic events in a shorter amount of time; (2) a greater number of hours spent in treatment in a shorter amount of time (massed practice), as opposed to the same amount of treatment delivered in a longer total amount of time (distributed practice); or (3) a greater number of total hours spent in treatment. Warren, Fey, and Yoder (2007) define a set of dosage terms that may be helpful in aphasia treatment to identify dosing effects. These terms include *dose form*, or the therapeutic task or activity that delivers the teaching episodes; *dose*, or the number of times a teaching episode or active ingredient occurs per session; *dose frequency*, or the number of intervention sessions per unit of time; *total intervention duration*, or the total period of time in which a particular intervention is provided; and *cumulative intervention intensity*, or the product of dose × dose frequency × total intervention duration. Documenting these dosage parameters, Harnish et al. (2014) demonstrated the feasibility of creating an intensive aphasia treatment session without extending the amount of daily time a person spends in treatment by saturating practice so that multiple teaching episodes or therapeutic events occurred per session. Six of eight participants achieved significant gains from baseline after 400 teaching episodes, or approximately 1 hour of treatment, and all eight participants showed significant increases from baseline after 1200 teaching episodes, or approximately 3 hours of treatment. Additional research is necessary to determine the optimal dosage for a variety of word retrieval treatments to facilitate acquisition, generalization, and maintenance.

Generalization of Naming Treatment Effects

Response generalization refers to transfer of a trained skill to untrained items using the same task (e.g., better picture naming for untrained pictures) whereas stimulus generalization refers to generalization to untrained tasks using the same items (e.g., better naming to definition for items trained using picture naming). Investigations of response generalization have found mixed results (Raymer et al., 2008), but have yielded principles that seem to guide this form of generalization. Specifically, complexity of trained items (e.g., typicality) and semantic relationships between trained and untrained items seem to play a role in generalization of word retrieval gains to untrained items (Kiran, 2007; Kiran & Thompson, 2003). When more complex items, such as atypical prototypes in a category, are trained, they tend to generalize to simpler, typical prototypes (Kiran, 2007). However, the reverse is not true. When simpler items are trained, they do not generalize as well to more complex items. A caveat noted by Wambaugh et al. (2013) is that studies investigating typicality (Kiran, 2008; Kiran & Johnson, 2008; Kiran & Thompson, 2003) have primarily included individuals with fluent aphasia. Two participants with nonfluent aphasia showed less clear typicality effects (Kiran, 2008). A subsequent study by Wambaugh and colleagues (2013) investigating generalization effects of semantic feature analysis in individuals with nonfluent aphasia found that naming of typical and atypical trained items improved in eight of nine participants, but generalization to untrained items was limited. Hence, more research is needed to investigate the interaction between the typicality of trained and untrained items and the degree of fluency in individuals with aphasia.

There is conflicting evidence about whether phonological treatments prompt generalization to untrained items. Miceli, Amitrano, Capasso, and Caramazza (1996) reported that if semantic representations are spared, and anomia results from a deficit in linking semantics to phonological form, then generalization of trained items to untrained items typically does not occur. However, there have been other reports that participants who learn to adopt a phonological strategy for self-cueing, such as better phonological sequence knowledge, may be able to apply this strategy to untrained items (Kendall et al., 2008; Vitali et al., 2010). The key between these two views may be the degree to which a person

is able to adjust a strategy to fit new situations (e.g., rote memorization versus strategy utilization).

Semantic treatments, such as Semantic Feature Analysis, sometimes show generalization to untrained items that share semantic features with trained items (Boyle, 2004; Boyle & Coelho, 1995; Coelho et al., 2000; Conley & Coelho, 2003). As previously noted, two theories of therapeutic actions of semantic feature analysis have been proposed (Boyle, 2004; Wambaugh et al., 2013). The first is to repair the semantic network. If the process of repeated productions of semantic features and labels of items strengthens or repairs the semantic network, then trained items within that same semantic category and network should benefit from the treatment, whereas items that are not in the same semantic category would be unlikely to benefit. The other proposed therapeutic action of Semantic Feature Analysis is that it is a mediating strategy to assist the individual with aphasia with naming. If the individual with aphasia is successful at implementing the mediating strategy, it is plausible that untrained items in the same semantic category as trained items, as well as items in different semantic categories from trained items, would respond to training. Studies investigating Semantic Feature Analysis have shown inconsistent generalization within and between semantic categories (Boyle, 2004; Lowell et al., 1995; Rider et al., 2008), which may indicate that the ability to generalize using this treatment depends on which therapeutic action most applies to each participant: repairing the semantic network or adopting a mediating semantic strategy.

Although generalization of trained items to untrained items is relatively uncommon, there is preliminary evidence that when treatment effects generalize to untrained items, they share neural correlates, possibly reflecting generalization of the trained cognitive strategy to untrained material (Vitali et al., 2010). Vitali et al. (2010) found delayed generalization of trained to untrained items. They investigated the effects of a phonological training program on naming performance of two individuals with chronic aphasia. Results indicated that the training yielded immediate behavioral gains on trained items and delayed generalization (6 months later) on untrained items. A connectivity analysis using structural equation modeling showed immediate coupling in connectivity for areas involved in naming trained items and delayed coupling in connectivity among regions involved in naming untrained items. The authors' interpretation of these results is that the participant may have learned to use a compensatory phonological strategy for lexical retrieval, as indicated by the immediate behavioral gains in naming trained pictures as well as the connectivity between the left pars triangularis and left supramarginal gyrus, an area that is important in phonological processing. Vitali et al. (2010) noted that although the naming performance and connectivity analysis of untrained items did not show the same patterns immediately after training, they did approximate these patterns 6 months after training (e.g., improved performance and increased coupling of the pars triangularis and left supramarginal gyrus), possibly suggesting the participant began adopting the phonological strategy to untrained items.

Stimulus generalization is for trained items to untrained tasks. Functionally, it is important to know that items trained in therapy can be used in other contexts. There are limited examples of this type of generalization in the literature. Typically, measures of discourse, such as picture description or story retell, are used to assess generalization of word retrieval treatment to a functional skill (Conroy et al., 2009; Rider et al., 2008). The difficulty in evaluating narrative speech after word retrieval training is that in order to directly assess the word retrieval abilities of trained items, the target for the narrative speech sample should incorporate the words trained in treatment; however, deficits are specific to the individual and items are often chosen based on words the individual was unable to retrieve prior to treatment. Therefore, choosing a discourse target that will provide an opportunity for trained words for a given individual to be used in narrative speech becomes a challenging endeavor. An example is Rider et al. (2008), who investigated generalization effects of Semantic Feature Analysis treatment for word retrieval using story retelling and procedural explanation. They found that all three individuals improved naming for trained items and showed an increased number of target words produced in narrative. Prior studies of this treatment technique showed no generalization to connected speech tasks (Boyle & Coelho, 1995; Coelho et al., 2000), possibly due to the methodological difficulties in assessing narrative for word retrieval generalization.

Although picture naming is often a useful training tool for word retrieval, it produces limited generalization and maintenance, potentially due to direct activation between the visual stimulus and the phonological form (sounds) without access to word meaning[4] (Maher & Raymer, 2004; Raymer &

Kohen, 2006). Conroy et al. (2009) investigated generalization of gains produced in picture-naming treatment to connected speech (i.e., picture-supported retell of a narrative and unsupported narrative) in seven individuals with aphasia. They found that picture naming elicited the most correct responses, followed by picture-supported narratives and finally unsupported narratives. However, additional research is needed to address generalization issues more robustly.

Kleim and Jones (2008) reviewed principles of experience-dependent neuroplasticity that play a role in rehabilitation after injury. The principle of "specificity" refers to neural and behavioral changes that depend on specific types of experiences. A limited subset of the neural circuitry may change in response to specific skilled training, which may not translate to a change in more general function (Kleim & Jones, 2008). The result of this is that the context in which items are trained likely determines the context in which they will best be retrieved. Functionally, picture naming has limited utility in social communication. Thus, the ability to retrieve an item in a variety of word-retrieval conditions is necessary for communicative activities of daily living.

Conclusions

A variety of treatments for anomia have been developed to address the underlying psycholinguistic causes of the impairment. A given treatment can work in different ways for different people. Semantic treatments may assist with word retrieval even when a person has good semantic abilities and performs well on semantic tasks. Phonological tasks are appropriate for individuals with and without phonological impairments, as they may assist by enhancing activation at the lemma level, which is often disrupted in individuals with semantic impairment due to weak semantic representations (Nickels, 2002). Multicomponent or combination treatment approaches using semantic and/or phonological cueing may be most promising for people with anomia (Drew & Thompson, 1999; Nickels, 2002).

Notes

1. It is worth noting that some accounts of lexical retrieval do not include a lemma stage, but indicate that phonological code is mapped directly onto semantic information. Once semantic activation reaches a threshold then phonological encoding occurs. The fact that some individuals with anomia are able to access information about sound structure, such as the first sound of the word or the number of syllables, but

are unable to identify the correct word from among competitors, can be seen as support for direct access to phonological information from semantics, without an intermediate lemma or lexical access stage.

2. Word meaning deafness is when a person is unable to understand a spoken word despite a preserved ability to repeat it and understand it in written form (Ellis & Young, 1996).

3. Note that although theoretically the nature of the treatment task and the targeted process should be similar (e.g., deficits in semantic knowledge may be best treated by semantic treatment tasks), it should not be assumed that they are always the same (Nickels, 2002).

4. The alternative view is that semantics are always accessed in picture naming by virtue of visual processing of a real object (Nickels, 2002).

References

Antonucci, S.M., Beeson, P., Labiner, D.M., & Rapcsak, S.Z. (2008). Lexical retrieval and semantic knowledge in patients with left inferior temporal lobe lesions. *Aphasiology*, 22(3), 281–304. doi: 10.1080/02687030701294491.

Antonucci, S.M., Beeson, P., & Rapcsak, S.Z. (2004). Anomia in patients with left inferior temporal lobe lesions. *Aphasiology*, 567, 543–554.

Baker, E.H. (2012). Optimal intervention intensity. *International Journal of Speech-Language Pathology*, 14(5), 401–409. doi: 10.3109/17549507.2012.700323.

Bartels, C., & Wallesch, C. (1996). Nineteenth-century accounts of the nature of the lexicon and semantics: Riddles posed by the case of Johann Voit. In C. Code, C. Wallesch, Y. Joanette, & A. Lecours (Eds.), *Classic cases in neuropsychology* (pp. 53–68). East Sussex, UK: Psychology Press.

Benjamin, M., Towler, S., Garcia, A., Park, H., Sudhyadhom, A., Harnish, S., ... Crosson, B. (2014). A behavioral manipulation engages right frontal cortex during aphasia therapy. *Neurorehabilitation and Neural Repair*, 28(6), 545–553.

Best, W., Herbert, R., Hickin, J., Osborne, F., & Howard, D. (2002). Phonological and orthographic facilitation of word-retrieval in aphasia: Immediate and delayed effects. *Aphasiology*, 16(1/2), 151–168.

Bhogal, S.K., Teasell, R., & Speechley, M. (2003). Intensity of aphasia therapy, impact on recovery. *Stroke*, 34(4), 987–993. doi: 10.1161/01.STR.0000062343.64383.

Bock, K., & Levelt, W. (1994). *Language production: Grammatical encoding*. San Diego, CA: Academic Press.

Boyle, M. (2004). Semantic feature analysis treatment for anomia in two fluent aphasia syndromes. *American Journal of Speech-Language Pathology*, 13(3), 236–249. doi: 10.1044/1058-0360(2004/025).

Boyle, M. (2010). Semantic feature analysis treatment for aphasic word retrieval impairments: What's in a name? *Topics in Stroke Rehabilitation*, 17(6), 411–422. doi: 10.1310/tsr1706-411.

Boyle, M., & Coelho, C.A. (1995). Application of semantic feature analysis as a treatment for aphasic dysnomia. *American Journal of Speech-Language Pathology*, 4, 94–98.

Brambati, S.M., Myers, D., Wilson, A., Rankin, K.P., Allison, S.C., Rosen, H.J., ... Gorno-Tempini, M.L. (2006). The anatomy of category-specific object naming in neurodegenerative diseases. *Journal of Cognitive Neuroscience*, 18(10), 1644–1653. doi: 10.1162/jocn.2006.18.10.1644.

Breier, J.I., Juranek, J., Maher, L.M., Schmadeke, S., Men, D., & Papanicolaou, A.C. (2009). Behavioral and neurophysiologic response to therapy for chronic aphasia. *Archives of Physical Medicine and Rehabilitation*, 90(12), 2026–2033. doi: 10.1016/j.apmr.2009.08.144.

Breitenstein, C., Kamping, S., Jansen, S., Schomacher, M., & Knecht, S. (2004). Word learning can be achieved without feedback: Implications for aphasia therapy. *Restorative Neurology and Neuroscience*, 22(6), 445–458.

Brookshire, R., Nicholas, L., Redmond, K., & Krueger, K. (1979). Effects of clinician behaviors on acceptability of patients' responses in aphasia treatment sessions. *Journal of Communication Disorders*, 12(5), 369–384.

Bruce, C., & Howard, D. (1988). Why don't Broca's aphasics cue themselves? An investigation of phonemic cueing and tip of the tongue information. *Neuropsychologia*, 26(2), 253–264.

Budd, M.A., Kortte, K., Cloutman, L., Newhart, M., Gottesman, R., Davis, C., ... Hillis, A.E. (2010). The nature of naming errors in primary progressive aphasia versus acute post-stroke aphasia. *Neuropsychology*, 24(5), 581–589. doi: 10.1037/a0020287.

Cabeza, R. (2002). Hemispheric asymmetry reduction in older adults: The HAROLD model. *Psychology and Aging*, 17(1), 85–100.

Capitani, E., Laiacona, M., Mahon, B., & Caramazza, A. (2003). What are the facts of semantic category-specific deficits? A critical review of the clinical evidence. *Cognitive Neuropsychology*, 20(3), 213–261. doi: 10.1080/02643290244000266.

Caramazza, A. (1997). How many levels of processing are there in lexical access? *Cognitive Neuropsychology*, 14, 177–208.

Catani, M., & ffytche, D.H. (2005). The rises and falls of disconnection syndromes. *Brain*, 128(Pt 10), 2224–2239. doi: 10.1093/brain/awh622.

Cherney, L.R. (2012). Aphasia treatment: Intensity, dose parameters, and script training. *International Journal of Speech-Language Pathology*, 14(5), 424–431.

Cherney, L.R., Patterson, J.P., & Raymer, A.M. (2011). Intensity of aphasia therapy: Evidence and efficacy. *Current Neurology and Neuroscience Reports*, 11(6), 560–569. doi: 10.1007/s11910-011-0227-6.

Cherney, L.R., Patterson, J.P., Raymer, A., Frymark, T., & Schooling, T. (2008). Evidence-based systematic review: Effects of intensity of treatment and constraint-induced language therapy for individuals with stroke-induced aphasia. *Journal of Speech, Language, and Hearing Research*, 51(5), 1282–1299.

Chouinard, P.A., & Goodale, M.A. (2010). Category-specific neural processing for naming pictures of animals and naming pictures of tools: An ALE meta-analysis. *Neuropsychologia*, 48(2), 409–418. doi: 10.1016/j.neuropsychologia.2009.09.032.

Classen, J., Schnitzler, A., Binkofski, F., Werhahn, K.J., Kim, Y.S., Kessler, K.R., & Benecke, R. (1997). The motor syndrome associated with exaggerated inhibition within the primary motor cortex of patients with hemiparetic. *Brain*, 120(Pt 4), 605–619.

Cloutman, L., Gottesman, R., Chaudhry, P., Davis, C., Kleinman, J.T., Pawlak, M., ... Hillis, A.E. (2009). Where (in the brain) do semantic errors come from? *Cortex*, 45(5), 641–649. doi: 10.1016/j.cortex.2008.05.013.

Code, C. (1996). Speech from the isolated right hemisphere? Left hemispherectomy cases. In C. Code, C. Wallesch, Y. Joanette, & A. Lecours (Eds.), *Classic cases in neuropsychology* (pp. 319–335). East Sussex, UK: Psychology Press.

Coelho, C.A., McHugh, R., & Boyle, M. (2000). Semantic feature analysis as a treatment for aphasic dysnomia: A replication. *Aphasiology*, 14, 133–142.

Conley, A., & Coelho, C.A. (2003). Treatment of word retrieval impairment in chronic Broca's aphasia. *Aphasiology*, 17, 203–211.

Conroy, P., Sage, K., & Ralph, M.L. (2009). Improved vocabulary production after naming therapy in aphasia: Can gains in picture naming generalize to connected speech? *International Journal of Language and Communication Disorders*, 44(6), 1036–1062.

Cornelissen, K., Laine, M., Tarkiainen, A., Jarvensivu, T., Martin, N., & Salmelin, R. (2003). Adult brain plasticity elicited by anomia treatment. *Journal of Cognitive Neuroscience*, 15(3), 444–461. doi: 10.1162/089892903321593153.

Cotelli, M., Manenti, R., Cappa, S.F., Zanetti, O., & Miniussi, C. (2008). Transcranial magnetic stimulation improves naming in Alzheimer disease patients at different stages of cognitive decline. *European Journal of Neurology*, 15(12), 1286–1292. doi: 10.1111/j.1468-1331.2008.02202.x.

Crosson, B., Benefield, H., Cato, M.A., Sadek, J.R., Moore, A.B., Wierenga, C.E., . . . Briggs, R.W. (2003). Left and right basal ganglia and frontal activity during language generation: Contributions to lexical, semantic, and phonological processes. *Journal of the International Neuropsychological Society*, 9(7), 1061–1077. doi: 10.1017/S135561770397010X.

Crosson, B., Fabrizio, K.S., Singletary, F., Cato, M.A., Wierenga, C.E., Parkinson, B.R., ... Rothi, L.J. (2007). Treatment of naming in nonfluent aphasia through manipulation of intention and attention: A phase 1 comparison of two novel treatments. *Journal of the International Neuropsychological Society*, 13(4), 582–594. doi: 10.1017/S1355617707070737.

Crosson, B., McGregor, K., Gopinath, K., Conway, T., Benjamin, M., Chang, Y.L., ... White, K.D. (2007). Functional MRI of language in aphasia: A review of the literature and the methodological challenges. *Neuropsychology Review*, 17(2), 157–177. doi: 10.1007/s11065-007-9024-z.

Crosson, B., Moore, A.B., McGregor, K., Chang, Y.L., Benjamin, M., Gopinath, K., ... White, K.D. (2009). Regional changes in word-production laterality after a naming treatment designed to produce a rightward shift in frontal activity. *Brain and Language*, 111(2), 73–85. doi: 10.1016/j.bandl.2009.08.001.

Damasio, H., Grabowski, T.J., Tranel, D., Hichwa, R.D., & Damasio, A.R. (1996). A neural basis for lexical retrieval. *Nature*, 380(6574), 499–505. doi: 10.1038/380499a0.

Davis, A., & Pring, T. (1991). Therapy for word-finding deficits: More on the effects of semantic and phonological approaches to treatment with dysphasic patients. *Neuropsychological Rehabilitation*, 1, 135–145.

Dell, G.S. (1986). A spreading-activation theory of retrieval in sentence production. *Psychology Review*, 93(3), 283–321.

Drew, R.L., & Thompson, C.K. (1999). Model-based semantic treatment for naming deficits in aphasia. *Journal of Speech, Language, and Hearing Research*, 42(4), 972–989.

Edmonds, L.A., Nadeau, S.E., & Kiran, S. (2009). Effect of verb network strengthening treatment (VNeST) on lexical retrieval of content words in sentences in persons with aphasia. *Aphasiology*, 23(3), 402–424.

Ellis, A.W., & Young, A.W. (1996). *Human cognitive neuropsychology: A textbook with readings*. East Sussex, UK: Lawrence Erlbaum.

Eyler, L.T., Sherzai, A., Kaup, A.R., & Jeste, D.V. (2011). A review of functional brain imaging correlates of successful cognitive aging. *Biological Psychiatry*, 70(2), 115–122. doi: 10.1016/j.biopsych.2010.12.032.

Fillingham, J.K., Hodgson, C., Sage, K., & Lambon Ralph, M.A. (2003). The application of errorless learning to aphasic disorders: A review of theory and practice. *Neuropsychological Rehabilitation*, 13, 337–363.

Fillingham, J.K., Sage, K., & Lambon Ralph, M.A. (2006). The treatment of anomia using errorless learning. *Neuropsychological Rehabilitation*, 16(2), 129–154. doi: 10.1080/09602010443000254.

Fillingham, J.K., Sage, K., & Ralph, M.A. (2005). Treatment of anomia using errorless versus errorful learning: Are frontal executive skills and feedback important? *International Journal of Language & Communication Disorders*, 40(4), 505–523. doi: 10.1080/13682820500138572.

Finger, S. (1994). *The origins of neuroscience: A history of explorations into brain function*. New York: Oxford University Press.

Fink, R.B., Schwartz, M.F., Sobel, P.R., & Myers, J.L. (1997). Effects of multilevel training on verb retrieval: Is more always better? *Brain and Language*, 60, 41–44.

Foundas, A.L., Daniels, S.K., & Vasterling, J.J. (1998). Anomia: Case studies with lesion localization. *Neurocase*, 4, 35–43.

Freed, D., & Marshall, R.C. (1995). The effect of personalized cueing on long-term naming of realistic visual stimuli. *American Journal of Speech-Language Pathology*, 4, 105–108.

Fridriksson, J. (2010). Preservation and modulation of specific left hemisphere regions is vital for treated recovery from anomia in stroke. *Journal of Neuroscience*, 30(35), 11558–11564. doi: 10.1523/JNEUROSCI.2227-10.2010.

Fridriksson, J., Baker, J.M., & Moser, D. (2009). Cortical mapping of naming errors in aphasia. *Human Brain Mapping*, 30(8), 2487–2498. doi: 10.1002/hbm.20683.

Fridriksson, J., Bonilha, L., Baker, J.M., Moser, D., & Rorden, C. (2010). Activity in preserved left hemisphere regions predicts anomia severity in aphasia. *Cerebral Cortex*, 20(5), 1013–1019. doi: 10.1093/cercor/bhp160.

Fridriksson, J., Holland, A., Beeson, P., & Morrow, L. (2005). Spaced retrieval treatment of anomia. *Aphasiology*, 19(2), 99–109. doi: 10.1080/02687030444000660.

Fridriksson, J., Morrow-Odom, L., Moser, D., Fridriksson, A., & Baylis, G.C. (2006). Neural recruitment associated with anomia treatment in aphasia. *NeuroImage*, 32(3), 1403–1412. doi: 10.1016/j.neuroimage.2006.04.194.

Fridriksson, J., Moser, D., Bonilha, L., Morrow-Odom, L., Shaw, H., Fridriksson, A., ... Rorden, C. (2007). Neural correlates of phonological and semantic-based anomia treatment in aphasia. *Neuropsychologia*, 45(8), 1812–1822. doi: 10.1016/j.neuropsychologia.2006.12.017.

Geschwind, N. (1967). The varieties of naming error. *Cortex*, 3, 96–112.

Geschwind, N., & Fusillo, M. (1966). Color-naming defects in association with alexia. *Archives of Neurology*, 15(2), 137–146.

Gonnerman, L.M., Andersen, E.S., Devlin, J.T., Kempler, D., & Seidenberg, M.S. (1997). Double dissociation of semantic categories in Alzheimer's disease. *Brain and Language*, 57(2), 254–279. doi: 10.1006/brln.1997.1752.

Guidotti Breting, L.M., Tuminello, E.R., & Duke Han, S. (2012). Functional neuroimaging studies in normal aging. *Current Topics in Behavioral Neurosciences*, 10, 91–111. doi: 10.1007/7854_2011_139.

Gupta, P., Martin, N., Abbs, B., Schwartz, M.F., & Lipinski, J. (2006). New word learning in aphasic patients: Dissociating phonological and semantic. *Brain and Language*, 99, 218–219.

Harnish, S.M., Morgan, J., Lundine, J.P., Bauer, A., Singletary, F., Benjamin, M.L., ... Crosson, B. (2014). Dosing of a cued picture-naming treatment for anomia. *American Journal of Speech-Language Pathology*, 23(2), S285–299. doi: 10.1044/2014_AJSLP-13-0081.

Harnish, S.M., Neils-Strunjas, J., Lamy, M., & Eliassen, J.C. (2008). Use of fMRI in the study of chronic aphasia recovery after therapy: A case study. *Topics in Stroke Rehabilitation*, 15(5), 468–483. doi: 10.1310/tsr1505-468.

Hebb, D.O. (1949). *The organization of behavior: A neuropsychological theory*. New York: Wiley.

Hillis, A.E. (1998). Treatment of naming disorders: New issues regarding old therapies. *Journal of the International Neuropsychological Society*, 4, 648–660.

Hillis, A.E., & Caramazza, A. (1991). Category-specific naming and comprehension impairment: A double dissociation. *Brain*, 114(Pt 5), 2081–2094.

Hillis, A.E., & Caramazza, A. (1995). The compositionality of lexical semantic representations: Clues from semantic errors in object naming. *Memory*, 3(3–4), 333–358. doi: 10.1080/09658219508253156.

Hillis, A.E., Gold, L., Kannan, V., Cloutman, L., Kleinman, J.T., Newhart, M., ... Gottesman, R. (2008). Site of the ischemic penumbra as a predictor of potential for recovery of functions. *Neurology*, 71(3), 184–189. doi: 10.1212/01.wnl.0000317091.17339.98.

Hillis, A.E., Kleinman, J.T., Newhart, M., Heidler-Gary, J., Gottesman, R., Barker, P.B., ... Chaudhry, P. (2006). Restoring cerebral blood flow reveals neural regions critical for naming. *Journal of Neuroscience*, 26(31), 8069–8073. doi: 10.1523/JNEUROSCI.2088-06.2006.

Hodges, J.R., Patterson, K., Oxbury, S., & Funnell, E. (1992). Semantic dementia. Progressive fluent aphasia with temporal lobe atrophy. *Brain*, 115(Pt 6), 1783–1806.

Jefferies, E., & Lambon Ralph, M.A. (2006). Semantic impairment in stroke aphasia versus semantic dementia: A case-series comparison. *Brain*, 129(Pt 8), 2132–2147. doi: 10.1093/brain/awl153.

Jokel, R., Rochon, E., & Anderson, N.D. (2010). Errorless learning of computer-generated words in a patient with semantic dementia. *Neuropsychological Rehabilitation*, 20(1), 16–41. doi: 10.1080/09602010902879859.

Jokel, R., Rochon, E., & Leonard, C.M. (2002). Therapy for anomia in semantic dementia. *Brain and Cognition*, 49(2), 241–244.

Kaplan, E., Goodglass, H., & Weintraub, S. (2001). *Boston Naming Test*. Philadelphia, PA: Lea & Febiger.

Kay, J., Lesser, R., & Coltheart, M. (1992). *Psycholinguistic assessments of language processing in aphasia*. Hove, UK: Erlbaum.

Kendall, D.L., Nadeau, S.E., Conway, T., Fuller, R.H., Riestra, A., & Gonzalez Rothi, L.J. (2006). Treatability of different components of aphasia—insights from a case study. *Journal of Rehabilitation Research and Development*, 43(3), 323–336.

Kendall, D.L., Rodriguez, A., Rosenbek, J.C., Conway, T., & Gonzalez Rothi, L.J. (2006). Influence of intensive phonomotor rehabilitation on apraxia of speech. *Journal of Rehabilitation Research and Development*, 43(3), 409–418.

Kendall, D.L., Rosenbek, J.C., Heilman, K.M., Conway, T., Klenberg, K., Rothi, L.J.G., & Nadeau, S.E. (2008).

Phoneme-based rehabilitation of anomia in aphasia. *Brain and Language*, 105(1), 1–17. doi: 10.1016/j.bandl.2007.11.007.

Kertesz, A. (2007). *Western aphasia battery-revised*. San Antonio, TX: Harcourt Assessment, Inc.

Kiran, S. (2007). Complexity in the treatment of naming deficits. *American Journal of Speech-Language Pathology*, 16(1), 18–29. doi: 10.1044/1058-0360(2007/004).

Kiran, S. (2008). Typicality of inanimate category exemplars in aphasia treatment: Further evidence for semantic complexity. *Journal of Speech, Language, and Hearing Research*, 51(6), 1550–1568. doi: 10.1044/1092-4388(2008/07-0038).

Kiran, S., & Johnson, L. (2008). Semantic complexity in treatment of naming deficits in aphasia: Evidence from well-defined categories. *American Journal of Speech-Language Pathology*, 17(4), 389–400. doi: 10.1044/1058-0360(2008/06-0085).

Kiran, S., & Thompson, C.K. (2003). The role of semantic complexity in treatment of naming deficits: Training semantic categories in fluent aphasia by controlling exemplar typicality. *Journal of Speech, Language, and Hearing Research*, 46(3), 608–622.

Kleim, J.A., Barbay, S., Cooper, N.R., Hogg, T.M., Reidel, C.N., Remple, M.S., & Nudo, R.J. (2002). Motor learning-dependent synaptogenesis is localized to functionally reorganized motor cortex. *Neurobiology of Learning and Memory*, 77(1), 63–77.

Kleim, J.A., Hogg, T.M., VandenBerg, P.M., Cooper, N.R., Bruneau, R., & Remple, M. (2004). Cortical synaptogenesis and motor map reorganization occur during late, but not early, phase of motor skill learning. *Journal of Neuroscience*, 24(3), 628–633. doi: 10.1523/JNEUROSCI.3440-03.2004.

Kleim, J.A., & Jones, T.A. (2008). Principles of experience-dependent neural plasticity: Implications for rehabilitation after brain damage. *Journal of Speech, Language, and Hearing Research*, 51(1), S225–239. doi: 10.1044/1092-4388(2008/018).

Lambon Ralph, M. A., Sage, K., & Roberts, J. (2000). Classical anomia: A neuropsychological perspective on speech production. *Neuropsychologia*, 38(2), 186–202.

Leger, A., Demonet, J.F., Ruff, S., Aithamon, B., Touyeras, B., Puel, M., ... Cardebat, D. (2002). Neural substrates of spoken language rehabilitation in an aphasic patient: An fMRI study. *NeuroImage*, 17(1), 174–183.

Levelt, W.J. (1992). Accessing words in speech production: Stages, processes and representations. *Cognition*, 42(1–3), 1–22.

Lowell, S., Beeson, P., & Holland, A. (1995). The efficacy of a semantic cueing procedure on naming abilities of adults with aphasia. *American Journal of Speech-Language Pathology*, 4(4), 109–114.

Lucchelli, F., & De Renzi, E. (1992). Proper name anomia. *Cortex*, 28(2), 221–230.

Luke, L.M., Allred, R.P., & Jones, T.A. (2004). Unilateral ischemic sensorimotor cortical damage induces contralesional synaptogenesis and enhances skilled reaching with the ipsilateral forelimb in adult male rats. *Synapse*, 54, 187–199.

Maher, L.M., & Raymer, A.M. (2004). Management of anomia. *Topics in Stroke Rehabilitation*, 11(1), 10–21.

Marangolo, P., Rinaldi, M., & Sabatini, U. (2004). Modality-specific naming deficit: Cognitive and neural mechanisms implicated in naming to definition. *Neurocase*, 10(4), 280–289. doi: 10.1080/13554790490507597.

Marcotte, K., & Ansaldo, A.I. (2010). The neural correlates of semantic feature analysis in chronic aphasia: Discordant patterns according to the etiology. *Seminars in Speech and Language*, 31(1), 52–63. doi: 10.1055/s-0029-1244953.

Marshall, J., Pound, C., White-Thompson, M., & Pring, T. (1990). The use of picture/word matching tasks to assist word retrieval in aphasic patients. *Aphasiology*, 4, 167–184.

Marshall, J., Pring, T., & Chiat, S. (1998). Verb retrieval and sentence production in aphasia. *Brain and Language*, 63(2), 159–183. doi: 10.1006/brln.1998.1949.

Martin, N., Fink, R.B., Renvall, K., & Laine, M. (2006). Effectiveness of contextual repetition priming treatments for anomia depends on intact access to semantics. *Journal of the International Neuropsychological Society*, 12(6), 853–866. doi: 10.1017/S1355617706061030.

Martin, N., & Saffran, E.M. (1999). Effects of word processing and short-term memory deficits on verbal learning: Evidence from aphasia. *International Journal of Psychology*, 34, 330–346.

McGregor, K., Zlatar, Z., Kleim, E., Sudhyadhom, A., Bauer, A., Phan, S., ... Crosson, B. (2011). Physical activity and neural correlates of aging: A combined TMS/fMRI study. *Behavioural Brain Research*, 222(1), 158–168. doi: 10.1016/j.bbr.2011.03.042.

McKissock, S., & Ward, J. (2007). Do errors matter? Errorless and errorful learning in anomic picture naming. *Neuropsychological Rehabilitation*, 17(3), 355–373. doi: 10.1080/09602010600892113.

Meinzer, M., Seeds, L., Flaisch, T., Harnish, S., Cohen, M.L., McGregor, K., ... Crosson, B. (2012). Impact of changed positive and negative task-related brain activity on word-retrieval in aging. *Neurobiology of Aging*, 33(4), 656–669. doi: 10.1016/j.neurobiolaging.2010.06.020.

Mesulam, M. (2008). Representation, inference, and transcendent encoding in neurocognitive networks of the human brain. *Annals of Neurology*, 64(4), 367–378. doi: 10.1002/ana.21534.

Mesulam, M., Rogalski, E., Wieneke, C., Cobia, D., Rademaker, A., Thompson, C.K., & Weintraub, S. (2009). Neurology of anomia in the semantic variant of primary progressive aphasia. *Brain*, 132(Pt 9), 2553–2565. doi: 10.1093/brain/awp138.

Miceli, G., Amitrano, A., Capasso, R., & Caramazza, A. (1996). The treatment of anomia resulting from output lexical damage: Analysis of two cases. *Brain and Language*, 52(1), 150–174. doi: 10.1006/brln.1996.0008.

Middleton, E.L., & Schwartz, M.F. (2011). Density pervades: An analysis of phonological neighbourhood density effects in aphasic speakers with different types of naming impairment. *Cognitive Neuropsychology*, 27(5), 401–427. doi: 10.1080/02643294.2011.570325.

Middleton, E.L., & Schwartz, M.F. (2012). Errorless learning in cognitive rehabilitation: A critical review. *Neuropsychological Rehabilitation*, 22(2), 138–168.

Mink, J.W. (1996). The basal ganglia: Focused selection and inhibition of competing motor programs. *Progress in Neurobiology*, 50(4), 381–425.

Monti, A., Cogiamanian, F., Marceglia, S., Ferrucci, R., Mameli, F., Mrakic-Sposta, S., ... Priori, A. (2008). Improved naming after transcranial direct current stimulation in aphasia. *Journal of Neurology, Neurosurgery, and Psychiatry*, 79(4), 451–453. doi: 10.1136/jnnp.2007.135277.

Naeser, M.A., Martin, P.I., Nicholas, M., Baker, E.H., Seekins, H., Kobayashi, M., ... Pascual-Leone, A. (2005). Improved picture naming in chronic aphasia after TMS to part of right Broca's area: An open-protocol study. *Brain and Language*, 93(1), 95–105. doi: 10.1016/j.bandl.2004.08.004.

Nickels, L. (2002). Therapy for naming disorders: Revisiting, revising, and reviewing. *Aphasiology*, 16(10/11), 935–979.

Nickels, L., & Best, W. (1996). Therapy for naming disorders (Part II): Specifics, surprises, and suggestions. *Aphasiology*, 10, 109–136.

Norris, D., McQueen, J.M., & Cutler, A. (2000). Merging information in speech recognition: Feedback is never necessary. *Behavioral Brain Science*, 23(3), 299–325; discussion 325–370.

Nudo, R.J. (2011). Neural bases of recovery after brain injury. *Journal of Communication Disorders*, 44, 515–520.

Obler, L.K., Rykhlevskaia, E., Schnyer, D., Clark-Cotton, M.R., Spiro, A., 3rd, Hyun, J., ... Albert, M.L. (2010). Bilateral brain regions associated with naming in older adults. *Brain and Language*, 113(3), 113–123. doi: 10.1016/j.bandl.2010.03.001.

Oomen, C.C., Postma, A., & Kolk, H.H. (2001). Prearticulatory and postarticulatory self-monitoring in Broca's aphasia. *Cortex*, 37(5), 627–641.

Ousset, P.J., Viallard, G., Puel, M., Celsis, P., Demonet, J.F., & Cardebat, D. (2002). Lexical therapy and episodic word learning in dementia of the Alzheimer type. *Brain and Language*, 80(1), 14–20. doi: 10.1006/brln.2001.2496.

Oxbury, J.M., Oxbury, S.M., & Humphrey, N.K. (1969). Varieties of colour anomia. *Brain*, 92(4), 847–860.

Parkinson, B.R., Raymer, A.M., Chang, Y.L., Fitzgerald, D.B., & Crosson, B. (2009). Lesion characteristics related to treatment improvement in object and action naming for patients with chronic aphasia. *Brain and Language*, 110(2), 61–70. doi: 10.1016/j.bandl.2009.05.005.

Poldrack, R.A., Clark, J., Pare-Blagoev, E.J., Shohamy, D., Creso Moyano, J., Myers, C., & Gluck, M.A. (2001). Interactive memory systems in the human brain. *Nature*, 414(6863), 546–550. doi: 10.1038/35107080.

Ramsberger, G., & Marie, B. (2007). Self-administered cued naming therapy: A single-participant investigation of a computer-based therapy program replicated in four cases. *American Journal of Speech-Language Pathology*, 16(4), 343–358. doi: 10.1044/1058-0360(2007/038).

Rapp, B., & Goldrick, M. (2006). Speaking words: Contributions of cognitive neuropsychological research. *Cognitive Neuropsychology*, 23(1), 39–73. doi: 10.1080/02643290542000049.

Raymer, A.M., Beeson, P., Holland, A., Kendall, D.L., Maher, L.M., Martin, N., ... Rothi, L.J.G. (2008). Translational research in aphasia: From neuroscience to neurorehabilitation. *Journal of Speech, Language, and Hearing Research*, 51(1), S259–275. doi: 10.1044/1092-4388(2008/020).

Raymer, A.M., Foundas, A.L., Maher, L.M., Greenwald, M.L., Morris, M., Rothi, L.J., & Heilman, K.M. (1997). Cognitive neuropsychological analysis and neuroanatomic correlates in a case of acute anomia. *Brain and Language*, 58(1), 137–156. doi: 10.1006/brln.1997.1786.

Raymer, A.M., & Kohen, F. (2006). Word-retrieval treatment in aphasia: Effects of sentence context. *Journal of Rehabilitation Research and Development*, 43(3), 367–378.

Raymer, A.M., Kohen, F.P., & Saffell, D. (2006). Computerized training for impairments of word comprehension and retrieval in aphasia. *Aphasiology*, 20, 257–268.

Raymer, A.M., McHose, B., Smith, K.G., Iman, L., Ambrose, A., & Casselton, C. (2012). Contrasting effects of errorless naming treatment and gestural facilitation for word retrieval in aphasia. *Neuropsychological Rehabilitation*, 22(2), 235–266. doi: 10.1080/09602011.2011.618306.

Raymer, A.M., Thompson, C.K., Jacobs, B., & LeGrand, H.R. (1993). Phonological treatment of naming deficits in aphasia: Model-based generalisation analysis. *Aphasiology*, 7, 27–53.

Rider, J.D., Wright, H.H., Marshall, R.C., & Page, J.L. (2008). Using semantic feature analysis to improve contextual discourse in adults with aphasia. *American Journal of Speech-Language Pathology*, 17(2), 161–172. doi: 10.1044/1058-0360(2008/016).

Roelofs, A. (1992). A spreading-activation theory of lemma retrieval in speaking. *Cognition, 42*, 107–142.

Rose, M., Douglas, J., & Matyas, T. (2002). The comparative effectiveness of gesture and verbal treatments for a specific phonologic naming impairment. *Aphasiology*, 16, 1001–1030.

Rothi, L.J., Raymer, A.M., Maher, L.M., Greenwald, M.L., & Morris, M. (1991). Assessment of naming failures in neurological communication disorders. *Clinics in Communication Disorders*, 1(1), 7–20.

Sage, K., Snell, C., & Lambon Ralph, M.A. (2011). How intensive does anomia therapy for people with aphasia need to be? *Neuropsychological Rehabilitation* 21, 26–41.

Shallice, T. (1988). *From neuropsychology to mental structure*. New York: Cambridge University Press.

Silkes, J.P., Dierkes, K.E., & Kendall, D.L. (2013). Masked repetition priming effects on naming in aphasia: A phase I treatment study. *Aphasiology*, 27(4), 381–397.

Silkes, J.P., & Rogers, M.A. (2012). Masked priming effects in aphasia: Evidence of altered automatic spreading activation. *Journal of Speech, Language, and Hearing Research*, 55(6), 1613–1625. doi: 10.1044/1092-4388(2012/10-0260).

Thompson, C.K. (2011). *Northwestern assessment of verbs and sentences*. Evanston, IL: Northwestern University.

Thompson, H.E., & Jefferies, E. (2013). Semantic control and modality: An input processing deficit in aphasia leading to deregulated semantic cognition in a single modality. *Neuropsychologia*, 51, 1998–2015.

Tremblay, S., Shiller, D.M., & Ostry, D.J. (2003). Somatosensory basis of speech production. *Nature*, 423(6942), 866–869. doi: 10.1038/nature01710.

Tyler, L.K., & Moss, H.E. (2001). Towards a distributed account of conceptual knowledge. *Trends in Cognitive Sciences*, 5(6), 244–252.

Vallila-Rohter, S., & Kiran, S. (2013). Non-linguistic learning and aphasia: Evidence from a paired associate and feedback-based task. *Neuropsychologia*, 51(1), 79–90. doi: 10.1016/j.neuropsychologia.2012.10.024.

van Hees, S., Angwin, A., McMahon, K., & Copland, D. (2013). A comparison of semantic feature analysis and phonological components analysis for the treatment of naming impairments in aphasia. *Neuropsychological Rehabilitation*, 23(1), 102–132. doi: 10.1080/09602011.2012.726201.

Vitali, P., Abutalebi, J., Tettamanti, M., Danna, M., Ansaldo, A.I., Perani, D., ... Cappa, S.F. (2007). Training-induced brain remapping in chronic aphasia: A pilot study. *Neurorehabilitation and Neural Repair*, 21(2), 152–160. doi: 10.1177/1545968306294735.

Vitali, P., Tettamanti, M., Abutalebi, J., Ansaldo, A.I., Perani, D., Cappa, S.F., & Joanette, Y. (2010). Generalization of the effects of phonological training for anomia using structural equation modelling: A multiple single-case study. *Neurocase*, 16(2), 93–105. doi: 10.1080/13554790903329117.

Wambaugh, J.L., Mauszycki, S., Cameron, R., Wright, S., & Nessler, C. (2013). Semantic feature analysis: Incorporating typicality treatment and mediating strategy training to promote generalization. *American Journal of Speech-Language Pathology*, 22(2), S334–369. doi: 10.1044/1058-0360(2013/12-0070); 10.1044/1058-0360(2013/12-0070).

Warren, S.F., Fey, M.E., & Yoder, P.J. (2007). Differential treatment intensity research: A missing link to creating optimally effective communication interventions. *Mental Retardation and Developmental Disabilities Research Reviews*, 13(1), 70–77.

Warrington, E.K. (1975). The selective impairment of semantic memory. *Quarterly Journal of Experimental Psychology*, 27(4), 635–657. doi: 10.1080/14640747508400525.

Warrington, E.K., & McCarthy, R.A. (1983). Category specific access dysphasia. *Brain*, 106, 859–878.

Warrington, E.K., & McCarthy, R.A. (1994). Multiple meaning systems in the brain: A case for visual semantics. *Neuropsychologia*, 32(12), 1465–1473.

Warrington, E.K., & Shallice, T. (1979). Semantic access dyslexia. *Brain*, 102, 43–63.

Warrington, E.K., & Shallice, T. (1984). Category specific semantic impairments. *Brain*, 107(Pt 3), 829–854.

World Health Organization. (2001). *International Classification of Functioning, Disability and Health (ICF)*. Geneva.

Broca's Aphasia and Grammatical Processing

Lynn M. Maher

Abstract

Broca's aphasia serves as a platform for discussions of the cognitive and neural mechanisms of sentence production and how those systems break down in individuals with damage in left inferior frontal regions beyond Broca's area, suggesting a role for such regions in syntactic processing. Standardized and nonstandardized diagnostic tools facilitate assessment of comprehension and production of grammatical functions that can be impaired in Broca's aphasia. Several treatment approaches address impairment in sentence production that emanates across various processes in sentence formulation. The nomenclature surrounding Broca's aphasia provides a launching pad to guide analysis and intervention for the communication impairments experienced by these individuals.

Key Words: Broca's aphasia, agrammatism, syntactic processing, morphosyntax, Broca's area

Introduction

In 1861, Pierre Paul Broca studied Leborgne, a patient who retained all of his mental faculties and showed no signs of physical impairment but was unable to utter any word except "tan," with varying intonation (Broca, 1861). Following his patient's death and subsequent autopsy, Broca described a lesion located in the left inferior frontal lobe. That same year, a second patient named Lelong with the same characteristics of intact comprehension but severely impaired speech came under Broca's care. Similar to Leborgne, Lelong's speech was limited to a total of five words: *oui* ("yes"), *non* ("no"), *tois* (a mispronunciation of *trois* or "three"), *toujours* ("always"), and *Lelo* (a mispronunciation of "Lelong"). Lelong's death and subsequent autopsy by Broca also revealed a lesion in the left lateral frontal lobe, suggesting the localization of speech in this area (Dronkers, Plaisant, Iba-Zizen, & Cabanis, 2007). Broca's focus was on the inferior frontal convolution in the left hemisphere, an area that came to be known as *Broca's area*. The speech and language

impairment of such a lesion came to be known as *Broca's aphasia*.

Research since Broca's seminal works have refined our understanding of the classical profile of Broca's aphasia. In general, people with Broca's aphasia have limited spoken production capabilities. Their speech is halting and effortful, often characterized as apraxic (Goodglass, Kaplan, & Barresi, 2001). What language output they have is nonfluent, limited in vocabulary, and characterized by the use of more nouns than verbs (Bastiaanse & Edwards, 2004; Goodglass, Christiansen, & Gallagher, 1994; Lee & Thompson, 2004; Miceli, Silveri, Villa, & Caramazza, 1984; Zingeser & Berndt, 1990). When they do use verbs, they tend to omit or misuse inflections; articles, pronouns, and adjectives may be eliminated altogether, giving the impression that speech is "telegraphic," sometimes referred to as *agrammatism* (Goodglass et al., 1994). Broca's aphasia is not confined to morphological errors, however; sentences produced by people with Broca's aphasia may be misordered and lacking in syntactic structure as well as morphological detail, resulting in confused output (Goodglass et al., 1994).

Schwartz, Saffran, and Marin (1980b) demonstrated that people with agrammatic Broca's aphasia lacked the ability to map thematic relations (e.g., agent, action, patient) onto sentence arguments (e.g., subject, verb, object) and instead generated word order in sentences based on the semantic properties of animacy and potency. An example of speech produced by someone with Broca's aphasia is "man . . . letter . . . box." The speaker may be trying to convey the notion that the mailman has delivered the mail. Or, the speaker may be trying to indicate that he or she would like to put correspondence in the mailbox for the mailman to pick up during his route. Yet another potential meaning of the utterance is that the speaker wishes to say someone other than the mailman deposited or removed mail from the mailbox.

Typically, the sentence-processing deficit in Broca's aphasia extends beyond sentence production to comprehension of sentences. Individuals with Broca's aphasia may also may be impaired in understanding speech as it is difficult for them to interpret the order of words in complex sentences (Caramazza & Zurif, 1976; Heilman & Scholes, 1976). Not only are noncanonical sentences problematic for people with Broca's aphasia to understand (e.g., "It was the dog with the red collar that was chased by the cat") (Thompson, 2003), but also canonical sentences, particularly when they are reversible (that is, when either noun may plausibly be used in the agent position), present receptive difficulties (e.g., "The cat chased the dog") (Schwartz, Saffran, & Marin, 1980a).

A review by Caramazza, Capitani, Rey, and Berndt (2001) indicated that no single pattern of auditory comprehension performance can be ascribed to Broca's aphasia, underscoring the variability of the syndrome. Caramazza, Capasso, Capitani, and Miceli (2005) reported similar findings, suggesting that the auditory comprehension of actives versus passives in Broca's aphasia may range from chance performance for both to excellent performance for both or somewhere in between. It is clear, then, that individual differences must be taken into account when discussing the syndrome of Broca's aphasia.

The syndrome of Broca's aphasia, while represented by a variety of symptoms, provides a unique opportunity to examine linguistic theories of syntactic processing and their neural correlates. In this chapter we discuss; the behavioral characteristics of Broca's aphasia; some theories on how language-processing occurs, in particular sentence-level language processing; some current considerations of the neuroanatomical underpinnings of grammatical processing; and clinical implications for assessment and treatment of this complex syndrome.

Incidence and Prevalence

The incidence and prevalence of Broca's aphasia are somewhat difficult to track due to factors such as spontaneous recovery, language differences, individual differences that may result in ambiguous diagnoses, and improvements in language abilities over time that may alter the original diagnosis (Code, 2010). Despite these limitations, the incidence of Broca's aphasia in patients hospitalized for cerebrovascular insult resulting in acute aphasia is estimated as 23% (Brkić, Sinanović, Vidović, & Dževdet, 2009). Brkić and colleagues noted that Broca's aphasia occurs more frequently than Wernicke's aphasia (8%), but less frequently than global aphasia (49%). Greater incidence of "nonfluent" aphasia, of which Broca's aphasia would be a subset, was confirmed in a prospective study by Engelter and colleagues (2006); nonfluent aphasia accounted for 60% of the cases compared to 29% with fluent aphasia, irrespective of gender, age, or severity.

Pederson, Vinter, and Olsen (2004) tracked consecutive strokes in the evolution and recovery of Broca's aphasia from 1 week to 1 year poststroke onset. The incidence of Broca's aphasia within first-ever ischemic strokes was 12%. Recovery of Broca's aphasia occurred in the majority of individuals to fully recovered (36%) or anomic aphasia (36%), suggesting improvements in fluency and repetition; transcortical motor aphasia (9%), suggesting improvement in repetition; or no change (18%). At 1 year poststroke, the incidence of Broca's aphasia was about the same at 13%, as 36% of those classified initially as having global aphasia evolved to other types of aphasia, such as Broca's aphasia with recovery.

These figures differ somewhat from those of Kertesz (1979), who reported that while individuals classified as having Broca's aphasia when assessed within 45 days of stroke onset yielded the greatest amount of recovery, most will remain classified as having Broca's aphasia at 6 months postonset. Finally, El Hachioui and colleagues (2013) described different recovery patterns for specific linguistic components in aphasia recovery, with syntax showing the most improvement in the first 6 weeks.

Models of Grammatical Production

Before we can understand how the language output of people with Broca's aphasia is impaired, we must first understand the complexities of unimpaired language processing. While there are a number of models that attempt to capture the components and stages of processing in sentence processing (e.g. Bock & Levelt, 1994; Dell, 1986; Garrett, 1984), typically they include stages that encompass cognition, pragmatics, semantics, syntax, and phonology. Each component adds a facet of meaning that creates a message that fully communicates the thoughts of the speaker. Garrett's (1984) model of sentence production (Figure 8.1) has been widely applied to typical sentence processing as well as to the speech of people with aphasia and continues to serve as a basis for discussions of this topic (Thompson,

Faroqi-Shah, & Lee, 2015). Developed by studying speech errors made by unimpaired speakers, the simplicity of Garrett's hierarchical model and the similarity of everyday "slips of the tongue" by typical speakers to the impaired output produced by people with aphasia makes Garrett's model ideal for identifying breakdowns in the speech of people with aphasia (Berndt, 2001; Buckingham, 1991; Garrett, 1984; Schwartz et al., 1980a, 1980b).

The first level of Garrett's (1975, 1984) model is the *message level*. It is arrived at by inferential processes that determine the content of the future utterance. It is at the message level that the mind decides what it would like to say; that is, conceptually the idea is developed but has yet to achieve any linguistic representation. Once a conceptual message has been generated, the next step of the

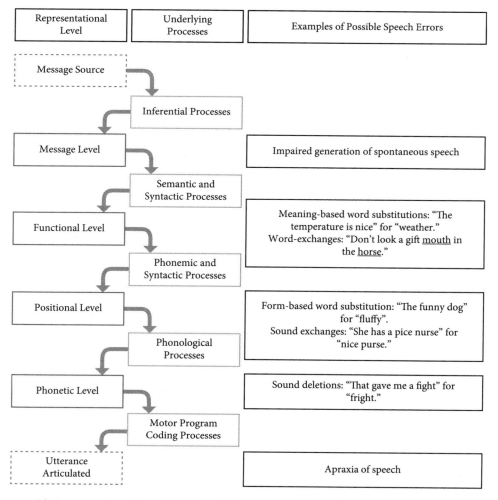

Figure 8.1 Modified representation of Garrett's (1984) model of sentence production, indicating level of representation, processes occurring at each level, and examples of possible errors caused by impairments at each level.

hierarchy is developed; it engages semantic and syntactic processes to represent the intended message. Semantic factors determine lexical selection, and the selected verb assigns these lexical items a thematic role, which will determine their structural placement. These processes yield an abstract representation of the arguments of the sentence. The product of these processes makes up the *functional-level representation*. Following this level, syntactic and phonological processes act to specify phonemes for lexical segments (including suprasegmentals, such as stress and duration) and to arrange those segments into a grammatical structure. The product of these processes, *the positional-level representation*, is then acted on by phonological processes, which specify the phonetic components of the message. Finally, *the phonetic-level representation* is acted on by motor coding processes, which allow the utterance to be articulated.

Theoretically, the errors produced by someone with agrammatic Broca's aphasia will depend on which level or levels of representation are affected and how the levels interact. There are a number of theories on how the stages of sentence-processing unfold, a few of which are presented next. As all theories of language processing include semantic, pragmatic, syntactic, and phonetic processes similar to those provided by Garrett (1984), his levels of representation are referenced when discussing specific levels of processing.

Theories of Grammatical Sentence Production

Several theories have been proposed as a way of understanding how language is produced in the brain. Evidence for how exactly abstract representations are created and manipulated prior to manifestation is difficult to obtain. Nevertheless, there is value in having a general understanding of how the prevailing theories describe the mechanisms of language processing. Theories of language production are categorized based on the type of processing that occurs to take the idea from the message level to the phonetic level (i.e., serial or interactive), as well as the number of lexical items transferred from one level of production to another (i.e., single product or cascaded).

In serial models of language processing, each component of the uttered or heard sentence is encapsulated in a distinct and separate process that does not share information with other processes; efficiency is improved because interference from other prior and subsequent processes is eliminated.

Processes occur in a hierarchical arrangement, with information flowing from higher levels to lower levels in a set order. As the system moves from one level to the next, it must deactivate the previous level, activate the current one, and prepare to activate the subsequent level, a system that has been described as one that "looks to the future and does not dwell on the past" (Dell, Burger, & Svec, 1997, p. 123). Serial systems of language production have been proposed by Mackay (1970), Garrett (1984; see Figure 8.1), and Levelt, Roelofs, and Meyer (1999).

In contrast, the language system is said to be interactive when the phonological units interact with the lexical ones, resulting in levels of processing that flow not only forward but also backward (Cutting & Ferreira, 1999; de Zubicaray, McMahon, Eastburn, & Pringle, 2006). Therefore, the phonological form of a word, which exists at the phonological encoding level of language processing, affects the probability of that word being selected during lexicalization, a level occurring much earlier. In noninteractive models (i.e., modular), semantic overlap is the factor that determines which of the activated lexical items is ultimately selected (Peterson & Savoy, 1998).

Unlike in single-product models, the processes of cascading models of sentence production select, or "activate," multiple lexical items. All activated items are passed from process to process until a single one is selected at the phonological encoding level. As each item moves from one stage of processing to the next, its level of activation diminishes (Peterson & Savoy, 1998).

Theories of Sentence Deficit

Just as there are theories that explain how language is processed in an unimpaired brain, there are theories that account for how and why disordered language is processed and produced. There are two theories in particular that bear relevance to grammatical processing in particular: trace deletion theory and working memory theory.

Trace Deletion Theory

In transformational grammar, a generative grammar in the tradition of Chomsky's Minimalist Program, traces exist as placeholders for linguistic units that have been moved during sentence generation (Chomsky, 1995). Theoretically, a deep structure exists that is the structural starting point of every sentence. Once all of the necessary words have populated that structure, they are then moved into their final positions, thus forming the surface structure that is ultimately the form that is expressed.

Traces allow for the mind to encode words with their appropriate thematic roles despite their having moved to different locations in the sentence, locations that may not be the canonical position for a subject or object of a sentence (in passive sentence constructions, for example). Grodzinsky (2000) proposed that Broca's area is where the manipulation of traces is localized and that Broca's aphasia directly results from the brain's inability to create and track traces.

Working Memory Theory

Keeping track of the various components of a sentence to inflect and position them while ensuring all thematic requirements are met for each verb requires a storage system that temporarily holds the linguistic units while they are processed. Martin and Slevc (2011) differentiated three types of memory in language processing: short-term memory, long-term memory, and working memory. Short-term and long-term memory are passive storage systems that retain linguistic information; short-term memory houses phonological and semantic information associated with words, while long-term memory houses the representations of word meanings and the language's grammatical rules. Working memory (Baddeley, 2007) is the process by which short-term and long-term memory information is placed at each level of language comprehension and production while the necessary processing takes place.

There is general consensus that individuals with aphasia present with impaired working memory, and that this deficit potentially contributes to impairments of sentence processing (Caspari, Parkinson, LaPointe, & Katz, 1998; Martin & Slevc, 2011; Wright & Fergadiotis, 2012). The nature of that contribution differs in part by the theoretical framework of working memory that is used, how it is assessed, and the extent to which attentional or control processes are included in that framework (Caplan & Waters, 1999; Hula & McNeil, 2008; Murray, 1999). Evidence exists for separate short-term memory stores for phonological representations, lexical-semantic/syntactic features, syntactic structure, and propositions (Caplan & Waters, 1999; Martin & Romani, 1994). Individuals with semantic short-term memory impairment have difficulty with sentence comprehension and production when semantic information must be retained in working memory before it is integrated with the verb, whereas individuals with phonologic short-term memory impairment do not (Martin & Freedman, 2001).

A number of studies have suggested that individuals with agrammatism have challenges with specific types of linguistic processing, that is, with specific types of sentences (e.g., object cleft sentences) or the number of arguments that are dictated by a particular verb (e.g., unaccusative verbs vs. unergative verbs) (Kemmerer & Tranel, 2000; Kim & Thompson, 2000; Thompson, 2003; Thompson et al., 1997). Others have suggested that performance on different syntactic forms is task dependent, and the deficit is a result of the greater demand complex syntax places on working memory, which is understood to be limited (Caplan, Michaud, & Hufford, 2013; Caplan & Waters, 1999). Regardless of which of these explanations is correct, it has been well described that a variety of patterns of syntactic performance may emerge in the context of Broca's aphasia, and these patterns may be associated with breakdown at different levels of sentence production.

Types of Errors in Grammatical Processing in Broca's Aphasia
Level of Conceptualization

Individuals who are unable to initiate message conceptualization are considered to have adynamic aphasia, an aphasia characterized by lack of initiated speech due to impaired concept generation (Nadeau, 2008). While a form of transcortical motor aphasia, areas of cortical damage overlap with that of Broca's aphasia (see Chapter 10 in this volume).

Level of Functional Processing

Derivational Errors: Derivational morphemes are affixes that are added to words that change their grammatical category, that is, their part of speech. For example, the suffix "er" can be added to verbs to create nouns (e.g., "bake" to "baker"). In a study measuring the response time of five Greek speakers with Broca's aphasia, Tsapkini, Peristeri, Tsimpli, and Jarema (2014) found that response time was increased by words exhibiting erroneous stem changes (i.e., derivational inflections).

Inflectional Errors: Inflection is the process by which endings are added to word roots to express meaning. For example, in English a noncomprehensive list of inflections includes the possessive (i.e., genitive) 's, the plural -s, the third-person singular -s, and the past tense -ed. Gleason and colleagues

(Gleason & Goodglass, 1984; Gleason, Goodglass, Green, Ackerman, & Hyde, 1975) suggested that whether the affix was stressed or unstressed had an effect on whether the inflection was produced accurately by people with Broca's aphasia, and they went on to describe a hierarchy of inflections based on the likelihood of error. Although considered a grammatical process, the addition of inflections to words is also considered to be a semantic process as the understanding of specific concepts, such as past tense, is required for a word to be correctly inflected. Research has indicated that people with Broca's aphasia have difficulty combining affixes with stem words due to either a slower-than-normal lexical activation of morphosyntactic information or an underspecification (i.e., the omission of features from underlying representations) of the grammatical requirements of specific inflections (Jonkers & de Bruin, 2009; Miceli & Caramazza, 1988; Tsapkini et al., 2014).

Level of Positional Processing

Grammatical processing impairment at the sentence level entails an impairment that extends beyond merely understanding the meaning of words. People with Broca's aphasia have expressive and receptive difficulty with sentences that deviate from a language's unmarked, canonical (i.e., simplest, more common form) sentence structure. In English, the unmarked sentence structure is subject-verb-object. When confronted with a sentence that deviates from that structure (a passive construction, for example), people with Broca's aphasia are unable to determine which of the two nouns in the sentence is the actor and which is the one being acted on (Berndt, 2001; Saffran et al., 1980; Schumacher, 2009). Noncanonical word order, as seen in passive sentence constructions, requires an ability to recognize the thematic role of a word even after it has moved from its deep structure placement, particularly in the case of reversible sentences where both nouns could assume agency. For example, take the following two sentences:

The girl chased the boy.
The boy was chased by the girl.

Despite which noun comes first in the sentence, they have the same meaning; the girl is the actor (agent) who chases the boy, (the patient). A person with Broca's aphasia would have difficulty determining the meaning of the passive construction, interpreting the second sentence to mean the boy was the actor of the sentence, based on the word's placement in the grammatical subject position. Because both nouns could be the agent in the sentence, the first sentence might also be difficult for some people with Broca's aphasia.

Despite the number of grammatical processing theories that have been proposed, data exist that support them all, making it difficult to distinguish which single theory best accounts for how sentences are constructed in the mind. Regardless of whether a single theory or combination of theories encapsulates the reality of grammatical processing most accurately, clinicians must treat the symptoms with which a client presents to help the individual attain as functional a level of aided or unaided speech as possible. The variability in performance for comprehension of canonical and noncanonical sentences in people with Broca's aphasia makes it imperative that clinicians not rely on assumptions or unidimensional theories when treating clients with aphasia. Subtle differences in lesion localization and neural activation likely contribute to this variability. Individualized assessment across the levels of processing is likely necessary to accurately capture the expressive and receptive language abilities of each person with Broca's aphasia.

Neuroanatomical Correlates of Broca's Aphasia

There has been a considerable amount of research on left hemisphere dominance for language and the regions in the left hemisphere that are critical to language production and comprehension since Broca presented Leborgne's lesion at the *Société de Anthropologie* in Paris (Dronkers et al., 2007). However, studies documenting the lesion locations in individuals with the same speech characteristics as Leborgne and Lelong have demonstrated damage to a wider left cortical area (Kertesz, Lesk, & McCabe, 1977), and a lesion confined to Broca's area is typically not sufficient to yield a syndrome of Broca's aphasia (Kearns, 2005; Mohr, 1976). Indeed, others have demonstrated that a lesion in Broca's area is not necessary to produce the syndrome of Broca's aphasia (Fridriksson, Bonilha, & Rorden, 2007).

The plethora of studies targeting individuals with Broca's aphasia and the use of advanced imaging techniques have built on Broca's early work and established more precise anatomical descriptions of the affected regions. Keeping in mind individual differences, Broca's aphasia is generally thought to conform to lesions in the superior branch of the middle cerebral artery, involving large portions of the frontal and parietal lobes, including Broca's area (i.e., the pars opercularis and the pars triangularis of the inferior frontal gyrus [IFG]), posteriorly and superiorly adjacent premotor and motor regions, the basal ganglia, and the insula extending to the anterior portions of the supramarginal gyrus (Davis et al., 2008; Kertesz et al., 1977).

While Broca first discovered Broca's region and gave the area its moniker, it was Carl Wernicke who, a decade later, posited the first large-scale network model of language using information gleaned from cadaver dissections. By comparing deficits with lesions, he attributed motor representations of words to the IFG (Wernicke, 1874). When Brodmann later published his cytoarchitectonic maps of the brain, "Broca's area" correlated with Brodmann's areas (BAs) 44 and 45 (Schlaug, Marchina, & Norton, 2008). Taubner, Raymer, and Heilman (1999) examined a gentleman with a left hemisphere lesion limited to pars opercularis. His language breakdown included some characteristics of Broca's aphasia, namely, syntactic impairment in speech production. Studies of individuals with lesions isolated to pars triangularis, on the other hand, showed that impairments are confined to articulatory phonetic difficulties in the absence of syntactic breakdown (Mohr, 1976). To develop the full constellation of symptoms of Broca's aphasia, the lesion needs to extend beyond Broca's area to include surrounding regions and subcortical white matter (Dronkers et al., 2007).

More recently, diffusion tensor imaging (DTI) studies focused on connectivity-based parcellation, that is, the segregation of white cortical matter with the same connectivity profile into a distinct area, further delineated the segregation of the surface portion of BAs 44 and 45 and the deep inferior frontal operculum, as well as a segmentation of the surface portions of BAs 44 and 45 (Anwander, Tittgemeyer, von Cramon, Friederici, & Knosche, 2007; Axer, Klingner, & Prescher, 2013; Hickok, 2009; Hickok & Poeppel, 2004). These findings support the differential contributions of segments of Broca's area and deep inferior frontal operculum to dorsal and ventral language pathways for grammatical processing.

Beyond Broca's Area

As integral as Broca's area is to the successful production of language, it is not the only area affected in Broca's aphasia. Broca's area is part of a language network that is connected to the frontal lobes via white matter bundles (Davis et al., 2008; Friederici,

2009; Friederici & Gierhan, 2013; Gierhan, 2013; Kümmerer et al., 2013; Vigneau et al., 2006). The dorsal part of Broca's area is connected to the superior temporal region of the brain through these tracts; and the superior temporal region is connected via white matter tracts to the frontal cortex (Davis et al., 2008). This lateral complex of neuronal fibers and brain cells responsible for transferring is known as the "local syntax" pathway and is responsible for processing local syntactic transitions (e.g., wh-movement) (Friederici, 2009).

The lateral connection between Broca's area, the temporal lobes, and the frontal cortex area is not the only pathway between Broca's area and the frontal cortex. A second pathway, which is ventrally oriented, connects the operculum of the IFG to the posterior portion of the left superior temporal cortex. This second pathway is known as the "hierarchical syntax" pathway and is responsible for more complex syntactic transitions (e.g., multiple relative clauses) (Friederici, 2009).

These pathways are significant in understanding the symptomatology of Broca's aphasia. In particular, damage to the arcuate fasciculus (AF) results in the inability to process complex sentences or to understand the passive tense, as had been previously described (Goodglass & Kaplan, 1983). Recent evidence indicates more specifically that the anterior regions of the left AF are implicated in nonfluent verbal production (Fridriksson, Guo, Fillmore, Holland, & Rorden, 2013). Research has also revealed that the uncinate fasciculus is connected to the superior temporal gyrus, and together these structures are involved in understanding and generating hierarchically structured sentences (Griffiths, Marslen-Wilson, Stamatakis, & Tyler, 2013).

Hierarchical syntax is understood to encompass the process of recursive syntactic structures, as well as processing word order derivation at the sentence level, while local syntax is understood to be involved in processing a combination of elements at the phrase level, that is, a determiner and a noun and perhaps simple verbs and adjectives. These sentences do not have to make sense or be meaningful; they only need to be syntactically correct. To imbue meaning to the phrases and ideas, the left IFG requires activation and must play a role in the development of the sentence as it is being created from origin to final expression. However, disruptions at the hierarchical level can result in more severe confusion and inability to comprehend word order, hierarchical structure, if/then statements, and cause-and-effect statements (Griffiths et al., 2013).

As stated, the left IFG is involved in comprehending complex sentences. As comprehension demands increase, the activation of the IFG increases in normal subjects. In people with Broca's aphasia, the IFG may not activate or may activate incompletely, which is evidenced by reduced understanding of even mildly complex sentences (Friederici, 2009). Recruitment of various brain structures does not result in either on or off activity; rather, there are various gradients of activation and recruiting of brain regions under different language comprehension requirements. This results in a gradual, and sequential, activation of neural tracks along an anterior-posterior frontal cortex, as seen on functional magnetic resonance imaging (fMRI) and DTI (Bornkessel-Schlesewsky & Schlesewsky, 2012). Highly local sequencing cues (or simpler speech) elicit activation along the most posterior frontal regions (premotor cortex and the cytoarchitechtonically corresponding frontal operculum) in individuals with expressive impairments in aphasia.

Other studies also have shown gradual activation of brain regions as they are challenged with more and more demanding comprehension. The greater the demand to focus as complexity of the statements increases, the more these structures are recruited, revealing higher activity under positron emission tomographic (PET) imaging. Furthermore, in Broca's area particularly, the pars opercularis and pars triangularis are implicated in understanding word order (Bornkessel-Schlesewsky & Schlesewsky, 2012). Individuals with damage or disruption to these areas via oxygen reduction demonstrated a lack of or diminished word order comprehension (Bornkessel-Schlesewsky & Schlesewsky, 2012; Davis et al., 2008).

Methods for the Assessment of Grammatical Processing

Assessing grammatical processing errors in a person with Broca's aphasia is the first step in designing a treatment plan that will maximize current abilities while targeting impairments to improve communication functionality. Evaluation of both how an individual's language is impaired and how that impairment affects daily living is best accomplished through a combination of formal and informal testing procedures. Standardized tests will elicit a wide variety of specific sentence and morpheme types, allowing for a more comprehensive assessment of an individual's language capabilities than spontaneously generated conversation can elicit. Likewise, nonstandardized testing will provide the clinician with a more

thorough knowledge of how the individual's communicative functionality is affected and what specific needs the person requires to be met by intervention.

In addition to standardized comprehensive aphasia batteries, there are several specialized aphasia batteries that prove useful when conducting a formal evaluation of grammatical processing. The *Northwestern Assessment of Verbs and Sentences* (*NAVS*; Thompson, 2011) is a standardized test used with people with acquired neurogenic language disorders for evaluating the production of verb arguments in sentences (i.e., the production of noun phrases that are semantically and syntactically related to a verb) and expressive and receptive language abilities regarding action verbs and marked and unmarked sentence structures. The *Verb and Sentence Test* (*VAST*; Bastiaanse, Edwards, & Rispens, 2002) is another test that specifically focuses on evaluating verb and sentence comprehension and production, grammaticality judgments, and sentence anagram tasks in people with aphasia. Additional tests that include subtests that evaluate grammatical processing are subtests of the *Boston Diagnostic Aphasia Examination* (*BDAE*, 3rd ed.; Goodglass et al., 2001) (e.g., the cookie-theft picture; supplemental subtests of syntactic processing); *Psycholinguistic Assessments of Language Processing in Aphasia* (*PALPA*; Kay, Lesser, & Coltheart, 1992); and the *Western Aphasia Battery–Revised* (*WAB-R*; Kertesz, 2007) (e.g., the Grammatical Competence score of the Spontaneous Speech subtest). The *Quantitative Production Analysis* (Berndt, Wayland, Rochon, Saffran, & Schwartz, 2000) allows for coding of grammatical elements of utterances in a systematically elicited narrative discourse with the Cinderella story. Because grammatical processes act on words, lexical access is important to assess as well. Tests like the *Northwestern Naming Battery* (Thompson, Lukic, King, Mesulam, & Weintraub, 2012) specifically evaluate lexical access for nouns and verbs in people with aphasia.

Grammatical Targets for Testing

A single standardized test or a combination of specialized batteries can be used to assess grammatical processing in people with suspected Broca's aphasia. Regardless of the approach used, it is important that information regarding expressive and receptive skills of the following targets is obtained:

- Verb usage (accuracy and variety of tenses)
- Inflections (accuracy and variety)
- Pronouns (accuracy and variety) (e.g., subjective, objective, genitive)
- Prepositions (accuracy and variety)

- Articles (accuracy and variety)
- Syntax (accuracy and variety) of sentences and phrases (passive construction, wh-movement)

Informal evaluation of the client's receptive and expressive skills is necessary for developing a complete picture of the capabilities, especially regarding the functional communication tasks that he or she will engage in on a daily basis. An ecological assessment that observes the client's level of functioning in a variety of real-life environments and situations will yield the most accurate picture of a client's needs; however, this type of assessment is often not feasible due to time constraints. In lieu of an ecological assessment, the clinician should attempt to collect information regarding a variety of communicative contexts. This information can be obtained through family interviews/questionnaires and role-playing specific scenarios with the client (e.g., how effectively the client can communicate through a telephone when receiving and placing calls). Observations obtained from standardized and informal assessment will be used to develop a treatment plan to address patterns of breakdown for syntactic comprehension and production.

Treatment of Grammatical Processing in Broca's Aphasia

The model of syntactic processing reviewed previously (Figure 8.1) has implications for treatment in Broca's aphasia. We review treatments devised to target specific elements of linguistic breakdown that tend to address different stages of sentence processing. We then review other treatments that have a more global focus on verbal expression and sentence production that are relevant to individuals with Broca's aphasia. A growing body of evidence indicates that language changes can be induced following effective implementation of a variety of treatment approaches.

Level of Conceptualization/Message

Treating grammatical processing that is unable to be initiated is difficult. Crosson and colleagues (see Chapter 10 in this volume), in their discussion of transcortical motor aphasia, review several approaches that attempt to address this deficit. Behavioral and pharmacological interventions have had limited success (Barrett & Eslinger, 2007; Raymer, 2003), and further research is warranted to establish the clinical efficacy of such interventions.

Level of Functional Processing

To address impairments in grammatical processing at the level of functional processing, treatment must focus on improving the selection and assignment of lemmas to specific syntactic functions (Garrett, 1975). Treatments target the assignment of thematic roles, that is, "who does what to whom." As thematic roles are assigned by the verb, treatments that emphasize verb retrieval within the context of sentence production are presumably used to improve representations at the functional level. Several treatments that tend to focus on this stage of sentence generation have been studied.

Selection of a verb is crucial to development of the sentence structure. Therefore, some researchers have focused on studies of verb retrieval, expecting that sentence production abilities might improve as a consequence (Mitchum, 2001; Raymer & Ellsworth, 2002). For example, Schneider and Thompson (2003) trained verb picture naming in two paradigms: a semantic treatment and an argument-structure treatment. Both treatments led to improvements in retrieval of trained verbs and in the ability to construct sentences using the trained verbs. Little significant improvement was noted in narrative analyses and there was no generalized increase in untrained verb retrieval for words selected to share semantic or argument structure attributes of trained verbs. Not all individuals trained in a picture-naming paradigm have shown such positive outcomes in sentence production, and Mitchum (2001) suggested that verb retrieval would be best trained in a sentence context.

Faroqi-Shah (2008) was concerned with training production of verbs with proper inflections in individuals with Broca's aphasia. She compared two training paradigms, one centered on morphosemantic context (verb naming, sentence comprehension and judgments, sentence completion, and sentence construction) and another targeting morphophonologic context (verb naming, recognition and production of inflected verbs). Both treatments led to improvements in use of correctly inflected verbs, but the morphosemantic training led to better outcomes for use of those verbs in sentence contexts and some generalized use of inflections in untrained verbs. Faroqi-Shah (2013) followed up with a study of a morphosemantic training protocol in which she compared outcomes for regular and irregularly inflected verbs. Again, all trained words improved, including their use in sentences. Generalized use of inflections was seen for untrained regular verbs.

Other treatment approaches have centered on the thematic role assignments that are generated by the verb. Clients are trained to engage the thematic roles of agent (the person who acts) and patient (the person/thing acted on), specifically, by presenting the client with a verb and asking the client to generate agents and patients that correspond with that verb (Bastiaanse, Hurkmans, & Links, 2006; Edmonds & Babb, 2011; Edmonds, Nadeau, & Kiran, 2009; Fink, Martin, Schwartz, Saffran, & Myers, 1992; Links, Hurkmans, & Bastiaanse, 2010; Loverso, Prescott, & Selinger, 1988). Studies differed in whether clients were required to verbally utter the agent, verb, and patient or whether only the thematic roles were spoken; however, Edmonds and colleagues (2009), using *verb network strengthening treatment* (*VNeST*) with people with agrammatic Broca's aphasia reported gains in single-word noun and verb retrieval, limited generalization to semantically related untrained items, improvements in spontaneous speech consisting of a higher percentage of complete sentences, and gains persisting at least 5 months posttreatment.

Edmonds and Babb (2011) found in a subsequent study that an individual with more severe Broca's aphasia required approximately twice as long to achieve the treatment criterion as the moderately impaired individuals. Edmonds, Mammino, and Ojeda (2014) tested VNeST in a larger sample of 11 individuals with aphasia, again showing positive outcomes for verb retrieval, sentence production, and discourse informativeness measures.

Sentence-level treatments also have been developed to address weaknesses at the functional level of sentence generation. *Treatment of underlying forms* (*TUF*) (Thompson, 2001; Thompson & Shapiro, 2005), also known as linguistic-specific treatment (Murray, Ballard, & Karcher, 2004), focuses exclusively on improving the production and comprehension of syntactically complex sentence structures through the use of spoken or written sentence models delivered in training. The client is guided through training with written word cards to arrange into complex sentences to be read aloud or repeated. The clinician then instructs the client on the roles of the words in the sentence array, such as verb, agent, or theme. Cards are added and moved to create a new sentence structure, such as a wh-question or a passive, and again the client is instructed on the roles of the word in the new location in the sentence. Detailed instructions for the TUF protocol can be found in Thompson's work (2001).

A series of studies have shown that by training complex syntactic structures first (e.g., object cleft sentences: "It was the dog that the cat chased"), TUF results in generalization to syntactically related untrained structures (e.g., wh-questions: "Who did

the cat chase?") (Ballard & Thompson, 1999; Murray et al., 2004), a finding Thompson, Shapiro, Kiran, and Sobecks (2003) called the complexity account of treatment efficacy (CATE). Neuroimaging studies have noted increased activity in Broca's area and the right hemisphere homologue of Wernicke's area (Thompson, Fix, Gitelman, Parrish, & Mesulam, 2000) and a general shift of activation to the bilateral posterior perisylvian and superior parietal cortices (Thompson, Den Ouden, Bonakdarpour, Garibaldi, & Parrish, 2010) as a result of treatment. These findings suggest that, individual differences aside, TUF increases activation of damaged cortical areas or recruits previously nonactivated cortical areas to aid in sentence processing.

Thompson, Choy, Holland, and Cole (2010) have developed a software program called Sentactics® that provides TUF through a computer and requires minimal clinician supervision. Their research found it comparable to face-to-face therapy in number of sessions required to meet criterion, accuracy of trained forms, and amount of generalization to untrained forms, making it a viable alternative treatment for those clients with transportation or financial considerations.

Another treatment that targets impairments at the functional level is *mapping therapy* (Schwartz, Saffran, Fink, Myers, & Martin, 1994). Specifically, mapping therapy is a treatment approach that targets functional processing of sentence syntax by training clients to recognize the number of arguments a verb may take (i.e., agent, action, patient); how those roles map onto the syntactic role in the sentence (i.e., subject, verb, object); as well as the location of phrase boundaries within a sentence. Treatment can focus on impairments in comprehension (Schwartz et al., 1994) or production (Harris, Olson, & Humphreys, 2012). Study participants completing production tasks not only acquired all trained morphological and syntactic structures, but also demonstrated generalization to trained and untrained morphological and syntactic structures in novel stimuli (Harris et al., 2012; Rochon, Laird, Bose, & Scofield, 2005). Wierenga and colleagues (2006) examined fMRI scans of the effect of mapping therapy on two individuals with Broca's aphasia and revealed increased activity in Broca's area in one individual and less-diffuse neural activity in the other individual posttreatment.

Level of Positional Processing

Impairments at the positional level of grammatical processing involve the inaccurate ordering of words within constituent structures and the inaccurate or lack of grammatical morphemes, bound (e.g., the possessive "s"), free-standing (e.g., articles, prepositions), or both. The *Sentence Production Program for Aphasia* (originally called *Helm Elicited Language Program for Syntax Stimulation* or *HELPSS*) (Helm-Estabrooks, Fitzpatrick, & Barresi, 1981; Helm-Estabrooks & Nicholas, 2000) is a treatment for people with chronic Broca's aphasia and agrammatism; the program presumably targets impairments at the positional level. In a story-completion format, the individual is trained to produce eight different sentence constructions in the order indicated by Gleason and colleagues' (1975) hierarchy of difficulty for people with Broca's aphasia (e.g., from imperative intransitive ["Come over."] to future ["She will come."]). Researchers have found that once a sentence construction is mastered, its production is generalized to untrained exemplars of that type (Doyle & Bourgeois, 1986; Fink et al., 1995; Helm-Estabrooks et al., 1981). Completion of the program through mastery of all sentence constructions is highly variable and can take between 24 and 113 therapy sessions, each lasting 30 minutes (Helm-Estabrooks & Ramsberger, 1986).

General Treatment Approaches

Some treatment approaches for verbal expression in aphasia, although not specifically designed to treat grammatical processing, can be used to target language-processing impairments at the sentence level.

Constraint-Induced Language Therapy

Constraint-induced language therapy (*CILT*) is a treatment approach motivated by knowledge of principles of neuroplasticity by incorporating treatment intensity (i.e., massed practice) and shaping of verbal responses (i.e., forced use), while restraining use of nonverbal communication modalities (Pulvermüller et al., 2001). Typically, treatment involves group therapy of people with aphasia interacting through a language game (such as Go Fish) for at least 24 hours of intervention over 10 days (Breier, Maher, Novak, & Papanicolaou, 2006). Recently, Difrancesco, Pulvermüller, and Mohr (2012) recoined the approach *intensive language-action therapy* (*ILAT*) to avoid the misunderstandings that the use of the term *constraint* may create and to highlight the required intensive schedule of the treatment.

Across several studies that have examined effects of CILT in aphasia, most participants had nonfluent forms of aphasia, including Broca's aphasia (Cherney, Patterson, & Raymer, 2011). Faroqi-Shah and Virion (2009) reported positive language gains in morphosyntactic and lexical measures in four participants with chronic Broca's aphasia who were treated with CILT; two participants received a traditional protocol informed by previously published CILT protocols (see Maher et al., 2006), and two participants received a modified CILT protocol that included additional shaping of verbal productions and judgment of tense morphology. Follow-up testing at 3 months posttreatment revealed that three of the four participants not only maintained but also increased the gains made during therapy. Breier and colleagues (2006) reported improvement in verbal production measures for four of six people with Broca's and conduction aphasia when treated with CILT.

Kirmess and Lind (2011) found large effect sizes ($d \geq 0.8$) of CILT treatment on three participants (two nonfluent and one fluent) as they improved in sentence construction and mean length of utterances, although some verb measures decreased significantly posttreatment. However, Goral and Kempler (2009) used a modified CILT protocol that emphasized the production of verbs within narratives and found significant increases in number of verbs produced. Imaging using magnetoencephalography of participants who responded and did not respond to CILT treatment indicated that a favorable response to CILT was dependent on preserved brain activity in left hemisphere posterior language areas and homotopic areas within the right hemisphere (Breier et al., 2006). While participants treated with CILT have made lexical gains in verbal speech production and on standardized tests, further research is needed to determine if CILT improves grammatical processing in comprehension and production tasks.

Melodic Intonation Therapy

An observation that the singing capabilities of people with Broca's aphasia remained intact even as their expressive speech was impaired led to the development of an aphasia treatment that utilizes rhythmic tapping and intoned speech (speech that is musically stylized by exaggerating the prosody of normal speech) to engage the right hemisphere in language production (Helm-Estabrooks, Nicholas, & Morgan, 1989; Sparks, 2008). *Melodic intonation therapy* (*MIT*) translates the prosodic patterns of normal speech into intoned speech by employing two pitches (high and low) and two durations (short and long). Naturally accented syllables are sung using the high pitch, with treatment progressing hierarchically through three levels of difficulty. Ultimately, the level of exaggeration of natural prosody is faded until speech resembles normal production. In addition to using intoned speech, MIT requires that each syllable be accompanied by a tap using the left hand. The underlying theory of the treatment is that the use of rhythm and intonation activates unaffected homotopic areas in the right hemisphere and recruits them to aid in language production (Zumbansen, Peretz, & Hébert, 2014).

Several early studies showed small improvements in spoken production after participating in MIT (Martin, Kubitz, & Maher, 2001). Schlaug and colleagues (2008) treated two patients with MIT and *speech repetition therapy* (SRT), which was identical in all aspects to MIT except that intoned speech and hand tapping were not utilized. After treatment, greater improvement on all language outcomes in the individual treated with MIT was accompanied by increased right hemisphere activation in fMRI analysis. Imaging of the individual treated with SRT showed changes only in the left hemisphere. Further research by Schlaug, Marchina, and Norton (2009) using DTI on six participants who received MIT found a significant increase after treatment in the number of fiber tracts in the right AF. Due to the extensive damage to the left AF in all patients, imaging was restricted to the right AF. In contrast, Breier, Randle, Maher, and Papanicolaou (2010) performed DTI on two individuals treated with MIT and found, in the responding participant, a steady decrease in right hemisphere activation proportional to an increase in activation of homotopic left hemisphere areas posttreatment.

The effect MIT has on grammatical processing in expressive language is currently unknown; while researchers have examined the effect of treatment on repetition and responsiveness (Conklyn, Novak, Boissy, Bethoux, & Chemali, 2012) and formal standardized tests (Schlaug et al., 2008), few studies have looked at the effect of treatment on specific morphological and syntactic structures. Springer, Willmes, and Haag (2007) compared the use of wh-questions and prepositions in dialogue after treating individuals with a stimulation approach utilizing many of the elements of MIT and a linguistically oriented approach, which provided participants with written multiple-choice sets. They found that,

while participants made improvement, partially correct answers could not be further improved with the stimulation approach.

It should be noted that many studies allegedly using MIT to treat participants, in fact, modified the original protocol (e.g., Wilson, Pearsons, & Reutens, 2006). As procedural variations in clinical research studying the effects of MIT may change the fundamental mechanisms at work (Zumbansen et al., 2014), future research is needed that clearly differentiates modifications from the original MIT program and studies the effects of treatment on morphological structures.

Summary

The syndrome of Broca's aphasia serves as a platform for discussions of normal processes of sentence production and how those systems break down in individuals with left hemisphere damage. Analyses of the neural correlates of Broca's aphasia indicate that damage extends to left inferior frontal regions beyond Broca's area, suggesting a role for such regions in syntactic processing. Formal and informal diagnostic tools facilitate assessment of both comprehension and production of grammatical functions that can be impaired in Broca's aphasia. Several treatment approaches have been described that address impairment in sentence production that emanates across various processes in sentence formulation. Overall, whereas some variation exists among individuals who present with the general pattern of Broca's aphasia, the nomenclature provides a launching pad to guide analysis and intervention for the communication impairments experienced by these individuals.

Acknowledgments

The author would like to acknowledge Carmen Seitan for her contributions to an early draft of this chapter.

References

Anwander, A., Tittgemeyer, M., von Cramon, D.Y., Friederici, A.D., & Knosche, T.R. (2007). Connectivity-based parcellation of Broca's area. *Cerebral Cortex, 17*, 816–825.

Axer, H., Klingner, C.M., & Prescher, A. (2013). Fiber anatomy of dorsal and ventral language streams. *Brain and Language, 127*(2), 192–204.

Baddeley, A. (2007). *Working memory, thought and action.* New York, NY: Oxford University Press.

Ballard, K.J., & Thompson, C.K. (1999). Treatment and generalization of complex sentence production in agrammatism. *Journal of Speech, Language, and Hearing Research, 42*, 690–707.

Barrett, A.M., & Eslinger, P.J. (2007). Amantadine for adynamic speech: Possible benefit for aphasia? *American Journal of Physical Medicine & Rehabilitation, 86*(8), 605–612.

Bastiaanse, R., & Edwards, S. (2004). Word order and finiteness in Dutch and English Broca's and Wernicke's aphasia. *Brain and Language, 89*, 91–107.

Bastiaanse, R., Edwards, S., & Rispens, S. (2002). *The verb and sentences test*. Bury St. Edmunds, England: Thames Valley Test.

Bastiaanse, R., Hurkmans, J., & Links, P. (2006). The training of verb production in Broca's aphasia: A multiple-baseline across-behaviours study. *Aphasiology, 20*, 298–311.

Berndt, R.S. (2001). More than just words: Sentence production in aphasia. In R.S. Berndt (Ed.), *Handbook of neuropsychology* (2nd ed., pp. 173–187). Amsterdam, the Netherlands: Elsevier Science.

Berndt, R.S., Wayland, S., Rochon, E., Saffran, E., & Schwartz, M. (2000). *Quantitative production analysis: A training manual for the analysis of aphasia sentence production*. New York, NY: Psychology Press.

Bock, K., & Levelt, W.J.M. (1994). Language production: Grammatical encoding. In M.A. Gernsbacher (Ed.), *Handbook of psycholinguistics* (pp. 945–984). San Diego, CA: Academic Press.

Bornkessel-Schlesewsky, I., & Schlesewsky, M. (2012). Linguistic sequence processing and the prefrontal cortex. *The Open Medical Imaging Journal, 6*(Suppl. 1-M2), 47–61.

Breier, J., Randle, S., Maher, L.M., & Papanicolaou, A.C. (2010). Changes in maps of language activity activation following melodic intonation therapy using magnetoencephalography: Two case studies. *Journal of Clinical and Experimental Neuropsychology, 32*(3), 309–314.

Breier, J.I., Maher, L.M., Novak, B., & Papanicolaou, A.C. (2006). Functional imaging before and after constraint-induced language therapy for aphasia using magnetoencephalography. *Neurocase, 12*, 322–331.

Brkić, E., Sinanović, O., Vidović, M., & Dževdet, S., (2009). Incidence and clinical phenomenology of aphasic disorders after stroke. *Medical Archives, 63*(4), 197–199.

Broca, P.P. (1861). Remarks on the seat of the faculty of articulated language, following an observation of aphemia (loss of speech). *Bulletin de la Société Anatomique, 6*, 330–357.

Buckingham, H.W. (1991). The psycholinguistics of microgenesis: The nature of paraphasia. In R.E. Hanlon (Ed.), *Cognitive microgenesis* (pp. 150–179). New York, NY: Spinger-Verlag.

Caplan, D., Michaud, J., & Hufford, R. (2013). Short-term memory, working memory, and syntactic comprehension in aphasia. *Cognitive Neuropsychology, 30*, 77–109.

Caplan, D., & Waters, G.S. (1999). Verbal working memory and sentence comprehension. *Behavioral and Brain Sciences, 22*, 77–94.

Caramazza, A., Capasso, R., Capitani, E., & Miceli, G. (2005). Patterns of comprehension performance in agrammatic Broca's aphasia: A test of the trace deletion hypothesis. *Brain and Language, 94*, 43–53.

Caramazza, A., Capitani, E., Rey, A., & Berndt, R.S. (2001). Agrammatic Broca's aphasia is not associated with a single pattern of comprehension performance. *Brain and Language, 76*, 158–184.

Caramazza, A., & Zurif, E.B., (1976). Dissociation of algorithmic and heuristic processes in language comprehension: Evidence from aphasia. *Brain and Language, 3*, 572–582.

Caspari, I., Parkinson, S.R., LaPointe, L.L., & Katz, R.C. (1998). Working memory and aphasia. *Brain and Cognition, 37*, 205–223.

Cherney, L., Patterson, J., & Raymer, A.M. (2011). Intensity of aphasia therapy: Evidence and efficacy. *Current Neurology and Neuroscience Reports, 11*, 560–569.

Chomsky, N. (1995). *The minimalist program*. Cambridge, MA: MIT Press.

Code, C. (2010). Aphasia. In J.S. Damico, N. Müller, & M.J. Ball (Eds.), *The handbook of language and speech disorders* (pp. 317–338). Chichester, England: Wiley-Blackwell.

Conklyn, D., Novak, E., Boissy, A., Bethoux, F., & Chemali, K. (2012). The effects of modified melodic intonation therapy on nonfluent aphasia: A pilot study. *Journal of Speech, Language, and Hearing Research, 55*, 1463–1471.

Cutting, J.C., & Ferreira, V.S. (1999). Semantic and phonological information flow in the production lexicon. *Journal of Experimental Psychology: Learning, Memory, and Cognition, 25*, 345–361.

Davis, C., Kleinman, J.T., Newhart, M., Gingis, L., Pawlak, M., & Hillis, A.E. (2008). Speech and language functions that require a functioning Broca's area. *Brain and Language, 105*(1), 50–58.

Dell, G.S. (1986). A spreading-activation theory of retrieval in sentence production. *Psychological Review, 93*(3), 283–321.

Dell, G.S., Burger, L.K., & Svec, W.R. (1997). Language production and serial order: A functional analysis and a model. *Psychological Review, 104*(1), 123–147.

de Zubicaray, G., McMahon, K., Eastburn, M., & Pringle, A. (2006). Top-down influences on lexical selection during spoken word production: A 4T fMRI investigation of refractory effects in picture naming. *Human Brain Mapping, 27*, 864–873.

Difrancesco, S., Pulvermüller, F., & Mohr, B. (2012). Intensive language-action therapy (ILAT): The methods. *Aphasiology, 26*(11), 1317–1351.

Doyle, P.J., & Bourgeois, M.S. (1986). The effect of syntax training on "adequacy" of communication in Broca's aphasia: A social validation study. In R.H. Brookshire (Ed.), *Clinical aphasiology* (Vol. 16, pp. 123–131). Minneapolis, MN: BRK.

Dronkers, N.F., Plaisant, O., Iba-Zizen, M.T., & Cabanis, E.A. (2007). Paul Broca's historic cases: High resolution MR imaging of the brains of Leborgne and Lelong. *Brain, 130*, 1432–1441.

Edmonds, L.A., & Babb, M. (2011). Effect of verb network strengthening treatment in moderate-to-severe aphasia. *American Journal of Speech-Language Pathology, 20*, 131–145.

Edmonds, L.A., Mammino, K., & Ojeda, J. (2014). Effect of verb network strengthening treatment (VNeST) in persons with aphasia: Extension and replication of previous findings. *American Journal of Speech-Language Pathology, 23*(2), S312–S329.

Edmonds, L.A., Nadeau, S.E., & Kiran, S. (2009). Effect of verb network strengthening treatment (VNeST) on lexical retrieval of content words in sentences in persons with aphasia. *Aphasiology, 23*(3), 402–424.

El Hachioui, H., Lingsma, H.F., van de Sandt-Koenderman, M.E., Dippel, D.W.J., Koudstaal, P.J., & Visch-Brink, E.G. (2013). Recovery of aphasia after stroke: A 1-year follow-up study. *Journal of Neurology, 260*, 166–171.

Engelter, S.T., Gostynski, M., Papa, S., Frei, M., Born, C., Ajdacic-Gross, V., . . . Lyrer, P.A. (2006). Epidemiology of aphasia attributable to first ischemic stroke: Incidence, severity, fluency, etiology, and thrombolysis. *Stroke, 37*, 1379–1384.

Faroqi-Shah, Y. (2008). A comparison of two theoretically driven treatments for verb inflection deficits in aphasia. *Neuropsychologia, 46*, 3088–3100.

Faroqi-Shah, Y. (2013). Selective treatment of regular versus irregular verbs in agrammatic aphasia: Efficacy data. *Aphasiology, 27*(6), 678–705.

Faroqi-Shah, Y., & Virion, C.R. (2009). Constraint-induced language therapy for agrammatism: Role of grammaticality constraints. *Aphasiology, 23*(7–8), 977–988.

Fink, R.B., Martin, N., Schwartz, M.F., Saffran, E.M., & Myers, J.L. (1992). Facilitation of verb retrieval skills in aphasia: A comparison of two approaches. *Clinical Aphasiology, 21*, 263–275.

Fink, R.B., Schwartz, M.F., Rochon, E., Myers, J.L., Socolf, S., & Bluestone, R. (1995). Syntax stimulation revisited: An analysis of generalization of treatment effects. *American Journal of Speech Language Pathology, 4*, 99–104.

Fridriksson, J., Bonilha, L., & Rorden, C. (2007). Severe Broca's aphasia without Broca's area damage. *Behavioural Neurology, 18*, 237–238.

Fridriksson, J., Guo, D., Fillmore, P., Holland, A., & Rorden, C. (2013). Damage to the anterior arcuate fasciculus predicts non-fluent speech production in aphasia. *Brain, 136*, 3451–3460.

Friederici, A.D. (2009). Pathways to language: Fiber tracts in the human brain. *Trends in Cognitive Sciences, 13*(4), 175–181.

Friederici, A.D., & Gierhan, S.M. (2013). The language network. *Current Opinion in Neurobiology, 23*(2), 250–254.

Garrett, M.F. (1975). Syntactic process in sentence production. In G. Bower (Ed.), *Psychology of learning and motivation: Advances in research and theory* (Vol. 9, pp. 133–177). New York, NY: Academic Press.

Garrett, M.F. (1984). The organization of processing structure for language production: Applications to aphasic speech. In D. Caplan, A.R. Lecours, & A. Smith (Eds.), *Biological perspectives on language* (pp. 172–193). London, England: MIT Press.

Gierhan, S.M. (2013). Connections for auditory language in the human brain. *Brain and language, 127*(2), 205–221.

Gleason, J.B., & Goodglass, H. (1984). Some neurological and linguistic accompaniments of the fluent and nonfluent aphasias. *Topics in Language Disorders, 4*(3), 71–81.

Gleason, J.B., Goodglass, H., Green, E., Ackerman, N., & Hyde, M.K. (1975). The retrieval of syntax in Broca's aphasia. *Brain and Language, 24*, 451–471.

Goodglass, H., Christiansen, J.A., & Gallagher, R.E. (1994). Syntactic constructions used by agrammatic speakers: Comparison with conduction aphasics and normal. *Neuropsychology, 8*(4), 598–613.

Goodglass, H., & Kaplan, E. (1983). *The assessment of aphasia and related disorders*. Philadelphia, PA: Lea & Febiger.

Goodglass, H., Kaplan, E., & Barresi, B. (2001). *The assessment of aphasia and related disorders* (3rd ed.). Philadelphia, PA: Lippincott Williams & Wilkins.

Goral, M., & Kempler, D. (2009). Training verb production in communicative context: Evidence from a person with chronic non-fluent aphasia. *Aphasiology, 23*(12), 1383–1397.

Griffiths, J.D., Marslen-Wilson, W.D., Stamatakis, E.A., & Tyler, L.K. (2013). Functional organization of the neural language system: Dorsal and ventral pathways are critical for syntax. *Cerebral Cortex, 23*, 139–147.

Grodzinsky, Y. (2000). The neurology of syntax: Language use without Broca's area. *Behavioral Brain Science, 23*, 1–21.

Harris, L., Olson, A., & Humphreys, G. (2012). Rehabilitation of past tense verb production and non-canonical sentence production in left inferior frontal non-fluent aphasia. *Aphasiology, 26*(2), 143–161.

Heilman, K.M., & Scholes, R. (1976). The nature of comprehension errors in Broca's, conduction, and Wernicke's aphasics. *Cortex, 12*, 258–265.

Helm-Estabrooks, N., Fitzpatrick, P. M., & Barresi, B. (1981). Response of an agrammatic patient to a syntax stimulation program for aphasia. *Journal of Speech and Hearing Disorders, 46*, 422–427.

Helm-Estabrooks, N., & Nicholas, M. (2000). *Sentence production program for aphasia: Administration manual* (2nd ed.). Austin, TX: Pro-Ed.

Helm-Estabrooks, N., Nicholas, M., & Morgan, M. (1989). *Melodic intonation therapy program*. Austin, TX: Pro-Ed.

Helm-Estabrooks, N., & Ramsberger, G. (1986). Treatment of agrammatism in long-term Broca's aphasia. *British Journal of Disorders of Communication, 21*, 39–45.

Hickok, G. (2009). The functional neuroanatomy of language. *Physics of Life Reviews, 6*(3), 121–143.

Hickok, G., & Poeppel, D. (2004). Dorsal and ventral streams: A framework for understanding aspects of the functional anatomy of language. *Cognition, 92*(1), 67–99.

Hula, W.D., & McNeil, M.R. (2008). Models of attention and dual-task performance as explanatory constructs in aphasia. *Seminars in Speech and Language, 29*(3), 169–187.

Jonkers, R., & de Bruin, A. (2009). Tense processing in Broca's and Wernicke's aphasia. *Aphasiology, 23*(10), 1252–1265.

Kay, J., Lesser, R., & Coltheart, M. (1992). *Psycholinguistic assessments of language processing in aphasia*. Hove, England: Erlbaum.

Kearns, K.P. (2005). Broca's aphasia. In L.L. LaPointe (Ed.), *Aphasia and related neurogenic language disorders* (3rd ed., pp. 117–141). New York, NY: Thieme.

Kemmerer, D., & Tranel, D. (2000). Verb retrieval in brain-damaged subjects: 1. Analysis of stimulus, lexical, and conceptual factors. *Brain and Language, 73*, 347–392.

Kertesz, A. (1979). *Aphasia and associated disorders: Taxonomy, localization, and recovery*. Orlando, FL: Grune & Stratton.

Kertesz, A. (2007). *Western aphasia battery–revised*. San Antonio, TX: Psychological Corporation.

Kertesz, A., Lesk, D., & McCabe, P. (1977). Isotope localization of infarcts in aphasia. *Archives of Neurology, 100*, 1–18.

Kim, M., & Thompson, C.K. (2000). Patterns of comprehension and production of nouns and verbs in agrammatism: Implications for lexical organization. *Brain and Language, 74*, 1–25.

Kirmess, M., & Lind, M. (2011). Spoken language production as outcome measurement following constraint induced language therapy. *Aphasiology, 25*, 1207–1238.

Kümmerer, D., Hartwigsen, G., Kellmeyer, P., Glauche, V., Mader, I., Klöppel, S., . . . Saur, D. (2013). Damage to ventral and dorsal language pathways in acute aphasia. *Brain, 136*(2), 619–629.

Lee, M., & Thompson, C.K. (2004). Agrammatic aphasia production and comprehension of unaccusative verbs in sentence context. *Journal of Neurolinguistics, 17*, 315–330.

Levelt, W.J.M., Roelofs, A., & Meyer, A.S. (1999). A theory of lexical access in speech production. *Behavioral and Brain Sciences, 22*, 1–75.

Links, P., Hurkmans, J., & Bastiaanse, R. (2010). Training verb and sentence production in agrammatic Broca's aphasia. *Aphasiology, 24*(11), 1303–1325.

Loverso, F.L., Prescott, T.E., & Selinger, M. (1988). Cueing verbs: A treatment strategy for aphasic adults (CVT). *Journal of Rehabilitation Research and Development, 25*(2), 47–60.

Mackay, D.G. (1970). Spoonerisms: The structure of errors in serial order of speech. *Neuropsychologia, 8*, 323–350.

Maher, L.M., Kendall, D., Swearingin, J.A., Rodriquez, A., Leon, S.A., Pingel, K., . . . Rothi, L.J.G. (2006). A pilot study of use-dependent learning in the context of constraint induced language therapy. *Journal of the International Neuropsychological Society, 12*, 843–852.

Martin, R.C., & Freedman, M.L. (2001). Short term retention of lexical-semantic representations: Implications for speech production. *Memory, 9*, 261–280.

Martin, R.C., & Romani, C. (1994). Verbal working memory and sentence comprehension: A multiple-components view. *Neuropsychology, 8*, 506–523.

Martin, R.C., & Slevc, L.R. (2011). Memory disorders and impaired language and communication. In R.K. Peach & L.P. Shapiro (Eds.), *Cognition and acquired language disorders: An information processing approach* (pp. 183–201). St. Louis, MO: Elsevier Mosby.

Martin, V.C., Kubitz, K.R., & Maher, L.M. (2001, October). Melodic intonation therapy. *Perspectives in Neurophysiology and Neurogenic Speech and Language Disorders, 11*(3), 33–37.

Miceli, G., & Caramazza, A. (1988). Dissociation of inflectional and derivational morphology. *Brain and Language, 35*, 24–65.

Miceli, G., Silveri, M.C., Villa, G., & Caramazza, A. (1984). On the basis for the agrammatic's difficulty in producing main verbs. *Cortex, 20*, 207–220.

Mitchum, C.C. (2001). Verbs and sentence production in aphasia: Evidence-based intervention. *Perspectives in Neurophysiology and Neurogenic Speech and Language Disorders, 11*(3), 4–13.

Mohr, J.P. (1976). Broca's area and Broca's aphasia. In H. Whitaker & H.A. Whitaker (Eds.), *Studies in neurolinguistics* (Vol. *1*, pp. 201–235). New York, NY: Academic Press.

Murray, L. (1999). Review attention and aphasia: Theory, research and clinical implications. *Aphasiology, 13*(2), 91–111.

Murray, L., Ballard, K., & Karcher, L. (2004). Linguistic specific treatment: Just for Broca's aphasia? *Aphasiology, 18*(9), 785–809.

Nadeau, S.E. (2008). Subcortical language mechanisms. In B. Stemmer & H.A. Whitaker (Eds.), *Handbook of the neuroscience of language* (pp. 329–340). Burlington, MA: Academic Press.

Pederson, P.M., Vinter, K., & Olsen, T.S. (2004). Aphasia after stroke: Type, severity and prognosis. The Copenhagen Aphasia Study. *Cerebrovascular Disease, 17*, 35–43.

Peterson, R.R., & Savoy, P. (1998). Lexical selection and phonological encoding during language production: Evidence from cascading processing. *Journal of Experimental Psychology, 24*(3), 539–557.

Pulvermüller, F., Neininger, B., Elbert, T., Mohr, B., Rockstroh, B., Koebbel, P., & Taub, E. (2001). Constraint-induced therapy of chronic aphasia after stroke. *Stroke, 32*(7), 1621–1626.

Raymer, A.M. (2003). Treatment of adynamia in aphasia. *Frontiers in Bioscience, 8*, s845–s851.

Raymer, A.M., & Ellsworth, T.A. (2002). Response to contrasting verb retrieval treatments in aphasia: A case study. *Aphasiology, 16*, 1031–1045.

Rochon, E., Laird, L., Bose, A., & Scofield, J. (2005). Mapping therapy for sentence production impairments in nonfluent aphasia. *Neuropsychological Rehabilitation, 15*(1), 1–36.

Saffran, E.M., Schwartz, M.F., & Marin, O.S. (1980). The word order problem in agrammatism. II. Production. *Brain and Language, 10*, 249–262.

Schlaug, G., Marchina, S., & Norton, A. (2008). From singing to speaking: Why singing may lead to recovery of expressive language function in patients with Broca's aphasia. *Music Perception: An Interdisciplinary Journal, 25*(4), 315–323.

Schlaug, G., Marchina, S., & Norton, A. (2009). Evidence for plasticity in white-matter tracts of patients with chronic Broca's aphasia undergoing intense intonation-based speech therapy. *Annals of the New York Academy of Sciences, 1169*, 385–394.

Schneider, S.L., & Thompson, C.K. (2003). Verb production in agrammatic aphasia: The influence of semantic class and argument structure properties on generalization. *Aphasiology, 17*, 213–241.

Schumacher, P.B. (2009). Real-time comprehension in agrammatic aphasia. In G. Ibanescu & S. Pescariu (Eds.), *Aphasia: Symptoms, diagnosis, and treatment*. Hauppauge, NY: Nova Science.

Schwartz, M.F., Saffran, E.M., Fink, R.B., Myers, J.L., & Martin, N. (1994). Mapping therapy: A treatment programme for agrammatism. *Aphasiology, 8*, 19–54.

Schwartz, M.F., Saffran, E.M., & Marin, O.S. (1980a). The word order problem in agrammatism: Comprehension. *Brain and Language, 10*, 249–262.

Schwartz, M.F., Saffran, E.M., & Marin, O.S. (1980b). The word order problem in agrammatism: Production. *Brain and Language, 10*, 263–280.

Sparks, R.W. (2008). Melodic intonation therapy. In R. Chapey (Ed.), *Language intervention strategies in aphasia and related neurogenic communication disorders* (4th ed., pp. 837–851). Baltimore, MD: Lippincott, Williams, & Wilkins.

Springer, L., Willmes, K., & Haag, E. (2007). Training in the use of wh-questions and prepositions in dialogue: A comparison of two different approaches in aphasia therapy. *Aphasology, 7*(3), 251–270.

Taubner, R.W., Raymer, A.M., & Heilman, K.M. (1999). Frontal-opercular aphasia. *Brain and Language, 70*, 240–261.

Thompson, C.K. (2001). Treatment of underlying forms: A linguistic specific approach for sentence production deficits in agrammatic aphasia. In R. Chapey (Ed.), *Language intervention strategies in adult aphasia* (4th ed., pp. 605–628). Baltimore, MD: Lippincott, Williams, & Wilkins.

Thompson, C.K. (2003). Unaccusative verb production in agrammatic aphasia: The argument structure complexity hypothesis. *Journal of Neurolinguistics, 16*, 151–167.

Thompson, C.K. (2011). *Northwestern assessment of verbs and sentences*. Evanston, IL: Northwestern University.

Thompson, C.K., Choy, J.W.J., Holland, A., & Cole, R. (2010). Sentactics: A computer automated treatment of underlying forms. *Aphasiology, 24*(10), 1242–1266.

Thompson, C.K., Den Ouden, D.B., Bonakdarpour, B., Garibaldi, K, & Parrish, T.B. (2010). Neural plasticity and treatment-induced recovery of sentence processing in agrammatism. *Neuropsychologia, 48*, 3211–3227.

Thompson, C.K., Faroqi-Shah, Y., & Lee, J. (2015). Models of sentence production. In A.E. Hillis (Ed.), *The handbook of adult language disorders* (pp. 328–354). New York, NY: Psychology Press.

Thompson, C.K., Fix, S.C., Gitelman, D.R., Parrish, T.B., & Mesulam, M.M. (2000). FMRI studies of agrammatic sentence comprehension before and after treatment. *Brain and Language, 74*, 387–391.

Thompson, C.K., Lukic, S., King, M.C., Mesulam, M.M., & Weintraub, S. (2012). Verb and noun deficits in stroke-induced and primary progressive aphasia: The Northwestern naming battery. *Aphasiology, 26*, 632–655.

Thompson, C.K., & Shapiro, L.P. (2005). Treating agrammatic aphasia within a linguistic framework: Treatment of underlying forms. *Aphasiology, 19*, 1021–1036.

Thompson, C.K., Shapiro, L.P., Ballard, K.J., Jacobs, B.J., Schneider, S.S., & Tait, M.E. (1997). Training and generalized production of wh- and NP-movement structures in agrammatic aphasia. *Journal of Speech, Language, and Hearing Research, 40*, 228–244.

Thompson, C.K., Shapiro, L.P., Kiran, S., & Sobecks, J. (2003). The role of syntactic complexity in treatment of sentence deficits in agrammatic aphasia: The complexity account of treatment efficacy (CATE). *Journal of Speech, Language, and Hearing Research, 46*, 591–607.

Tsapkini, K., Peristeri, E., Tsimpli, I. M., & Jarema, G. (2014). Morphological decomposition in Broca's aphasia. *Aphasiology, 28*(3), 296–319.

Vigneau, M., Beaucousin, V., Herve, P.Y., Duffau, H., Crivello, F., Houde, O., . . . Tzourio-Mazoyer, N. (2006). Meta-analyzing left hemisphere language areas: Phonology, semantics, and sentence processing. *Neuroimage, 30*(4), 1414–1432.

Wernicke, C. (1874/1969). The aphasic symptom-complex. A psychological study on the anatomical basis. In R.S. Cohen & M.W. Wartofsky (Eds.), *Boston studies in the philosophy of science* (pp. 34–97). Dordrecht, the Netherlands: Reidel.

Wierenga, C.E., Maher, L.M., Moore, A.B., Swearengin, J., Soltysik, D.A., Peck, K., . . . Crosson, B. (2006). Neural substrates of syntactic mapping treatment: An fMRI study of two cases. *Journal of the International Neuropsychological Society, 12*(1), 132–146.

Wilson, S.J., Pearsons, K., & Reutens, D.C. (2006). Preserved singing in aphasia: A case study of the efficacy of melodic intonation therapy. *Music Perception, 24*(1), 23–36.

Wright, H.H., & Fergadiotis, G. (2012). Conceptualizing and measuring working memory and its relationship to aphasia. *Aphasiology, 26*(3–4), 258–278.

Zingeser, L.B., & Berndt, R.S. (1990). Retrieval of nouns and verbs in agrammatism and anomia. *Brain and Language, 39*, 14–32.

Zumbansen, A., Peretz, I., & Hébert, S. (2014). Melodic intonation therapy: Back to basics for future research. *Frontiers in Neurology, 5*(7), 1–11.

Global Aphasia

Elizabeth E. Galletta *and* A. M. Barrett

Abstract

Global aphasia is a language disorder that involves the breakdown of all aspects of oral and written language, typically associated with an extensive left hemisphere lesion that involves cortical and subcortical areas as well as white matter tracts. The characteristics of global aphasia include severe auditory comprehension and oral expression deficits with some spared conceptual knowledge and spared comprehension of emotional prosody. The implications for clinical assessment and treatment are described, and recommendations for clinicians and family members are provided.

Key Words: Global aphasia, Stroke, Emotion, Prosody, Functional communication, Gesture

Introduction

Many different definitions of aphasia have been proposed over the years. From a neurological perspective, aphasia is an acquired language impairment resulting from focal brain damage in the absence of other cognitive, motor, or sensory impairments. From a cognitive psycholinguistic perspective, aphasia is the breakdown of information processing relevant to language and communication, including underlying perceptual, representational, and motor-intentional skills, and/or of important cognitive information-processing capacity, resulting from focal brain damage. From a functional perspective, aphasia is a breakdown in linguistic abilities resulting from an acquired focal lesion that causes functional disability in communication. According to the British neurologist Hughlings Jackson (1878), aphasia is a disorder of intentional speech, thus affecting intended acts of communication much more than nonpropositional speech acts, which can be produced when emotion and language become intertwined. Most definitions of aphasia do not comment on emotional aspects of language and how emotion and language are connected. Yet this specific point, the intertwining of

emotion and language, and the intimate interrelationship of conative (generative, intentional) mental processes with language, is inherently relevant to our discussion of *global aphasia.*

Global aphasia is a language disorder that involves the breakdown of all aspects of oral and written language, typically associated with an extensive left hemisphere lesion (Alexander, Naeser, & Palumbo, 1987; Goodglass, Kaplan, & Barresi, 2001). A person with global aphasia has severe difficulties in auditory language comprehension and their oral expressive use of language is often limited to single words, whether in spontaneous expression or when naming objects or repeating words. These impairments of verbal language are usually accompanied by significant problems with reading and writing as well. Synonyms for the word *global* include *comprehensive, total,* and *large-scale,* with Lichtheim (as cited in Compston, 2006) describing a syndrome of *total aphasia* for what today is referred to as *global aphasia.* Global aphasia represents a pattern of comprehensive or total disruption of language-processing abilities.

When considering the best methods for the assessment and treatment of a person affected by global aphasia, the clinician takes into account the individual's specific characteristics as well as the anatomical and etiological factors that led to the global aphasia. It is useful to recognize that within this encompassing language disorder there may be relative strengths and weaknesses that are very important to consider. Moreover, the assessment environment in and of itself (context effect) and the specific method used to evaluate intended speech acts may negatively affect speech and language productions of people with global aphasia. This may explain why a person who has global aphasia, while performing poorly in a formal aphasia assessment, can at times inject a yes/no response into a complex group conversation that seems to reflect understanding of the stream of communication, or why a person with global aphasia may blurt out an appropriate sentiment such as "*I love your dress*" to a family member, an utterance with emotional valence. Considering and capitalizing on preserved emotional capacity are crucial to the assessment and treatment of individuals with global aphasia. That is, an examination of the strengths of individuals with global aphasia can provide a window into the contributions of the intact right hemisphere of the brain to communication attempts.

Characteristics

Language and communication can be described in terms of modality (auditory, oral, visual, gestural, orthographic), domain of linguistic processing (phonology, morphology, syntax, semantics), or cognitive skills relevant to functional performance beyond pure linguistic abilities (emotional communication, pragmatics, self-monitoring, theory of mind or perspective taking, aesthetics, and humor). Regardless of the level of focus, all aspects of purely linguistic competence are severely impaired in global aphasia. Specifically, the individual is typically unable to speak using words other than one or two "stereotypic utterances" (Helm-Estabrooks & Albert, 1991), which are repeated, sometimes often and in every attempt to speak. These utterances may not be real words, and do not have one specific meaning (e.g., an utterance such as *tan-tan* or *op-po*). These utterances are generally well articulated and may be produced with a range of prosodic variation. In addition, auditory comprehension is impaired at the single word and sentence levels (Peach, 2008). Most often, the individual with global aphasia has difficulty reading single words and cannot write words.

Although language and communication in its formal sense are severely impaired, comprehension of emotions and emotional prosody may be spared. Yet comprehension of emotional prosody and its effect on communication are often not considered when characterizing global aphasia. Rather, most of the research on emotions and prosody of speech focuses on individuals who experienced a right hemisphere stroke. Several studies report that production and comprehension of emotional prosody are mediated, respectively, by the right prefrontal and temporal regions (Adolphs, Damasio, & Tranel, 2002; Heilman, Bowers, Speedie, & Coslett, 1984; Pell, 1998; Ross & Monnot, 2008). Therefore in the case of a left hemisphere stroke, emotional prosody is presumably spared. Yet, although spared production and comprehension of emotional prosodic communication may be a strength after left hemisphere stroke, this ability is often not the clinical focus of intervention for individuals recovering from left hemisphere stroke. However, characterizing cognitive strengths and spared functions makes it possible to plan for person-centered rehabilitation care, and also provides for increased information about aphasia rehabilitation to foster wellness and function. For example, in a case report Barrett, Crucian, Raymer, and Heilman (1999) described an individual with global aphasia who had spared comprehension of emotional prosody, supporting the notion that verbal and emotional systems are independent and that spared emotional prosody is a characteristic of individuals with global aphasia. Specifically, Barrett and colleagues (1999) tested a 31-year-old woman who had suffered a probable carotid blockage resulting in an infarction in the distribution of the left middle cerebral artery. The woman was attentive and motivated during extended speech and language testing via a standardized aphasia assessment. However, she was unable to express any words other than "yes" and "no" and she expressed these unreliably. Auditory comprehension was severely impaired. She followed 4/10 simple commands and could not follow written commands. This woman clearly presented with a global aphasia. In contrast to language assessment, on the Florida Affect Battery (Bowers, Blonder, & Heilman, 1991) the woman performed well on nonverbal affect recognition tasks. She was able to match sentences spoken with a variety of intonation patterns representing different emotions to emotional faces with 83% accuracy. This case illustrates the need to consider spared right hemisphere functions and their effect on communication for people with global aphasia. Unfortunately, this case report did not investigate whether sparing of emotional processing had any practical benefit with respect to functional communication in the home and for social activities. Whether the degree of sparing in emotional communication relates to caregiver burden, family coping, and return to community activities would be important to investigate in future studies.

A group study that examined the effects of emotionality on auditory comprehension in aphasia tested comprehension of emotional and nonemotional words (Reuterskiold, 1991). Eight individuals with global aphasia were included in this study. The results showed significantly better performance on emotional words supporting the concept of spared emotional processing in people with global aphasia. This study is consistent with the findings by Landis, Graves, and Goodglass (1982) who reported that people with global aphasia read words such as "fear" and "love" that contain emotional value better than neutral words such as "lake" and "bird."

Metalinguistic abilities may also be severely impaired in people with global aphasia, in parallel with linguistic impairment. However, some people with global aphasia demonstrate areas of metalinguistic and pragmatic competence. We and other clinicians have observed that some individuals with global aphasia actively attempt to predict and respond to the actions and intentions of others (an aspect of theory of mind, Siegal & Varley, 2006). Enjoyment of humor and nonverbal jokes can also be spared, particularly in communication with family or close friends. We often have noticed that some people with global aphasia carefully adhere to rules of conversational interaction (appropriate length of eye contact, speaking distance, physical contact or lack of same with the conversation partner), whereas others no longer demonstrate knowledge of these rules of social interaction.

Lastly, it is well understood that people with global aphasia may have varying levels of awareness of their deficit and ability to self-monitor the success of their attempts to communicate. This may be linked to spared emotional processing resulting from distinct neural networks for emotional compared to neutral information (Ofek et al., 2013). In working with individuals who have global aphasia, it is important to note and acknowledge areas of spared metalinguistic competence and to acknowledge these cognitive strengths. Recognizing and capitalizing upon these spared abilities may improve

the quality of life and social functional competence in individuals with global aphasia, an area that demands further examination in systematic studies.

In summary, despite severe linguistic breakdown that crosses all expressive and receptive modalities, both emotional communication and metalinguistic abilities may be relatively spared in people with global aphasia after left brain stroke. Rather than focusing on the impaired left hemisphere, considering the strengths of the right hemisphere may provide clinicians with windows of potential treatment.

Neural Correlates

Almost all people with global aphasia have left hemisphere lesions involving all of the perisylvian speech and language cortex (surrounding the sylvian fissure) as well as the subcortical white matter underlying these regions (e.g., Gold & Kertesz, 2000). The most common etiology for this damage is a left middle cerebral artery or internal carotid artery stroke. As all of the perisylvian speech and language areas fall within the middle cerebral artery territory, including Broca's area and Wernicke's area, the white matter underlying these regions as well as the related cortical and subcortical areas including the insula, and other subcortical structures, people with global aphasia almost invariably have large volume strokes affecting these regions, and in general the damage to all of these areas occurs simultaneously as a result of the identified stroke event. Although nonfluent speech is a symptom of both Broca's aphasia and global aphasia, the extent of the lesion in two subcortical pathways, the medial and rostral portions of the subcallosal fasciculus, plus the periventricular white matter near the body of the lateral ventricle, has been shown to differentiate Broca's aphasia and global aphasia such that individuals with global aphasia have more extensive lesions in both pathways compared to individuals with Broca's aphasia (Naeser, Palumbo, Helm-Estabrooks, Stiassny-Edner, & Albert, 1989). More recently Fridriksson and colleagues (Fridriksson, Guo, Fillmore, Holland, & Rorden, 2013) considered the relationship between white matter tracts and nonfluent speech production. They reported that damage to the anterior arcuate fasciculus predicts nonfluent speech production in people with aphasia. More specifically, greater involvement of the uncinate fasciculus was a predictor of auditory comprehension impairment, resulting in global aphasia. Although Fridriksson and colleagues (2013) acknowledge that continued research with more subjects will better support this work, it is a relatively recent consideration in work in the area of neural correlates of speech fluency in aphasia.

Rarely, multiple embolic events occur that may separately affect anterior and posterior speech and language areas, or one embolic or thrombotic event may affect anterior cortical or subcortical regions supporting speech production (caudate and putamen, white matter underlying Broca's area and the insula), whereas a second event affects temporal regions critical to language comprehension. The speech and language syndrome affecting these individuals may not differ significantly from the global aphasia in people who have had a single, large stroke. However, people with global aphasia as a result of more than one episode of brain ischemia may have a higher risk of recurrent stroke, and thus may have experienced multiple, small cortical or subcortical events affecting other eloquent regions. In these people, the cooccurrence of memory deficit, problems with behavioral self-regulation and planning, stroke-related mood disorders, and speech and language deficits may create greater challenges to effective management and therapy.

Although stroke is generally considered to be the major etiology of aphasia, including global aphasia, there are no organized studies to track how many people with acquired aphasia have symptoms as a result of encephalitis, brain tumor, traumatic brain injury, and neurodegenerative diseases such as primary progressive aphasia. As noted above, global aphasia can be the result of either cortical, subcortical and cortical, or, rarely, subcortical stroke alone, usually affecting the thalamus or basal ganglia (Naeser et al., 1982). We have repeatedly observed in our clinical work that in people with global aphasia as a result of isolated subcortical stroke, a severe adynamic syndrome may mask comprehension or pragmatic communication abilities.

Clinical Assessment

As reviewed by Patterson (in this volume), clinical assessment of aphasia typically involves standardized and nonstandardized language measures. Standardized tests of aphasia include the assessment of auditory comprehension and verbal expression skills [e.g., the Boston Diagnostic Aphasia Examination (BDAE), Goodglass et al., 2001; the Western Aphasia Battery (WAB)–Revised, Kertesz, 2007]. Yet, given the severity of the language impairment in people with global aphasia, standardized tests frequently can be too difficult to complete and provide insufficient information identifying areas of strengths that may serve as the basis of a rehabilitation program for these individuals. The Boston Assessment of Severe Aphasia (BASA) (Helm-Estabrooks, Ramsberger, Morgan, & Nicholas, 1989) is a test that was designed to identify the preserved abilities of individuals with global aphasia. The stimuli and test materials include items that were motivated by the clinical experiences of the authors as well as research evidence suggesting that language performance of people with global aphasia is positively affected by stimuli with emotional value and personal implications. For example, the previously mentioned study by Landis and colleagues (1982) reported that people with global aphasia read words such as "fear" and "love" that contain emotional value better than neutral words such as "lake" and "bird." Therefore, in the BASA, the authors included items that had emotional value in order to assess whether this is spared in the individual with global aphasia. In addition to considering stimuli that contain emotional value, scoring of the BASA is different from other language assessments of people with aphasia. In the BASA, individuals can receive full credit for nonverbal responses, suggesting that communication of the message, rather than the specific form of the message, is what is important.

In 2001, the World Health Organization (WHO) proposed a biopsychosocial model of health and disease, the International Classification of Functioning Disability and Health (ICF; World Health Organization, 2001). In this model, there are three domains that define a health condition: body structures and function, activity, and participation. In terms of aphasia, an example of body structures and function or an impairment level assessment might include focus on a naming task and involve naming pictured items such as those included in the Boston Naming Test (Kaplan, Goodglass, & Weintraub, 2001). In addition, the traditional aphasia assessments such as the BDAE and the WAB include a scoring system based on the impairment domain, whereas in the BASA, scoring criteria are different. The BASA includes nonverbal responses as allowable and accurate answers, and indicates that the ability to communicate a message and participate in an exchange is what is valued more than the specific form of the utterance. In terms of the ICF, the BASA is an aphasia assessment instrument that includes the domains of activity and participation as relevant areas of assessment.

Functional Assessments

In addition, other functional measures assessing independence and activities of daily living add to the clinician's ability to tailor assessment to the individual strengths and goals of people with global aphasia. Functional measures are integral to considering preserved strengths. For example, the Modified Rankin Scale (Van Swieten, Koudstaal, Visser, Schouten, & Van Gijn, 1988) is a measure of the degree of independence in the daily activities of people who have suffered a stroke. It is used for rating the degree of disability in activities of daily living on a scale from 0 to 5. Van Swieten and colleagues (1988) reported that interobserver agreement among physicians using a version of this modified scale could be implemented in people with global aphasia for degree of independence in communication interactions.

Similar to a Modified Rankin Scale, the Barthel Index (Mahoney & Barthel, 1965) is an evaluation of functional independence poststroke generally completed by clinicians. Although the Barthel includes activities of daily living (ADLs) such as walking and transferring, specific items in the area of communication are not included in this assessment. Yet the development of an instrument that addresses functional independence of communication, similar to the focus of the Barthel Index for ADLs, would allow for characterization of communication at the functional level for people with global aphasia.

In addition to ratings made by clinical observations, self-report is often used as an outcome measure to document the quality of life in stroke survivors (e.g., Williams, Weinberger, Harris, Clark, & Biller, 1999). However, because self-report measures involve processing language (typically a clinician asks the patient a question) and a verbal response, people with global aphasia are often excluded from such assessments (e.g., Edwards, Hahn, Baum, & Dromerick, 2006; Townsend, Brady, & McLaughlan, 2007) even though there is literature suggesting that people with moderate to severe aphasia can participate in communication exchanges in the presence of supported conversation (Kagan, 1995). This is relevant to an assessment instrument that addresses activity and participation, the Activity Card Sort, for which there are administration instructions adapted for people with aphasia (Tucker, Edwards, Mathews, Baum, & Connor, 2012). The Activity Card Sort allows the person with aphasia to indicate activities he or she enjoyed before being affected by stroke

or neurological disorder, using language-free cards and indicators, and can be used to plan life-relevant, social goals for communication therapy. To consider the abilities of people with aphasia to participate in self-report assessments, Tucker et al. (2012) administered modified measures to individuals with a range of severity of aphasia. The modified measures included the Stroke Impact Scale (Duncan et al., 1999), the Reintegration to Normal Living Scale (RNL; Wood-Dauphinee, Opzoomer, Williams, Marchand, & Spitzer, 1988), and the Activity Card Sort (Baum & Edwards, 2008). Each measure was adapted in terms of administration based on a five-step hierarchy of examiner support. Examples of adaptation included repeating the question, simplifying the syntax and restating the question, and reexplaining the choices. In addition, to indicate the degree of support an individual required to complete a measure, a seven-point scale based on the Functional Independence Measure (FIM) typically used in rehabilitation settings was completed (Smith, Illig, Fielder, Hamilton, & Ottenbacher, 1996). Tucker et al. (2012) reported that individuals with varied aphasia severity are able to participate in surveys about their personal situations given external support. Individuals with more severe aphasia, such as what is expected in global aphasia, understandably had lower ratings on the independence scale and required more support. However, this suggests that making the generalization that people with aphasia are unable to participate in self-report assessments is an error we need to correct. Another important purpose of performing an assessment that includes self-report is to evaluate self-monitoring and awareness of deficit. Although many people with global aphasia are distressed by their impairments and the impact of aphasia on their daily life functions, information collected from other groups of people with aphasia suggests that they may perceive their level of disability differently than those around them (unawareness of deficit or anosognosia; Barrett, Eslinger, Ballentine, & Heilman, 2005). This difference between self-perceived communication competence and the level of communication competence perceived by other family members can create conflict within the family and socially isolate the person with global aphasia. In a study of people with less-severe aphasia, Maniscalco, Williamson, and Barrett (2011) used the Communication Effectiveness Index (Lomas et al., 1989) to confirm that people with aphasia self-estimate their communication competence better than do their caregivers. In addition, they reported that caregivers and people with aphasia estimated different kinds of activities as most impaired. People with aphasia reported that their greatest difficulties occurred in communicating with strangers; in contrast, caregivers reported that their greatest difficulties occurred in conversation with family and people well-known to them. Rather, we need to consider people with aphasia as individuals and provide the support needed to allow people with global aphasia to actively participate in their rehabilitation programs and communication interactions with those around them. Studies focused on optimal methods to integrate information from self-report measures, especially those assessing activity and participation, to planning rehabilitation in people with global aphasia and achieve improved outcomes are not yet available, and are needed.

Advocacy

After all the assessments are said and done, and sometimes months or even years after these have been completed, professionals involved in the assessment of individuals with global aphasia, and aphasia in general, are sometimes asked to review medical records and make a statement regarding competency for decision making. Often this comes up after the stroke survivor is deceased and a family member is challenging a will that was altered by the stroke survivor. Competency for decision making is an important question that can have legal ramifications. Clinicians involved in the assessment of individuals with aphasia do not include a statement regarding competency for decision making as a standard; competence is ultimately determined by legal judgment. Yet, offering an opinion and advice on the ability of the person to contribute to decision making for himself or herself and others is an important contribution to care, and attention should be given to discussing this issue at the time of diagnosis. In addition, a statement of competency should be periodically reevaluated as an individual with global aphasia makes progress in therapy. Discussing with family members and loved ones what contributing to a decision means, and how a person with aphasia might participate in a medical, financial, or other important decision, even if he or she is not the final decision maker, is extremely important and useful.

Treatment

Although the prognosis for improvement of speech and language with traditional behavioral therapy is guarded, speech and language therapy for global aphasia is the main form of treatment that is currently available following stroke. Although behavioral interventions are the most common treatment for aphasia, biological interventions in the form of pharmacological therapy and noninvasive brain modulation techniques are explored in the research literature as well (Galletta, Rao, & Barrett, 2011).

One of the greatest challenges to behavioral treatment for global aphasia is severely reduced auditory comprehension and impaired linguistic semantics. Therefore, initial therapy tends to focus on matching tasks in order to model for the individual what is expected as a response. An auditory comprehension activity first involves an object-to-object matching task in which the selection field varies from a field of one to four objects. Initially, hand-over-hand cueing may be necessary to model the appropriate response. After this, written word matching to objects and pictures and spoken word matching to pictures would then be included. The goal of these types of activities is to work toward improved auditory comprehension of single words (Alexander & Loverso, 1992).

A different approach to improving functional communication in individuals with global aphasia involves utilizing involuntary productions for purposeful communication. The basic premise relies on capitalizing on the involuntary expressions and incorporating these productions into voluntary speech (see Goda, 1962). Helm and Barresi (1980) described this treatment approach, "Voluntary Control of Involuntary Utterances," and provided a specific protocol that involves reading single words aloud that were previously not produced in a volitional manner.

In an early study of global aphasia, Gardner, Zurif, Berry, and Baker (1976) documented that although auditory comprehension and oral verbal expression are severely impaired in individuals with global aphasia, there may be some spared conceptual information that is not accessible for communication purposes. Therefore, training gestures to improve communication was initially explored for the purposes of improving communication (Helm & Benson, 1978), and subsequently Visual Action Therapy (VAT) was designed to train severely impaired individuals to produce gestures for purposes of functional communication (Helm-Estabrooks, Fitzpatrick, & Barresi, 1982). Although the evidence base for VAT is fairly limited, some individuals may respond positively to aspects of the treatment (Conlon & McNeil, 1991). In addition to gesture, individuals with global aphasia may be encouraged to communicate with alternative modalities, such as drawing or communication boards (Peach, 2008).

Because people with global aphasia often understand social and emotional communication and nonverbal cues, it is important to structure therapy tasks to a mature, adult level to maintain dignity and an atmosphere of mutual respect. Creating social equity in the therapeutic relationship may foster better communication on the part of the person with global aphasia. This may result from diction or communication conventions appropriate for a formal interaction that restrict the acceptable range of emotional expression—as noted previously, emotionally inflected discourse may be easier for people with global aphasia. Because success with this type of task is variable among people with global aphasia, the treatment targets should be relevant to the individual's environment. Choosing treatment items for people with aphasia that are relevant to their life experiences is an important aspect of treatment and reflects the philosophy of the ICF promoted by the World Health Organization (2001), as described earlier.

In addition to individual treatment, group therapy as well as family educational sessions are often also integrated into behavioral intervention for people with global aphasia. At times, working with family members is a main focus of rehabilitation to promote successful communication, as in communication partner training (Simmons-Mackie, Raymer, Armstrong, Holland, & Cherney, 2010). Certainly it is important to educate family members, cosurvivors, and caregivers so that they are aware of spared metalinguistic and emotional right hemisphere processes in the presence of severe communication impairment. Because people with global aphasia have spared comprehension of emotional prosody (Barrett et al., 1999), the intonation of speech expressed by people in the environment of the individual with global aphasia may have a significant impact on the person, and is also a focus of intervention. Direct work on emotion and spared right hemisphere prosody is not common in the treatment of global aphasia. However, combining emotional cues, intonation of speech, and emotional material for therapy sessions (e.g., a happy face, a sad face, an angry face) to promote nonverbal expression is potentially an area that could enhance communication attempts in treatment. It may also be useful to employ materials likely to evoke an emotional response (e.g., use a picture of an infant grandchild instead of a generic picture

to illustrate the word "baby"). Choosing dramatic, emotional words (for example, "screeching" instead of "calling") may also support better comprehension as a result of emotional coprocessing of this kind of language. In any event, training the people who interact with a person with global aphasia to use intonation of speech, broadly emotional facial expressions and body gestures, and other nonverbal cues in their interactions may be worthwhile.

Biological Approaches to Treatment

Biological approaches to aphasia treatment focus on promoting repair of neural circuits for language and associated functions at the molecular, cellular, and systems level (Small & Llano, 2009). However, given that it is well known that plasticity does not occur in isolation, biological interventions without behavioral interventions might not be enough to foster improved function. Therefore much of the research focus in this area combines biological and behavioral interventions. One area of biological intervention for aphasia is pharmacotherapy. Many different drugs (e.g., amantadine, bromocriptine, or methylphenidate) have been used in aphasia clinical trials. A widely cited study (Walker-Batson et al., 2001) reported that individuals with aphasia enrolled in speech-language therapy who received dextroamphetamine performed better on the Porch Index of Communicative Ability (PICA) (Porch, 2001) than those who received speech-language therapy alone. This study has fostered much interest in the use of pharmacotherapeutic agents in conjunction with behavioral intervention for aphasia. In a review that considered the evidence supporting the use of drug therapy for people with aphasia, Berthier, Pulvermuller, Davila, Casares, and Gutierrez (2011) reported that the use of pharmacological agents to promote the production of neurotransmitters disrupted after stroke, in conjunction with intensive behavioral treatment, may prove worthwhile for the treatment of aphasia. A key component cited was the behavioral intervention. Pharmacological intervention paired with behavioral speech-language treatment has not been systematically examined in individuals with global aphasia, however.

Along with drug treatments, noninvasive brain stimulation techniques in the form of transcranial magnetic stimulation (TMS) and transcranial direct current stimulation (tDCS) are increasingly being studied as methods used for the improvement of language poststroke. TMS is a noninvasive method used to stimulate the brain by inducing a magnetic field outside of the head on the scalp. This penetrates the skull and induces electrical current that depolarizes neurons, promoting either an excitatory or inhibitory effect on neuronal firing. Naeser et al. (2005) published a case report of an individual with global aphasia who received repetitive TMS (rTMS). In this example, a 57-year-old woman with global aphasia that had persisted for 6 years was treated with rTMS. Following the application of a series of rTMS treatments (without behavioral intervention), improved naming was reported at 2 months and 8 months. This was the first case to note improved naming over time after rTMS. Given that the woman had global aphasia and stable deficits for several years prior to this intervention, the findings were striking and encouraging for the use of noninvasive brain stimulation techniques for the improvement of language poststroke.

Different from TMS, tDCS is a neuromodulation technique that involves applying low-voltage electrical current transcranially by placing electrodes on the scalp. An advantage to tDCS over TMS is the feasibility of combining tDCS with behavioral therapy. The first study that employed tDCS for aphasia (Monti et al., 2008) did not combine tDCS with behavioral intervention, whereas currently several studies (see Elsner, Kugler, & Mehrholz, 2013, for a review) have reported on the use of tDCS with behavioral treatments. The majority of the research using tDCS includes individuals with nonfluent aphasia, although some with fluent aphasia have also been included (e.g., Fridriksson, Richardson, Baker, & Rorden, 2011), and one study included individuals with global aphasia (Kang, Kim, Sohn, Cohen, & Paik, 2011).

People with global aphasia are underrepresented in research overall, and specifically in research that includes biological interventions such as medications, TMS, and tDCS. Given that an individual with global aphasia may often face major challenges in giving informed consent to participate in research trials, this understandably reduces the participation of people with global aphasia in aphasia research. In addition, because of relatively smaller changes in linguistic impairment that may occur in these individuals, researchers face a practical obstacle in recruiting these participants, because larger groups will be needed to obtain a reportable treatment effect. Thus, incentives to encourage researchers to recruit these underserved and vulnerable people to aphasia research may be needed and appropriate. Ethical consideration and caution need to be addressed in order to ensure that individuals with global aphasia who do assent to research participation are truly aware of what they are agreeing to as well as the risks and benefits associated with research participation.

Theoretical Implications

Global aphasia is different from other aphasia syndromes in that the preserved traditional strengths in terms of speech and language are limited. Considering alternatives to the speech and language pathologist's traditional assessment and treatment approaches for use in individuals with stroke-induced global aphasia gives us tools to create a new treatment model for enhancing care and quality of life in other groups who are severely language challenged, such as developmentally disabled individuals, people with dementia, and people with other terminal illnesses. This is consistent with other care philosophies that focus on ways of living rather than on traditional healthcare, such as the Eden Alternative (Brownie, 2011), an approach to elder care that promotes companionship and the opportunity to give care to other living things as relevant to health and well-being. In fostering richer life circumstances, clinicians managing the care of people with global aphasia can include family members, cosurvivors, and caregivers in the assessment and treatment as part of standard and customary clinical care.

Conclusions/Recommendations

People with global aphasia may sustain longstanding and profound speech and language deficits many years after stroke. Moreover, the recovery process is variable, and although many people do not make significant improvements in language impairment after the first year poststroke, recovery is life long and improvements have been reported many years after stroke onset (Smania et al., 2010). Focusing a treatment plan on spared abilities and life-relevant issues, and creating specific goals for return to activity and participation can be helpful ways of supporting community reintegration for individuals with global aphasia. Lastly, it is very important for individuals with global aphasia to maintain social connectedness, dignity, and a contributing family role. Therefore the involvement of loved ones in the intervention process, the active counseling of management strategies, and the use of nonverbal communication can help optimize communication within the family and social unit in the context of severe language impairment. Educating family members regarding preserved abilities in the areas of emotional processing and potential communication strategies as well as possibly incorporating alternatives into global aphasia care such as the principles of the Eden alternative may be worthwhile practices for the treatment of global aphasia.

References

Adolphs, R., Damasio, H., & Tranel, D. (2002). Neural systems for recognition of emotional prosody: A 3-D lesion study. *Emotion, 2*(1), 23–51.

Alexander, M. P., & Loverso, F. (1992). A specific treatment for global aphasia. *Clinical Aphasiology, 21,* 277–289.

Alexander, M. P., Naeser, M. A., & Palumbo, C. L. (1987). Correlations of subcortical CT lesion sites and aphasia profiles. *Brain, 110,* 961–991.

Barrett, A. M., Crucian, G. P., Raymer, A. M., & Heilman, K. M. (1999). Spared comprehension of emotional prosody in a patient with global aphasia. *Neuropsychiatry, Neuropsychology, and Behavioral Neurology, 12*(2), 117–120.

Barrett, A. M., Eslinger, P. J., Ballentine, N. H., & Heilman, K. M. (2005). Unawareness of cognitive deficit (cognitive anosognosia) in probable AD and control subjects. *Neurology, 64,* 693–699.

Baum, C. M., & Edwards, D. F. (2008). *Activity card sort* (2nd ed.). Bethesda, MD: AOTA Press.

Berthier, M. L., Pulvermüller, F., Dávila, G., Casares, N. G., & Gutiérrez, A. (2011). Drug therapy of post-stroke aphasia: A review of current evidence. *Neuropsychology Review, 21*(3), 302–317.

Bowers, D., Blonder, L. X., & Heilman, K. M. (1991). *Florida affect battery.* Center for Neuropsychological Studies. University of Florida, Gainsville, FL.

Brownie, S. (2011). A culture change in aged care: The Eden alternative. *Australian Journal of Advanced Nursing, 29*(1), 63–68.

Compston, A. (2006). On aphasia: By L. Lichtheim, MD, Professor of Medicine in the University of Berne. *Brain, 129,* 1347–1350.

Conlon, C. P., & McNeil, M. R. (1991). The efficacy of treatment for two globally aphasic adults using Visual Action Therapy. *Clinical Aphasiology, 19,* 185–195.

Duncan, P. W., Wallace, D., Lai, S. M., Johnson, D., Embretson, S., & Laster, L. J. (1999). The Stroke Impact Scale Version 2.0: Evaluation of reliability, validity, and sensitivity to change. *Stroke, 30,* 2131–2140. doi: 10. 1161/01.STR.30.10.2131.

Edwards, D. F., Hahn, M. G., Baum, C. M., & Dromerick, A. W. (2006). The impact of mild stroke on meaningful activity and life satisfaction. *Journal of Stroke and Cerebrovascular Diseases, 15,* 151–157.

Elsner, B., Kugler, J., & Mehrholz, J. (2013). Transcranial direct current stimulation (tDCS) for improving aphasia in patients after stroke (Review). *Cochrane Library, 6,* 1–45.

Fridriksson, J., Guo, D., Fillmore, P., Holland, A., & Rorden, C. (2013). Damage to the anterior arcuate fasciculus predicts non-fluent speech production in aphasia. *Brain, 136,* 3451–3460.

Fridriksson, J., Richardson, J. D., Baker, J. M., & Rorden, C. (2011). Transcranial direct current stimulation improves naming reaction time in fluent aphasia: A double-blind, sham-controlled study. *Stroke, 42,* 819–821.

Galletta, E. E., Rao, P. R., & Barrett, A. M. (2011). Transcranial magnetic stimulation (TMS): Potential progress for language improvement in aphasia. *Topics in Stroke Rehabilitation, 18*(2), 87–91.

Gardner, H., Zurif, E. B., Berry, T., & Baker, E. H. 1976). Visual communication in aphasia. *Neuropsychologia, 14,* 275–292.

Goda, S. (1962). Spontaneous speech, a primary source of therapy material. *Journal of Speech and Hearing Disorders, 27,* 190–192.

Gold, B. T., & Kertesz, A. (2000). Preserved visual lexicosemantics in global aphasia: A right hemisphere contribution? *Brain and Language, 75,* 359–375.

Goodglass, H., Kaplan, E., & Barresi, B. (2001). *The Boston Diagnostic Aphasia Examination* (3rd ed.). Philadelphia: Lippincott Williams & Wilkins.

Heilman, K. M., Bowers, D., Speedie, L., & Coslett, H. (1984). Comprehension of affective and nonaffective prosody. *Neurology, 34,* 917–920.

Helm, N. A., & Barresi, B. (1980). Voluntary control of involuntary utterances: A treatment approach for severe aphasia. In R. Brookshire (Ed.), *Clinical aphasiology conference proceedings,* 308–314. Minneapolis, MN: BRK Publishers.

Helm, N. A., & Benson, D. F. (1978, October). *Visual action therapy for global aphasia.* Paper presented at the annual meeting of the Academy of Aphasia, Chicago, IL.

Helm-Estabrooks, N., & Albert, M. L. (1991). *Manual of aphasia and aphasia therapy* (p. 54). Austin, TX: Pro-Ed.

Helm-Estabrooks, N., Fitzpatrick, R., & Barresi, B. (1982). Visual action therapy for global aphasia. *Journal of Speech and Hearing Disorders, 14,* 385–389.

Helm-Estabrooks, N., Ramsberger, G., Morgan, A. R., & Nicholas, M. (1989). *Boston assessment of severe aphasia.* Austin, TX: Pro-Ed.

Hughlings Jackson, J. (1878). On the affections of speech from disease of the brain. *Brain, 1,* 304–330.

Kagan, A. (1995). Revealing the competence of aphasic adults through conversation: A challenge to health professionals. *Topics in Stroke Rehabilitation, 2,* 15–28.

Kang, E. K., Kim, Y. K., Sohn, H. M., Cohen, L. G., & Paik, N. J. (2011). Improved picture naming in aphasia patients treated with cathodal tDCS to inhibit the right Broca's homologue area. *Restorative Neurology and Neuroscience, 29,* 141–152.

Kaplan, E., Goodglass, H., & Weintraub, S. (2001). *The Boston naming test.* Philadelphia: Lippincott Williams & Wilkins.

Kertesz, A. (2007). *The Western aphasia battery–revised.* New York: Pearson.

Landis, T., Graves, R., & Goodglass, H. (1982). Aphasic reading and writing: Possible evidence for right hemisphere participation. *Cortex, 18,* 105–112.

Lomas, J., Pickard, L., Bester, S., Elbard, H., Finlayson, A., & Zoghaib, C. (1989). The communicative effectiveness index: Development and psychometric evaluation of a functional communication measure for adult aphasia. *Journal of Speech and Hearing Disorders, 54,* 113–124.

Mahoney, F. I., & Barthel, D. (1965). Functional evaluation: The Barthel index. *Maryland State Medical Journal, 14,* 56–61.

Maniscalco, J., Williamson, D., & Barrett, A. M. (2011). Stroke survivors with aphasia may overestimate communication skills: Survivor versus caregiver report. [Abstract] *Archives of Physical Medicine and Rehabilitation, 92*(10), 1720.

Monti, A., Cogiamanian, F., Marceglia, S., Ferrucci, F., Mameli, F., Mrakic-Sposta, S., ., . . Priori, A. (2008). Improved naming after transcranial direct current stimulation in aphasia. *Journal of Neurology, Neurosurgery, and Psychiatry, 79,* 451–453.

Naeser, M. A., Alexander, M. P., Helm-Estabrooks, N., Levine, H. L., Laughlin, S. A., & Geschwind, N. (1982). Aphasia with predominantly subcortical lesion sites. *Archives of Neurology, 39*(2), 14.

Naeser, M. A., Martin, P. I., Nicholas, M., Baker, E. H., Seekins, H., Helm-Estabrooks, N., . . . Pascual-Leone, A. (2005). Improved naming after TMS treatments in a chronic, global aphasia patient—case report. *Neurocase, 11*(3), 182–193.

Naeser, M. A., Palumbo, C. L., Helm-Estabrooks, N., Stiassny-Eder, D., & Albert, M. L. (1989). Severe nonfluency in aphasia. Role of the medial subcallosal fasciculus and other white matter pathways in recovery of spontaneous speech. *Brain, 112,* 1–38.

Ofek, E., Purdy, S. C., Ali, G., Webster, T., Gharahdaghi, N., & McCann, C. M. (2013). Processing of emotional words after stroke: An electrophysiological study. *Clinical Neurophysiology, 124*(9), 1771–1778.

Peach, R. (2008). Global aphasia: Identification and management. In R. Chapey (Ed.), *Language intervention strategies in aphasia and related neurogenic communication disorders* (5th ed., pp. 565–594). Baltimore: Lippincott Williams & Wilkins.

Pell, M. D. (1998). Recognition of prosody following unilateral brain lesion: Influence of functional and structural attributes of prosodic contours. *Neuropsychologia, 36*(8), 701–715.

Porch, B. E. (2001). *Porch index of communicative ability.* Palo Alto, CA: Consulting Psychologists Press.

Reuterskiold, C. (1991). The effects of emotionality on auditory comprehension in aphasia. *Cortex, 7,* 595–604.

Ross, E. D., & Monnot, M. (2008). Neurology of affective prosody and its functional-anatomic organization in right hemisphere. *Brain and Language, 104,* 51–74.

Siegal, M., & Varley, R. (2006). Aphasia, language, and theory of mind. *Social Neuroscience, 1*(3–4), 167–174.

Simmons-Mackie, N., Raymer, A., Armstrong, E., Holland, A., & Cherney, L. R. (2010). Communication partner training in aphasia: A systematic review. *Archives of Physical Medicine and Rehabilitation, 91,* 1814–1837.

Small, S. L., & Llano, D. A. (2009). Biological approaches to aphasia treatment. *Current Neurology and Neuroscience Reports, 9*(6), 443–450.

Smania, N., Gandolfi, M., Aglioti, S. M., Girardi, P., Fiaschi, A., & Girardi, F. (2010). How long is the recovery of global aphasia? Twenty-five years of follow-up in a patient with left hemisphere stroke. *Neurorehabilitation and Neural Repair, 24*(9), 871–875.

Smith, P. M., Illig, S. B., Fielder, R. C., Hamilton, B. B., & Ottenbacher, K. J. (1996). Intermodal agreement of follow-up telephone functional assessment using the Functional Independence Measure in patients with stroke. *Archives of Physical Medicine and Rehabilitation, 77,* 431–435.

Townsend, E., Brady, M., & McLaughlan, K. (2007). Exclusion and inclusion criteria for people with aphasia in studies of depression after stroke: A systematic review and future recommendations. *Neuroepidemiology, 29,* 1–17.

Tucker, F. M., Edwards, D. F., Mathews, L. K., Baum, C. M., & Connor, L. T. (2012). Modifying health outcome measures for people with aphasia. *American Journal of Occupational Therapy, 66*(1), 42–50.

Van Swieten, J. C., Koudstaal, P. J., Visser, M. C., Schouten, H. J., & Van Gijn, J. (1988). Interobserver agreement for the assessment of handicap in stroke patients. *Stroke, 19*(5), 604–607.

Walker-Batson, D., Curtis, S., Natarajan R., Ford, J., Dronkers, N., Salmeron, E., . . . Unwin, D. H. (2001). A double-blind, placebo-controlled study of the use of amphetamine in the treatment of aphasia. *Stroke, 32,* 2093–2098.

Williams, L. S., Weinberger, M., Harris, L. E., Clark, D. O., & Biller, J. (1999). Development of a stroke-specific quality of life scale. *Stroke, 30,* 1362–1369.

Wood-Dauphinee, S. L., Opzoomer, M. A., Williams, J. I., Marchand, B., & Spitzer, W. O. (1988). Assessment of global function: The reintegration to normal living index. *Archives of Physical Medicine and Rehabilitation, 69*(8), 583–590.

World Health Organization. (2001). *International Classification of Functioning, Disability, and Health.* Geneva, Switzerland: Author.

Transcortical Motor Aphasia

Bruce A. Crosson, Anastasia Bohsali, *and* Anastasia M. Raymer

Abstract

The defining symptoms of transcortical motor aphasia (TCMA) are nonfluent verbal output with relatively preserved repetition. Other symptoms, such as naming difficulties, agrammatic output, or even some paraphasias, may occur, but these are not cardinal symptoms defining TCMA and are not necessary for the diagnosis. The core anatomy involved in TCMA is a lesion of the medial frontal cortex, especially the left presupplementary motor area (pre-SMA) and adjacent Brodmann's area 32; a lesion of the left posterior inferior frontal cortex, especially pars opercularis and ventral lateral premotor cortex; or a lesion of the pathways between these frontal structures. TCMA occasionally has been reported with a lesion of the left basal ganglia, the left thalamus, or the ascending dopaminergic pathways. From a cognitive standpoint, TCMA can be conceptualized as a disorder of intention, in other words, as a disorder of initiation and continuation of spoken language that is internally motivated. The medial frontal cortex provides the impetus to speak; this impetus to speak is conveyed to lateral frontal structures through frontal–subcortical pathways where it activates various language production mechanisms. The influence of the ascending dopaminergic pathways may occur either through their heavy connections with the pre-SMA region or through their influence on the basal ganglia. The influence of the basal ganglia and thalamus probably occurs through their connections with the medial frontal cortex. Assessments for TCMA should involve a thorough evaluation of conversational or narrative language output and repetition. New treatments are available that attempt to engage right-hemisphere intention mechanisms with left-hand movements and may be effective in TCMA. Although dopamine agonists have also shown some positive effects in increasing verbal output in TCMA, trials have been small, and some caution must be exercised in interpreting these findings.

Key Words: aphasia, intention, adynamic aphasia, transcortical motor aphasia, frontal lobes, nonfluent language, pre-SMA, Broca's area, frontal–subcortical white matter, thalamus, basal ganglia, ascending dopaminergic pathways

Syndrome Description and Unique Characteristics

The first description of transcortical motor aphasia (TCMA) is usually attributed to Lichtheim (1885). Descriptions of this syndrome since that time have varied somewhat in the literature, but today there is a fair degree of consensus regarding the description. Benson and Ardila (1996) refer to the extrasylvian aphasias, those transcortical aphasias that occur when, despite acquired brain damage to the left cerebral hemisphere, the perisylvian

cortex remains intact and allows for the remarkable ability to repeat complete sentences almost in parrot-like fashion, sometimes termed echolalia. That classical view of transcortical aphasias by itself does not account for the rather substantial difference between transcortical motor and transcortical sensory aphasia, and other mechanisms must be invoked to explain the differences between these syndromes. In this regard, Goldberg's (1985) concept of the role of the medial versus lateral frontal cortex in language is worth considering. He surmised that the supplementary motor area (SMA) was primarily involved in internally generated language and actions, whereas the lateral premotor cortex was involved in language or actions that are externally referenced. In any event, the defining pattern of TCMA is intact repetition abilities that are accompanied by nonfluent verbal expression. Despite such restricted spontaneous verbal output, some individuals with TCMA may be able to repeat even lengthy sentences correctly, and they may be able to produce lengthy material that is highly over-learned, for example, saying the alphabet or a familiar prayer (Alexander, 2003).

TCMA falls into the category of nonfluent aphasias. Nonfluent forms of aphasia are characterized by limited verbal output during attempts at spontaneous speech, usually reducing verbal production to less than 50 words per minute, whereas neurologically normal English-speaking adults produce approximately 150–180 words per minute (Berndt, Wayland, Rochon, Saffran, & Schwartz, 2000). Nonfluency can emanate from a number of sources, including failures in grammatical, phonetic-articulatory, word retrieval, and prosodic aspects of verbal production as well as failure to initiate and elaborate upon those linguistic mechanisms (Goodglass, Kaplan, & Barresi, 2001). Whereas nonfluency in a subset of individuals with TCMA may arise due to linguistic disturbances at a grammatical level (Alexander, Benson, & Stuss, 1989), including a stage of recovery from Broca's aphasia (Taubner, Raymer, & Heilman, 1999), the quintessential TCMA is characterized by difficulty in initiating and carrying out a verbal message, that is, in a reduction in the intentional, dynamic aspects of verbal expression. For that reason TCMA is sometimes referred to as "dynamic aphasia" (Bormann, Wallesch, & Blanken, 2008; Costello & Warrington, 1989; Crescentini, Lunardelli, Mussoni, Zadini, & Shallice, 2008; Luria, 1970; Robinson, Blair, & Cipolotti, 1998; Robinson, Shallice, & Cipolotti, 2005, 2006) or perhaps more appropriately, "adynamic aphasia" (Gold et al., 1997). This adynamic nonfluency can lead to short, effortful attempts to produce utterances, often responding to questions with words spoken in a prior question or statement as if to "turn on" or jumpstart verbal production. The utterances can also have a perseverative quality, yet they usually are produced with clear articulation and prosody.

In conjunction with the nonfluent verbal expression seen in sentence generation in conversation, individuals with TCMA are often evaluated for their ability to retrieve words in picture-naming, sentence completion, or word list generation tasks. Most commonly individuals with TCMA are remarkably able to retrieve words in confrontation picture-naming tasks or in sentence completion for highly predictable contexts, that is, when the words are evoked by an external visual or auditory stimulus (Bormann et al., 2008; Crescentini et al., 2008; Raymer, Rowland, Haley, & Crosson, 2002; Robinson et al., 1998). In contrast, significant difficulty emerges in word list generation tasks, such as letter category (e.g., FAS) or semantic category (e.g., animals) generation tasks, in which lexical items must be evoked through an internal search process (Cox & Heilman, 2011; Gold et al., 1997; Robinson et al., 1998).

Auditory comprehension abilities in those with TCMA are better preserved than verbal expression abilities (Crescentini et al., 2008; Raymer et al., 2002). These individuals have little difficulty recognizing the lexical content of messages, although they can at times struggle to understand grammatically complex utterances such as passives or embedded clause constructions (Heilman & Scholes, 1976). Some report that individuals with TCMA may be disinclined to respond to an auditory stimulus that is not due to lack of understanding of the information (Benson & Ardila, 1996).

Reading and writing abilities tend to parallel the patterns seen in auditory comprehension and verbal expression in TCMA. That is, reading abilities are largely intact except for difficulty understanding syntactically complex sentences. Writing is limited by the adynamic quality of written output. Some may refer to this pattern as "agraphia without alexia" (Benson & Ardila, 1996). Although spontaneous writing is limited, writing to dictation can be relatively intact (Alexander, 2002).

Consideration of the literature suggests some relationship between the syndrome of akinetic mutism and TCMA. Akinetic mutism is a syndrome often associated with medial frontal lesions. Individuals with this syndrome show few attempts at spontaneous communication and demonstrate a lack of spontaneous behavior in general. However, unlike TCMA, repetition is impaired in this syndrome, although those with akinetic mutism may be able to repeat single words with considerable coaxing (Damasio & Anderson, 2003). It is not uncommon for individuals with TCMA to be completely mute initially and to evolve into the TCMA syndrome over days or weeks (Alexander, 2003; Kertesz, 1999). We will discuss the anatomical and cognitive relationships between TCMA and akinetic mutism below.

In his original description, Lichtheim (1885) conceptualized TCMA as an interruption of the pathways between the conceptual center for language and the center for motor output of language (see Chapter 2 by Heilman for more details). Indeed, there is some evidence that semantic content can affect repetition in TCMA. For example, McCarthy and Warrington (1984) gave participants with aphasia sentences that ended in uncommon three-syllable words; in half of the sentences, the final word made sense and in the other half it did not. Participants had to repeat the final word of the sentence and indicate whether it made sense. Under these conditions, the repetition of an individual with TCMA deteriorated compared to repetition of the words in isolation. Persons with conduction aphasia, on the other hand, showed improved repetition when forced to attend to semantic content in this fashion. Gold and colleagues (1997) also reported a case of TCMA (adynamic aphasia) in which the patient was unable to sort closely related items into categories without prior cuing as to the nature of the categories. This individual also failed to use semantic strategies in recall.

Although there are some reports of adynamic aphasia occurring in individuals with progressive supranuclear palsy (Robinson et al., 2005, 2006), most often TCMA is seen following a left hemisphere stroke, sometimes involving a segment of the left middle cerebral artery (MCA) distribution (Bormann et al., 2008), or alternatively, as a result of disruption of vascular flow in the regions supplied by the anterior cerebral artery (ACA) (Raymer et al., 2002). The implications for the neural correlates of TCMA will be elaborated below. In several retrospective reviews of records, the number of cases of TCMA has ranged from 2% to 11% of all cases of aphasia following acute stroke (Kertesz, 2007; Pedersen, Vinter, & Olsen, 2004; Yang, Zhao, Wang, Chen, & Zhang, 2008). In the acute stage of recovery from the stroke, individuals may present with mutism for a period of several days, until verbal expression begins to recover to a stage in which the few, limited verbal responses are spoken with a hypophonic quality. Other accompanying cognitive, motor, and sensory impairments depend on the vascular distribution involved (Benson & Ardila, 1996). In TCMA associated with an MCA stroke, the lack of dynamic intentional input can also lead to a sense of apathy and decreased drive to engage in daily activities. Although these individuals usually do not have limb weakness, they may lack the inclination to move the right upper limb. In contrast, ACA strokes often lead to right hemiparesis of the lower limb (Kumral, Bayulkem, Evyapan, & Yunten, 2002).

Neuroanatomical Correlates of the Syndrome

The next two sections of this chapter are closely linked. In the current section, we will discuss the underlying anatomy of transcortical motor aphasia. In the subsequent section, we will discuss the cognitive constructs related to this anatomy. A good place to start the anatomy is with the work of Alexander and his colleagues. Alexander (2002) maintained that there are three anatomic substrates for TCMA. (1) Freedman, Alexander, and Naeser (1984) showed that the frontal operculum of the language-dominant hemisphere, specifically pars opercularis, and the lower third of the premotor region were important in TCMA. Specifically, a lesion in this region was sufficient to produce TCMA, and individuals with lesions that extended beyond this region could have involuntary repetition, prolongation, or arrest of speech sounds in addition to the core features of TCMA. (2) Lesions of the deep frontal white matter of the language-dominant hemisphere including the periventricular white matter also produce a variant of TCMA (Mega & Alexander, 1994). In the initial phase of TCMA in these lesions, there may be mutism. Other symptoms in addition to the core features of TCMA include dysarthria if the motor cortex (M1) or descending motor pathways are involved (Freedman et al., 1984). Larger lesions expanding into the white matter and surrounding cortex from the frontal operculum can lead to transient agrammatism acutely, and/or phonemic paraphasias, but with recovery the agrammatism clears (Alexander, 2002). (3) Lesions involving the region around the SMA (right or left) are sometimes seen as causing TCMA, except that after extensive recovery, these individuals may simply be unable to speak at length as opposed to having classical aphasia (Alexander & Schmitt, 1980; Freedman et al., 1984). In the paragraphs that follow, we will deal with each of these areas separately. Then we will argue, based on recent studies from our laboratory, that these areas simply constitute different loci within the same system and that the variations in symptoms simply represent involvement of structures adjacent to this system.

According to Alexander (2002), a lesion of pars opercularis and the inferior third of the lateral premotor cortex in the language-dominant hemisphere is sufficient to cause TCMA, albeit with additions to the core symptoms. Although acutely individuals with lesions confined to pars triangularis and pars opercularis in the language-dominant hemisphere may briefly exhibit Broca's aphasia, Mohr and colleagues (1978) showed that the lesions are much larger than that in chronic Broca's aphasia, covering a large extent of the middle cerebral artery distribution. Indeed, based on the lesion and functional imaging literatures, the concept of Broca's region has recently gained traction. Broca's region (or, alternatively, Broca's complex) is thought to be involved in phonological processing, in semantic processing, in syntactic processing, and in language production. In addition to pars triangularis and pars opercularis, which together are considered to be Broca's area, Broca's region includes pars orbitalis, the ventral portion of the lateral premotor cortex, and a portion of the cortex at the boundary of the inferior and middle frontal gyri (Brodmann's area 46). At this time, there appears to be some rough functional division of Broca's region such that the ventral premotor cortex and pars opercularis are involved in phonology, pars orbitalis and pars triangularis are involved in semantic functions, and pars triangularis, pars orbitalis, and Brodmann's area 46 are involved in syntactic functions (Hagoort, 2006). The importance of this division for TCMA will be discussed shortly.

Lesions of the deep frontal white matter of the language-dominant hemisphere are also thought to produce TCMA. The most common site of these lesions is in the white matter anterolateral to the frontal horn of the lateral ventricle, sometimes extending to the opercular cortex, and damage primarily to this site leads mainly to the cardinal symptoms of TCMA (Freedman et al., 1984). Duffau and colleagues (Duffau, Gatignol, Mandonnet, Capelle, & Taillandier, 2008; Duffau, 2012) have shown that intraoperative stimulation of white matter in this area leads to temporary TCMA. They attributed this behavior to stimulation of the subcallosal fasciculus, although fibers from medial frontal cortex to Broca's area are only a few millimeters from the subcallosal fasciculus (see the discussion of Ford, McGregor, Case, Crosson, & White, 2010 below).

Involvement of the medial frontal cortex in akinetic mutism has been known since the early 1950s when Nielsen and Jacobs (1951) and Barris and Schuman (1953) reported cases with large medial frontal lesions. The presence of this syndrome with lesions in this area has since been confirmed (Jonas, 1981; Tijssen, Tavy, Hekster, Bots, & Endtz,

1984). These lesions are rather large, however, and it was difficult to know exactly what portion of the medial frontal cortex was involved in language initiation. As noted by Alexander (2002), akinetic mutism with lesions of this area can evolve into a TCMA-like syndrome with intact repetition and limited language output. Subsequent studies have further narrowed down the critical cortex, at least for word generation. A review by Picard and Strick (1996) indicated that simple language functions involved SMA (the posterior portion of the medial premotor cortex) and that more complex language functions, such as word generation, involved more pre-SMA (the anterior portion of medial premotor cortex), as well as portions of the paracingulate gyrus (supracallosal Brodmann's area 32) beneath it. A subsequent study by Crosson and colleagues (1999) indicated that the critical area for category member generation was in the paracingulate sulcus beneath the pre-SMA when it existed and in the cingulate sulcus when there was no paracingulate sulcus. The paracingulate sulcus, when it exists, runs superior and parallel to the cingulate sulcus and is the dividing line between pre-SMA and supracallosal Brodmann's area 32. It should be noted that the distinction between pre-SMA and SMA was not made at the time that Freedman et al. (1984) studied TCMA or at the time Goldberg (1985) wrote his seminal paper on medial and lateral frontal contributions to language and behavior.

To this point, it would seem that there are three separate sites that can yield TCMA when damaged. It has been proposed that the primary reason for TCMA is any lesion severing connections between medial frontal cortex and anterior perisylvian language cortices (Alexander, 2003). Indeed, if we knew the trajectory of these connections, it might clarify the picture. Ford and colleagues (2010) have used diffusion weighted imaging and probabilistic tractography to image these pathways. They traced pathways from SMA, pre-SMA, medial Brodmann's area 8, and medial Brodmann's area 9 to Broca's area (pars triangularis and pars opercularis) in neurologically normal adults (Figure 10.1). Generally, these fibers descend inferiorly from these medial frontal areas to a point adjacent to the corpus callosum, where they turn more laterally to avoid the corpus callosum, lateral ventricle, and basal ganglia (Figure 10.1a, 10.1b, and 10.1d). They pass over the insula posteriorly, then continue in a lateral direction toward Broca's area. The more anterior portions of these pathways (from Brodmann's area 9; Figure 10.1a and 10.1b) do not have to pass over the insula;

rather, they pass anterior to it. At the point at which the fibers from the pre-SMA turn laterally near the corpus callosum and the frontal horn of the lateral ventricle, they are in close proximity to the subcallosal fasciculus (Figure 10.1d). Consideration of Ford and colleagues' (2010) data suggests an alternative to the "three-area" interpretation for the genesis of TCMA. Instead, we proposed that there is a system consisting of the medial frontal cortex, Broca's area, and the fibers between them, and that a substantial lesion in any one or more of these components will cause TCMA. Indeed, mutism is caused acutely by a lesion in either the medial frontal cortex or the fiber system between the medial frontal and lateral frontal cortices. The symptoms in addition to the

core TCMA symptoms that were mentioned above involving Broca's region (Alexander, 2002) most likely come when the cortex surrounding Broca's area is damaged. For example, temporary agrammatism might be caused by lesion to pars opercularis, ventral premotor cortex, and Brodmann's area 46 (Hagoort, 2006). Thus, an examination of the connections between the medial and lateral frontal cortex suggests a parsimonious explanation for the topography of lesions causing TCMA.

However, it should be noted that there is an alternative explanation for TCMA, that is, damage of dopaminergic pathways ascending from the midbrain may play a role in TCMA. The impetus for this explanation comes primarily from the observation

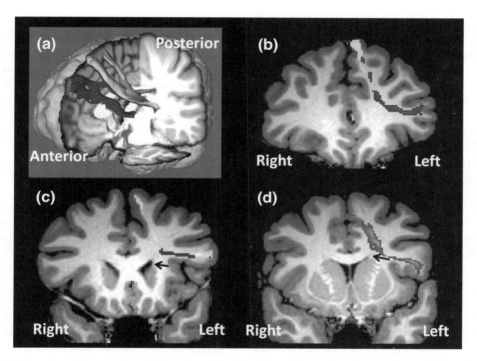

Figure 10.1 Fiber pathways between the medial frontal cortex and Broca's area. Fiber pathways between the medial frontal cortices and Broca's area were traced with probabilistic tractography using FSL in a neurologically normal participant from Ford et al. (2010). These images were created specifically for this chapter to demonstrate the relationship between the fiber pathways and other subcortical and cortical structures. **(a)** Fiber pathways between Broca's area and Brodmann's area 9 (most anterior pathway in this image, blue in color insert), Brodmann's area 8 (the middle pathway in this image, orange in the color insert), and pre-SMA (the most posterior pathway in this image and green in the color insert) are shown in relation to the position of the left caudate nucleus (red). A block consisting of the frontal and superior temporal lobes has been "cut away" so that the course of the pathways between medial frontal cortices and Broca's area can be clearly seen. **(b)** A relatively anterior coronal section demonstrates the fiber pathway between Brodmann's area 9 and Broca's area as it courses inferiorly, laterally, and somewhat posteriorly toward Broca's area. White in this image (orange in the color insert) represents fibers from Brodmann's area 8. **(c)** A coronal section posterior to **(b)** shows fibers from Brodmann's area 8 to Broca's area in white in this image (orange in the color insert); dark gray in this image (blue in the color insert) represents some overlap with fibers from Brodmann's area 9. The black arrow shows the approximate position of the subcallosal fasciculus. Fibers course over the insula to approach Broca's area. **(d)** The pathway shown (green in the color insert) represents fibers from pre-SMA to Broca's area in this coronal section posterior to **(c)**. The black arrow shows the approximate position of the subcallosal fasciculus. Note how closely the pathway from pre-SMA to Broca's area passes to the subcallosal fasciculus at this point. Fibers course over the insula to approach Broca's area.

that dopamine agonists can mitigate the symptoms of TCMA (see Raymer, 2003, for a review). It should be noted that pre-SMA is the area of macaque prefrontal cortex most heavily innervated by ascending dopamine pathways (Williams & Goldman-Rakic, 1993). As we have indicated above, pre-SMA, along with supracallosal Brodmann's area 32, appears to be the medial frontal area of greatest importance for word generation in humans (Crosson et al., 1999). Hence, dopamine activity is linked to the system anatomically implicated in TCMA. It should be noted, however, that the improvement in TCMA symptoms with dopamine agonists, although significant, is incomplete (e.g., Barrett & Eslinger, 2007). The real question is what dopaminergic agonists are accomplishing that allows them to mitigate symptoms of TCMA. Perhaps they increase the efficiency of the remaining medial to lateral frontal pathways, allowing them to compensate to some degree for the damaged portion of these pathways. As Ford and colleagues (2010) have shown, a wide expanse of medial frontal cortex from SMA through medial Brodmann's area 9 sends fibers to Broca's area (pars triangularis and pars opercularis). Hence, it appears likely that some medial frontal fibers remain intact in all but the largest medial frontal lesions. In any event, the distribution of dopamine afferents in the medial frontal cortex suggests that the success of dopamine agonists in mitigating the symptoms in TCMA is linked to the medial frontal portion medial to Broca's area system described above. However, Yang et al. (2007) have shown that as akinetic mutism from bilateral medial frontal lesions abated during the 6 months after a medial frontal infarction, levels of dopamine activity in the basal ganglia (striatum) bilaterally returned from decreased to more normal levels.

Hence, a final observation about TCMA and subcortical lesions should be made. TCMA or TCMA-like symptoms (i.e., limited verbal output with relatively spared repetition and comprehension) also have been reported with thalamic lesions (e.g., Cox & Heilman, 2011). Most frequently, these are ischemic lesions in the paramedian artery territory (e.g., Nicolai & Lazzarino, 1991; Raymer, Moberg, Crosson, Nadeau, & Rothi, 1997). However, these thalamic cases frequently involve prominent semantic paraphasias, which are infrequently described in TCMA. Paramedian infarcts involve large portions of the dorsomedial nucleus, which projects to both the medial and lateral frontal cortices (Goldman-Rakic & Porrino, 1985). Hence, the TCMA-like symptoms in these cases may be related to medial or lateral frontal connectivity, but the

centromedian–parafascicular complex of the intralaminar thalamic nuclei is also in the paramedian territory and projects to the basal ganglia (see below). TCMA (adynamic aphasia) has also been reported in cases of basal ganglia lesion (e.g., Crescentini et al., 2008; Gold et al., 1997). Given the relationship of the frontal lobes to the basal ganglia (Middleton & Strick, 2000), the involvement of the basal ganglia in endo-evoked intention (Heilman, Watson, & Valenstein, 2003), and the return of dopamine activity to more normal levels as symptoms from akinetic mutism abate (Yang et al., 2007), such reports are not too surprising. However, caution must be exercised because these lesions involve surrounding white matter, and fibers pass close to the caudate nucleus on their way from the medial frontal cortex to Broca's area (see Figure 10.1). Furthermore, it should be noted that there is evidence that neither lesions of the left basal ganglia nor Parkinson's disease produce TCMA on a chronic basis, although they do affect a number of complex language functions (Copland, Chenery, & Murdoch, 2000). At the same time, cases of TCMA (dynamic aphasia) have been reported in progressive supranuclear palsy (Robinson et al., 2005, 2006), which involves the basal ganglia (as well as other structures).

Cognitive Neuropsychological Underpinnings

To understand the cognitive underpinnings of TCMA, it is necessary to understand two things: (1) the anatomical nature of the lesions leading to TCMA (described in the section above), and (2) the concept of intention. In 1874, the Russian neuroanatomist Vladimir Alekseyevich Betz made a cogent observation. He noted that from the standpoint of functional organization, the brain is an elaboration of the spinal cord. Specifically, the anterior portion of the spinal cord deals with motor functions and the posterior portion with sensory information. With the brain being more elaborate than the spinal cord, this dichotomy can be conceptualized as follows: the anterior portions of the cerebral cortex (the frontal lobes) are largely devoted to action, and the posterior portions (occipital, temporal, parietal lobes) are largely devoted to perceptual processing.

This observation may seem simple, but it has profound implications for attention systems. In short, there are two broad attention systems: a posterior attention system that governs perceptual processing, and an anterior system that governs action. Hereafter, we shall refer to processes in the posterior system as attention and processes in the anterior system as intention. Attention involves the ability to select one from many competing sensory sources of information for further processing. This definition is similar to that of William James (1890). This selection mechanism is necessary because it keeps the limited capacity of our cognitive systems from being completely overwhelmed with all of the potentially available information they could not possibly process at once. At any moment there are hundreds of stimuli we could potentially process, and attention pares these down to a manageable level.

Because intention is the most relevant system for TCMA, we will concentrate mostly on it. Intention involves the ability to select one potential action among several competing actions for execution. Intention allows us to use our limited capacity for action by prioritizing and initiating actions most relevant to our current goals. Fuster (2003) has referred to this as "executive attention," but it is essentially the same construct as intention. Intention systems deal with the selection, initiation, and continuation of actions, and also with stopping actions and switching to new ones as appropriate. The frontal lobes and basal ganglia are involved in intention (Heilman et al., 2003). However, intention is not entirely a monolithic system. Heilman et al. (2003) have noted an important division in intentional systems regarding those actions that are evoked by endogenous motivations and cognitive systems (endo-evoked intention) and those evoked exogenously by external stimulation (exo-evoked intention).

The constructs of endo- and exo-evoked intention can be applied to language. Indeed, Goldberg (1985) suggested that the lateral frontal cortex is involved in language that is triggered by external contingencies, whereas the medial frontal cortex is more involved in language triggered by internal contingencies. We tested this assumption by varying the amount of internal versus external input that was given in word-generation paradigms during functional magnetic resonance imaging (fMRI) (Crosson et al., 2001). In the most internally evoked paradigm, young neurologically normal participants were given a category (e.g., birds) and asked to generate as many items in that category as possible for several seconds. A paced generation task added some degree of external constraint during a similar time period, and cuing production with an adjective describing only one or a few category members (e.g., "red" for the category of birds) added a greater degree of external constraint. Finally, word repetition was primarily externally driven. SMA activity showed no systematic variation across

tasks, that is, it showed the same extent of activity in unconstrained category member generation as it did in repetition. However, we had previously shown that it was pre-SMA/Brodmann's area 32 that was important in category-member generation (Crosson et al., 1999). Pre-SMA/Brodmann's area 32 showed a monotonic decrease in extent of activity as participants progressed from the most to the least internally evoked activity, consistent with Goldberg's (1985) theory. Of interest is that Broca's area also showed such a monotonic decrease in activity from most to least internally evoked word production, which is not consistent with Goldberg's concept of medial and lateral frontal activity in language. Yet, it is consistent with the idea that pre-SMA/Brodmann's area 32 and Broca's area form a system and is further consistent with the idea that damage in the vicinity of Broca's area would cause TCMA, leaving repetition relatively intact. Activity at the border of Broca's area, that is, along the inferior frontal sulcus, increased monotonically from unconstrained category-member generation, to paced category-member generation, to cued category-member generation, which generally is consistent with Goldberg's (1985) theory. However, there was no activity in this latter area during repetition, indicating that it is not involved with repetition, which can be done primarily on the basis of lexical representations with little semantic input. Finally, our data suggest that endo-evoked intention and exo-evoked intention are better conceptualized as a continuum than a strict dichotomy.

These observations lead us to the following questions: What does the pre-SMA- to-Broca's area system do for language? And how is it relevant to TCMA? We will address these questions by structure, starting with the medial frontal cortex. Cohen and colleagues (e.g., Botvinick, Braver, Barch, Carter, & Cohen, 2001; Botvinick, Cohen, & Carter, 2004; Forster, Carter, Cohen, & Cho, 2011) have advocated that the medial frontal cortex around pre-SMA/Brodmann's area 32 (which they call the anterior cingulate cortex) is involved in monitoring for conflict in competing response pathways and signaling for greater resources in the presence of high conflict. This would confer a role in response selection to the medial frontal cortex, which is an intention construct. However, if this were the sole function of the medial frontal cortex, we would expect merely a failure to adequately monitor potential conflicts in response pathways as a result of medial frontal lesions. Such a failure might lead to an inability to suppress competing responses in high conflict situations because of inadequate conflict monitoring. Returning to the observations of Nielson and Jacobs (1951) and Barris and Schuman (1953) and observations that have followed them (e.g., Jonas, 1981; Tijssen et al., 1984), akinetic mutism is clearly a more profound syndrome than a loss of conflict monitoring. Indeed, the defining symptom is lack of initiation of any behavior, including language. Initiation is also an intention construct. Hence, the medial frontal cortex in general seems to be a critical component of intention systems, and is involved in initiation, especially of internally driven behaviors, including language, as well as playing a role in monitoring conflict in response pathways. Even in the more profound syndrome of akinetic mutism, these individuals may be coaxed to repeat single words, and as noted by Alexander (2002), this mutism can evolve into a TCMA-like syndrome, with sparse language output and intact repetition. Thus, there appears to be a continuum between these two conditions.

The function of the pathways between the medial frontal cortices and Broca's area can be conceptualized as conveying the impetus for the initiation of behavior from medial frontal structures to Broca's area. This would mean that lesions confined to this subcortical white matter should cause a behavior very similar to medial frontal lesions. Indeed, such lesions often cause mutism lasting for days or weeks initially, and this behavior evolves over time into a syndrome described as a classical or pure TCMA, that is, difficulty initiating and continuing spoken output with intact or minimally impaired repetition (Alexander, 2002; Freedman et al., 1984). Although some have questioned whether individuals with medial frontal lesions have aphasia or just reduced output (e.g., Alexander, 2002), this question has not been so prominent for the frontal subcortical white matter lesions. However, a more detailed comparison between symptoms of medial frontal lesions and subcortical white matter lesions would be welcome.

The function of Broca's area in this medial and lateral frontal language production system is an interesting question. As noted above, Broca's area is part of a larger inferior lateral frontal region, Broca's region, which plays a role in semantic, phonological, and syntactic aspects of language. The similar pattern of activity decrease from more internally generated to more externally generated word production (Crosson et al., 2001) appears to be an indication that Broca's area and pre-SMA/Brodmann's area 32 are a part of the same system,

as noted above. Hence, one function, but probably not the only function, of Broca's area seems to be translating the medial frontal impetus to produce language into the phonological, semantic, and syntactic processes necessary to do so. As noted above, there may be agrammatic or other aspects to the language for individuals whose TCMA results from a lesion to Broca's area. This is probably because of the additional language functions of Broca's area or surrounding cortex in Broca's region that is also damaged.

It is also worth considering why individuals with TCMA at times have difficulty in comprehending complex sentences. To this point, we have treated intention and attention as separate constructs, but it is clear that these systems interact. Put simply, what we intend to do affects the things to which we attend. If we are carrying on a conversation, we must attend to what our conversation partner is saying. Hence, disturbances in intention will lead to disturbances in attention. If attention wanes during the perception of more complex sentences because the intention to listen is not maintained, problems in comprehending the sentence will result. However, complex sentence comprehension can also be affected by two other processes. First, if lesions in the lateral frontal structures extend into structures responsible for processing syntax, these individuals as a result may have difficulty in comprehending sentences with complex syntactic structures. Second, difficulties in comprehending complex syntax may be a function of working memory limitations. Such limitations could result from a failure of medial frontal structures to adequately engage lateral frontal mechanisms involved in working memory or even from damage to those lateral frontal structures. Wingfield and Grossman (2006) have suggested that both changes in frontal syntactic processing mechanisms and frontal working memory deficits are involved in difficulty comprehending complex sentences for neurologically normal older adults, and it seems likely that both mechanisms sometimes may be involved in TCMA as well.

Finally, with respect to dopaminergic and thalamic mechanisms and their involvement in TCMA, we have already noted that their involvement may be related to a connection with medial frontal mechanisms. However, it is unclear at the present time what the nature of these mechanisms might be from a cognitive standpoint. Like the medial frontal cortex, the basal ganglia appears to be involved in endo-evoked intention.

Assessment Issues in TCMA

Given the complexity of the cognitive and neural mechanisms of TCMA, assessment of individuals with suspected TCMA should respect the contributions of these left frontal regions. The pattern of TCMA often emerges in individuals who undergo standardized aphasia assessment and demonstrate nonfluent verbal output accompanied by remarkably intact repetition and good auditory comprehension abilities (Goodglass et al., 2001; Kertesz, 2007). To further characterize the nature of the nonfluency in TCMA, which may be suggestive of the neurological site of lesion, additional language testing may need to take place. Tasks that place demands on internally generated intentional elements of verbal expression versus externally driven verbal expression are useful to distinguish the characteristics of TCMA (see Table 10.1).

Beyond standardized aphasia testing, verbal expression should be assessed further in TCMA by using sentence and discourse production tasks that

Table 10.1 Standardized and Nonstandardized Tasks to Implement in Assessment of Individuals with Suspected Transcortical Motor Aphasia (TCMA)

Single Word Generation Tasks:

Semantic category generation (e.g., animals)

Letter category generation (e.g., FAS)

Sentence completion with open contexts (e.g., The man asked the lady if he could . . .)

Sentence Generation Tasks: Define spoken words

Sentence generation to polysemous word (e.g., bank, goal)

Sentence generation to pictured scene—"What would happen next?"

Discourse Generation Tasks:

Conversational discourse

Procedural discourse (e.g., how to change a tire)

Retell a familiar story (e.g., Cinderella, Noah's Ark)

Other Neuropsychological Measures:

Trails

Wisconsin Card Sort

Stroop Test

systematically contrast the nature of input used to generate the verbal production, that is whether through exogenous pictorial or written word stimuli or endogenous internally generated spontaneous verbal searches (Robinson et al., 2005). A number of clinical tasks can be implemented to assess the ability of these individuals to construct grammatically correct sentences, including describing pictured scenes, producing sentences for polysemous words (e.g., bank, step) or word pairs, and defining spoken words (Raymer et al., 2002; Robinson & Cipolotti, 2004). Individuals with TCMA are likely to have no difficulty generating a grammatical utterance given a picture or familiar written word (Robinson & Cipolotti, 2004; Crescentini et al., 2008). Likewise, some persons with TCMA have performed well on the Reporter's Test, in which the clinician moves around colored tokens for the individual to describe the action (Costello & Warrington, 1989; Robinson et al., 1998). They are likely to have tremendous difficulty generating an appropriate utterance in other types of language tasks, however. For example, although the participant in the study by Robinson et al. (2005) was able to describe what was happening in a given picture, he was unable to tell what might happen next for the same picture. Similarly, when individuals with TCMA were given a sentence scenario, they had difficulty producing a sentence about what would be appropriate to say in that scenario (Costello & Warrington, 1989; Crescentini et al., 2008; Robinson et al., 1998). In a task requiring individuals with TCMA to produce two sentences corresponding to the contrasting meanings of polysemous words, participants were likewise impaired in constructing two appropriate sentences (Raymer et al., 2002; Bormann et al., 2008). In clinical tasks, it is necessary to note not only the linguistic quality of the utterances generated, but also the time it takes to initiate the utterances. Raymer et al. (2002) reported that their participant was able to produce correct sentences in 95% of trials when given a written noun or verb, yet many of those sentences took more than 1 minute to generate.

Considerably more difficulty will be evident in discourse level verbal production tasks. Although it is possible for some individuals with TCMA to provide accurate, verbal output when describing a picture or a series of pictures depicting a story (Raymer et al., 2002; Robinson et al., 2005), verbal expression tends to be limited in tasks requiring spontaneous generation of verbal responses with little external prompting, such as when participating in conversational discourse or when asked to provide procedural discourse (e.g., describing how to perform certain activities) (Gold et al., 1997). Thus, a relevant comparison would be performance on the Quantitative Production Analysis (Berndt et al., 2000), comparing the ability to tell the Cinderella story when prompted with a series of story cards, compared to spontaneous telling of the story without cards present. At times, the individual with TCMA may not have sufficient verbal output for the Cinderella story, thus the QPA procedures might be implemented for pictorial descriptions for complex pictures, such as the Cookie Theft (Robinson et al., 2005), or for a story that is more familiar to the person, such as the story of Noah's ark (Raymer et al., 2002). Once a sufficient number of words is sampled, the QPA procedures may be used to analyze the linguistic characteristics and amount of speech. Whereas some linguistic elements may be within normal limits, individuals with TCMA will have a greatly reduced rate of speech (Bormann et al., 2008; Raymer et al., 2002; Robinson et al., 2005).

At this point, a comment about evaluating non-fluency in narrative output or discourse is in order. Some gross attempts to quantify fluency have been made as in the Boston Diagnostic Aphasia Examination (Goodglass et al., 2001) or the Western Aphasia Battery (Kertesz, 2007). Yet even these attempts have involved a degree of subjectivity in rating fluency. Park et al. (2011) developed a method that assessed five aspects of fluency: speech rate, syllable type token ratio, speech productivity, audible struggle, and filler ratio. Three experts (experienced speech pathologists) blind to participant diagnosis rated 61 narrative speech samples elicited by the Cookie Theft picture of the Boston Diagnostic Aphasia Examination. Samples were elicited from individuals with both fluent and nonfluent output, as well as from neurologically normal participants. Use of speech rate, speech productivity, and audible struggle in a regression model classified 95% of the speech samples into the fluent or nonfluent categories used by the raters. This system represents a more quantitative approach to fluency and could be useful in clinical and research evaluations of fluency, including evaluations of TCMA.

Tasks requiring lexical retrieval can also be informative in some individuals with TCMA. Although these individuals are usually accurate in standardized confrontation picture-naming tests (e.g., Boston Naming Test), studies uniformly report considerable impairment in word list generation tasks

(Bormann et al., 2008; Costello & Warrington, 1989; Cox & Heilman, 2011; Crescentini et al., 2008; Raymer et al., 2002; Robinson et al., 1998). Individuals with TCMA have difficulty in word search tasks, whether listing items in a semantic category, such as animals, or in letter fluency tasks, such as providing words beginning with the letter F. Sentence completion can also be difficult for sentences with an unpredictable or open context (e.g., The gentleman asked the lady if he could . . .), as compared to a highly predictable context (e.g., The man parked the car and opened the . . .). In summary, lexical retrieval tasks in which intentional search of the lexicon must take place are particularly effective in revealing difficulties in the person with TCMA.

Finally, because TCMA is associated with damage affecting the frontal lobe, neuropsychological measures that tap into frontal functions can be useful in clinical assessment. Trails A/B, Wisconsin Card Sort, and the Stroop Test all may be impaired in individuals with TCMA (Bormann et al., 2008; Crescentini et al., 2008; Gold et al., 1997; Robinson et al., 1998). In contrast, in a nonverbal design fluency task, unlike verbal fluency, performance may be intact (Bormann et al., 2008). Across standardized and nonstandardized tests, individuals with TCMA will be particularly impaired when internally generated searches of language and cognitive processes are required. The amount of verbal output produced will be limited, if not in accuracy, in the latency to produce the sparse output. These tools then may be useful to implement as outcome measures when individuals with TCMA take part in rehabilitation to improve their verbal expression abilities (Raymer et al., 2002).

Treatment of Verbal Expression in TCMA
Behavioral Treatments

Few experimental studies have examined behavioral treatments specifically to address the verbal production impairments seen in individuals with TCMA. Benson and Ardila (1996) noted that individuals with TCMA often use some kind of motor activity, whether movements of the head, hands, or whole body, to facilitate initiation of verbal utterances. It is this motor facilitation that has been explored as a form of behavioral treatment for the impaired fluency of TCMA and other nonfluent aphasias. Crosson et al. (2007) developed a picture-naming treatment for nonfluent aphasia that involves initiating picture-naming trials with a complex, nonsymbolic left-hand movement.

The complex movement was lifting the lid of a box in the participant's left hemispace with his or her left hand and finding and pushing the correct button on a button device to bring up a picture to name on a computer monitor. If the person named the picture correctly, she or he advanced to the next trial. However, if the person made an error on a trial, she or he repeated the correct response after the clinician while performing a nonsymbolic circular left-hand gesture. The conceptual motivation behind this treatment was that the left-hand movements would activate intention mechanisms in the right hemisphere, which in turn would activate right lateral frontal mechanisms that could either facilitate transfer of language production to the right frontal cortex or facilitate efficiency in right-hemisphere mechanisms already in use and potentially critical for word production. Preliminary case studies (Richards, Singletary, Rothi, Koehler, & Crosson, 2002) indicated that the therapy improved picture-naming performance in three nonfluent aphasia patients. A subsequent phase 1 clinical trial was conducted (Crosson et al., 2007) in which participants received the intentional naming treatment for 5 days per week for 6 weeks for a total of 30 sessions. The comparison treatment was an attention treatment in which the picture to be named was presented 45 degrees to participants' left, but no hand movement was used to initiate trials. Both treatments were administered in a cross-over design to all participants, and order of treatment was counterbalanced. For those with moderate-to-severe chronic naming deficits, both treatments led to improved naming, but the intention treatment (with the left-hand movement) led to faster relearning of words than the attention comparison treatment. Crosson et al. (2007) reasoned that if the treatment would lead to relateralization of word finding, effects would generalize from treated to untreated words. Of the participants with moderate to severe naming deficits, 89% showed significant improvement during this intention treatment and 85% showed generalization of treatment effects to untrained items. For those with profound naming deficits, there was no difference in response to the two treatments, and about half of the participants improved in each treatment. Although the intention underpinnings of the treatment suggest that it could be used in TCMA, the authors did not indicate whether individuals with TCMA were included in their sample.

Raymer et al. (2002) developed a variant of this intention treatment for sentence production and administered it to an individual with TCMA. During training, the participant tapped with his left hand in his left hemispace as he practiced production of sentences for words with multiple meanings (e.g., bank: money, river). In daily probes, percent correct sentences generated and time to produce correct sentences were measured for trained and untrained multiple meaning words. Number of words generated per minute in a control letter fluency task was also measured. Sentence-generation accuracy improved in two trained sets and one untrained set of multiple meaning words when movement was included during treatment, but not when movement was excluded in treatment. Little change was evident in the control letter fluency task. Following training, the participant produced increased numbers of words and well-formed utterances in connected speech samples as well. These findings suggest that incorporating a left-hand intentional movement into treatment can be useful in TCMA.

It is worth asking whether the actual reorganization that occurred in these participants' brain systems supports the original theory behind this treatment. Crosson et al. (2009) used fMRI of word production (category-member generation) in five individuals who received their intention treatment that incorporated the complex left-hand movement to initiate picture-naming trials. The four who improved on this treatment showed no greater right-sided lateralization of lateral frontal activity than age-matched normal controls before treatment. However, these individuals showed a significant increase in right-sided lateralization of lateral frontal activity posttreatment compared to pretreatment and greater lateralization of activity to the right lateral frontal lobe posttreatment than normal controls. Hence, the treatment was successful in relateralizing frontal activity to the right lateral frontal lobe. Given the role of the medial frontal lobe in initiating language, it is worth asking whether medial frontal mechanisms relateralized, and there was no evidence that they did. This finding leaves some doubt as to whether the intention mechanism is relateralizing. At least, the medial frontal component did not seem to change in lateralization. Furthermore, an alternative explanation for the relateralization of lateral frontal activity during word production is that hand movements and language are closely linked (Arbib, 2006) and that the hand movement relateralizes lateral frontal word production mechanisms through the more direct linkage between hand gesture and language.

Further investigation of how this treatment relateralizes frontal mechanisms would be useful, particularly in individuals with TCMA.

In addition to direct behavioral treatment, such as intentional verbal output treatment, compensatory methods may be implemented to promote verbal communication abilities in individuals with TCMA (Raymer, 2003). For example, exploiting the tendency of these persons to be echolalic in conversational interchanges, communication partners can be trained to provide them with a simple phrase that gives the individual a running start (e.g., I was thinking that . . .) to turn on the sentence production system and evoke words to express ideas appropriate to the context. Likewise, individuals with TCMA may be given prepared scripts for common daily communication scenarios to which they can refer and draw upon in the context of conversational interchanges. Although these methods have not been empirically validated systematically, they are commonly used clinically as compensatory strategies to facilitate communication in individuals with TCMA.

Pharmacological Intervention

In stroke-induced aphasia, neurotransmitter pathways feeding from subcortical and brainstem regions to left cortical language regions can be disrupted (Berthier, Pulvermuller, Davila, Casares, & Gutierrez, 2011). Because the nonfluency in TCMA seems to arise in association with reduced dopaminergic input to the left frontal lobe, dopaminergic agents have been explored for their impact on promoting recovery of verbal abilities in some individuals with nonfluent aphasias, including TCMA. The drug that has been examined most frequently is bromocriptine (Raymer, 2003; Berthier et al., 2011). In fact, the first report of the use of bromocriptine by Albert, Bachman, Morgan, and Helm-Estabrooks (1988) was in a person with TCMA.

Several early case studies and small trials of bromocriptine in individuals with nonfluent aphasia, including some with TCMA, reported improvements in latency of verbal responses, reduction in pauses and hesitations in sentence production, and improved initiation of verbal responses (Albert et al., 1988; Gold, Van Dam, & Silliman, 2000; Gupta, Mlcoch, Scolaro, & Moritz, 1995; MacLennan, Nicholas, Morley, & Brookshire, 1991; Raymer et al., 2001; Sabe, Leiguarda, & Starkstein, 1992). When bromocriptine was tested in more rigorous double-blind placebo-controlled investigations, however, the verbal production outcomes were more limited for the persons with nonfluent aphasia (Ashtary, Janghorbani, Chitsaz, Reisi, & Bahrami, 2006; Sabe, Salvarezza, Garcia Cuerva, Leiguarda, & Starkstein, 1995). Berthier et al. (2011) noted that several factors may have influenced the lack of positive outcomes in the more rigorous clinical trials, including variations in dosages that were used and the participant selection criteria for the studies. Raymer (2003) noted that bromocriptine's effects might be more robust in nonfluent TCMA, which occurs due to loss of dopaminergic input to intact frontal language regions, and not in nonfluent Broca's aphasia in which the language-specific cortex is compromised.

Findings were also mixed in two recent double-blind controlled trials in which levodopa was administered as an adjuvant to speech therapy in individuals with aphasia. In one trial, the effects of levodopa + speech therapy were greater than those of a placebo in those with frontal lesions (Seniow, Litwin, Litwin, Lesniak, & Czlonkowska, 2009). In another study, there was no benefit of levodopa as compared to placebo when administered in conjunction with a computerized aphasia treatment for a mixed group of individuals with aphasia (Leemann, Laganaro, Chetelat-Mabillard, & Schnider, 2011). This latter trial would again be subject to the criticism that the participant inclusion criteria were not selective to those for whom the neural mechanisms of aphasia are most appropriate for a dopaminergic effect.

An alternative dopaminergic drug, amantadine, has also been studied in early open-label trials with small numbers of participants with aphasia (Arciniegas, Frey, Anderson, Brousseau, & Harris, 2004). Barrett and Eslinger (2007) reported that amantadine paired with speech therapy led to improvement in a letter category word fluency measure in four individuals with TCMA.

Although some evidence suggests that pharmacological intervention with drugs such as bromocriptine and amantadine may promote aspects of verbal recovery in TCMA, these have been small clinical trials and results have not held up in rigorous clinical trials. Moreover, the adjuvant role that drug treatment may play to enhance the effects of behavioral speech–language treatment alone has not been sufficiently examined in controlled clinical trials (Berthier et al., 2011). This appears to be a direction for future research in the treatment of TCMA. To make this research most fruitful, however, participants need to be carefully selected to represent those individuals with nonfluent aphasia for whom a dopaminergic treatment is a motivated pharmacological intervention, paired with a theoretically motivated behavioral treatment, such as the intentional sentence production treatment reviewed earlier.

References

Albert, M. L., Bachman, D., Morgan, A., & Helm-Estabrooks, N. (1988). Pharmacotherapy of aphasia. *Neurology*, 38, 877–879.

Alexander, M. P. (2002). Disorders of language after frontal lobe injury: Evidence for the neural mechanisms of assembling language. In D. T. Stuss & R. T. Knight (Eds.), *Principles of frontal lobe function* (pp. 159–167). New York, NY: Oxford University Press.

Alexander, M. P. (2003). Aphasia: Clinical and anatomic issues. In T. E. Feinberg & M. J. Farah (Eds.), *Behavioral neurology & neuropsychology* (2nd ed., pp. 147–164). New York, NY: McGraw-Hill.

Alexander, M. P., Benson, D. F., & Stuss, D. T. (1989). Frontal lobes and language. *Brain and Language*, 37, 656–691.

Alexander, M. P., & Schmitt, M. A. (1980). The aphasia syndrome of stroke in the left anterior cerebral artery territory. *Archives of Neurology*, 37, 97–100.

Arbib, M. (2006). Broca's area in system perspective: Language in the context of action oriented perception. In Y. Grodzinsky & K. Amunts (Eds.), *Broca's region* (pp. 153–168). New York, NY: Oxford University Press.

Arciniegas, D. B., Frey, K. L., Anderson, C. A., Brousseau, K. M., & Harris, S. N. (2004). Amantadine for neurobehavioral deficits following delayed post-hypoxic encephalopathy. *Brain Injury*, 18, 1309–1318.

Ashtary, F., Janghorbani, M., Chitsaz, A., Reisi, M., & Bahrami, A. (2006). A randomized, double blind trial of bromocriptine efficacy in nonfluent aphasia after stroke. *Neurology*, 66, 914–916.

Barrett, A. M., & Eslinger, P. J. (2007). Amantadine for adynamic speech: Possible benefit for aphasia? *American Journal of Physical Medicine and Rehabilitation*, 86, 605–612.

Barris, R. W., & Schuman, H. R. (1953). Bilateral anterior cingulate gyrus lesions; syndrome of the anterior cingulate gyri. *Neurology*, 3, 44–52.

Benson, D. F., & Ardila, A. (1996). *Aphasia: A clinical perspective*. New York, NY: Oxford University Press.

Berndt, R. S., Wayland, S., Rochon, E., Saffran, E., & Schwartz, M. (2000). *Quantitative production analysis*. East Sussex, England: Psychology Press.

Berthier, M. L., Pulvermuller, F., Davila, G., Casares, N. G., & Gutierrez, A. (2011). Drug therapy of post-stroke aphasia: A review of current evidence. *Neuropsychology Review*, 21, 302–317.

Betz, V. A. (1874). Anatomischer Nachweis zweier Gehirncentra. *Centralblad fur die Medizinische Wissenschaft*, 12, 578–580, 595–599.

Bormann, T., Wallesch, C.-W., & Blanken, G. (2008). Verbal planning in a case of "dynamic aphasia": An impairment at the level of macroplanning. *Neurocase*, 14, 431–450.

Botvinick, M. M., Braver, T. S., Barch, D. M., Carter, C. S., & Cohen, J. D. (2001). Conflict monitoring and cognitive control. *Psychological Review*, 108, 624–652.

Botvinick, M. M., Cohen, J. D., & Carter, C. S. (2004). Conflict monitoring and anterior cingulate cortex: An update. *Trends in Cognitive Science*, 8, 539–546.

Copland, D. A., Chenery, H. J., & Murdoch, B. E. (2000). Persistent deficits in complex language function following dominant nonthalamic subcortical lesions. *Journal of Medical Speech-Language Pathology*, 8, 1–14.

Costello, A. L., & Warrington, E. K. (1989). Dynamic aphasia: The selective impairment of verbal planning. *Cortex*, 25, 103–114.

Cox, D. E., & Heilman, K. M. (2011). Dynamic-intentional thalamic aphasia: A failure of lexical-semantic self-activation. *Neurocase*, 17, 313–317.

Crescentini, C., Lunardelli, A., Mussoni, A., Zadini, A., & Shallice, T. (2008). A left basal ganglia case of dynamic aphasia or impairment of extra-language cognitive processes? *Neurocase*, 14, 184–203.

Crosson, B., Bacon Moore, A., McGregor, K. M., Chang, Y.-L., Benjamin, M., Gopinath, K., . . . White, K. D. (2009). Regional changes in word-production laterality after a naming treatment designed to produce a rightward shift in frontal activity. *Brain and Language*, 111, 73–85.

Crosson, B., Fabrizio, K. S., Singletary, F., Cato, M. A., Wierenga, C. E., Parkinson, R. B., . . . Rothi, L. J. G. (2007). Treatment of naming in nonfluent aphasia through manipulation of intention and attention: A phase 1 comparison of two novel treatments. *Journal of the International Neuropsychological Society*, 13, 582–594.

Crosson, B., Sadek, J. R., Bobholz, J. A., Gökçay, D., Mohr, C. M., Leonard, C. M., . . . Briggs, R. W. (1999). Activity in the paracingulate and cingulate sulci during word generation: An fMRI study of functional anatomy. *Cerebral Cortex*, 9, 307–316.

Crosson, B., Sadek, J. R., Maron, L., Gökçay, D., Mohr, C. M., Auerbach, E. J., . . . Briggs, R. W. (2001). Relative shift in activity from medial to lateral frontal cortex during internally versus externally guided word generation. *Journal of Cognitive Neuroscience*, 13, 272–283.

Damasio, A. R., & Anderson, S. W. (2003). The frontal lobes. In K. M. Heilman & E. Valenstein (Eds.), *Clinical neuropsychology* (4th ed., pp. 404–446). New York, NY: Oxford University Press.

Duffau, H. (2012). The "frontal syndrome" revisited: Lessons from electrostimulation mapping studies. *Cortex*, 48, 120–131.

Duffau, H., Gatignol, S. T., Mandonnet, E., Capelle, L., & Taillandier, L. (2008). Intraoperative subcortical stimulation mapping of language pathways in a consecutive series of 115 patients with Grade II glioma in the left dominant hemisphere. *Journal of Neurosurgery*, 109, 461–471.

Ford, A., McGregor, K. M., Case, K., Crosson, B., & White, K. D. (2010). Structural connectivity of Broca's area and medial frontal cortex. *NeuroImage*, 52, 1230–1237.

Forster, S. E., Carter, C. S., Cohen, J. D., & Cho, R. Y. (2011). Parametric manipulation of the conflict signal and control-state adaptation. *Journal of Cognitive Neuroscience*, 23, 923–935.

Freedman, M., Alexander, M. P., & Naeser, M. A. (1984). Anatomic basis of transcortical motor aphasia. *Neurology*, 34, 409–417.

Fuster, J. (2003). *Cortex and mind: Unifying cognition*. New York, NY: Oxford University Press.

Gold, M., Nadeau, S. E., Jacobs, D. H., Adair, J. C., Rothi, L. J. G., & Heilman, K. M. (1997). Adynamic aphasia: A transcortical motor aphasia with defective semantic strategy formation. *Brain and Language*, 57, 374–393.

Gold, M., Van Dam, D., & Silliman, E. R. (2000). An open-label trial of bromocriptine in nonfluent aphasia: A qualitative analysis of word storage and retrieval. *Brain and Language*, 74, 141–156.

Goldberg, G. (1985). Supplementary motor area structure and function: Review and hypotheses. *Behavioral and Brain Sciences*, 8, 567–616.

Goldman-Rakic, P. S., & Porrino, L. J. (1985). The primate mediodorsal (MD) nucleus and its projection to the frontal lobe. *Journal of Comparative Neurology*, 242, 535–560.

Goodglass, H., Kaplan, E., & Barresi, B. (2001). *The assessment of aphasia and related disorders* (3rd ed.). Philadelphia, PA: Lippincott Williams & Wilkins.

Gupta, S. R., Mlcoch, A. G., Scolaro, C., & Moritz, T. (1995). Bromocriptine treatment of nonfluent aphasia. *Neurology*, 45, 2170–2173.

Hagoort, P. (2006) On Broca, brain, and binding. In Y. Grodzinsky & K. Amunts (Eds.), *Broca's region* (pp. 242–253). New York, NY: Oxford University Press.

Heilman, K. M., & Scholes, R. (1976). The nature of comprehension errors in Broca's, conduction, and Wernicke's aphasia. *Cortex*, 12, 258–265.

Heilman, K., Watson, R., & Valenstein, E. (2003). Neglect and related disorders. In K. Heilman & E. Valenstein (Eds.), *Clinical neuropsychology* (4th ed., pp. 296–346). New York, NY: Oxford University Press.

James, W. (1890). *Principles of psychology* (Vol. 2). New York, NY: Holt.

Jonas, S. (1981). The supplementary motor region and speech emission. *Journal of Communication Disorders*, 14(5), 349–373.

Kertesz, A. (1999). Language and the frontal lobes. In B. L. Miller & J. L. Cummings (Eds.), *The human frontal lobes* (pp. 261–276). New York, NY: Guilford Press.

Kertesz, A. (2007). *Western aphasia battery-revised*. San Antonio, TX: PsychCorp.

Kumral, E., Bayulkem, G., Evyapan, D., & Yunten, N. (2002). Spectrum of anterior cerebral artery territory infarction: Clinical and MRI findings. *European Journal of Neurology*, 9, 615–624.

Leemann, B., Laganaro, M., Chetelat-Mabillard, D., & Schnider, A. (2011). Crossover trial of subacute computerized aphasia therapy for anomia with the addition of either levodopa or placebo. *Neurorehabilitation and Neural Repair*, 25, 43–47.

Lichtheim, L. (1885). On aphasia. *Brain*, VII, 433–484.

Luria, A. R. (1970). *Traumatic aphasia*. Oxford, England: Mouton.

MacLennan, D. L., Nicholas, L. E., Morley, G. K., & Brookshire, R. H. (1991). The effects of bromocriptine on speech and language functions in a man with transcortical motor aphasia. In T. E. Prescott (Ed.), *Clinical Aphasiology* (Vol. 20, pp. 145–156). Austin, TX: Pro-Ed.

McCarthy, R., & Warrington, E. K. (1984). A two-route model of speech production. Evidence from aphasia. *Brain*, 107, 463–485.

Mega, M. S., & Alexander, M. P. (1994). Subcortical aphasia: The core profile of capsulostriatal infarction. *Neurology*, 44, 1824–1829.

Middleton, F. A., & Strick, P. L. (2000). Basal ganglia and cerebellar loops: Motor and cognitive circuits. *Brain Research Reviews*, 31, 236–250.

Mohr, J. P., Pessin, M. S., Finkelstein, S., Funkenstein, H. H., Duncan, G. W., & Davis, K. R. (1978). Broca aphasia: Pathologic and clinical. *Neurology*, 28, 311–324.

Nicolai, A., & Lazzarino, L. G. (1991). Language disturbances from paramedian thalamic infarcts: A CT method for lesion location. *Rivista di Neurologia*, 61, 86–91.

Nielsen, J. M., & Jacobs, L. L. (1951). Bilateral lesions of the anterior cingulated gyri: Report of a case. *Bulletin of the Los Angeles Neurological Society*, 16, 231–234.

Park, H., Rogalski, Y., Rodriguez, A. D., Zlatar, Z., Benjamin, M., Harnish, S., . . . Reilly, J. (2011). Perceptual cues used by listeners to discriminate fluent from nonfluent narrative discourse. *Aphasiology*, 25, 998–1015.

Pedersen, P. M., Vinter, K., & Olsen, T. S. (2004). Aphasia after stroke: Type, severity and prognosis. The Copenhagen aphasia study. *Cerebrovascular Disease*, 17, 35–43.

Picard, N., & Strick, P. L. (1996) Motor areas of the medial wall: A review of their location and functional activation. *Cerebral Cortex*, 6, 342–353.

Raymer, A. M. (2003). Treatment of adynamia in aphasia. *Frontiers in Bioscience*, 8, s845–s851.

Raymer, A. M., Bandy, D., Schwartz, R. L., Adair, J. C., Williamson, D. J. G., Rothi, L. J. G., & Heilman, K. M. (2001). Effects of bromocriptine in a patient with crossed nonfluent aphasia: A case report. *Archives of Physical Medicine and Rehabilitation*, 82, 139–144.

Raymer, A. M., Moberg, P., Crosson, B., Nadeau, S., & Rothi, L. J. G. (1997). Lexical-semantic deficits in two patients with dominant thalamic infarction. *Neuropsychologia*, 35, 211–219.

Raymer, A. M., Rowland, L., Haley, M., & Crosson, B. (2002). Nonsymbolic movement training to improve sentence generation in transcortical motor aphasia: A case study. *Aphasiology*, 16, 493–506.

Richards, K., Singletary, F., Rothi, L. J. G., Koehler, S., & Crosson, B. (2002). The activation of intentional mechanisms through utilization of nonsymbolic movements in aphasia rehabilitation. *Journal of Rehabilitation Research and Development*, 39, 445–454.

Robinson, G., Blair, J., & Cipolotti, L. (1998). Dynamic aphasia: An inability to select between competing verbal responses? *Brain*, 121, 77–89.

Robinson, G., & Cipolotti, L. (2004). Dynamic aphasia and the generation of language. *Brain and Language*, 91, 49–50.

Robinson, G., Shallice, T., & Cipolotti, L. (2005). A failure of high level verbal response selection in progressive dynamic aphasia. *Cognitive Neuropsychology*, 22, 661–694.

Robinson, G., Shallice, T., & Cipollotti, L. (2006). Dynamic aphasia in progressive supranuclear palsy: A deficit in generating a fluent sequence of novel thought. *Neuropsychologia*, 44, 1344–1360.

Sabe, L., Leiguarda, R., & Starkstein, S. E. (1992). An open-label trial of bromocriptine in nonfluent aphasia. *Neurology*, 42, 1637–1638.

Sabe, L., Salvarezza, F., Garcia Cuerva, A., Leiguarda, R., & Starkstein, S. (1995). A randomized, double-blind, placebo-controlled study of bromocriptine in nonfluent aphasia. *Neurology*, 45, 2272–2274.

Seniow, J., Litwin, M., Litwin, T., Lesniak, M., & Czlonkowska, A. (2009). New approach to the rehabilitation of post-stroke focal cognitive syndrome: Effect of levodopa combined with speech and language therapy on functional recovery from aphasia. *Journal of Neurological Sciences*, 28, 214–218.

Taubner, R. W., Raymer, A. M., & Heilman, K. M. (1999). Frontal-opercular aphasia. *Brain and Language*, 70, 240–261.

Tijssen, C. C., Tavy, D. L., Hekster, R. E., Bots, G. T., & Endtz, L. J. (1984). Aphasia with a left frontal interhemispheric hematoma. *Neurology*, 34, 1261–1264.

Williams, S. M., & Goldman-Rakic, P. S. (1993). Characterization of the dopaminergic innervation of the primate frontal cortex using a dopamine-specific antibody. *Cerebral Cortex*, 3, 199–222.

Wingfield, A., & Grossman, M. (2006). Language and the aging brain: Patterns of neural compensation revealed by functional brain imaging. *Journal of Neurophysiology*, 96, 2830–2839.

Yang, C. P., Huang, W. S., Shih, H. T., Lin, C. Y., Lu, M. K., Kao, C. H., et al. (2007). Diminution of basal ganglia dopaminergic function may play an important role in the generation of akinetic mutism in a patient with anterior cerebral arterial infarct. *Clinical Neurology and Neurosurgery*, 109, 602–606.

Yang, Z. H., Zhao, X. Q., Wang, C. X., Chen, H. Y., & Zhang, Y. M. (2008). Neuroanatomic correlation of the post-stroke aphasias studied with imaging. *Neurological Research*, 30, 356–360.

Mixed Transcortical Aphasia: Repetition without Meaning

Annette Baumgaertner

Abstract

Although mixed transcortical aphasia (MTA) is a rare syndrome, it constitutes an interesting case for modern neuroanatomically driven language models. This is because its existence may be seen as congruent with the assumption of an independently operating "dorsal stream" in language processing. Predicted by the earliest models of language processing in the brain, the syndrome also pushes the boundaries of neurolinguistic model building because its symptoms arise from an interplay between partially preserved linguistic functions and partially disrupted amodal higher-order cognitive control mechanisms. In summarizing 15 case reports of persons with MTA, this chapter provides details about neurobiological underpinnings, performance during standard language assessments, and speech characteristics of persons diagnosed as having MTA. The chapter raises critical issues, such as the question of how to operationalize "spared repetition," and the difficulty of clearly differentiating between volitional repetition and nonvolitional echolalia. Data on the evolution of the syndrome are included, and assessment as well as treatment of MTA are discussed.

Key Words: Echolalia, Controlled processing, Concept, Repetition, Volition, Isolation of the speech area, Language processing, Watershed infarction, Comprehension, Language assessment

Introduction

The syndrome of mixed transcortical aphasia (MTA, or "isolation of the speech area" syndrome) likely constitutes the rarest among the aphasia syndromes, and its practical significance may be low. In theoretical terms, however, it is one of the most interesting syndromes. First, its existence is predicted by the earliest models of language processing in the brain, which in the past years have received empirical support by modern brain imaging techniques. Recent functional imaging studies provide a plausible account of the mechanisms underlying this syndrome; in effect, it is possible to argue that the existence of MTA provides a case for modern neuroanatomically driven models of language processing in the brain. Second, the syndrome of MTA pushes the boundaries of neurolinguistic language processing models, because its symptoms arise from

an interplay between partially preserved core language functions and partially disrupted amodal higher-order cognitive control mechanisms. Both aspects will be discussed in some detail below.

Simply put, the neurolinguistic classification of MTA is made when relatively intact repetition is observed in the presence of poor comprehension ability and, apart from echolalic responses, markedly reduced spontaneous speech. There is some uncertainty about the amount of spared repetition necessary to make a diagnosis of MTA, however, and although most standardized aphasia tests provide cut-off values for the classification of the syndrome, many of the case reports in the literature justify their classification of MTA by the occurrence of a constellation of aphasic symptoms "strongly suggestive" of MTA. Some authors simply use the criterion of "good repetition performance," compared to all other language functions. This circumstance complicates a comparison of the few cases reported in the literature.

Etiologies vary widely. As put by Duffy (2005), in MTA "the left perisylvian language area is relatively spared but is surrounded by widespread areas of infarction or degeneration of the anterior and posterior association cortex, as may occur in widespread border zone strokes, medial frontoparietal infarction in the area of the anterior cerebral artery, carbon monoxide poisoning, or dementia" (p. 360). MTA also has been described in viral disease (i.e., progressive multifocal leukoencephalopathy; Silveri & Colosimo, 1995) and after a drug overdose (Chenery & Murdoch, 1986).

This chapter profits from earlier in-depth case descriptions and overviews by Berthier (1999) and Cimino-Knight, Hollingsworth, and Rothi (2005), who discuss etiology, symptoms, and assessment of MTA, and provide a summary of relevant treatment approaches. Although briefly discussing all of these areas, this chapter focuses on potential neuroanatomical correlates of MTA and their historical basis, as well as the neuropsychological basis of this syndrome.

Syndrome Description and Unique Characteristics

Symptoms

In their spontaneous speech, individuals with MTA show markedly reduced verbal output, which typically is produced without effort and with relatively normal articulation and prosody. Often, spontaneous utterances consist of automatisms or stereotyped speech, such as "oh boy," "hi daddy," or "that's hot." Propositional speech is almost absent. Some persons with MTA have been described as occasionally producing single words, whereas others make no attempts at all at spontaneously producing speech. When spoken to, individuals with MTA typically react by producing echolalic responses, apparently without any awareness. Most of the time, persons with MTA do not write spontaneously; if they do, their writing is distorted and difficult to decipher. (See Table 11.1; also see Appendix A and Appendix B for details of case reports.)

Comprehension of auditory and written verbal material is severely impaired; often there are no signs of comprehension even for yes/no questions or simple spoken commands (e.g., Carota, Annoni, & Marangolo, 2007). In contrast to a markedly reduced verbal output and severely impaired comprehension ability, repetition is remarkably preserved, even though it remains limited in terms of length and complexity, and is often below normal levels. When repeating, individuals with MTA may or may not correct grammatical or semantic errors contained in the model stimuli.

Occasionally, individuals with MTA also can read aloud, but often they do so without showing signs of comprehension (e.g., Bogousslavsky, Regli, & Assal, 1988; Heilman, Tucker, & Valenstein, 1976; Rapcsak, Krupp, Rubens, & Reim, 1990). There are few reports of persons with MTA who were able to write to dictation (Bogousslavsky et al., 1988; Rapcsak et al., 1990, Case 2). However, the written production may be distorted, or they may stop writing after one or two letters. Confrontation naming may occasionally be spared, although most individuals with MTA are not able to name objects. In the few cases of spared naming, the naming response was immediate, and occurred in an automatic fashion (Silveri & Colosimo, 1995; Trojano, Fragassi, Postiglione, & Grossi, 1988).

During testing, individuals with MTA may spontaneously complete overlearned phrases. When presented with the phrase "ask me no questions," a person with MTA responded "I'll tell you no lies" (Geschwind, Quadfasel, & Segarra, 1968). Thus, when prompted with the beginning of an idiom, proverb, or serial speech, some individuals may continue the phrase or series to completion. Also, some persons with MTA are able to sing along. Remarkably, they have been observed to continue singing, with the correct melody and words, even after the model is faded out (Heilman et al., 1976; Geschwind et al., 1968; Trojano et al., 1988).

Frequency of Occurrence

More often than not, the classification of "mixed transcortical aphasia" appears to have been based on the circumstantial observation that in the presence of reduced spontaneous speech output and poor comprehension, repetition is relatively spared. Case reports rarely specify the criteria according to which MTA was classified [but see Berthier et al., 1991, who applied the classification criteria provided by the Western Aphasia Battery (WAB-Revised, Kertesz, 2007)].

Leaving aside this potential constraint, published data suggest that MTA is a rare syndrome. Among 270 patients with acute first stroke, only 1% (i.e., four patients) were diagnosed on the WAB as presenting with MTA; on repeated aphasia assessment 1 year after stroke, none of the 112 persons with aphasia showed MTA (Pedersen, Vinter, &

Table 11.1 Mixed Transcortical Aphasia: Performance on Language Assessments (+ = Preserved; − = Impaired; n/a = Not Reported)

Author/s, YOP	Spontaneous Speech	Spontaneous Writing	Repetition	Writing (to Dictation)	Confrontation Naming	Reading Aloud	Comprehension
Bogousslavsky et al., 1988							
Case 1	Markedly reduced, no sentences with >3 words	− only own name	+ fully preserved; phonemes and sentences with up to 10 words	+ rare letter omissions	− (semantic paraphasias)	+	− severely disturbed
Case 2	Isolated words	−	+ for short items (phonemes, words, sentences); in words with >5 phonemes and sentences with >5 words, only the last part is repeated	+ up to 5-word sentences	− or semantic paraphasias	+ slowed, no comprehension	−
Case 3	No sentences of >4 words, meaningless	−	+ for isolated phonemes or words or "sequences (3–8 items)"	+	− or semantic paraphasias	+ even texts, without comprehension	− only simple commands such as "Close your eyes"
Case 4	None	−	+ for series of up to 5 phonemes or words; with longer series, only 4 or 5 last items repeated	+	− or semantic paraphasias ("elephant" for watch)	+ but only with strong stimulation, without comprehension	− only simple commands
Carota et al., 2007	Completely abolished, no attempts to communicate; echolalic responses almost every time someone spoke to him	− distorted by nonsense graphic perseverations	+ words and short sentences, no comprehension	− distorted by nonsense graphic perseverations	− "compromised"	+ without comprehension	− no signs of comprehension for simple commands, yes/ no questions, contextual cues in conversational speech; no gesture comprehension
Chenery and Murdoch, 1986	"Very limited", occurring mostly in response to questions; few requests (e.g., "take me back"); nonfluent, restricted to <4 words	−	+ length of sentences that could be repeated successfully limited to 6–7 words; generally below normal	− severely impaired	− seriously impaired	− impaired; some letters (e.g., L) and words (such as "duck" or "pig") could be read, but not sentences	− could follow simple commands such as "Close your eyes"; unable to answer with yes/no to stimuli such as "Judy was pulled by Sue – was Sue pulled?"

(continued)

Table 11.1 Continued

Author/s, YOP	Spontaneous Speech	Spontaneous Writing	Repetition	Writing (to Dictation)	Confrontation Naming	Reading Aloud	Comprehension
Geschwind et al., 1968	Limited to stereotyped phrases or few words that are perseverated ("hi daddy," "mother," "dirty bastard"), and unrecognizable words; no propositional speech	–	+ repeated questions over and over again	n/a	n/a	n/a	– no evidence of comprehension
Grossi et al., 1991							
Case 1 (see Trojano et al., 1988)							
Case 2	"Few automatic profanities"	–	+ with relatively few articulatory and paraphasic errors, correct for 33% of words and 17% of nonwords	–	–	–	– not even simple spoken commands
Heilman et al., 1976	"Patient usually did not speak unless spoken to"; attempts to speak spontaneously result in incomplete phrases such as "the one," "that the," "but the," "it's about to"; no concrete nouns or verbs, phrases of 3–4 words	n/a	"Excellent," sentences of various complexity, up to 5 words (as judged by example given)	– poor, patient would write one or two letters, then stop	+ "spontaneously," when objects were held before the patient	+ without comprehension	Severely impaired
Maeshima et al., 1996	Markedly reduced	–	+ phonemes and short sentences (5–6 words)	–	–	– (unclear whether aloud or silent)	–
Maeshima et al., 2002	Remarkably reduced; "little of his own volition"	–	+ phonemes and short sentences of 4–5 words	–	–	+	–

McFarling et al., 1982							
Case 1	Little or no spontaneous speech; either no response to questions or monosyllabic words or short phrases	n/a	+ words, phrases, and sentences containing up to 9 words "without difficulty"	n/a	– impaired	n/a	Fluctuating, from almost total loss to brief periods of near normal performance
Pulvermüller and Schönle, 1993	–	–	+ for single words, pronounceable pseudowords, and phrases and sentences of 5–7 words	–	–	–	50/50 on TT, lexical decision correct on 112/120 written words
Rapcsak et al., 1990							
Case 1	Initially recurring utterances; after 4 days, spontaneous speech still "virtually absent"	n/a	+ words and sentences	n/a	– (4 of first 30 items of BNT)	+ "without evidence of comprehension"	– severely impaired even for single words
Case 2	propositional speech "virtually absent"	–	+ words, sentences, meaningless utterances	+ several words, no indication of comprehension	– occasionally, a few items on BNT can be correctly named; however, patient would soon start to perseverate	+ words and sentences, no indication of comprehension	– severely impaired even for single words, but could follow axial commands
Ross, 1980	"Exceedingly nonfluent"; restricted to single words except when producing echolalic response	n/a	Words, phrases, full sentences, such as "no ifs, ands, or buts"	–	– erratic responses, even in forced choice tasks or after tactile presentation	+ "fair," but without comprehension	+ for simple commands such as "point to the window," but impaired for more complex commands such as "point to the entrance to this room"

(continued)

Table 11.1 Continued

Author/s, YOP	Spontaneous Speech	Spontaneous Writing	Repetition	Writing (to Dictation)	Confrontation Naming	Reading Aloud	Comprehension
Silveri and Colosimo, 1995	Virtually absent (except for echolalia); markedly nonfluent; occasionally short spontaneous utterances ("give me some bread," "that's hot")	–	+ for words, nonwords, and sentences of 4–5 words	–	+ immediate response, apparently compulsory	–	– word–picture verification possible
Speedie et al., 1984							
Case 1	Initially effortful; 2 months p.o. "almost mute"	n/a	+ relatively preserved for phrases and sentences; no comprehension	n/a	– moderately impaired for objects, body parts, colors	n/a	– poor; could obey simple commands; could follow all but complicated tasks with nonverbal cues
Case 2	Greatly reduced; primarily a few short phrases (e.g., "oh boy")	–	+ relatively preserved for phrases and sentences; no comprehension	–	– poor for objects, body parts, colors	–	– simple one-step commands; responded to simple questions with gestures and occasional words
Trojano et al., 1988	Few automatic expressions, otherwise "only repetition"	Few words, difficult to decipher, which were produced automatically; "mamma," "casa"	+ but only words, never whole sentences	–	– patient "spontaneously and automatically named the first figure shown"	–	No comprehension for verbal material; some gesture comprehension

Olsen, 2004). Of 114 patients with acute (i.e., less than 2 months postonset) infarction or intracerebral hemorrhage, 4.4% (i.e., four patients) were classified as having MTA using the WAB criteria (Berthier et al., 1991). Of 211 patients with a contiguous vascular lesion in the middle cerebral artery (MCA) territory examined within the first 6 months after symptom onset, only 1.4% (i.e., three of the patients) presented with mixed transcortical aphasia using the operational criteria of the Aachen Aphasia Test (Willmes & Poeck, 1993). Similar percentages, namely 8% of 119 patients with aphasia in the acute stage after stroke who were screened with a Swedish adaptation of the WAB, were found to present with "mixed nonfluent" aphasia (Laska, Hellblom, Murray, Kahan, & Von Arbin, 2001), the authors' description for types of aphasia that did not fit the major nonfluent aphasia syndrome categories of Broca's and global aphasia, and that may or may not have subsumed individuals with MTA.

Terminology and the Emergence of the "Concept"

At the heart of the first models describing the speech mechanism was the "reflex arc," a pathway for routing speech in and out of the brain via two centers: one contained the acoustic images of words, one contained their motor images, and a connection between the two centers served to strengthen the association between acoustic and motor images during speech development (Wernicke, 1874; Lichtheim, 1885a) (see Chapter 2 for an overview). The reflex arc was thought to enable the imitation of words that both Wernicke (1874) and Lichtheim (1885a) believed was the defining mechanism of language acquisition. As Wernicke stated, "the pathway a-a_1-b is most critical of all for speech development because it provides the means by which the child learns speech. The major task of a child in speech acquisition is mimicry of the spoken word. . . . The word is essentially a reproduction of the auditory image" (Keyser, 1994, p. 76). Wernicke "envisaged that incoming sounds were conveyed via the acoustic nerve (a) to the centre for acoustic images located in the cortex of the posterior temporal lobe (a_1). This sensory centre was connected by major subcortical fibre tracts to the centre for motor images located in the inferior frontal region (b) and its efferent pathways concerned with speech (b_1)" (Berthier, 1999, p. 2). Interestingly, Wernicke's diagram depicts a strictly sensorimotor pathway; the elaboration of word meanings occurs elsewhere in the brain, via an "association system" that bonds together the images employed for speech, and the "memory images" that are generated in or near the primary sensory areas by the feel, smell, or sound of an object (such as, for example, a bell). According to Wernicke, damage to area "a_1," the center for acoustic images, would result in a loss of object names; the individual would no longer be able to repeat because the "acoustic imagery" was lost. In addition, because the association with other sensory regions would be disrupted by damage to center "a_1," the person would no longer be able to comprehend spoken words—the words could be heard, but the sounds would be meaningless. Importantly, Wernicke noted that although center "a_1" may be damaged, the concepts themselves may still be fully preserved. This is because in most cases, it is the sensory memory images that are pivotal to the concepts of objects, whereas the acoustic images of the objects' names are of secondary importance (Wernicke, 1874; see also Keyser, 1994).

Whereas Wernicke's (1874) first speech processing model consisted of a basic sensorimotor pathway (i.e., the "reflex arc" proper), his contemporaries who studied the mechanisms leading to aphasia put forward illustrative diagrams that specifically incorporated a component dedicated to processing the concepts associated with the word forms. Three years before Wernicke published his 1874 treatise, Baginsky (1871) proposed a first schematic diagram of language centers and their connections. Apart from three centers for sound perception, sound memory, and coordinated movements, this diagram specified a "main centre" for "concept construction," "to which the 'memory centres' of all sensory nerves send their fibres" and that "can form concepts by connecting the separate sensory impressions" (Eling, 2005, p. 305; see also Boller, 1978). This notion was espoused by Kussmaul (1877), whose diagram of the centers and pathways for language incorporated a central node "I" for the "ideagenic" or "concept centre." This center represented the entirety of cortical cell assemblies in which concepts are created by the influx of sensory impressions. Still a few years later, Lichtheim (1885a), who was strongly influenced by the work of Wernicke (1874), incorporated parts of "the excellent work of Kussmaul" (p. 206), such as center "B" ("B" for *Begriff [German]* = concept), the "generative site for concepts," into his model of the connections and innervation pathways supporting language. Lichtheim (1885b) noted that the "concept centre" B, in contrast to the relatively well localizable centers "A" and "M," cannot be localized in a specific anatomical site, but instead can be conceptualized "to result from the combined action of the whole sensory sphere" (p. 477).

The conceptual separation of a (more or less localizable) "concept centre" from the "reflex arc" proper mediating the most elemental language functions had important ramifications for the development of language processing models. First, given that meaning is elaborated in areas outside of the "reflex arc" proper, the function of the arc itself may be presumed to subserve more automatic language functions. As Berthier (1999) put it, "while Lichtheim accepted that the 'reflex arc' created by Wernicke was sufficient for simple language repetition and monitoring correct speech, he was convinced that other brain areas had to be used when less automatic aspects such as volition and intelligence are incorporated into language function" (p. 4). Second, it enabled Lichtheim (1885a) to predict several new forms of aphasia. These new forms differed from the three forms already predicted by Wernicke's (1874) model in that language production or language comprehension could be selectively impaired while repetition was basically spared. Thus, Lichtheim (1885a) predicted that a disruption of the pathway linking the concept center "B" to the center containing the motor images would result in a "loss of volitional speech and writing with preserved understanding of spoken and written language as well as . . . repetition" (Berthier, 1999, p. 6); this syndrome was termed by Lichtheim (1885a) "centrale Leitungsaphasie" (p. 256) or "inner-commissural aphasia" (Berthier, 1999). A disruption of the pathway connecting the center containing the acoustic images with concept center "B" would lead to a "sensory aphasia with fluent paraphasic speech, echolalia, and impaired understanding of spoken and written language" (Berthier 1999, p. 7), a form of aphasia termed "centrale Leitungssprachtaubheit" (Lichtheim, 1885a, p. 256), or "inner-commissural word-deafness" (Berthier, 1999). Because both forms of "inner-commissural" disruption would leave the reflex arc proper intact, Lichtheim (1885a) predicted that repetition should be spared. In addition, if the commissural disruption affected the pathway between the center for auditory images and the concept center, repetition should proceed without any comprehension of what is being repeated. Lichtheim (1885a) also argued that both pathways leading to and from concept center "B" may be disrupted simultaneously, leading to a syndrome in which comprehension and spontaneous speech are markedly reduced while repetition (without

processing meaning) should be spared. However, Lichtheim (1885a) cautioned that his prediction of the existence of "combination forms" of aphasia was hypothetical. He himself had not yet encountered a patient with such a "combination form," and potentially illuminating case reports by his contemporaries (for example, by Kussmaul, 1877) were considered to be "fragmentary" by Lichtheim (1885a, p. 244).

In promptly commenting on Lichtheim's (1885a) proposal, Wernicke (1885/1886) acknowledged Lichtheim's "great astuteness" in further developing his (Wernicke's) model, and adopted Lichtheim's (1885a) model, including a concept center, which predicted seven different forms of aphasia (leaving aside potential "combination forms" resulting from concurrent disruptions of the various pathways). He rejected the terminology proposed by Lichtheim (1885a), however, and instead suggested the terms "cortical" aphasia (to describe aphasias resulting from lesions to the centers for auditory and motor images), "subcortical" aphasia to describe damage to the peripheral afferent (leading into the center for auditory images) and efferent (leading out of the center for motor images) pathways, and "transcortical" aphasia, to denote disruptions to pathways connecting the centers for auditory and motor images with the concept center "B."

According to Berthier (1999), Hübner (1889) was the first to publish an account of a syndrome combining the motor and sensory varieties of transcortical aphasia. Goldstein (1917) expanded on this concept and coined the term "mixed transcortical aphasia" to describe a syndrome characterized by "paucity of speech and severe comprehension deficits with excellent preservation of repetition" (Geschwind et al., 1968, p. 327). This syndrome, also called "isolation of the speech area" by Goldstein (1917; see also Geschwind et al., 1968), was thought to result from a disconnection of the classical speech region (i.e., Broca's area, Wernicke's area, as well as the pathways connecting the two) from posterior parietal association cortex outside of the central speech region, the "concept fields" or "ideational fields" (in German: Begriffsfelder). As described by Geschwind and colleagues (1968) in their case report, "the patient can repeat because of the intactness of the speech areas, but does not comprehend because Wernicke's area cannot arouse associations in other parts of the brain" (p. 328). Another association area, the "frontal ideational field," lying anteriorly to Broca's area, was considered to provide the impetus for spontaneous speech.

A lesion of the frontal ideational field would result in a loss of volitional spontaneous speech, together with an increase in the degree of immediate, uninhibited repetition (i.e., echolalia; Goldstein, 1917; Geschwind et al., 1968). Although it has undergone substantial modification, the basic premise of this notion still holds more or less, as will be shown in the following sections.

Neuroanatomical Correlates of the Syndrome

Although MTA is a rare syndrome, its existence was predicted in the earliest neuroanatomical models of speech processing (e.g., Lichtheim, 1885a). Current studies using structural and functional brain imaging techniques have lent substantial plausibility to the early assumptions regarding the neuroanatomical basis of MTA.

Among the explanations that have been forwarded for the striking symptom of spared repetition in the presence of otherwise markedly reduced language function in MTA, Goldstein's (1917) account of an "isolation of the speech area" may be the most prominent (Bogousslavsky et al., 1988; Geschwind et al., 1968; Goldstein, 1917, 1948; Heilman et al., 1976; Maeshima et al., 1996; Speedie, Coslett, & Heilman, 1984). Goldstein (1917, 1948) "posited that the anatomical region of the left hemisphere that mediated the elementary expressive and receptive components of language, although separated from other brain areas (isolation of the speech area), was incompletely or not damaged at all and could be utilized to subserve language repetition even in the absence of spontaneous speech, auditory comprehension, or both" (p. 120; Berthier, 1999). According to Goldstein (1917, 1948), a syndrome of MTA may arise when core perisylvian language regions are disconnected from or unable to communicate with "peripheral parts of the brain important for nonlanguage mental processes" (p. 120; Berthier, 1999), mental processes such as the volitional impulse to speak, or the ability to infer the meaning of auditorily presented words and sentences. As Geschwind et al. (1968) pointed out, Goldstein's notion of the mechanism underlying MTA builds upon the less elaborate model by Lichtheim (1885a), who "thought that the transcortical aphasias were due to lesions between the motor or sensory speech areas and those parts of the brain important for non-language mental functions" (p. 329). Thus, just as had been proposed by Lichtheim (1885a), the "isolation of the speech area" account attributes the preserved repetition

ability in MTA to a lesion that spares the "reflex arc" proper, leaving intact only its bare and "slavish" (Compston, 2006, p. 1347) information transfer activities via perisylvian posterior superior temporal and posterior inferior frontal cortex, the subcortical fiber tracts connecting these two cortical areas, and their respective afferent and efferent nervous pathways (e.g., Wise et al., 2001).

In the literature, various etiologies have resulted in a condition described as "isolation of the speech area." Geschwind and colleagues (1968) presented a case of a patient who developed MTA after experiencing anoxia due to carbon monoxide poisoning. Autopsy revealed widespread bilateral cortical and subcortical necrosis with selective sparing of the opercular perisylvian cortex of the frontal, parietal, and temporal regions including the insula, the hippocampus and surrounding structures, and the occipital lobes, essentially cutting off the "classic" perisylvian language areas and their connection from the rest of the brain (except for hippocampal structures). The authors noted that perisylvian regions were better preserved in the left than in the right hemisphere. Other cases of MTA described in the literature as representing a pattern of "isolation of the speech area" are suggestive of (watershed) infarction due to hemodynamic failure, sometimes accompanied by a second embolic cortical infarction due to internal carotid artery occlusion (Bogousslavsky et al., 1988; Heilman et al., 1976; Speedie et al., 1984, case 1). In cases with focal infarction resulting in partial anatomic "isolation" of the speech area (e.g., Maeshima et al., 1996, 2002; Speedie et al., 1984, case 2; Rapcsak et al., 1990), the symptom cluster typical of MTA may have been caused by concomitant widespread hypoperfusion sparing the perisylvian region as evidenced by SPECT scans, leading to a "functional isolation" of the core language region (Maeshima et al., 1996, 2002; Rapcsak et al., 1990).

However, MTA has also been described after infarction restricted to subcortical areas (Berthier et al., 1991; McFarling, Rothi, & Heilman, 1982; Nagaratnam, McNeil, & Gilhotra, 1999; Nagaratnam & Gilhotra, 1998), as in an individual with a left thalamic lesion (McFarling et al., 1982, case 1). The authors pointed out that due to the close connections between thalamic regions and dorsolateral and medial frontal lobe regions, aphasic disorders following thalamic infarctions may closely resemble those that typically result from lesions in cortical areas to which the thalamic nuclei project. Among many other sources of supportive evidence, this interpretation is bolstered by a comprehensive review of aphasia after left subcortical lesions (Demonet, Puel, Celsis, & Cardebat, 1991). In their review, Demonet et al. (1991) concluded that "thalamic lesions are typically characterized by an aphasia with aspontaneity and lexico-semantic disorders, as well as by a rCBF pattern with a frontal and retrorolandic hypoperfusion and normal rCBF in the Sylvian region" (p. 337), a neuropathological pattern that may, under certain circumstances, result in transcortical aphasia with preserved repetition ability.

While the above reports attribute intact repetition in MTA to the spared function of the left perisylvian language areas that are disconnected from brain areas involved in comprehension and propositional speech, several case reports of individuals presenting with symptoms characteristic of MTA after extensive infarction of the MCA territory in the left hemisphere, including the perisylvian region, have led to the proposal that intact repetition is mediated by the unaffected right hemisphere (Berthier et al., 1991; Grossi et al., 1991; Pulvermüller & Schönle, 1993). Direct evidence consistent with an involvement of the right hemisphere in repetition comes from a case of a right-handed woman who developed the classic symptoms of MTA after a left frontal infarction, damaging Broca's area, premotor and prefrontal regions, and the lower aspect of the precentral gyrus (Rapcsak et al., 1990, case 1). The woman's severely impaired comprehension ability was explained by an area of low perfusion in the left parietal convexity. Four weeks postonset, a second stroke affecting the right frontoparietal areas in the MCA territory completely abolished her ability to repeat word and sentence stimuli, suggesting that her previously spared repetition ability must have been mediated by the right hemisphere. This report is somewhat qualified, however, by the fact that transient deactivation of the left hemisphere by the WADA test about 4 weeks postonset led to a functional disruption in repetition performance in a right-handed individual with an infarct in the left frontal and parietooccipital regions (Maeshima et al., 2002). For about 5 minutes following the injection, the patient was not able to repeat, before he recovered his repetition ability. Apparently, in this individual, left hemisphere structures were involved in repetition, which was disabled during the WADA procedure. An important difference between these two cases, however, is the fact that in the case report of Rapcsak et al. (1990), the right hemisphere may have been able to gradually adapt to the loss of the left frontal areas involved in repetition by shifting the repetition function to the right hemisphere, whereas WADA testing does not allow an observation of dynamic adaptive changes in the brain due to the short duration of the (functional) disruption. This explanation seems plausible as a longitudinal functional imaging study of individuals recovering from aphasia after left hemispheric infarction has demonstrated a fast and dynamic recruitment of right hemispheric areas within a few days poststroke which correlated with functional improvement (Saur et al., 2006). The woman described by Rapcsak et al. (1990) initially was unable to repeat and did not show echolalia; this ability developed 4 days poststroke, perhaps indicating a shift of function into the right hemispheric homologous perisylvian language areas.

Leaving aside for the moment the question of whether repetition function in MTA is governed by the left or, in the case of left perisylvian damage, the right hemisphere, brain imaging studies in healthy participants have provided further support consistent with Wernicke's (1874) and Lichtheim's (1885a) original assumption of a "reflex arc" subserving repetition. Functional imaging studies examining areas of increased regional metabolism during overt repetition have congruently demonstrated the involvement of a perisylvian network of areas, in particular the posterior superior temporal and posterior inferior frontal areas, as well as the primary motor and sensory cortices (Ohyama et al., 1996; Peschke, Ziegler, Kappes, & Baumgaertner, 2009; Saur et al., 2008; Shuster & Lemieux, 2005; Warren, Wise, & Warren, 2005; see also Hickok, 2009). Perisylvian areas were activated in a "shadowing" paradigm in which participants repeated meaningless syllable strings as quickly as possible, often while model stimuli were still playing (Peschke et al., 2009). Behavioral analyses showed that participants successfully performed the task, as both error rates (i.e., 86% on average; a high accuracy rate given the ambient noise in the scanner environment) and latencies, measured from stimulus onset, were low (i.e., on average 485 ms). Peschke and colleagues' (2009) finding of an involvement of the perisylvian areas during fast repetition, which should be relatively free from verbal working memory demands because it does not require any explicit phonological processing, concurs with Lichtheim's (1885a) original presumption that the engagement of the reflex arc can occur rather automatically in a healthy brain, without recourse to semantics and without requiring much cognitive effort. An additional analysis performed by Peschke et al. (2009) revealed that a region located in the posterior superior temporal plane in the posterior aspect of the Sylvian fissure at the temporoparietal boundary was more engaged as response latency increased, suggesting that this perisylvian region halfway between the auditory association and language production areas may be involved in the actual auditory–motor transformation process (because it responded to increasing auditory-to-motor transfer demand). Recently, Saur et al. (2008; see also references therein), using fiber tractography with diffusion-weighted imaging, demonstrated that the auditory association areas in the caudal end of the Sylvian fissure are connected to frontal areas via long-distance association fiber tracts that run in the white matter of the parietal lobe to the premotor cortex. This finding in essence completes the so-called "dorsal pathway" for language, a network of superior temporal, inferior parietal, and inferior frontal cortical and subcortical areas subserving repetition.

In keeping with Lichtheim's original (1885a) proposal, the question is whether the dorsal pathway may be able to operate independently of other brain areas, for example those that mediate higher level language comprehension and semantic integration. A series of functional imaging studies using positron emission tomography (PET) (Blank, Scott, Murphy, Warburton, & Wise, 2002; Scott, Blank, Rosen, & Wise, 2000; Wise et al., 2001; for a review see Scott & Wise, 2004) and functional magnetic resonance imaging (fMRI) (Saur et al., 2008) provide convincing evidence that in fact there exist separable pathways for the lexical–semantic processing of meaningful speech stimuli (i.e., the "ventral stream" in the middle and anterior temporal lobe), and for the sublexical processing of pronounceable speech stimuli (i.e., the "dorsal stream"). When meaningful stimuli are repeated, both streams may participate; however, sublexical processing may proceed on its own in a fast and automatic manner during repetition, as already suggested in the well-known two-route model of speech production (McCarthy & Warrington, 1984). In addition, different neural systems for propositional and nonpropositional speech were identified (Blank et al., 2002). Interestingly, both propositional (i.e., talking about personal experiences such as describing the place where you grew up) and nonpropositional speech (i.e., counting or reciting nursery rhymes) commonly activated perisylvian speech areas in the primary motor cortex and lateral parts of the superior temporal sulci bilaterally, as well as the most posterior part of the supratemporal plane (in the depths of the Sylvian sulcus), in the posterior inferior frontal gyrus, and the anterior insula in the left hemisphere; areas described as a "lower-order system" by Blank et al. (2002). In contrast, a widely distributed, predominantly left-lateralized, extrasylvian network of areas became active during propositional speech, including the dorsal superior frontal gyrus, the ventrolateral temporal cortex, the posterior cingulate cortex, and the angular gyrus bilaterally. Apparently, normal communicative speech relies on a number of left hemisphere regions remote from the core perisylvian regions of Broca's and Wernicke's areas (Blank et al., 2002).

Although fast and effortless repetition appears to rely preferably on left hemisphere perisylvian structures (e.g., Hickok, 2009; Scott & Wise, 2004; Warren et al., 2005), right hemisphere perisylvian structures may be able to participate in or even take over repetition function when much of the left hemisphere is damaged (Ohyama et al., 1996), a notion already forwarded by Goldstein (1917). It is noteworthy, however, that most of the individuals with MTA who were reported in the literature as "repeating with their right hemisphere" due to large infarctions of the left hemisphere including the perisylvian area showed a somewhat poorer repetition performance than those with MTA after partial or no damage of the left perisylvian areas (e.g., Berthier et al., 1991, case 8, whose performance lay at about 50% correct; Grossi et al., 1991, whose case 2 could repeat only 33% of the words and only 16% of the nonword stimuli; Trojano et al., 1988, whose case could repeat words but not whole sentences; but see Pulvermüller & Schönle, 1993, whose participant suffered a large stroke resulting in widespread damage in the left perisylvian areas and was able to repeat words, pseudowords, and sentences of five to seven words).

Cognitive Neuropsychological Underpinnings

Apart from displaying classic aphasic symptoms such as impaired comprehension ability and reduced verbal output interspersed with automatisms and stereotyped speech, the syndrome of MTA is characterized to a large degree by nonlinguistic higher-order cognitive deficits such as nonvolitional or even compulsory verbal behavior. Potential underlying mechanisms for these symptoms will be discussed after examining in more detail the function considered spared in MTA, namely repetition.

Spared Repetition

In mixed transcortical aphasia, repetition typically occurs without access to the meaning of what is being repeated. As detailed earlier, spared repetition in MTA may best be explained by a preservation of perisylvian structures of the dorsal stream system, either in the left and/or the right hemisphere, which according to current neuroanatomical models (Hickok, 2009; Peschke et al., 2009; Saur et al., 2008) supports sensorimotor integration for auditory–verbal stimuli. Repetition without comprehension is possible even in aphasia, as demonstrated by a study in which 44 individuals with various lesion sites and aphasic syndromes repeated verbal material of up to eight syllables (Gardner & Winner, 1978). No difference in accuracy was found when the performance of participants with high comprehension scores was compared to those with low comprehension scores, suggesting that "the ability to repeat is relatively unaffected by the ability to comprehend" (Gardner & Winner, 1978, pp. 174–175; see also Berthier et al., 1991). In MTA, repetition usually proceeds without comprehending the meaning of the model utterances. Without hesitation or external signs of reprocessing, these individuals may respond by repeating the question when asked a question, or will fluently repeat sentences that contain mismatches, violations, and semantic or syntactic errors or that are incomplete (e.g., Heilman et al., 1976; Pulvermüller & Schönle, 1993; but see Ross, 1980).

Repetition may be able to proceed independently of comprehension, but it still requires perceptual auditory processing, matching to stored auditory templates, auditory–motor transformation, articulatory planning, and actual execution (e.g., Peschke et al., 2009; Warren et al., 2005; Wise et al., 2001). Each of these processes has been associated with specific neurobiological substrates (for a summary, see Hickok, 2009). Although functional imaging evidence suggests that temporofrontal perisylvian regions may suffice to mediate the repetition of basic word, pseudoword, and sentence stimuli (Hickok, 2009; Peschke et al., 2009; Saur et al., 2008, Fig. S1A), it would be an oversimplification to assume that in MTA the capability to repeat is universally preserved, given the variability in etiology and lesion location. Indeed, there is strong evidence to suggest that in MTA, repetition performance depends on process and stimulus factors such

as relative demands on verbal short-term memory, the degree of volitional control required, and specific linguistic characteristics of the model stimuli. Two individuals with MTA were perfectly able to repeat syntactically simple sentences such as "The boy went to the store" in a neutral tone of voice (Speedie et al., 1984). However, they were not able to imitate variations in affective prosody (such as a happy, sad, or angry tone), but instead continued to apply neutral prosody in nearly all of the sentences, suggesting that the additional application of affective prosody during repetition is not done in an automatic fashion, but instead requires volitional regulation and coordination, which may have been beyond the participants' control. Geschwind et al. (1968) proposed that some persons with echolalia may repeat (or "echo") stimuli in their native language, but may not be able to repeat pseudowords or stimuli in a foreign language. In fact, in an individual with widespread frontoparietotemporal infarction, Trojano et al. (1988; see also Grossi et al., 1991) found less accurate reproduction for pseudowords than for real words matched for length and phonemic complexity, as well as a length effect that was more pronounced for pseudoword stimuli. This finding suggests that with increasing stimulus length, the participant's performance was affected by verbal short-term memory limitations. For the real word, but not the pseudoword stimuli, repetition performance may have been alleviated by drawing on the residual function of the phonological input lexicon. In a similar vein, an individual with MTA after subcortical infarction of the basal ganglia was able to repeat real words and pseudowords; however, accuracy was significantly higher for real word than for pseudoword stimuli (Carota et al., 2007), again suggesting lexical influences on repetition performance.

In the study by Gardner and Winner (1978), individuals with transcortical aphasia showed almost no errors during repetition, regardless of whether stimuli were long or short, concrete or abstract, nouns or prepositions, and real or pseudowords. None of the stimuli exceeded a length of eight syllables, however. In another study, participants with transcortical (motor) aphasia showed near normal performance when asked to repeat single words and high-probability sentences consisting of up to seven words (Ardila & Rosselli, 1992). However, accuracy dropped to 68% correct when low-probability sentences were repeated, suggesting that as stimulus length increased, more redundant and predictable semantic content facilitated repetition performance in the high-probability sentences. In some instances, participants were observed to omit sentence elements in the low-probability condition "to make them more normal and more simpler [*sic*]" (Ardila & Rosselli, 1992, p. 108). This may either indicate short-term memory limitations or reflect unintended, automatic modification toward a more prototypical and more overlearned sentence structure (see the section below, "Automatic Completion and Continuation Phenomena").

These observations may be summarized as follows: repetition is feasible as long as it does not tax the resources of verbal working memory and proceeds in a relatively automated fashion without being influenced by volitional manipulation and control during repeating. If the core perisylvian language areas involved in sensorimotor integration are unaffected, familiar verbal material of normal frequency and up to a certain length may be repeated normally. But with increasing length and grammatical complexity and decreasing frequency and familiarity, taxing executive and verbal working memory functions, repetition performance may decline. This is also demonstrated by the fact that in several case reports of persons with MTA, successful repetition was confined to strings of up to four to five words (Bogousslavsky et al., 1988; Maeshima et al., 2002; Silveri & Colosimo, 1995; Trojano et al., 1988).

Verbal Perseveration

Verbal perseveration is a frequent symptom in MTA. Perseveration as well as echolalia are considered involuntary (i.e., nonvolitional) behaviors that may coexist (Christman, Boutsen, & Buckingham, 2004; Wallesch, 1990). They differ, however, with respect to the source of the stimulus that triggers the behavior. While echolalia is characterized by "an inability to ignore the reproduction of a stimulus that is external to oneself" (Christman et al., 2004, p. 301), in perseveration our own previous productions cannot be inhibited even when context or task demands change. According to Christman et al. (2004), perseverations may be "intentional attempts at fully propositional utterances" (p. 300), which end up as a verbal response that may be repeated over and over again, irrespective of the given context or the nature of the stimulus. The underlying mechanism, according to the authors, may be that the intention to produce a legitimate utterance is translated into a "reflex-like cognitive response" that may be characterized as an expression of "modular cognitive processing which is fast, automatic, cognitively impenetrable, and . . . not readily localizable"

(Christman et al., 2004, p. 300). It was proposed that once a perseveration has been uttered, "the utterance enters into working memory and interferes with the successful retrieval of another word form" (Christman et al., 2004, p. 303, and references therein; see also Wallesch, 1990). Perseverations are symptoms that may be particularly common in aphasia, and may in principle be generated by any lesion site causing aphasia. However, they are often associated with lesions to cortical and/or subcortical anterior motor systems (Christman et al., 2004).

Echolalia and Echo Phenomena

Presumably, some of the successful "repetition" reactions in the various case reports on MTA may represent an involuntary response to external verbal stimuli rather than an expression of volitional and cognitively controlled repetition. Such involuntary, unsolicited repetitions of another person's utterances are termed "echolalia" (e.g., Christman et al., 2004; Duffy, 2005). Geschwind and colleagues (1968), on observing that their participant was not able to produce any propositional speech (except for highly automatized one- or two-word utterances such as "hi daddy" or "dirty bastard"), but promptly responded to external stimulation, reported that the person showed "uninhibited" (p. 328) or "echolalic repetition" (p. 338). Similarly, Heilman et al. (1976) pointed out that their participant occasionally showed echolalia for questions asked during comprehension testing that consisted of up to eight words, making it difficult to clearly distinguish between an echolalic response and repetition performance unaffected by echolalia.

Echolalia may be effortless, automatic, and even compulsive in quality, without comprehending the meaning of an utterance (Duffy, 2005). One example of such an "inevitable" response may be seen in the behavior of an individual with MTA who, when tested for his digit span, "frequently started to repeat the digits before the examiner had finished reading the series" (Heilman et al., 1976, p. 419). Geschwind and colleagues (1968) observed a very pronounced form of echolalia in a person with MTA after carbon monoxide poisoning and extensive bilateral damage, which spared the left (and most of the right) perisylvian cortex. The authors reported that this individual, instead of answering questions, "generally repeated questions in a normal voice without dysarthria" (Geschwind et al., 1968, p. 330). Apparently, the echolalia extended to ambient stimuli, because she sang along with songs or musical commercials that were being played on the radio, or recited prayers together with the priest during religious broadcasts.

In less pronounced forms of echolalia, a response may contain only some of the verbal material of the original utterance, or may undergo modification before production (Christman et al., 2004; Duffy, 2005). For example, Geschwind and colleagues (1968) noted that some individuals may omit the instruction in an echolalic response (i.e., when asked "Say: San Francisco" the response is "San Francisco"), suggesting some residual lexical processing. According to Geschwind et al. (1968), however, this apparent awareness of language rules may be reconciled with the assumption of an isolated speech system that is cut off from those areas important for "non-language mental function" (p. 329) such as the processing of meaning. This is because modifications such as the ones mentioned above, according to Geschwind et al. (1968), are carried out within the confines of the isolated speech area via "purely auditory associations" (p. 339) between temporal and frontal speech areas. Davis, Foldi, Gardner, and Zurif (1978) reported a related finding in a study of repetition of correct sentences and sentences that contained semantic and syntactic violations. They asked whether participants' spontaneous syntactic corrections during repetition reflected potential influences of lexical–semantic processing. Of particular interest were two conditions: grammatically incorrect sentences with violations of semantic selection restriction rules (e.g., "The milk drank the cat") and sentences with minor syntactic deviations (e.g., "The cats drinks milk"). The results showed a dissociation between the two conditions. While most of the semantically deviant sentences were repeated verbatim (or with changes that did not render them semantically more acceptable), the majority of the syntactically deviant sentences were spontaneously corrected during repetition. In addition, participants showed no signs of having noticed any deviance in the sentence stimuli. Davis and colleagues (1978) hypothesized that the spontaneous corrective syntactic changes "reflect the automatic or spontaneous operation of on-line language-processing components" (p. 233), changes apparently made without recourse to semantic information to which individuals with MTA supposedly have no or only limited access.

With respect to the underlying neuropsychological mechanisms giving rise to echolalia secondary to MTA, it has been suggested that echolalia is the expression of the "perisylvian repetition circuitry" (Christman et al., 2004, p. 300) operating in isolation from the wider distributed areas in the brain that in a task-dependent fashion support cognitively controlled and more elaborated language processes. As Duffy (2005) put it, "lesions associated with echolalia often preserve basic input and output circuits for spoken language, thus permitting repetition, but they isolate input and output channels from cognitive processes necessary for comprehension and language formulation" (p. 360). Duffy further noted that "It has been suggested that echolalia reflects an inability to propositionize, in combination with a lowered threshold to react to external stimuli. In contrast to palilalia, in which lower-level motor mechanisms appear disinhibited, echolalia seems more strongly tied to higher-level cognitive deficits" (Duffy, 2005, p. 360). As put by Geschwind and colleagues (1968), "Goldstein [1917] thought that for the production of fully developed echolalia it was necessary to have a lesion of the frontal 'ideational field,' i.e. of those parts of the frontal lobes lying anterior to Broca's area, whose destruction would lead to a loss of spontaneous speech together with a heightened degree of uninhibited repetition" (p. 328). Framed in modern neurobiological terms, "the phenomenon of echolalia ... in frontal lobe disease could be the consequence of autonomous activity of the dorsal pathway in the absence of executive control" (Warren et al., 2005, p. 640).

Compulsory Verbal Behavior Other Than Echolalia

Several case reports suggest that in MTA, an increased readiness to provide a spoken response immediately upon presentation of an (external) cue may hold not only for auditory stimulation (as in echolalia) but also for visual stimulation, as in confrontation naming (e.g., when a picture is shown that the participant is asked to name; Heilman et al., 1976; Silveri & Colosimo, 1995; Trojano et al., 1988). An individual with MTA was said to show "compulsory automatic naming" in that "when single pictures of objects were presented, he immediately named them; when he was requested to point to one of two pictures in a word-picture matching task, he named both of them, pointing at random" (Silveri & Colosimo 1995, p. 4). In a similar case, picture naming was impeded by the fact that the individual "spontaneously and automatically" named the first item shown, and then proceeded to continuously perseverate this word (Trojano et al., 1988, p. 634). When asked "Is this a rose?," an individual with MTA and a widespread lesion including extensive frontal lobe damage responded with "roses are red, violets are blue, sugar is sweet, and so are you." This response suggests that the last word of the question ("rose") triggered an inappropriate response that could not be inhibited and that occurred without self-awareness (Geschwind et al., 1968). As Geschwind and colleagues (1968) put it, "frontal lesions may cause a loss of spontaneous activity although the immediate response to stimulation may be increased" (p. 328).

Automatic Completion and Continuation Phenomena

Some individuals with MTA have been described as able to provide a fitting completion or response to highly familiar phrases. Typically, these completions cannot be produced volitionally, but occur only when prompted by the examiner. An example of such a nonvolitional verbal behavior is the response "Go to sleep" given by a person with MTA after being asked to "Close your eyes" (Geschwind et al., 1968). Several authors point out that singing (with words) is possible (Geschwind et al., 1968; Heilman et al., 1976; Trojano et al., 1988), and that some persons may continue to sing even when the music or the model is faded out. Again, singing is never initiated spontaneously; instead, the person is able to "join in" only when given an external cue such as songs on the radio (Geschwind et al., 1968) or songs sung by the examiner (Heilman et al., 1976; Trojano et al., 1988). Similarly, an individual with MTA reportedly was able to count or recite the alphabet or the days of the week, but only when the examiner started the series (Heilman et al., 1976). Persons with MTA have been described to be able to complete well-learned sentences. For example, when prompted with the beginning of a greeting phrase (i.e., "Buon . . . [= Good]), a person with otherwise severely reduced spontaneous speech responded with the correct completion (i.e., ". . . giorno" [= morning]; Trojano et al., 1988). Heilman et al. (1976) observed a dissociation between sentence completion (which the participant with MTA could not do) and continuation of automated series, such as days of the week (which he could do). Interestingly, Carota et al. (2007) observed the opposite pattern in a person with MTA after a left subcortical infarction. While spontaneous speech was "completely abolished," the individual could complete a few proverbs and well-known phrases. However, he was unable to complete an automatic series (such as counting and reciting the months in the year), suggesting that (automatic) sentence completion uses neural circuits that are different from those engaged by completing automatic series.

Assessment

Cimino-Knight and colleagues (2005) pointed out the need to assess MTA in a systematic fashion, using standardized language examinations that test spontaneous language production, repetition, and comprehension, among other language functions. Standardized test batteries such as the Western Aphasia Battery-Revised (WAB, Kertesz, 2007) or the Aachen Aphasia Test (original language: German; Huber, Poeck, Weniger, & Willmes, 1983) provide taxonomic criteria that enable examiners to differentiate MTA from transcortical sensory, transcortical motor, and global aphasia. In the WAB, for example, classification of the transcortical aphasias is made on the basis of fluency, comprehension, and repetition subtest scores. Thus, because the symptom of spared repetition is also a hallmark feature of transcortical sensory and transcortical motor aphasia, the differential neurolinguistic diagnosis of MTA focuses on the fluency of spontaneous language output (which should be relatively preserved in transcortical sensory aphasia, but reduced in MTA) and comprehension ability (which should be relatively intact in transcortical motor aphasia, but reduced in MTA). Furthermore, because spontaneous language output is often markedly reduced and comprehension is poor, MTA needs to be differentiated from global aphasia by examining the degree to which repetition is spared.

More in-depth neurolinguistic diagnostic procedures may be performed to examine the underlying deficient mechanisms constraining communication in persons with suspected MTA. During repetition, responses to systematically varied model stimuli may indicate whether performance is limited by verbal working memory constraints, or whether repetition function may be permeable to lexical–semantic processing or modifiable by higher-level cognitive control. For example, to test influences of verbal working memory function, model items may include words of increasing stimulus length, or may contrast word and sentence stimuli. Lexical–semantic influences on repetition may be tested by comparing performance for word and nonword stimuli, by using model stimuli composed of different word classes, by contrasting frequent with infrequent, concrete with abstract, or regular with irregular word stimuli, or by asking participants to repeat words in isolation versus within a sentence context. Speech motor programming and articulatory capability may be examined by using model items of similar frequency but varying phonetic complexity. The degree of automaticity during repetition might be tested by contrasting idioms or similarly over-learned phrases (which may be assumed to consist of a single lexical entry, McCarthy & Warrington, 1984) with more "propositional," unique types of phrases (which require more planning with respect to the surface and deep structure of the utterance than overlearned phrases). In addition, the degree of volitional control over speech output may be examined by asking participants to delay their responses during repetition.

Differential diagnosis also may need to consider neuropsychiatric syndromes, because echolalia, often the most prominent symptom in MTA, also occurs in different neuropsychiatric disorders. It may be associated with degenerative disorders such as frontotemporal dementia, corticobasal degeneration, or systemic lupus erythematosus, and may be one of the symptoms associated with Tourette's syndrome. Furthermore, echolalia has been noted in the language of psychosis or when emerging from coma (Christman et al., 2004; Duffy, 2005; Mendez, 2002). Thus, differential diagnosis with respect to neuropsychiatric disorders will include pathological signs indicative of a stroke syndrome, such as acute symptom onset.

Treatment

Due to the variety of underlying neurological disorders, etiologies, and sites of lesion associated with MTA, its course of recovery may vary. MTA has been reported to result from acute ischemic stroke within the first few days post-onset (Bogousslavsky et al., 1988; Carota et al., 2007; Flamand-Roze et al., 2011; Maeshima et al., 2002; McFarling et al., 1982; Rapcsak et al., 1990; Speedie et al., 1984, case 2). Other cases of MTA were observed in the subacute stage, between 2 and 8 weeks postonset (Maeshima et al., 1996; Rappaport, Gil, Ring, & Schechter, 1999; Speedie et al., 1984, case 1; Trojano et al., 1988), suggesting that MTA may have evolved from a more severe initial aphasic disorder such as global aphasia. In several of the above cases, language function in individuals with MTA was reported to improve rapidly over the course of several weeks (e.g., Bogousslavsky et al., 1988; Maeshima et al., 2002; Rapcsak et al., 1990, case 2) or months (Rappaport et al., 1999).

Only a few studies systematically examined the evolution of the syndrome, including repeat language examinations over the course of several months (Flamand-Roze et al., 2011; Rappaport et al., 1999) or years (Pulvermüller & Schönle, 1993; see also Geschwind et al., 1968, who reported incidental observations over the course of 7 years). Flamand-Roze et al. (2011) described the course of recovery in eight right-handed individuals who had developed MTA within 2 days after border zone infarcts in the left hemisphere. At the time of discharge from the stroke unit, three individuals had completely recovered, whereas the remaining individuals presented with either transcortical motor or transcortical sensory aphasia. At least 6 months postonset, none of the participants showed any signs of aphasia on a standardized aphasia assessment, although attentional deficits and reduced working memory span were noted. The authors did not note whether the participants received any language therapy after discharge. Rappaport and colleagues (1999) followed several individuals from the subacute phase after infarction over the course of at least 3 and up to nearly 8 months, during which time they received daily "intensive" multimodal language therapy. Of the eight individuals who received the initial diagnosis of MTA, five developed transcortical sensory aphasia, and in two others (who had received daily treatment for about 4 and 7 months, respectively), MTA had evolved into amnestic aphasia (Rappaport et al., 1999).

Still fewer studies report the outcomes of systematic targeted language intervention in individuals with MTA. With respect to the potential for improvement of language functions in MTA, Alexander and Schmitt (1980, cited in Cimino-Knight et al., 2005) cautioned that "treatment programs relying on repetition skill will not produce significant results because they address a function that is preserved and performed almost automatically in these patients" (p. 181). Thus, treatment approaches that aim to gradually shift language processing away from rather automatic toward more intentional, controlled processing are most likely to be beneficial in MTA (Cimino-Knight et al., 2005). In fact, such a treatment program has been reported by Pulvermüller and Schönle (1993). Their case may be the only detailed report of an intervention tailored specifically to the person's symptoms, which were typical of MTA. This right-handed individual had suffered a large stroke that entirely destroyed the left perisylvian language areas. Until 1 year poststroke, the person had global aphasia. Between 1 and 5 years poststroke, repetition function gradually improved whereas other language functions remained essentially unchanged. Therapy, which began 5 years postonset, was intended to enable the participant to use his single preserved language function, repetition, to perform speech acts. This was done by asking him to produce requests by "selective repetition." During a card game, the clinician offered choices such as "Do you want X [a pictured object on a card] or Y [another pictured object]?" and the participant had to repeat the item that best fit the communicative needs. Choices were always binary (i.e., the hit rate was 50%), apparently in order to make the task doable. Although the authors did not explicitly mention it, the description of the procedure suggests that due to echolalia, it was difficult for the participant to suppress repeating the entire utterance and select only one of the two items offered.

To counter the echolalia, Pulvermüller and Schönle (1993) devised a strategy that the person was able to use, namely to place stress on the respective word chosen while simultaneously looking at the therapist. This part of training, which allowed the participant to produce speech volitionally, was complemented by auditory comprehension training, in which the person had to select (out of several cards) the card requested by the therapist. After 3 weeks of five 1-hour sessions per week, the participant's ability to selectively repeat one of the two words offered as a choice had improved to above chance, regardless of whether it had occurred in the first or second position. Concurrently, there was first a marginally significant increase and then a marked decrease in reaction times. Comprehension performance also had improved significantly. The authors' explanation of the treatment gains is well in line with early language processing models. According to Pulvermüller and Schönle (1993), over the course of 5 years the participant had gradually developed the ability to repeat (despite a lesion that destroyed the left perisylvian area) because repeated and simultaneous activation (i.e., the man spoke and heard himself speak) had led to synaptic strengthening in the right hemispheric perisylvian areas. The initial speed–accuracy trade-off during therapy may indicate a shift in strategy, which may have enabled the man to develop the ability to monitor his output. According to the authors, the ensuing improvement in response times in both the production and comprehension tasks suggests improved connectivity between phonological representations in spared right perisylvian areas and semantic representations located in various cortical areas, both in the unaffected right hemisphere and in the spared left hemispheric areas.

Apart from being able to repeat, individuals with MTA are often able to complete auditorily presented sentence fragments (e.g., Carota et al., 2007; Geschwind et al., 1968; Grossi et al., 1991, case 2; Rapcsak et al., 1990, case 2; Silveri & Colosimo, 1995). Geschwind et al. (1968) noticed that their participant with MTA sang along correctly when a familiar song was played to her. If the music was stopped, she would continue to sing correctly both melody and words for a few lines before she would stop. If the examiner continued to hum the melody without words, she was able to continue the song correctly until the end. Upon this observation, Geschwind and his colleagues (1968) attempted to train her in new songs that she did not know before her long-standing illness. After a few cycles, the woman showed evidence of having learned the new songs, as suggested by her ability to continue the song without a model to imitate after the examiner had stopped the music. To explain this limited yet verifiable form of verbal learning, Geschwind and colleagues argued that "it would seem reasonable that for verbal learning to take place, not only should Wernicke's area be intact but also at least the left hippocampal region and the connections between these two areas" (p. 339); these are regions that were spared in this woman. This explanation is supported by a recent imaging study showing a positive correlation between verbal learning ability and integrity of the left hippocampus and surrounding white matter in 10 individuals with chronic stroke-induced aphasia (Meinzer et al., 2010).

The treatment approaches described above build on the (few) capacities that are spared in MTA. Other symptoms common in MTA, such as verbal perseveration and echolalia, have detrimental effects on attempts at successful communication. Thus, treatment should aim at inhibiting these behaviors. With respect to the management of verbal perseveration, Christman and colleagues (2004) appeared rather sceptical. As they stated, "one hopes that the mechanisms underlying perseveration are not completely modular because the hope of intervention is that, with recovery (particularly as word finding improves), perseveration can more easily be brought under volitional control" (p. 300). In reference to echolalia, Duffy (2005) noted that "the associated language and other cognitive deficits represent the true barriers to the formulation and expression of speech. In a sense, echolalia in such patients [with diffuse or cortical pathology and severe aphasia] represents a residual, relatively intact ability, even though its expression in most circumstances is inappropriate. When behavioral management is appropriate for such patients and echolalia is pervasive, it may be necessary to inhibit or reduce the echolalia before the underlying language and other cognitive deficits can be addressed" (p. 528).

Finally, Silveri and Colosimo (1995) proposed a compensatory strategy to circumvent compulsive, automatic (naming) behavior sometimes observed in MTA (Heilman et al., 1976; Silveri & Colosimo, 1995; Trojano et al., 1988). Silveri and Colosimo's (1995) participant could not help but name pictures of objects "immediately" upon presentation; when given a choice in a word–picture matching task, he named both of them, while pointing at random. The authors hypothesized that the impaired word–picture matching performance was caused by a competition for limited working memory resources between the "uncontrollable tendency to name pictorial stimuli" (Silveri & Colosimo, 1995, p. 3) and resource-demanding comprehension processes. Silveri and Colosimo (1995) reasoned that more working memory resources would be available to perform the word–picture matching task if the compulsion to name could be inhibited or reduced, for example, by making the naming task more difficult. In other words, the authors' expectation was that the more "difficult" items would be less likely to trigger compulsive naming. This hypothesis was examined in a series of specially designed language tests, and by manipulating name, familiarity, frequency, and visual complexity of the depicted objects. Results indeed showed that comprehension performance on the word–picture matching task improved with increasing naming difficulty. Silveri and Colosimo (1995) concluded that increasing the naming difficulty may have forced the participant to actively search for an adequate label for the depicted object, taking one step toward more "voluntary" naming and away from the rather involuntary, "automatic" naming.

Conclusions

Mixed transcortical aphasia is a syndrome that may be used to make significant contributions to our understanding of the organization, the mechanisms, and the neuronal correlates of language. However, for individual case studies of MTA to be instructive and comparable to other reports, it seems imperative that all levels of speech, especially the spontaneous speech output, be examined

in a formalized setting and described in detail. The integrity of repetition should be examined for stimuli of varying length, familiarity, and complexity, and the influence of context should be tested. An increasingly better understanding of the impairments of linguistic and nonlinguistic functions in MTA will generate more efficient treatment programs, which may, in some cases, have to focus first on treatment goals that target nonlinguistic functions and processes. For example, a first phase of treatment may aim to reduce the degree of automaticity in verbal behavior and increase the amount of voluntary control.

Future Directions

• Does the ability to repeat longer (e.g., more than seven words) sentences compellingly demonstrate that storage capacity (i.e., phonological working memory) is unimpaired? Which kind of working memory processes need to be unimpaired for sentence repetition; which need to be unimpaired for sentence comprehension?

• How can the fact be explained that within the group of individuals with MTA, some are able to repeat pseudowords at the same level of performance as real words, whereas others show a performance decrement for pseudowords?

• In a repetition task, how could we reliably distinguish between an echolalic response and a controlled and volitional repetition response?

• Might it be possible that in the most pronounced form of echolalia, stimulus-inherent characteristics that have an effect on performance during volitional, controlled repetition, such as lexicality, regularity, frequency, familiarity, and concreteness, do not have an effect?

References

Alexander, M. P., & Schmitt, M. A. (1980). The aphasia syndrome of stroke in the left anterior cerebral artery territory. *Archives of Neurology, 37*, 97–100.

Ardila, A., & Rosselli, M. (1992). Repetition in aphasia. *Journal of Neurolinguistics, 7*, 103–113.

Baginsky, A. (1871). Aphasie in Folge schwerer Nierenerkrankungen. *Berliner Klinische Wochenschrift: Organ für praktische Ärzte, 8*, 439–443.

Berthier, M. L. (1999). *Transcortical aphasias.* Hove: Psychology Press.

Berthier, M. L., Starkstein, S. E., Leiguarda, R., Ruiz, A., Mayberg, H. S., Wagner, H., ... Robinson, R. G. (1991). Transcortical aphasia: Importance of the nonspeech dominant hemisphere in language repetition. *Brain, 114*, 1409–1427.

Blank, S. C., Scott, S. K., Murphy, K., Warburton, E., & Wise, R. J. (2002). Speech production: Wernicke, Broca and beyond. *Brain*, 125, 1829–1838.

Bogousslavsky, J., Regli, F., & Assal, G. (1988). Acute transcortical mixed aphasia. A carotid occlusion syndrome with pial and watershed infarcts. *Brain*, 111, 631–641.

Boller, F. (1978). Comprehension disorders in aphasia. *Brain and Language*, 5, 149–165.

Carota, A., Annoni, J. M., & Marangolo, P. (2007). Repeating through the insula: Evidence from two consecutive strokes. *Neuroreport*, 18, 1367–1370.

Chenery, H. J., & Murdoch, B. E. (1986). A case of mixed transcortical aphasia following drug overdose. *British Journal of Disorders of Communication*, 21, 381–392.

Christman, S. S., Boutsen, F. R., & Buckingham, H. W. (2004). Perseveration and other repetitive verbal behaviors: Functional dissociations. *Seminars in Speech and Language*, 25, 295–307.

Cimino-Knight, A. M., Hollingsworth, A. L., & Rothi, L. J. G. (2005). The transcortical aphasias. In L. L. LaPointe (Ed.), *Aphasia and related neurogenic language disorders* (3rd ed., pp. 169–185). New York: Thieme Medical Publishers.

Compston, A. (2006). From the archives. [Editorial]. *Brain*, 129, 1347–1350.

Davis, L., Foldi, N. S., Gardner, H., & Zurif, E. B. (1978). Repetition in the transcortical aphasias. *Brain and Language*, 6, 226–238.

Démonet, J.-F., Puel, M., Celsis, P., & Cardebat, D. (1991). "Subcortical" aphasia: Some proposed pathophysiological mechanisms and their rCBF correlates revealed by SPECT. *Journal of Neurolinguistics*, 6, 319–344.

Duffy, J. R. (2005). *Motor speech disorders: Substrates, differential diagnosis, and management*. St. Louis: Elsevier Mosby.

Eling, P. (2005). Baginsky on aphasia. *Journal of Neurolinguistics*, 18, 301–315.

Flamand-Roze, C., Cauquil-Michon, C., Roze, E., Souillard-Scemama, R., Maintigneux, L., Ducreux, D., ... Denier, C. (2011). Aphasia in border-zone infarcts has a specific initial pattern and good long-term prognosis. *European Journal of Neurology*, 18, 1397–1401.

Gardner, A., & Winner, E. (1978). A study of repetition in aphasic patients. *Brain and Language*, 6, 168–178.

Geschwind, N., Quadfasel, F. A., & Segarra, J. M. (1968). Isolation of the speech area. *Neuropsychologia*, 6, 327–340.

Goldstein, K. (1917). *Die transkortikalen Aphasien*. Jena: Gustav Fischer.

Goldstein, K. (1948). *Language and language disturbances: Aphasic symptom complexes and their significance for medicine and theory of language*. New York: Grune & Stratton.

Grossi, D., Trojano, L., Chiacchio, L, Soricelli, A., Mansi, L., Postiglione, A., & Salvatore, M. (1991). Mixed transcortical aphasia: Clinical features and neuroanatomical correlates. A possible role of the right hemisphere. *European Neurology*, 31, 204–211.

Heilman, K. M., Tucker, D. M., & Valenstein, E. (1976). A case of mixed transcortical aphasia with intact naming. *Brain*, 99, 415–426.

Hickok, G. (2009). The functional neuroanatomy of language. *Physics of Life Reviews*, 6, 121–143.

Huber, W., Poeck, K., Weniger, D., & Willmes, K. (1983). *Aachener Aphasie Test*. Göttingen: Hogrefe.

Hübner, O. (1889). Über Aphasie. *Schmidt's Jahrbücher*, 224, 220–222.

Kertesz, A. (2007). *The Western aphasia battery-Revised*. San Antonio, TX: Harcourt Assessment.

Keyser, A. (1994). Carl Wernicke. In P. Eling (Ed.), *Reader in the history of aphasia: From Franz Gall to Norman Geschwind* (pp. 59–98). Amsterdam: John Benjamins.

Kussmaul, A. (1877). *Die Störungen der Sprache. Versuch einer Pathologie der Sprache*. Leipzig: Vogel.

Laska, A. C., Hellblom, A., Murray, V., Kahan, T., & Von Arbin, M. (2001). Aphasia in acute stroke and relation to outcome. *Journal of Internal Medicine*, 249, 413–422.

Lichtheim L. (1885a). Über Aphasie. Aus der medicinischen Klink Bern. *Deutsches Archiv für Klinische Medicin*, 36, 204–268.

Lichtheim, L. (1885b). On aphasia. *Brain*, 7, 433–484.

Maeshima, S., Toshiro, H., Sekiguchi, E., Okita, R., Yamaga, H., Ozaki, F., ... Roger, P. (2002). Transcortical mixed aphasia due to cerebral infarction in left inferior frontal lobe and temporo-parietal lobe. *Neuroradiology*, 44, 133–137.

Maeshima, S., Uematsu, Y., Terada, T., Nakai, K., Itakura, T., & Komai, N. (1996). Transcortical mixed aphasia with left frontoparietal lesions. *Neuroradiology*, 38, S78–S79.

McCarthy, R., & Warrington, E. K. (1984). A two-route model of speech production. Evidence from aphasia. *Brain*, 107, 463–485.

McFarling, D., Rothi, L. J. G., & Heilman, K. M. (1982). Transcortical aphasia from ischaemic infarcts of the thalamus: A report of two cases. *Journal of Neurology, Neurosurgery, and Psychiatry*, 45, 107–112.

Meinzer, M., Mohammadi, S., Kugel, H., Schiffbauer, H., Flöel, A., Albers, J., ... Deppe, M. (2010). Integrity of the hippocampus and surrounding white matter is correlated with language training success in aphasia. *Neuroimage*, 53, 283–290.

Mendez, M. F. (2002). Prominent echolalia from isolation of the speech area. *Journal of Neuropsychiatry and Clinical Neurosciences*, 14, 356–357.

Nagaratnam, N., & Gilhotra, J. S. (1998). Acute mixed transcortical aphasia following an infarction in the left putamen. *Aphasiology*, 12, 489–493.

Nagaratnam, N., McNeil, C., & Gilhotra, J. S. (1999). Akinetic mutism and mixed transcortical aphasia following left thalamo-mesencephalic infarction. *Journal of the Neurological Sciences*, 163, 70–73.

Ohyama, M., Senda, M., Kitamura, S., Ishii, K., Mishina, M., & Terashi, A. (1996). Role of the nondominant hemisphere and undamaged area during word repetition in poststroke aphasics: A PET activation study. *Stroke*, 27, 897–903.

Pedersen, P. M., Vinter, K., & Olsen, T. S. (2004). Aphasia after stroke: Type, severity and prognosis. The Copenhagen aphasia study. *Cerebrovascular Disease*, 17, 35–43.

Peschke, C., Ziegler, W., Kappes, J., & Baumgaertner, A. (2009). Auditory-motor integration during fast repetition: The neuronal correlates of shadowing. *Neuroimage*, 47, 392–402.

Pulvermüller, F., & Schönle, P. W. (1993). Behavioral and neuronal changes during treatment of mixed transcortical aphasia: A case study. *Cognition*, 48, 139–161.

Rapcsak, S. Z., Krupp, L. B., Rubens, A. B., & Reim, J. (1990). Mixed transcortical aphasia without anatomic isolation of the speech area. *Stroke*, 21, 953–956.

Rappaport, Z., Gil, M., Ring, H., & Schechter, I. (1999). Isolation of speech area syndrome (ISAS): A follow-up study—a rehabilitative approach. *Disability and Rehabilitation*, 21, 181–186.

Ross, E. D. (1980). Left medial parietal lobe and receptive language functions: Mixed transcortical aphasia after left anterior cerebral artery infarction. *Neurology*, 30, 144–151.

Saur, D., Kreher, B. W., Schnell, S., Kümmerer, D., Kellmeyer, P., Vry, M. S., ... Weiller, C. (2008). Ventral and dorsal pathways for language. *Proceedings of the National Academy of Sciences USA*, 105, 18035–18040.

Saur, D., Lange, R., Baumgaertner, A., Schraknepper, V., Willmes, K., Rijntjes, M., & Weiller, C. (2006). Dynamics of language reorganization after stroke. *Brain*, 129, 1371–1384.

Scott, S. K., Blank, S. C., Rosen, S., & Wise, R. J. S. (2000). Identification of a pathway for intelligible speech in the left temporal lobe. *Brain*, 123, 2400–2406.

Scott, S. K., & Wise, R. J. S. (2004). The functional neuroanatomy of prelexical processing in speech perception. *Cognition*, 92, 13–45.

Shuster, L. I., & Lemieux, S. K. (2005). An fMRI investigation of covertly and overtly produced mono- and multisyllabic words. *Brain and Language*, 93, 20–31.

Silveri, M. C., & Colosimo, C. (1995). Hypothesis on the nature of comprehension deficit in a patient with transcortical mixed aphasia with preserved naming. *Brain and Language*, 49, 1–26.

Speedie, L. J., Coslett, H. B., & Heilman, K. M. (1984). Repetition of affective prosody in mixed transcortical aphasia. *Archives of Neurology*, 41, 268–270.

Trojano, L., Fragassi, N. A., Postiglione, A., & Grossi, D. (1988). Mixed transcortical aphasia. On relative sparing of phonological short-term store in a case. *Neuropsychologia*, 26, 633–638.

Wallesch, C. W. (1990). Repetitive verbal behaviour: Functional and neurological considerations. *Aphasiology*, 4, 133–154.

Warren, J. E., Wise, R. J., & Warren, J. D. (2005). Sounds doable: Auditory-motor transformations and the posterior temporal plane. *Trends in Neurosciences*, 28, 636–643.

Wernicke, C. (1874). *Der aphasische Symptomencomplex. Eine psychologische Studie auf anatomischer Basis.* Breslau: Cohn & Weigert.

Wernicke, C. (1885/1886). Einige neuere Arbeiten zur Aphasie. *Fortschritte der Medizin*, 3, 824–830, and 4, 371–377, 463–469.

Willmes, K., & Poeck, K. (1993). To what extent can aphasic syndromes be localized? *Brain*, 116, 1527–1540.

Wise, R. J., Scott, S. K., Blank, S. C., Mummery, C. J., Murphy, K., & Warburton, E. A. (2001). Separate neural subsystems within "Wernicke's area." *Brain*, 124, 83–95.

Appendix A. Case Reports of Mixed Transcortical Aphasia

Author/s, YOP	MPO	MTA Identified by	Etiology	Lesion Location	Identified by	Other Observations
Bogousslavsky et al., 1988						
Case 1	Acute	A priori definition: nonfluent aphasia with impaired comprehension and "good repetition"	Infarct	2 infarct zones, one in precentral artery territory, one posterior parietal	CT	Tendency to repeat every word or sentence said by the examiner
Case 2	4 days	See Case 1	Infarct	2 infarct zones, one in superior posterior frontal, one posterior parietal	CT	
Case 3	2 days	See Case 1	Infarct	2 infarct zones, one posterior prefrontal, one posterior parietal	CT	Word finding difficulties
Case 4	Acute	See Case 1	Infarct	2 infarct zones, one in middle posterior frontal lobe, one posterior parietal	CT	
Carota et al., 2007	Acute–10 days post	Constellation of aphasic signs suggestive of MTA	New onset atrial fibrillation, L ICA occlusion	Complete "MCA syndrome" due to extensive subcortical stroke affecting the basal ganglia and corona radiata	DWI	Completion of few proverbs and well-known phrases possible; but no completion of automatic series (counting, months of the year); most agrammatical sentences "passively repeated" without changes

(continued)

Appendix A. Continued

Author/s, YOP	MPO	MTA Identified by	Etiology	Lesion Location	Identified by	Other Observations
Chenery and Murdoch, 1986	4 months	Various standardized tests, e.g., WAB and BNT	Anoxic brain damage due to heroin overdose	Mild dilation of ventricular system with prominence of cortical sulci, indicating cerebral atrophy	CT	Establishing a syntactic frame appeared difficult; when asked "Do you like dancing to rock and roll?" the response was "dancing, dancing, a lot, like rock"; digit span forward = 4; backward not feasible; sentences with syntactic and phonologic errors and words with incorrect stress patterns corrected during repetition, but not sentences with semantic errors ("The apple was eaten by a stone")
Geschwind et al., 1968	11 months– 9 years post	Observation: nonfluent spontaneous speech in the presence of "echolalic repetition with excellent articulation"	Carbon monoxide poisoning	Sparing of Wernicke's area and auditory pathways including Heschl's and Broca's area, as well as lower end of rolandic cortex and motor outflow plus connections between them	Autopsy, histopathology	Hippocampi spared, singing with words and completion of proverbs or titles of songs possible; in addition, idiom completion observed
Grossi et al., 1991						
Case 1		See Trojano et al. (1988)	See Trojano et al. (1988)	CBF reduced in LH except for two small areas in prefrontal and temporal region	SPECT	Assessment of verbal span difficult because the woman repeated the first item given
Case 2	10 months		Thromboendarterectomy surgery after ulcerated stenosis in ICA was found; symptoms developed after surgery; markedly reduced blood flow in LH	L hemisphere, with partial sparing of frontal and occipital polar regions	Arteriography, CT, SPECT	Could sing old songs when prompted (some of the words replaced by stereotyped expressions while keeping the tune), completion of idiomatic expression

Study	Time	Assessment	Lesion (etiology)	Lesion location / CBF	Imaging	Language findings
Heilman et al., 1976	15 and 16 months, and 2 years and 8 months postonset			Complete block at the bifurcation of the left carotid artery; excellent cross-filling of LH circulation from the right	Arteriography	No completion when incomplete sentences are presented; patient echos incomplete sentence
Maeshima et al., 1996	6 weeks postonset	WAB criteria	Aneurysm at the junction of L ICA and PCA; after neck-clipping period of unconsciousness due to vasospasm of L ICA	L frontal and basal ganglia infarction; decreased CBF in the entire L hemisphere except for L perisylvian area (6 weeks post)	angiography, SPECT	
Maeshima et al., 2002	Few days postonset (acute)		Infarction; SPECT: wide area of low perfusion over entire LH except for part of perisylvian language area	L frontal and parietooccipital infarcts; SPECT revealed wider area of low perfusion over entire L hemisphere except for part of perisylvian region	CT, MRI, SPECT	
McFarling et al., 1982						
Case 1	7 days poststroke	WAB (modified)	Infarct	Left internal capsule and adjacent posterior-lateral aspect of left thalamus	CT	Partly correct sentence completion; inability to generate words in phonemic fluency task
Pulvermüller and Schönle, 1993	5 years	Language tests (improved repetition concurrent with increased echolalia)	Infarction of left internal carotid artery	Widespread cortical and subcortical perisilesional areas as well as insula in the LH	CT	No spontaneous correction of minor grammatical errors and no completion of incomplete sentences during repetition
Rapczak et al., 1990						
Case 1	4 days post	Not given	L frontal infarct	MCA and ACA distribution: Broca's area and premotor/prefrontal regions, plus lower precentral gyrus; area of low CBF in L frontal areas but also in parietal convexity	CT (day 4), MRI (2 weeks post), SPECT (3 weeks post)	Able to sing; 4 weeks post, R frontoparietal infarction in MCA territory, leading to abolition of repetition ability

(continued)

Appendix A. Continued

Author/s, YOP	MPO	MTA Identified by	Etiology	Lesion Location	Identified by	Other Observations
Case 2	4 days post		Large L frontal infarct	MCA territory, Broca's area, and dorsolateral premotor and prefrontal cortex		Completion of open-ended sentences
Ross, 1980	3–5 months	Language testing (nonformal?): preserved repetition in the presence of markedly nonfluent spontaneous speech and "very poor" comprehension	Infarction secondary to clipping of a berry aneurysm of left anterior communicating artery	Large ACA infarct extending beyond rolandic fissure into medial portions of left parietal lobe; destruction of anterior half of corpus callosum	CT	Automatic speech (counting, reciting days of the week) "very poor"; at 5 months p.o. sentence completion possible (the grass is. . .? "the grass is green"); 5 months p.o. puzzled reaction to ungrammatical phrases such as "We came there back," and refusal to repeat
Silveri and Colosimo, 1995	Gradual onset		Progressive multifocal leukoencephalopathy	Multiple lesions in L anterior frontal, frontoparietal, and posterior temporal white matter; markedly decreased perfusion in whole L hemisphere	MRL, SPECT	Pat. cooperative, fluctuating performance; completion of proverbs possible
Speedie et al., 1984						
Case 1	2 months poststroke	WAB and clinical impression	Watershed infarction	White matter, maximal superior and lateral to left lateral ventricle	CT	During repetition, spontaneous correction of errors of tense, pronoun usage, number agreement, but not obvious semantic inconsistencies

		WAB and clinical impression	Infarct		CT	
Case 2	3 days poststroke			Left parietooccipital	CT	During repetition, intermittently correction of grammatical errors of tense and pronoun usage
Trojano et al., 1988	1 month	Severely reduced spontaneous speech, few automated expressions, few fragmentary syllables, neologisms, few dialectal expressions used iteratively	Myocardial infarct, 10 days later stroke leading to cortical and subcortical atrophy mainly in LH	Hypodensity in L fronto-temporoparietal region	CT	Singing with words possible, even when only beginning is given; compulsory naming; comprehension of gestures

Note: CT, computed tomography; MTA, mixed transcortical aphasia; LH, left hemisphere; ICA, internal carotid artery; DWI, diffusion weighted imaging; WAB, Western Aphasia Battery; BNT, Boston Naming Test; CBF, cerebral blood flow; SPECT, single photon emission computed tomography; MCA, middle cerebral artery; MRI, magnetic resonance imaging.

Appendix B. Mixed Transcortical Aphasia: Neurolinguistic Characteristics during Speech Production (+ = Impairment; − = No Impairment; n/a = Not Reported)

Author/s, YOP	Articulatory Disturbances	Prosodic Impairment	Echolalia	Semantic Paraphasias	Phonemic Paraphasias	Dysarthria	Apraxia	Other Cognitive Deficits Reported?
Bogousslavsky et al., 1988								
Case 1	n/a	n/a	+	+	−	−	n/a	Perseveration
Case 2	n/a	n/a	+	+	−	−	n/a	n/a
Case 3	n/a	n/a	+	+	−	−	n/a	n/a
Case 4	n/a	n/a	+	+	−	−	n/a	n/a
Carota et al., 2007	n/a	n/a	+ almost every time when spoken to	n/a	n/a	n/a	n/a	n/a
Chenery and Murdoch, 1986	−	n/a	+	+	n/a	−	−	Spatial disorientation
Geschwind et al., 1968	−	−	+	n/a	n/a	−	n/a	Perseveration (continuous), sang songs, and completed idioms such as *"Ask me no questions . . ."* *"I'll tell you no lies,"* or proverbs or titles of songs
Grossi et al., 1991								
Case 1 (see Trojano et al., 1988)								
Case 2	"Some disturbances"	n/a	+	+	n/a	n/a	n/a	Completion for idiomatic expression, could sing old songs when prompted (some words replaced by stereotyped expressions while keeping the tune), testing of verbal span not feasible; after gestural explanation Corsi block span = 3

Heilman et al., 1976	–	n/a	+ in response to conversational speech or direct questions, occasionally echoing of complete questions of up to 8 words; more frequently, only part of a sentence echoed, usually the last part (for example, the last 3–4 words)	n/a	–	n/a	–	n/a	Joining in singing is possible, even when examiner had stopped; copying of meaningful and nonsense sentence ok
Maeshima et al., 1996	n/a	n/a	+ (often)	n/a	n/a	n/a	n/a	n/a	n/a
Maeshima et al., 2002	+ clear	n/a	+ when questioned	–	+	n/a	+	n/a	n/a
Case 1									
McFarling et al., 1982	n/a	n/a	+	–	–	+ moderate	n/a	n/a	Irritability, uncooperativeness
Pulvermueller and Schoenle, 1993	n/a	n/a	+	n/a	n/a	n/a	n/a	n/a	n/a
Rapcsak et al., 1990									
Case 1	n/a	n/a	+ words and sentences	n/a	n/a	n/a	n/a	n/a	Completion of sentences and singing possible
Case 2	n/a	n/a	+ occasional echolalic repetition	n/a	n/a	n/a	n/a	n/a	Completion of open-ended sentences possible

(continued)

Appendix B. Continued

Author/s, YOP	Articulatory Disturbances	Prosodic Impairment	Echolalia	Semantic Paraphasias	Phonemic Paraphasias	Dysarthria	Apraxia	Other Cognitive Deficits Reported?
Ross, 1980	–	–	+	n/a	n/a	–	Could not be tested due to comprehension difficulties; at 5 months p.o. constructional apraxia	"Lability of affect"; further cognitive testing not possible
Silveri and Colosimo, 1995	–	–	+	–	–	–	+	Fluctuating performance
Speedie et al., 1984								
Case 1	–	n/a	n/a	n/a	n/a	n/a	+	Affective intonation (neutral, sad, happy, angry) in sentences with neutral semantic content not realized during repetition
Case 2	–	n/a	n/a	n/a	n/a	n/a	+	Affective intonation (neutral, sad, happy, angry) in sentences with neutral semantic content not realized during repetition
Trojano et al., 1988	Some "disturbances"	n/a	+ the last word spoken by examiner	n/a	n/a	n/a	n/a	Several traditional Neapolitan and religious songs could be sung, and even "recent songs"; also able to recite prayers (unclear whether prompted, but presumably so); could complete common phrases; compulsory naming

Acquired Alexias: Mechanisms of Reading

Ellyn A. Riley, C. Elizabeth Brookshire, *and* Diane L. Kendall

Abstract

Reading is one of the most important cognitive skills an individual can acquire and the process of reading has been debated much in the psycholinguistic, neurolinguistic, and educational literature for many years now. Much of this literature has discussed the process of reading, proposed theoretical models to describe its components, and identification of neuroanatomic underpinnings. In this chapter we have attempted to provide a review of both dual-route and connectionist models of alexia, outline specific types of peripheral and central alexias, provide a brief overview of the neural substrates linked with reading processes, and finally offer diagnostic and treatment strategies.

Key Words: Alexia, Dyslexia, Stroke, Treatment, Rehabilitation

Introduction

Models of reading involve some variation of processes for perceiving a printed word, analyzing the components of a printed word, understanding the meaning of the word, and in the case of reading aloud, orally producing the word. Some reading models specify the process of print analysis in more detail by defining separate processes for recognizing specific features of letters, recognizing letters from those features, and recognizing graphemes from the letters. Other models define separate processes for accessing the lexical entry of a word and accessing the word's meaning. For oral word reading, some theoretical models define separate processes for accessing the sounds composing the word and articulating those sounds to produce it.

Dual-Route Models

Although reading models are designed to represent the reading process in both typical and disordered readers, some of the first models of reading evolved from examining reading patterns in individuals with acquired alexias. In 1973, Marshall and Newcombe described a model of oral reading

that offered an interpretation for various types of acquired alexia. This model was a precursor to the current Dual-Route Cascaded (DRC) model of reading, a model that conceptualizes oral reading as a serial process with two separate routes: one for lexical and one for nonlexical reading processes (see Figure 12.1) (Beeson & Henry, 2008; Coltheart, Rastle, Perry, & Langdon, 2001). For each of these reading routes, the model conceptualizes the reading process as a series of modules, each specified for a particular task in the reading process. The *visual feature analysis* module is involved in analyzing the individual visual parts of each letter (e.g., the letter P consists of a single vertical line attached to a single line curved to the right). The *letter analysis* module is involved in identifying the letter, identifying the letter's position in relation to other letters, and identifying the graphemes in the word (e.g., *bush* contains four letters, b-u-s-h, but only three graphemes, b-u-sh). Within the lexical reading route, the *orthographic input lexicon* contains a store of the visual forms of known, familiar words (e.g., the visual word form of *candle* would be accessed at this level, but the visual form of the pseudoword *tandle* would not be accessed here). The *semantic system* is involved in associating the visual form of the word with the meaning of the word (e.g., the visual form *cat* is associated with a small furry animal with four legs that meows). The *phonological output lexicon* contains a store of the phonological forms of known, familiar words (e.g., the phonological form /tɪp/ would be accessed at this level, but the pseudoword /fɪp/ would not be accessed here). The *grapheme–phoneme conversion* module that is fundamental to the nonlexical reading process involves translating the graphemes in a word with their corresponding phonemes (e.g., the graphemes t-i-p would be translated to the phonemes /t/, /ɪ/, /p/). The *phonological assembly* module shared by both lexical and nonlexical reading routes involves breaking down the phonological form into individual phonemes for speech production (e.g., the phonological form of *keep*, that is, /kip/, would be broken down to /k/, /i/, /p/ for later speech execution. In this model, the *visual feature analysis, letter analysis, orthographic input lexicon,* and *grapheme–phoneme conversion* modules are hypothesized to be involved only in the reading process whereas the *semantic system, phonological output lexicon,* and *phonological assembly* modules are hypothesized to be involved in language processes other than reading, such as spontaneous speech production and repetition.

Whereas this model's fundamental distinction lies between lexical and nonlexical reading processes, within lexical reading, two routes are proposed: a lexical–semantic route and a lexical–nonsemantic route (Raymer & Berndt, 1996). When reading a familiar word via the lexical–nonsemantic route, the results of letter analysis activate the word's entry in the *orthographic input lexicon*, which activates the corresponding word entry in the *phonological output lexicon*, which activates the word's phonemes. This route could be used only for oral reading and not reading comprehension because the meaning of the word is never accessed. In contrast, the lexical–semantic route could be used for oral reading as well as reading comprehension. The lexical–semantic route would operate similarly to the lexical–nonsemantic route except that the *semantic system* (i.e., word meaning) would be accessed between the *orthographic input lexicon* and the *phonological output lexicon*. According to this model, when reading a pseudoword or an unfamiliar word with regular spelling-to-sound rules (e.g., fip), the nonlexical or sublexical route would be used. In this route, the letter string is converted into a phoneme string, assembled in a serial fashion with each grapheme

converted to its corresponding phoneme (i.e., more commonly known as "sounding out the word") for pronunciation. In contrast, a word with an exceptional spelling must be read by way of lexical processes as the pronunciation derived in nonlexical reading would not be correct (e.g., *yacht* read as "yatcht" /jætʃt/).

Connectionist Models

In contrast to the serial processing of dual-route models, the connectionist triangle model explains oral reading as a single-route process involving bidirectional connections between orthography, meaning, and phonology units (Figure 12.2) (Harm & Seidenberg, 1999; Plaut, 1999; Plaut, McClelland, Seidenberg, & Patterson, 1996; Seidenberg & McClelland, 1989). Proponents of this model argue that word reading is accomplished by the interaction of orthographic, semantic, and phonological information that is not specified only for the reading process, but is used for all types of language processing. Instead of postulating that the language system is made up of "rules" governing processing as the dual-route models do, connectionists argue that language knowledge is graded and that learning language involves a process of statistical learning, or learning based on the probability of grapheme or phoneme patterns occurring in different contexts. This connectionist model would predict that in any language modality, processing occurs by comparing language input (via orthography or phonology) to information previously acquired, looking for consistency between the two.

In the connectionist model, a specific distinction is not made between lexical and nonlexical reading; however, because orthography, semantics, and phonology all interact in this model and processing can proceed bidirectionally, the model can still explain both types of reading. In the case of oral word reading and processing the word's meaning (i.e., lexical–semantic reading), the connectionist model would predict that grapheme representations would be accessed first by searching for similarity among previously observed orthographic contexts, followed by access to the semantic information associated with the word, finally ending with accessing the phoneme pattern previously associated with this grapheme pattern and using the phonological representation to produce the word. In the case of orally reading a word without processing the word's meaning (i.e., lexical–nonsemantic reading), this model would predict that the grapheme representation would be accessed first, followed by directly accessing the word's corresponding phonological representation. Pseudoword reading is more difficult to explain with a connectionist model and computational versions of the model have thus far experienced limited success in achieving accurate pseudoword reading (Plaut, 1999). Theoretically, however, a process similar to lexical–nonsemantic reading would be involved in pseudoword reading, comparing grapheme patterns in the pseudoword to previously observed grapheme patterns followed by accessing the phoneme pattern previously associated with this grapheme pattern.

Syndrome Description—Cognitive Neuropsychological Underpinnings

Acquired alexia is a reading disorder caused by injury to the central nervous system associated with neurological disease such as stroke or traumatic brain injury. Acquired alexia results from damage to the mature reading system and is manifested as an impairment in the comprehension of written language. Although several subtypes of acquired alexia have been discussed in the literature, acquired reading disorders can be divided into peripheral and central alexias, each category representing deficits in different stages of the reading process. Peripheral subtypes affect early stages of the reading process and involve difficulty perceiving the written word. Peripheral alexias include pure alexia, neglect alexia, attentional alexia, and visual alexia (Ellis & Young, 1988). Central subtypes affect later stages of the reading process and involve impairments in lexical or sublexical processing. Central alexias include surface alexia, deep alexia, and phonological alexia (Beeson & Henry, 2008; Ellis & Young, 1988).

Peripheral Alexia Subtypes

PURE ALEXIA

Pure alexia involves an impairment in the way written words are perceived and analyzed during reading, specifically manifesting as an impairment in the simultaneous, parallel identification and processing of letters in a written word (Patterson & Kay, 1982; Warrington & Shallice, 1980). In an unimpaired system, the perception and processing of the letters in most words can be accomplished simultaneously (e.g., in the word *dog*, the initial letter *d* can be perceived and processed in relatively the same time-frame as the final letter *g*). In pure alexia, however, letters are perceived and processed in a serial fashion (e.g., in the word *dog*, the initial letter *d* must be perceived, processed, and identified before the second letter *o* can be processed, which is

perceived, processed, and identified before the final letter *g*). This process, known as *letter-by-letter* reading, is extremely slow as the individual identifies each letter (e.g., d-o-g) to slowly build the word. In other words, the person essentially needs to spell out the entire word before being able to read it.

Pure alexia can be explained in dual-route reading models by an impairment at an early level of visual orthographic analysis, possibly occurring between the levels of *visual feature analysis* and *letter analysis*. Although most letters are perceived and identified correctly, the exchange of information between these processing levels is limited, with resources reduced to processing a single letter at a time. Although dual-route models present a plausible explanation for pure alexia, connectionist models do not really present a specific explanation for this or other peripheral subtypes. Connectionist models combine all orthographic analysis into a single processing stage and do not differentiate between the analysis of single letters and overall orthographic patterns. Although the connectionist model contains an orthographic processing stage, it could be argued that pure alexia as well as other peripheral alexia subtypes occur due to impairment prior to the level of orthographic processing represented in the model and are therefore not relevant to discuss in the context of connectionist models.

NEGLECT ALEXIA

Neglect alexia involves an impairment in the way written words are perceived and analyzed spatially during reading, specifically manifesting as an impairment in correctly identifying initial or final letters in words (Ellis, Flude, & Young, 1987). It is important to note that this impairment is specific to the perception of orthographic forms and is not the same as a general visual neglect. In neglect alexia, individuals produce spatially consistent errors at either end of a word. For example, an individual who exhibits a left-sided neglect alexia will produce errors at the beginning of words in single-word oral reading tasks while reading remains relatively unimpaired at the end of the word (e.g., *cat* produced as "bat"; *book* produced as "look"). In contrast, an individual who exhibits a right-sided neglect alexia will produce the beginning of the word correctly, but the end of the word will be produced incorrectly or omitted (e.g., *cat* produced as "car"; *book* produced as "boot" or "boo"). Left-sided neglect alexia following a right hemisphere lesion is more common than right-sided neglect alexia following a left hemisphere lesion.

Neglect alexia can be explained in dual-route reading models by an impairment at the level of visual orthographic analysis, likely to occur specifically at the level of *letter analysis*. In this case, either before or after the point of neglect, the person would be unable to correctly identify the printed orthographic symbol (e.g., in a left-sided neglect alexia, the letter *c* in the word *cat* could be identified as *b*), resulting in activating an inaccurate target *bat* in all subsequent reading processes. Although the parts of the model following *letter analysis* would be intact, because *letter analysis* processing is impaired, the inaccurate information would be passed to all of the following modules for processing, resulting in an inaccurate production. As with pure alexia, although dual-route models present a plausible explanation for neglect alexia, connectionist models do not really present a specific explanation for this alexia subtype.

ATTENTIONAL ALEXIA

Attentional alexia involves an impairment in the way written words are perceived and analyzed during reading, specifically manifesting as incorrect productions of letters in a word as the result of interference from other letters in the word (Shallice & Warrington, 1977). An individual who exhibits attentional alexia will produce errors due to the influence of other letters occurring in the written context (e.g., *river bank* produced as *biver bank; hot meal* produced as *hot heal; butterfly* produced as *flutterfly; bare* produced as *rare*).

Attentional alexia can be explained in dual-route reading models by an impairment at the level of visual orthographic analysis, likely to occur specifically at the level of *letter analysis*. In this case, the individual would be unable to identify correctly the spatial orientation of some letters in relation to others (e.g., for the word *bad*, the presence of the letter *d* could influence the perception of other letters, resulting in the person perceiving the word *dad*), resulting in activation of an inaccurate target *dad* in all subsequent reading processes. As with pure and neglect alexia, although dual-route models present a plausible explanation for attentional alexia, connectionist models do not really present a specific explanation for this alexia subtype.

VISUAL ALEXIA

Visual alexia involves an impairment in the way written words are perceived and analyzed during reading, specifically manifesting as the production of a word that is visually similar to the target word (Marshall & Newcombe, 1973). The error patterns demonstrated in visual alexia are similar to those of neglect alexia except that the errors in visual alexia do not demonstrate a pattern of spatial consistency and errors almost always represent real-word substitutions. The errors observed in visual alexia are also not specific to consonants or vowels, but could occur at any point in the word on any type of letter and appear as letter or syllable substitutions, additions, or omissions (e.g., *butter* produced as *better; applause* produced as *applesauce; prince* produced as *price*).

Visual alexia can be explained in dual-route reading models by an impairment at the level of *letter analysis* or at the level of the *orthographic input lexicon*. If the impairment originated from *letter analysis*, the individual would be unable to correctly perceive all the letters in the word (e.g., for the word *butter*, the misperception of the first vowel could result in perceiving the word *better*), resulting in activating an inaccurate target *better* in the *orthographic input lexicon, semantic system*, and *phonological output lexicon*, leading to processing of inaccurate phonemes at the level of *phonological assembly (/bɛrə/)*.

If the impairment originated from the *orthographic input lexicon*, the individual would visually perceive the word correctly, but when similar words were activated in the *orthographic input lexicon*, selection of a visually similar word form would occur, resulting in inaccurate activation for the remaining parts of the process. As with other peripheral alexias, although dual-route models present a plausible explanation for visual alexia, if it is considered a problem with perceiving the written form of the word, connectionist models do not really present a specific explanation for this alexia subtype. If visual alexia is conceptualized as an impairment in selecting an appropriate orthographic form, however, connectionist models could explain it as a reduced ability to activate correct forms or to inhibit incorrect forms at the level of orthographic processing.

Central Alexia Subtypes

SURFACE ALEXIA

Surface alexia involves an impairment in the way written words are processed during lexical reading, specifically manifesting as impaired reading of irregularly spelled words with relatively intact reading of regularly spelled real words and pseudowords (Marshall & Newcombe, 1973). For example, the word *yacht* is considered an irregular word because it is pronounced /jɑt/ in American English, although it would be pronounced /jætʃt/

if regular spelling rules were applied; the word *bike* is considered a regular word because it is pronounced using a specific and predictable spelling rule (if the word ends in "e" the preceding vowel is pronounced as a long vowel). In surface alexia, the individual would produce regular words such as *bike* more accurately than irregular words such as *yacht*. The errors produced by persons with surface alexia can consist of visual errors (e.g., *blank* produced as *bank*), regularization errors (e.g., *pint* produced as /pɪnt/), and sometimes errors with visual and semantic overlap with the target (e.g., *car* produced as *cab*).

Surface alexia can be explained in dual-route reading models by an impairment at the level the *orthographic input lexicon*, impairment in accessing the *semantic system*, or impairment in selection at the level of the *phonological output lexicon*. If errors are predominately visual in nature, dual-route models would explain them as occurring due to an inappropriate selection at the level of the *orthographic input lexicon*, resulting in the subsequent activation of the semantic and phonological information for the visually similar word (e.g., for the word *blank*, other visually similar words would be activated and the incorrect word *bank* could be selected instead of the correct target, resulting in access to the semantic and phonological information for the word *bank*). If the lexical reading route is impaired, dual-route models would predict that one possibility would be to use the unimpaired nonlexical route for reading. Regularization errors can be explained by a dual-route model as an overreliance on the *grapheme–phoneme conversion* process in reading due to impairment in selection at the level of the *phonological output lexicon* (e.g., if the person is unable to select the correct phonological form for the word *pint*, the *grapheme–phoneme conversion* route could be used to produce the word, resulting in the word pronounced using regular spelling rules—/pɪnt/). Errors with both visual and semantic overlap with the target word are explained by dual-route models as an impairment in accessing the *semantic system* from the *orthographic input lexicon*. In this case, a correct orthographic form could have been selected at the *orthographic input lexicon*, but incorrect selection would occur in the *semantic system* (e.g., the word *car* would be selected in the *orthographic input lexicon* along with other visually similar words such as *cab* and *cat*; in the *semantic system*, other semantically related words would be activated such as *cab* and

truck; at this point, inaccurate selection could occur for *cab* because it was first active in the *orthographic input lexicon* and then active again in the *semantic system*).

In contrast to the dual-route approach of providing separate explanations for different types of reading errors, connectionist models explain surface dyslexia as a symptom of a general semantic impairment that is not specific to reading. Evidence for this explanation stems primarily from reports of individuals who demonstrate reading patterns consistent with surface alexia as well as co-occurring symptoms of semantic dementia, a type of dementia associated with the decline of semantic memory (Woollams, Ralph, Plaut, & Patterson, 2007). For connectionist models, all reading errors associated with surface alexia stem from weakened activations at the level of semantic processing.

DEEP ALEXIA

Deep alexia involves an impairment in the way written words are processed during lexical and nonlexical reading (Marshall & Newcombe, 1973; Patterson & Marcel, 1977; Shallice & Warrington, 1975). Although the literature offers varying descriptions of deep alexia, these individuals exhibit several hallmark symptoms, including (1) severely impaired pseudoword reading (e.g., an inability to orally read *blik*), (2) semantic errors in oral reading (e.g., *apple* produced as *banana*; *window* produced as *door*), (3) visual errors in oral reading (e.g., *table* produced as *cable*; *goal* produced as *goat*), (4) morphological errors in oral reading (e.g., *baking* produced as *baked*; *drives* produced as *drive*), and (5) an imageability effect in word reading with greater success in reading concrete, imageable words (e.g., higher accuracy reading *horse* in comparison to *freedom*).

Dual-route models have traditionally explained deep alexia as a dual impairment of nonlexical and lexical reading routes. In this explanation, errors in pseudoword reading can be explained as an impairment in *grapheme–phoneme conversion*, and lexical errors (especially semantic errors) can be explained as an impairment somewhere along the lexical route, either in semantic access, semantic processing, or phonological processing. One proposed theory (Failure of Inhibition Theory, FIT) suggests that symptoms of deep alexia (most specifically the production of semantic errors) result from a failure to inhibit selection of inappropriate targets at the level of the *phonological output lexicon* (Colangelo & Buchanan, 2006, 2007). However, other evidence indicates that individuals with deep alexia demonstrate differences in semantic processing that are not limited to reading, suggesting that semantic errors may be due to impairment occurring prior to phonological processing (Riley & Thompson, 2010).

Although the Failure of Inhibition Theory (Colangelo & Buchanan, 2006, 2007) and evidence from Riley and Thompson (2010) most directly address the question of lexical–semantic errors in deep alexia raised by dual-route model explanations, both are also compatible with connectionist model explanations of deep alexia. In a connectionist model, deep alexia can be explained either by a weakened phonological system (compatible with FIT) or by weakened connections between semantic and phonological processing (compatible with evidence from Riley & Thompson, 2010).

PHONOLOGICAL ALEXIA

Phonological alexia involves an impairment in the way written words are processed during non-lexical reading, specifically manifesting as impaired pseudoword reading in conjunction with the absence of semantic reading errors (Beauvois & Dérouesné, 1979; Dérouesné & Beauvois, 1979; Ellis & Young, 1988). In pseudoword oral reading, lexicalization errors (e.g., the pseudoword *blaf* produced as the real word *black*) are common in phonological alexia. In addition to this hallmark symptom of phonological alexia, in more recent years studies have recognized that individuals with phonological alexia often demonstrate several overlapping symptoms with deep alexia, including visual errors and imageability effects, with semantic errors as the only consistent differentiating symptom between the two disorder subtypes (Crisp & Lambon Ralph, 2006; Friedman, 1996; Glosser & Friedman, 1990).

Dual-route models have traditionally explained phonological alexia as an impairment of the nonlexical reading route. More specifically, in this model, errors in pseudoword reading can be explained as an impairment in *grapheme–phoneme conversion*. Lexicalization and visual errors are explained in a dual-route model as an overreliance on lexical route reading (e.g., due to nonlexical route impairment, the pseudoword *tavder* would be processed using the lexical route and read as the real word *ladder*, which is both a lexicalization error and is visually similar to the pseudoword target); however, imageability effects are more difficult to explain using a

dual-route model as they are generally associated with semantic processing and dual-route models do not explicitly conceptualize an interaction between semantic processing and nonlexical reading. Connectionist models explain phonological alexia primarily as a general weakening of phonological processing. Although some evidence would suggest that individuals with phonological alexia do not demonstrate a general phonological impairment (Coltheart, 1996; Tree & Kay, 2006), others have argued that growing evidence would suggest that phonological impairment in these individuals exists beyond the realm of reading and overlaps in spelling as well as other tasks not involving orthographic processing (Patterson & Lambon Ralph, 1999; Rapcsak et al., 2009; Welbourne & Lambon Ralph, 2007).

DEEP AND PHONOLOGICAL ALEXIA: TWO SIDES OF THE SAME COIN?

Most existing literature treats phonological and deep alexia as separate subtypes of acquired alexia. However, some have suggested that phonological and deep alexia are not really separate disorders, but simply lie along a severity continuum of reading deficit, with phonological alexia representing the mild end and deep alexia representing the severe end of the continuum (Crisp & Lambon Ralph, 2006; Friedman, 1996; Glosser & Friedman, 1990). This view is based on evidence of significant symptom overlap between the diagnoses of phonological or deep alexia as well as reading recovery patterns (Crisp & Lambon Ralph, 2006). Friedman (1996) reported five individuals whose reading deficits appeared to change over their recovery period, with symptoms of deep alexia eventually evolving into symptoms of phonological alexia. For all the participants reviewed in this study, the first sign of recovery was a significant decrease and eventual disappearance of semantic reading errors. The last symptom affected was pseudoword reading, which significantly improved, but did not fully recover in any of the participants, suggesting that deep and phonological alexia are not independent disorders, but represent differing levels of severity (Friedman, 1996). Proponents of the continuum theory have provided some rather convincing evidence. One possible explanation as to why previous studies did not adopt a spectral view of alexia may be that published research studies present a disproportionate number of cases from opposite ends of the continuum (i.e., more intermediary cases existed, but went unreported).

Associations between Alexia and Aphasia

Typically, individuals with peripheral alexia do not have a co-occurring aphasia; however, the two language disorders are not mutually exclusive. In pure alexia, the most-studied peripheral alexia subtype, writing and spelling are usually intact and language is fairly unimpaired with occasional cases of anomia (Friedman & Hadley, 1992). Typically, central alexias tend to co-occur with aphasia. Brookshire, Wilson, Nadeau, Rothi, and Kendall (2014) investigated the frequency and nature of alexia in a convenience sample of 100 persons with aphasia. They also wanted to see if the severity of aphasia and level of education were predictive of oral reading abilities. The results showed that 68% of people with aphasia had alexia, and the alexia type tended to be sublexical in nature. Furthermore, aphasia severity was significantly predictive of oral reading performance and education achievement was trending toward significance. Although the current evidence is not conclusive, cases of surface alexia have often reported fluent aphasia (Friedman & Hadley, 1992), cases of deep alexia have often reported nonfluent (often Broca's) aphasia (Coltheart, Patterson, & Marshall, 1980), and cases of phonological alexia have either reported no aphasia or mild aphasia (Coltheart, 1996).

Neuroanatomical Correlates of Reading

Neuroanatomical correlates of reading have been examined and tested using functional imaging techniques [e.g., positron emission tomography (PET) and functional magnetic resonance imaging (fMRI)] in normal controls and individuals with brain lesions (see Price, 2012, for a comprehensive review). As in other areas of language processing, lesion-deficit correlation studies to date have yet to identify a single cortical area essential for reading, which has led some investigators to propose that neural substrates for reading may indeed be reliant on a number of cortical regions that are components of a distributed neural network (Henry, Beeson, Stark, & Rapcsak, 2007; Rapcsak et al., 2009; Rapcsak & Beeson, 2002). One common approach to investigating neuroanatomical correlates of reading has been to separate the reading process into two distinct stages: (1) early visual processing and (2) mapping orthography to phonology (with and without a semantic component). Early visual processing is associated with peripheral alexias, whereas mapping orthography to phonology is associated with central alexias.

Regarding early visual processing, research has primarily focused on identifying areas of the brain that are more active during written word processing as compared to other kinds of stimuli (e.g., words versus pictures, words versus strings of symbols, written words versus spoken words). Early work in this area lead to the discovery of what has been termed the "visual word form area" (VWFA), a label that was applied to the left occipitotemporal cortex (e.g., Dehaene et al., 2001; Fiez & Peterson, 1998; Leff et al., 2001). Some argued that the role of the left occipitotemporal cortex was to store abstract representations of visual words, hence the name "visual word form area" (Cohen et al., 2000; Dehaene et al., 2001). However, later studies investigating the activation of the left occipitotemporal cortex indicated that its role was not to store visual forms of words, but instead to integrate low-level visual information with higher-level processing (Price & Devlin, 2003; Price & Friston, 2005). More recent work has expanded the evidence in support of this view and replicated findings of similar patterns of left occipitotemporal cortex activation across letter, word, and object processing tasks (e.g., Shinkareva, Malave, Mason, Mitchell, & Just, 2011; Turkeltaub, Flowers, Lyon, & Eden, 2008; Wright et al., 2008). From the contributions of these and other studies, an even more specific hypothesis of the role of the left occipitotemporal cortex has been proposed, suggesting that this area is involved in processing generic visual features of any visual stimuli (Barton, Fox, Sekunova, & Iaria, 2010; Braet, Wagemans, & de Beeck, 2011).

In individuals with peripheral alexia, lesions have been identified in areas of the brain associated with visual processing, including the left occipitotemporal cortex. Lesions in the left occipital lobe and the splenium of the corpus callosum have been identified as areas of damage typically associated with pure alexia (Friedman & Glosser, 1998; Friedman & Hadley, 1992). However, because lesion sites extensively vary across individuals, more research is necessary before definitive correlations can be made between lesion site and behavioral symptoms/alexia diagnosis.

Regarding later processes involved in reading, research has primarily focused on identifying areas of the brain that are more active during tasks that require mapping orthography to phonology as compared to other tasks (e.g., reading pseudowords versus real words with irregular spellings). Several studies that compared real words with pseudowords have found evidence of greater activation in the left posterior or inferior frontal cortex for pseudowords, presumably due to the increased requirement to map orthography to phonology for pseudowords (e.g., Hagoort et al., 1999; Pugh et al., 1996) or perhaps due to the increased difficulty of the task (Fiez & Petersen, 1998). Expanding on this work, Mechelli and colleagues (2005) found activation of anterior ventral occipitotemporal cortex and left ventral inferior frontal cortex for words with irregular spellings, suggesting that these areas are involved in lexicosemantic reading. More recently, reports have suggested that not all reading involves activation of the left ventral occipitotemporal cortex (Levy et al., 2008; Richardson, Seghier, Leff, Thomas, & Price, 2011). Levy and colleagues (2009) proposed that the left posterior occipitotemporal cortex is required only for pseudoword reading and is primarily involved in directly mapping phonology onto orthography, whereas reading familiar words does not require activation of this area. Interestingly, several studies have also demonstrated a large degree of variability across subjects in the cortical networks that are most active during reading. For instance, using a familiar word reading task, Seghier, Lee, Schofield, Ellis, and Price (2008) were able to classify skilled readers into two groups: (1) those who showed more activation in the anterior occipitotemporal and inferior frontal areas, and (2) those who showed more activation in the left posterior occipitotemporal and right inferior parietal areas.

With regard to central alexia, lesion sites also vary across individuals and across subtypes. Several studies have reported left perisylvian or left superior temporal lesions in phonological alexia (Beeson, Rising, Kim, & Rapcsak, 2010; Friedman & Glosser, 1998), left-temporal or temporoparietal lesions in surface alexia (Friedman & Hadley, 1992), and large left hemisphere lesions in deep alexia (Coltheart et al., 1980; Friedman & Glosser, 1998). Rapcsak and colleagues (2009) reported computed tomography (CT) and MRI results in 31 individuals who showed damage to one or more perisylvian cortical regions implicated in phonological processing. These neuroanatomical areas included the posterior inferior frontal gyrus/Broca's area (BA 44/45), precentral gyrus (BA 4/6), insula, superior temporal gyrus/ Wernicke's area (BA 22), and supramarginal gyrus (BA 40). Given the evidence of premorbid reading variability in combination with the variability of lesion sites, establishing a strong correlation between lesion site and behavioral symptoms of central alexia is likely to be a challenging task and more research is needed before lesion/symptom relationships become clear.

Assessment

To determine the type of alexia, severity, and underlying psycholinguistic mechanisms contributing to the reading disorder, it is necessary to conduct a sensitive and specific assessment. Screening tests of reading that are embedded as subtests of classic aphasia testing are included in the Boston Diagnostic Aphasia Examination (Goodglass, Kaplan, & Barresi, 2001) and the Western Aphasia Battery-revised (Kertesz, 2007). A detailed assessment can also be conducted using standardized, research experimental assessments, or unstandardized stimuli.

Standardized Assessments

Psycholinguistic Assessments of Language Processing in Aphasia (PALPA; Kay, Lesser, & Coltheart, 1992) is intended to be used for clinical and research purposes. The *PALPA* is modeled within current cognitive models of language and includes a set of resource materials enabling the user to select language tasks that can be tailored to the investigation of an individual's impaired and intact abilities. The *PALPA* consists of 60 subtests of components of language structure such as orthography and phonology, word and picture semantics, and morphology and syntax. Many of the subtests have normative data and many are devoted to written language. Although the *PALPA* is one of the most comprehensive assessments of reading function, there are drawbacks of the test, such as original norms only for British English and the brevity of the stimulus word lists.

Reading Comprehension Battery for Aphasia, 2nd Edition (RCBA; LaPointe & Horner, 1998) provides a systematic evaluation of the nature and degree of reading impairment in adults with aphasia, including oral reading comprehension. The RCBA can be individually administered in 30 minutes with 20 subtests covering single-word comprehension for visual confusions, auditory confusions, and semantic confusions; functional reading; synonyms; sentence comprehension; short paragraph comprehension; paragraphs; and morphosyntactic reading with lexical controls.

Gray Oral Reading Test—4 (Wiederholt & Bryant, 2001) is intended for use for individuals 6 years–18 years to assess oral reading rate, fluency, and comprehension. The test stimuli include 13 passages that are controlled for a variety of features of words and sentences.

Gates-MacGinitie Reading Test (GMRT; Gates & MacGinitie, 1978) is intended for use for individuals aged 6–18 years to measure reading achievement. The GMRT is a timed multiple-choice test administered in groups. It provides scores in five areas including literacy concepts, oral language concepts, and letters and letter–sound correspondences.

Woodcock-Johnson III Diagnostic Reading Battery (*WJ-III DRB*; Woodcock, Mather, & Schrank, 2004) includes several subtests, such as word identification, passage comprehension, nonword reading, reading fluency, and sound awareness. This battery provides normative values for individuals from age 2 to 90 years.

Research experimental assessments for reading include the Battery of Adult Reading Function (Rothi, Coslett, & Heilman, 1984), the Maryland Reading Battery (Berndt, Haendiges, Mitchum, & Wayland, 1996), and the Johns Hopkins University Dyslexia Battery (Goodman & Caramazza, 1986, presented in Beeson & Henry, 2008).

Nonstandardized Assessment
PERIPHERAL ASSESSMENT

To ascertain that the reading deficit is not due to early visual perception or peripheral mechanisms, an assessment of shape/letter matching and abstract letter identification can be used. For shape/letter matching, the individual can be asked to select two identical shapes from an array of nonsense shapes or to match letters of the same case and font. Abstract letter identities can be assessed with a task of letter matching across case and/or font and with a letter recognition task such as a forced choice task in which the individual must distinguish correct letters from mirror-reversed letters.

CENTRAL ASSESSMENT

Visual word recognition: To assess if there is activation of the lexeme from orthography, a visual lexical decision task can be used. In this task, equal numbers of real words and nonwords are presented randomly and the person is asked to determine whether the stimulus is a real word or not. Depending upon the severity of the individual's reading impairment, stimuli can be manipulated to include nonwords comprised of legal and illegal phonotactic orthographic structure (e.g., flig and flvg), high- and low-frequency real words, and irregularly spelled real words (e.g., yacht, shoe).

Semantic processing: To assess the access to semantics from visual orthography, several tasks can be conducted. A *category sorting task*, for example, includes written words belonging to several semantic categories (e.g., tools, fruits, vegetables, transportation). The person is given randomly ordered written words on index cards and is asked to sort the cards into the appropriate categories. Another semantic processing task is *cross-modality matching* in which a single written word is matched with a corresponding picture or object from several choices. A *semantic associate matching task* can be also used to assess semantic activation in which a picture is shown and the person is asked to match the picture to an associated word from among semantically related written words (e.g., picture: tree; written word stimuli: leaf, grass, flower). A final task that can be used to detect the integrity of the orthographic to semantic network is to *match a written word with a written definition,* again from among several choices.

Nonlexical processing: An evaluation of the aspects of the reading process that do not involve the lexical–semantic system includes an assessment of *graphemic parsing, grapheme to phoneme letter conversion, and phonological blending.* To assess *graphemic parsing,* real and nonword stimuli can be visually presented and the individual must segment the word into smaller units such as syllables or phonemes. For example, the real word "boxcar" would be segmented into two real words, box + car. A nonword such as "drislee" would be segmented into dris + lee. A *grapheme-to-phoneme letter conversion* can be assessed by presenting individual written letters and asking the person to produce the corresponding sound. *Pseudohomophone verification* may also be used. In this task pairs of phonetically identical letter strings are presented in which one string is a word and the other is a nonword (e.g., groan/grone and crane/crain). The individual decides whether the two letter strings can be pronounced the same way. Finally, *phonological blending* could be elicited for individual graphemes (b + e + d = bed) and syllables (ba + by = baby) that need to be blended into one pronunciation.

Treatment
Impairment-Based Reading Approaches and Strategies

To determine the most appropriate treatment approach for an individual with alexia, it is essential to link the behaviors observed in the standardized and/or nonstandardized assessment with the underlying mechanism of impairment, as described earlier in this chapter. At that point, the treatment programs listed below, as well as others in the literature, can be evaluated for appropriateness to match the level of severity and stimulability for the individual with alexia. To that end, we will first provide an overview of the common treatment approaches for each alexia subtype, and then selected, recent, efficacious treatment studies will be more thoroughly described in regard to research design, lesion location of participants, targeted behavior, stimuli, procedure, treatment intensity/frequency, and outcomes. Finally, in addition to the alexia treatment studies described in this chapter, the reader is encouraged to visit resources such as the Academy of Neurologic Communication Disorders and Sciences (ANCDS) aphasia treatment website (http://aphasiatx.arizona.edu/) created as part of the ANCDS Evidence-Based Practice (EBP) guidelines project (Golper et al., 2001). The goal of the project is "... to improve quality of services to individuals with neurologic communication disorders by assisting clinicians in decision-making about the management of specific populations through guidelines based on research evidence" (p. 1).

The ANCDS aphasia treatment website contains summaries (in the form of composite tables) of aphasia treatment studies related to the rehabilitation of lexical retrieval, syntax, speech production, and written language impairment (reading and writing). The studies were evaluated and coded for type of design (between group, within group, single subject, and case study), class of study (strongest, intermediate, weakest), and phase of treatment research (1–5) (Robey & Schultz, 1998). In direct relation to this chapter, the section of the ANCDS website concerning reading impairment (http://aphasiatx.arizona.edu/written_reading) contains reviews of 70 alexia treatment studies completed between 1964 and 2010 targeting different alexia subtypes utilizing varied treatment approaches, some of which will be reviewed below.

PURE ALEXIA

The rehabilitation of pure alexia focuses on either improving the hallmark compensatory letter-by-letter reading strategy used by individuals with pure alexia, or training the use of whole word reading (while discouraging the use of segmental letter reading). Letter-level treatments generally focus on improving single letter identification (e.g., cross-case matching tasks, speeded letter matching) and letter naming, often via tactile–kinesthetic tasks (e.g., trace the letters, copy the letter on the palm)

in an attempt to make the letter-by-letter reading strategy more efficient. Word-level treatments tend to focus on rapid recognition of words and parallel grapheme processing in an attempt to help the person reacquire a whole word reading strategy. An individual who has difficulty naming letters might tend to receive treatment focused on letter identification, whereas a person with intact letter naming, but impaired letter integration, would likely be better suited for word-level treatment (Ablinger & Domahs, 2009). Some researchers have had success combining letter-level and word-level treatments (Harris, Olson, & Humphreys, 2013; Sage, Hesketh, & Lambon Ralph, 2005). Regardless of which approach, or combination of approaches, is used, pure alexia treatments aim to improve impairment in the early stages of reading (i.e., impaired visual feature analysis/letter analysis) (see Figure 12.1) and do not typically focus on semantics or phonology, although at least one study experimented with including these types of tasks (Viswanathan & Kiran, 2005).

Table 12.1 provides a description of five recent pure alexia treatment studies. The studies ranged in sample size from one to three participants and employed case study, case series, or single-subject research designs. Participants across all five studies demonstrated some degree of injury in the occipital lobe, which is likely related to difficulties with visual analysis and reliance on a letter-by-letter reading strategy. Treatment strategies included limited exposure whole word reading (Ablinger & Domahs, 2009), tactile–kinesthetic letter reading (Lott, Carney, Glezer, & Friedman, 2010; Sage et al., 2005), comparison of word-level and letter-level treatment (Harris et al., 2013), and sublexical conversion and semantic feature analysis (Viswanathan & Kiran, 2005). See Table 12.1 for details concerning stimuli type, treatment procedures, and outcomes.

SURFACE ALEXIA

The rehabilitation of surface alexia typically focuses on improving the hallmark symptoms of impaired irregular word reading (e.g., yacht) and homophone confusion (e.g., peek–peak) via lexical (whole word) treatment approaches. According to the dual-route theory, surface alexia treatments aim to improve reading impairments located in the lexical route at the level of the orthographic input lexicon, semantic system, and/or phonological output lexicon (see Figure 12.1). The connectionist theory would support a surface alexia treatment aimed

Table 12.1 Description of Recent Pure Alexia Treatment Studies

Reference	Design	Site of Lesion(s)	Treatment Type	Target Behavior	Stimuli	Procedure	Intensity and Frequency	Outcome
Ablinger & Domahs (2009)	Case study (n = 1)	L MCA/PCA CVA	Whole word (limited exposure)	Word reading and letter ID	160 real words (80 trained, 80 control) between 1 and 3 syllables. Words contained "difficult" letters the pt had difficulty naming.	Training began with *auditory–visual verification tasks* (pt decided if written word matched spoken word) to familiarize pt with stimuli. Then, *whole-word recognition training* began. Pt briefly (1,000 ms) saw the target word on screen and was asked to read it. Each word was randomly seen 4 times/session. Feedback was provided if pt was unable to correctly read the target.	2 sessions/day, 5 days/week for 4 weeks	Improved speed and accuracy of cross-case matching and reading of words and text
Harris et al. (2013)	ABACA single subject design (n = 2)	L occipitotemporal abscess; L temporal and insular CVA	Word-level vs. letter-level	Word reading	40, 4- to 5-letter words (20 with high letter confusability and 20 with low letter confusability)	Target words were presented individually on cards. *Word-level txt:* (1) therapist read aloud word 5 times while pt listened, (2) pt repeated word 5 times while looking at word; *Letter-level txt:* (1) word presented one letter at a time with "moving window." Therapist named each letter and pt repeated letter name and traced letter shape with finger; (2) pt read each letter name before reading whole word. If error occurred, repeated Step 1.	20 weeks; 1 hour/week in clinic, plus home training	Word txt improved reading of low confusability words; letter txt improved both high and low confusability words
Lott et al. (2010)	Case series (n = 3)	L CVA; L parietal-occipital hemorrhage; L occipital CVA	Tactile-kinesthetic at letter level	Reading of untrained words in "free vision"	*Phase 1:* 26 alphabetic letters; *Phase 2:* 450 nonpronounceable letter strings and 450 words 4–8 letters in length matched for orthographic similarity; *Untrained list:* 40, 6-letter, 2-syllable low-frequency regularly spelled words	*Phase 1 (letter naming):* (1) traced each letter with and without pen strokes provided, (2) copied each letter onto palm, (3) copied on palm and named it; *Phase 2a (rapid letter naming):* (1) named letters in isolation and then in letter strings as fast as possible; *Phase 2b (rapid letter by letter word reading):* named each letter in the word and then read the word as fast as possible; 3 blocks of 25 letter strings or words presented each session.	1 hour/day, 3 times/week; plus home practice 3 times/day during Phase 1 only	Phase 1 did not improve reading; continued practice (Phase 2) improved reading speed and accuracy of untrained words without overt use of trained strategy

(continued)

Table 12.1 Continued

Reference	Design	Site of Lesion(s)	Treatment Type	Target Behavior	Stimuli	Procedure	Intensity and Frequency	Outcome
Sage et al. (2005)	Case study (n = 1)	L parietal-temporal CVA followed 2 months later by L occipital hemorrhage	Tactile-kinesthetic at whole word and letter level	Word reading	3, 30-word lists matched for length, frequency, imageability, and AOA; lists consisted of triads (first 3 letters are identical), words related to ADLs, and words of personal interest to the pt	Family trained to deliver txt and therapist visited 1 time/week. *Treatment 1 (Word Txt):* (1) pt traced around the shape of the word focusing on visual features, (2) looked at final 3 letters (in red font), (3) looked and listened to word read aloud by family member, (4) looked, listened, and then repeated word 5 times; *Treatment 2 (Letter Txt):* (1) family member read aloud each target word one letter at a time and traced the letter onto pt's palm. Pt repeated word. (2) Same as Step 1 except pt read word aloud after letters were traced, (3) cards were shuffled and Step 2 repeated, (4) Pt read aloud each letter and said word. Errorless learning feedback was provided.	*Word therapy:* 10 words/week for 7 weeks; *Letter therapy:* 30-item word list trained over 7 weeks	Improved accuracy and speed on treated items; attempted use of whole word reading instead of letter-by-letter strategy; decreased omissions and increased semantic and visual errors; letter ID remained impaired
Viswanathan & Kiran (2005)	Case study (n = 1)	L occipitotemporal-parietal CVA	Sublexical conversion and semantic feature analysis	Word reading	22 regularly spelled words matched for frequency, familiarity, and number of letters and syllables divided into trained and untrained lists; each word in one list was semantically related to a word in the other list	11 regularly spelled words were trained using the following steps: (1) oral reading of target word, (2) written spelling, (3) identify letters of the word from phonological and orthographic distracters, (4) identify randomly presented letters of target word, (5) read aloud letter names of target word, (6) description of semantic features of the target word, and (7) oral reading of the target word.	2 baseline sessions and 20 probe sessions	Improved oral reading accuracy for trained and untrained words; generalization to spelling of untrained words

Note: pt, participant; txt, treatment; L, left; CVA, cerebrovascular accident; MCA, middle cerebral artery; PCA, posterior cerebral artery; AOA, age of acquisition; ADLs, activities of daily living; ID, identification.

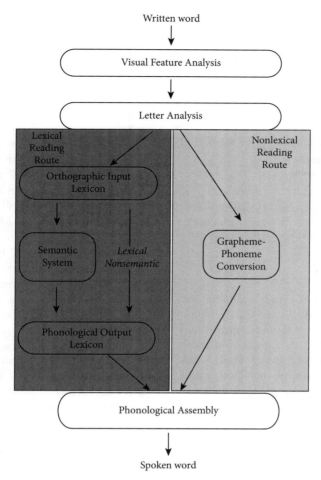

Figure 12.1 Dual-route model adopted from Coltheart, Rastle, Perry, and Langdon (2001). The lexical reading route (dark box) is divided into lexical–semantic reading and lexical–nonsemantic reading while the light gray box represents the nonlexical reading route.

at training semantic processing and connections between semantic processing and orthographic processing (see Figure 12.2). Surface alexia treatments often pair pictures with words to provide a boost to the semantic system. Phonology is generally not targeted in surface alexia treatments as sublexical reading skills (e.g., grapheme–phoneme conversion, nonword reading) are thought to be mostly intact, at least relative to lexical reading skills.

Table 12.2 provides a description of seven recent surface alexia treatment studies. All are case studies by design and the participants demonstrated various lesion etiologies, including semantic dementia, closed head injury, and stroke. All of the studies used a lexical treatment, and strategies employed included word reading with mnemonic support (Coltheart & Byng, 1989), homophone recognition

(Scott & Byng, 1989), reading words with ambiguous vowel patterns (Friedman & Robinson, 1991), speeded presentation of irregular words and homophone selection (Moss, Rothi, & Fennell, 1991), mixed irregular word reading and homophone spelling with mnemonic support (Weekes & Coltheart, 1996), acronym reading (Playfoot, Tree, & Izura, 2014), and picture naming and single-word reading (Ellis, Lambon Ralph, Morris, & Hunter, 2000). See Table 12.2 for details concerning stimuli type, treatment procedures, and outcomes.

PHONOLOGICAL AND DEEP ALEXIA

The rehabilitation of phonological and deep alexia commonly focuses on improving the hallmark symptom of impaired grapheme-to-phoneme correspondence (GPC) knowledge evidenced by

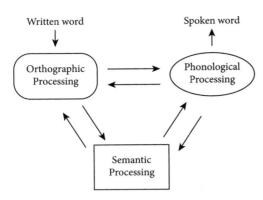

Figure 12.2 Connectionist Triangle Model adapted from Seidenberg and McClelland (1989). This model represents a distributed connectionist network of orthographic, semantic, and phonological processing.

poor reading of nonwords and unfamiliar real words. According to the dual-route theory, phonological/deep alexia treatment should target the non-lexical route (Figure 12.1). A connectionist theory interpretation of phonological/deep alexia would support a treatment targeting phonological processing more generally (beyond reading) and connections from phonology to orthographic and semantic processing (Figure 12.2). Typically, in phonological/deep alexia treatment, sublexical reading skills are the target behavior. In the past, GPC training was the main focus of phonological/deep alexia treatment (de Partz, 1986; Mitchum & Berndt, 1991). More recently, however, a combination of GPC training in the context of more general phonological skills training (e.g., phoneme parsing and blending, minimal pair discrimination) has come into favor (Brookshire, Conway, Hunting Pompon, Oelke, & Kendall, 2014; Kendall, Conway, Rosenbek, & Rothi, 2003; Yampolsky & Waters, 2002). Targeting sublexical skills both within *and* outside the context of orthography supports the notion that the source of reading impairment in phonological/deep alexia is related to a general underlying impairment of phonology, not limited to the domain of reading (Beeson et al., 2010).

For individuals with deep alexia, treatment usually contains a component focused on semantics, in addition to phonology, to target their coexisting semantic impairments. Purely visual tasks (i.e., letter matching) are typically not used in phonological/deep alexia treatments given that the early reading stages (i.e., visual feature and letter analysis) are thought to be intact for individuals with phonological and deep alexia.

Table 12.3 provides a description of eight recent phonological/deep alexia treatment studies. The studies ranged in sample size from one to eight participants and employed case study, case series, single subject design, or single group pretreatment/posttreatment research designs. All participants experienced left hemisphere damage due to stroke, except for two participants who experienced unspecified left hemisphere "craniocerebral injury" (Ablinger, Huber, & Radach, 2014) and left hemisphere injury due to skull fracture (Lacey, Lott, Snider, Sperling, & Friedman, 2010). Treatment strategies included bigraph–biphone correspondence training (Bowes & Martin, 2007), phonological self-cueing with mnemonic support (Lott, Sample, Oliver, Lacey, & Friedman, 2008), eye movement-based reading therapy (Ablinger et al., 2014), sublexical/lexical interactive therapy (Beeson et al., 2010), multimodal phonology treatment (phonomotor; Brookshire et al., 2014), multiple oral rereading (MOR; Lacey et al., 2010), sublexical conversion and semantic feature analysis (Kiran & Viswanathan, 2008), and phonological complexity (sonority) training (Riley & Thompson, 2015). See Table 12.3 for details concerning stimuli type, treatment procedures, and outcomes.

MULTIPLE ORAL REREADING (MOR; MOYER, 1979)

The MOR reading treatment has been used with individuals across the alexia subtypes with varying degrees of success. In the MOR technique, individuals with alexia practice reading aloud simple text passages multiple times for a set number of days. The speed of reading is recorded. Although MOR has improved text reading for individuals with pure alexia, it has also been used with some degree of success in individuals with other reading and language impairments (Cherney, 1995). The underlying mechanism influenced by MOR is unclear (Lacey, Lott, Sperling, Snider, & Friedman, 2007; Beeson, Magloire, & Robey, 2005); however, it is understood that with this technique text reading aloud facilitates both bottom-up and top-down whole word processing. Eleven studies for rehabilitation of alexia using MOR, or a treatment similar to MOR, were reviewed for the EBP project mentioned previously, of which seven were evaluated to be a Phase I research study (Beeson, 1998; Cherney, Merbitz, & Grip, 1986; Cherney, 2004; Friedman, Sample, & Lott, 2002; Mayer & Murray, 2002; Moody, 1988; Moyer, 1979) and four were Phase II (Beeson et al., 2005, Cherney, 1995; Lacey et al., 2010; Toumainen & Laine, 1991). All but one

Table 12.2 Description of Recent Surface Alexia Treatment Studies

Reference	Design	Site of Lesion(s)	Treatment Type	Target Behavior	Stimuli	Procedure	Intensity and frequency	Outcome
Coltheart & Byng (1989)	Case study (n = 1)	R temporal and L temporal-parietal s/p skull fx	Whole word with mnemonic support	Txt 1: irregular word reading; Txt 2 and 3: high-frequency words	Txt 1: 24 irregular words containing "-ough" (e.g., cough); Txt 2: 54 high-frequency words; Txt 3: 101 high-frequency words	Txt 1: Each word was printed on a card alongside a picture representing the word. Pt read aloud each word and recorded progress in a daily log. Txt 2 and 3: Words were accompanied by symbols selected by pt and therapist. Pt used mnemonic to assist in reading aloud each word.	Txt 1: 15 minutes/day at home for 5 weeks; Txt 2: 15 minutes/day at home for 1 week; Txt 3: not specified	Txt 1: 100% oral reading accuracy of all 24 words and maintained 1 year later; Txt 2 and 3: improved reading of trained words with some generalization to untrained words
Ellis et al. (2000)	Case study (n = 1)	L parietal craniotomy to evacuate intracerebral hematoma	2 treatments: picture naming and whole word reading	Picture naming and single word reading	52 pictures and 52 words the pt had difficulty naming and reading on 2 or 3 prior occasions; each set split into 26 trained and 26 untrained	Txt 1 (naming therapy): Pt given a booklet with 4 pages per target word: (1) picture only, (2) picture plus first letter, (3) picture plus first half of written name, (4) picture plus full written name. Pt started on page 1 and tried to name the picture using page 4 to check work. Txt 2 (reading therapy): Pt given worksheets with printed target words and corresponding audio tapes. Pt first tried to read aloud from worksheet, then listened to tape. If incorrect he "looked hard," repeated the correct pronunciation several times, and thought of the meaning of the target word.	Daily home practice for 20 minutes for 3 weeks for naming txt and 2 weeks for reading txt with weekly visits by clinician	Improved naming accuracy for trained pictures and improved reading accuracy for trained words; no generalization to untrained pictures or words

(continued)

Table 12.2 Continued

Reference	Design	Site of Lesion(s)	Treatment Type	Target Behavior	Stimuli	Procedure	Intensity and frequency	Outcome
Friedman & Robinson (1991)	Case study ($n = 1$)	L temporal-occipital CVA	Whole word	Reading of words with ambiguous vowels	16 vowel groups with inconsistent vowels (e.g., ow- cow, row) and words with and without the "rule of e" (e.g., rate, rat) were represented in 253 words; the words were divided into treatment and control groups	Each vowel group (e.g., -ow) was represented on a card with the top half representing words with one pronunciation (e.g., cow) and the lower half another pronunciation (e.g., row). One to three vowel groups were trained each session. Pt read aloud each word independently and repeated clinician or wife example when necessary.	7 sessions over 13 weeks, plus daily home practice 15–30 minutes	Improved reading of trained words, with poor generalization to untrained words with the same ambiguous vowels
Moss et al. (1991)	Case study ($n = 1$)	R frontal craniotomy and L frontotemporal contusion	Whole word	Oral reading and reading comprehension	*Task 1*: 100 words, 10 per session; *Task 2*: 10 irregularly spelled words; *Task 3*: 5-sentence paragraphs containing homographic pairs	Treatment consisted of 3 tasks: *Task 1*: Forced semantic analysis (pt saw a word for 1 second and named the semantic category); *Task 2*: Rapid reading aloud of irregular words; *Task 3*: Homophone selection (pt read paragraph silently and selected appropriate homophone based on context (e.g., flower/flour).	10, 1-hour sessions over 2-week period	Increased reading rate while maintaining or improving accuracy

Study	Design	Etiology	Focus	Task	Stimuli	Procedure	Dosage	Outcome
Playfoot et al. (2014)	Case study (n = 1)	Semantic dementia (area of cerebral atrophy not specified)	Context effects of acronym reading	Oral reading of acronyms	20 ambiguous acronyms (contain vowels and consonants, e.g., "NASA," "HIV"); 80 unambiguous acronyms (contain only consonants, e.g., "NPR"); 80 regularly spelled words, 3–5 letters in length	Pt read aloud stimuli from two lists. *List 1:* 20 ambiguous acronyms (e.g., "AOL," "NATO") were randomly embedded in the list of regular words (e.g., "ACT"). *List 2:* The same 20 ambiguous acronyms were embedded in the list of unambiguous acronyms (e.g., "CBS"). Pt was instructed to read aloud each stimulus, which was typed in all uppercase letters on the computer screen.	One experimental training session; 10-minute break provided between reading lists	In list of regular words, pt read all acronyms as if they were words (using GPC conversion). In the context of unambiguous acronyms (NPR), pt read the ambiguous acronyms (NASA) by naming each letter and did not pronounce it as a word. Greater overall accuracy for those acronyms pronounced letter by letter (HIV) than as a word (NATO).
Scott & Byng (1989)	Case study (n = 1)	L temporal lobe s/p car accident	Recognition and comprehension of written homophones	Homophones	135 homophone pairs: divided into 68 pairs trained and 67 untrained	Pt shown a sentence on the screen with a missing word (e.g., "The ladies served cream ____") and was required to choose from a set of 6 words that contained the following: correct word, homophone, NW homophone, and 3 visual distractors (e.g., "teas, tease, teeze, tens, team, tenze"). Pt then typed in the correct word. Visual and auditory feedback provided by the computer program.	29 sessions over 10 weeks	Improved homophone sentence judgment for treated and untreated pairs; improved homophone recognition for treated pairs only; writing homophones to dictation did not improve

(continued)

Table 12.2 Continued

Reference	Design	Site of Lesion(s)	Treatment Type	Target Behavior	Stimuli	Procedure	Intensity and frequency	Outcome
Weekes & Coltheart (1996)	Case study (n = 1)	R frontal contusion, L occipital fx, L postparietal extradural hematoma s/p car accident	2 treatments: whole word reading and spelling with mnemonic support	*Txt 1*: reading "exception" words; *Txt 2*: homophone spelling	*Txt 1*: 80 exception words (e.g., choir) divided into trained and untrained groups matched for word length and frequency; *Txt 2*: 62 homophones divided into trained and untrained groups	*Txt 1*: Each target word was presented on a card with the corresponding picture and the "conventional letter-sound rule pronunciation" printed below. Pt read aloud treated words with feedback from the clinician. *Txt 2*: Each target word (e.g., peak) was shown with a picture and the correct spelling. On a separate card, the corresponding homophone (e.g., peek) was presented for the pt to make a comparison between the spellings and associate the mnemonics with the word.	*Txt 1*: 15 minutes/day for 7 days; *Txt 2*: 3 hours/day for 3 days	*Txt 1*: improved reading accuracy of trained and some untrained words; spelling of trained words did not improve; *Txt 2*: improved spelling of trained words; no generalization to spelling of untrained words

Note: pt, participant; tx, treatment; L, left; R, right; CVA, cerebrovascular accident; fx, fracture; s/p, status post; GPC, grapheme-to-phoneme conversion; NW, nonword.

Table 12.3 Description of Recent Phonological/Deep Alexia Treatment Studies

Reference	Design	Site of Lesion(s)	Treatment Type	Target Behavior	Stimuli	Procedure	Intensity and Frequency	Outcome
Ablinger et al. (2014)	Single group pre/post txt (*n* = 5)	4 pts with L CVAs; 1 pt with L craniocerebral injury	Eye movement-based reading therapy	Reading strategy (lexical or segmental)	150 nouns ranging from 6 to 9 letters	Target words were presented on screen 8 at a time similar to sentence reading. Pt fixated on a cross. In *lexical approach*, forced fixation on word center and if eye movement outside of center was detected, those letters were masked to encourage whole word reading. In *segmental approach*, word was presented gradually in 2–3 segments to encourage segmental reading and then complete, unmasked word remained on screen for 3,000 ms.	Not specified. took place during a 7-week stay at an "aphasia ward" in Germany	3 of 5 pts adopted a segmental reading strategy and 2 pts maintained a lexical reading strategy. All pts showed improved accuracy for reading RWs but not NWs. Error analysis showed reduction of omissions and increase in phonological errors. Error type did not indicate the reading strategy (lexical or segmental) utilized.
Beeson et al. (2010)	Single subject design (*n* = 2)	L CVA in perisylvian cortical regions	2-stages: phonological and then interactive (sublexical and lexical)	Sound–letter correspondences; nonword spelling	*Stage 1:* 20 consonants, 12 vowels and corresponding "key" words (e.g., pie for /p/); *Stage 2:* regular and irregular words	*Stage 1:* Cueing hierarchy was used to train phoneme–grapheme correspondence: (1) write the letter that goes with the target phoneme, (2) think of a "key" word paired to target phoneme and try to write it, (3) show picture of key word, write the word, and underline the target phoneme, (4) copy the key word. Phonological tasks (e.g., segmentation) using RWs and NWs were also trained. *Stage 2:* Trained a spelling problem-solving strategy: (1) attempt plausible spelling using phoneme–grapheme knowledge, (2) check spelling using lexical knowledge, (3) use electronic device to check and correct spelling errors.	1 hour/day, 3 days/week for 12–14 weeks; homework 45 minutes/day, 5 days/week	Improved phonological processing; improved reading and spelling of untrained RWs and NWs; improved spelling with use of an electronic spelling aid

(continued)

Table 12.3 Continued

Reference	Design	Site of Lesion(s)	Treatment Type	Target Behavior	Stimuli	Procedure	Intensity and Frequency	Outcome
Bowes & Martin (2007)	Longitudinal case study (*n* = 1)	L CVA involving frontal and parietal lobes and insular cortex	Bigraph-biphone segment blending	Reading and writing of nonwords, words, and phrases	*Txt 1:* 30, 1-syllable NWs; with CVC, CCVC, CVCC structure; *Txt 2:* 80, 2-syllable RWs with CVCVC, CVVCVC, CVCCVC structure; *Txt 3:* 48 noun/verb and verb/noun phrases	*Txt 1: 1-syllable reading:* read bigraphs and then blended together into whole word; *1-syllable writing:* repeat and write spoken biphones and then write each bigraph to spell whole word; *Txt 2: 2-syllable reading:* progress from reading bigraphs to syllables to whole word (e.g., CA-ME-EL, CA-ME-EL, CAMEL); *2-syllable writing:* write spoken bigraphs, then spoken syllable, and then whole word; *Txt 3: reading phrases:* nouns and verbs read syllable by syllable and then as a phrase; *writing phrases:* each word spelled by emphasizing syllable-by-syllable strategy.	1 hour/day, 2–3 days/week over 3 years	Pt improved from impaired 1-syllable word reading to accurate reading and writing at phrase level
Brookshire et al. (2014)	Single group pre/post txt (*n* = 8)	All pts had L CVAs	Phonomotor treatment (multimodal txt of phonology)	Oral reading of untrained real words and nonwords; comprehension of single words and text	English phonemes; 42, 1- to 2-syllable RWs and 72, 1- to 2-syllable NWs with low phonotactic probability and high neighborhood density	*Stage 1* (about 20 hours): train all English phonemes in isolation via multimodal tasks including motor description, perception, production, and sound-to-letter correspondences; *Stage 2* (about 40 hours): train phonological sequence knowledge in NWs and then RWs via tasks, such as repetition, minimal pair discrimination, phoneme parsing and blending, reading, and spelling.	2 hours/day, 5 days/week for 6 weeks	Improved NW repetition of trained and untrained items and improved reading accuracy of untrained regular and irregular RWs and NWs for all 8 pts with maintenance at 3 months; only 1 pt showed improved single word and text comprehension

Study	Design	Lesion	Treatment	Outcome measures	Stimuli	Procedure	Dose	Results
Kiran & Viswanathan (2008)	Case study (n = 1)	L occipito-temporal-parietal CVA	Combination of sublexical conversion and semantic feature tasks	Oral reading, written naming, and visual lexical decision	22 regularly spelled words (11 trained) matched for frequency, letter/syllable length, imageability, and semantic relatedness	Trained 11 regularly spelled words following these steps: (1) oral reading of target word, (2) spelling while saying the letter and sound, (3) selecting letters from distractors, (4) identifying letters presented randomly, (5) saying the sound while pointing to the letter, (6) identifying 6 semantic features when presented with picture, (7) oral reading of target word.	2 hours/day, 2 days/week for 18 sessions	Improved oral reading of trained and semantically related untrained words; improved spelling of trained and untrained words; maintenance of reading skills at 2 year follow-up
Lacey et al. (2010)	Case-series (n = 6; 4 phonological and 2 pure)	5 pts with L CVA; 1 pt with skull fx with L hemorrhage	Multiple Oral Rereading (MOR)	Oral text reading	300-word text passages that were either trained, untrained with 60–80% overlap, or control with minimal overlap with trained passages	Each session trained a different passage. Pt read the passage aloud as fast and as accurately as possible. Clinician pointed to incorrect word(s) and prompted pt to reread, and if necessary provided repetition. Pt read passage 3 times/session and then 5 times/day at home and called in 1 time/week to read aloud over the phone so clinician could provide feedback.	2 hours/day, 1 day/week for 8 weeks; plus homework	MOR improved reading accuracy and rate of untrained passages that contained overlap with the trained passages; no generalization to untrained passages that did not have overlap of words with trained passages
Lott et al. (2008)	Single subject multiple baseline (n = 1)	L frontoparietal CVA	Expanded paired association (phonological priming)	Oral reading of functor words	120, 1- to 2-syllable functors divided into 8 lists; 4 lists were experimental, 3 control, and 1 untrained	Target words were paired with relay word(s) that shared initial phonemes but varied on how closely the phonology and orthography were related (e.g., "else"–"elk"; "former"–"four mermaids"). A picture accompanied the relay word(s). Pt was asked to name the relay first and then read the target word. If incorrect, repetition was provided.	1.5 hours/day, 2 days/week over 17 months; plus home practice	Improved reading accuracy of trained grammatical words, but no generalization to untrained items; the closer the phonological relationship between target and relay, the faster the pt reached training criterion

(continued)

Table 12.3 Continued

Reference	Design	Site of Lesion(s)	Treatment Type	Target Behavior	Stimuli	Procedure	Intensity and Frequency	Outcome
Riley & Thompson (2015)	Single subject multiple baseline (n = 5)	All pts had L CVAs	Phonological complexity (sonority) training	Oral reading of initial consonant clusters in real and nonwords	Initial clusters with large (pl) and small (gl) sonority differences with a list of 20 RWs and 20 NWs per cluster	2 consonant clusters (one simple, one complex) were selected for each pt; 3 pts trained on the complex cluster and 2 pts trained on the simple cluster. Pt was asked to read aloud a target word and then complete 3 phonological tasks: (1) phoneme segmentation, (2) grapheme–phoneme matching, and (3) phoneme blending.	Maximum of 10 weeks (20 sessions) per consonant cluster	All pts improved on trained clusters; 2 out of 3 pts in the "complex" (e.g., "gl-") training showed generalization to the untrained "simple" cluster ("kl-"); pts in the "simple" condition (e.g., "pl-") did not show generalization to the "complex" cluster ("gl-")

Note: pt, participant; txt, treatment; L, left; CVA, cerebrovascular accident; RW, real word; NW, nonword; fx, fracture; CV, consonant vowel.

(Lacey et al., 2010) of the studies was judged to be Class 3 (weakest strength). The studies mentioned above implemented MOR with positive outcomes in individuals with pure alexia or individuals on the phonological/deep alexia continuum; however, it is unknown at this time which alexia subtype is most responsive to this treatment.

Future Directions

Directions for future research needs in acquired disorders of reading are proposed in the areas of assessment, treatment, and elucidating neural substrates.

Assessment: Although few standardized assessments exist to assess acquired reading disorders, most are lacking in support of essential standardization criteria such as content validity, construct validity, specificity, and sensitivity. Furthermore, assessment to understand reading abilities as related to the International Classification of Functioning, Disability and Health (ICF) model (World Health Organization, 2001) is essential. As it stands now, most available tools that assess reading are directed at the level of impairment, and items/stimuli need to be created to assess reading performance for social participation.

Treatment: When conducting clinical research in the field of alexia rehabilitation, a clear foundation must be set in order to develop knowledge that can later support inferences of causality as well as conclusions that can be generalized to the larger population being sampled. To date, essentially all published rehabilitation studies for acquired reading disorders have focused on Phases I and II research methods (Robey, 2004). Future research is needed to extend existing knowledge of Phase II treatment protocols into Phase III efficacy studies.

Neural substrates: Although it is widely agreed that reading entails multiple cognitive processes, there is little consistent evidence for localization of these processes. Further research combining functional and structural neuroimaging with behavioral performance is needed to determine the precise mechanisms that account for the alexias.

References

Ablinger, I., & Domahs, F. (2009). Improved single-letter identification after whole-word training in pure alexia. *Neuropsychological Rehabilitation*, 19(3), 340–363.

Ablinger, I., Huber, W., & Radach, R. (2014). Eye movement analyses indicate the underlying reading strategy in the recovery of lexical readers. *Aphasiology*, 28(6), 640–657.

Barton, J. J., Fox, C. J., Sekunova, A., & Iaria, G. (2010). Encoding in the visual word form area: An fMRI adaptation study of words versus handwriting. *Journal of Cognitive Neuroscience*, 22, 1649–1661.

Beauvois, M. F., & Dérouesné, J. (1979). Phonological alexia: Three dissociations. *Journal of Neurology, Neurosurgery, and Psychiatry*, 42(12), 1115–1124.

Beeson, P. M. (1998). Treatment for letter-by-letter reading: A case study. In N. Helm-Estabrooks & A. Holland (Eds.), *Approaches to the treatment of aphasia* (pp. 153–177). San Diego: Singular Publishing Group.

Beeson, P. M., & Henry, M. L. (2008). Comprehension and production of written words. In R. Chapey (Ed.), *Language intervention strategies in aphasia and related neurogenic communication disorders* (5th ed., pp. 654–688). Baltimore, MD: Lippincott Williams & Wilkins.

Beeson, P., Magloire, J., & Robey, R. (2005). Letter-by-letter reading: Natural recovery and response to treatment. *Behavioural Neurology*, 16(4), 191–202.

Beeson, P., Rising, K., Kim, E. S., & Rapcsak, S. Z. (2010). A treatment sequence for phonological alexia/agraphia. *Journal of Speech, Language and Hearing Research*, 53, 450–468.

Berndt, R. S., Haendiges, A. N., Mitchum, C. C., & Wayland, S. C. (1996). An investigation of non-lexical reading impairments. *Cognitive Neuropsychology*, 13, 763–801.

Bowes, K., & Martin, N. (2007). Longitudinal study of reading and writing rehabilitation using a bigraph-biphone correspondence approach. *Aphasiology*, 21(6), 687–701.

Braet, W., Wagemans, J., & de Beeck, H. O. (2011). The visual word form area is organized according to orthography. *Neuroimage*, 59(3), 2751–2759.

Brookshire, C. E., Conway, T., Hunting Pompon, R., Oelke, M., & Kendall, D. (2014). Effects of intensive phonomotor treatment on reading in eight individuals with aphasia and phonological alexia. *American Journal of Speech-Language Pathology*, 23, S300–S311.

Brookshire, C. E., Wilson, J., Nadeau, S., Rothi, L. J., & Kendall, D. (2014). Frequency, nature, and predictors of alexia in a convenience sample of individuals with chronic aphasia. *Aphasiology*, 28(12), 1464–1480. http://dx.doi.org/10.1080/02687038.2014.945389.

Cherney, L. (2004). Aphasia, alexia, and oral reading. *Topics in Stroke Rehabilitation*, 11(1), 22–36.

Cherney, L. R. (1995). Efficacy of oral reading in the treatment of two patients with chronic Broca's aphasia. *Topics in Stroke Rehabilitation*, 2, 57–67.

Cherney, L. R., Merbitz, C. T., & Grip, J. C. (1986). Efficacy of oral reading in aphasia treatment outcome. *Rehabilitation Literature*, 47, 112–118.

Cohen, L., Dehaene, S., Naccache, L., Lehericy, S., Dehaene-Lambertz, G., Henaff, M.A., & Michel, F. (2000). The visual word form area: Spatial and temporal characterization of an initial stage of reading in normal subjects and posterior split-brain patients. *Brain*, 123, 291–307.

Colangelo, A., & Buchanan, L. (2006). Implicit and explicit processing in deep dyslexia: Semantic blocking as a test for failure of inhibition in the phonological output lexicon. *Brain and Language*, 99, 258–271.

Colangelo, A., & Buchanan, L. (2007). Localizing damage in the functional architecture: The distinction between implicit and explicit processing in deep dyslexia. *Journal of Neurolinguistics*, 20(2), 111–144.

Coltheart, M. (1996). Phonological dyslexia: Past and future issues. *Cognitive Neuropsychology*, 13(6), 749–762.

Coltheart, M., & Byng, S. (1989). A treatment for surface dyslexia. In X. Seron & G. Deloche (Eds.), *Cognitive approaches in neuropsychological rehabilitation* (pp. 159–174). London: Lawrence Erlbaum.

Coltheart, M., Patterson, K., & Marshall, J. (1980). *Deep dyslexia*. London: Routledge & Kegan Paul.

Coltheart, M., Rastle, K., Perry, C., & Langdon, R. (2001). DRC: A dual route cascaded model of visual word recognition and reading aloud. *Psychological Review*, 108(1), 204–256.

Crisp, J., & Lambon Ralph, M. (2006). Unlocking the nature of the phonological-deep dyslexia continuum: The keys to reading aloud are in phonology and semantics. *Journal of Cognitive Neuroscience*, 18(3), 348–362.

Dehaene, S., Naccache, L., Cohen, L., Bihan, D. L., Mangin, J. F., Poline, J. B., & Riviere, D. (2001). Cerebral mechanisms of word masking and unconscious repetition priming. *Nature Neuroscience*, 4, 752–758.

De Partz, M. (1986). Re-education of a deep dyslexic patient: Rationale of the method and results. *Cognitive Neuropsychology*, 3, 149–177.

Dérouesné, J., & Beauvois, M. F. (1979). Phonological processing in reading: Data from alexia. *Journal of Neurology, Neurosurgery, and Psychiatry*, 42(12), 1125–1132.

Ellis, A. W., Flude, B. M., & Young, A. W. (1987). "Neglect dyslexia" and the early visual processing of letters in words. *Cognitive Neuropsychology*, 4, 439–464.

Ellis, A. W., Lambon Ralph, M. A., Morris, J., & Hunter, A. (2000). Surface dyslexia: Description, treatment, and interpretation. In E. Funnell (Ed.), *Case studies in the neuropsychology of reading* (pp. 85–122). Hove, East Sussex, UK: Psychology Press.

Ellis, A. W., & Young, A. W. (1988). *Human cognitive neuropsychology*. Hove, UK: Lawrence Erlbaum Associates.

Fiez, J. A., & Petersen, S. E. (1998). Neuroimaging studies of word reading. *Proceedings of the National Academy of Sciences USA*, 95, 914–921.

Friedman, R. (1996). Recovery from deep alexia to phonological alexia: Points on a continuum. *Brain and Language*, 52, 114–128.

Friedman, R., & Glosser, G. (1998). Aphasia, alexia, and agraphia. In H. S. Friedman (Ed.), *Encyclopedia of mental health* (pp. 137–148). San Diego: Academic Press.

Friedman, R., & Hadley, J. (1992). Letter-by-letter surface alexia. *Cognitive Neuropsychology*, 9(3), 185–208.

Friedman, R. B., & Robinson, S. R. (1991). Whole-word training therapy in a stable surface alexic patient: It works. *Aphasiology*, 5, 521–527.

Friedman, R. B., Sample, D. M., & Lott, S. N. (2002). The role of level of representation in the use of paired associate learning for rehabilitation of alexia. *Neuropsychologia*, 40, 223–234.

Gates, A., & MacGinitie, W (1978). *Gates-MacGinitie reading tests*. New York: Teachers College Press.

Glosser, G., & Friedman, R. (1990). The continuum of deep/phonological alexia. *Cortex*, 26(3), 343–359.

Golper, L., Wertz, R., Frattali, C., Yorkston, K., Myers, P., Katz, R., et al. (2001). *Evidence-based practice guidelines for the management of communication disorders in neurologically impaired individuals: Project Introduction*. Retrieved from Academy of Neurologic Communication Disorders and Sciences website: http://www.ancds.org/pdf/practiceguidelines.pdf.

Goodglass, H., Kaplan, E., & Barresi, B. (2001). *The assessment of aphasia and related disorders* (3rd ed.). Philadelphia: Lippincott Williams & Wilkins.

Goodman, R., & Caramazza, A. (1986). *Johns Hopkins University dyslexia battery*. Baltimore, MD: The Johns Hopkins University.

Hagoort, P., Indefrey, P., Brown, C., Herzog, H., Steinmetz, H., & Seitz, R. J. (1999). The neural circuitry involved in the reading of German words and pseudowords: A PET study. *Journal of Cognitive Neuroscience*, 11, 383–398.

Harm, M., & Seidenberg, M. (1999). Phonology, reading acquisition, and dyslexia: Insights from connectionist models. *Psychological Review*, 106(3), 491–528.

Harris, L., Olson, A., & Humphreys, G. (2013). Overcoming the effect of letter confusability in letter-by-letter reading: A rehabilitation study. *Neuropsychological Rehabilitation*, 23(3), 429–462.

Henry, M., Beeson, P., Stark, A., & Rapcsak, S. (2007). The role of left perisylvian cortical regions in spelling. *Brain and Language*, 100, 44–52.

Kay, J., Lesser, R., & Coltheart, M. (1992). *Psycholinguistic assessments of language processing in aphasia (PALPA)*. Hove, UK: Lawrence Erlbaum Associates Ltd.

Kendall, D., Conway, T., Rosenbek, J., & Rothi, L. J. G. (2003). Phonological rehabilitation of acquired phonologic alexia. *Aphasiology*, 17(11), 1073–1095.

Kertesz, A. (2007). *Western aphasia battery-revised*. San Antonio, TX: PsychCorp.

Kiran, S., & Viswanathan, M. (2008). Effect of model-based treatment on oral reading abilities in severe alexia: A case study. *Journal of Medical Speech-Language Pathology*, 16(1), 43–59.

Lacey, E., Lott, S., Snider, S., Sperling, A., & Friedman, R. (2010). Multiple oral re-reading treatment for alexia: The parts may be greater than the whole. *Neuropsychological Rehabilitation*, 20(4), 601–623.

Lacey, E., Lott, S., Sperling, A., Snider, S., & Friedman, R. (2007). Multiple oral re-reading treatment for alexia: It works, but why? *Brain and Language*, 103, 115–116.

LaPointe, L. L., & Horner, J. (1998). *Reading comprehension battery for aphasia* (2nd ed.). Tigard, OR: C.C. Publications.

Leff, A. P., Crewes, H., Plant, G. T., Scott, S. K., Kennard, C., & Wise, R. J. (2001). The functional anatomy of single-word reading in patients with hemianopic and pure alexia. *Brain*, 124, 510–521.

Levy, J., Pernet, C., Treserras, S., Boulanouar, K., Aubry, F., Demonet, J. F.,. . . Celsis, P. (2009). Testing for the dual-route cascade reading model in the brain: An fMRI effective connectivity account of an efficient reading style. *PLoS One*, 4(8), e6675.

Levy, J., Pernet, C., Treserras, S., Boulanouar, K., Berry, I., Aubry, F.,. . . & Celsis, P. (2008). Piecemeal recruitment of left-lateralized brain areas during reading: A spatio-functional account. *Neuroimage*, 43, 581–591.

Lott, S., Carney, A., Glezer, L., & Friedman, R. (2010). Overt use of a tactile/kinaesthetic strategy shifts to covert processing in rehabilitation of letter-by-letter reading. *Aphasiology*, 24(11), 1424–1442.

Lott, S., Sample, D., Oliver, R., Lacey, E., & Friedman, R. (2008). A patient with phonologic alexia can learn to read "much" from "mud pies." *Neuropsychologia*, 46, 2515–2523.

Marshall, J., & Newcombe, F. (1973). Patterns of paralexia: A psycholinguistic approach. *Journal of Psycholinguistic Research*, 2(3), 175–199.

Mayer, J. F., & Murray, L. L. (2002). Approaches to the treatment of alexia in chronic aphasia. *Aphasiology*, 16, 727–744.

Mechelli, A., Crinion, J. T., Long, S., Friston, K. J., Lambon Ralph, M. A., Patterson, K.,... & Price, C. J. (2005). Dissociating reading processes on the basis of neuronal interactions. *Journal of Cognitive Neuroscience*, 17, 1753–1765.

Mitchum, C. C., & Berndt, R. S. (1991). Diagnosis and treatment of the non-lexical route in acquired dyslexia: An illustration of the cognitive neuropsychological approach. *Journal of Neurolinguistics*, 6, 103–137.

Moss, S. E., Rothi, L. J. G., & Fennell, E. B. (1991). Treating a case of surface dyslexia after closed head injury. *Archives of Clinical Neuropsychology*, 6, 35–47.

Moody, S. (1988). The Moyer reading technique re-evaluated. *Cortex*, 24, 473–476.

Moyer, S. (1979). Rehabilitation of alexia: A case study. *Cortex*, 15, 139–144.

Patterson, K. E., & Kay, J. (1982). Letter-by-letter reading: Psychological descriptions of a neurological syndrome. *Quarterly Journal of Experimental Psychology*, 34A, 411–441.

Patterson, K. E., & Lambon Ralph, M. (1999). Selective disorders of reading? *Current Opinion in Neurobiology*, 9, 235–239.

Patterson, K. E., & Marcel, A. J. (1977). Aphasia, dyslexia and the phonological coding of written words. *Quarterly Journal of Experimental Psychology*, 29, 307–318.

Plaut, D. (1999). A connectionist approach to word reading and acquired dyslexia: Extension to sequential processing. *Cognitive Science*, 23(4), 543–568.

Plaut, D., McClelland, J. L., Seidenberg, M. S., & Patterson, K. (1996). Understanding normal and impaired word reading: Computational principles in quasi-regular domains. *Psychological Review*, 103(1), 56–115.

Playfoot, D., Tree, J., & Izura, C. (2014). Naming acronyms: The influence of reading context in skilled reading and surface dyslexia. *Aphasiology*, 28(12), 1448–1463. http://dx.doi.org/10.1080/02687038.2014.939517.

Price, C. J. (2012). A review and synthesis of the first 20 years of PET and fMRI studies of heard speech, spoken language, and reading. *Neuroimage*, 62(2), 816–847.

Price, C. J., & Devlin, J. T. (2003). The myth of the visual word form area. *Neuroimage*, 19, 473–481.

Price, C. J., & Friston, K. J. (2005). Functional ontologies for cognition: The systematic definition of structure and function. *Cognitive Neuropsychology*, 22, 262–275.

Pugh, K. R., Shaywitz, B. A., Shaywitz, S. E., Constable, R. T., Skudlarski, P., Fulbright, R. K.,... & Gore, J. C. (1996). Cerebral organization of component processes in reading. *Brain*, 119(Pt 4), 1221–1238.

Rapcsak, S. Z., & Beeson, P. M. (2002). Neuroanatomical correlates of spelling and writing. In A. E. Hillis (Ed.), *Handbook of adult language disorders: Integrating cognitive neuropsychology, neurology and rehabilitation* (pp. 71–99). Philadelphia: Psychology Press.

Rapcsak, S., Beeson, P., Henry, M., Leyden, A., Kim, E., Rising, K.,... Cho, H. (2009). Phonological dyslexia and dysgraphia: Cognitive mechanisms and neural substrates. *Cortex*, 45(5), 575–591.

Raymer, A. M., & Berndt, R. S. (1996). Reading lexically without semantics: Evidence from patients with probable Alzheimer's disease. *Journal of the International Neuropsychological Society*, 2, 340–349.

Richardson, F. M., Seghier, M. L., Leff, A. P., Thomas, M. S., & Price, C. J. (2011). Multiple routes from occipital to temporal cortices during reading. *Journal of Neuroscience*, 31, 8239–8247.

Riley, E. A., & Thompson, C. K. (2010). Semantic typicality effects in acquired dyslexia: Evidence for semantic impairment in deep dyslexia. *Aphasiology*, 24, 802–813.

Riley, E. A., & Thompson, C. K. (2015). Training pseudoword reading in acquired dyslexia: A phonological complexity approach. *Aphasiology*, 29(2), 129–150. http://dx.doi.org/10.1080/02687038.2014.955389.

Robey, R. R. (2004). A five-phase model for clinical-outcome research. *Journal of Communication Disorders*, 37, 401–411.

Robey, R. R., & Schultz, M. C. (1998). A model for conducting clinical-outcome research: An adaptation of the standard protocol for use in aphasiology. *Aphasiology*, 12, 787–810.

Rothi, L. J. G., Coslett, H. B., & Heilman, K. M. (1984). *Battery of adult reading function, experimental edition*. Unpublished test.

Sage, K., Hesketh, A., & Lambon Ralph, M. (2005). Using errorless learning to treat letter-by-letter reading: Contrasting word versus letter-based therapy. *Neuropsychological Rehabilitation*, 15, 619–642.

Scott, C., & Byng, S. (1989). Computer assisted remediation of a homophone comprehension disorder in surface dyslexia. *Aphasiology*, 3, 301–320.

Seghier, M. L., Lee, H. L., Schofield, T., Ellis, C. L., & Price, C. J. (2008). Inter-subject variability in the use of two different neuronal networks for reading aloud familiar words. *Neuroimage*, 42, 1226–1236.

Seidenberg, M., & McClelland, J. (1989). A distributed, developmental model of word recognition and naming. *Psychological Review*, 96(4), 523–568.

Shallice, T., & Warrington, E. (1975). Word recognition in a phonemic dyslexic patient. *Quarterly Journal of Experimental Psychology*, 27, 187–199.

Shallice, T., & Warrington, E. (1977). The possible role of selective attention in acquired dyslexia. *Neuropsychologia*, 15, 31–41.

Shinkareva, S. V., Malave, V. L., Mason, R. A., Mitchell, T. M., & Just, M. A. (2011). Commonality of neural representations of words and pictures. *Neuroimage*, 54, 2418–2425.

Toumainen, J., & Laine, M. (1991). Multiple oral rereading technique in rehabilitation of pure alexia. *Aphasiology*, 5, 401–409.

Tree, J., & Kay, J. (2006). Phonological dyslexia and phonological impairment: An exception to the rule? *Neuropsychologia*, 44(14), 2861–2873.

Turkeltaub, P. E., Flowers, D. L., Lyon, L. G., & Eden, G. F. (2008). Development of ventral stream representations for single letters. *Annals of the New York Academy of Sciences*, 1145, 13–29.

Viswanathan, M., & Kiran, S. (2005). Treatment for pure alexia using a model based approach: Evidence from one acute aphasic individual. *Brain & Language*, 95, 204–206.

Warrington, E., & Shallice, T. (1980). Word-form dyslexia. *Brain*, 30, 99–112.

Weekes, B., & Coltheart, M. (1996). Surface dyslexia and surface dysgraphia: Treatment studies and their theoretical implications. *Cognitive Neuropsychology*, 13, 277–315.

Welbourne, S. R., & Lambon Ralph, M. A. (2007). Using parallel distributed processing models to simulate phonological dyslexia: The key role of plasticity-related recovery. *Journal of Cognitive Neuroscience*, 19, 1125–1139.

Wiederholt, J. L., & Bryant, B. R. (2001). *GORT 4: Gray oral reading tests examiner's manual*. Austin, TX: PRO-ED.

Woodcock, R. W., Mather, N., & Schrank, F. A. (2004). *The Woodcock-Johnson III diagnostic reading battery*. Rolling Meadows, IL: Riverside Publishing.

Woollams, A., Ralph, M., Plaut, D., & Patterson, K. (2007). SD-squared: On the association between semantic dementia and surface dyslexia. *Psychological Review*, 114(2), 316–339.

World Health Organization. (2001). *International classification of functioning, disability, and health*. Geneva, Switzerland. http://www.who.int/classifications/icf/en/.

Wright, N. D., Mechelli, A., Noppeney, U., Veltman, D. J., Rombouts, S. A., Glensman, J., ... Price, C. J. (2008). Selective activation around the left occipito-temporal sulcus for words relative to pictures: Individual variability or false positives? *Human Brain Mapping*, 29, 986–1000.

Yampolsky, S., & Waters, G. (2002). Treatment of single word oral reading in an individual with deep dyslexia. *Aphasiology*, 16, 455–471.

Acquired Dysgraphias: Mechanisms of Writing

Pélagie M. Beeson *and* Kindle Rising

Abstract

Acquired dysgraphia refers to disorders of spelling or writing due to neurological damage in individuals with normal premorbid literacy skills. Dysgraphia can result from the disruption of central cognitive processes that also support spoken language and reading, so that spelling impairments frequently co-occur with aphasia and acquired alexia. The ability to produce written words can also be affected by damage to peripheral processes necessary to plan and execute the appropriate hand movements for letter generation or typing. In this chapter, we review the cognitive processes that support spelling and writing, and the characteristic dysgraphia syndromes that reflect differential impairment to specific central and peripheral components. We also review assessment procedures for writing and spelling that are structured to clarify the status of component processes and to guide rehabilitation planning. Treatment procedures and sequences are described with a focus on lexical-semantic, phonological, and interactive treatments. The nature and treatment of dysgraphia are illustrated by case examples of global dysgraphia, phonological dysgraphia, and surface dysgraphia.

Key Words: agraphia, dysgraphia, writing, spelling, writing disorders, spelling disorders, phonological agraphia, surface agraphia

Introduction

Acquired dysgraphia (or agraphia) refers to disorders of spelling or writing that are caused by neurological damage in individuals with normal premorbid literacy skills. The functional consequences of written language impairment have always been significant for literate adults, but the recent, dramatic shift to electronic media for professional and personal communication certainly increases the consequent disability associated with dysgraphia for many individuals. In this chapter, we review the cognitive processes and neural substrates that support written communication, as well as the nature and treatment of recognized dysgraphia syndromes.

Dysgraphia often results from impairments to central cognitive processes that also support spoken language and reading, so that spelling impairments frequently co-occur with aphasia and acquired dyslexia. Writing (or typing/keyboarding) can also be affected by disruption of the processes that support the planning and implementation of the necessary hand movements, so the peripheral, as well as central, components of written communication may be affected by brain damage (Hillis & Rapp, 2004; Rapcsak & Beeson, 2002; Rapp & Caramazza, 1997). As with aphasia and acquired dyslexia, there is a principled relationship between lesion location, the nature of the impairment, and the dysgraphia profile (Henry, Beeson, & Stark, 2007; Hillis et al., 2002; Rapcsak & Beeson, 2004; Rapcsak et al., 2009). Furthermore, certain dysgraphia subtypes can be expected to occur in the presence of specific aphasia and dyslexia subtypes, as described in this chapter.

Overview of Cognitive Processes and Neural Underpinnings of Written Language

Understanding the underlying cognitive processes and neural substrates of written language provides a useful framework for diagnosis and treatment planning for the acquired dysgraphias. From a neurocognitive perspective, speech comprehension and production rely on interactions among cortical networks involved in processing the sounds of the language (phonology) and word meanings (semantics). These relations develop as young children learn spoken language, and are well underway by the time they begin learning to read and write. Orthographic knowledge is gained as visual representations of individual letters (graphemes) become associated with corresponding speech sounds (phonemes), and specific letter strings (written words) become linked to phonology and lexical–semantics. These lexical (whole word) and sublexical (sound-to-letter) correspondences are depicted in the cognitive model of single word processing presented in Figure 13.1. It is evident that written language skills reflect interactive processing of semantics, orthography, and phonology, and the latter two components involve both lexical and sublexical relations. Even as adults, our lexical knowledge continues to expand based on what we hear and read. As we add to our vocabulary, new phonological, orthographic, and semantic links are established, and we often rely on sublexical skills to decode or produce written words that are new to us.

As noted by Riley and Kendall in Chapter 12, language processing has been conceptualized by two "opposing" models: a triangle (connectionist) model with the fundamental components of semantics, phonology, and orthography (Plaut, McClelland, Seidenberg, & Patterson, 1996), and a dual route model with the same central components but inclusion of a sublexical processing route that is distinct from lexical processing (Coltheart, Rastle, Perry, Langdon, & Zeigler, 2001). To date, there is no empirical evidence to clearly adjudicate between the two models. We present a blended model in Figure 13.1 that provides a means to characterize differential impairment of lexical and sublexical processes, as well as the interactive use of lexical and sublexical information that is apparent in individuals with impaired written language (Beeson, Rewega, Vail, & Rapcsak, 2000; Greenwald, 2004; Rapp, Epstein, & Tainturier, 2002).

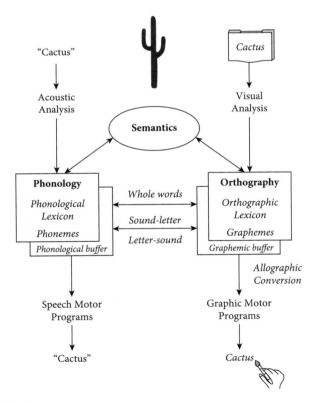

Figure 13.1 A cognitive model of language processing.

Converging evidence regarding the neural substrates that support written language comes from lesion-deficit correlations in individuals with neurological disease and functional imaging studies in healthy individuals. It is well established that the phonological system that supports both spoken and written language performance depends on a left hemisphere *perisylvian* cortical network (i.e., Broca's area, Wernicke's area, and supramarginal gyrus and the associated white matter connections) (Fiez, Tranel, Seager-Frerichs, & Damasio, 2006; Jobard, Crivello, & Tzourio-Mazoyer, 2003; Rapcsak et al., 2009; Vigneau et al., 2006). By contrast, semantic processing for both written and spoken language tasks depends on the integrity of a distributed left hemisphere *extrasylvian* neural network that includes the anterior and ventral temporal lobe (encompassing the middle and inferior temporal gyri), the angular gyrus, and the anterior–inferior frontal gyrus (Binder, Desai, Graves, & Conant, 2009; Vigneau et al., 2006). Written language processing is supported by the functional specialization of cortical areas involved in visual object recognition (Cohen & Dehaene, 2004; Schlaggar & McCandliss, 2007). In particular, the region referred to as the visual word form area (VWFA) in the left ventral occipitotemporal cortex plays a critical role in processing orthographic information during both reading and spelling (Philipose et al., 2007; Purcell, Turkeltaub, Eden, & Rapp, 2011; Rapcsak & Beeson, 2004; Rapp & Lipka, 2011; Tsapkini & Rapp, 2010). Damage to any of these critical left hemisphere regions that support semantics, phonology, or orthography can result in dysgraphia.

At a more peripheral level, writing requires knowledge of abstract letter codes that are converted to specific letter shapes (allographs). This transcoding process requires that orthographic information be held in short-term working memory, referred to as the graphemic buffer (Buchwald & Rapp, 2009; Caramazza, Miceli, Vill, & Romani, 1987). From a neural perspective, the translation of orthographic representations into letter shapes has been associated with the left posterior middle and superior frontal gyri (Hillis & Rapp, 2004), but allographic conversion difficulties have also been associated with damage to left temporoparieto-occipital regions (Lubrano, Roux, & Demonet, 2004; Rapcsak & Beeson, 2002; Tohgi, Saitoh, & Sasaki, 1995). In many cases, letter selection errors or impaired knowledge of letter shape is concomitant with central spelling impairments, rather than occurring in isolation.

Graphomotor planning and implementation of the appropriate hand movements to produce writing rely on a left lateralized cortical network that involves the superior parietal lobule/intraparietal sulcus, the premotor area for the hand (Exner's area), and the primary motor strip for the hand (Beeson, Rapcsak et al., 2003; Magrassi, Bongetta, Bianchini, Berardesca, & Arienta, 2010; Rapcsak & Beeson, 2002). Of course, bimanual typing also requires motor control of the nondominant hand, but the motor planning is left lateralized, even when both hands are used (Purcell, Napoliello, & Eden, 2011).

Dysgraphia Subtypes

Acquired dysgraphia syndromes can be separated into central and peripheral subtypes, with the former affecting the processing of phonology, orthography, or semantics, and the latter affecting aspects of letter shape knowledge, graphomotor planning, and implementation of hand movements. The central dysgraphias can be broadly categorized into those with phonological impairment versus those with preserved phonological skills (Table 13.1).

Central Dysgraphia Syndromes with Phonological Impairment

It is well established that damage to the left perisylvian language zone typically results in one of the classic aphasia syndromes (Broca's, Wernicke's, conduction, or global). Although the characteristic features of spoken language in these aphasia types are quite different from one another, they share a common deficit in phonological processing (Fiez et al., 2006; Rapcsak et al., 2009). The disruption of phonology is evident on tasks that require the segmentation and manipulation of sounds of the language, such as those used to test phonological awareness (Patterson & Marcel, 1992; Rapcsak et al., 2009). This fundamental impairment of phonology is also evident on written language tasks that require sublexical manipulation of sounds and transcoding to their associated orthography. An easy way to document phonological impairment as it affects spelling is to ask individuals to spell/write pseudowords, that is, plausible nonwords, such as "glope." In the case of perisylvian damage, sublexical skills are notably impaired on nonword spelling tasks relative to performance on familiar words, which can be spelled in a lexical manner. There is a range in the severity of the phonological impairment, as well as the status of lexical–semantic knowledge, resulting in several dysgraphia syndromes with phonological

Table 13.1 Characteristic Features of Central Dysgraphia Subtypes, Associated Lesion Location, and Aphasia and Dyslexia Subtypes

	Dysgraphia Subtype	Characteristic Features	Location of Damage	Associated Aphasia Types	Associated Dyslexia Types
Impaired Phonology	Phonological	Lexicality effect (disproportionately poor nonword vs. real word spelling) Grammatical class effects (e.g., nouns better than functors) Agrammatic or paragrammatic written sentences	L perisylvian Large or focal	Broca's Wernicke's Conduction Anomic Logopenic PPA	Deep dyslexia Phonological dyslexia Phonological text alexia
	Deep	Semantic errors (e.g., orange for apple) Lexicality effect (disproportionately poor nonword vs. real word spelling) Grammatical class effects Agrammatic sentences	L perisylvian Typically large lesions	Broca's Conduction Wernicke's	Deep dyslexia Phonological dyslexia
	Global	Few words spelled correctly (<30%) Markedly impaired nonword spelling Typically unable to write sentences	L perisylvian Typically large lesions	Global Broca's Wernicke's Conduction	Global dyslexia Deep dyslexia Phonological dyslexia
Preserved Phonology	Surface	Regularity effect disproportionately poor spelling of irregular vs. regular words and nonwords Syntactically appropriate written sentence constructions, but may be empty if semantics impaired	L extrasylvian Ventral temporooccipital cortex Anterior temporal atrophy	Anomic Transcortical sensory Semantic PPA Alzheimer's	Letter-by-letter reading Surface dyslexia

PPA = primary progressive aphasia.

impairment: phonological dysgraphia, deep dysgraphia, and global dysgraphia.

PHONOLOGICAL DYSGRAPHIA

Phonological dysgraphia is characterized by difficulty generating spellings on the basis of sound-to-letter correspondences. As noted above, this problem is particularly evident during clinical evaluation when an individual is asked to generate plausible spellings for nonwords. The disproportionate difficulty in spelling nonwords compared to familiar words gives rise to an exaggerated **lexicality effect** (Fiez, Balota, Raichle, & Petersen, 1999; Henry et al., 2007; Rapcsak et al., 2009; Rapp, 2002; Shallice, 1981). Considered from a dual-route perspective, poor nonword spelling in phonological dysgraphia is attributable to damage to the sublexical route, whereas better-preserved real-word spelling reflects the residual functional capacity of the lexical–semantic route. The vulnerability of nonwords is related to the fact that these unfamiliar items cannot benefit from top-down lexical–semantic support, and accurate reading/spelling must rely on phoneme–grapheme conversion that requires the identification, manipulation, and maintenance of sublexical phonological information.

In phonological dysgraphia, spelling accuracy for words (both regular and irregular) is better preserved than spelling of nonwords; however, real-word performance may also be degraded to some extent relative to premorbid abilities, leading to functional spelling difficulties. Due to the reliance on lexical processing with limited sublexical input, real-word spelling is typically influenced by lexical–semantic variables such as word frequency (high better than low frequency) and imageability (concrete better than abstract words) (Shallice, 1981). A grammatical class effect is also typical, in that content words (e.g., nouns, verbs) are better preserved than functors, presumably reflecting greater reliance on phonology for spelling words with minimal semantic weight (Shallice, 1981).

There is evidence to suggest that phonological dysgraphia reflects a central impairment of phonological processing ability that is also apparent on reading tasks; however, the spelling impairment is typically of greater severity owing to the increased demands for spelling compared to reading (Rapcsak et al., 2009). Even in the mildest cases, where single-word spelling is relatively preserved, written composition is often impoverished and agrammatic in phonological dysgraphia (Shallice, 1981). This may be observed in individuals who recover to the extent that their spoken language profiles evolve to anomic aphasia, but written narratives still reveal vulnerability with regard to grammatical construction and morphosyntax (Beeson, Rising, DeMarco, Foley, & Rapcsak, 2016).

DEEP DYSGRAPHIA

The **deep dysgraphia** syndrome includes all of the characteristic features of phonological dysgraphia, but is distinguished from the latter by the production of semantic errors when spelling words (e.g., *brother* written as *sister*) (Bub & Kertesz, 1982; Rapcsak & Beeson, 1991). There are no strict criteria regarding what proportion of semantic errors is necessary to constitute the classification of deep dysgraphia (or deep dyslexia, for that matter), but the presence of even 3–5% semantic errors is notable and is likely to warrant the diagnostic label of "deep dysgraphia." The severity of the spelling impairment for real words in deep dysgraphia is often greater than that observed in phonological dysgraphia. Poor phonological monitoring is evident by the fact that there tends to be a lack of awareness of the phonological mismatch between target words and the semantic error. For example, the mismatch between "sister" beginning with /s/ and "brother" beginning with /b/ is likely to go unnoticed. Like phonological dysgraphia, deep dysgraphia is typically encountered in individuals with aphasia syndromes characterized by phonological impairment including Broca's, conduction, and Wernicke's aphasia. The left hemisphere damage tends to be more extensive than that associated with phonological dysgraphia, and it has been hypothesized that the right hemisphere may be responsible for the deep dysgraphia profile (Bub & Kertesz, 1982; Rapcsak & Beeson, 1991). The right hemisphere hypothesis is consistent with the more coarse encoding of semantics by the right hemisphere, leading to within-class semantic errors, such as writing *beer* for "wine" (Coslett & Saffran, 1998).

GLOBAL DYSGRAPHIA

In many instances, left hemisphere damage results in such marked impairment of written language that very few meaningful words are spelled correctly. We refer to this profile as **global dysgraphia** (Beeson & Hillis, 2001), and use the criterion of accuracy less than 30% for the spelling of real words in our standard battery, the *Arizona Battery for Reading and Spelling* (Beeson, 2010). Written language performance in global dysgraphia may be far more impaired than spoken language or reading.

Recent research suggests that one-third to one-half of all individuals with significant damage to the left perisylvian cortex have severely impaired written language abilities (Rapcsak et al., 2009). When attempting to write single words, individuals with global dysgraphia often fail to respond, or they produce unrelated errors that may be perseverative or phonologically implausible nonwords. On a spelling-to-dictation task, error responses may reflect partial word-form knowledge (e.g., *shamoon* for *shampoo*) or may be implausible nonwords totally unrelated to the target (e.g., *emorge* for *mile*). Performance is typically influenced by word frequency and imageability, such that high frequency, imageable words are among the few words spelled correctly (Beeson, 1999; Beeson, Rising, & Volk, 2003).

The perisylvian damage associated with global dysgraphia is typically extensive. It may include predominantly the frontal lobe (associated with Broca's aphasia), superior temporal lobe (associated with Wernicke's aphasia), or supramarginal gyrus (associated with conduction aphasia), or the damage may extend throughout the perisylvian region (associated with global aphasia). As noted, in individuals with perisylvian damage it is not uncommon for spelling to be more impaired than reading, because it is the more difficult of the two tasks (Rapcsak et al., 2009). However, the reverse may be observed in individuals with marked impairment of speech production due to impaired motor control for speech (e.g., apraxia of speech) or those with marked difficulty with phonological assembly resulting in paraphasic errors seen in Wernicke's or conduction aphasia (e.g., Beeson, 1999; Hier & Mohr, 1977). For that reason, it is important to explore the potential for written communication in individuals with severe spoken language impairment.

Central Dysgraphia with Preserved Phonological Skills: Surface Dysgraphia

Written language impairment is also evident following damage to left hemisphere cortical regions outside of the perisylvian language zone. Phonological abilities are preserved in such cases, but written language is affected by degraded orthographic or semantic knowledge. **Surface dysgraphia** is the characteristic profile that reflects overreliance on a phonological spelling strategy, an approach that works well for regularly spelled words (e.g., *gate*), but poorly for irregular words (e.g., *cough*). The discrepancy by which regular words (and pseudowords) are spelled with significantly

better accuracy than irregular words is referred to as a **regularity effect** (Patterson, Marshall, & Coltheart, 1985; Roeltgen & Heilman, 1984). The predominant errors in surface dysgraphia are phonologically plausible misspellings, such as *serkit* for *circuit*. The surface dysgraphia profile is also referred to as lexical dysgraphia because it reflects a disruption of the lexical spelling route (Beauvois & Dérouesné, 1981; Behrmann & Bub, 1992; Roeltgen & Heilman, 1984).

Surface dysgraphia reflects weakened or failed access to orthographic representations (i.e., visual word forms) along with compensatory reliance on a phonological strategy for spelling. The underlying cause of the spelling impairment can be loss of word-specific orthographic knowledge (i.e., an orthographic impairment) or degraded semantic knowledge, so that orthography is not accessible via lexical–semantic activation. Orthographic impairment is most commonly associated with focal damage due to a left posterior cerebral artery infarct, whereas semantic degradation is most prevalent in cases of cortical atrophy affecting the anterior temporal lobes (Gorno-Tempini et al., 2011; Hodges, Patterson, Oxbury, & Funnell, 1992).

SURFACE DYSGRAPHIA ASSOCIATED WITH ORTHOGRAPHIC IMPAIRMENT

Surface dysgraphia associated with damage to (or impaired access to) the orthographic lexicon reflects reliance on a sublexical phoneme–grapheme conversion strategy (Behrmann & Bub, 1992; Rapcsak & Beeson, 2004). The typical consequence is the occurrence of phonologically plausible regularization errors on irregular words, a finding that is most pronounced on low-frequency items (e.g., *yot* for *yacht*). Focal lesions that give rise to surface dysgraphia have been documented in the left inferior occipitotemporal cortex, often due to vascular events in the distribution of the left posterior cerebral artery (Rapcsak & Beeson, 2004; Roeltgen & Heilman, 1984). This region includes a portion of the fusiform gyrus known as the visual word form area that has been shown in neuroimaging studies to be engaged in healthy adults during reading (Cohen et al., 2002) and spelling tasks (Beeson, Rapcsak et al., 2003; Purcell, Napoliello et al., 2011). In surface dygraphia, it is thought that orthographic representations are degraded in the face of well-preserved perisylvian cortical regions that support phonological processes. A less common lesion profile associated with surface dyslexia has been documented in some individuals with damage to the posterior, inferior frontal brain regions (Hillis et al., 2002; Hillis, Chang, Breese, & Heidler, 2004; Rapcsak, Arthur, & Rubens, 1988). Hillis and colleagues (2004) suggested that this lesion-deficit association may reflect impaired *access* to orthographic representations rather than degraded lexical orthography, and the problem may be particularly evident on spelling tasks that involve verbs or specific morphological forms.

Individuals with surface dysgraphia due to ventral occipitotemporal damage may demonstrate concomitant reading impairment consistent with letter-by-letter reading or surface dyslexia, or even a combination of the two profiles in which letter-by-letter decoding yields phonologically plausible errors (Hanley & Kay, 1992; Ingles & Eskes, 2007). Letter-by-letter reading refers to sequential identification of component letters of a word as a means to support word recognition. Although this compensatory reading strategy is most often associated with "pure alexia," when it cooccurs with surface dysgraphia, the reading impairment is clearly not "pure." The letter-by-letter reading approach reflects a serial left-to-right reading strategy that is adopted due to weakened top-down lexical support. In individuals who present with surface dyslexia concomitant with surface dysgraphia, it is not uncommon to observe resolution of the surface dyslexia over time, with a more persistent pattern of surface dysgraphia. This is likely due to improved self-monitoring of reading output that serves to block the production of phonologically plausible errors. In such cases, visually similar words are frequently produced rather than phonologically plausible nonwords. For spelling, however, there is greater tolerance for phonologically plausible errors, as this is not an uncommon approach when individuals are uncertain about spelling. The spoken language skills in individuals with surface dysgraphia are typically relatively preserved with word retrieval problems (anomia) as the characteristic feature.

SURFACE DYSGRAPHIA ASSOCIATED WITH SEMANTIC IMPAIRMENT

Damage to central semantic representations can also be associated with surface dysgraphia (and surface dyslexia), as is often observed in individuals with the semantic variant of primary progressive aphasia (semantic dementia; Graham, Patterson, & Hodges, 2000; Woollams, Lambon Ralph, Plaut, & Patterson, 2007) and individuals with moderate to advanced Alzheimer's disease (Patterson, Graham, & Hodges, 1994). The reduction in the ability to process lexical–semantic information results in overreliance on sublexical spelling procedures and regularization errors. Surface dysgraphia that is associated with degraded semantic knowledge is often accompanied by anomia and language comprehension difficulties, so that the aphasia profile is likely to progress from anomic to transcortical sensory aphasia as semantic knowledge declines but repetition skills remain strong. Writing at the text level is likely to result in semantically empty written narratives, despite relatively preserved syntactic structure.

Semantic dementia is associated with cortical atrophy of the anterior temporal lobes that is greater on the left (Gorno-Tempini et al., 2011; Hodges et al., 1992). Damage to semantic representations may also be responsible for surface dyslexia/dysgraphia in individuals with posterior temporoparietal damage involving the middle temporal/angular gyrus, as these areas frequently show activation in functional imaging studies of semantic processing in healthy individuals (Binder et al., 2009); however, the lesion-deficit data are limited because damage is rarely restricted to this region without also affecting perisylvian language regions.

Peripheral Dysgraphias

Deficits at the peripheral stages of processing include degraded ability to convert graphemes to their correct allographic form, or problems more specific to graphomotor planning and implementation. In some instances, there appears to be dysfunction at the interface between central and peripheral processes, so that orthographic information fails to persist in the graphemic buffer, and written output shows a pattern of short-term memory decay (Buchwald & Rapp, 2009; Caramazza et al., 1987). In individuals with aphasia, these more peripheral writing impairments may cooccur with their central linguistic difficulties. We review here the most common peripheral writing problems: allographic dysgraphia, apraxic dysgraphia, and issues related to right hemiparesis.

ALLOGRAPHIC DYSGRAPHIA

Allographic dysgraphia is an impairment of written spelling due to errors in letter selection or degraded knowledge of letter shapes. In some cases, incorrect letter selection may occur in the presence of correct spelling knowledge, so that the individual correctly spells a word aloud, but writes the wrong letter(s). If the problem relates to the generation of the letter shape knowledge per se, then typing or keyboarding may remain a useful means to write.

More commonly, however, errors in letter selection compound central impairments of spelling knowledge, so that the effects are additive. An assessment of allographic knowledge can be accomplished by requesting written production of lowercase letters in response to the uppercase forms, and vice versa.

Allographic disorders in which there appears to be impairment of letter-shape knowledge have been associated with damage to the temporoparietooccipital regions of the left hemisphere (Rapcsak & Beeson, 2002). Other cases in which there appears to be an impaired selection of the graphomotor programs for specific letters have been associated with infarcts restricted to the left inferior frontal cortex (Hillis et al., 2004). As noted, an allographic impairment can occur in relative isolation, but more commonly cooccurs with central impairments of written language. In such cases, degraded spelling knowledge is confounded by incorrect letter selection.

APRAXIC DYSGRAPHIA

Apraxic dysgraphia is a peripheral writing impairment that reflects damage to the graphic motor programs for handwriting. The impairment is not due to muscle weakness or incoordination, but rather the disruption of motor programming of the movements of the hand. The resulting written output is characterized by poorly formed letters that contain distortions, additions, or deletions of the expected strokes of the pen/pencil. In some cases the handwriting is completely illegible.

Apraxic dysgraphia results from damage to a network of cortical regions that supports the programming of handwriting movements. This includes the posterior–superior parietal cortex in the region of the intraparietal sulcus, the dorsolateral premotor cortex (i.e., the premotor region for the hand), and the supplementary motor area (Beeson, Rapcsak et al., 2003; Menon & Desmond, 2001; Purcell, Turkeltaub et al., 2011). Isolated cases of apraxic dysgraphia are relatively rare due to vascular causes. However, when such cases do occur, they typically arise from hemorrhagic strokes, as they do not respect vascular distributions (Otsuki, Soma, Arai, Otsuka, & Tsuji, 1999). Some instances of progressive limb apraxia and apraxic dysgraphia have been reported in association with cortical atrophy in the dominant superior parietal lobule (Heilman, Coenen, & Kluger, 2008).

WRITING WITH THE NONDOMINANT HAND

An additional challenge regarding written communication is presented to those individuals with aphasia who also have hemiparesis of the dominant hand. About half of all individuals who have nonfluent aphasia are likely to have significant right hemiparesis due to concomitant damage to the motor cortex for the hand or associated descending white matter tracks (Croquelois, Godefroy, & Bogousslavsky, 2007). In such cases, individuals typically shift to the nondominant (left) hand for handwriting, and if they choose to type on a keyboard, they do so using only the left hand. Although the transition is awkward at first, improvements in fine motor control of the nondominant hand typically occur relatively quickly for handwriting, and some individuals are able to keyboard functionally with only the left hand.

Assessment of Written Language

The evaluation of individuals with acquired dysgraphia is structured so that the status of the relevant component processes involved in spelling and writing is examined. The evaluation should provide insight into the nature of the impairment and the level of breakdown with reference to a cognitive model of spelling. It is equally important to document relatively spared abilities and the use of compensatory strategies, as this information is helpful in planning rehabilitation. Assessment tasks can range from direct copying of single words (to examine graphomotor control with limited linguistic demands) to self-generation of a written narrative paragraph that requires engagement of semantics, phonology, orthography, and syntax (Table 13.2).

Orthographic Assessment

Single word spelling can be evaluated using writing-to-dictation tasks, or written naming of pictured items. Writing to dictation has the benefit of isolating spelling and writing skills without requiring lexical retrieval. Controlled word lists can be used to examine spelling accuracy for words and nonwords, such as those found in the literature [e.g., Johns Hopkins Dyslexia/Dysgraphia Battery (published in Beeson & Henry, 2008); Arizona Battery for Reading and Spelling (published in Beeson, Rising, Kim, & Rapcsak, 2010)], in commercially available test batteries [e.g., *Psycholinguistic Assessments of Language Processing in Aphasia (PALPA);* Kay, Lesser, & Coltheart, 1992], or provided on research websites (Beeson, 2010; Medler & Binder, 2005). Spelling accuracy can be compared on real words versus pseudowords in order to calculate lexicality effects and regular versus irregular words to calculate a regularity effect. Error type analyses serve to

Table 13.2 Assessment of Spelling and Writing

Assessment Domain Task Description	Example Task/Stimuli
Peripheral Skills	
Visual processing	Detecting mirror reversed letters (*PALPA* 18) Lexical decision tasks (*PALPA* 24, 25, 27)
Graphomotor control	Direct copy of printed words Case conversion (uppercase → lowercase, vice versa)
Orthographic Knowledge	
Writing to dictation	Regularly and irregularly spelled words and nonwords *Arizona Battery for Reading & Spelling* (*ABRS*) Grammatical class list (*PALPA* 33) Word lists controlled for length
Written naming Written narrative	*Boston Naming Test* (written responses) Written naming of objects (e.g., *WAB*) Written picture description (e.g., *WAB* picnic scene)
Oral reading	Reading single words (*ABRS*) Reading reaction time Text-level reading
Phonological Skills	
Sound–letter correspondences	Sound–letter correspondences Single letters and CVC nonword spelling Letter–sound correspondences Single letters and CVC nonword reading
Phoneme segmentation	"Say 'cat.' Now say the first sound."
Phoneme deletion	"Say 'cat.' Now take away the /k/."
Phoneme blending	/b/–/æ/–/t/ "What do those sounds make?"
Phoneme replacement	"Say 'cat.' Now change the /k/ to /h/."
Semantic Knowledge	
Picture–picture match	*Pyramids & Palm Trees Test* (pictures) *Arizona Semantic Test* (pictures)
Phonology → semantics	Spoken word–picture match (*PALPA* 47) Auditory synonym judgment (*PALPA* 49)
Orthography → semantics	Written word–picture match (*PALPA* 48) *Pyramids & Palm Trees Test* (written)

confirm the nature of the impairment. For example, phonologically plausible errors (e.g., *tuff* for *tough*) are typical of surface agraphia, semantic errors (e.g., *strong* for *tough*) are the defining feature of deep dysgraphia, and phonologically implausible spellings (e.g., *tofg* for *tough*) are common in phonological agraphia. Lists that control for word length are also useful to determine whether performance declines with longer words, which place greater requirements on the graphemic buffer (Buchwald & Rapp, 2009; Caramazza et al., 1987).

To test for grammatical class effects, performance should be compared for nouns, verbs, adjectives, and functors. Retrieval and spelling of words across a range of grammatical categories can be examined in the context of written descriptions of standard picture scenes, such as the picnic scene from the *Western Aphasia Battery–Revised* (Kertesz, 2007). Written narratives can be analyzed using procedures that are traditionally used to analyze spoken narratives, such as the Quantitative Production Analysis (QPA) (Berndt, Wayland, Rochon, Saffran, & Schwartz, 2000).

Writing requires visual processing as well as graphomotor control. If there is concern regarding visual perception or visual–orthographic processing abilities, then several tasks that test letter recognition and visual lexical decision can be administered, such as those included in the *PALPA* (Kay et al., 1992). Specifically, the stimuli in *PALPA* 18 require detection of correct versus mirror reversal of printed letters, whereas subtests such as *PALPA* 25 require more complex visual processing for making lexical decisions, that is, determining whether letter strings are real words or not. Peripheral writing abilities can be screened using a direct copying task (printed words) and a letter case conversion task (uppercase to lowercase and vice versa). Standard stimuli are not necessary for these tasks, but are also available in the PALPA subtests.

Phonological Assessment

A comprehensive assessment of phonological skills provides insight regarding the nature and severity of the phonological impairment. Tasks should include those that require phonological manipulation (with and without phonology–orthography relations), such as those listed in Table 13.2. Performance across a range of phonological tasks can be combined into one or more composite scores to provide an overall estimate of phonological skills that provides a metric for comparison across and within individuals (see, for example, Beeson et al., 2010; Rapcsak et al., 2009).

Semantic Assessment

It is important to assess the integrity of semantic representations using nonverbal tests of conceptual knowledge, such as the picture version of the *Pyramids and Palm Trees Test* (*PPTT*) (Howard & Patterson, 1992). Tests of spoken/written word comprehension further evaluate semantic knowledge, but also place varying demands on auditory or visual processing of single words (e.g., *PALPA* 47 and 48).

Treatment Procedures for Written Language Impairment

Treatment of written language is logically integrated into the larger rehabilitation plan that addresses spoken language and the individual's functional communication needs. Three treatment approaches are reviewed here that serve to strengthen central written language processing skills: lexical–semantic treatment, phonological treatment, and interactive processing of residual (or retrained) lexical and sublexical skills. When appropriate, treatment for the peripheral aspects of handwriting can be implemented concurrent with these treatments. Ideally, treatment can advance from one stage to the next as skills are strengthened.

Lexical–Semantic Treatment

Lexical spelling treatment involves retraining the spellings for specific words. It is an appropriate starting point for the treatment of global and deep dysgraphia. Implementation of lexical writing treatment, wherein spellings are trained for a corpus of specific words, inherently provides structured training for the reading of those words as well. A number of researchers have documented the value of lexical spelling treatment that involves repeated copying and delayed recall of targeted words (e.g., Beeson et al., 2003; Rapp & Kane, 2002; Raymer, Cudworth, & Haley, 2003). Copy and Recall Treatment (CART), described in Table 13.3, is an example of lexical spelling treatment. Target words selected for treatment should be of functional value to the individual, because the response to treatment is often item specific. Of course, treatment should be implemented in a manner that links the orthographic representations to their meaning, so that it is truly lexical–semantic treatment. In most instances, this approach is implemented using handwriting; however, a recent case report documented successful relearning of spelling using typing via a cell phone keyboard (Beeson, Higginson, & Rising, 2013). It was noteworthy, however, that the participant's long-term memory was better for words retrained with handwriting versus texting, suggesting that spelling treatment benefits from the inclusion of handwritten practice.

Lexical spelling treatment can easily incorporate spoken repetition of target words in training, and spoken production for those words may improve as well. When speech production is limited, as in cases of severe apraxia of speech or paraphasic output, single-word writing can be used as a means of "conversational" interaction. It is often necessary to provide pragmatic training to establish the use of written words to request and provide information

Table 13.3 Lexical Spelling Treatment

Lexical Spelling Treatment (Copy and Recall Treatment: CART)	
Goal	To strengthen orthographic representations for specific words to reestablish a functional written vocabulary and/or prepare for phonological treatment
Stimuli	• Personally relevant words or "key words" to be used for phonological treatment. • Picturable items such as favorite foods, family members' names, and household items (e.g., *computer*). Start with 20 items, grouped into four sets of 5.
Procedure	Implement the following cueing hierarchy to train the spelling of target words: 1. Present picture for target word; ask "What's this? Can you say the name?" • Correct spoken name: "Yes, it's a computer. Can you write *computer*?" • Incorrect spoken name: "It's a computer. Try to say *computer*. Now, try to spell *computer*." • Correct spelling: Provide feedback and move to the next item. • Incorrect spelling: Move to step 2. 2. Show handwritten model of the word. "Copy this word: *computer*." • Correct copying: Provide feedback and prompt copying two more times. • Incorrect copying: Refer back to written model. "Try to copy *computer* again." 3. Cover all written models of the target word. Present picture and prompt spelling recall. "Can you remember how to spell *computer*? Try to write it again." • Correct: Prompt recall twice more, then move on to next word. • Incorrect: Repeat copy sequence with model. 4. If correct recall is not achieved after several trials, move on to another word. Return to difficult words during the session if there is time. 5. As target words become established, implement activities to encourage use of the words in various contexts, such as in cloze phrases or conversational interactions.
Homework	• Provide daily homework packets consisting of labeled pictures from the target set(s) and multiple lines for copying each word. • Include a "test" page at the end of each day's packet with each picture and a line for written recall (no written model). • For practice with spoken naming of target words, a talking photo album can be used. Place a picture in the album, provide the written label for copying, and record the spoken name of the target word. The patient can push the button to hear the name and practice verbal repetition along with repeated copying.

(Clausen & Beeson, 2003; Robson, Marshall, Chiat, & Pring, 2001). Another potential benefit of lexical spelling treatment is the use of self-generated written words to stabilize phonology for speech production, as in cases of conduction aphasia (Beeson & Egnor, 2006).

Lexical treatment can also be used to retrain the spellings of specific words in individuals with surface dysgraphia (Beeson et al., 2000; Behrmann, 1987; Hillis & Caramazza, 1987). Difficult words are likely to be those with irregular spellings because such words are often misspelled due to overreliance on phonology. Several investigators have shown

positive effects when lexical treatment is accompanied by visual imagery of the components of the word (de Partz, Seron, & Van der Linden, 1992; Schmalzl & Nickels, 2006).

Phonological Treatment

Phonological treatment is intended to reestablish sound–letter and letter–sound correspondences, as well as strengthen phonological skills in general. Various phonological treatment protocols have been shown to result in improved performance on sublexical and lexical reading and spelling tasks (Beeson et al., 2010; Greenwald,

Table 13.4 Phonological Treatment

Phonological Treatment	
Goal	Retrain phoneme–grapheme correspondences and phonological manipulation skills.

Stimuli	Establish phonemes to be trained. May begin with the most frequently occurring consonants and progress to less frequently occurring consonants.
	• Example training sequence:
	  • Set 1: r, t, s, l, n
	  • Set 2: k, d, m, p, f
	  • Set 3: b, sh, v, g, z
	  • Set 4: j, ch, th, h, w
	• Establish "key words" for targeted phonemes
	• Key word characteristics:
	  • Each key word should begin with one of the targeted phonemes.
	  • Select words the patient can spell correctly (train if necessary).
	  • Picturable key words are useful for treatment and homework procedures.
	  • Patients do not have to be able to verbally produce key words for phonological treatment to be successful.
	  • Example key words for Set 1 consonants: rug, top, safe, leaf, net

Procedure	Implement the following cueing hierarchy to train phoneme–grapheme correspondences: 1. Model the target phoneme: /t/. "Say /t/. Can you write the letter that makes the sound /t/?" • Correct: Proceed to the next sound • Incorrect: Go to step 2. 2. "Try to write your key word for /t/" • Correct: "Yes, *top* is your key word for /t/. Which letter in top makes the sound /t/?" Proceed to the next sound. • Incorrect: Go to step 3. 3. "Here is your key word for /t/ (show picture). *Top*. Write *top*. Which letter in the word top makes the sound /t/?" • Correct: Proceed to the next sound. • Incorrect: Provide the written model for the key word and proceed through the rest of step 3. 4. As phoneme sets become established, implement additional phonological training activities such as identification and segmentation of phonemes in words and nonwords. (Example: What is the last sound in the word *cat*?)

Homework	• Using a talking photo album, or DVD/video, record each phoneme and provide a picture of the corresponding key word.
	  • The patient plays the recorded phonemes, repeats, and writes the graphemes on a sheet of paper.
	• Provide "flash cards" with the grapheme on one side and key word on the other.
	  • Patient says the key words and tries to isolate the target phoneme.

2004; Luzzatti, Colombo, & Frustaci, 2000). For individuals with marked phonological impairment, it is often useful to employ a "key word" approach in which a set of words is used to assist in the recall of sound–letter correspondences, as described in Table 13.4. For example, "tape" might be the key word to assist in the recall of the letter *t* for the /t/ sound. Consonant training typically precedes vowel training because the latter tends to be particularly difficult (Beeson et al., 2010). Phonological training involves strengthening phonology and its relation to orthography, and improvements are often evident on nonword spelling tasks.

Interactive Treatment

Another spelling treatment approach involves strategic training to facilitate interactive use of residual lexical and sublexical knowledge in a problem-solving manner, along with the use of an electronic speller (see Table 13.5). The premise of the approach is based on the assumption of interactive activation models that postulate simultaneous bottom-up and top-down influences occurring at multiple levels within the hierarchically organized language processing system (i.e., sublexical, lexical, and sentence levels). Interactive treatment has been shown to result in improved spelling for untrained words as well as successful use of the electronic speller for independent self-correction of errors (Beeson et al., 2000, 2010).

Peripheral Writing Impairments

There is evidence that allographic skills can improve in the context of treatment for central spelling impairments (Beeson et al., 2010). In other words, the stimulation provided by structured writing treatments that include supported, repeated production of letter shapes often serves to strengthen allographic knowledge (or access to such knowledge). When writing is accomplished with the nondominant hand due to hemiparesis of the dominant hand, it is also evident that repeated written production with the nondominant hand results in improved graphomotor control. In cases of apraxic dysgraphia, anecdotal evidence suggests that when apraxic dysgraphia is mild to moderate, individuals may benefit from behavioral treatment that focuses on deliberate and feedback-dependent practice copying written words. Severe forms of apraxic agraphia appear to be resistant to treatment, and therefore modalities other than written language may be more appropriate.

Case Examples of Treatment for Acquired Dysgraphia

We present three individuals who received treatment for acquired dysgraphia. Initial assessment provided direction regarding the starting point for treatment, and the cases illustrate a treatment progression intended to maximize language recovery.

Global Dysgraphia

Mrs. T was a 53-year-old, right-handed woman who experienced a left middle cerebral artery stroke following surgical removal of a glioblastoma. At 2 years poststroke, her spoken language performance was consistent with relatively severe Broca's aphasia,

characterized by single word utterances, phonemic paraphasias, and moderately impaired auditory comprehension. On the *Western Aphasia Battery* (*WAB*; Kertesz, 1982), her Aphasia Quotient was 36.6. She demonstrated considerable difficulty with lexical retrieval, as indicated by a score of 10/60 on the *Boston Naming Test* (*BNT*; Kaplan, Goodglass, & Weintraub, 2001). Semantic knowledge was relatively intact, but performance on a battery of phonological tests indicated severe impairment, with a composite score of 22% (calculated in a manner consistent with Beeson et al., 2010). Mrs. T demonstrated globally impaired reading and spelling abilities with 10% accuracy for oral reading of real words and 0% accuracy on writing to dictation tasks for both real and nonwords (Figure 13.2). Although she wrote with her nondominant left hand, she had adequate motor control for copying words and adequate letter-shape (allographic) knowledge.

Mrs. T received lexical spelling treatment (CART) for 6 weeks, during which time she relearned the spellings for 24 words, and also demonstrated improved spoken naming of these same words (Figure 13.2). The improvement in spelling did not generalize to untrained words, but Mrs. T was able to relearn additional items and thus expand her written vocabulary using this technique. She also demonstrated functional use of the trained items in communication interactions.

Following lexical treatment, Mrs. T went on to participate in phonological treatment. Over the course of 10 weeks, she relearned sound–letter and letter–sound correspondences, attaining 95% and 83% accuracy, respectively (Figure 13.2). Following completion of phonological treatment, Mrs. T demonstrated improved use of phonology to spell untrained real words. She then moved on to interactive treatment for approximately 5 weeks, after which she was able to use retrained lexical and sublexical skills along with an electronic spell checker to spell untrained single words with 55% accuracy (Figure 13.2). Additionally, her phonological skills continued to improve as evidenced by her increased ability to spell nonwords following interactive treatment, and her overall improvement on the Arizona phonological test battery (see Beeson et al., 2010) was indexed by a composite score of 56%, compared to 22% before treatment.

Of note, Mrs. T's naming performance on the *Boston Naming Test* also improved by 7 points after the treatment sequence, despite the treatment focus on phonology and written language rather than lexical retrieval. Following this written language

Table 13.5 Interactive Treatment

Interactive Treatment (Problem-Solving Approach)	
Goal	Promote the interactive use of residual (or retrained) phonology and orthography skills to improve the detection and self-correction of spelling errors.
Stimuli and Materials	Generate a list of irregularly spelled words for use in treatment and homework tasks. An electronic spell checker is used in this protocol. Spell checker features include: • Sensitivity to phonologically plausible spelling errors (e.g., will correct "serkit" to "circuit"). • Spoken output. • A large keypad and screen may be helpful for some. • The Franklin Speaking Language Master˚ is an example of an electronic spell checker that is appropriate for this approach; however, there may be other brands and models that will work as well.
Procedure	Train the use of spell checker device, ensuring ability to: • Turn device on and off. • Manipulate the keyboard without assistance. • See the words on the screen and adjust the screen quality. • Hear the voice output and adjust the volume independently.
	Verbally present an irregularly spelled word. Train the following problem-solving strategy: 1. "Sound out" the word and write it down. 2. Look carefully at the word. If it does not look correct, try to spell it again. 3. Type the best spelling attempt into the spell checker. 4. Scroll through the list of options to find the correct spelling. 5. Look and listen to the words on the list to verify the correct spelling. 6. Copy the correct word.
	For those who are able to write at text level, therapy tasks can include writing sentences to dictation and generating written sentences. Encourage the detection and correction of errors in all words within the sentence, regular and irregular, using the spell checker as needed.
Homework	• Record 5–10 irregular words (per homework day) in a talking photo album or on another recordable device. • Patient generates spellings for the words, using the procedure established during treatment sessions. • As treatment progresses, include sentence and paragraph level writing. Provide irregular words to generate sentences, or a general topic (e.g., favorite vacation) for paragraph writing. • Always encourage editing of text-level writing and correction of spelling errors using problem-solving techniques.

treatment, she went on to successfully participate in a lexical retrieval treatment that capitalized on her ability to use retrained phonology and orthography skills in addition to residual semantic skills to self-cue naming.

Phonological Dysgraphia

Mr. G was a right-handed, 37-year-old man who had no overt risk factors to explain his left middle cerebral artery stroke, which occurred 6 months prior to his initial assessment in our research laboratory. At the time of the evaluation, his spoken language was consistent with anomic aphasia: fluent with mildly impaired repetition and naming on the *Western Aphasia Battery* (Aphasia Quotient = 88.4).

His performance on a battery of phonological tests indicated moderately impaired phonological skills, with a composite score of 69%. Phonological difficulties were also apparent in Mr. G's performance on pseudoword reading and spelling. Although real word performance on both tasks was better than 90% accurate, he showed a clear lexicality effect, reading nonwords with 55% accuracy and spelling them with 15% accuracy (see examples in Figure 13.3). He also demonstrated a slow reading rate for text (approximately 48 words per minute for second-grade level text) and reduced grammatical complexity in text-level writing, which was not consistent with the relatively normal grammatical complexity of his spoken language.

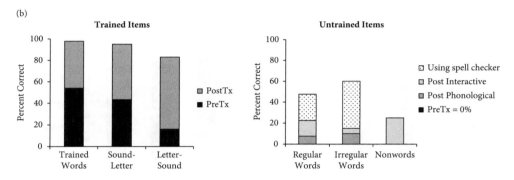

(a)

Global Dysgraphia

Regular Words		Irregular Words		Nonwords	
Target	*Response*	Target	*Response*	Target	*Response*
mile	*emorge*	sword	*rorgus*	flig	*heal*
drive	*stroug*	choir	*choley*	dringe	*quenh*
shampoo	*shamoon*	subtle	*share*	barcle	*duleg*
grill	*goush*	ghost	*donlde*	trad	*clse*

Figure 13.2 (a) Individual with global dysgraphia (Mrs. T). Lesion location and example spelling errors on writing-to-dictation task prior to treatment. (b) Response to treatment. Performance before and after treatment sequence (lexical → phonological → interactive treatment). Left: Spelling of trained words, sound–letter, and letter–sound correspondences. Right: Performance on untrained items before and after treatment.

Mr. G participated in phonological treatment for approximately 10 weeks, including retraining of sound–letter/letter–sound correspondences as well as work directed toward phonological manipulation in the context of nonword spelling. After successfully meeting the criterion for completion of phonological treatment, his nonword spelling performance for untrained items reflected a marked improvement in sublexical skills (Figure 13.3). Following phonological training, Mr. G went on to interactive spelling treatment, concurrent with a text-level reading treatment. After approximately 3 months, posttesting revealed continued improvement in sublexical skills, with nonword spelling performance at 85% accuracy (compared to 15% before treatment) and verbal phonology composite scores at 89% (up 20% from pretesting). Additionally, Mr. G demonstrated improved formulation of text-level writing, as evidenced by his pre- and posttreatment written descriptions of the picnic scene from the *Western Aphasia Battery*. After treatment, his written sentences showed improved use of function words and grammatical morphemes, resulting in a greater percentage of sentences that were well formed and complete according to the production analysis (Berndt et al., 2000) (see Figure 13.3).

On a self-rating measure, both Mr. G and his wife indicated that they thought his written language had improved considerably, and he expressed greater confidence in overall communication abilities (speaking, reading, writing) following his treatment course.

Surface Dysgraphia

Mr. F was a 73-year-old male who experienced a left posterior artery stroke 8 years prior to his first visit to our clinic. Although he reported being ambidextrous, Mr. F wrote with his right hand both before and after his stroke. He had a prior right-sided occipital lobe lesion that caused left hemianopia, and the addition of the left hemisphere lesion and corresponding right hemianopia gave him "tunnel" vision. However, his vision was functional for most activities of daily living, including reading and writing.

Mr. F's spoken language was consistent with mild anomic aphasia on the *Western Aphasia Battery* (Aphasia Quotient = 89.4), and he demonstrated mildly to moderately impaired confrontation naming on the *Boston Naming Test* (42/60). Single word spelling was characterized by better performance on regularly spelled words and

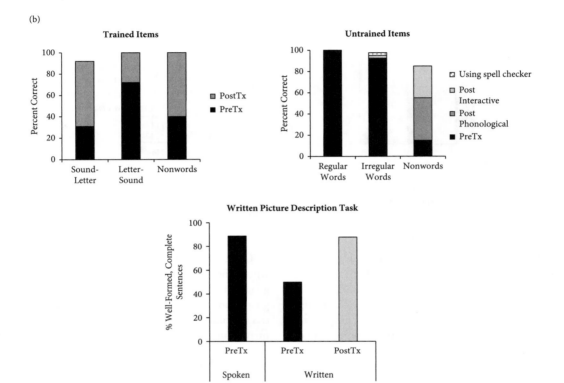

(a)

Phonological Dysgraphia

Regular Words		Irregular Words		Nonwords	
Target	*Response*	Target	*Response*	Target	*Response*
broom	+	circuit	+	hoach	*host*
grumble	+	castle	+	wape	*wipat*
sister	+	tomb	+	barcle	*burnger*
fresh	+	yacht	*yact*	snite	+

(b)

Figure 13.3 (a) Individual with phonological dysgraphia (Mr. G.). Lesion location and example spelling responses on writing-to-dictation task before treatment. (b) Response to treatment. Performance before and after treatment sequence (phonological → interactive treatment). Left: Performance on sound–letter, and letter–sound correspondence tasks and nonword spelling. Right: Performance on untrained items before and after treatment. Lower Middle: Performance on spoken and written picture descriptions indicated by percent of sentences that were well formed and complete.

nonwords compared to irregular words, resulting in a regularity effect consistent with a profile of surface dysgraphia (Figure 13.4). He also demonstrated a significantly slower than average reading rate for single words (1.5–2.0 seconds/word) and text (approximately 60 words per minute for second-grade level text).

Mr. F participated in interactive spelling treatment and a concurrent oral reading treatment for approximately 30 sessions over the course of several months. He successfully learned strategies for detecting and correcting spelling errors, demonstrating improved real-word spelling after treatment and near normal single-word spelling performance when using an electronic spell checker (Figure 13.4). On a self-rating form posttreatment, Mr. F and his wife both indicated that they felt his overall spelling ability was better, and they indicated his confidence in his communication abilities had improved.

(a)

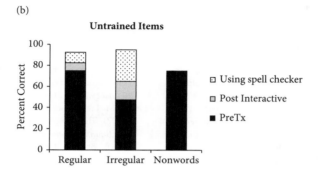

Surface Dysgraphia	Regular Words		Irregular Words		Nonwords	
	Target	*Response*	Target	*Response*	Target	*Response*
	broom	+	routine	*rutine*	hoach	+
	plastic	+	castle	*casal*	nace	+
	chant	+	choir	*quaire*	trad	*trade*
	fresh	+	yacht	*yat*	merber	+

(b)

Untrained Items

Percent Correct

□ Using spell checker
▦ Post Interactive
■ PreTx

Regular   Irregular   Nonwords

Figure 13.4 (a) Individual with surface dysgraphia (Mr. F). Lesion location and example spelling responses on writing-to-dictation task before treatment. (b) Mr. F's spelling performance before and after interactive treatment. Spell checker was available to help self-correct spelling errors after treatment.

Summary

Acquired impairments of written language production are common following left hemisphere damage. The goal of behavioral treatment is to strengthen the weakened skills and to take advantage of residual abilities. As demonstrated in this chapter, written language skills are dependent upon central language processes that are common to spoken language (semantics and phonology) and reading (orthography). Therefore, it is not surprising that the interventions for written language can simultaneously advance reading and spelling skills. Individual case studies demonstrate that overall language performance can be maximized by sequential treatments that promote interactive use of relearned, strengthened, and preserved cognitive processes. Participants and their families confirm the functional benefits of these treatments, suggesting that the long-term rehabilitation efforts are worth the effort.

Acknowledgments

This work was supported by Grants DC007646 and DC 008286 from the National Institute on Deafness and Other Communication Disorders.

References

Beauvois, M. F., & Dérouesné, J. (1981). Lexical or orthographic agraphia. *Brain*, 104, 21–49.

Beeson, P. M. (1999). Treating acquired writing impairment: Strengthening graphemic representations. *Aphasiology*, 13(9–11), 767–785.

Beeson, P. M. (2010). Arizona battery for reading and spelling. http://web.me.com/pelagie1/Aphasia_Research_Project/Assessment_Materials.html.

Beeson, P. M., & Egnor, H. (2006). Combining treatment for written and spoken naming. *Journal of the International Neuropsychological Society*, 12(6), 816–827.

Beeson, P. M., & Henry, M. L. (2008). Comprehension and production of written words. In R. Chapey (Ed.), *Language intervention strategies in aphasia and related neurogenic communication disorders* (5th ed., pp. 654–688). Baltimore, MD: Lippincott Williams & Wilkins.

Beeson, P. M., Higginson, K., & Rising, K. (2013). Writing treatment for aphasia: A text messaging approach. *Journal of Speech, Language, and Hearing Research*, 56, 945–955.

Beeson, P. M., & Hillis, A. (2001). Comprehension and production of written words. In R. Chapey (Ed.), *Language intervention strategies in aphasia and related neurogenic communication disorders* (4th ed., pp. 572–604). Baltimore, MD: Lippincott Williams & Wilkins.

Beeson, P., Rapcsak, S., Plante, E., Chargualaf, J., Chung, A., Johnson, S., & Trouard, T. (2003). The neural substrates of writing: A functional magnetic resonance imaging study. *Aphasiology*, 17(6–7), 647–665.

Beeson, P. M., Rewega, M. A., Vail, S., & Rapcsak, S. Z. (2000). Problem-solving approach to agraphia treatment: Interactive use of lexical and sublexical spelling routes. *Aphasiology*, 14, 551–565).

Beeson, P. M., Rising, K., DeMarco, A., Foley, T. H., & Rapcsak, S. Z. (2016). The nature and treatment of phonological text agraphia. *Neuropsychological Rehabilitation*, 26, 1–21.

Beeson, P. M., Rising, K., Kim, E. S., & Rapcsak, S. Z. (2010). A treatment sequence for phonological alexia/agraphia. *Journal of Speech, Language, and Hearing Research*, 53, 450–468.

Beeson, P. M., Rising, K., & Volk, J. (2003). Writing treatment for severe aphasia: Who benefits? *Journal of Speech, Language, and Hearing Research*, 46(5), 1038–1060.

Behrmann, M. (1987). The rites of righting writing: Homophone remediation in acquired dysgraphia. *Cognitive Neuropsychology*, 4(3), 365–384.

Behrmann, M., & Bub, D. (1992). Surface dyslexia and dysgraphia: Dual routes, single lexicon. *Cognitive Neuropsychology*, 9(3), 209–251.

Berndt, R. S., Wayland, S., Rochon, E., Saffran, E., & Schwartz, M. (2000). *Quantitative production analysis: A training manual for the analysis of aphasic sentence production*. Philadelphia, PA: Psychology Press.

Binder, J. R., Desai, R. H., Graves, W. W., & Conant, L. L. (2009). Where is the semantic system? A critical review and meta-analysis of 120 functional neuroimaging studies. *Cerebral Cortex*, 19(12), 2767–2796.

Bub, D., & Kertesz, A. (1982). Deep agraphia. *Brain and Language*, 17, 146–165.

Buchwald, A., & Rapp, B. (2009). Distinctions between orthographic long-term memory and working memory. *Cognitive Neuropsychology*, 26(8), 724–751.

Caramazza, A., Miceli, G., Villa, G., & Romani, C. (1987). The role of the graphemic buffer in spelling: Evidence from a case of acquired dysgraphia. *Cognition*, 26(1), 59–85.

Clausen, N., & Beeson, P. (2003). Conversational use of writing in severe aphasia: A group treatment approach. *Aphasiology*, 17(6), 625–644.

Cohen, L., & Dehaene, S. (2004). Specialization within the ventral stream: The case for the visual word form area. *Neuroimage*, 22(1), 466–476.

Cohen, L., Lehéricy, S., Chochon, F., Lemer, C., Rivaud, S., & Dehaene, S. (2002). Language-specific tuning of visual cortex? Functional properties of the visual word form area. *Brain*, 125(5), 1054–1069.

Coltheart, M., Rastle, K., Perry, C., Langdon, R., & Zeigler, J. (2001). DRC: A dual route cascaded model of visual word recognition and reading aloud. *Psychological Review*, 108, 204–256.

Coslett, H. B., & Saffran, E. M. (1998). Reading and the right hemisphere: Evidence from acquired dyslexia. In M. Beeman & C. Chiarello (Eds.), *Right hemisphere language comprehension* (pp. 105–132). Mahwah, NJ: Lawrence Erlbaum Associates.

Croquelois, A., Godefroy, O., & Bogousslavsky, J. (2007). Acute vascular aphasia. In O. Godefroy & J. Bogousslavsky (Eds.), *The behavioural and cognitive neurology of stroke* (pp. 75–85). Cambridge, England: Cambridge University Press.

de Partz, M., Seron, X., & Van der Linden, M. (1992). Reeducation of a surface dysgraphia with a visual imagery strategy. *Cognitive Neuropsychology*, 9(5), 369–401.

Fiez, J. A., Balota, D. A., Raichle, M. E., & Petersen, S. E. (1999). Effects of lexicality, frequency, and spelling-to-sound consistency on the functional anatomy of reading. *Neuron*, 24, 205–218.

Fiez, J. A., Tranel, D., Seager-Frerichs, D., & Damasio, H. (2006). Specific reading and phonological processing deficits are associated with damage to the left frontal operculum. *Cortex*, 42(4), 624–643.

Gorno-Tempini, M. L., Hillis, A. E., Weintraub, S., Kertesz, A. E., Mendez, M. D., Cappa, S. F., . . . Grossman, M. (2011). Classification of primary progressive aphasia and its variants. *American Academy of Neurology*, 76(11), 1006–1014.

Graham, N. L., Patterson, K., & Hodges, J. R. (2000). The impact of semantic memory impairment on spelling: Evidence from semantic dementia. *Neuropsychologia*, 38(2), 143–163.

Greenwald, M. (2004). "Blocking" lexical competitors in severe global agraphia: A treatment of reading and spelling. *Neurocase*, 10(2), 156–174.

Hanley, J. R., & Kay, J. (1992). Does letter-by-letter reading involve the spelling system? *Neuropsychologia*, 30(3), 237–256.

Heilman, K. M., Coenen, A., & Kluger, B. (2008). Progressive asymmetric apraxic agraphia. *Cognitive and Behavioral Neurology*, 21(1), 14–17.

Henry, M. L., Beeson, P. M., & Stark, A. J., & Rapcsak, S. Z. (2007). The role of left perisylvian cortical regions in spelling. *Brain and Language*, 100(1), 44–52.

Hier, D. B., & Mohr, J. D. (1977). Incongruous oral and written naming: Evidence for a subdivision of Wernicke's aphasia. *Brain and Language*, 4, 115–126.

Hillis, A. E., & Caramazza, A. (1987). Model-driven treatment of dysgraphia. In R. H. Brookshire (Ed.), *Clinical aphasiology* (pp. 84–105). Minneapolis, MN: BRK.

Hillis, A. E., Chang, S., Breese, E., & Heidler, J. (2004). The crucial role of posterior frontal regions in modality specific components of the spelling process. *Neurocase*, 10(2), 175–187.

Hillis, A. E., Kane, A., Tuffiash, E., Beauchamp, N. J., Barker, P. B., Jacobs, M. A., & Wityk, R. J. (2002). Neural substrates of the cognitive processes underlying spelling: Evidence from MR diffusion and perfusion imaging. *Aphasiology*, 16(4–6), 425–438.

Hillis, A., & Rapp, B. (2004). Cognitive and neural substrates of written language comprehension and production. In M. Gazzaniga (Ed.), *The cognitive neurosciences* (3rd ed., pp. 775–788). Cambridge, MA: Bradford Books.

Hodges, J. R., Patterson, K., Oxbury, S., & Funnell, E. (1992). Semantic dementia. Progressive fluent aphasia with temporal lobe atrophy. *Brain*, 115, 1783–1806.

Howard, D., & Patterson, K. E. (1992). *The Pyramids and Palm Trees Test: A test of semantic access from pictures and words*. Bury St. Edmunds, Suffolk: Thames Valley Test Company.

Ingles, J. L., & Eskes, G. A. (2007). Temporal processing deficits in letter-by-letter reading. *Journal of the International Neuropsychological Society*, 13(01), 110–119.

Jobard, G., Crivello, F., & Tzourio-Mazoyer, N. (2003). Evaluation of the dual route theory of reading: A metanalysis of 35 neuroimaging studies. *Neuroimage*, 20(2), 693–712.

Kaplan, E., Goodglass, H., & Weintraub, S. (2001). *Boston Naming Test* (2nd ed.). Philadelphia, PA: Lippincott Williams & Wilkins.

Kay, J. M., Lesser, R., & Coltheart, M. (1992). *PALPA. Psycholinguistic assessments of language processing in aphasia*. East Sussex, England: Lawrence Erlbaum Associates Ltd.

Kertesz, A. (1982). *Western aphasia battery (WAB)*. San Antonio, TX: The Psychological Corporation.

Kertesz, A. (2007). *Western aphasia battery-revised (WAB-R)*. Boston, MA: Pearson Education.

Lubrano, V., Roux, F. E., & Demonet, J. F. (2004). Writing-specific sites in frontal areas: A cortical stimulation study. *Journal of Neurosurgery*, 101(5), 787–798.

Luzzatti, C., Colombo, C., & Frustaci, M. (2000). Rehabilitation of spelling along the sub-word-level routine. *Neuropsychological Rehabilitation*, 10(3), 249–278.

Magrassi, L., Bongetta, D., Bianchini, S., Berardesca, M., & Arienta, C. (2010). Central and peripheral components of writing critically depend on a defined area of the dominant superior parietal gyrus. *Brain Research*, 1346, 145–154.

Medler, D. A., & Binder, J. R. (2005). MCWord: An on-line orthographic database of the English language. http://www.neuro.mcw.edu/mcword/.

Menon, V., & Desmond, J. E. (2001). Left superior parietal cortex involvement in writing: Integrating fMRI with lesion evidence. *Cognitive Brain Research*, 12, 337–340.

Otsuki, M., Soma, Y., Arai, T., Otsuka, A., & Tsuji, S. (1999). Pure apraxic agraphia with abnormal writing stroke sequences: Report of a Japanese patient with a left superior parietal hemorrhage. *Journal of Neurology, Neurosurgery & Psychiatry*, 66(2), 233–237.

Patterson, K., Graham, N., & Hodges, J. R. (1994). Reading in dementia of the Alzheimer type: A preserved ability? *Neuropsychology*, 8(3), 395–412.

Patterson, K., & Marcel, A. (1992). Phonological alexia or phonological alexia? In J. Alegria, D. Holender, J. Junca de Moras, & M. Radeau (Eds.), *Analytic approaches to human cognition* (pp. 259–274). Oxford, England: North-Holland.

Patterson, K., Marshall, J. C., & Coltheart, M. (1985). *Surface dyslexia: Neuropsychological and cognitive studies of phonological reading*. Hillsdale, NJ: Erlbaum Associates.

Philipose, L. E., Gottesman, R. F., Newhart, M., Kleinman, J. T., Herskovits, E. H., Pawlak, M. A., . . . Hillis, A. E. (2007). Neural regions essential for reading and spelling of words and pseudowords. *Annals of Neurology*, 62(5), 481–492.

Plaut, D. C., McClelland, J. L., Seidenberg, M. S., & Patterson, K. (1996). Understanding normal and impaired word reading: Computational principles in quasi-regular domains. *Psychological Review*, 103(1), 56–115.

Purcell, J. J., Napoliello, E. M., & Eden, G. F. (2011). A combined fMRI study of typed spelling and reading. *Neuroimage*, 55, 750–762.

Purcell, J. J., Turkeltaub, P. E., Eden, G. F., & Rapp, B. (2011). Examining the central and peripheral processes of written word production through meta-analysis. *Frontiers in Psychology*, 2, 1–16.

Rapcsak, S., Arthur, S., & Rubens, A. (1988). Lexical agraphia from focal lesion of the left precentral gyrus. *Neurology*, 38(7), 1119.

Rapcsak, S. Z., & Beeson, P. M., & Rubens, A. B. (1991). Writing with the right hemisphere. *Brain and Language*, 41, 510–530.

Rapcsak, S. Z., & Beeson, P. M. (2002). Neuroanatomical correlates of spelling and writing. In A. Hillis (Ed.), *The handbook of adult language disorders* (pp. 71–99). New York, NY: Psychology Press.

Rapcsak, S. Z., & Beeson, P. M. (2004). The role of left posterior inferior temporal cortex in spelling. *Neurology*, 62, 2221–2229.

Rapcsak, S. Z., Beeson, P. M., Henry, M. L., Leyden, A., Kim, E., Rising, K., . . . Cho, H. (2009). Phonological dyslexia and dysgraphia: Cognitive mechanisms and neural substrates. *Cortex*, 45(5), 575–591.

Rapp, B. (2002). Uncovering the cognitive architecture of spelling. In A. Hillis (Ed.), *The handbook of adult language disorders* (pp. 47–69). New York, NY: Psychology Press.

Rapp, B., & Caramazza, A. (1997). From graphemes to abstract letter shapes: Levels of representation in written spelling. *Journal of Experimental Psychology: Human Perception and Performance*, 23(4), 1130–1152.

Rapp, B., Epstein, C., & Tainturier, M. J. (2002). The integration of information across lexical and sublexical processes in spelling. *Cognitive Neuropsychology*, 19(1), 1–29.

Rapp, B., & Kane, A. (2002). Remediation of deficits affecting different components of the spelling process. *Aphasiology*, 16, 439–454.

Rapp, B., & Lipka, K. (2011). The literate brain: The relationship between spelling and reading. *Journal of Cognitive Neuroscience*, 23(5), 1180–1197.

Raymer, A., Cudworth, C., & Haley, M. (2003). Spelling treatment for an individual with dysgraphia: Analysis of generalisation to untrained words. *Aphasiology*, 17, 607–624.

Robson, J., Marshall, J., Chiat, S., & Pring, T. (2001). Enhancing communication in jargon aphasia: A small group study of writing therapy. *International Journal of Language and Communication Disorders*, 36(4), 471–488.

Roeltgen, D. P., & Heilman, K. M. (1984). Lexical agraphia. Further support for the two-system hypothesis of linguistic agraphia. *Brain*, 107(Pt 3), 811–827.

Schlaggar, B. L., & McCandliss, B. D. (2007). Development of neural systems for reading. *Annual Review of Neuroscience*, 30(1), 475–503.

Schmalzl, L., & Nickels, L. (2006). Treatment of irregular word spelling in acquired dysgraphia: Selective benefit from visual mnemonics. *Neuropsychological Rehabilitation*, 16(1), 1–37.

Shallice, T. (1981). Phonological agraphia and the lexical route in writing. *Brain*, 104(3), 413–429.

Tohgi, H., Saitoh, K., & Sasaki, T. (1995). Agraphia and acalculia after a left prefrontal (F1, F2) infarction. *Journal of Neurology, Neurosurgery & Psychiatry*, 58(5), 629–632.

Tsapkini, K., & Rapp, B. (2010). The orthography-specific functions of the left fusiform gyrus: Evidence of modality and category specificity. *Cortex*, 46(2), 185–205.

Vigneau, M., Beaucousin, V., Herve, P., Duffau, H., Crivello, F., Houde, O., . . . Tzourio-Mazoyer, N. (2006). Meta-analyzing left hemisphere language areas: Phonology, semantics, and sentence processing. *Neuroimage*, 30(4), 1414–1432.

Woollams, A. M., Ralph, M. A. L., Plaut, D. C., & Patterson, K. (2007). SD-squared: On the association between semantic dementia and surface dyslexia. *Psychological Review*, 114(2), 316–339.

PART 3

Language and Right Hemisphere Damage

Discourse and Social Cognition Disorders Affecting Communication Abilities

Maximiliano A. Wilson, Bernadette Ska, *and* Yves Joanette

Abstract

This chapter offers an overview of the pragmatic and social communication disorders that can occur after an alteration of the brain, as best exemplified by individuals with right hemisphere damage. It also discusses the theoretical approaches developed to explain indirect speech act comprehension and inference impairments affecting conversational and narrative comprehension. Similar deficits have been described in other brain-damaged populations such as individuals with traumatic brain injuries, early dementia, and some forms of aphasia. Taken together, deficits of discourse and social aspects of communication abilities show they depend upon the integrity of brain networks that are widely distributed over the brain. These deficits need to be better recognized and described with reference to the underlying cognitive processes involved in order to move toward a more efficient way of helping these individuals participate in society again.

Key Words: Pragmatics, Social cognition, Right-brain damage, Prosody, Inference, Theory of mind

Introduction

Language is a privileged tool for communication, but communicating is more than the ability to produce the sounds that form the words of a sentence. It implies the ability to think about a message to be communicated and, at the other end, to interpret a message that has been expressed, including the speaker/writer's intention. In that sense, communication is more than the sum of sentences; it has a particular structure that goes beyond the meaning of the utterances that compose it.

Because of the complex nature of communication, its study is by definition a cross-disciplinary field that involves linguistics, psychology, sociology, and philosophy, among other disciplines. Two disciplines in particular have studied communication, its social role, and its impairments: social communication and pragmatics. The seminal works of theorists such as Grice (1969, 1975) and Searle (1979) (for further references, see Cummings, 2007) laid the foundations for further theoretical developments

and are still influential. The idea that language is used with a purpose and that this purpose is social in nature puts the language user at the center of research interest.

Pragmatics can be conceived of as the study of meaning in context or, in other words, how context contributes to meaning. The word "context" refers not only to the particularities of the communication situation, such as the time and place of the utterance, but also to the subjective state of the communication partners, that is, their shared knowledge, their intentions, and their emotional states (Joanette & Ansaldo, 1999; Joanette, Goulet, & Hannequin, 1990).

The results of experiments by Gibbs and Moise (1997) also stress the role of context. According to these authors, listeners do not necessarily analyze the literal meaning of an utterance, but they will analyze whether what the speaker meant is equal to what he or she said, depending on the context. This led Gibbs (1999) to propose that different aspects of pragmatics are used when a listener understands what the speaker said and when the listener understands what the speaker meant. Gibbs proposes that there are two types of pragmatic knowledge:

• primary pragmatic knowledge provides default knowledge to interpret what the speaker said;
• secondary pragmatic knowledge is related to specific contextual information to interpret what the speaker intended.

These inferences are based on the particular features of the context and on the common shared background between the speaker and the listener. For example, if John says to Robert "The telephone is ringing," their shared knowledge of the world indicates that telephones ring when they are receiving a call (primary pragmatic knowledge), but this utterance could also mean that John wants Robert to pick up the telephone (secondary pragmatic knowledge). This will be interpreted by Robert according to the context and their shared background (e.g., it could be that Robert is the one who answers the phone in their office).

Gibbs (1999) admits that there are no a priori criteria to disentangle what belongs to primary and what belongs to secondary pragmatic knowledge. In Gibbs' description, primary pragmatic knowledge seems very similar to the classical semantic processing used to understand the literal meaning of an utterance.

Accordingly, another key element in pragmatics is the concept of "intention": meaning is based on what the speaker intended to communicate and not necessarily on what he or she actually said. Grosz and Sidner (1986) developed a theory in which discourse intentions form a general structure that the author of the utterance aims to convey and the receiver of the utterance must decode. This primary purpose or intention guides discourse choice and the contents to be communicated and is achieved by means of subordinate purposes in different discourse segments (Gordon, 1993). Traditionally, interpreting what a speaker said was considered part of semantics, whereas interpretating what the speaker meant belonged to the domain of pragmatics. Gibbs (1999) questions this assumption by pointing out that pragmatics is used to determine both what the speaker says and what the speaker means.

Thus, the classical lexicosemantic language approach has obvious limitations when we focus on communicative abilities, leaving room for the multidisciplinary approach of pragmatics. The ability to access pragmatic information is crucial for communication and this is one of the reasons why many communicative disorders have been related to pragmatic deficits (Gibbs, 1999). Pragmatic problems can be found in various populations suffering from an alteration of the brain, such as individuals with right brain damage, traumatic brain injuries, early dementia, and even some cases of aphasia.

In the field of aphasiology, little attention was paid to discourse and pragmatic deficits before the late 1970s. Research focused mostly on impaired linguistic processing in individuals with aphasia, because they were thought to have unimpaired discourse abilities (Ulatowska & Streit Olness, 2007). Consequently, the study of language and aphasia was centered almost exclusively on phonology, morphosyntax, and the semantics of single words. Pragmatic difficulties were not classically considered to be part of any aphasic syndrome in particular. Nevertheless, in some brain-damaged populations, such as right hemisphere-damaged (RHD) individuals, pragmatic deficits are at the core of the possible language problems patients present with; however, they are not classically considered as manifestations of aphasia.

To resolve this apparent contradiction, Joanette and Ansaldo (1999) reminded us that pragmatics is an aspect inherently linked to language, as much as morphosyntax or phonology (Stemmer, 1999). As such, communication problems cannot be divided into aphasic or nonaphasic in nature. Moreover, the relationship between these aspects of language and other cognitive domains, such as working memory or executive functions, should be similar. Consequently, in the past 20 years, the study of pragmatic abilities and their impairment has given rise to clinical pragmatics as a field of study—a field that mainly focuses on the RHD population (Cummings, 2007).

The RHD population does not usually show the flagrant language impairments found after left hemisphere damage (LHD) resulting in aphasia (Molloy, Brownell, & Gardner, 1990). In spite of their unimpaired ability to understand sentences and name pictures, individuals with RHD usually have been described as presenting with difficulties making relevant and appropriate contributions, maintaining topic coherence, understanding metaphors and humor, making inferences, and interpreting other people's intentions.

In the first part of this chapter, we will critically assess some studies that addressed narrative and conversational discourse impairments in RHD individuals and the theories developed to explain such difficulties. In the second part, we will introduce a number of studies that focused on social cognition impairment, specifically Theory of Mind (ToM) deficits in this population.

Discourse

Discourse can be considered as a sequence of natural language expressions that represent a piece of knowledge that a speaker or writer wants to communicate to a listener or reader (Chantraine, Joanette, & Cardebat, 1998a). There are different types of discourse, such as narrative, conversational, and argumentative. However, it is narrative discourse that has been the most systematically studied and theorized about.

Probably the most influential model of discourse comprehension was developed by Kintsch and van Dijk (1978; van Dijk & Kintsch, 1983). It distinguishes four levels of narrative discourse comprehension: (1) microstructural, (2) macrostructural, (3) superstructural, and (4) conceptual.

In this narrative discourse model, the microstructure is made up of a list of propositions (a predicate and one or more arguments) linked together based on shared arguments that represent the different ideas of the text, whereas the macrostructure represents the main ideas—the general structure or gist of a text. Because short-term memory has a limited capacity, the processing of a text is done by cycles. Each cycle roughly corresponds to one clause (more or less a sentence). The most important propositions are held in short-term memory for more cycles and are normally better recalled afterward (see Fayol & Lemaire, 1993, for further details). As text processing proceeds, the arguments are hierarchically organized.

Coherence is linked to cooccurrence in van Dijk and Kintsch's (1983) model: two propositions are related if they share the same arguments and cooccur in working memory. When two propositions do not share an argument, the reader might create a link that does not explicitly exist between them, that is, an inference. This is an important part of the model, because in normal discourse not all of the information is made available explicitly and the reader/listener must complete the missing parts. Let us consider the following sentences:

John put the groceries in the fridge. The ice cream was almost completely melted.

In this case, the reader/listener must infer that the ice cream was among the groceries John bought, because the link between the two sentences is not explicit. Thus, the model assumes that readers will make inferences to try and link two propositions that do not overlap before creating a new hierarchy with a new nonlinked proposition. Consequently, the more inferences a reader must make, the more difficult the comprehension of a text becomes (Fayol & Lemaire, 1993).

The macrostructure generates the global structure or essence of the text by the application of certain rules that generalize the arguments of redundant propositions, depending on a schema, and delete irrelevant ones (Gordon, 1993). For instance, a sentence such as the following:

John took the car, went to the supermarket, picked up some groceries for dinner, and then came back home.

could be simplified to:

John went shopping.

The macrostructure thus deals with global coherence at the discourse level. It consists of semantic units that are based on the sentences of a text (Mross, 1990).

The superstructural level is an abstract cognitive structure that captures the conventions and invariabilities of the type of discourse in question, such as narrative, argumentative, or conversational. It is related to the global organization or structural framework of discourse that facilitates the categorization of information.

The conceptual level corresponds to the "situational" or "mental" model a person creates from the narrative he or she listens to/reads and, as such, it is linguistic independent and is related to the person's previous knowledge of the world. This model can be either propositional or nonpropositional (for example, a spatial distribution of elements we get after reading a text).

In the following sections, we will focus on the two most studied types of discourse and its impairment in RHD subjects: conversational and narrative (Chantraine, Joanette, & Ska, 1998b). The first part will present studies of conversational discourse and the second part will present studies of narrative production and comprehension. The third section will focus on the theoretical approaches developed to explain the role of the right hemisphere in discourse comprehension and production.

Conversational Discourse

Conversation is not merely another type of discourse. It is almost invariably the first to be developed and the most frequently used in everyday life (Levelt, 1989). Consequently, impaired conversational abilities are one of the most disabling situations for brain-damaged individuals. The main difference between conversation and the other types of discourse, such as narrative discourse, is the online interaction between the participants in the speech act. Indeed, it involves an alternating cooperative interaction, directed to a goal, between two or more interspeakers who share the same spatial and temporal context (Chantraine et al., 1998a). This shared context becomes another key feature of this online interaction because the interpretation of what is said and what is implied depends on context.

Grice (1975) proposed the cooperative principle for conversation: the speaker should cooperate to produce sentences that a listener can easily understand and interpret and that are in accordance with the goal of the conversation. Grice also put forward four conversational maxims (i.e. Quantity, Quality, Relation, and Manner) that provide the common ground for conversational partners. In other words, a speaker should provide a contribution with the right amount of information (Quantity) that is true (Quality), that is relevant for the purpose of the conversation (Relation), and that is said in a clear way, avoiding ambiguities (Manner).

Some studies of conversation in RHD individuals show that the performance of this population does not always differ significantly from that of healthy participants, especially if the task is set in a naturalistic conversational context (see Barnes & Armstrong, 2010, for a review). For instance, Kennedy, Strand, Burton, and Peterson (1994) studied turn-taking and topic generation during first-encounter interactions in 12 RHD individuals and 11 age- and education-matched controls. Their results showed that the RHD individuals did not differ significantly from normal controls in topic management, but they made fewer requests for information, took more speech turns, and produced fewer words per turn during conversation. Along the same lines, Brady, Mackenzie, and Armstrong (2003) analyzed coherence and topic maintenance in structured conversation in 17 RHD individuals and 51 normal controls. They failed to find any significant differences between the two groups of participants, except for fillers and repetitions, which were used more frequently by controls (see also Brady, Armstrong, & Mackenzie, 2005).

These more ecological studies suggest that interactional competence is relatively preserved in at least some RHD individuals. In that regard, Chantraine et al. (1998b) used a naturalistic referential communication task to investigate verbal communication impairment in RHD individuals. Participants sat in front of a screen and saw a series of unfamiliar visual stimuli in a predetermined order. Their task consisted in instructing a second person, sitting on the other side of the screen, on how to order the visual stimuli in the same way as the participant's. Their results highlight the heterogeneity of abilities in individuals with RHD: some of them showed unimpaired performance on the task, whereas others had referential difficulties.

Prosody has also been described as impaired in RHD participants' conversation. Hird and Kirsner (2003) analyzed 6-minute-long recordings of informal social conversations by nine individuals with RHD and eight controls. The results showed reduced or absent use of prosody to alert listeners to changes in discourse structure in the RHD group. RHD individuals gave their conversational partners less information and introduced fewer topics than normal controls. This means that individuals with RHD took less responsibility for developing and maintaining conversation.

The studies reported in this section share a naturalistic approach in which participants are engaged in interactive tasks or real-life topic conversations. Taken as a whole, they show that some aspects of conversation are preserved, at least in some RHD individuals, whereas other aspects, such as prosody, are impaired. These differences seem to depend not only on the study (cf. Brady et al., 2003, and Hird & Kirsner, 2003, for instance) but also on the heterogeneity of the RHD population (see Chantraine et al., 1998b).

Narrative Discourse

In this section, we will present studies of narrative discourse processing in RHD individuals. It is noteworthy that most—if not all—of the studies reported used experimental, fictional, noninteractive tasks and not actual interaction, such as conversation. Barnes and Armstrong (2010) argue that some previously reported deficits in individuals with RHD should be revisited in light of ecological everyday interactions that are also relevant for clinical assessment and rehabilitation.

Many studies have addressed the topic of narrative discourse comprehension abilities in the RHD population (see Molloy et al., 1990, for a review). However, only a few of them have examined narrative production. Joanette and Goulet (1990) used a series of vignettes that formed a story to elicit narrative production in 36 RHD individuals and 20 normal controls, matched by age, education, and gender. They analyzed several aspects of participants' production, such as formal (lexical and syntactic) cohesion and coherence, as well as content (story schema and informative content). Their results showed no differences between the two groups in the lexical–syntactic aspects of narrative production. The total number of words produced and the number of nouns, verbs, and adverbs produced were not significantly different in RHD participants and normal controls; only adjective production and the adjective/noun ratio were significantly lower in the RHD group. Even though RHD individuals made more cohesion–coherence errors on average, their production did not differ significantly from that of normal controls. This seems to contrast with previously reported results showing coherence difficulties in RHD narrative comprehension (see Kaplan, Brownell, Jacobs, & Gardner, 1990, for instance). Conversely, the content aspects were impaired in the RHD group. They produced less information that was also different in nature from that produced by the controls. In general, the results reported in Joanette and Goulet's (1990) study showed that content is more affected than form after RHD. Moreover, the heterogeneity of the RHD population should be emphasized, given that not all of the participants presented impaired content in narrative production.

The study of narrative discourse comprehension has focused mostly on indirect requests, irony, jokes, and simple inference processing. The first two—indirect requests and irony—are considered to be figurative language because a listener must distinguish between the literal meaning of the sentences and what the speaker actually intends or means.

Most of the time, speakers explicitly convey what they mean in an utterance. Nevertheless, it is not unusual for meaning to be conveyed indirectly. For instance, if Robert says to John "It's hot in here," he might simply want to inform John of how he feels about the room temperature, which would constitute a direct speech act. It could also mean that John should open the window or turn on the air conditioning. This would be an indirect speech act. Figuring out the speaker's intent is not always simple, and individuals with RHD usually have difficulties interpreting indirect speech acts.

An early explanation of the interpretation of indirect speech acts (consider Searle, 1979, for instance) assumed that listeners would first construct a literal meaning of the utterance (e.g., in the preceding example, that Robert is expressing how he feels about the weather). If this interpretation is not coherent with the speakers' discourse, then, later in processing, the listener would construct another possible interpretation of the speaker's utterance, usually an indirect one (e.g. that Robert wants John to open the window). This model has the advantage of explaining why people do not always pay attention to the indirect meaning of a phrase. However, because the indirect interpretation is built only after the direct one proves to be inappropriate, the model cannot explain why, for many sentences, we do not process the direct meaning but go directly to the indirect interpretation (Murphy, 1990). For example, if Robert asks John "Can you open the window?" it is hardly likely that John will think of the direct interpretation, that is to say, that Robert is asking him whether he has the ability to open the window. Instead, John would interpret this question indirectly: Robert is asking him to open the window. Thus, an indirect request, such as "Can you open the window?" may be interpreted either as a literal question about ability (i.e. whether the person is physically capable of opening the window) or as a figurative request for an action to be carried out (i.e. the person is being asked to open the window). Because both interpretations are plausible, context helps to disentangle the expressed literal question and the intended messages in a top-down manner.

A different account was put forward by Clark (1979), who argued that listeners activate the direct, the indirect, or both interpretations depending on context. In line with this claim, Gibbs (1979) found that participants sometimes understand indirect meanings faster than direct interpretations, depending on the situation in which the sentence is embedded. Gibbs (1999) interpreted this finding as evidence of the limited psychological validity of a theory that states that indirect language is a sort of ornament that requires further processing to be interpreted. Thus, there should be no distinction between what a speaker says and what he or she implies.

Weylman, Brownell, Roman, and Gardner (1989, Study 2) compared the performance of 12 RHD and 12 LHD participants in a task that consisted of a set of paragraph-length vignettes that described two people performing an activity. Participants heard the paragraph and they also had a written transcription of the text, which they could read at the same time. After each vignette, a question that could be interpreted as either a direct or an indirect request was presented visually and also read aloud. In half of the vignettes, context was biased to favor a direct literal interpretation, whereas in the other half, the indirect request interpretation was favored. To avoid the influence of wording conventions—for example, the formula "Could you . . . ?" is typically associated with indirect requests—the experimenters also used other, less conventional, beginnings, such as "Is it possible for you to . . . ?," which can be associated with direct requests as well. Participants had to choose among four options: an appropriate indirect interpretation, an appropriate direct interpretation, and two incorrect distractor responses. RHD participants were significantly impaired at making judgments based on contextual information, as compared to normal controls (Weylman et al., 1989, Study 1). In addition, both RHD and LHD groups showed a tendency to select the appropriate interpretation when the wording of questions was very prototypical ("Could you . . . ") and could be used as a cue to interpretation. Interestingly, the RHD group performed comparably to the LHD group in the use of context and conventionality. According to the authors, these results highlight the difficulties RHD individuals have in using contextual information in less prototypical contexts and interpreting indirect requests.

Irony, like indirect requests, demands contextual information to be interpreted. However, irony has something that indirect requests lack, namely affective content. Irony is meant to be sarcastic or funny. Irony is a violation of Grice's (1969) maxim of Quality (i.e. a speaker should not say something that is false) that a speaker uses to reinforce the opposite unspoken statement. For example, two friends, Robert and John, are talking. Robert is telling his friend John the details of his most recent practical joke on a co-worker and John says "You really are a nice person to work with!" In the context of their conversation, John's comment means exactly the opposite, that is to say, that Robert is a bad co-worker.

This is also a good example of an inference. Because what people communicate is more than what is being said in a sentence—what Grice (1969) calls *implicature*—listeners should infer what the speaker really means. Finding the right implicature requires knowledge of the world (e.g. practical jokes are no fun for the butt of the joke), knowledge of the speaker (e.g. Robert plays practical jokes all the time), and knowledge of linguistic conventions (e.g. irony is expressed with a particular intonation) (Murphy, 1990).

Kaplan et al. (1990) studied the ability to interpret conversational utterances in RHD participants and normal controls by means of narrative vignettes similar to those used in the study reported above. Each vignette described two characters engaged in an activity. One of the characters was always depicted as good or bad and the other character made a positive or a negative comment about the first one. Half of the stimuli were coherent, that is to say, the performance of the first character, whether good or bad, was in agreement with the second character's statement (whether positive or negative). In the other half of the stimuli, performance and comments differed, allowing for a figurative, nonliteral interpretation. Participants had to choose from among five possibilities concerning the intent of the second character's utterance: he was telling the truth, he was joking, he was being sarcastic, he was saying something wrong by mistake, or he was telling a lie on purpose. The results showed no significant differences between RHD and normal control groups for the congruent, literally interpreted stimuli; both groups would say that the second character was telling the truth. Nevertheless, RHD participants performed significantly worse on the nonliteral stimuli. Normal participants paid attention to the character's actions and the relationship between the two characters, whereas those with RHD had problems using the information derived from the relationship between the characters. These results reveal the difficulty individuals with RHD have in understanding the internal state of a person and his or her intentions. Along the same lines, Shamay-Tsoory, Tomer, Berger, Goldsher, and Aharon-Peretz (2005b) studied irony processing in RHD according to lesion site (anterior vs. posterior). They presented brief recorded stories at the end of which there was either an ironic or a neutral statement. Participants had to identify the negative meaning of the sarcastic comment. They found that individuals with prefrontal ventromedial RHD had impaired irony interpretation as compared to those with posterior RHD and normal controls. These results are in line with studies of social cognition problems, a topic presented in the following section.

In the case of joke interpretation and simple inferences, unlike indirect requests and irony, it is the sentence that changes context in a bottom-up fashion. As we accommodate new information, our previous assumptions are altered by the new information conveyed, for instance, by the punch line in a joke that disconfirms the previous interpretation and makes the joke surprising and funny. Thus, a listener must be able to revise his or her assumptions (i.e. repair and update the conversation) in order to understand the story. The role of the right hemisphere (RH) in normal joke processing was studied by Coulson and Williams (2005) using event-related brain potentials (ERPs). Their findings show that joke comprehension is facilitated by the semantic activation of the RH in normal individuals.

Brownell, Michel, Powelson, and Gardner (1983) examined RHD participants' sensitivity to coherence and surprise in narrative jokes. Participants heard narrative jokes and were asked to choose which sentence from four options would be the best punch line for the joke. To test sensitivity to coherence and surprise, one of the options had a straightforward ending that was coherent with the rest of the narrative but lacked the surprise factor needed in a joke; and another of the options was not coherent with the narrative but introduced the element of surprise because it was an unexpected line. RHD patients were significantly more likely to choose the noncoherent surprising ending than normal controls. This means that even though the RHD patients realized that a surprising ending was necessary for a joke, they had difficulties processing that requirement while retaining congruency with the joke's opening.

In a subsequent study that included narrative jokes and nonverbal cartoons as stimuli, and both RHD and LHD patients, Bihrle, Brownell, Powelson, and Gardner (1986) confirmed the results of their previous study. RHD patients showed a preserved sensitivity to surprise but not to coherence, whereas LHD patients showed the opposite pattern, preserved coherence and impaired surprise processing. These results indicate that the ability to integrate new information (coherence) is generally impaired in RHD individuals. Likewise, RHD patients have also demonstrated an impaired ability to revise their assumptions for inferences in simple two-sentence narratives (Brownell, Potter, Bihrle, & Gardner, 1986).

Taken together, these studies suggest that RHD patients have a preference for literal meanings and find it difficult to convey the nonliteral or intended meaning of an utterance. RHD individuals have problems interpreting new information by considering the narrative context and they also seem to have an impaired ability to alter their initial assumptions in light of new information in narrative comprehension (Molloy et al., 1990).

Some Explanatory Hypotheses

So far, we have presented evidence that shows that, in general, individuals with RHD have difficulties processing messages that require indirect, nonliteral inferences. But how are these difficulties to be explained theoretically? They have been interpreted, at least partially, in terms of underlying lexicosemantic deficits. In this view, the unimpaired RH is normally responsible for "coarse coding," that is to say, it activates a diffuse network of remote associates and secondary meanings of the words that are being processed (Beeman, 1993, 1998). The left hemisphere, on the other hand, focuses on strong associates or on a narrow range of dominant interpretations from the very early stages of word processing. This "coarse coding" is thought to be responsible for nonliteral language interpretation and inferences. Beeman (1993, 1998) proposed that a "coarse semantic impairment" could explain RHD individuals' interpretive deficits: they would be unable to activate the distant semantic associates necessary to make an inference or a nonliteral interpretation. However, according to Tompkins, Scharp, Meigh, and Fassbinder (2008b), this explanation does not directly link the comprehension problems of individuals with RHD to their possible lexicosemantic (or coarse coding) deficit.

The multiple activation hypothesis is an alternative explanation developed by Tompkins and colleagues (Tompkins, Fassbinder, Lehman Blake, Baumgaertner, & Jayaram, 2004; Tompkins, Lehman Blake, Baumgaertner, & Fassbinder, 2001). It states that RHD and normal individuals generate multiple inferences when confronted with stimuli that allow them to do so. Normal controls suppress a contextually inappropriate inference if it is disconfirmed by context, but individuals with RHD are unable to suppress the contextually inappropriate meaning and this leads to poor discourse comprehension.

To test their hypothesis, Tompkins et al. (2004) designed five-sentence narratives that elicited two types of inferences: (1) a bridging inference (BI), that is, an inference that links the different elements in a narrative to each other or to people's knowledge of the world, and (2) an alternative inference (AI) that was plausible but incompatible with the rest of the narrative. Each narrative led to a single BI that made the final sentence coherent with the rest of the story. However, this final sentence, considered alone, was ambiguous and biased toward an AI that was incompatible with the BI and the rest of the text. The authors tested 37 RHD participants and 34 normal controls, matched by age, education, gender, and estimated premorbid IQ, on three experimental tasks: (1) an auditory lexical decision task, in which participants had to decide whether a stimulus was a real word or not and in which the words were chosen to represent either the BI or the AI of each story; (2) a gender judgment task presented after the lexical decision task, in which participants were asked about the gender of the characters in the story; and (3) a text comprehension task with yes–no questions to test participants' comprehension of the narratives. First, participants heard the first sentence of the narrative, followed by one of the stimuli from the lexical decision task (initial position). They then heard the other four sentences. After that, they were presented with another word for lexical decision. In the end, participants were presented with one of the yes–no questions from the gender judgment task. The yes–no questions from the comprehension task were administered in a separate session. The "coarse semantic coding" deficit explanation (Beeman, 1993, 1998) would predict that the BIs should have no effect on the lexical decision task for the RHD group because they would not activate such inferences. Contrary to this prediction, a main effect of BIs was found for both RHD and normal control groups' response times (RTs). On the other hand, the prediction of the multiple activation hypothesis would be that the RHD group should activate both the BIs and the AIs. This did not happen either. AIs did not affect RTs in the lexical decision task in either group. However, this study showed that under certain conditions—notably, less demanding tasks than those of Beeman's (1993) study—individuals with RHD are as capable as normal controls of using the contextual information necessary to produce inferences (Tompkins et al., 2004).

In another study, Tompkins et al. (2008b) further tested the coarse coding impairment and its link with comprehension difficulties in RHD. Thirty-two RHD individuals and 38 normal controls were recruited for the study, the two groups being matched for sociodemographic variables. A measure of coarse coding was taken from participants' performance (accuracy) on a lexical decision task similar to that used by Tompkins et al. (2004) with peripheral semantic features of concrete nouns as the targets (e.g., "rotten" was presented in the lexical decision task after previous presentation of the noun "apple" in a sentence such as "He had an apple" in a narrative). The target words were presented at a short interval—the word "rotten" was presented 175 milliseconds after the noun (e.g., "apple") was

heard in the narrative, or at a long interval—the target word was presented 1000 milliseconds after the noun. A lack of activation in the short interval condition for the RHD group would be interpreted as an early impairment of distant semantic activation, as claimed by the coarse coding impairment explanation (Beeman, 1993, 1998). On the other hand, a lack of activation in the long interval condition would provide evidence for poor *maintenance* of the activation of peripheral semantic features. The authors also administered two discourse comprehension tasks: one was derived from the Discourse Comprehension Test (DCT, Brookshire & Nicholas, 1993) that targeted comprehension of implied information; the second task, high-level inference questions, was based on Winner, Brownell, Happé, Blum, and Pincus's (1998) study, which assessed the ability of participants with RHD to deal with competing interpretations (see Tompkins et al., 2008b, for further details). Their hypothesis was that if coarse coding and comprehension are linked, the measure of coarse semantic coding should be associated with narrative comprehension performance in RHD adults.

Their results showed that the RHD group performed significantly worse than controls on all measures, but there was no reliable association between the coarse coding measure and the discourse comprehension tasks. However, after the RHD participants were divided into poor and good comprehenders based on their performance on the high-level inference task, poor RHD comprehenders were found to be less accurate at making lexical decisions about semantically distant features but only at long (1000 milliseconds) intervals. Tompkins et al. (2008b) found that poor comprehension in RHD individuals was associated with poor maintenance, and not poor activation, of peripheral semantic features. Thus, their results indicate a link between a form of coarse coding impairment and discourse comprehension. However, this impairment does not affect early processing, as Beeman (1993) claimed, but makes it difficult for poor RHD comprehenders to maintain semantic peripheral activation (see Lehman Blake & Tompkins, 2001, for similar results).

There is another possible explanation for the apparent failure of individuals with RHD to sustain inferences over time: the slowed selection hypothesis (Lehman Blake, 2009). This explanation suggests that the RHD participants did generate inferences, but they could not integrate them into their mental model. Still, the inferences remained available for later selection in long-term memory. Once these inferences are confirmed by context, it may take longer for RHD individuals to retrieve them from memory and, consequently, the inferences could not be detected at the time the experimental measures took place.

To test the slowed selection hypothesis, Lehman Blake (2009) used a sample of 14 individuals with RHD and 14 normal controls to determine whether predictive inferences are indeed generated but take longer to process in RHD. A predictive inference is a guess about what is going to happen next in a story. For example, after the sentences "There was a spider on the balcony. Susan took out a shoe," a predictive inference would be "Susan killed the spider with the shoe." Once a predictive inference is generated, it may be integrated into the mental representation of the text after being brought into working memory. It may also remain activated in long-term memory until further information is gathered to confirm it, for instance with the sentence "Susan killed the spider." Finally, it can be deactivated from long-term memory if a sentence such as "Susan polished her shoe" appears next in the story, disconfirming the inference.

Lehman Blake (2009) used the same stimuli as Lehman Blake and Tompkins (2001), with the addition of a sixth sentence that aimed to test the slowed selection hypothesis. Thus, stories with six sentences each were used. Four sentences described a common scene (e.g., house cleaning); the predictive sentence was either the second sentence (distant position condition) or the fourth sentence (recent position condition). The fifth sentence (target) disconfirmed the predicted outcome (e.g., "Susan polished her shoe"). The sixth sentence was neutral regarding the inference but consistent with the story. The generation of inferences was measured by comparing sentence reading times for the fifth (target) sentence in the recent position condition and an equivalent sentence in the control condition, which did not include any predictions. The maintenance of inferences was calculated by comparing reading times for the target sentence in the distant position and the sentence from the control condition. The results showed no significant differences between the RHD group and the control groups for either generation or maintenance of inferences. Examination of individual data revealed that most of the participants in both groups maintained inferences active over time. Among those who did not maintain inferences, normal subjects always deactivated the inference, whereas RHD participants either deactivated it or showed slowed selection. Because slowed selection

appeared only in the RHD group, it is interpreted as being an aberrant process (Lehman Blake, 2009). These results conflict with the finding that inference maintenance of individuals with RHD was affected in Lehman Blake and Tompkins's (2001) study and challenge the maintenance deficit hypothesis.

However clear it seems that individuals with RHD have inference deficits, no consensus has been reached so far as to the explanation for these deficits. Some studies suggest that the cause of inference difficulties resides in the activation of alternative inferences (Beeman, 1993, 1998), others studies suggest that it resides in the maintenance of inferences (Lehman Blake & Tompkins, 2001), and finally, some authors claim that RHD inference deficits can be explained by a slowed selection of inferences from memory (Lehman Blake, 2009).

Social Cognition

Social cognition can be defined as a person's knowledge of the social world in which he or she lives, acts, and communicates (Condor & Antaki, 1997). As such, it includes the interpretation of sarcasm and its social communicative function (Shamay-Tsoory, Tomer, & Aharon-Peretz, 2005a), and the reactions of one individual to the observed experiences of another, usually called "empathy" (Shamay-Tsoory, Tomer, Berger, & Aharon-Peretz, 2003). Social cognition is also related to the ability to form representations of other people's mental states (beliefs, intentions, shared knowledge) and to use those representations to interpret and predict their behavior; that is to say, ToM (Champagne-Lavau & Joanette, 2009; Tompkins, Scharp, Fassbinder, Meigh, & Armstrong, 2008a). This section will focus on ToM processing in individuals with RHD.

It has been stated that pragmatic interpretation, for example, nonliteral language interpretation, involves the generation of inferences about the mental state of the speaker (Champagne-Lavau & Joanette, 2009; Grice, 1969). Consequently, a deficit in interpreting the speaker's mental state, that is, a ToM deficit, would have consequences for pragmatic interpretation and could explain, at least partially, pragmatic problems of individuals with RHD. It has been shown that some individuals with RHD have difficulties correctly inferring the intentions of a speaker if they have to reconcile a specific kind of language encoding with certain contextual variables (Stemmer, Giroux, & Joanette, 1994), such as distinguishing a lie from a joke (Winner et al., 1998).

Executive function disturbances, such as lack of inhibition or flexibility, and communication deficits have also been described as being associated in individuals with RHD (Champagne-Lavau, Stip, & Joanette, 2007). Because communication abilities are complex, it seems reasonable to assume that they depend on the integrity of other high-level capacities. However, the interpretation of communication deficits in terms of ToM or executive dysfunctions is still a matter for debate (Champagne-Lavau & Joanette, 2009; Stemmer, 1999).

Champagne-Lavau and Joanette (2009) investigated the coexistence of pragmatic, ToM, and executive function deficits in individuals with RHD. They examined 15 participants with RHD between 1 and 4 months after a stroke and 15 normal controls, matched by age and educational level, using two tasks that assess pragmatics, the metaphor comprehension and indirect request comprehension subtests of the Montreal d'Evaluation de la Communication (MEC) protocol (Joanette, Ska, & Côté, 2004). The participants were also given a ToM task that assessed false belief attribution as well as executive function tasks such as the Stroop test (Stroop, 1935), the Hayling test (Burgess & Shallice, 1997), and the Wisconsin Card Sorting Test (Heaton, 1981). As a general result, the RHD participants performed significantly worse on all the tasks than normal controls. Based on their performance on the pragmatic tasks, and by means of a hierarchical cluster analysis, participants were divided into three groups: (1) no pragmatic deficits or executive dysfunctions ($n = 6$); (2) impaired nonliteral processing (metaphors and indirect requests), ToM deficits, and lack of inhibition ($n = 3$); and (3) impaired literal interpretation, ToM deficits, and lack of flexibility ($n = 5$). The remaining person, whose performance was impaired on all the tests, constituted another group that was not further analyzed. These results emphasize the heterogeneity of the RHD population. Interestingly, only one group (group 2) had difficulties processing nonliteral language, which is traditionally described as one of the characteristic deficits of RHD patients. Moreover, the two groups that presented with problems processing pragmatic aspects of language (groups 2 and 3) also showed associated ToM and executive deficits. The association between pragmatic and ToM difficulties seems to confirm that pragmatic interpretation requires attribution of the speaker's mental state. It was concluded that some shared mechanisms involved in both pragmatics and ToM might depend on the

RH (see Gallagher et al., 2000, for data on neuroimaging) and that executive deficits alone cannot account for pragmatic impairments in individuals with RHD.

Tompkins et al. (2008a) argued that inadequate stimulus control (i.e., number of characters, number of perspective changes involved) that made non-mental-state inferences easier than mental-state ones may have been responsible for the apparent ToM deficits in processing mental-state inferences in the RHD population. The authors used the same ToM stimuli as those used by Happé, Brownell, and Winner (1999), who reported a significant advantage for non-mental-state as compared to mental-state inferences in RHD individuals. Tompkins et al. (2008a) developed new control stimuli matched with the ToM stimuli for number and mention of characters, number of perspective shifts, and syntactic complexity. These control texts had an explicit conflict that could be resolved with a non-mental-state inference. The authors hypothesized that once these possible differential processing demands were eliminated, there would be no discrepancy between ToM mental-state and non-mental-state inferences in individuals with RHD. They assessed 22 RHD participants and 38 normal controls with auditorily presented narratives that targeted either a mental-state (ToM) or a non-mental-state inference. Target inference comprehension was assessed by means of true–false sentences. Results on accuracy and RTs showed an advantage for ToM stimuli over non-mental-state ones, but this difference disappeared once the easiest ToM item was removed, suggesting that the difference was due only to that item. RTs showed a main effect of group as well. Participants in the control group responded significantly faster than the RHD group. When mental-state (ToM) and non-mental-state stimuli were matched for a number of important variables, no evidence of disadvantage was found for RHD individuals' ToM inferences, contrary to the results found by Happé et al. (1999). However, the Happé et al. study used an explicit question to assess inference accuracy (i.e. "Why did this happen?"), whereas Tompkins and colleagues (2008a) used an implicit true–false statement. Although the authors dismissed this difference as a possible explanation for the interstudy discrepancy, it is arguable that these implicit measures improved the performance of the RHD group enough to account for these divergent findings.

In sum, the studies reviewed in this section highlight the relationship between RHD and the impaired ability to form representations of other people's mental states. Nevertheless, certain confounding factors, such as type of task, the nature of the inferences, and the influence of other cognitive functions, especially executive functions, cast some doubt on the usefulness of studying ToM as an example of social cognition impairment in the RHD population (Tompkins et al., 2008a).

Explanatory Conceptual Frameworks

The ability to access and use pragmatic information, such as the speaker's intentions and context, among others, is crucially important for communication (Gibbs, 1999). That is why communication impairments after brain damage are extremely disabling and decrease the person's quality of life. Pragmatic deficits can be found in different neuropsychological populations, such as people with aphasia or dementia. However, the most studied neuropsychological population, by far, has been individuals with RHD (Cummings, 2007). RHD individuals are described in the literature as individuals who may present with problems to make relevant and appropriate contributions to conversation, understanding humor, metaphors, and indirect speech acts in general, or interpreting other people's intentions.

The literature on conversation shows that RHD individuals take less responsibility for developing and maintaining conversation and they fail to use prosody appropriately. In more ecological production tasks in which performance differs notably from one individual to another, not all of the participants have been found to have impaired conversational abilities. This pattern of results is also found in narrative production, where content seems to be more affected than form, but not all RHD individuals have problems with narrative production (Joanette & Goulet, 1990). These studies stress the heterogeneity of the RHD population. This is seen in almost all such studies, whether they rely on production or comprehension of discourse (Chantraine et al., 1998a; Murphy, 1990).

The studies on nonliteral language comprehension highlight the problems RHD individuals have using contextual information in less prototypical contexts and interpreting indirect requests. Pragmatic deficits in RHD have been the focus of interest for researchers in recent decades. Studies have focused on this population's deficits in understanding indirect speech acts, inference, irony, and sarcasm. Studies of irony comprehension highlight difficulties of individuals with RHD in understanding people's internal states and intentions. The results of studies of joke understanding reveal

their difficulties revising their assumptions and integrating the new information needed to understand the punch line of a joke (Brownell et al., 1986). In general, individuals with RHD show a preference for literal interpretations and have comprehension problems when an utterance requires a nonliteral interpretation.

Even though it seems indisputable that RHD individuals can have problems processing inferences, the nature of these problems remains unclear. Some studies suggest that they could be explained by inference activation deficits, whereas other results point to inference sustaining or slowed selection. To date, no consensus has been reached on how to account for these different and sometimes contradictory results.

When it comes to higher-level capacities, such as the ability to represent other people's intentions and mental states, individuals with RHD tend to show ToM impairments. This impairment is manifested in greater difficulties with mental-state inferences than with non-mental-state inferences. Nevertheless, such ToM difficulties seem to be associated with the complexity of narratives—which tend to be more complex for mental-state-inducing stories—as well as the type of task or question—explicit or implicit—that participants are asked to perform or answer (Tompkins et al., 2008a).

It is noteworthy that tasks and stimuli vary greatly from one study to another (Lehman & Tompkins, 2000; Tompkins et al., 2008a). This lack of consistency demands caution when attempts at generalization to the RHD population as a whole are made. Nevertheless, stimuli and tasks are not the only factors that are heterogeneous. Individuals with RHD are very different from one another, not only in terms of lesion site but also in their profile of impairment (Chantraine et al., 1998b; Murphy, 1990). Efforts are being made to better classify the RHD population into different communication performance profiles (for a good example, see Côté, Payer, Giroux, & Joanette, 2007).

Finally, it has been argued that some RHD difficulties can be explained by other high-level deficits, such as executive dysfunctions or working memory problems (e.g., Douglas, 2010). In that regard, Joanette and Ansaldo (1999) maintain that the relationship between the pragmatic aspects of language and other cognitive domains, such as working memory or executive functions, should be similar to that found in phonological or lexicosemantic impairments.

Conclusions

The pragmatic and social cognitive components of interindividual communication are particularly complex and multidimensional. These abilities, which are fundamental to an individual's normal participation in society, rely on a multitude of other abilities, which, in turn, depend on many basic cognitive processes sustained by widely distributed neural networks. This characteristic makes these abilities particularly vulnerable to alterations of the brain. At the same time, these abilities can become early markers of the loss of integrity of these neural networks, as in the early phases of dementia. In any case, it is clear that the pragmatic and social cognition components of communication abilities cannot be conceived of as a unitary cognitive component. Their complexity requires a truly interdisciplinary approach, fed by many complementary theoretical frameworks and making the link with basic cognitive processes such as executive functions, including flexibility and inhibition.

Pragmatic and social cognition components of communication abilities are only beginning to be understood. One way to better understand these deficits will be to stratify the brain-damaged population in order to allow for a better understanding of the underlying altered processes. This is starting to be done for individuals with RHD (Côté et al., 2007). The stratified population will then have to be better understood with the help of advances both at the level of the theoretical cognitive frameworks and in functional neuroimaging, which allows for the description of functional and anatomical connectivity (see, for instance, the work of Agosta et al., 2010, on semantic dementia).

Ultimately, any better understanding we gain of these disabilities and their theoretical and neurofunctional bases should result in the introduction of clinical assessment tools (e.g. Bryan, 1994; Gardner & Brownell, 1986; Joanette et al., 2004; Pimental & Kingsbury, 2000; Ross-Swain, 1996) and, especially, systematic therapeutic procedures in order to help individuals suffering from pragmatic and social cognition communication impairments to reintegrate into society, because language constitutes the most important tool for socialization.

Future Directions

In the field of discourse and social cognition impairment in brain-damaged populations, it would be desirable for future studies to address the many questions that still remain unanswered, and in particular the following:

- How does the striking heterogeneity of RHD individuals in terms of their performance and impairments affect possible generalizations to the entire RHD population? Is it the same among traumatic brain injury (TBI) patients?
- Is it possible to establish stable profiles of pragmatic and communication problems in RHD or TBI patients?
- What is the nature of RHD/TBI patients' inference problems? Do they affect inference maintenance, integration, or reactivation, or a mixture of several of these factors?
- What is the relationship between executive functions, such as inhibition and cognitive flexibility, and communicational impairments, and how might the former influence the latter?

References

Agosta, F., Henry, R. G., Migliaccio, R., Neuhaus, J., Miller, B. L., Dronkers, N. F., et al. (2010). Language networks in semantic dementia. *Brain*, 133, 286–299.

Barnes, S., & Armstrong, E. (2010). Conversation after right hemisphere brain damage: Motivations for applying conversation analysis. *Clinical Linguistics and Phonetics*, 24, 55–69.

Beeman, M. (1993). Semantic processing in the right hemisphere may contribute to drawing inferences from discourse. *Brain and Language*, 44, 80–120.

Beeman, M. (1998). Coarse semantic coding and discourse comprehension. In M. Beeman & C. Chiarello (Eds.), *Right hemisphere language comprehension: Perspectives from cognitive neuroscience* (pp. 255–284). Hillsdale, NJ: Lawrence Erlbaum Associates.

Bihrle, A. M., Brownell, H. H., Powelson, J. A., & Gardner, H. (1986). Comprehension of humorous and nonhumorous materials by left and right brain-damaged patients. *Brain and Cognition*, 5, 399–411.

Brady, M., Armstrong, L., & Mackenzie, C. (2005). Further evidence on topic use following right hemisphere brain damage: Procedural and descriptive discourse. *Aphasiology*, 19, 731–747.

Brady, M., Mackenzie, C., & Armstrong, L. (2003). Topic use following right hemisphere brain damage during three semi-structured conversational discourse samples. *Aphasiology*, 17, 881–904.

Brookshire, R. H., & Nicholas, L. E. (1993). *Discourse comprehension test*. Tucson, AZ: Communication Skill Builders.

Brownell, H. H., Michel, D., Powelson, J., & Gardner, H. (1983). Surprise but not coherence: Sensitivity to verbal humor in right-hemisphere patients. *Brain and Language*, 18, 20–27.

Brownell, H. H., Potter, H. H., Bihrle, A. M., & Gardner, H. (1986). Inference deficits in right brain-damaged patients. *Brain and Language*, 27, 310–321.

Bryan, K. L. (1994). *The right hemisphere language battery* (2nd ed.). Kibworth, UK: Far Communications.

Burgess, C., & Shallice, T. (1997). *The Hayling and Brixton tests*. Thurston, UK: Thames Valley Test Company.

Champagne-Lavau, M., & Joanette, Y. (2009). Pragmatics, theory of mind and executive functions after a right-hemisphere lesion: Different patterns of deficits. *Journal of Neurolinguistics*, 22, 413–426.

Champagne-Lavau, M., Stip, E., & Joanette, Y. (2007). Language functions in right-hemisphere damage and schizophrenia: Apparently similar pragmatic deficits may hide profound differences. *Brain*, 130, e67; author reply e68.

Chantraine, Y., Joanette, Y., & Cardebat, D. (1998a). Impairments of discourse-level representations and processes. In B. Stemmer & H. A. Whitaker (Eds.), *Handbook of neurolinguistics* (pp. 261–274). San Diego, CA: Academic Press.

Chantraine, Y., Joanette, Y., & Ska, B. (1998b). Conversational abilities in patients with right hemisphere damage. *Journal of Neurolinguistics*, 11(1–2), 21–32.

Clark, H. H. (1979). Responding to indirect speech acts. *Cognitive Psychology*, 11, 430–477.

Condor, S., & Antaki, C. (1997). Social cognition and discourse. In T. A. van Dijk (Ed.), *Discourse as structure and process: Discourse studies: A multidisciplinary introduction* (Vol. 1, pp. 320–347). London: Sage.

Côté, H., Payer, M., Giroux, F., & Joanette, Y. (2007). Towards a description of clinical communication impairment profiles following right-hemisphere damage. *Aphasiology*, 21, 739–749.

Coulson, S., & Williams, R. F. (2005). Hemispheric asymmetries and joke comprehension. *Neuropsychologia*, 43, 128–141.

Cummings, L. (2007). Pragmatics and adult language disorders: Past achievements and future directions. *Seminars in Speech and Language*, 28, 96–110.

Douglas, J. M. (2010). Relation of executive functioning to pragmatic outcome following severe traumatic brain injury. *Journal of Speech, Language, and Hearing Research*, 53, 365–382.

Fayol, M., & Lemaire, P. (1993). Levels of approach to discourse. In H. Brownell & Y. Joanette (Eds.), *Narrative discourse in neurologically impaired and normal aging adults* (pp. 3–21). San Diego, CA: Singular Publishing Group.

Gallagher, H. L., Happé, F., Brunswick, N., Fletcher, P. C., Frith, U., & Frith, C. D. (2000). Reading the mind in cartoons and stories: An fMRI study of "theory of mind" in verbal and nonverbal tasks. *Neuropsychologia*, 38, 11–21.

Gardner, H., & Brownell, H. H. (1986). *Right hemisphere communication battery*. Boston, MA: Psychology Service, VAMC.

Gibbs, R. W. (1979). Contextual effects in understanding indirect requests. *Discourse Processes*, 2, 1–10.

Gibbs, R. W. (1999). Interpreting what speakers say and implicate. *Brain and Language*, 68, 466–485.

Gibbs, R. W., & Moise, J. (1997). Pragmatics is understanding what is said. *Cognition*, 62, 51–74.

Gordon, P. C. (1993). Computational and psychological models of discourse. In H. Brownell & Y. Joanette (Eds.), *Narrative discourse in neurologically impaired and normal aging adults* (pp. 23–46). San Diego, CA: Singular Publishing Group.

Grice, H. P. (1969). Utterer's meaning and intentions. *Philosophical Review*, 78, 147–177.

Grice, H. P. (1975). Logic and conversation. In P. Cole & J. L. Morgan (Eds.), *Syntax and semantics* (Vol. 3: Speech acts, pp. 41–58). New York: Academic Press.

Grosz, B. J., & Sidner, C. L. (1986). Attention, intentions, and the structure of discourse. *Computational Linguistics*, 12, 175–204.

Happé, F., Brownell, H., & Winner, E. (1999). Acquired "theory of mind" impairments following stroke. *Cognition*, 70, 211–240.

Heaton, R. K. (1981). *Wisconsin card sorting test: Manual.* Odessa, FL: Neuropsychological Assessment Resources.

Hird, K., & Kirsner, K. (2003). The effect of right cerebral hemisphere damage on collaborative planning in conversation: An analysis of intentional structure. *Clinical Linguistics and Phonetics*, 17, 309–315.

Joanette, Y., & Ansaldo, A. I. (1999). Clinical note: Acquired pragmatic impairments and aphasia. *Brain and Language*, 68, 529–534.

Joanette, Y., & Goulet, P. (1990). Narrative discourse in right-brain-damaged right-handers. In Y. Joanette & H. H. Brownell (Eds.), *Discourse ability and brain damage: Theoretical and empirical perspectives* (pp. 131–153). New York: Springer-Verlag.

Joanette, Y., Goulet, P., & Hannequin, D. (1990). *Right hemisphere and verbal communication.* New York: Springer-Verlag.

Joanette, Y., Ska, B., & Côté, H. (2004). *Protocole Montreal d'Evaluation de la Communication MEC.* Isbergues, France: Ortho Editions.

Kaplan, J. A., Brownell, H. H., Jacobs, J. R., & Gardner, H. (1990). The effects of right hemisphere damage on the pragmatic interpretation of conversational remarks. *Brain and Language*, 38, 315–333.

Kennedy, M. R. T., Strand, E. A., Burton, W., & Peterson, C. (1994). Analysis of first-encounter conversations of right-hemisphere-damaged adults *Clinical Aphasiology*, 22, 67–80.

Kintsch, W., & van Dijk, T. A. (1978). Toward a model of text comprehension and text production. *Psychological Review*, 85, 363–394.

Lehman, M. T., & Tompkins, C. A. (2000). Inferencing in adults with right hemisphere brain damage: An analysis of conflicting results. *Aphasiology*, 14, 485–499.

Lehman Blake, M. (2009). Inferencing processes after right hemisphere brain damage: Maintenance of inferences. *Journal of Speech, Language, and Hearing Research*, 52, 359–372.

Lehman Blake, M. T., & Tompkins, C. A. (2001). Predictive inferencing in adults with right hemisphere brain damage. *Journal of Speech, Language, and Hearing Research*, 44, 639–654.

Levelt, W. J. M. (1989). *Speaking: From intention to articulation.* Cambridge, MA: MIT Press.

Molloy, R., Brownell, H., & Gardner, H. (1990). Discourse comprehension by right-hemisphere stroke patients: Deficits of prediction and revision. In Y. Joanette & H. Brownell (Eds.), *Discourse ability and brain damage: Theoretical and empirical perspectives* (pp. 113–130). New York: Springer-Verlag.

Mross, E. F. (1990). Text analysis: Macro- and microstructural aspects of discourse processing. In Y. Joanette & H. Brownell (Eds.), *Discourse ability and brain damage: Theoretical and empirical perspectives* (pp. 50–68). New York: Springer-Verlag.

Murphy, G. L. (1990). The psycholinguistics of discourse comprehension. In Y. Joanette & H. Brownell (Eds.), *Discourse ability and brain damage: Theoretical and empirical perspectives* (pp. 28–49). New York: Springer-Verlag.

Pimental, P. A., & Kingsbury, N. A. (2000). *Mini inventory of right brain injury* (2nd. ed.). Austin, TX: Pro-Ed.

Ross-Swain, D. G. (1996). *Ross information processing assessment.* Austin, TX: Pro-Ed.

Searle, J. (1979). Metaphor. In A. Ortony (Ed.), *Metaphor and thought* (pp. 92–123). New York: Cambridge University Press.

Shamay-Tsoory, S. G., Tomer, R., & Aharon-Peretz, J. (2005a). The neuroanatomical basis of understanding sarcasm and its relationship to social cognition. *Neuropsychology*, 19, 288–300.

Shamay-Tsoory, S. G., Tomer, R., Berger, B. D., & Aharon-Peretz, J. (2003). Characterization of empathy deficits following prefrontal brain damage: The role of the right ventromedial prefrontal cortex. *Journal of Cognitive Neuroscience*, 15, 324–337.

Shamay-Tsoory, S. G., Tomer, R., Berger, B. D., Goldsher, D., & Aharon-Peretz, J. (2005b). Impaired "affective theory of mind" is associated with right ventromedial prefrontal damage. *Cognitive Behavioural Neurology*, 18, 55–67.

Stemmer, B. (1999). Discourse studies in neurologically impaired populations: A quest for action. *Brain and Language*, 68, 402–418.

Stemmer, B., Giroux, F., & Joanette, Y. (1994). Production and evaluation of requests by right hemisphere brain-damaged individuals. *Brain and Language*, 47, 1–31.

Stroop, J. R. (1935). Studies of interference on serial verbal reaction. *Journal of Experimental Psychology*, 18, 643–662.

Tompkins, C. A., Fassbinder, W., Lehman Blake, M., Baumgaertner, A., & Jayaram, N. (2004). Inference generation during text comprehension by adults with right hemisphere brain damage: Activation failure versus multiple activation. *Journal of Speech, Language, and Hearing Research*, 47, 1380–1395.

Tompkins, C. A., Lehman Blake, M. T., Baumgaertner, A., & Fassbinder, W. (2001). Mechanisms of discourse comprehension impairment after right hemisphere brain damage: Suppression in inferential ambiguity resolution. *Journal of Speech, Language, and Hearing Research*, 44, 400–415.

Tompkins, C. A., Scharp, V. L., Fassbinder, W., Meigh, K. M., & Armstrong, E. M. (2008a). A different story on "theory of mind" deficit in adults with right hemisphere brain damage. *Aphasiology*, 22, 42–61.

Tompkins, C. A., Scharp, V. L., Meigh, K. M., & Fassbinder, W. (2008b). Coarse coding and discourse comprehension in adults with right hemisphere brain damage. *Aphasiology*, 22, 204–223.

Ulatowska, H. K., & Streit Olness, G. (2007). Pragmatics in discourse performance: Insights from aphasiology. *Seminars in Speech and Language*, 28, 148–158.

van Dijk, T. A., & Kintsch, W. (1983). *Strategies of discourse comprehension*. London: Academic Press.

Weylman, S. T., Brownell, H. H., Roman, M., & Gardner, H. (1989). Appreciation of indirect requests by left- and right-brain-damaged patients: The effects of verbal context and conventionality of wording. *Brain and Language*, 36, 580–591.

Winner, E., Brownell, H., Happé, F., Blum, A., & Pincus, D. (1998). Distinguishing lies from jokes: Theory of mind deficits and discourse interpretation in right-hemisphere brain damaged patients. *Brain and Language*, 62, 89–106.

Right Hemisphere Damage and Prosody

Susan A. Leon, Amy D. Rodriguez, *and* John C. Rosenbek

Abstract

Communication requires interdependent functioning of large portions of the brain, and damage to any of these systems can disrupt effective and appropriate communication. Damage to the right hemisphere or basal ganglia can result in difficulty using or understanding prosodic contours in speech. Prosody includes pitch, loudness, rate, and voice quality, and is used to convey emotional connotation or linguistic intent. A disorder in the comprehension or production of prosody is known as aprosodia; affective aprosodia is a specific deficit affecting emotional or affective prosodic contours. The right hemisphere has been shown to play a critical role in processing emotional prosody and aprosodia syndromes resulting from damage to right hemisphere areas have been proposed. These include an expressive aprosodia resulting from anterior damage and a receptive aprosodia resulting from more posterior damage. Assessment and diagnosis of aprosodia in clinical settings are often perceptually based; however, acoustic analyses of means and ranges of frequency, intensity, and rate provide an instrumented analysis of prosody production. The treatment of aprosodia following stroke has received scant attention in comparison to other disorders of communication, although a few studies investigating cognitive–linguistic and imitative treatments have reported some positive results.

Key Words: aprosodia, right hemisphere damage, rehabilitation, affective prosody, basal ganglia, emotional expression, aprosodia assessment, aprosodia treatment, emotional communication

Introduction

Human communication is as complex in its creation as it is rich in its effects. Large portions of the brain contribute to the cognitive, affective, linguistic, and prosodic networks necessary for normal communication. Predictably, damage to any portion of one or more of these overlapping networks can disrupt normal communication. Damage to language eloquent areas of the cortex in the left hemisphere can result in word finding errors and in difficulty with auditory and reading comprehension, verbal expression, and writing. Damage to areas of the right hemisphere can result in deficits in relevance and appropriateness of communication. Cortical and subcortical damage, usually to the right hemisphere and/or basal ganglia, can result in defects of emotional or affective prosody often called aprosodia (Ross, 1981). Aprosodia, with special emphasis on expressive aprosodia after right hemisphere stroke, is the subject of this chapter. Relevant definitions will be reviewed, followed by sections on the anatomic and physiological bases of emotional prosody, on the pathophysiology of aprosodia, and on the evaluation and treatment of expressive aprosodia.

Definitions

Normal communication depends on normal cognition as well as language, gestures (including facial expression), and prosody. The traditional components of language include phonology, semantics, and syntax. Disorders of these components are discussed elsewhere in this volume. Facial expression, despite the cues they may provide concerning a speaker's intent or affect, is not reviewed at length in this chapter, but the interested reader can consult Russell, Bachorowski, and Fernandez-Dols (2003) for a discussion of facial expression of emotion and its relationship to vocal expressions.

Normal prosody is the complex result of lawful changes in intonation, rate, rhythm, stress, and voice quality and is divisible into linguistic and affective (i.e., emotional) prosody. Linguistic prosody, or what Boutsen (2004) calls intrinsic prosody, refers to predictable changes in the timing of articulatory or speech movements such that, for example, some syllables have a longer duration than others. Intrinsic prosody can be used to denote stress or signal linguistic intent (i.e., a statement versus a question). Intrinsic prosody depends critically upon left hemisphere, subcortical, and cerebellar circuits, and is disrupted in a variety of disorders including Parkinson's disease, cerebellar disease, and speech–language abnormalities resulting from left frontal damage, including apraxia of speech and Broca's aphasia. Affective or emotional prosody, or what Boutsen (2004) calls extrinsic prosody, refers primarily to predictable alterations in intonation, intensity, rate, and voice quality that signal a person's affective state (e.g., angry, happy, fearful). Unlike intrinsic prosody, extrinsic or affective prosody primarily reflects changes over multiple linguistic units such as sentences or phrases. However, affective prosody can be conveyed in shorter utterances as well (e.g., anger can clearly be conveyed by the production of a single word such as "stop"). Affective prosody signals a speaker's intent as in "You got it done," spoken with positive affect (i.e., "way to go") or negative affect (i.e., "this is your fault"). Affective prosody depends critically upon right hemisphere and basal ganglia structures, although the left hemisphere may play a subordinate processing role, as the right hemisphere does in processing linguistic prosody.

Impaired prosody, whether linguistic or affective, can be called dysprosody, and Monrad-Krohn (1947) is generally credited with introducing this term into the list of speech–language disorders. However, observations of this deficit were noted decades earlier by Hughlings Jackson (1915), who asserted that the right hemisphere was critical for expressing emotion after noting that individuals with nonfluent aphasia following left hemisphere stroke were still able to express different emotional tones despite other language deficits. The suspected importance of the right hemisphere in affective prosody was later supported by reports of

persons with deficits in emotional expression and/or comprehension (Heilman, Scholes, & Watson, 1975; Ross & Mesulam, 1979; Ross, 1981; Tucker, Watson, & Heilman, 1977). Ross (1981) appears to have first used the term aprosodia specifically to describe disordered affective or emotional prosody following right hemisphere damage (RHD).

Signs and Symptoms

Myers (2004) described the perceptual signs of expressive aprosodia as "a flattened, monotonic, somewhat robotic, stilted prosodic production characterized by reduced variation in prosodic features and somewhat uniform intersyllabic pause time" (p. 108). Additionally, these individuals may experience some degree of receptive deficits affecting comprehension of affective prosody, as well as impairment in the ability to comprehend and produce facial expressions. As such, combined deficits in the production of facial expressions and emotional tones of voice often contribute to the perception of the "flattened affect" described by some. The overall impression is of blandness and apparent indifference, especially if the affect abnormality extends to facial expression and general physical inertia. However, it is worth stating that expressive aprosodia can occur in the absence of clinical depression. That is, individuals with aprosodia may experience the normal range of emotions, but be unable to reflect those emotions in their tone of voice (Tucker et al., 1977). However, it is important to recognize that post-stroke depression, although more commonly reported following left hemisphere lesions, can occur following a right hemisphere stroke (Hama, Yamashita, Yamawaki, & Kurisu, 2011), particularly if the lesion is more anteriorly located (for a review of emotional disorders following unilateral stroke, see Gainotti, 2003).

In addition to the affective deficits seen in expressive aprosodia, these individuals often experience other deficits. Among the most common is anosognosia, or the unawareness or denial of difficulties, which can occur after RHD. Anosognosia may be the principal reason why those with RHD often fail to report difficulties of prosody and even less subtle abnormalities such as hemiplegia. Caregivers or family members are often the ones to report that their loved one can no longer interpret what the caregivers are feeling, or that misinterpretations of intent are frequent, or that the person sounds sad or bored or angry, regardless of what is being said. As a result, impaired prosody can negatively impact interpersonal relationships (Heilman, 2002). Substantial caregiver stress and subsequent marital strain are frequent and may contribute to a decrease in the quality of life for individuals with aprosodia and their loved ones. Some persons with aprosodia may have a general insight into the flatness of their voices or the marital discord that has arisen, but may assign almost no importance to the difference or to its potential contribution to a spouse's unhappiness. Others may have normal insight into their difficulty and its impact on others, but are unable to alter it on their own. Because neglect and other attentional deficits are common in RHD, the presence of one or both of these deficits may contribute to the lack of self-initiated change in emotional communication. Aprosodia, however, does not result from neglect, despite the frequent cooccurrence of these two conditions.

Neuroanatomical Correlates of Prosodic Processing

Prosodic processing deficits may be seen following damage to the right hemisphere, the left hemisphere, and certain subcortical regions. Because this chapter focuses on affective prosody, we will cover only affective prosodic processing rather than prosodic processing as a whole. A number of theories address the issue of hemispheric laterality and emotional prosodic processing, including a right hemisphere dominance theory, a valence-specific laterality theory, and an acoustic laterality theory. Data exist in varying degrees of support and negation for each of these theories. More recent approaches consider that these theories may not be mutually exclusive and, in fact, may all have some explanatory power. The complexity of emotional prosodic processing and the widely differing stimuli and populations used to address these theoretical issues make a confident explanation of neuroanatomic correlates impossible. Nonetheless, the following section highlights a variety of possibilities.

Processing of affective prosody was attributed to the right hemisphere for many years (Heilman et al., 1975; Ross, 1981; Ross & Mesulam, 1979; Tucker et al., 1977) based on case studies of individuals who demonstrated reduced prosodic ability following RHD. However, deficits in affective prosody have also been reported following left hemisphere damage (LHD), both in individuals with aphasia (De Bleser & Poeck, 1985; Schlanger, Schlanger, & Gerstmann, 1976) and in individuals with mild

or no aphasia (Cancelliere & Kertesz, 1990; Ross, Thompson, & Yenkosky, 1997).

It has been proposed that affective prosodic deficits seen following left hemisphere damage are due to an impairment in interhemispheric temporal integration of the propositional message and prosodic processing (Ross & Monnot, 2008), rather than an indication of left hemisphere affective contribution. Studies examining aprosodia following LHD have shown that it is not associated with the degree of aphasic deficit but with lesion location (Ross & Monnot, 2008). Lesions producing affective aprosodia in LHD individuals are generally found in the deep white matter adjacent to the corpus callosum, the structure that enables interhemispheric communication. Additionally, individuals with aprosodia from LHD often show improvement in expression and comprehension of affective prosody if articulatory-linguistic content is reduced, thus reducing integrational demand. That is, individuals with LHD are better at recognizing or producing appropriate emotional prosodic contours layered onto utterances such as monosyllables or vowel prolongations, than propositional utterances (i.e., sentences). Individuals with aprosodia from RHD do not show improvement in recognition or production with such a reduction in linguistic load.

Ross and colleagues (Gorelick & Ross, 1987; Ross, 1981; Ross & Mesulam, 1979; Ross & Monnot, 2008) have suggested that aprosodia resulting from RHD occurs in syndromes analogous to the aphasias from damage to right hemisphere areas that are homologues of the areas commonly damaged in aphasia. Aprosodia, like aphasia, can affect expression, comprehension, or repetition. A person with expressive aprosodia would produce speech that was monotonous, flat, or affectless. A person with a receptive aprosodia would misunderstand or misinterpret a speaker's emotional prosody. A person with global aprosodia would fail to produce and understand prosodic signals. In a series of studies (including Ross et al., 1997; Ross & Monnot, 2008), neuroanatomical areas associated with expressive and receptive deficits have been demonstrated. The right posterior inferior frontal region is important for both the production and repetition of affective prosody, and injury to the right frontal operculum has been shown to result in deficits in spontaneous prosodic expression in early stages. The right posterior superior temporal region is essential for comprehension of affective prosody, and in particular, the right temporal operculum as well as thalamic lesions are associated with poor receptive prosodic ability.

As with the aphasias, Ross' (1981) types of aprosodia are derived from central tendencies. The person with expressive aprosodia typically has a more expressive than receptive deficit, and the reverse is true for receptive aprosodia. In our experience, the person with an isolated deficit is rare. Nonetheless, the search for pure types continues (Heilman, Leon, & Rosenbek, 2004). Reports of individuals with aprosodia resulting from lesions that do not fit into this anatomical classification, notably Cancelliere and Kertesz (1990), Breitenstein, Daum, and Ackermann (1998), and Adolphs, Damasio, and Tranel (2002), have also appeared. However, many of the cases reported in these studies had bilateral brain damage and/or damage from an etiology other than stroke (for a review see Ross & Monnot, 2008).

The valence laterality theory posits that the two hemispheres specialize in processing emotions differently, with the right hemisphere specializing in negative emotions (e.g., anger, fear) and the left hemisphere specializing in processing positive emotions (e.g., happiness). Although some studies have provided support for this theory (e.g., Canli, Desmond, Zhao, Glover, & Gabrieli, 1998; Gur, Skolnick, & Gur, 1994), others have not (Borod, 1993; Wager, Phan, Liberzon, & Taylor, 2003). Wildgruber, Pihan, Ackermann, Erb, and Grodd (2002) used functional imaging to investigate this theory in relation to emotional prosodic contours. They found that hemispheric activation did not lateralize according to the valence of the prosody.

The acoustic laterality theory states that the auditory cortices from both hemispheres are involved in the analysis of the acoustic cues that signal affective prosody, but that they differ in what cues they specialize in processing (Baum & Pell, 1999; Van Lancker & Sidtis, 1992). Schirmer and Kotz (2006) stated that the right hemisphere excels at processing lower temporal resolution cues such as the pitch contours of utterances, whereas the left hemisphere specializes in processing timing and duration cues.

The basal ganglia have also been increasingly implicated in the processing of prosody. However, the data are more frequently derived from neurodegenerative disease with basal ganglia involvement than from stroke, with its typically more restricted damage. Imaging as well as clinical studies have suggested that the basal ganglia are involved in processing prosody (Breitenstein, Van Lancker, Daum, & Waters, 2001; Kotz, Frisch, von Cramon, & Friederici, 2003; Pell & Leonard, 2003; Van Lancker Sidtis, Pachana, Cummings, & Sidtis, 2006). Cancelliere and Kertesz (1990) found in a study of 46 brain-damaged individuals, some of whom had suffered a stroke, that damage to the basal ganglia, when present in addition to cortical damage, was significantly associated with impaired prosody recognition. Evidence from studies investigating prosody processing in individuals with Parkinson's disease also shows that deficits in discrimination and identification of emotional prosody are common (e.g., Pell & Leonard, 2003). However, it is unclear whether the basal ganglia are uniquely necessary for prosodic processing or whether their role is an indirect result of the extensive connectivity between the basal ganglia, the thalamus, and the frontal lobes (as suggested by Adolphs et al., 2002; Ross & Monnot, 2008). The amygdala may also play a role in processing emotional prosody, particularly anger and fear, although the evidence is clearer in regard to facial emotional processing by the amygdala at this time.

Neurocognitive Theories of Emotional Expression

The bases of emotional expression continue to be elusive despite centuries of conjecture, observation, and experimentation. A dominating modern paradigm, still alive in clinical practice to at least a muted degree, is the notion attributed to Tomkins (1962) that a group of basic emotions such as fear and anger is represented in the nervous system as modules or subsystems. Thus an angry person displays that anger in posture, facial expression, and voice, and a listener recognizes those signs and reacts. These signs of anger are supported by distinct but overlapping areas of the nervous system as compared to other basic emotions. A product of this paradigm is the notion of an affect lexicon (Bowers, Bauer, & Heilman, 1993). Developed originally as a model for the reception and labeling of emotional cues by listeners, it was extended to explain the potential breakdown in expression of emotion as well. A central concept to this model is that the emotions are stored in the right hemisphere, similar to the way words are stored in the left. This theory posits that both receptive and expressive aprosodia may result when the affect lexicon is damaged. Ross and Monnot (2008) continue to adhere to this model at least for receptive aprosodia. Traditional clinical practice from the classification of subtypes of aprosodia and their localization primarily in the right hemisphere to their evaluation and treatment has been guided by this modular approach to the processing of emotion.

In a radical departure, Russell and colleagues (2003) concluded that "Emotion expressions may not be . . . related to emotions in any simple way" (p. 342). Their summary of "new conceptions of emotions" warrants quotation. "These conceptions include an emphasis on multicomponent dynamic processes laced with cognition . . . , with a looser, more malleable and context-dependent relation among the components . . . and with a role for broad primitive affective dimensions such as pleasure–displeasure and activation" (p. 331). The pleasure–displeasure continuum has been commonly referred to in emotion literature as "valence." Sidtis and Van Lancker Sidtis (2003) took a similar approach in formulating their neurobehavioral model of prosody. They proposed that prosody serves multiple functions (e.g., linguistic, emotional, attitudinal, pragmatic, and personal), and that each function is characterized by multiple dimensions and is served by elaborate nervous system networks. Numerous authors have attempted specification of all or a portion of these processes, their relationships, and underlying neural networks and the role of "broad primitive affective dimensions."

Scherer (1986) posited that the processing of emotional prosody depends upon both external conditions and internal neural networks and processes or conditions. Scherer created a "component patterning" model of prosodic processing linking the external stimuli for emotional responses and the internal physiological bases of those responses. The model is especially elegant on the external or antecedent events. Specifically, he identified five so-called stimulus evaluation checks whose outcome influences a person's emotional response. He called these novelty check, intrinsic pleasantness check, goal/need significance check, coping potential check, and norm/self compatibility check. The outcome of these checks, for example, whether the event is judged to be pleasant or unpleasant and whether the stimulus is relevant to a person's goals and needs, influences the person's "physiological arousal, and expression and feeling" (p. 146). Although not featured in the model, the burden these checks impose on cognitive processes such as attention, speed of processing, and working memory is obvious. He does, however, predict the physiological conditions of respiration, vocalization, articulation, and resulting prosodic features in response to different outcomes of these checks. For example, unpleasant events may lead to a narrowing and tensing of components of the vocal tract, whereas pleasant events may lead to more open and relaxed component states, resulting in a higher or lower fundamental frequency, respectively.

Schirmer and Kotz (2006) have a more limited model of perception of emotion. They posit three stages and specify the neuroanatomic and physiological correlates of each stage. Stage one comprises sensory processing; Stage Two represents the integration of cues important to emotion recognition; and Stage Three, labeled cognition, involves the labeling of the perceived emotion. Stages Two and Three are especially dependent on right hemisphere temporal and frontal regions. Schirmer and Kotz (2006) also emphasize that what Scherer (1986) called external factors, such as salience to the listener and whether the emotion is seen as pleasant or unpleasant, will influence attention, and therefore the accuracy of perception and what they call "increased processing efforts" (p. 29). These authors highlight the notion that the processing of affective prosody involves a widely distributed, bilateral network of sensory, emotional, and cognitive subprocesses.

What Russell and colleagues (2003), among numerous others, call valence (pleasant–unpleasant) and activation (muted–hyper) deserves special mention for their scientific and clinical implications. They speculate that much of perception depends upon recognizing or inferring with these "broad bipolar dimensions" (p. 334). Similarly, these dimensions influence the production of prosody. They speculate that it is these dimensions that are most readily perceived and that are basic drivers of the physiology important to the production of emotional utterances. Even this broad emphasis is not as bare bones as it might seem. For example, experience could influence our view of pleasantness and even the degree of activation.

Motor Theories of Prosodic Expression

The motor system obviously contributes to emotional prosody, particularly on the expressive side. Two components of motor performance are generally recognized. The first is motor programming and planning (see van der Merwe, 1997, for the differentiation of these two processes) and the second is execution. The traditional nomenclature in the neuropathologies of speech reserves the term apraxia for the programming/planning subcomponent and dysarthria for the execution. Dysarthrias, such as the hypokinetic speech impairment that results from Parkinson's disease (PD), can also cause deficits in prosodic production. The prosody deficit associated with

RHD (i.e., aprosodia), however, can occur in the absence of the strength, tone, and timing abnormalities responsible for the dysarthrias (Darley, Aronson, & Brown, 1975). In addition, some of the perceptual signs of aprosodia are distinct from those of the dysarthrias. Duffy (2005), for example, compared aprosodia with the perceptual speech characteristics of unilateral upper motor neuron (UUMN) dysarthria, which is most likely to occur after unilateral, including right, brain damage. He observed that articulatory imprecision is a cardinal feature of UUMN dysarthria, and in aprosodia, articulatory precision is preserved in the presence of the flat prosodic profile.

The prosodic disturbance of hypokinetic dysarthria bears a closer resemblance to the aprosodia of RHD (Kent & Rosenbek, 1982). The prosodic insufficiency seen in PD is generally considered to be attributable to muscle weakness or rigidity resulting in respiratory insufficiency and reduced range of movement as well as deficits in motor programming (Duffy, 2005; Spencer & Rogers, 2005). However, deficits in producing and understanding emotion in modalities other than prosodic intonation (e.g., facial) have been demonstrated in individuals with PD, as well as in individuals with other disorders affecting basal ganglia circuitry (Ariatti, Benuzzi, & Nichelli, 2008; Clark, Neargarder, & Cronin-Golomb, 2008; Nikolova, Fellbrich, Born, Dengler, & Schröder, 2011). A recent meta-analysis examining almost 1300 individuals with PD reported a robust link between PD and deficits in recognizing and identifying emotional cues from facial expressions and prosody (Gray & Tickle-Degnen, 2010). These reports provide increasing evidence for a concomitant nonmotoric dysfunction contributing to deficits in emotional prosodic processing in PD.

In apraxia of speech, strength, tone, and timing are preserved, as is language and cognition, but the selection and ordering of motor movements for the segmental (speech) or suprasegmental (prosodic) elements of speech are impaired. It can be hypothesized that expressive aprosodia following RHD may be a specific form of apraxic speech production primarily influencing respiratory/laryngeal movements essential to the changes in fundamental frequency (F_O) critical to signaling emotional prosody. Tone and strength are normal. Apraxia can also be conceptualized as a loss of skill, and our treatment developments, including the most recent, are based on the principles of skill learning, an approach that would appear to improve expressive aprosodia. We offer this argument with the knowledge that

treatment, especially behavioral treatment, may be the weakest possible test of an explanatory hypothesis. Other evidence, however, supports the apraxia hypothesis. As with speech apraxia, aprosodia is improved on imitation in which the model or motor program is provided by a clinician. Impairment of volitional motor performance that improves with, though is not normalized by, imitation is a portion of apraxia's classic definition (Goodglass, Kaplan, & Barresi, 2001).

Other admittedly indirect evidence supports the hypothesized importance of praxis to normal emotional prosodic profiles. For example, van der Merwe (1997) highlighted a basal ganglia–limbic system connection that she posits serves to support programming and planning functions. The role of the limbic systems in emotional response is widely recognized. In addition, the limbic system has connections specifically to the larynx, which is responsible in part for the changes in F_O that offer important, but admittedly incomplete, cues to the interpretation of emotional prosody. Finally, it is apparent that impaired emotional prosody can occur in speakers with no evidence of depression or other mental illness (Myers, 1999), and no measurable cognitive deficit and an intact executive motor system.

Assessment of Aprosodia

Experienced clinicians are typically able to recognize the perceptual signs of aprosodia. However, as stated previously, individuals with aprosodia themselves do not always acknowledge or complain of deficits in emotional communication, so initiation of evaluation and treatment is often dependent on reports from caregivers and family. Because the degree to which individuals express emotion through tone of voice is highly variable, particularly in males, information about the individual's emotional expression prior to RHD is useful.

Clinical Evaluation

Deficits in prosody can result from a number of disorders, including dysarthria, chronic alcoholism, psychiatric disorders (e.g., schizophrenia), disorders affecting subcortical structures (e.g., Parkinson's and Huntington's disease), and cortical lesions from stroke or injury in the left or right hemisphere. Deficits in prosodic expression can occur without any deficit in emotional comprehension or the two deficits can cooccur. The term "aprosodia," however, has historically been used to refer to the disorder resulting from RHD (Ross, 1981).

Individuals suffering from depression or apathy may also present with a flattened affect. A study examining prosodic abnormalities in individuals with a diagnosis of a major depressive disorder versus individuals with prosodic deficits from RHD revealed similar quantitative expressive prosodic disturbances (Naarding, van den Broek, Wielaert, & van Harskamp, 2003). Individuals with a major depressive disorder have also been shown to have altered perceptions of emotional prosody (Uekermann, Abdel-Hamid, Lehmkämper, Vollmoeller, & Daum, 2008). Because depression as well as apathy can accompany strokes or neurodegenerative disease, it is important to screen for these disorders before making a diagnosis of aprosodia. There are a number of depression screens available, such as the Geriatric Depression Scale (Yesavage et al., 1982), the Beck Depression Inventory (Beck, Steer, & Brown, 1996), and the Hamilton Rating Scale for Depression (Hamilton, 1980). Apathy screens are also available, for example, the Lille Apathy Rating Scale (Sockeel et al., 2006). Although a positive score on a rating scale for depression or apathy does not rule out concomitant aprosodia, this information can be useful in determining treatment focus.

The clinical presentation of receptive aprosodia is not as apparent. Often individuals with receptive emotional deficits are unaware of any problem. Family members may be able to provide insight into this issue as well. Often they report that the affected individual does not "seem to care" about the moods or emotional states of others. If anosognosia is present, the individual may deny any difficulty understanding emotional expression even when an assessment tool or family report indicates a deficit.

Aprosodia can be assessed informally or formally, at bedside or in a clinical setting. Similar to aphasia screenings, the person's receptive, expressive, and repetition abilities should be assessed. An informal screening can provide an indication of the presence of a deficit. Bedside screening measures could include asking a person to identify the emotional tone in a semantically neutral sentence (e.g., the sentence "She went to the store" spoken by the examiner in an angry voice), in a semantically congruent sentence (e.g., "All the puppies are dead" spoken in a sad voice), and in a semantically incongruent sentence (e.g., "All the puppies are dead" spoken in a happy tone of voice). These individuals can then be asked to produce similar types of sentences using emotional prosodic expression. Linguistic prosody (e.g., a declarative statement versus an interrogative statement) can also be requested to gauge a person's ability to produce variations in pitch and loudness without emotional content. Because emotional facial expression or comprehension is also often affected in aprosodia, clinicians may also consider evaluating this mode of communication.

A number of tools are available for formal assessment, but in the interest of brevity we will address only a selected few. The Aprosodia Battery was originally developed by Ross and colleagues (1997) as a bedside measure. It allows testing of prosody in individuals with or without concomitant speech or language deficits. The tasks in the battery range from very low articulatory demand tasks, such as the production of a prolonged vowel sound with a prosodic contour (e.g., "aaaahhh" said using a sad tone of voice), to full sentences. The Aprosodia Battery allows the assessment of repetition of affective prosody, identification of affective prosody, and discrimination between two stimuli produced using differing affective prosodic tones. It can also be used to assess the ability to understand gestures associated with emotional intent. Ratings of responses can be analyzed via acoustical measures as described by Ross et al. (1997) or by trained raters.

The Florida Affect Battery (FAB) (Bowers, Blonder, & Heilman, 1999) evaluates affective and linguistic prosody discrimination and identification, as well as the ability to discriminate and identify emotional facial expressions. This battery can be judged by the individual performing the assessment as it does not contain expressive tasks, making it a practical choice if independent trained raters are not available. Other tests for assessment of aprosodia include the Battery of Emotional Expression and Comprehension (Cancelliere & Kertesz, 1990) and the New York Emotion Battery (Borod, Welkowitz, & Obler, 1992). Both tests contain extensive tasks for the assessment of expressive and receptive emotional prosodic and facial processing.

Acoustic Evaluation

Although perceptual judgment is the cornerstone of clinical practice and an appropriate basis for a diagnosis, clinical science is most comfortable with instrumented analysis. Acoustic evaluation in which speech signals are analyzed for frequency, intensity, rate, and quality characteristics has the potential for providing that comfort. However, it is important to remember that acoustic or instrumented analysis is not necessarily a less subjective mode of analysis than perceptual. Nonetheless, more than one level or type of analysis strengthens any science including speech science; thus, acoustic analysis has featured prominently in the study of normal and abnormal prosody.

The search for a set of distinctive acoustic signs in support of a perceptual diagnosis of expressive aprosodia depends first on identifying acoustic signatures for the various emotions as produced by normal speakers. Unfortunately, distinct signatures for even basic emotions such as happiness are elusive (Russell et al., 2003). Experimental issues abound. First is the possible complication of differences in what might be called laboratory emotional expression and spontaneous emotional utterances. Emotional expressions produced by actors under laboratory conditions may well produce easily classifiable emotional utterances that are different acoustically and even perceptually from utterances occurring naturally. Role playing, recording in natural environments, and other procedural manipulations have been experimental responses to this challenge. Another issue is the typically small number of emotions studied. Banse and Scherer (1996) argued that many listening experiments are actually discrimination rather than recognition tasks in which listeners merely identify utterances as different and then assign them to the limited number of categories identified for the study. Their experimental work to be referenced below deals with this issue by employing 14 emotions. A third issue is that emotional expressions are not equally perceptually identifiable even by normal listeners.

Nonetheless, progress has been made in identifying what would appear to be overlapping profiles for a select group of emotions, including happy, sad, angry, and fearful. The results of a model-driven approach to the search for acoustic profiles of the basic emotions by Banse and Scherer (1996) is typical. Understanding their results requires familiarity with selected acoustic variables. Fundamental frequency (F_O) reflects the rate of vocal fold vibration, is perceived as pitch, and can vary in level and pattern and extent of change. Vocal intensity, perceived as loudness, results critically from the interaction of respiratory drive and vocal fold activity and can differ in absolute values, pattern of alteration, and distribution across the various frequencies present in the speech signal. Temporal changes perceived as rate include pause time or the amount of silence between identifiable portions of an utterance, and articulation time or the duration of consonants, vowels, and transitions among them. Based on data from 12 professional actors for 14 emotions Banse and Scherer (1996) concluded that "The . . . perceptually most prominent parameter

of voice is fundamental frequency" (p. 624). It was highest for what they classified as hot anger, panic fear, and elation, and lowest for contempt and boredom. Intensity similarly was greatest for despair, hot anger, panic fear, and elation, and lowest for shame and sadness. Results are more variable for speech rate, with sadness being among the slowest. They concluded that "The present results clearly demonstrate the existence of differential vocal profiles for a large number of emotions . . . " (p. 630). Typical of the profiles is the one for fear showing increases in F_O variability and increased intensity and rate.

Although the acoustic profiles of different emotions may differ with methodology, including stimuli, speakers, listeners, methods of acoustic analysis, and emotions tested, concurrence with the main findings from Banse and Scherer (1996) has occurred in other studies, including that of Hammerschmidt and Jurgens (2007). They were able to differentiate rage/hot anger, despair/lamentation, contempt/disgust, joyful surprise, voluptuous enjoyment/sensual satisfaction, and affection/tenderness using clusters of 15 acoustic parameters including the ratio of peak frequency to F_O. The lesson here is that combinations of features are most powerful in human differentiation of emotional states reflected in speech. Although the perceptual and acoustic features of different emotions are complex, an understanding of the characteristics of different emotional tones has clinical utility. Rosenbek and colleagues (2006), for example, used a set of descriptors for each of three emotions in a cognitive–linguistic treatment for expressive aprosodia. We now turn to treatment of expressive aprosodia after RHD.

Treatment

Treatment of expressive aprosodia following stroke has received little attention in comparison to other communication disorders. Several factors may contribute to the lack of research in this area. Among these are the aforementioned complexities of affective prosody, the presence of concomitant deficits that reduce the awareness of deficits or the desire to participate in treatment, and/or a focus on remediation of other cognitive–linguistic communication disorders associated with right hemisphere stroke. However, given the estimated incidence of aprosodia reported by Blake and colleagues (Blake, Duffy, Myers, & Tompkins, 2002; Blake, Duffy, Tompkins, & Myers, 2003), up to 94,500 individuals per year may suffer from this disorder with negative consequences for themselves and their loved ones. Moreover, it has been demonstrated that expressive aprosodia in some individuals following right hemisphere stroke does not spontaneously improve (Ross & Mesulam, 1979) and that their deficits may even worsen over time (Nakhutina, Borod, & Zgaljardic, 2006). As such, it is important for clinicians to consider the treatment of expressive aprosodia in the plan of care, when appropriate. This section will review the treatment approaches described in the literature and discuss behavioral accommodations that may need to be considered.

Treatment Approaches

Current treatments for aprosodia have applied two different approaches, imitative and cognitive–linguistic. Imitative approaches, in which clinicians provide a model of the target sentence, are based on the hypothesis that expressive aprosodia is due to a motor programming/planning deficit. Cognitive–linguistic approaches, in which individuals are provided cues about the perceptual characteristics for each emotional tone as well as pictures of the associated facial expressions, are based on the hypothesis that expressive aprosodia is due to the loss of affective representations in the nonverbal affect lexicon. These two treatment approaches will be discussed in turn.

IMITATIVE TREATMENT

The first treatment study for expressive aprosodia reported in the literature was a case study combining imitation and pitch feedback (Stringer, 1996). The patient, who had suffered a traumatic brain injury (TBI), was trained to produce emotional tones of voice and affective facial expressions either singly or simultaneously. The individual's verbal responses were captured and displayed by a computer program that provided feedback on the contour of her productions. Facial expressions were trained using a mirror for feedback. Treatment gains in affective production and facial expressions were evident and remained stable for 2 months after treatment. Although this study provided initial evidence that expressive aprosodia was amenable to imitative treatment, the methods were underspecified. As such, there were unanswered questions about the emotions that can or should be treated using imitation, ideal training stimuli, and tasks or analyses that best capture changes in emotional communication.

A decade later we employed an imitative treatment as one approach in a study comparing two treatments for expressive aprosodia (Rosenbek et al., 2006). Twelve individuals, 11 who had suffered a right hemisphere stroke and one who had suffered a

TBI, were trained to produce happy, angry, sad, and neutral tones of voice. The stimuli used for assessment and training were sentence-length utterances that were emotionally congruent with the verbal message (i.e., "I just won the lottery" was a sentence used to train HAPPY). The treatment was provided along a six-step continuum in which cues were gradually faded from Step 1 (modeling of production and facial expression) to Step 6 (independent production of the target sentence). The approach included production of the target sentence following imitation of the target tone of voice (Steps 1–3), a neutral tone of voice (Step 4), in response to a question (Step 5), and during a role-playing task (Step 6). The later steps, with spontaneous production in the context of a functional task, were incorporated to provide an opportunity for responding in a way that is more typical of natural communication. Eight of the 12 individuals with aprosodia demonstrated a significant change in their ability to express the trained emotions.

COGNITIVE–LINGUISTIC TREATMENT

As part of the comparison study of Rosenbek et al. (2006), we also employed a cognitive–linguistic approach with 13 patients who had suffered right hemisphere stroke, six of whom had previously received the imitative treatment. Again, the treated emotions were happy, sad, angry, and neutral and the stimuli were sentence-length, congruent sentences. Participants were provided with a list of perceptual characteristics related to the target emotion, the target emotion names, and pictures of target facial expressions (see Figure 15.1). A six-step continuum with fading cues was employed. In Step 1, the person read the cue card and paraphrased the perceptual characteristic to demonstrate understanding. In Step 2, the person chose the name of the emotion and the facial expression that matched the description. In Step 3, a written sentence was provided and the person was asked to produce it with the tone of voice and facial expression that matched the cue cards. In Steps 4–6, the person continued to produce the target sentence as cue cards were systematically removed one at a time (i.e., description removed in Step 4, emotion name removed in Step 5, facial expression removed in Step 6). Ten of 13 individuals demonstrated a significant change in their ability to express the trained emotion.

Although such a positive response to the cognitive–linguistic treatment may seem to provide evidence against the predominant theories of aprosodia as a motor-based deficit, it is possible that this

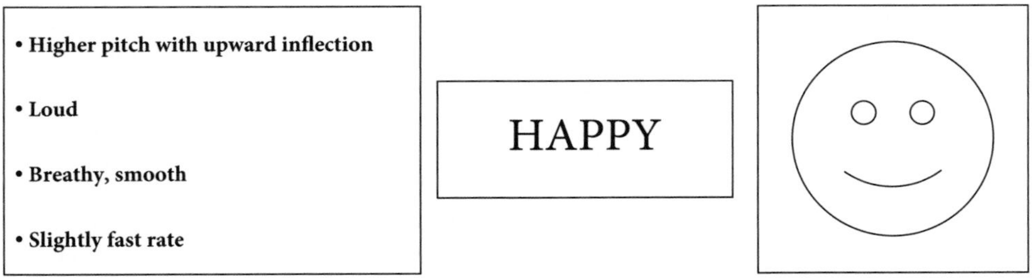

Figure 15.1 Depiction of the cue cards as part of the cognitive–linguistic treatment (Rosenbek et al., 2006).

treatment had a more significant motor component than expected. That is, in the absence of a clinician-provided model, individuals had to generate their own model (based on the written description of the voice), and then refine it on subsequent attempts. Approximations toward the target in repeated responses likely invoked aspects of motor learning used in learning other motor skills (e.g., throwing a ball at a target).

We offer two conclusions with respect to the imitative and cognitive–linguistic treatments discussed here. First, and most important, is that individuals with expressive aprosodia are able to improve their emotional communication skills with treatment. Second is that although a single approach may be successful, a combined approach may yield even greater benefit. The latter observation is based on the results of the study by Rosenbek et al. (2006) in which the imitative and cognitive–linguistic treatments were administered to 11 individuals, and seven responded favorably to both regardless of which treatment came first.

That is, the critical aspect of the imitation treatment was the clinician-provided model that individuals with aprosodia were able to use to guide their own production, and the critical aspect of the cognitive–linguistic treatment was the provision of written descriptions that provided the basis for the self-initiated model and subsequent refinement of each response. These observations led us to create a combined treatment approach that incorporates the critical aspects of both treatments with a feedback method known to enhance motor learning.

COMBINED TREATMENT

In the combined treatment approach currently under investigation, we focus on the type and frequency of feedback provided to individuals with aprosodia. To begin, consider the two types of feedback identified by Proctor and Dutta (1995). One is knowledge of results (KR) in which information

about the accuracy of the response is provided (i.e., right or wrong). The other is knowledge of performance (KP) in which information about the pattern of response is provided (i.e., why it is right or wrong). KP, a type of extrinsic feedback, has been identified as critical for the learning of complex behaviors, particularly when intrinsic information cannot be adequately processed (Schmidt & Wrisberg, 2004). When considering the complexity of overlaying emotion on speech, the prevalence of anosognosia in right hemisphere stroke, and the presence of receptive deficits in some individuals with expressive aprosodia, the use of KP appears to be well justified. However, Goodman and Wood (2004) suggested that individuals may become less engaged when specific feedback is provided, which, in turn, can reduce the retention of acquired skill, and studies have shown that the frequency and timing of KP are important for the acquisition and retention of skill. Results from a series of studies have suggested that optimal results are obtained when there is a systematic reduction in feedback over time (Weeks & Kordus, 1998; Winstein, Merians, & Sullivan, 1999; Winstein & Schmidt, 1990) and when delayed (as opposed to immediate) feedback is provided (Austermann-Hula, Robin, Maas, Ballard, & Schmidt, 2009; Knock, Ballard, Robin, & Schmidt, 2000; Swinnen, Schmidt, Nicholson, & Shapiro, 1990).

In our combined treatment approach, KP feedback is provided by a computer software program called VisiPitch IV˚, which Stringer (1996) also utilized in his study. The program displays the frequency, intensity, and duration of target sentences such that the model appears on the top half of the screen and the patient's response appears on the bottom half of the screen. This allows a direct comparison of the prosodic features of the model and the response. The treatment is set up along a seven-step continuum that reduces feedback in a systematic way. In Step 1, persons are provided with a written description of perceptual characteristics associated with the target tone of voice (as in the previous cognitive–linguistic treatment). The person is also provided with a recorded model of the target sentence for imitation. Use of recorded sentences (rather than a clinician-generated sentences) removes any effect related to the difficulty that clinicians may face in producing a consistent model, and it also ensures that these persons receive an age- and gender-appropriate model for production. In Step 2, the written description is removed. In the first two steps, KP is provided on each response by the participant. In Step 3, KP is reduced to alternating sentences. This means that the person is not able to see the computer screen showing the model and his or her response. In Step 4, KP is further reduced to every third sentence, and no KP is provided in Steps 5–7. Judgments about each response are made by the clinician and the person with aprosodia to facilitate self-monitoring of productions. Preliminary results from four individuals with expressive aprosodia secondary to right hemisphere stroke demonstrated that this combined approach that incorporates feedback in the form of KP significantly improves emotional expression (Rodriguez, Patel, Bashiti, Shrivastav, & Rosenbek, 2011). However, more investigation is necessary to determine its effect on each treated emotion.

Although the imitative, cognitive–linguistic, and combined treatments have yielded positive effects on emotional communication, the literature on valence and activation urges us to contemplate how these factors may be considered in future treatments. For example, it remains an empirical question whether larger treatment effects may be obtained if training is focused on increased activation generally and then on pleasant–unpleasant distinctions. Similarly, consideration of antecedent events (Scherer, 1986) may also enhance treatment effects. Although it is difficult to "create" emotion in a clinical setting, the use of scenarios as a prompt for target responses, or using other means of increasing perceptual salience, may evoke more emotion in persons undergoing the treatment, which according to Scherer (1986) would in turn change the physiology that subsequently affects speech production.

BEHAVIORAL CONSIDERATIONS

Due to the additional deficits often associated with expressive aprosodia following right hemisphere stroke previously discussed, clinicians must make some behavioral considerations when planning treatment. For example, the presence of neglect may require the clinician to place treatment materials in the person's right hemispace to facilitate attention. For individuals who demonstrate anosognosia and/or mixed receptive and expressive deficits, clinicians may need to strongly consider incorporating a visual model and visual feedback to circumvent perceptual difficulties in processing affective prosody. Additionally, as in the study by Rodriguez and colleagues (2011), it may be useful to incorporate participant judgment of responses to improve self-monitoring.

Conclusions

The physiology of emotion and the pathophysiology of impaired emotional processing are complex and only partly specified in the experimental literature. Peripheral sensory and motor mechanisms, a variety of cognitive functions including attention (Lane, Chua, & Dolan, 1999), affect, arousal, experience, and praxis, contribute in varying proportions to both the reception and expression of emotion. In addition, the type and strength of environmental stimuli are critical. Not surprisingly, portions of the entire neural axis, from cortex through subcortical regions and peripheral sensory and motor systems, have been implicated in the support of normal emotional processing. The clinical implications include the following: (1) deficits in emotional processing are not unitary; (2) evaluation ideally would measure the integrity of all components of normal emotional response; and (3) treatment to the degree possible should be tailored to each individual's specific pathophysiology and should use the most realistic and powerful available methods of stimulation. Research into the treatment of expressive aprosodia remains in its infancy. However, the available evidence demonstrates that some individuals with aprosodia can improve their emotional communication with training. Moreover, treatment approaches will continue to be refined as more comprehensive neuroanatomical and neuropsychological models of emotion processing are developed. It is important for clinicians and researchers to stay abreast of these developments, as the factors to be considered in the treatment of expressive aprosodia are as complex, and as important, as emotion itself.

References

Adolphs, R., Damasio, H., & Tranel, D. (2002). Neural systems for recognition of emotional prosody: A 3-D lesion study. *Emotion, 2,* 23–51.

Ariatti, A., Benuzzi, F., & Nichelli, P. (2008). Recognition of emotions from visual and prosodic cues in Parkinson's disease. *Journal of the Neurological Sciences, 29*(4), 219–227.

Austermann-Hula, S. N., Robin, D. A., Maas, E., Ballard, K. J., & Schmidt, R. A. (2009). Effects of feedback frequency and timing on acquisition and retention of speech skills in acquired apraxia of speech. *Journal of Speech, Language, and Hearing Research*, 18(4), 343–360.

Banse, R., & Scherer, K. R. (1996). Acoustic profiles in vocal emotion expression. *Journal of Personality and Social Psychology*, 70, 614–636.

Baum, S. R., & Pell, M. D. (1999). The neural bases of prosody: Insights from lesion studies and neuroimaging. *Aphasiology*, 13(8), 581–608.

Beck, A. T., Steer, R. A., & Brown, G. K. (1996). *Manual for Beck depression inventory II* (BDI-II). San Antonio, TX: Psychology Corporation.

Blake, M. L, Duffy, J. R., Myers, P. S., & Tompkins, C. A. (2002). Prevalence and patterns of right hemisphere cognitive/communicative deficits: Retrospective data from an inpatient rehabilitation unit. *Aphasiology*, 16, 537–547.

Blake, M. L., Duffy, J. R., Tompkins, C. A., & Myers, P. S. (2003). Right hemisphere syndrome is in the eye of the beholder. *Aphasiology*, 17, 423–432.

Borod, J. C. (1993). Cerebral mechanisms underlying facial, prosodic, and lexical emotional expression: A review of neuropsychological studies and methodological issues. *Neuropsychology*, 7, 445–463.

Borod, J. C., Welkowitz, J., & Obler L. K. (1992). *The New York emotion battery*. New York, NY: Mount Sinai Medical Center, Department of Neurology.

Boutsen, F. (2004). Aprosody: A right hemisphere dysarthria. *Journal of Medical Speech Language Pathology*, 12, 67–75.

Bowers, D., Bauer, R. M., & Heilman, K. M. (1993). The nonverbal affect lexicon: Theoretical perspectives from neuropsychological studies of affect perception. *Neuropsychology*, 7, 433–444.

Bowers, D., Blonder, L. X., & Heilman, K. M. (1999). *The Florida affect battery: A manual*. Gainesville, FL: University of Florida, Center for Neuropsychological Studies, Cognitive Neuroscience Laboratory. http://www.hp.ufl.edu/cogneuro/Bowers/Research/FAB/.

Breitenstein, C., Daum, I., & Ackermann, H. (1998). Emotional processing following cortical and subcortical brain damage: Contribution of the fronto-striatal circuitry. *Behavioral Neurology*, 11, 29–42.

Breitenstein, C., Van Lancker, D., Daum, I., & Waters, C. H. (2001). Impaired perception of vocal emotions in Parkinson's disease: Influence of speech time processing and executive functioning. *Brain and Cognition*, 45(2), 277–314.

Cancelliere, A., & Kertesz, A. (1990). Lesion localization in acquired deficits of emotional expression and comprehension. *Brain and Cognition*, 13, 133–147.

Canli, T., Desmond, J. E., Zhao, Z., Glover, G., & Gabrieli, J. D. (1998). Hemispheric asymmetry for emotional stimuli detected with fMRI. *NeuroReport*, 9, 3233–3239.

Clark, U. S., Neargarder, S., & Cronin-Golomb, A. (2008). Specific impairments in the recognition of emotional facial expressions in Parkinson's disease. *Neuropsychologia*, 46, 2300–2309.

Darley, F. L., Aronson, A. E., & Brown, J. J. R. (1975). *Motor speech disorders*. Philadelphia, PA: W.B. Saunders.

De Bleser, R., & Poeck, K. (1985). Analysis of prosody in the spontaneous speech of patients with recurring CV-utterances. *Cortex*, 21, 405–416.

Duffy, J. R. (2005). *Motor speech disorders: Substrates, differential diagnosis, and management* (2nd ed.). Philadelphia, PA: Elsevier Mosby.

Gainotti, G. (2003). Emotional disorders in relation to unilateral brain disorders. In T. E. Feinberg & M. J. Farah (Eds.), *Behavioral neurology and neuropsychology* (pp. 691–698). New York, NY: McGraw-Hill.

Goodglass, H., Kaplan, E., & Barresi, B. (2001). *The Boston diagnostic aphasia examination* (3rd ed.). Philadelphia, PA: Lippincott Williams & Wilkins.

Goodman, J. S., & Wood, R. E. (2004). Feedback specificity, learning opportunities, and learning. *Journal of Applied Psychology*, 89, 809–821.

Gorelick, P. B., & Ross, E. D. (1987). The aprosodias: Further functional-anatomical evidence for the organisation of affective language in the right hemisphere. *Journal of Neurology, Neurosurgery and Psychiatry*, 50, 553–560.

Gray, H. M., & Tickle-Degnen, L. (2010). A meta-analysis of performance on emotion recognition tasks in Parkinson's disease. *Neuropsychology*, 24(2), 176–191.

Gur, R. C., Skolnick, B. E., & Gur, R. E. (1994). Effects of emotional discrimination tasks on cerebral blood flow: Regional activation and its relation to performance. *Brain and Cognition* 25(2), 271–286.

Hama, S., Yamashita, H., Yamawaki, S., & Kurisu, K. (2011). Post-stroke depression and apathy: Interactions between functional recovery, lesion location, and emotional response. *Psychogeriatrics*, 11(1), 68–76.

Hamilton, M. (1980). Rating depressive patients. *Journal of Clinical Psychiatry*, 41, 21–24.

Hammerschmidt, K., & Jurgens, U. (2007). Acoustical correlates of affective prosody. *Journal of Voice*, 21, 531–540.

Heilman, K. M. (2002). *Matter of mind: A neurologist's view of brain-behavior relationships*. New York, NY: Oxford University Press.

Heilman, K. M., Leon, S. A., & Rosenbek, J. C. (2004). Affective aprosodia from a medial frontal stroke. *Brain and Language*, 89, 411–416.

Heilman, K. M., Scholes, R., & Watson, R. T (1975). Auditory affective agnosia. Disturbed comprehension of affective speech. *Journal of Neurology, Neurosurgery, and Psychiatry*, 38, 69–72.

Hughlings Jackson, J. (1915). On affectations of speech from diseases of the brain. *Brain*, 38, 107–174.

Kent, R., & Rosenbek, J. C. (1982). Prosodic disturbance and neurologic lesion. *Brain and Language*, 15, 259–291.

Knock, T. R., Ballard, K. J., Robin, D. A., & Schmidt, R. A. (2000). Influence of order of stimulus presentation on speech motor learning: A principled approach to treatment for apraxia of speech. *Aphasiology*, 14, 653–668.

Kotz, S. A., Frisch, S., von Cramon, D. Y., & Friederici, A. D. (2003). Syntactic language processing: ERP lesion data on the role of the basal ganglia. *Journal of the International Neuropsychological Society*, 9, 1053–1060.

Lane, R. D., Chua, P. M. L, & Dolan, R. J. (1999). Common effects of emotional valence, arousal and attention on neural activation during visual processing of pictures. *Neuropsychologia*, 37, 989–997.

Monrad-Krohn, G. H. (1947). Dysprosody or altered "melody of language." *Brain*, 70, 405–415.

Myers, P. (1999). *Right hemisphere damage: Disorders of communication and cognition*. San Diego, CA: Singular Publishing Group, Inc.

Myers, P. S. (2004). Aprosodia. In R. D. Kent (Ed.), *The MIT encyclopedia of communication disorders* (pp. 107–110). Cambridge, MA: The MIT Press.

Naarding, P., van den Broek, W. W., Wielaert, S., & van Harskamp, F. (2003). Aprosodia in major depression. *Journal of Neurolinguistics*, 16(1), 37–41.

Nakhutina, L., Borod, J. C., & Zgaljardic, D. J. (2006). Posed prosodic emotional expression in unilateral stroke patients: Recovery, lesion location, and emotional perception. *Archives of Clinical Neuropsychology*, 21(1), 1–13.

Nikolova, Z. T., Fellbrich, A., Born, J., Dengler, R., & Schröder, C. (2011). Deficient recognition of emotional prosody in primary focal dystonia. *European Journal of Neurology*, 18(2), 329–336.

Pell, M. D., & Leonard, C. L. (2003). Processing emotional tone from speech in Parkinson's disease: A role for the basal ganglia. *Cognitive, Affective and Behavioral Neuroscience*, 3(4), 275–288.

Proctor, R. W., & Dutta, A. (1995). *Skill acquisition and human performance*. Thousand Oaks, CA: Sage Publications.

Rodriguez, A. D., Patel, S., Bashiti, N., Shrivastav, R., & Rosenbek, J. C. (2011, May). The effect of incorporating knowledge of performance in the treatment of aprosodia. Presentation at the Clinical Aphasiology Conference, Fort Lauderdale, FL.

Rosenbek, J. C., Rodriguez, A. D., Hieber, B., Leon, S. A., Crucian, G. P., Ketterson, T. U., . . . Rothi, L. J. G. (2006). The effects of two treatments for aprosodia secondary to acquired brain injury. *Journal of Rehabilitation Research & Development*, 43, 379–390.

Ross, E. D. (1981). The aprosodias: Functional-anatomic organization of the affective components of language in the right hemisphere. *Archives of Neurology*, 38, 561–569.

Ross, E. D., & Mesulam, M. M. (1979). Dominant language functions of the right hemisphere? Prosody and emotional gesturing. *Archives of Neurology*, 36(3), 144–148.

Ross, E. D., & Monnot, M. (2008). Neurology of affective prosody and its functional-anatomic organization in right hemisphere. *Brain and Language*, 104, 51–74.

Ross, E. D., Thompson, R. D., & Yenkosky, J. (1997). Lateralization of affective prosody in the brain and the callosal integration of hemispheric language functions. *Brain and Language*, 56, 27–54.

Russell, J. A., Bachorowski, J. A., & Fernandez-Dols, J. M. (2003). Facial and vocal expressions of emotion. *Annual Review of Psychology*, 54, 329–340.

Scherer, K. R. (1986). Vocal affect expression: A review and a model for future research. *Psychological Bulletin*, 99, 143–165.

Schirmer, A., & Kotz, S. A. (2006). Beyond the right hemisphere: Brain mechanisms mediating vocal emotional processing. *Trends in Cognitive Sciences*, 10(1), 24–30.

Schlanger, B., Schlanger, P., & Gerstmann, L. (1976). The perception of emotionally toned sentences by right hemisphere damaged and aphasic subjects. *Brain and Language*, 3, 396–403.

Schmidt, R. A., & Wrisberg, C. A. (2004). *Motor learning and performance* (3rd ed.). Champaign, IL: Human Kinetics.

Sidtis, J. J., & Van Lancker Sidtis, D. (2003). A neurobehavioral approach to dysprosody. *Seminars in Speech and Language*, 24(2), 93–105.

Sockeel, P., Dujardin, K., Devos, D., Deneve, C., Destee, A., & Defebvre, L. (2006). The Lille apathy rating scale (LARS), a new instrument for detecting and quantifying apathy: Validation in Parkinson's disease. *Journal of Neurology, Neurosurgery, and Psychiatry*, 77, 579–584.

Spencer, K. A., & Rogers, M. A. (2005). Speech motor programming in hypokinetic and ataxic dysarthria. *Brain and Language*, 94(3), 347–366.

Stringer, A. Y. (1996). Treatment of motor aprosodia with pitch biofeedback and expression modeling. *Brain Injury*, 10(8), 583–590.

Swinnen, S. P., Schmidt, R. A., Nicholson, D. E., & Shapiro, D. C. (1990). Information feedback for skill acquisition: Instantaneous knowledge of results degrades learning. *Journal of Experimental Psychology: Learning, Memory, and Cognition*, 16, 706–716.

Tomkins, S. S. (1962). *Affect, imagery, consciousness, Vol. 1*. New York, NY: Springer.

Tucker, D. M., Watson, R. T., & Heilman, K. M. (1977). Discrimination and evocation of affectively intoned speech in patients with right parietal disease. *Neurology*, 27, 947–950.

Uekermann, J., Abdel-Hamid, M., Lehmkämper, C., Vollmoeller, W., & Daum, I. (2008). Perception of affective prosody in major depression: A link to executive functions? *Journal of the International Neuropsychological Society*, 14(4), 552–561.

van der Merwe, A. (1997). A theoretical framework for the characterization of pathological speech sensorimotor control. In M. R. McNeil (Ed.), *Clinical management of sensorimotor speech disorders* (pp. 1–25). New York, NY: Thieme.

Van Lancker, D., & Sidtis, J. J. (1992). The identification of affective-prosodic stimuli by left- and right-hemisphere-damaged subjects: All errors are not created equal. *Journal of Speech and Hearing Research*, 35, 963–970.

Van Lancker Sidtis, D., Pachana, N., Cummings, J. L., & Sidtis, J. J. (2006). Dysprosodic speech following basal ganglia insult: Toward a conceptual framework for the study of the cerebral representation of prosody. *Brain and Language*, 97, 135–153.

Wager, T. D., Phan, K. L., Liberzon, I., & Taylor, S. F. (2003). Valence, gender, and lateralization of functional brain anatomy in emotion: A meta-analysis of findings from neuroimaging. *NeuroImage 19*, 513–531.

Weeks, D. L., & Kordus, R. N. (1998). Relative frequency of knowledge of performance and motor skill learning. *Research Quarterly for Exercise and Sport*, 69, 224–230.

Wildgruber, D., Pihan, H., Ackermann, H., Erb, M., & Grodd, W. (2002). Dynamic brain activation during processing of emotional intonation: Influence of acoustic parameters, emotional valence and sex. *NeuroImage 15*, 856–869.

Winstein, C. J., Merians, A. S., & Sullivan, K. J. (1999). Motor learning after unilateral brain damage. *Neuropsychologia*, 37, 975–987.

Winstein, C. J., & Schmidt, R. A. (1990). Reduced frequency of knowledge of results enhances motor skill learning. *Journal of Experimental Psychology: Learning, Memory, and Cognition*, 16, 677–691.

Yesavage, J. A., Brink, T. L., Rose, T. L., Lum, O., Huang, V., Adey, M., & Leirer, V. O. (1982). Development and validation of a geriatric depression screening scale: A preliminary report. *Journal of Psychiatric Research*, 17(1), 37–49.

PART 4

Clinical Implications

16 Biological Markers of Aphasia Recovery after Stroke

Marcus Meinzer, Lena Ulm, *and* Robert Lindenberg

Abstract

Language recovery after stroke is often incomplete and residual symptoms may persist for many years. However, there is ample evidence for structural and functional reorganization of language networks after stroke that mediate recovery. This chapter reviews studies that investigated biological markers of language recovery by means of functional and structural imaging techniques. In particular, we discuss neural signatures associated with spontaneous and treatment-induced language recovery across the first year poststroke and in the chronic stage of aphasia, studies that aimed at predicting recovery and treatment outcome as well as recent developments in brain stimulation that may be suited to enhance the potential for functional recovery.

Key Words: Aphasia, Recovery, Functional imaging, Structural imaging, Rehabilitation, Reorganization, Brain stimulation

Introduction

Acquired language disorders may be caused by different types of neurological diseases. The most common cause of aphasia is cerebrovascular accident, or stroke, affecting perisylvian regions of the language-dominant left hemisphere. In approximately 80% of the affected individuals, aphasia is caused by occlusion of the middle cerebral artery (MCA). Depending on the location and size of the damage, language production or comprehension may be affected to different degrees (Nicholas, 2005). In addition, aphasia typically entails negative consequences for the affected individuals and their relatives (i.e., affecting vocational reintegration, social life, and psychological well-being) and places major burdens on the healthcare system (Code, 2001).

Initially after a stroke, approximately one-third of these individuals suffer from aphasia (Pedersen, Vinter, & Olsen, 2004). It is generally agreed that even without intervention, substantial spontaneous recovery occurs within the first few days ("acute stage") and weeks to months ("subacute stage") after the insult (Bakheit, 2007; Pedersen

et al., 2004; Wade, Hewer, David, & Enderby, 1986), which is explained by early physiological repair mechanisms (Cramer, 2008; Hillis & Heidler, 2002). During this time, recovery can be enhanced by additional rehabilitative treatment (Lazar & Antoniello, 2008; Robey, 1994, 1998). However, complete remission can be observed only in about one-third of the initially affected individuals with aphasia after 3 months (Pedersen et al., 2004). The degree of spontaneous recovery gradually flattens after the first 3 months poststroke (Laska, Hellblom, Murray, Kahan, & Von Arbin, 2001; Pedersen, Jorgensen, Nakayama, Raaschou, & Olsen, 1995; Poeck, Huber, & Willmes, 1989) and reaches a plateau after approximately 6–12 months (Robey, 1998). In about 40% of individuals with aphasia, the condition persists more than 1 year after the stroke. These chronic language impairments are among the most devastating sequelae of stroke (Pedersen et al., 2004). Even though it is generally agreed that across aphasic groups no further spontaneous improvement of language function occurs, there are anecdotal reports of spontaneous improvements even many years after stroke (Smania et al., 2010). Moreover, it has been shown in a large number of studies that specific and deficit-oriented speech therapy at high intensity and frequency (i.e., several days/week with a total of at least 6 hours/week; see Bhogal, Teasell, & Speechley, 2003) can further improve language function in chronic aphasia (for a review see Kelly, Brady, & Enderby, 2010).

In this chapter, we review studies that investigated neural mechanisms associated with recovery of language impairments from the acute to the chronic stage and predictors of recovery with a specific focus on functional and structural imaging studies. In addition, we discuss treatment-induced reorganization in the chronic stage of aphasia and highlight more recent developments in noninvasive brain stimulation that have been used to enhance the recovery potential in poststroke aphasia.

Biological Markers of Aphasia Recovery

A growing interest has emerged to explore the recovery potential from aphasia by means of different functional and structural imaging techniques. Brain function can be assessed with neurophysiological techniques such as electroencephalography (EEG) and magnetoencephalography (MEG), or blood flow-based techniques such as functional magnetic resonance imaging (fMRI) and positron emission tomography (PET). These techniques allow the in vivo assessment of brain functions during rest or task performance in healthy or brain-damaged individuals. In addition, cross-sectional morphological differences between groups (e.g., individuals with aphasia and healthy individuals) or longitudinal changes in brain structure due to learning or rehabilitation can be delineated using advanced structural imaging techniques (e.g., diffusion tensor imaging, DTI; see Crosson et al., 2010, for a review of common techniques).

In the past decade, insight in the neural substrates of language processing in healthy individuals has increased dramatically. At the same time, this yielded a knowledge increase in rehabilitation neuroscience, in which researchers are interested in assessing changes in brain systems during spontaneous or treatment-induced recovery from neurological injury. A greater understanding of the underlying mechanisms and patterns of brain reorganization is a necessary prerequisite to improve prognosis and may eventually foster the development of more effective and individually tailored treatments.

Predicting Aphasia Recovery

A large number of studies have aimed to determine predictors of aphasia recovery using patient and stroke-related variables (Plowman, Hentz, & Ellis, 2011). So far, there is little evidence that a single patient-related factor (e.g., age, gender, handedness, premorbid educational level, and intelligence) has predictive value for linguistic recovery in individuals with aphasia (for reviews see Lazar & Antoniello, 2008; Plowman et al., 2011). With regard to stroke-related factors, a number of potentially important variables have been identified. For example, it has been demonstrated that overall severity at baseline in individuals with mild-to-moderate aphasia predicted the degree of linguistic improvement at 3 months poststroke (Lazar, 2010; Lazar et al., 2010). Moreover, this relation was proportional in nature, that is, dependent on the maximal remaining recovery potential. As similar findings had been reported for poststroke motor recovery (Prabhakaran et al., 2008), this may point to a common mechanism underlying recovery of motor and language function early after stroke. In addition to the initial impairment level, lesion site and size have been shown to influence the potential for functional recovery. For example, Naeser, Palumbo, Helm-Estabrooks, Stiassny-Eder, and Albert (1989) demonstrated that lesions to certain white matter tracts (subcallosal fasciculus; middle part of the periventricular white matter) are associated with persistent nonfluent aphasia. However, the predictive value of lesion location and extent is still controversial, due to the large variability of aphasia recovery in individuals with similar lesion patterns (Lazar et al., 2010).

Other stroke-related factors, such as the classic aphasia subtypes described in other chapters, appear to have limited predictive value for recovery on an individual basis (Code, 2001). Moreover, disruption in the neural networks underlying the multiple cognitive processing steps involved in language tasks can give rise to different aphasia syndromes and the location and extent of lesions do not usually correspond to the size and shape of distinct functional areas. Therefore, lesions often overlap with different functional areas and functional deficits may comprise a number of cognitive, linguistic, and motor deficits. To tackle the problem of interindividual variability, Price, Seghier, and Leff (2010) established a database that currently is composed of anatomical images of >300 stroke patients as well as results of standardized language scores assessed longitudinally during recovery. This database allows predictions about language outcomes for new stroke patients by comparing their lesions to those of other individuals with aphasia with known outcomes in the database. With the continued implementation and growth of such databases, the predictions for aphasia recovery may improve in the near future.

In addition to structural imaging, there have been attempts to characterize the recovery potential of individuals with stroke based on early functional imaging activity patterns acquired during language tasks. Saur et al. (2010) investigated the predictive value of early functional MRI patterns to language recovery at 6 months poststroke in 21 individuals with aphasia. The participants were scanned with fMRI during an auditory comprehension task 2 weeks poststroke and a computer-based "supervised, multivariate classification method (SVM)" was used to determine if early poststroke fMRI activation patterns predicted good versus bad language outcome based on functional activity patterns and (known) language outcome in a different aphasia sample. Functional activity 2 weeks after stroke in combination with age and language scores predicted language recovery with 86% accuracy. If confirmed in subsequent studies, such algorithms may allow assigning individuals with a predicted unfavorable aphasia outcome to more intensive and specific treatment programs early after stroke.

Neural Mechanisms Associated with Functional Recovery from Aphasia

Recovery from poststroke aphasia occurs in three overlapping phases that rely on partially overlapping but also distinct neural mechanisms (Marsh & Hillis, 2006). Immediately after stroke, loss of oxygen results in an inflammatory reaction causing local tissue destruction that is nonreversible ("core infarct"). This core is surrounded by a structurally intact ischemic penumbra in which blood flow and neural functioning are compromised and eventually progresses to infarction through a biochemical chain reaction (Shisler, Baylis, & Frank, 2000).

Restoration of function in the penumbra by restoring blood flow is the main underlying mechanism for rapid recovery of language function immediately after stroke (Hillis & Heidler, 2002), which may be possible until several hours and even days after the initial insult (Shisler et al., 2000). Reperfusion and its impact on language functions can be investigated using perfusion-weighted imaging (PWI). PWI measures blood flow in brain tissue to obtain information about tissue viability and can be used to detect abnormal functioning of brain

areas that may appear normal on structural MRI or DTI scans (Crosson et al., 2010). Several studies have shown that individuals with reperfusion of language task-critical areas recover certain functions, whereas those who do not show reperfusion continue to exhibit symptoms (Hillis & Heidler, 2002). Moreover, interventions that restore reperfusion can result in immediate symptom resolution (Hillis et al., 2001).

However, as mentioned above, reperfusion of the penumbra is possible only in the acute stroke phase. Thus, different mechanisms must come into play in the subacute (even after the first few days poststroke) and chronic stage, as recovery continues. The main mechanisms responsible for functional recovery in the days and even months following the injury are regression from diaschisis and plastic reorganization within the language system (Marsh & Hillis, 2006). Diaschisis refers to hypometabolism and impaired information processing in structurally intact remote brain areas due to deafferentation and loss of input from the functionally connected lesioned area. Functional imaging studies of brain metabolism or perfusion have provided support for the notion that aphasia recovery may be mediated by regression from diaschisis in both cerebral hemispheres (for a review see Cappa, 2000; Pizzamiglio, Galati, & Committeri, 2001). For example, individuals with subcortical lesions may show hypoperfusion in remote cortical language areas initially after stroke, and in some studies aphasia recovery is correlated with reperfusion of these areas (Baron et al., 1986; Vallar et al., 1988). Similar results also have been reported for individuals with cortical lesions. Cappa et al. (1997) demonstrated that acute hypometabolism in structurally unaffected areas in both hemispheres returned to more normal levels after 6 months poststroke and this increase in metabolism was associated with improved language functions.

Plastic brain reorganization describes the lifelong adaptive structural and functional changes in response to experience, environmental input, or demands and is expressed at the synaptic (e.g., increased synaptic efficiency) and cortical network level ("cortical remapping"; Buonomano & Merzenich, 1998). There is ample evidence that spontaneous and treatment-induced brain reorganization plays a major role in stroke recovery. For instance, in their seminal study, Nudo, Wise, SiFuentes, and Milliken (1996) demonstrated that retraining of affected limb function after experimentally induced stroke in squirrel monkeys resulted in plastic reorganization at the cortical level. In particular, perilesional areas that were not involved in limb control prior to stroke participated in those movements after training. Similarly, functional imaging in humans provided evidence for plastic reorganization after successful motor training in persons following stroke (Liepert et al., 1998, 2000). The potential underlying neural mechanisms of this reorganization after stroke involve strengthening of the remaining connections within damaged cell assemblies, unmasking of silent pathways, and axonal sprouting to bridge disrupted connections (Taub, Uswatte, & Elbert, 2002). These mechanisms are also responsible for language recovery in the subacute and chronic stages after stroke. New functional and structural connections are established gradually over weeks, months, and even years after stroke. In particular, even in the chronic stage, individuals with aphasia may still be able to improve their language skills in the context of intensive and symptom-specific intervention programs (Kelly et al., 2010) and a number of studies have provided evidence for functional reorganization even in this late recovery stage (Meinzer, Harnish, Conway, & Crosson, 2011). However, although the potential for reorganization at the neural level may be exhausted at some point in time, further improvements of language may be possible by behavioral strategies, for example, by teaching different ways to perform the same function using intact skills (Marsh & Hillis, 2006).

In summary, immediate recovery of language function after stroke is mediated by reperfusion of structurally intact regions adjacent to the core infarct zone. Later on, regression from diaschisis and functional reorganization of the language network contribute to recovery. To elucidate patterns of functional reorganization in aphasia during spontaneous or treatment-induced recovery, we will discuss in the following sections studies that used functional imaging techniques and activation paradigms during language tasks.

Functional Activation Studies of Aphasia Recovery from the Acute to the Chronic Stage

A large number of studies have used functional imaging to investigate activity patterns associated with language processing and reorganization in individuals with aphasia (Heiss & Thiel, 2006; Pizzamiglio et al., 2001). These studies determined brain activity patterns during different language tasks in aphasia participants with favorable

recovery (Cao, Vikingstad, George, Johnson, & Welch, 1999; Weiller et al., 1995), compared brain activity patterns of those with good versus poor language recovery (Crinion & Price, 2005; Fridriksson, Bonilha, Baker, Moser, & Rorden, 2010; Perani et al., 2003), or used single-session intervention paradigms (Blasi et al., 2002; Musso et al., 1999). In most studies, task-related activity was found in both hemispheres of individuals with aphasia during language processing, even during tasks that are strongly bound to the left hemisphere in healthy participants. In particular, previous studies that used language production or syntactic paradigms usually found that reactivation of perilesional areas in the left hemisphere may be associated with better recovery (Heiss & Thiel, 2006). Even though right hemisphere regions can support recovery if homologous areas assume the functions of lesioned areas in the left hemisphere (Leff et al., 2002; Thompson, den Ouden, Bonakdarpour, Garibaldi, & Parrish, 2010), sustained right hemisphere activity appears to be linked to a less favorable outcome in most cases (Cao et al., 1999; Winhuisen, 2007). Moreover, this enhanced activity may represent inefficient or dysfunctional processing (Meinzer et al., 2006; Postman-Caucheteux et al., 2010) or disinhibition (Martin, Naeser, Ho, Treglia, et al., 2009; Naeser, 2005) and it is possibly associated with a larger lesion size and less preserved language eloquent cortex in the left hemisphere (Heiss et al., 1997).

A slightly different picture emerged for language comprehension tasks, where effective takeover of function by the right hemisphere in individuals with chronic aphasia has been demonstrated, at least for relatively simple tasks such as single word comprehension (e.g., Crinion & Price, 2005; also see below the study by Warren, Crinion, Lambon Ralph, & Wise, 2009).

In addition, a study by Saur et al. (2006) demonstrated that recovery across the first year poststroke is a highly dynamic process and involves three stages. The authors used fMRI during language tasks and scanned individuals with aphasia immediately after stroke, and again in the subacute and chronic stages. In line with previous studies that showed widespread hypometabolism immediately after stroke (Marsh & Hillis, 2006), task-related activity was largely reduced in perilesional as well as in homologous brain areas in the right hemisphere. In the subacute stage, functional recovery was paralleled by enhanced activity in both hemispheres, and the most successful language recovery in the chronic stage was related to a normalization of activity in perilesional areas of the language-dominant hemisphere.

This general pattern was largely confirmed by a recent quantitative meta-analysis of functional imaging studies of aphasia recovery. In this study, Turkeltaub, Messing, Norise, and Hamilton (2011) used an objective quantification procedure (voxel-wise activation likelihood, ALE analysis) to identify common patterns of reorganization evident in functional imaging studies of aphasia recovery in the chronic stage (>6 months poststroke) and their relation to lesion patterns. Across different imaging techniques (fMRI, PET) and language paradigms, task-related activity involved spared areas in the left hemisphere and homologous areas in the right hemisphere as well as new left hemisphere areas not recruited by healthy participants. The results indicated that spared nodes in the left hemisphere retained their function and regions active in individuals with aphasia, but not in healthy participants, assumed compensatory functions (e.g., left insula, pars orbitalis of the left inferior frontal gyrus, IFG) or reflected increased reliance on executive control processes (left middle frontal gyrus). Moreover, it was suggested that patterns of reorganization systematically varied with lesion location. In line with previous studies that used repetitive transcranial magnetic stimulation (Naeser, 2005) to temporarily inhibit the function of different subportions of the right IFG, a compensatory role of the right pars opercularis for phonological processing was evident. In contrast, lesions affecting the left pars triangularis resulted in a dysfunctional up-regulation of the right homologous area, potentially related to a lack of interhemispheric inhibition.

In summary, take-over of functions by perilesional areas plays an important role in functional reorganization of language networks and recovery after stroke. However, when regions adjacent to lesions are not capable of supporting functions in this new network, homologous right hemisphere regions assume the functions. Take-over of functions by the right hemisphere may be constrained by its limited capability to process important aspects of language.

Elaborating Functional Activity Changes at the System Level

Circumscribed neurological injury, such as a stroke, not only results in local dysfunction at the lesion site, but also affects remote brain regions. Different parts of a dysfunctional network contribute to behavioral impairments and neural

adaptations in the course of recovery may occur at different nodes of the network. More recent developments in functional imaging data analysis make it possible to investigate how different brain regions interact with each other during task performance and at rest. These so-called functional network approaches have the potential to allow cortical reorganization to be investigated in a more realistic way, as patterns of functional linkage between different areas (vs. activity in isolated brain areas) can be studied (see Price, Crinion, & Friston, 2006, and Margulies et al., 2010, for reviews of common techniques). For example, using a functional connectivity approach, Carter et al. (2010) showed that disruption of complex dorsal attention versus arm-related somatosensory networks in stroke patients predicted visual detection performance or upper extremity impairment, respectively.

A recent study in the language domain (Warren et al., 2009) assessed functional connectivity of the left anterior superior temporal lobe (STL) in individuals with chronic stroke and aphasia. STL is critically involved in speech processing so that, in a first step, the authors determined connectivity of this region in a group of healthy subjects. This analysis demonstrated strong interactions of the left STL with its homologous areas in the right hemisphere as well as left inferior frontal and basal temporal areas. In individuals with aphasia, connectivity of the right and left anterior superior temporal lobe was generally impaired, which correlated with the degree of behavioral impairment during a narrative sentence comprehension task. Moreover, in those individuals who exhibited intact functional connectivity of the right and left temporal areas, more pronounced activity in the functionally connected left inferior frontal lobe was found as compared to the control group. This area has been implicated in top-down modulation of language comprehension in previous studies (Thompson-Schill, D'Esposito, Aguirre, & Farah, 1997). In summary, this study highlighted the important interplay of remote but tightly interconnected brain areas in normal language comprehension and allowed unprecedented insights in the neural systems supporting language recovery after stroke.

Imaging Treatment Success in Chronic Aphasia

Neuronal correlates of treatment outcome in the chronic stage of aphasia are of particular interest because changes in imaging parameters during interventions can be attributed to the treatment itself in this otherwise stable condition. However, few studies have examined which brain regions mediate successful language recovery as a result of intense training in chronic aphasia. The majority of these studies involved case reports (N = 1–3 patients), which preclude generalization of the results (for a review of those studies see Meinzer & Breitenstein, 2008). Only recently, several group studies have been accomplished showing that treatment-induced improvements may be associated with specific neural signatures (Fridriksson, 2010; Meinzer, 2008; Meinzer et al., 2008; Raboyeau et al., 2008; Richter, Miltner, & Straube, 2008). Three distinct patterns have been identified that were associated with different degrees of behavioral improvement. Moreover, similar to the dynamic activity patterns described by Saur et al. (2006) across the first year poststroke, two studies have shown that short-term outcomes and the long-term consolidation of treatment effects may be associated with different types of activity patterns (Breier et al., 2009; Menke et al., 2009). We will describe these findings in more detail below.

Two fMRI studies suggested that increased activity in perilesional areas in the left hemisphere may be a good candidate for successful short-term intervention success. Fridriksson (2010) investigated 26 individuals with different degrees of anomia who received 2 weeks of phonemic and semantic cueing treatment. The individuals underwent pretraining/posttraining fMRI scanning using a picture naming task. A regression analysis showed that superior treatment outcome was correlated with increased activity in perilesional regions in the affected left hemisphere after training. Similarly, Meinzer et al. (2008) conducted repeated fMRI scans (overt picture naming task) and compared activity patterns before and after 2 weeks of Constraint-Induced Language Therapy (CILT) (Meinzer, Rodriguez, & Rothi, 2012). A regions-of-interest (ROI) analysis focused on individually determined brain regions exhibiting excessive slow-wave activity that were identified by MEG before the training had commenced. Excessive slow wave activity is a marker of dysfunctional information processing and is typically found in perilesional areas. A previous study of the same workgroup found that training-induced changes in slow wave activity after intensive language therapy were correlated with improved language functions (Meinzer, Elbert, Djundja, Barthel, & Rockstroh, 2004). In a more recent study, increased activity in perilesional areas, which exhibited excessive slow-wave activity

before training, was positively correlated with performance gains after therapy (Meinzer et al., 2008). Thus, both studies found that perilesional left-hemispheric recruitment is still possible in the late chronic stage of aphasia recovery and that successful reactivation of these areas may be associated with more pronounced improvement.

A different outcome parameter was used in two other studies (Raboyeau et al., 2008; Richter et al., 2008). Raboyeau et al. (2008) provided 10 individuals chronically suffering from word-retrieval difficulties (anomia) with daily lexical training (15 minutes/day) over the course of 4 weeks. Overt naming-related brain activity patterns of the participants were assessed using PET prior to and after the intervention. A correlation analysis was carried out in predefined ROIs in order to relate behavioral improvements to changes in brain activity. Naming performance in the participants with aphasia improved following training and the improvement correlated with increased activity in motor and attention-related areas in the right hemisphere (dorsolateral prefrontal cortex, supplementary motor area, insula, cingulate gyrus). In the second study, Richter et al. (2008) investigated language improvement in 16 individuals with chronic aphasia prior to and after CILT using a composite score that was composed of spontaneous speech and Token Test subscales of the Aachen Aphasia Test Battery (AAT) (Huber, Poeck, Weniger, & Willmes, 1983), and the auditory and semantic comprehensibility of speech subtests of the Amsterdam-Nijmegen Everyday Language Test (ANELT) (Blomert, Kean, Koster, & Schokker, 1994). In the Richter et al. (2008) study, improved performance was correlated with decreased activity assessed with two language tasks (word-reading; word-stem completion) in the frontotemporal areas of the right hemisphere (inferior frontal gyrus, insula, precentral gyrus, and middle temporal gyrus).

In summary, in line with previous longitudinal studies that assessed language-associated activity patterns across the first year poststroke (Heiss & Thiel, 2006), two of the above studies showed that perilesional areas in the left hemisphere mediated short-term treatment gains. Two other studies, however, implicated increased or decreased activity in the contralesional right hemisphere with treatment outcome. Some of these contradicting results are most likely explained by participant selection and design-related factors. For example, Raboyeau et al. (2008) and Richter et al. (2008) restricted their analyses to ROIs in the right hemisphere. Treatment gains were relatively moderate in both studies. Because right hemisphere involvement poststroke has been associated with a less favorable outcome in a number of longitudinal studies, increased activity in the right hemisphere (Raboyeau et al., 2008) and decreased activity in the right hemisphere (in the absence of increased left hemisphere recruitment; Richter et al., 2008) may be indicators of suboptimal task processing (Belin et al., 1996). Moreover, in one of these studies (Richter et al., 2008) the interpretation of the results is complicated by the unknown functional relationship between the fMRI tasks, which were unrelated to the treatment, and the lack of direct language performance measures due to the covert nature of the paradigm. In the future, more sufficiently sized group studies using appropriate fMRI designs to evaluate the impact of treatment on neural processing are needed in chronic aphasia.

Neural Correlates of Short-Term and Long-Term Language Therapy Outcome

Until recently, functional imaging group studies assessed only immediate treatment gains and associated activity changes (Meinzer & Breitenstein, 2008). However, studies that assessed activity patterns across the first year poststroke revealed a highly dynamic pattern associated with different stages of recovery (Saur et al., 2006). Similar findings were reported in two studies on short-term and long-term neural consequences of intensive treatment in chronic aphasia (Breier et al., 2009; Menke et al., 2009).

In the study by Menke et al. (2009), naming performance was assessed during fMRI using a picture-naming task immediately prior to and 2 weeks after intensive anomia training as well as 8 months after the training. Naming improvement was highly significant immediately after training (on average 65% above baseline) and those gains were retained in the follow-up after 8 months. Immediately after the intervention, a whole brain regression analysis revealed that task-related activity in brain areas associated with memory, attentional processes, and multimodal integration (e.g., bilateral hippocampal formation and fusiform gyrus, right precuneus, cingulate gyrus) were correlated with recovery: the greater the therapeutic gains, the higher the activity. Retention of the treatment gains during the follow-up scan, however, was correlated with increased activity in posterior parietotemporal areas of the right hemisphere and left temporal areas implicated in semantic processing. Thus, specific brain areas might be associated with an immediate treatment

response, whereas different areas are implicated in the consolidation of treatment gains over time.

Breier et al. (2009) used MEG to assess short-term and long-term language network plasticity in response to treatment. In this study, 23 individuals with moderate to severe chronic aphasia received CILT. Participants were assessed at three time points (prior to and after CILT and 3 months after the end of the treatment) using a word recognition task. Based on the immediate treatment response, the authors identified three groups for the MEG data analysis: (1) individuals who showed a positive treatment response and maintained these gains at the follow-up assessment, (2) individuals who improved after treatment but did not maintain these gains 3 months later, and (3) nonresponders. The first group exhibited a consistent increase in task-related activity in the left temporal areas at both posttreatment assessments, whereas nonresponders showed the opposite trend (i.e., reduced left temporal activity). In contrast, the small group of participants that benefited initially but did not maintain the gains had the most pronounced activity in the *right* temporal areas, a pattern that was sustained across both posttreatment scanning sessions. Thus, in line with the above mentioned fMRI study by Menke et al. (2009), this study by Breier et al. (2009) showed that specific patterns of task-related activity may be associated with different types of either short-term or long-term treatment outcomes. Moreover, the study is in line with previous functional imaging studies of spontaneous (Saur et al., 2006) or treatment-induced recovery (Fridriksson, 2010) showing that increased (perilesional) left hemisphere activity might be related to more pronounced and stable improvements.

In summary, the first few studies on neural correlates of aphasia treatment in the chronic stage confirm the importance of reintegration of perilesional areas in the left hemisphere for a favorable treatment outcome. In addition, sustained right hemisphere activity may contribute to treatment success in individuals with larger lesions and sustained severe aphasia.

Rehabilitation of Sentence Level Processing

Most studies that assessed the impact of treatment on functional activity patterns used word-retrieval paradigms (category generation, picture naming), which might be related to the fact that anomia is the most frequent symptom in chronic aphasia. On the other hand, residual syntactic impairments are also common in chronic aphasia but have rarely been assessed using functional imaging techniques in intervention studies (Meinzer & Breitenstein, 2008). One of the few functional imaging studies on treatment-induced recovery of syntax processing has been conducted by Thompson et al. (2010). The authors investigated six individuals with chronic aphasia who were treated with a linguistically based approach to improve sentence processing. They used fMRI during an auditory sentence verification task before and after treatment to assess treatment-induced activity changes in preselected ROIs in language-related regions in both hemispheres. In addition, arterial spin labeling (ASL; a noninvasive perfusion imaging technique that does not require an exogenous tracer) was performed to assess potential hypoperfusion and changes consequent upon treatment. Prior to treatment, a delayed hemodynamic response (task-specific fMRI) was associated with reduced perfusion (ASL) mainly in perilesional areas. More pronounced treatment gains were associated with a shift of activity from the left superior temporal regions toward bilateral posterior temporoparietal areas, which were also active in a healthy control group during the same task. Areas with changed fMRI activity after treatment evidenced higher perfusion levels and more normal time-to-peak (TTP) values (i.e., reduced latency). Thus, improved performance was associated with a normalization of activity (changed functional activity, reduced TTP, and increased perfusion) in brain areas activated during the same task in healthy controls. Similar to previous studies on anomia rehabilitation, reactivation of networks active during the same task in healthy participants predicted a favorable treatment outcome.

Functional Network Reorganization in Response to Therapy

Measures of connectivity have been shown to add important information about functional reorganization of the language network in cross-sectional studies of aphasia recovery (Warren et al., 2009) and may also have great value in aphasia treatment research. Two studies have demonstrated the feasibility of such a dynamic network approach in aphasia treatment research using different types of connectivity analyses (Abutalebi, Rosa, Tettamanti, Green, & Cappa, 2009; Vitali et al., 2010).

Abutalebi et al. (2009) assessed fMRI patterns of interregional connectivity in a formerly bilingual patient (L1: Spanish/L2: Italian) with anomia using an overt picture naming task before and after 6 weeks of daily phonological treatment in his second language. Follow-up assessments were conducted 4 months after the end of the treatment. Connectivity changes were assessed using dynamic causal modeling, a functional connectivity measure that requires a priori assumptions about the underlying effects of interest (Price et al., 2006). The authors focused on left hemisphere language areas [inferior temporal gyrus, Brodmann area (BA)19/37, and inferior frontal gyrus, BA 45/47] and areas associated with language control in bilinguals (head of the caudate nucleus, anterior cingulate gyrus). Behaviorally, the participants' previously less proficient second language that was targeted during treatment improved substantially at both post-assessments, which was mirrored by increased coupling of parts of the "naming network." In addition, parts of the control network became less connected over time at the post-assessments. This study demonstrated that complex network changes may constitute the underlying neural basis of intensive treatment.

In a second study, Vitali et al. (2010) addressed connectivity changes due to intensive phonological treatment in two individuals with chronic aphasia. Even though both individuals improved during the training, interindividually different patterns of network reorganization were observed. One participant with prefrontal cortex damage and additional white matter injury in posterior brain regions showed enhanced connectivity in the bilateral IFG and inferior parietal lobe (IPL) and left middle temporal gyrus (MTG). The second individual presented with a larger lesion that affected the left IFG and MTG and exhibited increased connectivity between the spared left IPL and right sided MTG and insula and other parts of the right hemisphere network. This study suggests that different types of functionally relevant connectivity changes may be associated with improved language function after treatment and that these changes seem to depend on the extent and location of the lesion. More recently, Marcotte, Perlbarg, Marrelec, Benali, and Ansaldo (2013) provided evidence from task-absent ("resting-state") fMRI that treatment may enhance integration of posterior aspects of the so-called default network, that is, areas not traditionally associated with language processing.

Together, these studies provide valuable information about complex patterns of interregional activity changes in response to treatment complementing previous studies that addressed local cortical functioning. The challenge for future studies will be to develop designs that allow researchers to address questions about favorable patterns of network reorganization, interactions with lesion patterns, and the impact of different treatments at the group level.

Treatment-Induced Structural Brain Plasticity

A recent study addressed structural plasticity in order to investigate the effects of aphasia treatment (Schlaug, Marchina, & Norton, 2009). The authors used DTI to assess the microstructural status of white matter (i.e., fiber tracts), which provides a measure of structural connectivity of different brain areas. As all participants had extensive lesions in the left hemisphere, the authors chose a treatment approach that is thought to facilitate right hemisphere compensatory mechanisms (Melodic Intonation Therapy). They assessed potential changes in the right arcuate fasciculus (AF), a fiber bundle connecting the anterior and posterior regions potentially involved in language recovery. Across the group, the "number of fibers" (i.e., a measure of structural connectivity between dedicated ROIs) in the AF increased significantly after treatment, which tended to correlate with the degree of language improvement. Specificity of this finding was assessed by a control ROI (i.e., the corticospinal tract) where no differences between assessment points were found. In addition, repeated baseline DTI scans were obtained for some participants prior to treatment and no changes in the AF were found as well. Thus, their findings point to a specific treatment-induced plasticity of white matter structures that may subserve compensatory functions of the right hemisphere.

Predicting Treatment Outcome in Chronic Aphasia

Previous studies pointed toward the importance of the hippocampal (memory) system in language learning in healthy subjects (Breitenstein et al., 2005) as well as language and motor recovery in stroke patients (Gauthier, 2008; Goldenberg & Spatt, 1994). Based on these findings, Meinzer et al. (2010) addressed the specific role of the hippocampus in language relearning in chronic aphasia after stroke due to middle cerebral artery (MCA) occlusion. The rationale for this study was that proximal occlusion of the MCA relative to the internal carotid artery may affect the integrity of the hippocampus or its surrounding white matter, which may impair explicit language relearning in individuals with aphasia (Goldenberg & Spatt, 1994). Proximity

was determined based on the lesion pattern in 10 individuals with chronic anomia. The integrity of the hippocampus was assessed using MR-based volumetry and the microstructural integrity of the surrounding white matter by fractional anisotropy derived from DTI. The authors found that more proximal infarcts, damage of the hippocampus in the left hemisphere, and impaired integrity of the white matter surrounding the left hippocampus predicted less favorable treatment gains immediately after 2 weeks of anomia training and 8 months after the end of the treatment. Thus, damage to brain areas involved in learning in healthy subjects may be important for explicit language relearning in aphasia.

Adjunct Treatment Approaches to Enhance Responsiveness to Treatment

As mentioned in the introduction, even short periods of intensive language therapy (i.e., several hours of daily treatment for 2–3 weeks) can significantly improve language functions, with excellent long-term stability of therapeutic outcome (Kelly et al., 2010). However, despite its general effectiveness, effect sizes are only low to moderate and highly variable even within the same study (Beeson & Robey, 2006). More recently, researchers have begun to explore new directions to enhance treatment efficacy using different types of noninvasive brain stimulation techniques such as transcranial direct current stimulation (tDCS) or repetitive transcranial magnetic stimulation (rTMS). Both techniques allow modifying cortical excitability with the goal of enhancing learning during therapy (Schlaug, Marchina, & Wan, 2011).

Transcranial Direct Current Stimulation

Noninvasive tDCS modulates brain activity by applying weak electrical currents to the scalp (typically 1–2 mA). Depending on the current polarity, the excitability of underlying brain areas is increased (anodal tDCS, atDCS) or decreased (cathodal tDCS) by modulating resting membrane potentials (Stagg & Nitsche, 2011). Beneficial effects on motor and cognitive performance in healthy subjects have mainly been reported for excitatory atDCS. In particular, a number of previous behavioral studies in healthy participants showed beneficial effects of atDCS on language processing, including word retrieval and grammar and vocabulary learning (Cattaneo, Pisoni, & Papagno, 2011; de Vries et al., 2010; Flöel, Rösser, Michka, Knecht, & Breitenstein, 2008; Meinzer et al., 2012; Meinzer, Lindenberg, Antonenko, Flaisch, & Flöel, 2013).

Moreover, these effects have convincingly been shown to be independent of unspecific (e.g., attentional) effects and participants can be blinded to the stimulation by comparison with a placebo ("sham") stimulation (Gandiga, Hummel, & Cohen, 2006). Safety for individuals following stroke has been established, and due to the portability of the stimulation device it can be applied during therapy to exploit its effect on cortical excitability and plasticity (Schlaug et al., 2011).

Several studies have used atDCS in combination with behavioral treatment and demonstrated additional beneficial effects on language relearning in individuals with aphasia compared to treatment alone. For example, based on previous fMRI studies showing increased perilesional activity in participants with aphasia who were responsive to treatment, two studies applied atDCS to perilesional brain areas in the left hemisphere (Baker, Rorden, & Fridriksson, 2010; Fridriksson, Richardson, Baker, & Rorden, 2011). In both studies, the stimulation site was individually determined based on a pretreatment fMRI scan. In the first study, Baker et al. (2010) demonstrated enhanced picture naming performance in individuals with nonfluent mild-to-moderate aphasia after 5 days of computerized anomia treatment with concomitant anodal tDCS compared to behavioral training alone. Similar results were found in individuals with fluent aphasia in which the combination of atDCS and treatment yielded reduced naming latency compared to treatment combined with sham stimulation (Fridriksson, 2011).

In both of the above studies, however, most participants were relatively well recovered and the results may not be easily translated to those with extensive left hemispheric lesions, little spared language eloquent cortex, and persistent moderate-to-severe language impairment. Indeed, the exact areas that contribute to language relearning are still controversial and it remains unclear which brain areas should be facilitated or inhibited. As mentioned above, although good recovery in longitudinal studies is usually associated with increased activity in left perilesional areas (Heiss & Thiel, 2006), interventional studies that included participants with larger lesions have shown that up-regulation of right hemisphere brain regions may also contribute to recovery (Crosson et al., 2005). In addition, another study implicated right temporoparietal areas with the long-term retention of anomia treatment success (Menke et al., 2009). In a crossover design, Flöel et al. (2011) explored whether atDCS

stimulation of the same temporoparietal areas can enhance the outcome of high-frequency short-term anomia training compared to inhibitory (cathodal) tDCS and sham stimulation. This study showed significantly more pronounced treatment gains after atDCS compared to sham stimulation, while the effects of cathodal tDCS were not different from sham stimulation.

In summary, the first few studies that used atDCS in combination with treatment showed promising additional gains when compared to treatment alone. However, future studies are necessary to determine the relevant parameters that affect treatment responsiveness (e.g., lesion size and site, aphasia severity, duration and frequency of stimulation) to maximize the benefits for individuals with aphasia.

Transcranial Magnetic Stimulation

Repetitive TMS is a brain stimulation technique during which a fluctuating magnetic field induces an electrical current in cortical regions. The magnetic field is produced by an electrical current discharged through a coil held to the scalp over a target brain region. The magnetic field penetrates the scalp and induces a depolarizing electrical current in the underlying cortical surface. Trains of stimulations can either decrease (low-frequency TMS) or increase (high-frequency TMS) the excitability of the underlying cortex (Pascual-Leone, Walsh, & Rothwell, 2000). Several previous studies in healthy subjects have shown that low-frequency rTMS to the left inferior frontal gyrus can interfere with language tasks (e.g., Thiel et al., 2005).

Most studies that applied rTMS in aphasia rehabilitation used low-frequency rTMS (1 Hz) to reduce the excitability of the right frontal brain regions, as functional imaging studies suggested that overactivation of the right frontal cortices may interfere with functioning of the (perilesional) left frontal areas (Belin et al., 1996). For example, Naeser (2005) and Barwood et al. (2011a) administered low-frequency rTMS across several consecutive days to the anterior portion of "Broca's area" (pars triangularis) and found beneficial effects on naming performance in chronic nonfluent aphasia that was sustained up to 8 months after treatment. Additional evidence that suppression of the right frontal brain regions may yield positive results has been provided by Martin, Naeser, Ho, Doron, et al. (2009). In this study, the authors assessed language network changes with fMRI prior to and after an rTMS intervention suggesting that restoration of left hemisphere activity may underlie the beneficial effects of individuals undergoing right frontal rTMS. Another study used a word–picture verification task and EEG to investigate the impact of rTMS treatment on the N400 event-related EEG component (Barwood et al., 2011b), in which N400 has been implicated with semantic access. After rTMS (vs. sham stimulation), more pronounced treatment effects were mirrored by higher N400 amplitudes 2 months posttreatment and interpreted as long-term neural consequences of improved semantic integration.

So far, most studies in aphasia rehabilitation have assessed only the impact of rTMS as a sole treatment. Only recently, rTMS interventions have been combined with behavioral treatment to assess the potentially mutual benefits on training outcome. In a dual-case crossover design, Naeser et al. (2010) investigated the effects of slow-frequency rTMS over right frontal areas and 2 weeks of CILT and compared the results with the effects of rTMS alone. In both participants, the combination of the two treatments produced more pronounced improvement of language functions than rTMS alone, which warrants future controlled clinical trials in larger patient samples.

Conclusions

In summary, as a result of the invention of functional imaging techniques and refinements in data acquisition and analysis, our knowledge about functional and structural language network reorganization associated with aphasia recovery increased dramatically in the past two decades. A large number of studies have used functional activation paradigms and assessed patterns of activity across the first year(s) after stroke and also in the context of intervention paradigms in the chronic stage. These studies highlight the importance of perilesional areas for successful recovery. However, as summarized above, the right hemisphere may also contribute to recovery of certain language functions. In summary, patterns of reorganization clearly depend on a complex interaction of stroke and participant-related factors and also on the specific language function that is studied. Studies in larger groups and even well-designed case series will continue to provide important information about recovery and brain reorganization. However, because of the complex interactions of the above mentioned factors in recovery, an emphasis should be placed

on establishing larger databases and the sharing of functional and structural datasets in combination with behavioral performance data. Moreover, meta-analytic techniques based on numerous datasets that are now readily available may be a valuable tool to elucidate common patterns of recovery. These two avenues of research may result in more general and comprehensive insights into the potential for aphasia recovery after stroke and will hopefully provide researchers and clinicians with important information to improve the prognosis for individuals with aphasia and allow for more specific and effective treatment decisions.

Additional insight into how the injured brain remodels itself to cope with structural damage may be gained by different types of functional connectivity analysis that have been shown to be a promising and powerful tool for understanding brain functions at the network level in groups of healthy participants. However, this has yet to be accomplished in larger groups of individuals with aphasia. Unraveling patterns of network reorganization in a more realistic (systemic) way across different stages of recovery or consequent upon treatment may represent one of the greatest endeavors of aphasia recovery research. In addition, new brain stimulation techniques may be suited to enhance the recovery potential in aphasia and treatment responsiveness. However, given the fact that only a few individuals with aphasia have been treated so far, future studies need to determine which areas should be targeted for facilitation (or inhibition) in individuals before they can become a standard tool in clinical environments.

Acknowledgments

This work was supported by the Bundesministerium für Bildung und Forschung (MM: 01EO0801), the Australian Research Council (M.M.: ARC FT120100608), the Else-Kröner Fresenius Stiftung (R.L.: 2011-119), and the Deutsche Forschungsgemeinschaft (U.L.: 423/1-1).

References

Abutalebi, J., Rosa, P. A., Tettamanti, M., Green, D. W., & Cappa, S. F. (2009). Bilingual aphasia and language control: A follow-up fMRI and intrinsic connectivity study. *Brain and Language*, 109(2–3), 141–156.

Baker, J. M., Rorden, C., & Fridriksson, J. (2010). Using transcranial direct-current stimulation to treat stroke patients with aphasia. *Stroke*, 41(6), 1229–1236.

Bakheit, A. M. (2007). A prospective, randomized, parallel group, controlled study of the effect of intensity of speech and language therapy on early recovery from poststroke aphasia. *Clinical Rehabilitation*, 21, 885–894.

Baron, J. C., D'Antona, R., Pantano, P., Serdaru, M., Samson, Y., & Bousser, M. G. (1986). Effects of thalamic stroke on energy metabolism of the cerebral cortex. A positron tomography study in man. *Brain*, 10(Pt 6), 1243–1259.

Barwood, C. H., Murdoch, B. E., Whelan, B. M., Lloyd, D., Riek, S., O'Sullivan, J. D., ... Wong, A. (2011a). Improved language performance subsequent to low-frequency rTMS in patients with chronic non-fluent aphasia post-stroke. *European Journal of Neurology*, 18(7), 935–943.

Barwood, C. H., Murdoch, B. E., Whelan, B. M., Lloyd, D., Riek, S., O'Sullivan, J. D., ... Wong, A. (2011b). Modulation of N400 in chronic non-fluent aphasia using low frequency repetitive transcranial magnetic stimulation (rTMS). *Brain and Language*, 116(3), 125–135.

Beeson, P. M., & Robey, R. R. (2006). Evaluating single-subject treatment research: Lessons learned from the aphasia literature. *Neuropsychology Review*, 16(4), 161–169.

Belin, P., Van Eeckhout, P., Zilbovicius, M., Remy, P., Francois, C., Guillaume, S., ... Samson, Y. (1996). Recovery from nonfluent aphasia after melodic intonation therapy: A PET study. *Neurology*, 47(6), 1504–1511.

Bhogal, S. K., Teasell, R., & Speechley, M. (2003). Intensity of aphasia therapy: Impact on recovery. *Stroke*, 34, 987–993.

Blasi, V., Young, A. C., Tansy, A. P., Petersen, S. E., Snyder, A. Z., & Corbetta, M. (2002). Word retrieval learning modulates right frontal cortex in patients with left frontal damage. *Neuron*, 36(1), 159–170.

Blomert, L., Kean, M. L., Koster, C., & Schokker, J. (1994). Amsterdam-Nijmegen everyday language test. *Aphasiology*, 8, 381–407.

Breier, J. I., Juranek, J., Maher, L. M., Schmadeke, S., Men, D., & Papanicolaou, A. C. (2009). Behavioral and neurophysiologic response to therapy for chronic aphasia. *Archives of Physical Medicine and Rehabilitation*, 90(12), 2026–2033.

Breitenstein, C., Jansen, A., Deppe, M., Foerster, A. F., Sommer, J., Wolbers, T., & Knecht, S. (2005). Hippocampus activity differentiates good from poor learners of a novel lexicon. *Neuroimage*, 25(3), 958–968.

Buonomano, D. V., & Merzenich, M. M. (1998). Cortical plasticity: From synapses to maps. *Annual Reviews of Neuroscience*, 21, 149–186.

Cao, Y., Vikingstad, E. M., George, K. P., Johnson, A. F., & Welch, K. M. (1999). Cortical language activation in stroke patients recovering from aphasia with functional MRI. *Stroke*, 30(11), 2331–2340.

Cappa, S. F. (2000). Recovery from aphasia: Why and how? *Brain and Language*, 71(1), 39–41.

Cappa, S. F., Perani, D., Grassi, F., Bressi, S., Alberoni, M., Franceschi, M., ... Fazio, F. (1997). A PET follow-up study of recovery after stroke in acute aphasics. *Brain and Language*, 56(1), 55–67.

Carter, A. R., Astafiev, S. V., Lang, C. E., Connor, L. T., Rengachary, J., Strube, M. J., ... Corbetta, M. (2010). Resting interhemispheric functional magnetic resonance imaging connectivity predicts performance after stroke. *Annals of Neurology*, 67(3), 365–375.

Cattaneo, Z., Pisoni, A., & Papagno, C. (2011). Transcranial direct current stimulation over Broca's region improves phonemic and semantic fluency in healthy individuals. *Neuroscience*, 183, 64–70.

Code, C. (2001). Multifactorial processes in recovery from aphasia: Developing the foundations for a multileveled framework. *Brain and Language*, 77(1), 25–44.

Cramer, S. C. (2008). Repairing the human brain after stroke. II. Restorative therapies. *Annals of Neurology*, 63(5), 549–560.

Crinion, J., & Price, C. J. (2005). Right anterior superior temporal activation predicts auditory sentence comprehension following aphasic stroke. *Brain*, 128(Pt 12), 2858–2871.

Crosson, B., Ford, A., McGregor, K. M., Meinzer, M., Cheshkov, S., Li, X., ... Briggs, R. W. (2010). Functional imaging and related techniques: An introduction for rehabilitation researchers. *Journal of Rehabilitation Research & Development*, 47(2), vii–xxxiv.

Crosson, B., Moore, A. B., Gopinath, K., White, K. D., Wierenga, C. E., Gaiefsky, M. E., ... Rothi, L. J. G. (2005). Role of the right and left hemispheres in recovery of function during treatment of intention in aphasia. *Journal of Cognitive Neuroscience*, 17(3), 392–406.

de Vries, M. H., Barth, A. C., Maiworm, S., Knecht, S., Zwitserlood, P., & Flöel, A. (2010). Electrical stimulation of Broca's area enhances implicit learning of an artificial grammar. *Journal of Cognitive Neuroscience*, 22(11), 2427–2436.

Flöel, A., Meinzer, M., Kirstein, R., Nijhof, S., Deppe, M., Knecht, S., & Breitenstein, C. (2011). Short-term anomia training and electrical brain stimulation. *Stroke*, 42(7), 2065–2067.

Flöel, A., Rosser, N., Michka, O., Knecht, S., & Breitenstein, C. (2008). Noninvasive brain stimulation improves language learning. *Journal of Cognitive Neuroscience*, 20(8), 1415–1422.

Fridriksson, J. (2010). Preservation and modulation of specific left hemisphere regions is vital for treated recovery from anomia in stroke. *Journal of Neuroscience*, 30(35), 11558–11564.

Fridriksson, J. (2011). Measuring and inducing brain plasticity in chronic aphasia. *Journal of Communication Disorders*, 44(5), 557–563.

Fridriksson, J., Bonilha, L., Baker, J. M., Moser, D., & Rorden, C. (2010). Activity in preserved left hemisphere regions predicts anomia severity in aphasia. *Cerebral Cortex*, 20(5), 1013–1019.

Fridriksson, J., Richardson, J. D., Baker, J. M., & Rorden, C. (2011). Transcranial direct current stimulation improves naming reaction time in fluent aphasia: A double-blind, sham-controlled study. *Stroke*, 42(3), 819–821.

Gandiga, P. C., Hummel, F. C., & Cohen, L. G. (2006). Transcranial DC stimulation (tDCS): A tool for double-blind sham-controlled clinical studies in brain stimulation. *Clinical Neurophysiology*, 117(4), 845–850.

Gauthier, L. V. (2008). Remodeling the brain: Plastic structural brain changes produced by different motor therapies after stroke. *Stroke*, 39, 1520–1525.

Goldenberg, G., & Spatt, J. (1994). Influence of size and site of cerebral lesions on spontaneous recovery of aphasia and on success of language therapy. *Brain and Language*, 47(4), 684–698.

Heiss, W. D., Karbe, H., Weber-Luxenburger, G., Herholz, K., Kessler, J., Pietrzyk, U., & Pawlik, G. (1997). Speech-induced cerebral metabolic activation reflects recovery from aphasia. *Journal of the Neurological Sciences*, 145(2), 213–217.

Heiss, W. D., & Thiel, A. (2006). A proposed regional hierarchy in recovery of post-stroke aphasia. *Brain and Language*, 98(1), 118–123.

Hillis, A., & Heidler, J. (2002). Mechanisms of early aphasia recovery. *Aphasiology*, 16(9), 885–895.

Hillis, A., Kane, A., Tuffiash, E., Ulatowski, J. A., Barker, P. B., Beauchamp, N. J., & Wityk, R. J. (2001). Reperfusion of specific brain regions by raising blood pressure restores selective language functions in subacute stroke. *Brain and Language*, 79(3), 495–510.

Huber, H., Poeck, K., Weniger, D., & Willmes, K. (1983). *Aachener Aphasie Test*. Göttingen: Hogrefe.

Kelly, H., Brady, M. C., & Enderby, P. (2010). Speech and language therapy for aphasia following stroke. *Cochrane Database Systematic Reviews*, 5, CD000425.

Laska, A. C., Hellblom, A., Murray, V., Kahan, T., & Von Arbin, M. (2001). Aphasia in acute stroke and relation to outcome. *Journal of Internal Medicine*, 249(5), 413–422.

Lazar, R. M. (2010). Improvement in aphasia scores after stroke is well predicted by initial severity. *Stroke*, 41, 1485–1488.

Lazar, R. M., & Antoniello, D. (2008). Variability in recovery from aphasia. *Current Neurology & Neuroscience Reports*, 8, 497–502.

Lazar, R. M., Minzer, B., Antoniello, D., Festa, J. R., Krakauer, J. W., & Marshall, R. S. (2010). Improvement in aphasia scores after stroke is well predicted by initial severity. *Stroke*, 41(7), 1485–1488.

Leff, A., Crinion, J., Scott, S., Turkheimer, F., Howard, D., & Wise, R. (2002). A physiological change in the homotopic cortex following left posterior temporal lobe infarction. *Annals of Neurology*, 51(5), 553–558.

Liepert, J., Bauder, H., Wolfgang, H. R., Miltner, W. H., Taub, E., & Weiller, C. (2000). Treatment-induced cortical reorganization after stroke in humans. *Stroke*, 31(6), 1210–1216.

Liepert, J., Miltner, W. H., Bauder, H., Sommer, M., Dettmers, C., Taub, E., & Weiller, C. (1998). Motor cortex plasticity during constraint-induced movement therapy in stroke patients. *Neuroscience Letters*, 250(1), 5–8.

Marcotte, K., Perlbarg, V., Marrelec, G., Benali, H., & Ansaldo, A. I. (2013). Default-mode network functional connectivity in aphasia: Therapy-induced neuroplasticity. *Brain and Language*, 124, 45–55.

Margulies, D. S., Bottger, J., Long, X., Lv, Y., Kelly, C., Schafer, A., . . . Villringer, A. (2010). Resting developments: A review of fMRI post-processing methodologies for spontaneous brain activity. *MAGMA*, 23(5–6), 289–307.

Marsh, E. B., & Hillis, A. (2006). Recovery from aphasia following brain injury: The role of reorganization. *Progress in Brain Research*, 157, 143–156.

Martin, P. I., Naeser, M. A., Ho, M., Doron, K. W., Kurland, J., Kaplan, J., . . . Pascual-Leone, A. (2009). Overt naming fMRI pre- and post-TMS: Two nonfluent aphasia patients, with and without improved naming post-TMS. *Brain and Language*, 111(1), 20–35.

Martin, P. I., Naeser, M. A., Ho, M., Treglia, E., Kaplan, E., Baker, E. H., & Pascual-Leone, A. (2009). Research with transcranial magnetic stimulation in the treatment of aphasia. *Current Neurology & Neuroscience Reports*, 9(6), 451–458.

Meinzer, M. (2008). Functional re-recruitment of dysfunctional brain areas predicts language recovery in chronic aphasia. *Neuroimage*, 39, 2038–2046.

Meinzer, M., Antonenko, D., Lindenberg, R., Hetzer, S., Ulm, L., Flaisch, T., & Flöel, A. (2012). Electrical brain stimulation improves cognitive performance by modulating functional connectivity and task-specific activation. *The Journal of Neuroscience*, 32, 1859–1866.

Meinzer, M., & Breitenstein, C. (2008). Functional imaging studies of treatment-induced recovery in chronic aphasia. *Aphasiology*, 22(12), 1251–1268.

Meinzer, M., Elbert, T., Djundja, D., Barthel, G., & Rockstroh, B. (2004). Intensive training enhances brain plasticity in chronic aphasia. *BMC Biology*, 2, 20.

Meinzer, M., Flaisch, T., Breitenstein, C., Wienbruch, C., Elbert, T., & Rockstroh, B. (2008). Functional re-recruitment of dysfunctional brain areas predicts language recovery in chronic aphasia. *Neuroimage*, 39(4), 2038–2046.

Meinzer, M., Flaisch, T., Obleser, J., Assadollahi, R., Djundja, D., Barthel, G., & Rockstroh, B. (2006). Brain regions essential for improved lexical access in an aged aphasic patient: A case report. *BMC Neurology*, 6, 28.

Meinzer, M., Harnish, S., Conway, T., & Crosson, B. (2011). Recent developments in functional and structural imaging of aphasia recovery. *Aphasiology*, 25, 271–290.

Meinzer, M., Lindenberg, R., Antonenko, D., Flaisch, T., & Flöel, A. (2013). Anodal transcranial direct current stimulation temporarily reverses age-associated cognitive decline and functional brain activity changes. *The Journal of Neuroscience*, 33, 12470–12478.

Meinzer, M., Mohammadi, S., Kugel, H., Schiffbauer, H., Flöel, A., Albers, J., . . . Deppe, M. (2010). Integrity of the hippocampus and surrounding white matter is correlated with language training success in aphasia. *Neuroimage*, 53(1), 283–290.

Meinzer, M., Rodriguez, A., & Rothi, L. G. (2012). The first decade of research on constrained-induced treatment approaches for aphasia rehabilitation. *Archives of Physical Medicine & Rehabilitation*, 93, S35–S45.

Menke, R., Meinzer, M., Kugel, H., Deppe, M., Baumgartner, A., Schiffbauer, H., . . . Breitenstein, C. (2009). Imaging short- and long-term training success in chronic aphasia. *BMC Neuroscience*, 10(1), 118.

Musso, M., Weiller, C., Kiebel, S., Muller, S. P., Bulau, P., & Rijntjes, M. (1999). Training-induced brain plasticity in aphasia. *Brain*, 122, 1781–1790.

Naeser, M. A. (2005). Improved picture naming in chronic aphasia after TMS to part of right Broca's area: An open-protocol study. *Brain and Language*, 93, 95–105.

Naeser, M. A., Martin, P. I., Treglia, E., Ho, M., Kaplan, E., Bashir, S., . . . Pascual-Leone, A. (2010). Research with rTMS in the treatment of aphasia. *Restorative Neurology and Neuroscience*, 28(4), 511–529.

Naeser, M. A., Palumbo, C. L., Helm-Estabrooks, N., Stiassny-Eder, D., & Albert, M. L. (1989). Severe nonfluency in aphasia. Role of the medial subcallosal fasciculus and other white matter pathways in recovery of spontaneous speech. *Brain*, 112(Pt 1), 1–38.

Nicholas, M. (2005). Aphasia and dysarthria after stroke. In M. Barnes, B. H. Dobkin, & J. Bogousslavsky (Eds.), *Recovery after stroke* (pp. 474–502). Cambridge: Cambridge University Press.

Nudo, R. J., Wise, B. M., SiFuentes, F., & Milliken, G. W. (1996). Neural substrates for the effects of rehabilitative training on motor recovery after ischemic infarct. *Science*, 272(5269), 1791–1794.

Pascual-Leone, A., Walsh, V., & Rothwell, J. (2000). Transcranial magnetic stimulation in cognitive neuroscience—virtual lesion, chronometry, and functional connectivity. *Current Opinion in Neurobiology*, 10(2), 232–237.

Pedersen, P. M., Jorgensen, H. S., Nakayama, H., Raaschou, H. O., & Olsen, T. S. (1995). Aphasia in acute stroke: Incidence, determinants, and recovery. *Annals of Neurology*, 38(4), 659–666.

Pedersen, P. M., Vinter, K., & Olsen, T. S. (2004). Aphasia after stroke: Type, severity and prognosis. The Copenhagen aphasia study. *Cerebrovascular Diseases*, 17(1), 35–43.

Perani, D., Cappa, S. F., Tettamanti, M., Rosa, M., Scifo, P., Miozzo, A., . . . Fazio, F. (2003). A fMRI study of word retrieval in aphasia. *Brain and Language*, 85(3), 357–368.

Pizzamiglio, L., Galati, G., & Committeri, G. (2001). The contribution of functional neuroimaging to recovery after brain damage: A review. *Cortex*, 37(1), 11–31.

Plowman, E., Hentz, B., & Ellis, C. (2011). Post-stroke aphasia prognosis: A review of patient-related and stroke-related factors. *Journal of Evaluation in Clinical Practice*, 18, 689–694.

Poeck, K., Huber, W., & Willmes, K. (1989). Outcome of intensive language treatment in aphasia. *Journal of Speech & Hearing Disorders*, 54(3), 471–479.

Postman-Caucheteux, W. A., Birn, R. M., Pursley, R. H., Butman, J. A., Solomon, J. M., Picchioni, D., . . . Braun, A. R. (2010). Single-trial fMRI shows contralesional activity linked to overt naming errors in chronic aphasic patients. *Journal of Cognitive Neuroscience*, 22(6), 1299–1318.

Prabhakaran, S., Zarahn, E., Riley, C., Speizer, A., Chong, J. Y., Lazar, R. M., . . . Krakauer, J. W. (2008). Inter-individual variability in the capacity for motor recovery after ischemic stroke. *Neurorehabilitation & Neural Repair*, 22(1), 64–71.

Price, C. J., Crinion, J., & Friston, K. J. (2006). Design and analysis of fMRI studies with neurologically impaired patients. *Journal of Magnetic Resonance Imaging*, 23(6), 816–826.

Price, C. J., Seghier, M. L., & Leff, A. P. (2010). Predicting language outcome and recovery after stroke: The PLORAS system. *Nature Reviews Neurology*, 6, 202–210.

Raboyeau, G., De Boissezon, X., Marie, N., Balduyck, S., Puel, M., Bezy, C., . . . Cardebat, D. (2008). Right hemisphere activation in recovery from aphasia: Lesion effect or function recruitment? *Neurology*, 70(4), 290–298.

Richter, M., Miltner, W. H., & Straube, T. (2008). Association between therapy outcome and right-hemispheric activation in chronic aphasia. *Brain*, 131(Pt 5), 1391–1401.

Robey, R. R. (1994). The efficacy of treatment for aphasic persons: A meta-analysis. *Brain and Language*, 47(4), 582–608.

Robey, R. R. (1998). A meta-analysis of clinical outcomes in the treatment of aphasia. *Journal of Speech, Language, Hearing Research*, 41(1), 172–187.

Saur, D., Lange, R., Baumgaertner, A., Schraknepper, V., Willmes, K., Rijntjes, M., & Weiller, C. (2006). Dynamics of language reorganization after stroke. *Brain*, 129(Pt 6), 1371–1384.

Saur, D., Ronneberger, O., Kummerer, D., Mader, I., Weiller, C., & Kloppel, S. (2010). Early functional magnetic resonance imaging activations predict language outcome after stroke. *Brain*, 133(Pt 4), 1252–1264.

Schlaug, G., Marchina, S., & Norton, A. (2009). Evidence for plasticity in white-matter tracts of patients with chronic Broca's aphasia undergoing intense intonation-based speech therapy. *Annals of the New York Academy of Sciences*, 1169, 385–394.

Schlaug, G., Marchina, S., & Wan, C. Y. (2011). The use of non-invasive brain stimulation techniques to facilitate recovery from post-stroke aphasia. *Neuropsychology Review*, 21(3), 288–301.

Shisler, R. J., Baylis, G. C., & Frank, E. M. (2000). Pharmacological approaches to the treatment and prevention of aphasia. *Aphasiology*, 14(12), 1163–1186.

Smania, N., Gandolfi, M., Aglioti, S. M., Girardi, P., Fiaschi, A., & Girardi, F. (2010). How long is the recovery of global aphasia? Twenty-five years of follow-up in a patient with left hemisphere stroke. *Neurorehabilitation & Neural Repair*, 24(9), 871–875.

Stagg, C. J., & Nitsche, M. A. (2011). Physiological basis of transcranial direct current stimulation. *Neuroscientist*, 17(1), 37–53.

Taub, E., Uswatte, G., & Elbert, T. (2002). New treatments in neurorehabilitation founded on basic research. *Nature Reviews Neuroscience*, 3(3), 228–236.

Thiel, A., Haupt, W. F., Habedank, B., Winhuisen, L., Herholz, K., Kessler, J., . . . Heiss, W. D. (2005). Neuroimaging-guided rTMS of the left inferior frontal gyrus interferes with repetition priming. *Neuroimage*, 25(3), 815–823.

Thompson-Schill, S. L., D'Esposito, M., Aguirre, G. K., & Farah, M. J. (1997). Role of left inferior prefrontal cortex in retrieval of semantic knowledge: A reevaluation. *Proceedings of the National Academy of Sciences USA*, 94(26), 14792–14797.

Thompson, C. K., den Ouden, D. B., Bonakdarpour, B., Garibaldi, K., & Parrish, T. B. (2010). Neural plasticity and treatment-induced recovery of sentence processing in agrammatism. *Neuropsychologia*, 48(11), 3211–3227.

Turkeltaub, P. E., Messing, S., Norise, C., & Hamilton, R. H. (2011). Are networks for residual language function and recovery consistent across aphasic patients? *Neurology*, 76(20), 1726–1734.

Vallar, G., Perani, D., Cappa, S. F., Messa, C., Lenzi, G. L., & Fazio, F. (1988). Recovery from aphasia and neglect after subcortical stroke: Neuropsychological and cerebral perfusion study. *Journal of Neurology, Neurosurgery, & Psychiatry*, 51(10), 1269–1276.

Vitali, P., Tettamanti, M., Abutalebi, J., Ansaldo, A. I., Perani, D., Cappa, S. F., & Joanette, Y. (2010). Generalization of the effects of phonological training for anomia using structural equation modelling: A multiple single-case study. *Neurocase*, 16(2), 93–105.

Wade, D. T., Hewer, R. L., David, R. M., & Enderby, P. M. (1986). Aphasia after stroke: Natural history and associated deficits. *Journal of Neurology, Neurosurgery, & Psychiatry*, 49(1), 11–16.

Warren, J. E., Crinion, J. T., Lambon Ralph, M. A., & Wise, R. J. (2009). Anterior temporal lobe connectivity correlates with functional outcome after aphasic stroke. *Brain*, 132(Pt 12), 3428–3442.

Weiller, C., Isensee, C., Rijntjes, M., Huber, W., Muller, S., Bier, D., . . . Diener, H. C. (1995). Recovery from Wernicke's aphasia: A positron emission tomographic study. *Annals of Neurology*, 37(6), 723–732.

Winhuisen, L. (2007). The right inferior frontal gyrus and poststroke aphasia: A follow-up investigation. *Stroke*, 38, 1286–1292.

Principles of Aphasia Rehabilitation

Anastasia M. Raymer *and* Leslie J. Gonzalez Rothi

Abstract

This chapter reviews the broad literature on approaches to treatment of aphasia. Behavioral interventions for aphasia are influenced by perspectives from neuroscience that emphasize that neuroplasticity in rehabilitation is experience-dependent and potent. Several principles of neuroplasticity are reviewed, and examples are described from the aphasia treatment literature. Additional principles are considered regarding influences of error production and feedback in aphasia rehabilitation outcomes. Adjuvant treatments then are described that are meant to enhance behavioral treatment outcomes through pharmacologic and neuromodulatory interventions. Finally, life participation approaches are highlighted that encourage use of multi-modality communication for daily life activities along with training of communication partners. An interdisciplinary process is emphasized in which many professionals work together to provide individuals with aphasia the maximum benefits in language recovery, communication skills, and meaningful social engagement and quality of life.

Key Words: aphasia, rehabilitation, neuroplasticity, communication, neuromodulation, pharmacology, participation

> One day out of the blue I had a stroke and in an instant my ability to talk was wiped out. I felt so isolated and confused because I could not communicate with people. I felt depressed and very anxious about how I could parent my children properly. I lost most of my old friends, as people lost patience with me. I felt trapped, with my confidence destroyed. I couldn't carry on with my old life . . . .
>
> *(Carol Griffiths, 2014, Living with Aphasia: www.UKConnect.com)*

Why Treat Aphasia?

Stroke is the single most disabling health condition in adulthood worldwide (Mozaffarian et al., 2016; Numminen et al., 2016; Wolfe, 2000; World Health Organization, 1997), and stroke survivors account for a substantial proportion of those living with aphasia (Berthier, 2005; Dickey et al., 2010; Laska, Hellblom, Murray, Kahan, & von Arbin, 2001). Further complicating this picture is the fact that, compared to stroke survivors who don't

have aphasia, those who have aphasia experience longer hospital stays and exhibit more intensive health service utilization (Ellis, Simpson, Bonilha, Mauldin, & Simpson, 2012). Fewer eventually return to work (Black-Schaffer & Osberg, 1990), and they participate in fewer activities and report lower quality of life as well as high distress (Hilari, 2011; Hilari, Needle, & Harrison, 2012). The social isolation of these persons with aphasia is profoundly life-altering and begins immediately upon aphasia onset and initial stroke hospitalization (O'Halloran, Grohn, & Worrall, 2012; O'Halloran, Worrall, & Hickson, 2011). The economic and social consequences are urgent and substantial, underscoring the need to place a premium on the development and delivery of treatments that can mitigate these debilitating outcomes (Pollock, St. George, Fenton, & Firkins, 2012).

Historical Perspective on Aphasia Treatment

Written descriptions of attempts to behaviorally treat aphasia can be traced back to the physician Galen (approx. 180 AD), who described bloodletting for aphasia, and to Celcus (approx. 100 BC) who recorded, among other ideas, that ". . . when one was unable to articulate . . . he must exercise himself to retain his breath, wash his head with cold water and then vomit . . ." (Finger, 1994, p. 418). Targets for treatment evolved from the spiritual (demonic possession) to the physiological (imbalance of four "humors"), with treatment modalities spanning from the wearing of charms to herbal potions, each attempting to address the purported mechanism of the deficit. Then and more recently, reports were anecdotal. For example, Goodglass (1985) cited an 1879 paper that describes a 49-year-old patient with aphasia who was treated repeatedly with applications of "a strong current to the man's skin with an electric brush" (p. 308).

Modern-day history of behavioral treatments for aphasia is much more data-substantive, with turn-of-the-century case series beginning to emerge, such as those of Bateman (1890), Franz (1905; 1924), and Mills (1904) recounting case attributes, treatment methods, and outcomes. More extensive reports surfaced as the result of caring for returning wounded troops after World War I, with the early experiences in Germany of Kurt Goldstein (1942, 1948), in Russia subsequent to World War II by Luria (1970), and many in the United States, including Franz (1924) and Wepman (1951). Since that time, a considerable literature has examined effects of behavioral treatments aimed at impaired language functions in order to improve communication abilities of individuals with aphasia.

Behavioral Treatments Versus Natural Recovery

The nervous system is malleable and continually changing in response to life experiences, a concept often referred to as *neuroplasticity*.

Neuroplasticity can be broadly defined as the ability of the nervous system to respond to intrinsic and extrinsic stimuli by reorganizing its structure, function and connections . . . and can occur during development, in response to the environment, in support of learning, in response to disease, or in relation to therapy. Such plasticity can be viewed as adaptive when associated with a gain in function or as maladaptive when associated with negative consequences . . . . (*Cramer et al., 2011, p. 1592*)

One example of the suspected contribution of experiential neuroplasticity to maladaptation can be found in discussions of addiction (e.g., Koob & Volkow, 2010). In contrast, most studies of adaptive neuroplasticity have focused on motor function recovery, which results in functional gains in both animals and humans (e.g., Adkins, 2015; Adkins et al., 2006; Buonomano & Merzenich, 1998; Johansson, 2000; Koski, Mernar, & Dobkin, 2004; Nudo, 2007, 2011; Nudo, Wise, SiFuentes, & Milliken, 1996). Evidence for restoration within cognitive (e.g., Corbetta, Kincade, Lewis, Snyder, & Sapir, 2005; Sturm et al., 2004) and affective (e.g., Eack et al., 2010) systems in humans can be found in the recent literature as well. What is clear from various strands of research is that experience is potent (Cramer, 2008). Carefully constructed experiences are needed to improve functions beyond what would happen through natural recovery alone. Because plasticity is experience-dependent, clinicians should attempt to provide rehabilitation experiences that contribute to adaptive and not maladaptive change (Cramer et al., 2011).

Adaptive Neuroplasticity Following Behavioral Aphasia Treatments

Do we have reason to believe that behavioral aphasia treatments can improve upon natural recovery after stroke by virtue of adaptive neuroplasticity? For more than 100 years, clinicians and researchers have contributed responses to this question, with the answer being a resounding "yes." In their insightful review of the history of aphasia treatment, Cherney and Robey (2001) noted that early in the 20th century, several elaborate case reports and case series described methods that seemed to effect some amount of improvement in language abilities of individuals with aphasia. The need for effective rehabilitation methods exploded following World Wars I and II, when massive numbers of soldiers survived brain injuries and flooded medical systems. The fortunate consequence of this unfortunate

Table 17.1 Results of Meta-analyses of Group Treatment Studies of Aphasia

Author	Number of studies included	Effect sizes	
		Treated	Untreated
Greenhouse et al., 1990	13	.80	
Whurr et al., 1992	45	.59	
Robey, 1994	21	1.25	.65
Robey, 1998	55	1.15 acute	
		.57 post-acute	
		.66 chronic	
Brady et al., 2012	19	.30	
Brady et al., 2016	27	.28	

circumstance was that larger numbers of individuals with aphasia participated in studies that reported that recovery was enhanced for those who engaged in some kind of behavioral therapy (Weisenburg & McBride, 1935). As scientific methods advanced in rigor, the era of group studies in medicine emerged, including those in behavioral aphasia treatment and recovery. Among the first controlled clinical trials were those of Wertz and colleagues (1981, 1986) who, with the support of the Veteran's Affairs Rehabilitation Research Service throughout the United States, showed that treatment led to significant gains on standardized aphasia test scores. Among the considerable number of clinical trials that have taken place in the past 40 years, the vast majority of studies have reported that aphasia treatment is associated with superior outcomes when compared to no-treatment conditions (e.g., Hagen, 1973; Marshall et al., 1989; Poeck, Huber, & Willmes, 1989; Shewan & Kertesz, 1984).

In the era of evidence-based medicine, efforts have been initiated to coalesce research evidence in the form of systematic reviews and meta-analyses. Whereas a literature review is conducted with general attempts to encompass a mass of literature, a systematic review is intended as a scientifically rigorous endeavor to identify every investigation that exists on a topic to address specific clinical questions (Grant & Booth, 2009). Several groups worldwide are now sponsoring efforts to synthesize research, including studies of rehabilitation for aphasia (e.g., Cochrane Reviews: www.cochrane.org/CD000425; American Speech-Language-Hearing Association: www.asha.org/public/Efficacy Summaries.htm; Academy of Neurologic Communication Disorders and Sciences: www.ancds.org/evidence-based-clinical-research; Speech Pathology Database for Best Interventions and Treatment Efficacy: www.speechpathologyaustralia.org.au/resources/speechbite). A number of systematic reviews have shown positive outcomes on standardized aphasia tests (Basso, 1992; Cherney, Patterson, Raymer, Frymark, & Schooling, 2008; Holland, Fromm, DeRuyter, & Stein, 1996). Of particular interest are meta-analyses that quantified the effects of aphasia treatments and reported medium to large effect sizes across reviews (Basso et al., 2011; Brady, Kelly, Godwin, & Enderby, 2012; Brady, Kelly, Godwin, Enderby, & Campbell, 2016; Greenhouse et al., 1990; Robey, 1994, 1998; Whurr, Lorch, & Nye, 1992). These findings (see Table 17.1) demonstrate the efficacy of aphasia treatment in general. The question thus evolved to *"What is the best treatment; for whom; under what circumstances?"*

Optimizing Relearning

Within this book, as chapters are organized by classical aphasia syndromes, a number of theoretically motivated, linguistically targeted treatments have been described as appropriate to the typical language impairments in each syndrome. We believe the advantage of this method in the overarching design of this book is that discussions by syndrome would allow the reader to recognize groupings through history; to share a common and accessible terminology that transcends time, settings, and professional perspectives; and to use the syndrome discussions to partition characteristic language attributes for more specific discussion (e.g., Broca's aphasia and a discussion of grammar processing and dysfunction). We also believe that understanding detailed characteristics of language breakdown and remaining capabilities through a comprehensive assessment help guide the selection of potential language targets and strategic choices of methods for a given individual with aphasia, again as described in the chapters of this volume.

Discussions relevant to the various psycholinguistic subsystems of language in the context of aphasia syndromes are described in each of the prior chapters as though they were unique and independent, but in fact, difficulties with grammar, phonology, semantic underpinnings of words, reading, spelling, and so forth can occur in unique constellations in each person with aphasia. Because human communication is a multifaceted phenomenon supported by a complex set of processes (from psychological/linguistic to neurological; macro- to microstructures), and because any event which might disrupt this complex would be unique to the individual, restorative behavioral strategies with the goal of regaining effective communication in any one person with aphasia would need to be individualized. This would involve possibly bundling as well as staging a variety of treatments targeting various impaired linguistic mechanisms. While the evidence for such combinations and individualization represents a largely unexplored frontier, at this point we can examine more overarching questions of how normal learning generally occurs, extract suspected principles of how such learning can be optimized within the context of the rehabilitation experience, and consider how to apply those principles to relearning in the context of restorative behavioral therapies for aphasia (Rothi, Musson, Rosenbek, & Sapienza, 2008).

As noted in the NIH Blueprint for Neuroscience Research sponsored workshop in 2009, a behavioral experience can be potent and is influenced by experience attributes, is time-sensitive, and is impacted by intrinsic factors such as attention and motivation (Cramer et al., 2011). Kleim (2011), Nudo (2013) and others appropriately challenge us to use knowledge of the neural and behavioral signals that drive neural plasticity in order to develop "performance-enhancing" behavioral therapies. Similar mechanisms of brain plasticity occur across the lifespan and across varying forms of central nervous system (CNS) injury (disease, trauma, etc.), and this consistency "suggests that plasticity . . . uses a limited repertoire of events across numerous contexts"

(Cramer et al., 2011, p. 1593). Kleim (2011) offers that, when relearning, "the brain will rely on the same fundamental neurobiological processes it used to acquire those behaviors initially. The basic rules governing how neural circuits adapt to encode new behaviors do not change after injury" (p. 522). Thus, a rehabilitation experience where individuals are expected to engage in linguistically rich activities might result in changed language behavior through learning-dependent, experiential neural plasticity; that is, relearning.

Accepting the premise that the act of verbal communication is an external representation of many underlying internal processes that can be examined from many levels of perspective, not least of which is a neural systems perspective, we looked to neural explanations of experience-dependent learning to seek principles of experience that might be applied to the context of restorative behavioral treatments for aphasia (Raymer et al., 2008). Turkstra, Holland, and Bays (2003) were among the first clinicians to draw attention to the implications of the neuroscience literature for clinical practice. Kleim and Jones (2008) were challenged to identify principles of experience-dependent neuroplasticity emanating from laboratory-based neuroscience studies using rodent models that they would recommend as "best candidates" for translation to humans. They offered ten possibilities, described in Table 17.2. While neuroscience studies in animal models surely have limits for the inferences that can be made for human language, principles garnered from these studies may have implications for aphasia rehabilitation practices. Some of these principles refer to factors that can be manipulated in the aphasia treatment context. Other principles guide outcomes that should be tracked in aphasia rehabilitation (transference and interference). Other possibilities exist beyond this set of ten principles, but this set often serves as a starting point for a discussion of principles emanating from neuroscience that have the potential to influence behavioral treatments in aphasia.

Use it, Use it, Use it

The first two principles offered by Kleim and Jones (2008) are "Use it or Lose it" and "Use it and Improve it" (see Table 17.2). Loss of function within the nervous system from disuse post–brain injury, or "learned non-use" as described by Taub, Uswatte, and Mark (2014), has been demonstrated for motor and sensory systems in animal models (Nudo, 2013). Compensatory skill-learning by the

Table 17.2 Principles of Experience-Dependent Plasticity (after Kleim & Jones, 2008)

Principle	Description
1. Use It or Lose It	Failure to drive specific brain functions can lead to functional degradation.
2. Use It and Improve It	Training that drives a specific brain function can lead to an enhancement of that function.
3. Specificity	The nature of the training experience dictates the nature of the plasticity.
4. Repetition Matters	Induction of plasticity requires sufficient repetition.
5. Intensity Matters	Induction of plasticity requires sufficient training intensity.
6. Time Matters	Different forms of plasticity occur at different times during training.
7. Salience Matters	The training experience must be sufficiently salient to induce plasticity.
8. Age Matters	Training-induced plasticity occurs more readily in younger brains.
9. Transference	Plasticity in response to one training experience can enhance the acquisition of similar behaviors.
10. Interference	Plasticity in response to one experience can interfere with the acquisition of other behaviors.

less-affected limb impedes later functional recovery in the more-affected limb (Allred & Jones, 2008; Allred, Maldonado, Hsu, & Jones, 2005; Jones et al., 2013; Kerr, Wolke, Bell, & Jones, 2013). These maladaptive effects were not seen in animals that were trained on a bimanual task (Kerr et al., 2013).

In humans, functional loss in the early post-injury period has been shown to occur in the cognitive system as well (e.g., Coslett & Saffran, 1989). Thus much of the rationale for the class of rehabilitation therapies known as "constraint induced" (CI) therapies is based upon the principle of optimizing this latent residual capacity left behind by "learned non-use." In parallel to optimizing this residual capacity using targeted post-injury activity/experience (Karni et al., 1998; Kleim, Barbay, & Nudo, 1998; Nudo Milliken, Jenkins, & Merzenich, 1996), recovery of function in the context of network changes incorporating inter- and intra-hemispheric adaptations is well documented (e.g., Jacquin-Courtois et al., 2013). Similar findings have been reported in humans in sensory (Taub et al., 2014), motor (Taub, Uswatte, & Morris, 2003), and cognitive (Corbetta et al., 2005; Saur et al., 2006) systems as well. An explosion of recent rehabilitation research has emphasized "use-dependent" or "experience-dependent" techniques based upon this principle of "use it," focusing on massed practice of purposeful activity at maximal/

optimal levels of an individual's performance capacity, done in a manner that closely approximates normal performance and avoids compensation.

For individuals with aphasia, constraint induced language therapy (CILT) was developed by Pulvermüller and colleagues (2001) as a behavioral approach to overcome learned non-use and to promote use of verbal communication. Later the approach was broadened to be referred to as intensive language-action therapy (ILAT; Pulvermuller & Berthier, 2008). Because the treatment focuses on engaging expressive verbal language skills in the context of communicative interactions with partners in training, it is especially implemented in individuals with nonfluent forms of aphasia, as noted in the chapter on Broca's aphasia (see Maher, Chapter 8). Systematic review of aphasia treatment studies has shown that the effects of CILT surpass those of comparison treatments on measures of general language, word retrieval, and auditory comprehension, as well as measures of communication participation (communication logs, rating scales) (Cherney et al., 2008; Cherney, Patterson, & Raymer, 2011).

In addition to CILT, any other aphasia treatments that facilitate language use during verbal production, auditory comprehension, reading, and writing activities can be conceived of as methods to overcome learned non-use. Thus many of the methods reviewed across the chapters in this book also would be considered as supporting use-dependent learning. Neuroscience evidence as well as evidence from aphasia rehabilitation suggest that language behavior must be engaged to overcome the natural propensity toward learned non-use.

Specificity in Training

Neuroscience researchers have shown that representational neural maps change in ways related to the specifics of the training experience (e.g., Wang, Conner, Rickert, & Tuszynski, 2011). In healthy human adults, expansions of hand, foot/ankle, or tongue motor maps have been shown to change in concert with skill learning in unilateral hand (Pascual-Leone, Wassermann, Sadato, & Hallett, 1995), leg (Perez, Lungholt, Nyborg, & Nielsen, 2004), or tongue movement task practice (Svensson, Romaniello, Arendt-Nielsen, & Sessle, 2003), respectively. Interestingly, the notion of the specificity of treatment effect has been borne out in the human stroke rehabilitation literature as well with Koski and colleagues (2004) showing expansion of motor maps correlated with motor improvements.

Additionally, researchers have shown that it is not as simple as repeating a behavior, but instead, that the effect of task practice is embellished when experiences are varied (Plautz, Milliken, & Nudo, 2000) and present opportunities for skill-building (Kleim et al., 2003), as opposed to repetitive or passively evoked responses. Thus it behooves the rehabilitation clinician to insure that the treatment plan is directed at achievement of carefully considered target behaviors. Kleim and Jones (2008) extend this notion by suggesting that in rehabilitation, one consideration might be that a specific modality of training may serve to influence subsequent training.

The concept of specificity in training can be applied to aphasia rehabilitation in several examples. Much of the extensive word-retrieval training literature employs picture-naming tasks where specific target vocabulary items are trained. Because the process of word retrieval engages both semantic and phonologic mechanisms for successful production of words, word-retrieval impairments can emanate from semantic or phonologic sources of breakdown (Harney in this volume; Reilly & Martin in this volume; Wilshire in this volume). Thus, word-retrieval treatments have been devised that focus on either semantic or phonologic attributes of words to target the impaired mechanism, a means to provide more specificity in training. The often-cited result across studies is that word-retrieval training effects are item-specific, as individuals with aphasia improve their ability to name trained pictures, with little

generalization to untrained vocabulary (Raymer, 2015). Wilshire notes that in order to enhance effects, word-retrieval training should take place in a sentence context rather than during picture naming, as is the case in typical language use. Broader language gains, including improvements for word retrieval, have been reported in the outcomes of CILT (Cherney et al., 2008) or verb network strengthening treatment (Edmonds, Mammino, & Ojeda, 2014), where individuals engage lexical access while producing sentence-length utterances, rather than simply naming pictures. Yet, training of a limited set of functional "survival" vocabulary may be necessary in individuals with severe aphasia.

Likewise, in the treatment of acquired alexia and agraphia, specificity in training is a consideration. Several treatment approaches have been devised to address the multi-faceted patterns of breakdown that can be observed with disruption of distinct lexical and sublexical processes engaged in reading and spelling. The reading treatments reviewed by Riley, Brookshire, and Kendall (in this volume) and the spelling treatments reviewed by Beeson and Rising (in this volume) emphasize the connection between impaired processes and treatment approach to maximize training effects. Further, as Greenwald (in this volume) noted, writing treatment used as a compensatory method of communication for individuals with Wernicke's aphasia may need to take place in a functional communicative context to encourage the use of writing as a communication modality.

Finally, the notion of specificity also implies that the outcomes measured following training should be specific to the intended goal. In studies of treatments such as CILT, in addition to treatment results documented in standardized aphasia test batteries or modality-specific tools (e.g., standardized tests of naming and auditory comprehension), outcomes pertaining to language use in daily communication activities, such as communication activity logs, discourse samples, or communication rating scales, also are documented (Maher et al., 2006; Meinzer, Djundja, Barthel, Elbert, & Rockstroth, 2005; Pulvermüller et al., 2001).

Repetition and Intensity Matter

When Kleim and Jones (2008) invoke the principle of repetition, they refer to the ongoing practice that takes place *over time*. The principle of intensity in training for them relates to the density or dosage of that practice *within* training sessions. In aphasia rehabilitation, CILT rehabilitation techniques are based upon the principle that relearning is optimized by repeated and intensive performances of target language behaviors (Pulvermüller et al., 2001).

To distinguish repetition and intensity in the context of aphasia rehabilitation, however, it is useful to consider the definitions of Warren, Fey, and Yoder (2007) as they discuss dosage as it pertains to intervention. "Dose" refers to "the number of properly administered teaching episodes during a single intervention session" (p. 71). The definition of episode varies across tasks, types of interventions implemented, and therapists. "Dose frequency" is the number of sessions per time span, typically reported as sessions per week. "Total intervention duration" is the total span in days, weeks or months over which interventions are administered. Together, dose over dose frequency over total intervention duration leads to a "cumulative intervention intensity." For example, a 30 minute session delivered 3 times per week for 12 weeks would equal a cumulative intervention intensity of 1080 minutes. The dose of episodes within a session is not often reported, however. In this parlance, "dose" is more of a corollary to Kleim and Jones's (2008) principle that intensity matters within training sessions, while repetition matters across time in dose frequency and intervention duration.

In order to invoke long-term changes, aphasia treatment must incorporate many opportunities for the target language behavior, what we might refer to as a *high-dose* intervention (see Harnish in this volume). In their meta-analysis of the word-retrieval treatment literature, Snell, Sage and Lambon Ralph (2010) reported on the relationship between the number of words trained and naming outcomes, noting some negative correlation. This observation speaks to dose, as larger sets typically have a lower dose of exposure in training than smaller training sets. Yet, two systematic investigations of size of training sets showed that the same *proportion* of words were learned regardless of the size of training set, indicating that more words are learned when larger training sets are employed (Laganaro, Di Pietro, & Schnider, 2006; Snell et al., 2010). Harnish et al. (2014) demonstrated that aphasia treatment sessions can be structured with what they call *saturated* practice, in which individuals with aphasia have hundreds of opportunities to produce target words, thereby leading to rapid improvement in their word-retrieval outcomes after only three hours of training.

In the aphasia treatment literature, high intensity dose frequency tends to be referred to as "massed practice," whereas lower intensity training is known as "distributed practice" (Dignam, Rodriguez, & Copland, 2016). As noted by Maher (in this volume), intensive training is a principle applied in CILT, as, not only are individuals with aphasia forced to use verbal utterances, but they are also provided training on an intensive massed schedule of 10–15 hours per week. In Robey's (1998) meta-analysis of the aphasia treatment literature, larger effect sizes were reported when treatment was provided two or more hours per week, compared to less than 1.5 hours per week. Since then, several studies have directly compared massed versus distributed treatment schedules to evaluate intensity effects in aphasia treatment (Cherney et al., 2008, 2011). Across studies, some have varied dose frequency (sessions per week) while controlling total intervention duration, thus leading to differences in cumulative intervention intensity (Bakheit et al., 2007; Hinckley & Carr, 2005; Hinckley & Craig, 1998). Other studies have compared dose frequency administered at different intervention durations to equate cumulative intervention intensity (Dignam et al., 2015; Pulvermüller et al., 2001; Raymer, Kohen, & Saffell, 2006; Sage, Snell, & Lambon Ralph, 2011). Dose frequency studies typically compare training delivered in 4–5 sessions per week versus 1–2 sessions per week. Treatment gains following a short course of treatment tend to show advantages for a massed dose frequency schedule. Yet a less intensive, distributed treatment schedule may have better *maintenance* of results at follow-up, a finding reminiscent of a pattern reported often in the motor learning literature (Dignam et al., 2015). Differences in cumulative intervention intensities across studies ranging from 10–100 hours of total training may explain divergent findings. Over larger cumulative intervention intensities of greater than 50 hours of training, it appears that results tend to equalize across massed and distributed dose frequencies. What is clear across the literature is that greater cumulative intervention is better.

Time Matters

Neuroscience studies demonstrate that the timing of an intervention has considerable impact on the outcomes of that intervention (Turkstra et al., 2003). Timing of interventions in aphasia rehabilitation has also been considered. Historically, the presumption in rehabilitation has been that restorative treatments are more appropriate during acute phases of recovery, with reorganization approaches being added in subacute phases, and compensatory approaches applied in chronic phases of recovery (Barrett & Rothi, 2002; Nouwens et al., 2015). Robey's (1998) meta-analysis seems to support that perspective, as treatment effects, while surpassing changes associated with no treatment, grow smaller over time from acute to chronic stages of aphasia recovery. But research examining patterns of aphasia recovery and treatment may refine that viewpoint.

Saur and colleagues (2006) showed through serial functional magnetic resonance imaging (fMRI) examinations of aphasia recovery (day 4 post-stroke, 2 weeks post-onset, greater than 4 months post-onset) that patterns of activation changed over time. The first epoch (day 4 post-stroke) showed complete breakdown of left hemisphere language-related activation. The second timeframe (2 weeks post-onset) showed activation of remaining left and newly formed right homologue language areas. Finally, in the chronic phase (4 months post-onset), participants showed normalization of language lateralization back to the left hemisphere. In their 2012 paper, Saur and Hartwigsen concluded that, with time, "aphasic patients may be able to resort to normative learning mechanisms in the chronic phase after stroke . . . (and) it can be assumed that model-based therapeutic strategies may be best applied in the chronic phase" (p. S21). Much of the aphasia treatment literature is conducted in the chronic phase of recovery, at least 4–6 months post–stroke onset and beyond, and impressive treatment effects are not uncommon in individuals who are years and even decades post–stroke onset (Kendall et al., 2007; Raymer et al., 2007). Less is known about the effects of aphasia treatment in the acute stage, as mixed findings are reported in several randomized controlled trials of aphasia treatment initiated within three days of stroke onset (Godecke et al., 2014; Laska, Kahan, Hellblom, Murray, & von Arbin, 2011). Further complicating this picture is the work of El Hachioui and colleagues (2013), who followed the language-recovery patterns of a group of individuals with aphasia at periodic time points, assessing different linguistic systems: semantics, syntax, and phonology. Findings indicated differing trajectories of recovery for the different linguistic systems, with phonology lagging significantly behind semantics and syntax. These observations suggest that the linguistically oriented treatments reviewed across chapters in this book might come into play at slightly different, as of yet unknown, timeframes in recovery.

Salience and Motivation Matters

Salience in human rehabilitation including that for aphasia can take on a number of different definitions. Things that are familiar, useful, functional, likeable, or interesting to the individual might be considered salient. Renvall, Nickels and Davidson (2013a,b) offer that functionality of words for aphasia treatment might be based upon how commonly they are used. Wilshire (in this volume) discusses the work of Marshall and Freed (2006), who demonstrated that personalized cues were more effective than generic cues in facilitating improvements in word retrieval. Beeson and Rising (in this volume) emphasize that target words for spelling treatments should have functional value for the person in training. In addition, how pleasant or unpleasant a stimulus may be to the individual can influence arousal and verbal expression, as noted by Leon, Rodriguez, and Rosenbek (in this volume).

Alternatively, salience may include the notion of reward and motivational state, which has a considerable influence on changes observed in the neuroscience training studies (Mosberger, de Clauser, Kasper, & Schwab, 2016). Less attention has been given to the influence of reward or motivation on aphasia treatment outcomes. Within right-hemisphere communication disorders, as noted by Leon and colleagues (in this volume), anosognosia, or lack of awareness of deficits, can be a detriment to rehabilitation outcomes. The type of feedback used during training may need to be adjusted to address the lower motivation to engage in treatment that might be seen in these individuals. Overall, reward and motivation are areas ripe for investigation for the effects on rehabilitation outcomes for aphasia and related communication disorders.

Age Matters

While neuroplasticity of the brain spans across the lifespan (Turkstra et al., 2003), there are limits to that potential as we age. Age of onset when a nervous system injury occurs has long been recognized for its influence on the prognosis for aphasia recovery, as children who incur brain injury with aphasia demonstrate considerably greater recovery than do adults (e.g., Bates et al., 2001). Within adulthood, age continues to be a potent mediating influence on stroke (Jorgensen et al., 1999), and aphasia recovery (Code, 2001), although the influence of age on aphasia treatment outcomes directly is not as evident (Ellis & Urban, 2016). Nevertheless, McClung, Rothi, and Nadeau (2010) included age, 50 years and younger vs. older than 50 years, as an intra-individual ambient factor that should be considered for its influence on rehabilitation outcomes.

Transference or Generalization

The corollary to what Kleim and Jones (2008) in neuroscience called *transference* is referred to in the aphasia literature as *generalization*. Transference has to do with effects of training that transcend the currently trained language stimuli, language behavior/task, or communicative context. As noted across chapters of this volume, to the extent that words or sentences engage common linguistic rules or principles, the likelihood of generalization of training effects is increased. Harney (in this volume) mentions the work of Kiran (Kiran, 2008; Kiran & Thompson, 2003), who has demonstrated that word-retrieval training for atypical category exemplars (e.g., *artichoke*) generalize to untrained typical category exemplars (e.g., *carrot*) because of common semantic features across stimuli. Maher (in this volume) refers to the work of Thompson and colleagues (Thompson & Shapiro, 2005; Thompson, Shapiro, Kiran, & Sobecks, 2003), who demonstrated that training of sentence production using syntactically complex stimuli (e.g., object cleft sentences) leads to improvements in untrained syntactically related stimuli (e.g., *wh*-questions) that share base syntactic structures.

Another form of generalization occurs across tasks that share psycholinguistic processing mechanisms. For example, Beeson and Rising (in this volume) mention the natural relationships in training involving writing and reading, such that training that focuses on spelling can generalize to improvements in reading or speech production for the trained words. Harnish (in this volume) described semantic treatments for anomia that influence both auditory comprehension and picture naming for the same words.

The overarching goal of aphasia treatment is transference or generalization from the immediate trained stimuli, tasks, or context to other untrained stimuli, tasks, or contexts, primarily to allow individuals with aphasia to engage in daily communication activities; that is, connected discourse. Many treatments discussed across chapters of this book lead to improvements in connected speech (e.g., CILT, Cherney et al., 2008; semantic feature analysis [SFA], Boyle, 2010; verb network strengthening treatment, Edmonds et al., 2014). As Harney notes (in this volume), some aphasia treatments lead to generalized improvements through remediation of the impaired language mechanism, while other approaches, such as SFA, have broader influence by teaching individuals a strategy to circumvent the impaired language system.

Interference

While a number of factors have potent positive influences on neuroplasticity, it is also possible for neuroplasticity to be maladaptive or harmful. Kolb, Muhammad, and Gibb (2011) note that pain, seizures, and drug addiction can be examples of maladaptive neuroplasticity. Perseverations so common in aphasia can be viewed as an interference phenomenon in this regard. As Greenwald (in this volume) noted, perseverations that are frequent in Wernicke's aphasia are at times viewed as the lack of deactivation of prior productions of words that act as competitors in future attempts to say other words (Cohen & Dehaene, 1998).

Kleim and Jones (2008) include interference as a form of maladaptive neuroplasticity seen in rehabilitation. Interference occurs when training on one skill is detrimental to the potential benefit of training for subsequent skills. When Wilshire (in this volume) discussed conduction aphasia treatments, she mentions that one side effect of contextual priming treatment with phonologically similar pairings is phonologic confusion (e.g., Fisher, Wilshire, & Ponsford, 2009), which we might consider a form of interference effect. Fisher et al. proposed that one reason contextual priming ultimately works as an intervention method is that individuals implement error-monitoring mechanisms to overcome the interfering phonologic confusions that are often reported during this treatment approach. Another example of interference seen in the aphasia treatment literature is provided by Keane and Kiran (2015), who reported that a trilingual speaker with aphasia was trained in one language, which impeded progress in an untrained language.

To avoid interference among a set of impaired language mechanisms, attention might be given to sequencing treatments. Beeson and Rising in their chapter discuss writing interventions that occur in sequence, as advances in one mechanism of spelling (e.g., phonological) may need to take place prior to implementing more advanced spelling methods (e.g., interactive), which would otherwise be interfered with by the impaired mechanism.

Other Principles of Rehabilitation

In addition to the principles espoused by Kleim and Jones (2008), there are other factors that might be considered for their impact on aphasia treatment outcomes. Many of these principles can be applied in conjunction with the variety of treatments described across the chapters of this volume.

Sufficient Abilities

Cramer (2011) noted that "a behavior whose underlying brain regions are destroyed is less likely to improve than a behavior whose underlying regions are accessible to a restorative therapy" (p. S6). It is notable that functional gains post–motor therapy for hemiplegia (upper extremity) are greatest for those who begin treatment with some residual voluntary movement (Duncan et al., 2003; Kwakkel, 2006). A minimum level of motor function is a requirement stipulated for admission to constraint-induced motor therapy (Taub et al., 1993). However, those with precious little movement do respond to targeted as opposed to functional practice approaches (Taub et al., 2014).

In aphasia rehabilitation, there is some indication that a sufficient ability must be present for progress to take place—*a leg to stand on*, so to speak. It is not uncommon to find that the more severe the aphasia, the more limited the progress following treatment. For example, Crosson, Bohsali, and Raymer (in this volume) reported the work of Crosson and colleagues (2007), where, following intentional treatment for word retrieval, greater improvements in naming for trained and untrained probes were evident for groups with moderate–severe naming impairment compared to profound impairment. In a recent meta-analysis of randomized controlled trials of aphasia treatment, there was considerable variability of treatment effects across studies with little relationship to aphasia severity, which was attributed to methodologic variations across studies conducted in many different countries (Brady et al., 2016).

Error Production in Training

While it is a decades-old principle of learning, Wilson and colleagues (Wilson, Baddeley, Evans, & Shiel, 1994; Wilson & Evans, 1996) moved the principle of "errorless learning" into neurorehabilitation circles. They reported that individuals with memory impairments associated with brain injury or dementia can remember facts better when trained in an errorless format as compared to errorful trial-and-error practice. One notion is that the Hebbian principle—*neurons that fire together wire together*—implies that error production during training may be counterproductive and reinforce errors (Fillingham, Hodgson, Sage, & Lambon Ralph, 2003). In brain injury, declarative memory mechanisms (i.e., mesial temporal lobe) through which one can "learn from one's mistakes" are often damaged. Errorless methods take advantage of intact neural networks (typically basal ganglia circuits) of implicit or procedural learning (Middleton & Schwartz, 2012) to improve memory for specific information.

The influence of error production on aphasia treatment outcomes also has been examined, especially in word-retrieval training paradigms. Chapters by Harnish and Greenwald (in this volume) both refer to errorless naming training studies by Fillingham, Sage, and Lambon Ralph (2005, 2006). When this effect has been examined systematically for naming treatments in aphasia, improvements are *comparable* in errorless and errorful training conditions, although participants often prefer errorless training methods perceived to be less frustrating. Likewise, in spelling remediation in individuals with acquired dysgraphia, errorless and errorful copy and recall approaches had similar positive outcomes, although some advantage was evident for errorful approaches at one-month follow-up (Raymer, Strobel, Prokup, Thomason, & Reff, 2010). This finding speaks to the integrity of declarative memory and frontal executive mechanisms that are integral to error awareness during aphasia rehabilitation.

Feedback Influences in Rehabilitation

The type of feedback provided during training events is another factor that has a potent influence on training outcomes, especially maintenance of those outcomes (Schmidt & Wrisberg, 2004). Feedback in the form of knowledge of performance (KP) provides information about why or how the response is in error, whereas knowledge of results (KR) feedback gives summary information about the accuracy of the performance. During acquisition phases of training, KP feedback is important and effective, but to promote maintenance of performance, feedback needs to evolve to KR. Harnish (in this volume) reviewed studies that showed that feedback has less effect on aphasia rehabilitation because associative learning takes place in language learning, although feedback increased the rate at which learning took place (Breitenstein, Kamping, Jansen, Schomacher, & Knecht, 2004). However, McKissock and Ward (2007) found that errorful naming training required KR feedback to be successful for improving naming performance compared to no feedback at all. In another example, Leon, Rodriguez and Rosenbek (in this volume) note that feedback played an important role in rehabilitation of prosodic impairments following right-hemisphere damage. In training individuals to overcome affective aprosodia, KP feedback was modified across steps of training to be delayed and intermittent in an effort to promote self-monitoring of prosodic productions and maintain training effects.

Adjuvants to Behavioral Training

An adjuvant is an agent, often pharmacologic, that acts to modify the effects of other agents. In aphasia rehabilitation, several drugs have been tried in an attempt to manipulate neurotransmitter systems needed to facilitate language recovery or to amplify behavioral language treatment effects (Berthier, Pulvermüller, Davila, Casares, & Gutierrez, 2011). Crosson, Bohsali, and Raymer (in this volume) report studies using the dopamine agonist bromocriptine administered to individuals with transcortical motor aphasia as an intervention to promote verbal generativity, with some positive findings in open-label trials (e.g., Albert et al., 1988; Gold, Van Dam, & Silliman, 2000; Raymer et al., 2001). Walker-Batson and colleagues (2001) reported that dextro-amphetamine, a noradrenergic agonist, enhanced aphasia treatment effects on a general test battery. In a systematic review of this literature, Greener, Enderby, and Whurr (2010) found few randomized controlled trials of pharmacologic interventions for aphasia. They reported the best results for a nootropic agent, piracetem, a drug that is not yet approved for use in the United States. Despite the unclear findings, some remain optimistic that drugs have the potential to enhance aphasia recovery when paired with intensive language treatment (Berthier et al., 2011).

Alternative adjuvants explored to enhance aphasia recovery are neuromodulators that use an electrical current in an effort to enhance treatment outcomes (Schlaug, Marchina, & Wan, 2011; Turkeltaub, 2015). The neuromodulatory approaches vary greatly in how, where (left or right hemisphere), when (before or after treatment), and how long they are administered, leading to a complex literature examining their impact on aphasia recovery or treatment effects. Turkeltaub's (2015) review contrasts the approaches and effects of two main neuromodulatory techniques, repetitive transcranial magnetic stimulation (rTMS) and transcranial direct current stimulation (tDCS).

In rTMS, a device is positioned above the skull to deliver a magnetic pulse that incites an electrical current over a targeted focal brain region in the left or right hemisphere. When administered at a low frequency, rTMS inhibits functions in the target brain region, whereas at a high frequency, it excites neuronal firing in the underlying region (Turkeltaub, 2015). Side effects can include headache, dizziness, or, in rare occasions, a seizure (Schlaug et al., 2011). Among the first to explore the influence of rTMS in aphasia rehabilitation were Naeser and colleagues (2012). Language treatment is administered before or after the rTMS session. Systematic reviews and meta-analyses of aphasia treatment studies employing rTMS demonstrate that improvements in language skills such as word-retrieval abilities occur when low frequency TMS is applied to right inferior frontal cortex (Gadenz, Moreira, Capobianco, & Cassol, 2015; Li, Qu, Yuan, & Du, 2015; Ren et al., 2014). Thus, the best effects are reported when rTMS is used to inhibit the right hemisphere during aphasia recovery.

An alternative portable, less expensive, and safe neuromodulator technique is tDCS, in which an electrical current is applied directly to the scalp to induce a broader signal. Anodal tDCS acts as an excitatory stimulus, and cathodal tDCS decreases the likelihood of cortical excitability (Schlaug et al., 2011). This technique can be administered before, during, or after language therapy. Reported side effects include tingling, burning, or itching sensations (Turkeltaub, 2015). A careful systematic review of 12 studies using tDCS for aphasia, including six studies incorporated in a meta-analysis of effects for a common picture-naming measure, showed little clear benefit of the technique (Elsner, Kugler, Pohl, & Mehrholz, 2015). In contrast, a meta-analysis of three tDCS studies administering cathodal tDCS to the right hemisphere reported positive improvements for naming in aphasia (Otal, Olma, Floel, & Wellwood, 2015). Cappon, Jahanshahi, and Bisiacchi (2016) conclude that more consistent methods need to be employed before any true benefits of tDCS for aphasia rehabilitation are known.

Life Participation Approaches in Aphasia Treatment

The World Health Organization International Classification of Functioning, Disability and Health (WHO ICF, 2001) integrates biomedical and psychosocial perspective on health and disability. The WHO ICF represents the interaction of three primary domains: body structure/function,

Table 17.3 Strategies to Enhance Communication in Individuals with Aphasia

Strategies when speaking to individuals with aphasia and auditory comprehension impairments:

1. Speak slowly, with pauses between phrases of a sentence.

2. Look directly at the person with aphasia; make eye contact.

3. Write down key words to help the person understand the main concepts.

4. Embellish speech with gestures, written words, or drawings.

5. Speak at a natural loudness level with natural intonation.

Strategies for individuals with expressive communication impairments:

1. Encourage the person to get out whatever words they can.

2. Encourage the use of circumlocutions.

3. Disregard mistakes as long as the idea is understood.

4. Encourage the person to use alternative modes of communication, such as gestures, writing, or drawing, to express ideas.

5. Write down what you think the person is trying to say to verify the message.

6. Repeat what is understood so far.

7. Provide a pointing board with pictures or letters to spell words they cannot say.

8. Give the person with aphasia options if they are struggling to utter a specific word.

9. Give the person with aphasia plenty of time to respond.

activity/participation, and contextual factors. Much of the focus across chapters of this volume has been on *language functions*, including their assessment and treatment. As Patterson (in this volume) reviews assessment tools developed to address the social context of communication guided by the WHO ICF, so, too, does that framework lead to treatments devised to promote life-participation approaches to aphasia (LPAA; Chapey et al., 2008). The LPAA approaches can be categorized generally as *functional/pragmatic* in which individuals with aphasia are trained to use effective communication strategies, or *social* in which intervention aims to remove barriers in the communication context, typically through communication partners (Worrall, Papathanasiou, & Sherratt, 2013). Principles of neuroplasticity reviewed throughout this chapter have a potent influence on learning, maintenance, and generalization of communication strategies trained within these LPAA treatments. Importantly, treatments for language functions and life participation should be integrated throughout the recovery continuum to maximize communication outcomes for individuals with aphasia.

Functional Approaches in Aphasia Treatment

The term *functional* in this context refers to the use of language for daily communication activities (Armstrong, Ferguson, & Simmons-Mackie, 2013; Frattali, 1998). A number of treatment techniques take a broader approach to facilitating communication for individuals with aphasia to take part in daily conversations. Such approaches may use role-playing (e.g., conversational coaching; Hopper, Holland, & Rewega, 2002), multi-modality training (Rose, Mok, Carragher, Katthagen, & Attard, 2016), and practice with discourse-level text (e.g., script training; Cherney, Kaye, & Van Vuuren, 2014). A common thread across many functional treatment approaches is that individuals with aphasia are encouraged to implement any strategies to communicate, not just auditory-verbal alone.

A number of compensatory strategies can be implemented either to facilitate comprehension in light of impaired auditory skills or to support expression of thoughts and ideas despite impaired verbal expression abilities. Table 17.3 lists a number of strategies that can be used by individuals speaking to persons with aphasia to support comprehension or circumvent expression impairments. However, intervention may be needed so that persons with aphasia can become skilled in the use of compensatory strategies. One natural context for this to take place is within group aphasia therapy.

Group Therapy

In group aphasia treatment, several individuals with aphasia work together to engage in communication activities (Elman, 2011). The key purpose is for the participants to have opportunities for interchanges in which they can implement compensatory strategies to express or comprehend language as needed, in a safe, supportive environment. A natural outgrowth of such groups is a psychosocial benefit when individuals with common communication struggles work together to support and accept the new identity and deal with the complex emotions that aphasia has generated.

A number of studies have systematically explored the outcomes associated with aphasia group treatment as compared to treatment provided to individuals with aphasia (e.g., Elman & Bernstein-Ellis, 1999; Wertz et al., 1981). Systematic reviews of the literature have summarized findings across studies and report that outcomes of group aphasia therapy are commensurate with those of individualized treatment for language, communication, and quality of life measures (Brady et al., 2016; Layfield, Ballard, & Robin, 2013). Aphasia group training can benefit participants in the size of their social networks and community access as well (Lanyon, Rose, & Worrall, 2013).

Social Support for Aphasia

The WHO ICF model includes the environment as a consideration for its impact for an individual recovering from or living with a health condition, such as aphasia. The environment of an individual with aphasia includes many communication partners (e.g., family members, friends, healthcare providers) who may or may not naturally know how to communicate effectively with someone with aphasia. Therefore, communication partner training may be helpful to embellish the communicative context. A number of investigations have explored ways to support communication with different groups of communication partners, including families (Rautakoski, 2011), volunteers (e.g., Kagan, Black, Duchan, Simmons-Mackie, & Square, 2001), and medical providers (Legg, Young, & Bryer, 2005). While many partner-training studies provide education and counseling about aphasia, the majority of studies incorporate dyads where individuals with aphasia and their partners are trained to use specific communication strategies to facilitate better comprehension, expression, and repair of communication breakdown. Simmons-Mackie and colleagues (Simmons-Mackie, Cherney, Raymer, Holland & Armstrong, 2010; Simmons-Mackie, Raymer, & Cherney, 2016), in their systematic reviews of this extensive literature, reported that communication partner training leads to considerable improvements in the use of effective communication strategies by partners of individuals with aphasia and successful communication by individuals with aphasia. No changes in language measures were noted for persons with aphasia following communication partner training, however.

Conclusions

Treatment for aphasia is a complex process that requires the participation of a number of professionals in an interprofessional synergism to assure the best outcomes for individuals with aphasia (van de Sandt-Koenderman, van der Meulen, & Ribbers, 2012). While many of the approaches reviewed across the chapters of this text are language-oriented methods that aim to promote neuroplastic language recovery, other approaches focus on optimizing life participation of individuals with aphasia, using multi-modality communication methods and effective communication partners. We emphasize that these varied approaches are complementary, such that all may be implemented in an individual with aphasia as indicated with a consideration of the patterns of impairment, stage of recovery, neurologic indications, and personal factors. A number of principles of neuroplasticity can be considered for their modulatory effects of behavioral treatments for aphasia.

Fortunately, advances in technology now allow individuals with aphasia to take part in ongoing activities apart from traditional face-to-face individualized therapy. Telehealth practices may allow individuals with aphasia to benefit from treatment at a distance (Woolf et al., 2016). Computer programs and mobile applications on tablets or smartphones allow individuals with aphasia to participate in activities independently or with guidance from clinicians (Des Roches, Balachandran, Ascenso, Tripodis, & Kiran, 2015). Virtual reality applications are advancing to engage individuals with aphasia in rich communication interactions (Marshall et al., 2016).

The challenge persists for clinicians who work with individuals with aphasia to provide interventions that optimize outcomes. Research continues to explore methods to enhance behavioral treatments, advance technological applications, understand pharmacologic and neuromodulatory options, and implement psychosocial life-participation approaches. Other influences on successful recovery from aphasia are under investigation, such as exercise and motivation. Progress will continue in efforts to identify optimum treatment combinations that lead to the greatest language-recovery possible, the most effective communication skills, and the best quality of life and engagement for individuals with aphasia.

References

Adkins, D.L. (2015). Cortical stimulation-induced structural plasticity and functional recovery after brain damage. In F.H. Kobeissy (Ed.), *Brain neurotrauma: Molecular, neuropsychological, and rehabilitation aspects* (Chapter 43). Boca Raton, FL: CRC Press/Taylor & Francis.

Adkins, D.L., Campos, P., Quach, D., Borromeo, M., Schallert, K., & Jones, T.A. (2006). Epidural cortical stimulation enhances motor function after sensorimotor cortical infarcts in rats. *Experimental Neurology, 200*, 356–370.

Albert, M. L., Bachman, D., Morgan, A., & Helm-Estabrooks, N. (1988). Pharmacotherapy of aphasia. *Neurology, 38*, 877–879.

Allred, R.P., & Jones, T.A. (2008). Maladaptive effects of learning with the less-affected forelimb after focal cortical infarcts in rats. *Experimental Neurology, 210*, 172–181.

Allred, R.P., Maldonado, M.A., Hsu, J.E., & Jones, T.A. (2005). Training the "less-affected" forelimb after unilateral cortical infarcts interferes with functional recovery of the impaired forelimb in rats. *Restorative Neurology and Neuroscience, 23*, 297–302.

Armstrong, E., Ferguson, A., & Simmons-Mackie, N. (2013). Discourse and functional approaches to aphasia. In I. Papathanasiou, P. Coppens, & C. Potages (Eds.), *Aphasia and related neurogenic communication disorders* (pp. 217–231). Burlington, MA: Jones & Bartlett Learning.

Bakheit, A. M. O., Shaw, S., Barrett, L., Wood, J., Carrington, S., Griffiths, S., . . . Koutsi, F. (2007). A prospective, randomized, parallel group, controlled study of the effect of intensity of speech and language therapy on early recovery from post-stroke aphasia. *Clinical Rehabilitation, 21*, 885–894.

Barrett, A.M., & Rothi, L.J.G. (2002). Theoretical bases for neuropsychological interventions. In P.J. Eslinger (Ed.), *Neuropsychological interventions: Clinical research and practice* (pp. 16–37). New York, NY: Guilford Press.

Basso, A. (1992). Prognostic factors in aphasia. *Aphasiology, 6*, 337–348.

Basso, A., Cattaneo, S., Girelli, L., Luzzatti, C., Miozzo, A., Modena, L., & Monti, A. (2011). Treatment efficacy of language and calculation disorders and speech apraxia: A review of the literature. *European Journal of Physical Rehabilitation, 47*, 101–121.

Bateman, F. (1890). *On aphasia or loss of speech and the localization of the faculty of articulate language.* London, UK: J. & A. Churchill.

Bates, E., Reilly, J., Wulfeck, B., Dronkers, N., Opie, M., Fenson, J., . . . Herbst, K. (2001). Differential effects of unilateral lesions on language production in children and adults. *Brain and Language, 79*, 223–265.

Berthier, M.L. (2005). Postroke aphasia—epidemiology, pathophysiology and treatment. *Drugs and Aging, 22*, 163–182.

Berthier, M.L., Pulvermüller, F., Davila, G., Casares, N.G., & Gutierrez, A. (2011). Drug therapy of post-stroke aphasia: A review of current evidence. *Neuropsychology Review, 21*, 302–317. doi:10.1007/s11065-011-9177-7

Black-Schaffer, R.M., & Osberg, J.S. (1990). Return to work after stroke: Development of a predictive model. *Archives of Physical Medicine and Rehabilitation, 71*(5), 285–290.

Boyle, M. (2010). Semantic feature analysis treatment for aphasia word retrieval impairments: What's in a name? *Topics in Stroke Rehabilitation, 17*(6), 411–422. doi:10.1310/tsr1706-411

Brady, M.C., Kelly, H., Godwin, J., & Enderby, P. (2012). Speech and language therapy for aphasia following stroke. *Cochrane Database of Systematic Reviews,* Issue 5. Art. No.: CD000425. doi:10.1002/14651858.CD000452.pub3

Brady, M.C., Kelly, H., Godwin, J., Enderby, P., & Campbell, P. (2016). Speech and language therapy for aphasia following stroke. *Cochrane Database of Systematic Reviews,* Issue 6. Art. No.: CD000425. doi:10.1002/14651858.CD000452.pub4

Breitenstein, C., Kamping, S., Jansen, A., Schomacher, M., & Knecht, S. (2004). Word learning can be achieved without feedback: Implications for aphasia therapy. *Restorative Neurology & Neuroscience, 22*(6), 445–458.

Buonomano, D.V., & Merzenich, M.M. (1998). Cortical plasticity: From synapses to maps. *Annual Review of Neuroscience, 21*, 149–186.

Cappon, D., Jahanshahi, M., & Bisiacchi, P. (2016). Value and efficacy of transcranial direct current stimulation in the cognitive rehabilitation: A critical review since 2000. *Frontiers in Neuroscience, 10*, Article 157. doi:10.3389/fnins.2016.00157

Chapey, R., Duchan, J.F., Elman, R.J., Garcia, L.J., Kagan, A., Lyon, J.G., & Simmons-Mackie, N. (2008). Life-participation approach to aphasia: A statement of values for the future. In R. Chapey (Ed.), *Language intervention strategies in aphasia and related neurogenic communication disorders* (5th ed., pp. 279–289). Baltimore, MD: Lippincott Williams &Wilkins.

Cherney, L.R., Kaye, R.C., & van Vuuren, S. (2014). Acquisition and maintenance of scripts in aphasia: A comparison of two cuing conditions. *American Journal of Speech-Language Pathology, 14*(5), 424–431.

Cherney, L.R., Patterson, J.P., Raymer, A.M., Frymark, T., & Schooling, T. (2008). Evidence-based systematic review: Effects of intensity of treatment and constraint-induced language therapy for individuals with stroke-induced aphasia. *Journal of Speech, Language, and Hearing Research, 51*, 1282–1299.

Cherney, L.R., Patterson, J.P., & Raymer, A.M. (2011). Intensity of aphasia therapy: Evidence and efficacy. *Current Neurology and Neuroscience Reports, 11*, 560–569.

Cherney, L., & Robey, R. (2001). Aphasia treatment: Recovery, prognosis and clinical effectiveness. In R. Chapey (Ed.), *Language intervention strategies in adult aphasia* (4th ed., pp. 148–172). Baltimore, MD: Williams & Wilkins.

Code, C., (2001). Multifactorial processes in recovery from aphasia: Developing the foundations for a multileveled framework. *Brain and Language, 77*(1), 25–44.

Cohen, L., & Dehaene, S. (1998). Competition between past and present: Assessment and interpretation of verbal perseverations. *Brain, 121*, 1641–1659.

Corbetta, M., Kincade, M.J., Lewis, C., Snyder, A.Z., & Sapir, A. (2005). Neural basis and recovery of spatial attention deficits in spatial neglect. *Nature Neuroscience, 8*, 1603–1610.

Coslett, H.B., & Saffran, E. (1989). Evidence for preserved reading in "pure alexia." *Brain, 112*(2), 327–359.

Cramer, S.C. (2008). Repairing the human brain after stroke. II. Restorative therapies. *Annals of Neurology, 63*, 549–560.

Cramer, S.C. (2011). An overview of therapies to promote repair of the brain after stroke. *Head & Neck, 33* (Suppl. 1), S5–S7.

Cramer, S.C., Sur, M., Dobkin, B.H., O'Brien, C., Sanger, T.D., Trojanowski, J.Q., . . . Vinogradov, S. (2011). Harnessing neuroplasticity for clinical applications. *Brain, 134*, 1591–1609.

Crosson, B., Fabrizio, K.S., Singletary, F., Cato, M.A., Wierenga, C.E., Parkinson, R.B., . . . Rothi, L.J.G. (2007). Treatment of naming in nonfluent aphasia through manipulation of intention and attention: A phase 1 comparison of two novel treatments. *Journal of the International Neuropsychological Society, 13*, 582–594.

Des Roches, C.A., Balachandran, I., Ascenso, E.M., Tripodis, Y., & Kiran, S. (2015). Effectiveness of an impairment-based individualized rehabilitation program using an iPad-based software platform. *Frontiers in Human Neuroscience, 8*, 1015. doi:10.3389/fnhum.2014.01015

Dickey, L., Kagan, A., Lindsay, M.P., Fang, J., Rowland, A., & Black, S. (2010). Incidence and profile of inpatient stroke-induced aphasia in Ontario, Canada. *Archives of Physical Medicine & Rehabilitation, 91*, 196–202.

Dignam, J., Copland, D., McKinnon, E., Burfein, P., O'Brien, K., Farrell, A., & Rodriguez, A.D. (2015). Intensive versus distributed aphasia therapy. *Stroke, 46*, 2206–2211. doi:10.1161/STROKEAHA.115.009522

Dignam, J.K., Rodriguez, A.D., & Copland, D.A. (2016). Evidence for intensive aphasia therapy: Consideration of theories from neuroscience and cognitive psychology. *Physical Medicine & Rehabilitation, 8*, 254–267.

Duncan, P., Studenski, S., Richards, L., Gollub, S., Lai, S.M., Reker, D., . . . Johnson, D. (2003). Randomized clinical trial of therapeutic exercise in subacute stroke. *Stroke, 34*, 2173–2180.

Eack, S.M., Hogarty, G.E., Cho, R.Y., Prasad, K.M., Greenwald, D.P., Hogarty, S.S., & Keshavan, M.S. (2010). Neuroprotective effects of cognitive enhancement therapy against gray matter loss in early schizophrenia: Results from a 2-year randomized controlled trial. *Archives of General Psychiatry, 67*, 674–682.

Edmonds, L.A., Mammino, K., & Ojeda, J. (2014). Effect of verb network strengthening treatment (VNeST) in persons with aphasia: Extension and replication of previous findings. *American Journal of Speech-Language Pathology, 23*(2), S312–S329.

El Hachioui, H., Lingsma, H.F., van de Sandt-Koenderman, M.E., Dippel, D.W.J., Koudstaal, P.H., & Visch-Brink, E.G. (2013). Recovery of aphasia after stroke: A 1-year follow-up study. *Journal of Neurology, 260*, 166–171.

Ellis, C., & Urban, S. (2016). Age and aphasia: A review of presence, type, recovery and clinical outcomes. *Topics in Stroke Rehabilitation, 23*(6), 430–439.

Ellis, C., Simpson, A.N., Bonilha, H., Mauldin, P.D., & Simpson, K.N. (2012). The one-year attributable cost of post stroke aphasia. *Stroke, 43*, 1429–1431.

Elman, R.J. (2011). Social and life participation approaches to aphasia intervention. In L.L. LaPointe (Ed.), *Aphasia and related neurogenic language disorders* (4th ed., pp. 171–184). New York, NY: Thieme.

Elman, R.J., & Bernstein-Ellis, E. (1999). The efficacy of group communication treatment in adults with chronic aphasia. *Journal of Speech, Language, and Hearing Research, 42*, 411–419.

Elsner, B., Kugler, J., Pohl, M., & Mehrholz, J. (2015). Transcranial direct current stimulation (tDCS) for improving aphasia in patients with aphasia after stroke. *Cochrane Database of Systematic Reviews, 5*, Art. No. CD009760. doi:10.1002/14651858.CD009760.pub3

Fillingham, J.K., Hodgson, C., Sage, K., & Lambon Ralph, M.A. (2003). The application of errorless learning to aphasic disorders: A review of theory and practice. *Neuropsychological Rehabilitation, 13*, 337–363.

Fillingham, J.K., Sage, K., & Lambon Ralph, M.A. (2005). Treatment of anomia using errorless and errorful learning: Are frontal executive skills and feedback important? *International Journal of Language & Communication Disorders, 40*, 505–523.

Fillingham, J.K., Sage, K., & Lambon Ralph, M. (2006). The treatment of anomia using errorless learning. *Neuropsychological Rehabilitation, 16*, 129–154.

Finger, S. (1994). *Origins of neuroscience: A history of explorations into brain function.* New York, NY: Oxford University Press.

Fisher, C.A., Wilshire, C.E., & Ponsford, J.L. (2009). Word discrimination therapy: A new technique for the treatment of a phonologically-based word-finding impairment. *Aphasiology, 23*(6), 676–693.

Franz, S.I. (1905). The reeducation of an aphasic. *Journal of Philosophy, Psychology and Scientific Methods, 2*, 589–597.

Franz, S.I. (1924). Studies in re-education: The aphasias. *The Journal of Comparative Psychology, 4*, 349–429.

Frattali, C.M. (1998). Assessing functional outcomes: An overview. *Seminars in Speech and Language, 19*(3), 209–220.

Gadenz, C.D., de Campos Moreira, T., Capobianco, D.M., & Cassol, M. (2015). Effects of repetitive transcranial magnetic stimulation in the rehabilitation of communication and deglutition disorders: Systematic review of randomized controlled trials. *Folia Phoniatrica et Logopaedica, 67*, 97–105. doi:10.1159/000439128

Godecke, E., Ciccone, N.A., Granger, A.S., Rai, T., West, D., Cream, A., Cartwright, J., & Hankey, G.J. (2014). A comparison of aphasia therapy outcomes before and after a very early rehabilitation programme following stroke. *International Journal of Language and Communication Disorders, 49*, 149–161.

Gold, M., Van Dam, D., & Silliman, E. R. (2000). An open-label trial of bromocriptine in nonfluent aphasia: A qualitative analysis of word storage and retrieval. *Brain and Language, 74*, 141–156.

Goldstein, K. (1942). *Aftereffects of brain injuries in war: Their evaluation and treatment.* New York: Grune & Stratton.

Goldstein, K. (1948). *Language and language disturbances.* New York: Grune & Stratton.

Goodglass, H. (1985). Aphasiology in the United States. *International Journal of Neuroscience, 25*(3–4), 307–311.

Grant, M.J., & Booth, A. (2009). A typology of reviews: An analysis of 14 review types and associated methodologies. *Health Information and Libraries Journal, 26*, 91–108, doi:10.1111/j.1471-1842.2009.00848.x

Greener, J., Enderby, P., & Whurr, R. (2010). Pharmacologic treatment for aphasia following stroke. *Cochrane Database of Systematic Reviews, 5.*

Greenhouse, J.B., Fromm, D., Iyengar, S., Dew, M.A., Holland, A.L., & Kass, R.E. (1990). The making of a meta-analysis: A quantitative review of the aphasia treatment literature. In K.W. Wachter & M.L. Straf (Eds.), *The future of meta-analysis* (pp. 29–46). New York, NY: Russell Sage Foundation.

Hagen, C. (1973). Communication abilities in hemiplegia: Effect of speech therapy. *Archives of Physical Medicine & Rehabilitation, 54,* 454–463.

Harnish, S.M., Morgan, J., Lundine, J.P., Bauer, A., Singletary, F., Benjamin, M.L., . . . Crosson, B. (2014). Dosing of a cued picture-naming treatment for anomia. *American Journal of Speech-Language Pathology, 23*(2), S285–S299. doi:10.1044/2014_AJSLP-13-0081

Hilari, K. (2011). The impact of stroke: Are people with aphasia different to those without? *Disability and Rehabilitation, 33,* 211–218.

Hilari, K., Needle, J.J., & Harrison, K.L. (2012). What are the important factors in health-related quality of life for people with aphasia? A systematic review. *Archives of Physical Medicine and Rehabilitation, 93*(Suppl. 1), S86–S95.

Hinckley, J. J., & Carr, T. H. (2005). Comparing the outcomes of intensive and non-intensive context-based aphasia treatment. *Aphasiology, 19,* 965–974.

Hinckley, J. J., & Craig, H. K. (1998). Influence of rate of treatment on the naming abilities of adults with chronic aphasia. *Aphasiology, 12,* 989–1006.

Holland, A.L., Fromm, D.S., DeRuyter, F., & Stein, M. (1996). Treatment efficacy: Aphasia. *Journal of Speech & Hearing Research, 39* (5), S27–S36.

Hopper, T., Holland, A., & Rewega, M. (2002). Conversational coaching: Treatment outcomes and future directions. *Aphasiology, 15*(7), 745–761. doi:10.1080/02687030244000059

Jacquin-Courtois, S., O'Shea, J., Luauté, J., Pisella, L., Revol, P., Mizuno, K., . . . Rossetti, Y. (2013). Rehabilitation of spatial neglect by prism adaptation: A peculiar expansion of sensorimotor after-effects to spatial cognition. *Neuroscience & Biobehavioral Reviews, 37*(4), 594–609.

Johansson, B.B. (2000). Brain plasticity and stroke rehabilitation. The Willis lecture. *Stroke, 31,* 223–230.

Jones, T.A., Allred, R.P., Jefferson, S.C., Kerr, A.L., Woodie, D.A., Cheng, S.Y., & Adkins, D.L. (2013). Motor system plasticity in stroke models: Intrinsically use-dependent, unreliably useful. *Stroke, 44*(6 Suppl. 1), S104–S106.

Jorgensen, H.S., Reith, J., Nakayama, H., Kammersgaard, L.P., Raaschou, H.O., & Olsen, T.S. (1999). What determines good recovery in patients with the most severe strokes? The Copenhagen Stroke Study. *Stroke, 30,* 2008–2012.

Kagan, A., Black, S., Duchan, J., Simmons-Mackie, N., & Square, P. (2001). Training volunteers as conversation partners using "supported conversation for adults with aphasia" (SCA): A controlled trial. *Journal of Speech, Language, Hearing Research, 44,* 624–638.

Karni, A., Meyer, G., Rey-Hipolito, C., Jezzard, P., Adams, M.M., Turner, R., & Ungerleider, L.G. (1998). The acquisition of skilled motor performance: Fast and slow experience-driven changes in primary motor cortex. *Proceedings of the National Academy of Sciences U.S.A., 95,* 861–868.

Keane, C., & Kiran, S. (2015). The nature of facilitation and interference in the multilingual language system: Insights from treatment in a case of trilingual aphasia. *Cognitive Neuropsychology, 32,* 169–194. doi: 10.1080/02643294.2015.1061982

Kendall, D.L., Nadeau, S.E., Conway, T., Fuller, R.H., Riestra, A., & Rothi, L.J.G. (2007). Treatability of different components of aphasia—Insights from a case study. *Journal of Rehabilitation Research & Development, 43,* 323–336.

Kerr, A.L., Wolke, M.L., Bell, J.A., & Jones, T.A. (2013). Post-stroke protection from maladaptive effects of learning with the non-paretic forelimb by bimanual home cage experience in C57BL/6 mice. *Behavioral and Brain Research, 252,* 180–187.

Kiran, S. (2008). Typicality of inanimate category exemplars in aphasia treatment: Further evidence for semantic complexity. *Journal of Speech, Language, and Hearing Research, 51,* 1550–1568.

Kiran, S., & Thompson, C.K. (2003). The role of semantic complexity in treatment of naming deficits: Training semantic categories in fluent aphasia by controlling exemplar typicality. *Journal of Speech, Language, and Hearing Research, 46,* 608–622.

Kleim, J.A. (2011). Neural plasticity and neurorehabilitation: Teaching the new brain old tricks. *Journal of Communication Disorders, 44,* 521–528.

Kleim, J.A., Barbay, S., & Nudo, R.J. (1998). Functional reorganization of the rat motor cortex following motor skill learning. *Journal of Neurophysiology, 80,* 3321–3325.

Kleim, J.A., Bruneau, R., VandenBerg, P., MacDonald, E., Mulrooney, R., & Pocock, D. (2003). Motor cortex stimulation enhances motor recovery and reduces peri-infarct dysfunction following ischemic insult. *Neurological Research, 25*(8), 789–793.

Kleim, J.A., & Jones, T.A. (2008). Principles of experience-dependent neural plasticity: Implications for rehabilitation after brain damage. *Journal of Speech, Language, Hearing Research, 51,* S225–S239.

Kolb, B., Muhammad, A., & Gibb, R. (2011). Searching for factors underlying cerebral plasticity in the normal and injured brain. *Journal of Communication Disorders, 44,* 503–516.

Koob, G.F., & Volkow, N.D. (2010). Neurocircuitry of addiction. *Neuropsycho-pharmacology, 35,* 217–238.

Koski, L., Mernar, T., & Dobkin, B. (2004). Immediate and long-term changes in corticomotor output in response to rehabilitation: Correlation with functional improvements in chronic stroke. *Neurorehabilitation and Neural Repair, 18,* 230–249.

Kwakkel, G. (2006). Impact of intensity of practice after stroke: Issues for consideration. *Disability and Rehabilitation, 28*(13–14), 823–830.

Laganaro, M., Di Pietro, M., & Schnider, A. (2006). Computerised treatment of anomia in acute aphasia: Treatment intensity and training size. *Neuropsychological Rehabilitation, 16*(6), 630–640.

Lanyon, L.E., Rose, M.L., & Worrall, L. (2013). The efficacy of outpatient and community-based aphasia group interventions: A systematic review. *International Journal of Speech-Language Pathology, 15*(4), 359–374. doi:10.3109/17549507.2012.752865

Laska, A.C., Hellblom, A., Murray, A., Kahan, T., & von Arbin, M. (2001). Aphasia in acute stroke and relation to outcome. *Journal of Internal Medicine, 249,* 413–422.

Laska, A.C., Kahan, T., Hellblom, A. Murray, V., & von Arbin, A.M. (2011). A randomized controlled trial on very early speech and language therapy in acute stroke patients with aphasia. *Cerebrovascular Diseases Extra, 1,* 66–74. doi:10.1159/000329835

Layfield, C.A., Ballard, K.J., & Robin, D.A. (2013). Evaluating group therapy for aphasia: What is the evidence? *EBP Briefs, 7*(5), 1–17.

Legg, C., Young, L., & Bryer, A. (2005). Training sixth-year medical students in obtaining case-history information from adults with aphasia. *Aphasiology, 19,* 559–575.

Li, Y., Qu, Y., Yuan, M., & Du, T., (2015). Low-frequency repetitive transcranial magnetic stimulation for patients with aphasia after stroke: A meta-analysis. *Journal of Rehabilitation Medicine, 47,* 675–681.

Luria, A.R. (1970). *Traumatic aphasia: Its syndromes, psychology, and treatment.* The Hague: Mouton de Gruyter.

Maher, L., Kendall, D., Swearengin, J., Rodriguez, A., Leon, S., Pingel, K., . . . Rothi, L. (2006). A pilot study of use-dependent learning in the context of constraint induced language therapy. *Journal of the International Neuropsychological Society, 12,* 843–852.

Marshall, J., Booth, T., Devane, N., Galliers, J., Greenwood, H., Hilari, K., . . . Woolf, C. (2016). Evaluating the benefits of aphasia intervention delivered in virtual reality: Results of a quasi-randomised study. *PLoS One, 11*(8), e0160381. doi:10.1371/journal.pone.0160381

Marshall, R.C., & Freed, D.B. (2006). The personalized cueing method: From the laboratory to the clinic. *American Journal of Speech-Language Pathology, 15,* 103–111.

Marshall, R.C., Wertz, R.T., Weiss, D.G., Aten, J.L., Brookshire, R.H., Garcia-Bunuel, L., . . . Goodman, R. (1989). Home treatment for aphasia patients by trained nonprofessionals. *Journal of Speech & Hearing Disorders, 54,* 462–470.

McClung, J.S., Rothi, L.J.G., & Nadeau, S.E. (2010). Ambient experience in restitutive treatment of aphasia. *Frontiers in Human Neuroscience, 4,* article 183, 1–19. . doi:10.3389/fnhum.2010.00183

McKissock, S., & Ward, J. (2007). Do errors matter? Errorless and errorful learning in anomic picture naming. *Neuropsychological Rehabilitation, 17,* 355–373.

Meinzer, M., Djundja, D., Barthel, G., Elbert, T., & Rockstroth, B. (2005). Long-term stability of improved language functions in chronic aphasia after constraint-induced aphasia therapy. *Stroke, 36,* 1462–1466.

Middleton, E.L., & Schwartz, M.F. (2012). Errorless learning in cognitive rehabilitation: A critical review. *Neuropsychological Rehabilitation, 22*(2), 138–168.

Mills, C.K. (1904). Treatment of aphasia by training. *Journal of the American Medical Association, 43,* 1940–1949.

Mosberger, A.C., de Clauser, L., Kasper, H., & Schwab, M.E. (2016). Motivational state, reward value, and Pavlovian cues differentially affect skilled forelimb grasping in rats. *Learning and Memory, 23*(6), 289–302.

Mozaffarian, D., Benjamin, E.J., Go, A.S., Arnett, D.K., Blaha, M.J., Cushman, M., . . . Turner, M.B. (Writing Group). (2016). Heart disease and stroke statistics—2016 update: A report from the American Heart Association. American Heart Association Statistics Committee; Stroke Statistics Subcommittee. *Circulation, 133*(4), e38–e360.

Naeser, M.A., Martin, P.I., Ho, M., Treglia, E., Kaplan, E., Bashir, S., & Pascual-Leone, A. (2012). Transcranial magnetic stimulation and aphasia rehabilitation. *Archives of Physical Medicine & Rehabilitation, 93*(Suppl. 1), S26–S34. doi:10.1016/j.apmr.2011.04.026

Nouwens, F., Visch-Brink, E.G., Van de Sandt-Koenderman, M.M., Dippel, D.W., Koudstaal, P.J., & de Lau, L.M. (2015). Optimal timing of speech and language therapy for aphasia after stroke: More evidence needed. *Expert Reviews in Neurotherapeutics, 15*(8), 885–893. doi:10.1586/14737175

Nudo, R.J. (2007). Postinfarct cortical plasticity and behavioral recovery. *Stroke, 38,* 840–845.

Nudo, R.J. (2011). Neural bases of recovery after brain injury. *Journal of Communication Disorders, 44,* 515–520.

Nudo, R.J. (2013). Recovery after brain injury: Mechanisms and principles. *Frontier in Human Neuroscience, 7,* 887. doi:10.3389/fnhum.2013.00887

Nudo, R.J., Milliken, G.W., Jenkins, W.M., & Merzenich, M.M. (1996). Use-dependent alterations of movement representations in primary motor cortex of adult squirrel monkeys. *Journal of Neuroscience, 16,* 785–807.

Nudo, R.J., Wise, B., SiFuentes, F., & Milliken, G. (1996). Neural substrates for the effects of rehabilitative training on motor recovery after ischemic infarct. *Science, 272,* 1791–1794.

Numminen, S., Korpijaakko-Huuhka, A.M., Parkkila, A.K., Numminen, H., Dastidar, P., & Jehkonen, M. (2016). Factors influencing quality of life six months after a first-ever ischemic stroke: Focus on thrombolyzed patients. *Folia Phoniatrica Logopedica, 68,* 86–91.

O'Halloran, R., Grohn, B., & Worrall, L. (2012). Environmental factors that influence communication for patients with a communication disability in acute hospital stroke units: A quantitative metasynthesis. *Archives of Physical Medicine and Rehabilitation, 93*(1), S77–S85.

O'Halloran, R., Worrall, L., & Hickson, L. (2011). Environmental factors that influence communication between patients and their healthcare providers in acute hospital stroke units: An observational study. *International Journal of Language and Communication Disorders, 46,* 30–47.

Otal, B., Olma, M.C., Floel, A., & Wellwood, I. (2015). Inhibitory non-invasive brain stimulation to homologous language regions as an adjunct to speech and language therapy in post-stroke aphasia: A meta-analysis. *Frontiers in Human Neuroscience, 9,* 236. doi:10.3389/fnhum.2015.00236

Pascual-Leone, A., Wassermann, E.M., Sadato, N., & Hallett, M. (1995). The role of reading activity on the modulation of motor cortical outputs to the reading hand in Braille readers. *Annals of Neurology, 38*(6), 910–915.

Perez, M.A., Lungholt, B.K., Nyborg, K., & Nielsen, J.B. (2004). Motor skill training induces changes in the excitability of the leg cortical area in healthy humans. *Experimental Brain Research, 159*(2), 197–205.

Plautz, E.J., Milliken, G.W., & Nudo, R.J. (2000). Effects of repetitive motor training on movement representations in adult squirrel monkeys: Role of use versus learning. *Neurobiology of Learning and Memory, 74*(1), 27–55.

Poeck, K., Huber, W., & Willmes, K. (1989). Outcomes of intensive language treatment in aphasia. *Journal of Speech and Hearing Disorders, 54,* 471–479.

Pollock, A., St. George, B., Fenton, M., & Firkins, L. (2012). Top ten research priorities relating to life after stroke. *The Lancet, 11,* 209.

Pulvermüller, F., & Berthier, M.L. (2008). Aphasia therapy on a neuroscience basis. *Aphasiology, 22*(6), 563–599.

Pulvermüller, F., Neininger, B., Elbert, T., Mohr, B., Rockstroh, B., Koebbel, P., & Taub, E. (2001). Constraint-induced therapy of chronic aphasia after stroke. *Stroke, 32,* 1621–1626.

Rautakoski, P. (2011). Training total communication. *Aphasiology, 25,* 344–365. doi:10.1080/02687038.2010.530671

Raymer, A.M. (2015). Clinical diagnosis and treatment of naming disorders. In A.E. Hillis (Ed.), *The handbook of adult language disorders* (2nd ed., pp. 161–183). New York, NY: Psychology Press.

Raymer, A. M., Bandy, D., Schwartz, R. L., Adair, J. C., Williamson, D. J. G., Rothi, L. J. G., & Heilman, K. M. (2001). Effects of bromocriptine in a patient with crossed nonfluent aphasia: A case report. *Archives of Physical Medicine and Rehabilitation, 82,* 139–144.

Raymer, A.M., Beeson, P., Holland, A., Kendall, D., Maher, L.M., Martin, N., . . . Rothi, L.J.G. (2008). Translational research in aphasia: From neuroscience to neurorehabilitation. *Journal of Speech, Language, and Hearing Research, 51,* S259–S279.

Raymer, A.M., Ciampitti, M., Holliway, B., Singletary, F., Blonder, L.X., Ketterson, T., . . . Rothi, L.J.G. (2007). Semantic-phonologic treatment for noun and verb retrieval impairments in aphasia. *Neuropsychological Rehabilitation, 17,* 244–270.

Raymer, A.M., Kohen, F.P., & Saffell, D. (2006). Computerised training for impairments of word comprehension and retrieval in aphasia. *Aphasiology, 20,* 257–268.

Raymer, A., Strobel, J., Prokup, T., Thomason, B., & Reff, K.-L. (2010). Errorless versus errorful training of spelling in individuals with acquired dysgraphia. *Neuropsychological Rehabilitation, 20*(1), 1–15.

Ren, C.-L., Zhang, G.-F., Xia, N., Jin, C.-H., Zhang, X.-H., Hao, J.-F., . . . Cai, D.-L. (2014). Effect of low-frequency rTMS on aphasia in stroke patients: A meta-analysis of randomized controlled trials. *PLoS ONE, 9*(7), e102557. doi:10.1371/journal.pone.0102557

Renvall, K., Nickels, L., & Davidson, B. (2013a). Functionally relevant items in the treatment of aphasia (part I): Challenges for current practice. *Aphasiology, 27*(6), 636–650.

Renvall, K., Nickels, L., & Davidson, B. (2013b). Functionally relevant items in the treatment of aphasia (part II): Further perspectives and specific tools. *Aphasiology, 27*(6), 651–677.

Robey, R.R. (1994). The efficacy of treatment for aphasic persons: A meta-analysis. *Brain and Language, 47*(4), 582–608.

Robey, R.R. (1998). A meta-analysis of clinical outcomes in the treatment of aphasia. *Journal of Speech, Language, and Hearing Research, 41,* 172–187.

Rose, M.L., Mok, Z., Carragher, M., Katthagen, S., & Attard, M. (2016). Comparing multi-modality and constraint-induced treatment for aphasia: A preliminary investigation of generalization to discourse. *Aphasiology, 30*(6), 678–698. doi:10.1080/02687038.2015.1100706

Rothi, L.J.G., Musson, N., Rosenbek, J.C., & Sapienza, C.M. (2008). Neuroplasticity and rehabilitation research for speech, language, and swallowing disorders. *Journal of Speech, Language, and Hearing Research, 51*(1), S222–S224.

Sage, K., Snell, C., & Lambon Ralph, M.A. (2011). How intensive does anomia therapy for people with aphasia need to be? *Neuropsychological Rehabilitation, 21,* 26–41.

Saur, D., & Hartwigsen, G. (2012). Neurobiology of language recovery after stroke: Lessons from neuroimaging studies. *Archives of Physical Medicine and Rehabilitation, 93*(1), S15–S25.

Saur, D., Lange, R., Baumgaertner, A., Schraknepper, V., Willmes, K., Rijntjes, J., & Weiller, C. (2006). Dynamics of language reorganization after stroke. *Brain, 129,* 1371–1384.

Schlaug, G., Marchina, S., & Wan, C.Y. (2011). The use of non-invasive brain stimulation techniques to facilitate recovery from post-stroke aphasia. *Neuropsychology Review, 21,* 288–301. doi:10.1007/s11065-011-9181-y

Schmidt, R.A., & Wrisberg, C.A. (2004). *Motor learning and performance.* Champaign, IL: Human Kinetics.

Shewan, C.M., & Kertesz, A. (1984). Effects of speech and language treatment in recovery from aphasia. *Brain and Language, 23,* 272–299.

Simmons-Mackie, N., Cherney, L., Raymer, A.M., Holland, A.L., & Armstrong, E. (2010). Communication partner training in aphasia: A systematic review. *Archives of Physical Medicine and Rehabilitation, 91,* 1814–1837.

Simmons-Mackie, N., Raymer, A., & Cherney, L.R. (2016). Communication partner training in aphasia: An updated systematic review. *Archives of Physical Medicine & Rehabilitation, 97,* 2202–2221.

Snell, C., Sage, K., & Lambon Ralph, M.A. (2010). How many words should we provide in anomia therapy? A meta-analysis and a case series study. *Aphasiology, 24,* 1064–1094.

Sturm, W., Longoni, F., Weis, S., Specht, K., Herzog, H., Vohn, R., . . . Willmes, K. (2004). Functional reorganization in patients with right hemisphere stroke after training of alertness: A longitudinal PET and fMRI study in eight cases. *Neuropsychologia, 42*(4), 434–450.

Svensson, P., Romaniello, A., Arendt-Nielsen, L., & Sessle, B.J. (2003). Plasticity in corticomotor control of the human tongue musculature induced by tongue-task training. *Experimental Brain Research, 152*(1), 42–51.

Taub, E., Miller, N.E., Novack, T.A., Cook, E.W., Fleming, W.C., Nepomuceno, C.S., . . . Crago, J.E. (1993). Technique to improve chronic motor deficit after stroke. *Archives of Physical Medicine & Rehabilitation, 74,* 347–354.

Taub, E., Uswatte, G., & Morris, D.M. (2003). Improved motor recovery after stroke and massive cortical reorganization following constraint-induced movement therapy. *Physical Medicine & Rehabilitation Clinics of North America, 14*(1 Suppl.), S77–S91.

Taub, E., Uswatte, G., & Mark, V.W. (2014). The functional significance of cortical reorganization and the parallel development of CI therapy. *Frontiers of Human Neurosciences, 8,* 396. doi:10.3389/fnhum.2014.00396

Thompson, C.K., Shapiro, L.P., Kiran, S., & Sobecks, J. (2003). The role of syntactic complexity in treatment of sentence deficits in agrammatic aphasia: The complexity account of treatment efficacy (CATE). *Journal of Speech, Language, and Hearing Research, 46,* 591–607.

Thompson, C.K., & Shapiro, L.P. (2005). Treating agrammatic aphasia within a linguistic framework: Treatment of underlying forms. *Aphasiology, 19,* 1021–1036.

Turkeltaub, P.E. (2015). Brain stimulation and the role of the right hemisphere in aphasia recovery. *Current Neurology and Neuroscience Reports, 15,* 72. doi:10:1007/s11910-015-0593.6

Turkstra, L.S., Holland, A.L., & Bays, G.A. (2003). The neuroscience of recovery and rehabilitation: What have we learned from animal research? *Archives of Physical Medicine & Rehabilitation, 84*(4), 605–612.

van de Sandt-Koenderman, M.E., van der Meulen, I., & Ribbers, G.M. (2012). Aphasia rehabilitation: More than treating the language disorders. *Archives of Physical Medicine and Rehabilitation, 93*(1), S1–S3.

Walker-Batson, D., Curtis, S., Natarajan, R., Ford, J., Dronkers, N., Salmeron, E., . . . Unwin, D.H. (2001). A double-blind, placebo-controlled study of the use of amphetamine in the treatment of aphasia. *Stroke, 32*, 2093–2098.

Wang, L., Conner, J.M., Rickert, J., & Tuszynski, M.H. (2011). Structural plasticity within highly specific neuronal populations identifies a unique parcellation of motor learning in the adult brain. *Proceedings of the National Academy of Sciences U.S.A., 108*, 2545–2550.

Warren, S.F., Fey, M.E., & Yoder, P.J. (2007). Differential treatment intensity research: A missing link to creating optimally effective communication interventions. *Mental Retardation and Developmental Disabilities, 13*, 70–77.

Weisenburg, T.S., & McBride, K.L. (1935). *Aphasia.* New York, NY: Hafner.

Wepman, J.M. (1951). *Recovery from aphasia.* New York, NY: The Ronald Press.

Wertz, R.T., Collins, M.J., Weiss, D., Kurtzke, J.F., Friden, T., Brookshire, R.H., . . . Resurreccion, E. (1981). Veterans Administration cooperative study on aphasia: A comparison of individual and group treatment. *Journal of Speech and Hearing Research, 24*, 580–594.

Wertz, R.T., Weiss, D.G., Aten, J.L., Brookshire, R.H., Garcia-Bunuel, L., Holland, A.L., . . . Brannegan, R. (1986). Comparison of clinic, home, and deferred language treatment for aphasia: a Veterans Administration cooperative study. *Archives of Neurology, 43*, 653–658.

Whurr, R., Lorch, M.P., & Nye, C. (1992). A meta-analysis of studies carried out between 1946 and 1988 concerned with the efficacy of speech and language therapy treatment for aphasic patients. *European Journal of Disorders of Communication, 27*(1), 1–17.

Wilson, B.A., Baddeley, A., Evans, J., & Shiel, A. (1994). Errorless learning in the rehabilitation of memory impaired people. *Neuropsychological Rehabilitation, 4*(3), 307–326.

Wilson, B.A., & Evans, J.J. (1996). Error-free learning in the rehabilitation of people with memory impairments. *Journal of Head Trauma Rehabilitation, 11*(2), 54–64.

Woolf, C., Caute, A., Haigh, Z., Galliers, J., Wilson, S., Kessie, A., . . . Marshall, J. (2016). A comparison of remote therapy, face to face therapy and an attention control intervention in people with aphasia: A quasi-randomised controlled feasibility study. *Clinical Rehabilitation, 30*(4), 359–373. doi:10.1177/0269215515582074

Worrall, L., Papathanasiou, I., & Sherratt, S. (2013). Therapy approaches to aphasia. In I. Papathanasiou, P. Coppens, & C. Potages (Eds.), *Aphasia and related neurogenic communication disorders* (pp. 93–111). Burlington, MA: Jones & Bartlett Learning.

World Health Organization (2001). *International Classification of Functioning, Disability and Health (ICF).* Geneva: WHO. Retrieved November 6, 2016 from http://www.who.int/classifications/icf/en/

World Health Organization (1997). *The World Health Report. Conquering Suffering, Enriching Humanity* (pp. 1–162). Geneva: WHO.

Wolfe, C.D. (2000). The impact of stroke. *British Medical Bulletin, 56*, 275–286.

INDEX

Page references followed by an "*f*" indicate figure; "*t*" indicate table.

JAMES BRIDIE LIBRARY
NEW VICTORIA HOSPITAL

This book is due for return on or before the last date shown below.